Path Through Catholicism

Mark Link, S.J.

Resource Manual

Revised Edition

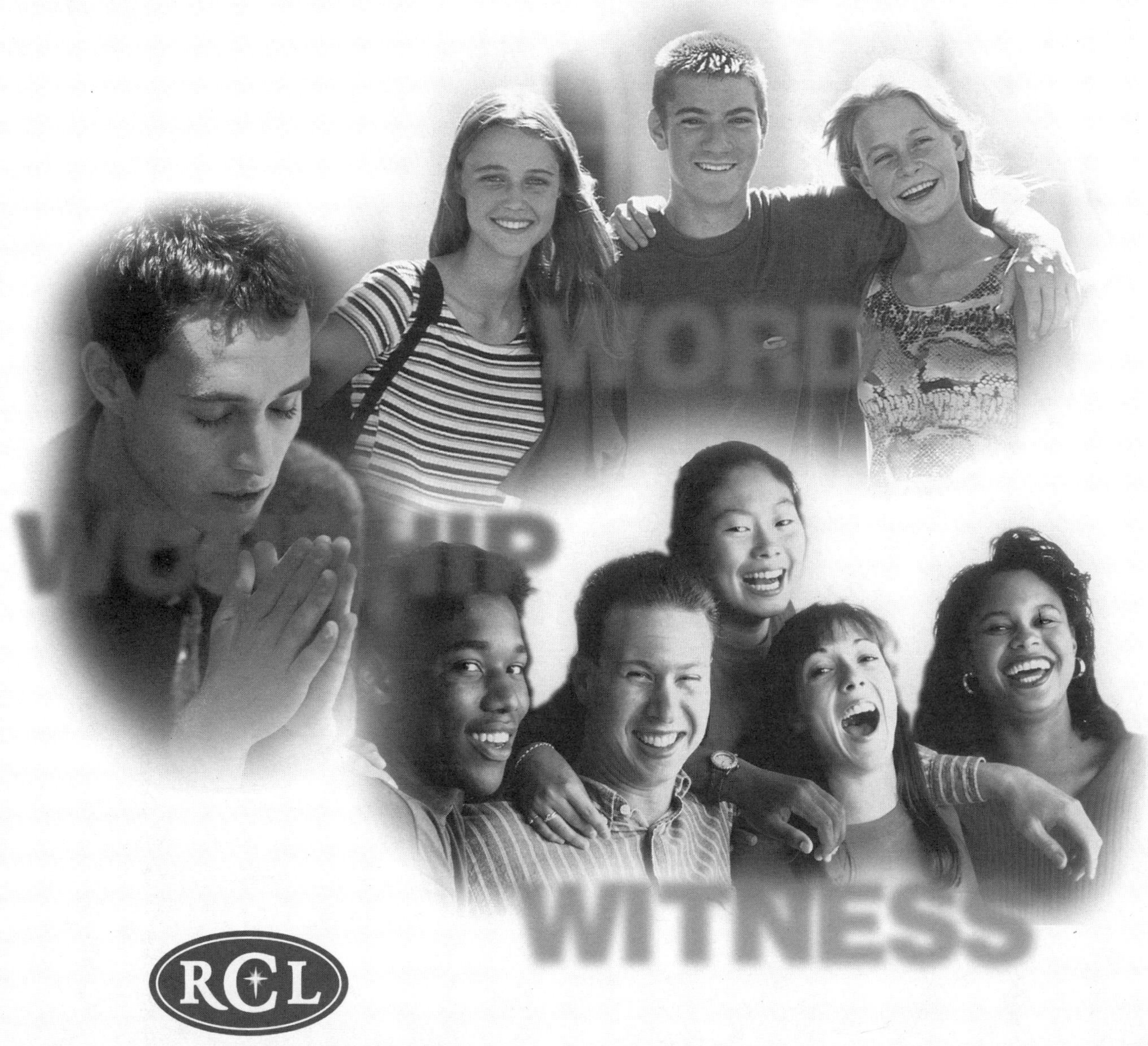

RCL

Resources for Christian Living®

Executive Editor:
John L. Sprague

Book and Cover Design:
Dennis Davidson

Production:
Kevin Fremder
Laura Fremder

Nihil Obstat:
Rev. Msgr. Glenn D. Gardner, J.C.D.
Censor Librorum

Imprimi Potest:
Richard J. Baumann, S.J.

Imprimatur:
† Most Rev. Charles V. Grahmann
Bishop of Dallas

May 12, 2000

The Nihil Obstat and Imprimatur are official declarations that the material reviewed is free of doctrinal or moral error. No implication is contained therein that those granting the Nihil Obstat and Imprimatur agree with the contents, opinions, or statements expressed.

ACKNOWLEDGMENTS

Unless otherwise noted, Scripture quotations are taken or adapted from the *Good News Bible: Today's English Version* (Catholic edition). Copyright © American Bible Society 1992, 1976, 1971, 1966. Used by permission.

Excerpts from the English translation of the *Rite of Baptism for Children* © 1969, International Committee on English in the Liturgy, Inc. (ICEL); excerpts from the English translation of *Rite of Marriage* © 1969, ICEL; excerpts from the English translation of *The Roman Missal* © 1973, ICEL; excerpts from the English translation of *Rite of Confirmation,* second edition © 1975, ICEL; excerpts from *Pastoral Care of the Sick: Rites of Anointing and Viaticum* © 1982, ICEL. All rights reserved.

Excerpts taken from the *Catechism of the Catholic Church* for the United States of America, copyright © 1994, United States Catholic Conference, Inc.—Libreria Editrice Vaticana.

Excerpts from the Vatican II documents are adapted from *The Documents of Vatican Council II,* copyright © 1966, Walter M. Abbott, S.J., Gen. Ed., America Press.

Photograph credits appear on page 319.

Send all inquiries to:
RCL • Resources for Christian Living®
200 East Bethany Drive
Allen, Texas 75002-3804
Toll free 800-822-6701
Fax 800-688-8356

Printed in the United States of America

20289 ISBN 0-7829-0975-2

2 3 4 5 6 06 05 04 03 02

About this resource manual

Teacher resources

This manual contains the following teacher resources:

1. A page-by-page reproduction (smaller, but highly readable) of each page of the student textbook;

2. A page-by-page teaching guide, placed alongside each page from the textbook;

3. Chapter-by-chapter suggestions for additional classroom resources (e.g., CD-ROM, video, film, books) appear at the end of each chapter in the manual.

4. A reproducible set of tests for each of the 23 chapters of the textbook;

5. A list of general resources along with a list of addresses, phone numbers, and fax numbers of publishers of resource material—and other prominent publishers.

Student materials

1. *Path Through Catholicism*

2. *Notebook:* Three-ring Binder

Have students do all work on 3-hole, 8½" x 11" paper. This permits them to insert written work in the proper section in their notebook:

- Section #1 Classwork
- Section #2 Homework
- Section #3 Prayer Journal
- Section #4 Scripture Journal

Assign each student a number depending on their seat assignment. (e.g., Mary Ellen, who sits in the third seat of the first row, is assigned #3.) Have students put their name and number in the upper right hand corner of all written assignments. This facilitates collecting and returning assignments.

3. *Good News Bible: Today's English Version* (Catholic edition)

If students do not have personal Bibles, make available a reserve shelf of Bibles in the classroom or the student library.

4. *Catechism of the Catholic Church: Second Edition*

The Second Edition has been revised in accordance with the official Latin text promulgated by Pope John Paul II and contains a new glossary and a new analytical index.

Teaching procedure

The author's teaching pattern for each lesson follows this general format:

1. *Review* Each new class begins with a review of the previous class. Review procedures vary depending on the content under discussion, for example:

    a. Questioning the students orally;
    b. Presenting an oral summary;
    c. Chalk talk from the board;
    d. Quiz of previous lesson.

2. *View* The new material to be presented. For example, it may be "Three Faith Stages," which is subdivided into "Childhood stage," "Adolescent stage," and "Adult stage." This means four segments are to be presented.

Before presenting and developing a given segment, it is read aloud by one or more students. This refreshes memories and improves the quality of the participation.

3. *Preview* The class ends with a brief preview of the material to be taken in the next class.

Contents

Stage 3 – Witness
We journey together

STAGE 1 WORD
God reaches out to us

CLARIFY—Before having someone read aloud the poem "I said to the man . . ." introduce it with the following background.

In September 1939, an army of a million Nazi soldiers invaded Poland. Two weeks later, Russia joined the invasion. Ten days later, Germany and Russia divided Poland.

Two months later, the Russians invaded Finland; and the Nazis drew up plans to invade all of Europe and England.

On Christmas Day, King George VI of England addressed the nation and counseled trust in God. He ended by quoting from the poem by Minnie Louise Haskins: "I said to the man who stood at the gate of the year."

DISCUSS—What does the phrase "gate of the year" refer to?

- *The start of the new year, Jan. 1, 1940.*

What "light" does the poet ask "the man at the gate of the year" to give him?

- *Light of reason. In other words, the poet is saying, "Show me what I should do in the difficult days ahead.*

What "light" does the "man of the gate of the year" counsel?

- *Light of faith. In other words, he is saying, "Trust God!"*

Why is faith the *better* and *safer* light?

- *When we put trust in God's infinite wisdom, we are in far better hands than if we would put trust in our finite wisdom.*

Corrie ten Boom expresses the supremacy of the "light of faith" over the "light of reason" this way: "Faith is like radar that sees through the fog, the reality of things at a distance that the human eye can't see."

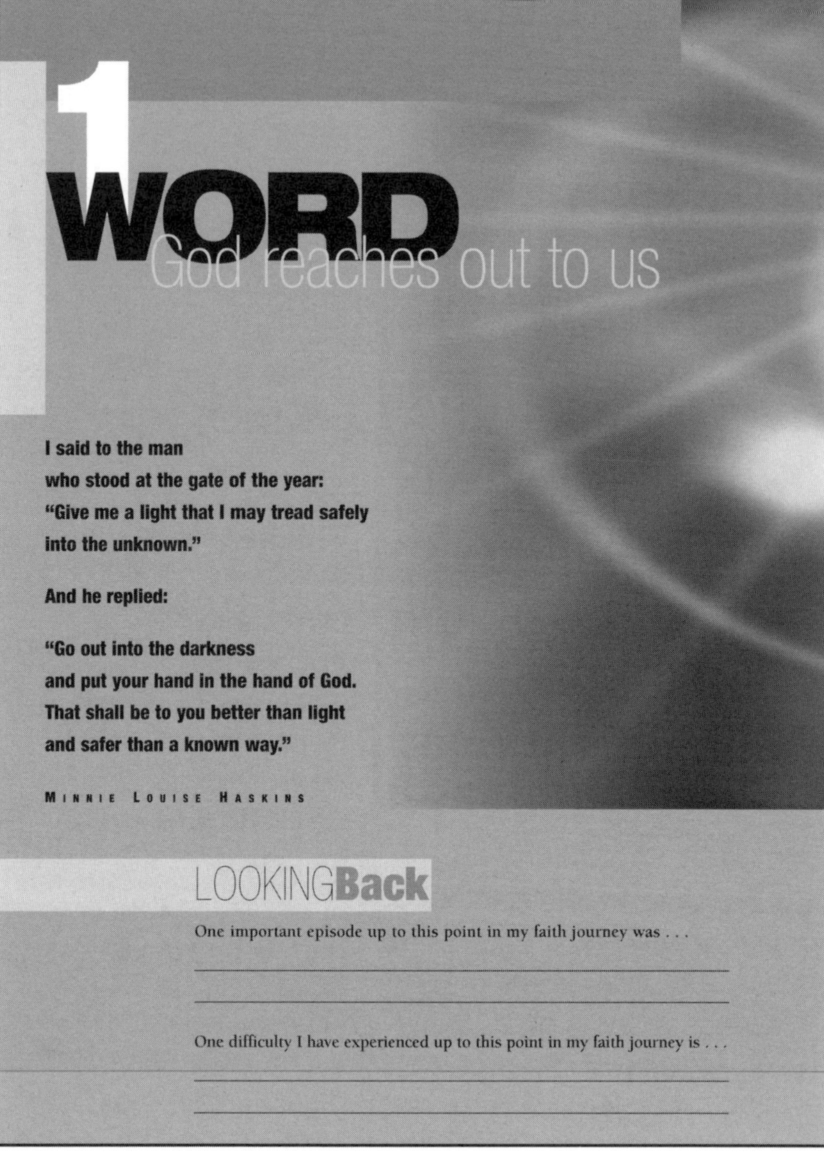

1
WORD
God reaches out to us
I said to the man
who stood at the gate of the year:
"Give me a light that I may tread safely
into the unknown."
And he replied:
"Go out into the darkness
and put your hand in the hand of God.
That shall be to you better than light
and safer than a known way."
MINNIE LOUISE HASKINS
LOOKINGBack
One important episode up to this point in my faith journey was . . .
One difficulty I have experienced up to this point in my faith journey is . . .

LOOKING**Back**

NOTEBOOK—Give the students a few minutes to reflect on the two questions before answering them in their notebooks. Before doing so, consider sharing with them your personal responses. For example, an "important episode" in the author's faith journey was a deeply prayerful experience of God's grandeur. It occurred in his sophomore year in high school while ice-skating alone under the stars on a beautiful winter's night. One "difficulty" the author experienced in his faith journey was a tendency to be overly critical of the faults and shortcomings of others.

After the students have responded, invite volunteers to share their responses. Get

NOTES

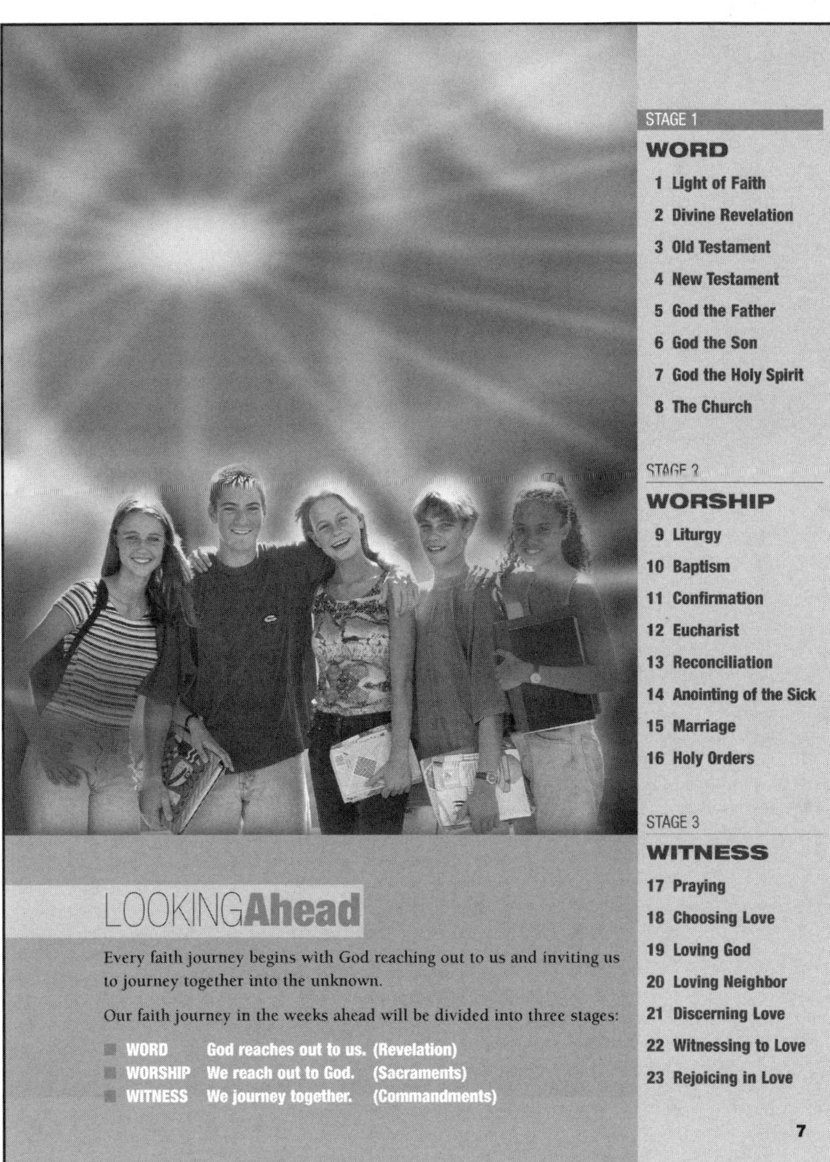

all the voluntary responses to the first question before going on to the second question.

LOOKINGAhead

***DISCUSS*—**What do we mean by the word "revelation"?

■ *It is God's personal word to us through Scripture and Tradition.*

How does "God reach out to us" in revelation?

■ *The same way a new friend reaches out to us. God reveals his love for us.*

How do we "reach out to God" in worship?

■ *By our loving response to God's revelation of his love for us.*

In what sense do we "journey together" with God when we keep the commandments?

■ *By trusting that God knows what is best for us. After all, God made us—and loves us more than we love ourselves.*

***CLARIFY*—**An example of trust in God is John Henry Newman (1801–1890). He was an Anglican priest, who felt drawn to the Catholic Church. He went to Rome to discern if this was what God wanted. Returning to England, he was still wondering what God wanted. That's when he penned the lyrics of the famous hymn, "Lead Kindly Light":

Lead, kindly Light,
amid the encircling gloom,
Lead thou me on;

The night is dark,
and I am far from home;
Lead thou me on.

Keep thou my feet;
I do not ask to see
The distant scene;
one step's enough for me.

***DISCUSS*—**Have the students explain the imagery of the hymn and how it relates: (1) to Newman's situation, (2) to the poem by Minnie Louise Haskins.

■ *Newman still wasn't sure—when he wrote it—whether he should become a Roman Catholic or not. He placed his trust in God to guide him. Once home, it became clear what he should do. So, in 1845, he entered the Church and became a great scholar and spiritual leader.*

■ *Similarly, the person in the poem by Minnie Louise Haskins wasn't sure what to do, so she put all her trust in God to guide her.*

***NOTEBOOK*—**You might have the students copy the lyrics of "Lead Kindly Light" into their notebooks. If you do, copy it on the chalkboard ahead of time or dictate it a line at a time.

CHAPTER 1
Light of Faith

CHAPTER at a Glance

The aim of this chapter is to give the students an overview of the "faith journey to God."

***DISCUSS*—**Have a student read aloud the introduction that begins: "It was faith that made Abraham . . ." Reread paragraph four and ask: What do we mean by a "personal relationship with Jesus" and how do we go about developing it?

■ *It's the kind of relationship we have with our best friend. We develop it the same way two people become best friends. We spend time together and learn as much as we can about each other.*

Tommy's faith journey

***DISCUSS*—**Explain the sentence: "Tommy was Fr. Powell's 'atheist in residence.'"

■ *Tommy was making the transition from childhood to adult faith. Sometimes this confuses people to the point they sometimes even question God's existence.*

***NOTEBOOK*—**List on the chalkboard the various "God positions" (left column). Have students fill the description (right column) and enter both columns into their notebooks:

Atheist	*Denies there is a God*
Agnostic	*Doesn't deny/affirm God*
Theist	*Affirms a personal God*
Deist	*Affirms impersonal God*
Monotheist	*Affirms only one God*
Polytheist	*Affirms many gods*

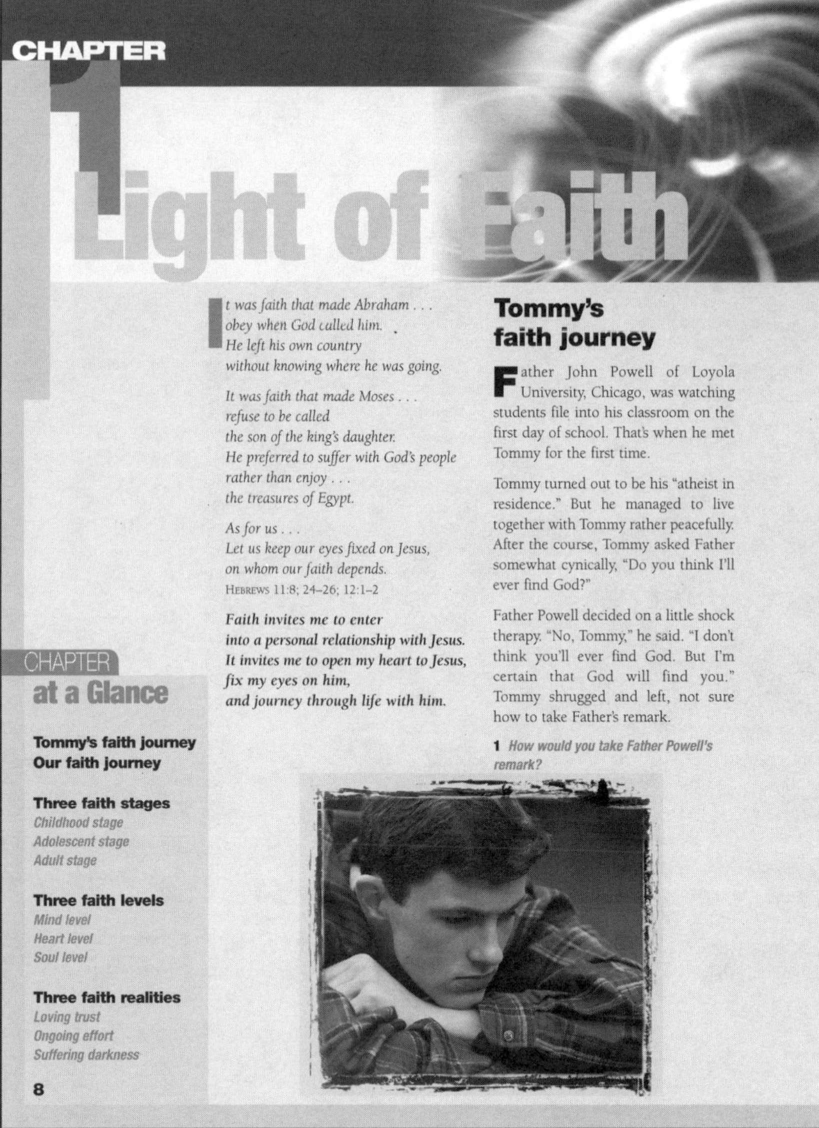
CHAPTER 1

Light of Faith

It was faith that made Abraham . . .
obey when God called him.
He left his own country
without knowing where he was going.

It was faith that made Moses . . .
refuse to be called
the son of the king's daughter.
He preferred to suffer with God's people
rather than enjoy . . .
the treasures of Egypt.

As for us . . .
Let us keep our eyes fixed on Jesus,
on whom our faith depends.
HEBREWS 11:8; 24–26; 12:1–2

Faith invites me to enter
into a personal relationship with Jesus.
It invites me to open my heart to Jesus,
fix my eyes on him,
and journey through life with him.

CHAPTER at a Glance

Tommy's faith journey
Our faith journey

Three faith stages
Childhood stage
Adolescent stage
Adult stage

Three faith levels
Mind level
Heart level
Soul level

Three faith realities
Loving trust
Ongoing effort
Suffering darkness

Tommy's faith journey

Father John Powell of Loyola University, Chicago, was watching students file into his classroom on the first day of school. That's when he met Tommy for the first time.

Tommy turned out to be his "atheist in residence." But he managed to live together with Tommy rather peacefully. After the course, Tommy asked Father somewhat cynically, "Do you think I'll ever find God?"

Father Powell decided on a little shock therapy. "No, Tommy," he said. "I don't think you'll ever find God. But I'm certain that God will find you." Tommy shrugged and left, not sure how to take Father's remark.

1 *How would you take Father Powell's remark?*

8

***CLARIFY*—**By an "impersonal" God, we mean a God who (so to speak) wound up the world like a clock, and is letting it tick down, not really caring what happens.

QUESTION **1** ***How would you take Father Powell's remark?***

■ *God never ceases to search for us. Like the Good Shepherd who went in search of the "lost sheep," when God finds us, he puts us on his shoulder and carries us back home.* LUKE 15:1

Recall, also, the biographical poem "The Hound of Heaven" by the English poet Francis Thompson.

Thompson (1859–1907) led a sinful life—fleeing God as a frightened rabbit flees a

NOTES

About a year later, Father Powell learned that Tommy had terminal cancer. Before he could get in touch with Tommy, Tommy got in touch with him. Father Powell writes:

When Tommy walked into my office,
his body was badly wasted. . . .
I blurted out,
"I've thought about you so often . . .
Can you talk about it?"
"Sure, what would you like to know?"

"What's it like to be only twenty-four
and know you are dying?"
"Well, it could be worse," Tommy said.
"Like what?" I asked.

"Well," said Tommy,
"like being fifty years old
and having no values and thinking
that booze and making money
are the real biggies in life.

"But what I really came to see you about
is something you said to me
the last day of class.
I asked if you thought I would ever
find God and you said, 'No!' which
surprised me. Then you said,
'But God will find you.'"

Tommy went on to say that after the doctors removed a malignant lump from his groin, he decided he'd start looking for God.

For the first time in his life, Tommy made a serious effort to reach out and search for the God that he had been avoiding:

"I really began banging
against the bronze doors of heaven.
But nothing happened. So I just quit."

2 ***How would you explain Tommy's failure to find God?***

Then one day Tommy remembered something else that Father had said in class:

The essential sadness
is to go through life without lovi
But it would be almost equally sad
to leave this world
without ever telling those you lov
that you loved them.

Tommy decided to spend the time he had left reaching out to those [illegible]. He began with his dad. One [illegible] said to him:

"'Dad, I love you.
I just wanted you to know that . . .'
Then my father did two things
I couldn't remember him doing before.

"First, he cried and hugged me.
Then we talked all night, even though
he had to go to work the next morning.

"It was easier with my mother and
little brother."

Tommy then explained what h[illegible] after he reached out to his [illegible] "I turned around and God w[illegible] You were right. God found m[illegible]

3 ***When we are lost, how does Go[d go] about finding us?***

dog. But God kept pursuing him, in spite of his life of sin.

Eventually, God caught up with him and Thompson's life ended up happily, the same way Tommy's did.

QUESTION **2** ***How would you explain Tommy's failure to find God?***

■ *Tommy was looking for a "quick fix"—not for a God to love. Unless he reached out to God in love, his faith would be short-lived and his spiritual growth negligible. God is not a 911 number that you call only in emergencies.*

***CLARIFY*—What two remarks by Powell inspired Tommy to reach out in love?**

1 *The essential sadness is to go through life without loving.*

2 *It would be almost equally sad to leave this world without ever telling those you loved that you loved them.*

***DISCUSS*—Why is it important to show our loved ones, by our deeds, that we love them?**

■ *Dr. Lee Salk's book* My Father, My Son *describes an interview with Mark Chapman, convicted slayer of Beatle John Lennon. Chapman says:*

"I don't think I ever hugged my father.
He never told me he loved me . . .
I needed emotional love and support.
I never got that.

Explain Chapman's comment: "I needed emotional love and support."

■ *We all need emotional love and support. Children need it from parents; and parents and siblings need it from each other.*

***ACTIVITY*—Have students respond anonymously and briefly to the following two questions:**

1 *Which member of your family do you find it easiest to talk to and why?*

2 *Which member of your family do you find it hardest to talk to and why?*

Collect and shuffle (to protect anonymity). Have two students read off the responses to the first question, while a third student tallies the responses to the family member (father-mother-brother-sister) on the chalkboard.

Do the same for the second question. After tallying up the results, read and discuss a few of the reasons given for finding it "easy" or "hard" to talk to this family member.

QUESTION **3** ***When we are lost, how does God go about finding us?***

■ *God finds us in the sense that God does not give up on us. Rather, God continually graces us to open our hearts to him as Tommy finally did).*

FAITH Connection

NOTEBOOK—Have students compose and copy the verses in their notebooks. When the students are finished, invite a few volunteers to copy one of their verses on the chalkboard.

ACTIVITY—You might consider having the class vote for the verse they like best.

Our faith journey

DISCUSS—Have a student read aloud the first three paragraphs under this heading. List on the board the three "knocks at the door of the heart" referred to:

- *Spiritual hunger,*
- *Call to love in the heart,*
- *Event that turns our world upside down.*

Have students give an example of each and explain which "knock" they think is the most common one—and why.

- Spiritual hunger: *Something is missing in my life; I'm unhappy, but don't know why.*
- Call to love: *Someone I admire inspires me to want to be a better person.*
- Some shattering event: *Death in family; Accident or sickness makes me realize how vulnerable I am. Breakup with someone I love.*

Three faith stages

CLARIFY—Whether we are born Muslim or Lutheran, we must eventually make the transition from a *faith by culture* to a *faith by conviction*. This means *reexamining* our cultural faith with a view to *reaffirming* or *rejecting* it. This involves study and prayer.

THINK about it

It's not dying for faith that's so hard, it's living up to it.

William Makepeace Thackeray

Our faith journey

Listen! I stand at the door and knock; if any hear my voice and open the door, I will come into their house and eat with them, and they will eat with me. Revelation 3:20

Every faith journey begins with a knock at the door of the heart. It may take the form of a spiritual hunger in the soul, a call to love in the heart, or some unforeseen event that turns our world upside down.

If we open the door, God will take us by the hand and lead us into the unknown. Then at some memorable moment, God will surprise and bless us beyond all of our expectations.

FAITH Connection

Doubt sees the obstacles—
Faith sees the way.

Doubt sees the darkest night—
Faith sees the day.

Doubt dreads to take a step—
Faith soars on high.

Doubt questions, "Who believes?"
Faith answers, "I."

Author Unknown

■ *Compose two or three verses of your own.*

Three faith stages

Most faith journeys follow a path that leads the believer through three faith stages:

- **Childhood stage** — **Cultural faith**
- **Adolescent stage** — **Transitional faith**
- **Adult stage** — **Convictional faith**

Childhood stage

The childhood stage is *cultural,* in the sense that, if we were born in Iran to Iranian parents, we'd probably begin life as a Muslim; if we were born of Lutheran parents, we would probably be Lutheran.

In other words, our childhood faith is conditioned by both our cultural situation and the faith—or lack of faith—of the family into which we are born and raised.

Adolescent stage

The adolescent stage is both the most critical and the most painful.

It is the most critical because it involves making the transition from receiving the "seed" of faith in baptism to "confirming" it by personal conviction. CCC 168

It is the most painful because our childhood faith must die before our adult faith can be born. That is, we must rid our faith of any simplistic or immature notions. This is what takes place in the adolescent stage. It is this process that causes the pain.

John Kirvan's book *The Restless Believers* contains a description of how the death of our childhood faith affects us. He quotes a young person as saying:

I don't know what's going wrong.
When I was in grade school,
and for the first couple of years
of high school I was real religious,
and now I just don't seem to care.

4 ***Have you ever felt this way? Explain.***

The death of our childhood faith can make us feel sick of heart—even guilty. This is unfortunate because the truth of the matter is that we are only experiencing growth pains, which are a part of every "faith journey."

Adolescent questioning

The adolescent stage of our faith involves a good deal of questioning. When this questioning is done constructively, it results in faith growth.

5 ***What do we mean by "constructive questioning"?***

10 Stage 1: Chapter 1

Adolescent stage

CLARIFY—The adolescent stage may be compared to the cutting of the umbilical cord and separating a baby from its mother.

Similarly, we must cut the spiritual umbilical cord that binds us to our *cultural faith* and begin living on our own. The pain we sometimes experience in this stage can be intense.

QUESTION **4** ***Have you ever felt this way? Explain.***

- *This question refers to Kirwin's quote.*

NOTES

First, constructive questioning fosters *faith clarity*. For example, we may have a view of God that needs to be revised. This was the case of a college student who told her professor, "I no longer believe in God." The professor said, "Good!" The student said, "Now what's that supposed to mean?"

The professor explained that many of us have childhood images of God that are simplistic and need to be clarified. CCC 158

Second, constructive questioning widens *faith horizons*. For example, we may think that science and the biblical story of creation are in conflict. Exploring the question, however, we learn that if the creation story and science are understood correctly, there is no conflict at all. CCC 159

6 ***How is the creation story often misunderstood by people?***

Third, constructive questioning deepens *faith commitment*. Take the case of God again. Before our questioning, we may have prayed to God out of habit or fear. After our questioning, we may begin praying to God out of conviction and love.

In brief, *destructive* questioning means we want to disprove a point, so we can do what we want. *Constructive* questioning means we want to learn the truth, so we can do what is right. Constructive questioning does the following:

- **Fosters faith clarity**
- **Widens faith horizons**
- **Deepens faith commitment**

7 ***What are some questions you have about your faith?***

Adult stage

The adult stage is clearly the important one. At this stage we appropriate the faith to ourselves. In other words, we move beyond an unexamined cultural faith to an examined, personal faith. An example is the Samaritan neighbors of the "woman at the well."

Many of the Samaritans in that town
believed in Jesus
because the woman had said,
"He told me everything I have ever done."
So when the Samaritans came to him,
they begged him to stay with them,
and Jesus stayed there two days.

Many more believed because of his message,
and told the woman, "We believe now,
not because of what you said,
but because we ourselves have heard him,
and we know that he is really
the Savior of the world. JOHN 4:39–42

8 ***How does this story illustrate what needs to take place at the adult stage of faith?***

Up Close & Personal

Dorothy Day

A convert to the Catholic faith, Dorothy Day dedicated her life to the poor, saying: "What you do for them you do for Jesus."

She was so active in seeking justice for the poor and in opposing war, that she was accused of being a Communist. She was denounced, shot at, jailed, and repeatedly investigated by the FBI.

In her book *From Union Square to Rome,* Dorothy describes a key episode in her faith journey. She writes:

Many a morning after
sitting all night in taverns . . .
I went to Saint Joseph's Church
on Sixth Avenue.

It was just around the corner
from where I lived, and
seeing people going
to an early weekday Mass
attracted me. . . .

So I used to go and kneel
in the back pew of Saint
Joseph's.

When she died in 1980 at the age of 83, the *New York Times* called her one of the most influential Catholics in America.

NOTEBOOK—Have the students think about the question before answering it in their notebooks. Invite volunteers to share their response with the class. Invite comments from the other students.

Adolescent questioning

CLARIFY—When adolescents question, it's a sign they care. It is by constructive questioning that our faith matures from a "faith by culture" to a "faith by conviction."

QUESTION **5** ***What do we mean by "constructive questioning"?***

■ *It is an honest search for truth.*

QUESTION **6** ***How is the creation story often misunderstood?***

■ Literalists *say creation took place as the Bible says. This rules out evolution.*

CLARIFY—The biblical story of creation and evolution deal with different questions: (1) Who created? (2) How created? Pius XII, in his encyclical *Humani Generis* (1950), said the theory of the evolutionary origin of the human body does not conflict with Catholic faith so long as it does not deny "that souls are immediately created by God." *America* 21/28/96

QUESTION **7** ***What are some questions you have about your faith?***

ACTIVITY—Have students write out their response. Collect and comment on them in the next class—or collect the responses and involve the class in commenting on them.

Adult stage

DISCUSS—Samaritans were Jews who compromised their faith through intermarriage with their Assyrian conquerors in 722 B.C.

QUESTION **8** ***How does this story illustrate what needs to take place at the adult stage of faith?***

■ *There must be a transition from* cultural *to* convictional *faith: "They told the woman, "We believe now . . . because we ourselves have heard him."*

Up Close & Personal

DISCUSS—A proverb says: "Not the *cry*, but the *flight* of the duck leads the flock to fly and *follow.*" How does it apply to what led Dorothy Day to become a Catholic?

■ *She was moved to faith by example, rather than words.*

Share Your meditation

***ACTIVITY*—**Invite students to take a *special* item, such as a poem, prayer, or photo, from their wallets and explain why they carry it.

Three faith levels

***CLARIFY*—**We may think of ourselves as having four layers: senses (sense), mind (conscious), heart (subconscious), soul (sanctuary).

Senses — Sense *layer at which we make contact with others: see, hear, feel, etc.*

Mind — Conscious *layer at which we process data gathered at the "sense" layer.*

Heart — Subconscious *layer at which we experience moods of joy, peace, love.*

Soul — Sanctuary *layer where the divine and the human meet and embrace. Jesus said "The Kingdom of God is within you."* LUKE 17:21 *Saint Paul said: "You are a temple of the Holy Spirit."* 1 CORINTHIANS 6:19

SHARE YOUR meditation

A reporter asked astronaut Ed White what personal items he took along with him on his Gemini-4 flight. He said one was a Saint Christopher medal, which Pope John XXIII gave each astronaut. White said: "I took it on the Gemini-4 flight to express my faith in myself, in Jim McDivitt, my partner, and especially in God." "Faith," he said, "was the most important thing I had going for me on the flight."

- *What do you carry or wear that expresses your faith?*
- *What faith do you find most challenging: faith in God, others, yourself? Explain.*

Our faith journey is the greatest adventure we will ever embark upon. This is because it takes us beyond the natural world to the supernatural. It leads us beyond material reality to spiritual reality.

We begin our faith journey by placing our hand in the hand of God and allowing ourselves to be led by both the light of reason and the light of faith, which is the safer light. CCC 154–55 Jesus spoke of this light when he said:

"I will ask the Father
and he will give you . . . the Spirit,
who will stay with you forever. . . .
He is the Spirit,
who . . . will teach you everything
and make you remember
all that I have told you." JOHN 14:16

And so our journey begins and moves forward toward that awesome faith encounter that brings us face to face with the mystery of the Holy Trinity. CCC 253–56

- **Father** — **Who created us**
- **Son** — **Who redeemed us**
- **Holy Spirit** — **Who graces us**

Three faith levels

The Holy Spirit graces and guides us every step of the faith journey. It unfolds gradually and throughout our lives at three levels:

- **Mind level** — **Openness to truth**
- **Heart level** — **Openness to love**
- **Soul level** — **Openness to grace**

THINK about it

Faith with works is a force.
Faith without works is a farce.

E. C. McKenzie

Mind level

At the *mind* level, the Holy Spirit helps us to better grasp the truths of our faith. For example, we deepen our knowledge of God. The Russian mystic, Leo Tolstoy, had this in mind, by saying:

When a savage
ceases to believe in his wooden God,
this does not mean there is no God,
but only that the true God
is not made of wood.

In other words, by opening our minds to truth, we get a better grasp of who God is and what God is really like.

Heart level

At the *heart* level, the Holy Spirit leads us beyond our childhood world—with its focus on love of self—to an adult world, which looks to love of other people. In other words, by opening our hearts to a love of other people, we open our hearts to God.

We discover what Tommy realized; namely, that a failure or inability to find God is often traceable to a failure or inability to open our hearts to love other people and to receive love from them.

9 ***What keeps me from opening my heart more fully to love—especially family love?***

Soul level

Lastly, there is the *soul* level. If our soul is open, the Holy Spirit will grace us abundantly, prepare us for faith, invite us to faith, and embrace us every step of the faith journey. CCC 153–54 This journey involves a mystery of:

Mind level

***DISCUSS*—**How does Tolstoy's point about God relate to the college professor's remark to the college girl? (page 6)

- *The savage had an immature image of God, just as the girl did. Both had to upgrade their image to a mature level.*

***CLARIFY*—**Tolstoy (1828–1910) was a Russian novelist. His *War and Peace* became a Hollywood movie. At 18 he left his faith. For the next ten years, he lived a life of sin.

Then one spring day, he was walking through a forest enjoying nature. Suddenly, he found himself opening his heart to God as never before. That experience sparked his return to his faith. He returned to it with the same intensity that he departed from it. He renounced his considerable wealth and lived the life of a simple peasant.

QUESTION **9** ***What keeps me from opening my heart more fully to love—especially family love?***

***DISCUSS*—**Have students respond anonymously in writing. Collect responses, read a sampling, and discuss.

***DISCUSS*—**Tommy took the initiative and reached out to his father. Mark Chapman waited for his father to reach out to him. The difference in approaches meant "life" for Tommy and "death" for Mark. Who should take the initiative and why?

NOTES

- **Gift** — **God's contribution**
- **Freedom** — **Our contribution**

Faith is a gift from God. It cannot be "merited" or "won." Jesus himself made this clear. One day he said:

JESUS *Who do people say I am?*

APOSTLES *Some say John the Baptist. . . .*

JESUS *What about you? Who do you say I am?*

PETER *You are the Messiah, the Son of the living God!*

JESUS *Good for you, Simon, son of John. For this truth did not come to you from any human being, but it was given to you directly by my Father.* MATTHEW 16:13–17

10 ***How does this dialogue make it clear that faith is a gift from God?***

Faith involves "freedom" on our part. Although God graces us and guides us on our faith journey, God does this in a way that respects our free will. In other words, God leaves us free to accept or to reject the gift.

Three faith realities

This leads us to three realities that we must be prepared to embrace on our faith journey:

- **Loving trust** — **Risk**
- **Ongoing effort** — **Recommitment**
- **Suffering darkness** — **Growth times**

Loving trust

An example of the kind of "loving trust" that faith requires is marriage. When two people join hands and promise to journey together on the road of life, there is no guarantee that each will remain faithful should a major crisis arise.

This is where loving trust comes in. Without it, there could be no marriage. Every marriage, by its very nature, involves a dimension of risk.

Faith is something like this. It too involves loving trust—not in the sense that God might be unfaithful (God is always faithful), but in the sense that we are not sure where our faith commitment to God will lead us. It is in this sense that faith involves risk and loving trust.

Abraham is a good example of the kind of risk and loving trust that a faith commitment to God involves. God said to Abraham:

"Leave your country,
your relatives,
and your father's home,
and go to a land
I am going to show you."
GENESIS 12:1

In other words, God was inviting Abraham to embrace a situation that involved both risk and loving trust. CCC 145–46

11 ***What risk might God be asking of you?***

PRAYER hotline

Dear Lord,
I believe in you
but I am so confused
about where I am going—
all I know
is where I've been.

I am so scared and
I have no one to talk to
but myself
and I hide my feelings
in my music.

Homeless youth. Quoted in *God, Please Save Me,* by Sr. Mary Rose McGready

STAGE 1: *CHAPTER 1* **13**

Soul Level

DISCUSS—Faith is a gift in the sense that God prepares us for faith, invites us to faith, and graces us with faith.

1. How did God prepare Tommy for faith?

■ *God brought him to the point (cancer) where he desired to connect with God.*

2. How did God invite and grace Tommy with faith?

■ *When he couldn't connect with God, he decided to open his heart to his family. The act of opening to his family in love, opened himself to God, as well.*

QUESTION **10** ***How does this dialogue make it clear that faith is a gift from God?***

■ *The revelation that Jesus is "the Messiah, the Son of the living God" came directly from the Father, not from Peter's own reasoning.*

Three faith realities

Loving trust

NOTEBOOK—Peter Drucker lists four kinds of risk. Write on the chalkboard, as follows:

1. One I can afford to take:

■ *I can afford to risk lending a dollar to someone who may not repay me. If they don't, it's not a big loss.*

2. One I can't afford to take:

■ *I can't afford to risk selling my car and spending every cent on $10-million lottery tickets. Too big a risk.*

3. One I can't afford not to take:

■ *George Burns starred as God in the film* Oh, God! *He appeared to John Denver with a message that would bring eternal happiness to millions. When John began preaching, his boss threatened to fire him. When John complained, God said to him, in effect: "That's a risk you cannot afford not to take: lose your job in exchange for bringing eternal happiness to millions.*

4. One I must take:

■ *Marriage involves this risk, e.g., my partner may be unfaithful. I must take the risk. If I don't, I'll never marry.*

DISCUSS—Which risk does faith involve?

■ *The fourth. If I want eternal life, I must trust Jesus, who promises it to those who believe in him and his Word.* JOHN 6:54

QUESTION **11** ***What risk might God be asking of you?***

■ *God may be asking me for a more (1) open mind (to truth), (2) open heart (to love), (3) open soul (to trust).*

Share Your meditation

CLARIFY—John Newton (1725–1807) left school at 11, went to sea, and lived a wild life. After his conversion, he became a minister in the village of Olney, England. There, he won renown as a preacher and hymn writer.

NOTEBOOK—Have students record the response to their meditation in their notebooks. If the spirit among the students is good, have them share their meditation in groups of three or four. Otherwise, have a few volunteers share their meditations with the class.

THINK about it

CLARIFY—The saying that "faith is like a toothbrush" is another way of saying that a time will come when we must cut the "spiritual" umbilical cord. We shouldn't try to build our spiritual lives on another's faith.

Ongoing effort

DISCUSS—What does the text mean when it says "we are constantly evolving and changing as persons"? Give examples.

Help the students out by asking: How are you different now in your attitude, values, goals, dreams, than you were in grade school?

QUESTION **12 *How would you answer these questions?***

■ *It's possible that the person was deluded. But it's more likely that the commitment was true. Because we are evolving as persons (sometimes more rapidly, because of a death, etc.), we may be significantly different from the person we were a year ago, or even a day ago. (Newton's conversion.)*

■ *Another example of how we evolve and change is Estlin Carpenter, a former Harvard University chaplain. During his own college days he was apathetic about God and religion. Then one afternoon, on a walk, he felt the presence of God as real as if someone suddenly began walking along with him. That experience had a profound effect on the rest of his life. He said of it, "I could now not only believe in God with my mind, but also love him with my heart."*

DISCUSS—Why does God often give a "spiritual experience" to people who seem to be "undeserving" of it?

■ *A spiritual experience is a pure gift. No one is "deserving" of it. God is free to give to anyone for any reason. Concerning God's gifts, Paul writes: "God purposely chose what the world considers nonsense in order to shame the wise and he chose*

SHARE YOUR meditation

John Newton was a British sea captain and slave trader. One night a great storm threatened his ship and his cargo of slaves. He promised to give up slave trade if his ship came through the storm. It did and he kept his promise. He wrote a hymn to celebrate his conversion. A part of it reads:

Amazing grace!
How sweet the sound,
that saved a wretch like me!
I once was lost
but now am found—
Was blind, but now I see. . . .

Through many dangers, toils, and snares
I have already come;
'Tis grace hath brought me
safe thus far,
and grace will lead me home.

■ *Describe a time when you felt God's grace at work in you in a special way.*

THINK about it

Faith is like a toothbrush. Everyone should have one and use it regularly, but he should not try to use someone else's.

J. G. Stipe

Ongoing effort

A misunderstanding that some people have is the idea that once we "get the faith" we don't have to worry about it again. This is not the case. An example will illustrate. A person writes:

I made a five-day retreat.
On it, I committed my life to Jesus
in a way that I had not anticipated.
This decision gave me deep peace and joy.

A week later,
I found myself doing something
that was contrary to my faith.
I was profoundly disturbed.
How can I explain this?
Had I really committed myself to Jesus
on the retreat?
Or had I merely deluded myself
into thinking that I had?

12 *How would you answer these questions?*

The person's retreat experience illustrates what psychologists have always told us. The greater part of ourselves lies beneath our consciousness. It surfaces slowly and only gradually with each new experience.

This explains why faith involves *ongoing effort.* It's because we are constantly evolving and changing as persons. As a result, we must constantly recommit ourselves to God in harmony with our change and evolvement. It is by this process of recommitment that faith grows and matures. CCC 162

Suffering darkness

Finally, our faith is like the sun. Sometimes it shines brightly and everything is clear and beautiful. At other times it seems to go behind a cloud and disappear in darkness. You begin to wonder if it is even there. CCC 164–65 This darkness is usually traceable to one of three sources:

- **Human nature**
- **Ourselves**
- **God**

Human nature

First, it may be caused by *human nature.* The darkness may simply reflect the natural mood swings of our human nature. On some days everything goes right and life is great. On other days everything goes wrong and life is a drag.

14 STAGE 1: CHAPTER 1

NOTES

Ourselves

Our faith follows similar mood swings. Such swings simply go with the territory of being human.

Second, the darkness of faith may be of our own making. We can cause it by neglecting our faith. That is, we can let our faith grow weak from sin or lack of spiritual nourishment. In other words, just as our body grows weak from abuse or lack of nourishment, our soul does the same thing.

God

Third, the darkness of faith may be traceable to God. Just as God can use our physical suffering—regardless of what caused it—to help us grow and mature in our faith, so can God use spiritual suffering—like darkness—to help our faith grow and mature.

Abraham

Take the case of Abraham, again: When he was told to sacrifice his son Isaac, he was absolutely thunderstruck. The spiritual suffering this caused must have been close to unbearable.

Just as painful to Abraham was the dilemma that God's command posed. How could Abraham have descendants through Isaac—as God had promised he would—if Isaac were sacrificed?

Suddenly, Abraham felt his faith being challenged to the breaking point. Had he relied solely on the light of reason, his faith would have died right there and then.

Instead, Abraham trusted God and—in God's providence—his faith grew to a level he never dreamed to be possible. When it reached this level, God could do great things through him; and he did.

13 ***Which of the three sources of darkness is the most common cause of darkness? Why?***

ART Connection

The great seventeenth-century Dutch painter Rembrandt spells out in living color God's command to Abraham:

"Take Isaac,
whom you love so much,
and offer him
as a sacrifice to me."
Genesis 22:2

LITERARY Connection

Faith darkness can cause deep spiritual agony. In his novel *The Devil's Advocate,* Morris West describes such an agony and the loss of faith that it occasioned. The character says:

I groped for God
and could not find God.
I prayed to God. . . .
God did not answer.
I wept at night
for the loss of God. . . .
Then one day,
God was there again. . . .
I had a parent
and God knew me. . . .
I had never understood
'til this moment
the meaning of the words
"gift of faith."
Slightly adapted

what the world considers weak in order to shame the powerful." 1 Corinthians 1:27

No one, not even the greatest saint, has a claim on God's generosity. That's the point of Jesus' Parable of the Workers. Matthew 20:15

Suffering darkness

Students need this message. A lot of them experience darkness acutely.

QUESTION **13** ***Which of the three sources of darkness is the most common cause of darkness? Why?***

NOTEBOOK—Have the students write out their responses in their notebooks.

Next, poll the class, tally the results on the chalkboard, and discuss the reasoning behind responses.

CLARIFY—Author Marion Bond gives an example of how God can use period of darkness for our growth. When she lost her father at age 4, her mother had to take a job to support her. She arranged for a neighbor to baby-sit Marion.

Each lunch hour she hurried home to eat with her. But when she left after lunch, Marion grew hysterical. Her mother stopped coming. Marion wondered, Did her mother stop loving her?

Years later, Marion learned that her mother still came each noon, sat at a window, ate lunch, and watched Marion play. She longed to hold her close, but she knew it was for Marion's own growth that she didn't.

God withdraws from us in a similar way for our own growth and good.

ART Connection

CLARIFY—When Rembrandt's wife died, he fell into depression and painted poorly. After he recovered, he painted with new passion and purpose.

Some critics think his wife's death raised him to a new artistic level. It shows how God uses the "darkness" of tragedy to fashion us into something better.

LITERARY Connection

CLARIFY—True faith requires the involvement of both the *head* and the *heart.*

When the character in West's novel said, "I never understood 'til this moment the meaning of the words 'gift of faith,'" he means he had a knowledge of "gift of faith," but not *heart* (personal experience) knowledge of it. Again, "darkness" leads to growth.

Recap

This section summarizes the key points of the chapter. An easy way to construct a quick "daily quiz" is to convert the "summary diagrams" (found here and in the text) into a "matching exercise." Here's an example:

1. The faith usually involves three stages. Match the "kind of faith" found at each stage:

c *1 Childhood stage*	*a. Transitional faith*
a *2 Adolescent stage*	*b. Convictional faith*
b *3 Adult stage*	*c. Cultural faith*

2. Constructive faith questioning leads to faith growth. Match the correct description to the kind of growth to which each leads:

b *1 Produces clarity*	*a. See more*
a *2 Widens horizons*	*b. See better*
c *3 Builds commitment*	*c. Act more lovingly*

Review

DAILY QUIZ—The review questions may be assigned (one or two at a time) for homework or as a brief daily quiz. For example:

1. Explain:

   a) The three stages through which faith passes as it grows

   b) Why the second stage is the most critical

CHAPTER TESTS—Reproducible chapter tests are found in Appendix A.
For consistency and ease in grading, quizzes are restricted to (1) "Matching," (2) "True/False," and (3) "Fill in the Blanks."

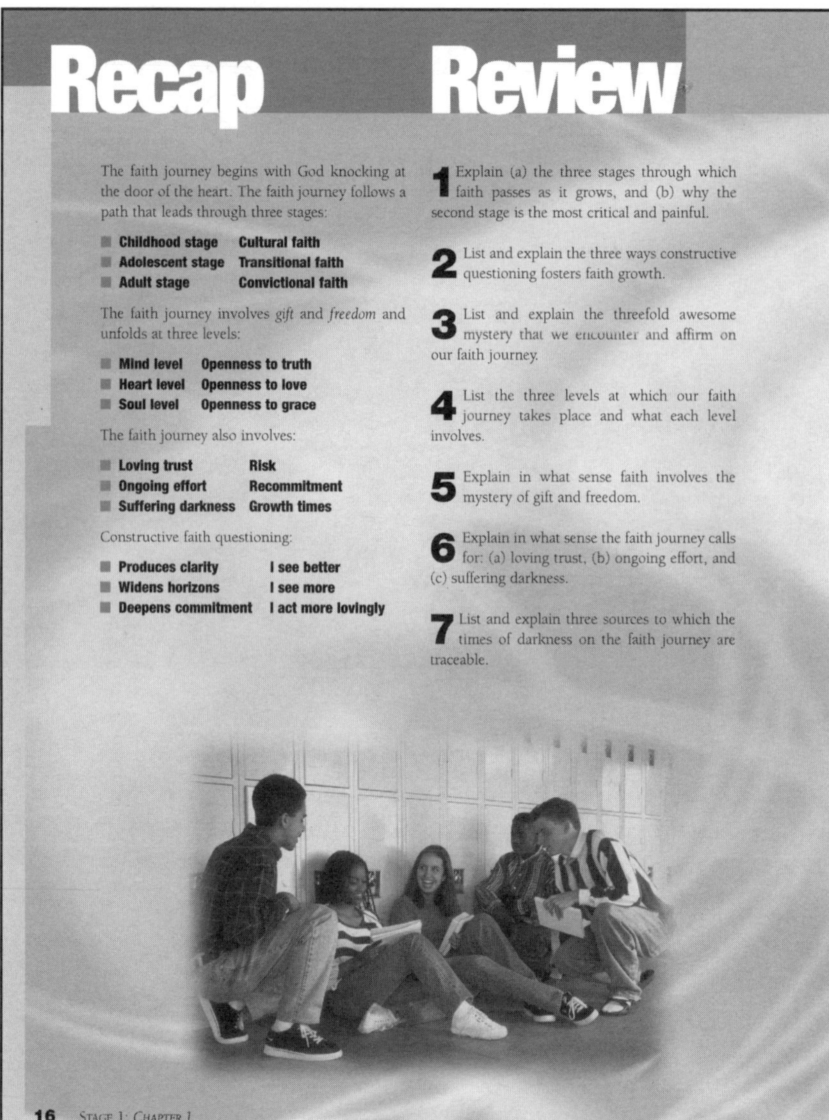

Recap Review

The faith journey begins with God knocking at the door of the heart. The faith journey follows a path that leads through three stages:

- **Childhood stage** **Cultural faith**
- **Adolescent stage** **Transitional faith**
- **Adult stage** **Convictional faith**

The faith journey involves *gift* and *freedom* and unfolds at three levels:

- **Mind level** **Openness to truth**
- **Heart level** **Openness to love**
- **Soul level** **Openness to grace**

The faith journey also involves:

- **Loving trust** **Risk**
- **Ongoing effort** **Recommitment**
- **Suffering darkness** **Growth times**

Constructive faith questioning:

- **Produces clarity** **I see better**
- **Widens horizons** **I see more**
- **Deepens commitment** **I act more lovingly**

1 Explain (a) the three stages through which faith passes as it grows, and (b) why the second stage is the most critical and painful.

2 List and explain the three ways constructive questioning fosters faith growth.

3 List and explain the threefold awesome mystery that we encounter and affirm on our faith journey.

4 List the three levels at which our faith journey takes place and what each level involves.

5 Explain in what sense faith involves the mystery of gift and freedom.

6 Explain in what sense the faith journey calls for: (a) loving trust, (b) ongoing effort, and (c) suffering darkness.

7 List and explain three sources to which the times of darkness on the faith journey are traceable.

16 STAGE 1: CHAPTER 1

TEST ANSWERS—The following are the answers to the test for Chapter 1. (See Appendix A, page 313.) All correct answers are worth four points.

Matching

1 = b	2 = a	3 = e	4 = d	5 = c

True/False

1 = T	2 = F	3 = T	4 = F
5 = F	6 = T	7 = T	8 = T
9 = F	10 = T	11 = F	

Fill in the Blanks

1:	a = Human nature	c = God
	b = Ourselves	
2:	a = Mind	b = Truth
	c = Heart	d = Love
	e = Soul	f = Faith

NOTES

Reflect

1 Ludolf Ulrich writes:

One night I was standing in the rain,
waiting for the bus. Up comes a man
who had had a bit too much to drink.
Tapping me on the chest
with an empty beer bottle, he asked,
"Do you believe in God?"

What a question to ask! Was it a joke?
Was he putting me on?
I ignored him, hoping he'd move on.
But he persisted.
Finally, I said, "Yes."
At this, I was ready for the worst—
a remark like, "Explain to me why!"

But he just stood there unsteadily,
looked me in the eye, and said,
"Man! Are you ever lucky!"
(Paraphrased)

■ ***In what sense was the man right in saying, "Man! Are you ever lucky!"?***
■ ***What are some reasons you believe in God?***

2 Dan Wakefield has won many awards for his writing (e.g., *TV Guide*, NBC TV, etc.). But none of these awards filled the void that he experienced after he had left God behind in college. To numb the pain caused by the void, he turned to drugs. When he began to turn back to God, the "return" road was not easy. A couple of times he turned back to drugs. In his book *Returning*, he writes:

Throughout all this I never lost faith in God,
never imagined he was not there.
It was just that his presence was obscured.
Then the storm broke like a fever,
and I felt in touch again. . . . I was grateful,
but I also knew that such storms . . .
would come again.

■ ***How do you explain the "faith storms" that so many Christians seem to experience?***
■ ***How are you handling your own storms?***

3 The final day of school had ended. The students had gone home, and the building was as quiet as a tomb. A teacher was in her classroom picking up a few books that had been carelessly left behind. Randomly, she picked up a book that still looked useable. It opened to this quote by Morris West:

The sanctions of being a man
are so horrendous,
that it seems madness to try to relate them
to any kind of divine plan.
A cancer will eat your guts . . .
a drunken fool with an automobile
will mow you down . . .
The believers are the lucky ones . . .
But belief is a gift . . .
If you have not the gift,
you are thrust back on reason.

In the margin the student wrote, "Tell me how to go about getting this gift. I really need it."

■ ***How would you answer the student?***

Reflect

1 a) *In what sense was the man right in saying, "Man! Are you lucky!"?*

■ *The man at the bus stop felt a "need to believe." But for some reason, he couldn't. Why?*

a) Maybe God could not yet give him the "gift of faith" because he would not yet opened himself to God.

b) Maybe, like the college girl in the text, he had an immature idea of God that needed to be upgraded.

c) Maybe he was involved in some behavior that was in conflict with his belief. To achieve inner peace, he had to resolve the conflict. So, he bent his belief to fit his behavior. Psychologists give the name cognitive dissonance *to the mental trick of twisting one's belief to fit one's behavior.*

b) *What are some reasons you believe in God?*

***NOTEBOOK*—**Have the students write out their responses in preparation for sharing them with the class.

2 a) *How do you explain the "faith storms" that so many Christians like Dan Wakefield seem to experience?*

■ *Recall that these "times of darkness" have as their source one of the following: human nature, God, or ourselves.*

b) *How are you handling your own storms?*

***ACTIVITY*—**Have the students copy the following questions on a sheet of paper and write out the answers to them.

1. Did your faith ever "go behind a cloud" for a rather long period of time?

2. If so, when (grade/high school)?

3. Do you recall what triggered the period of questioning, doubting, or darkness? Explain.

4. What things about your faith did you question or wonder about?

5. On a scale of 1 (low) to 5 (high), how would you evaluate your present faith in (a) God, (b) Jesus, (c) the Church?

Collect the responses. Tally them on the chalkboard, and discuss them.

You may wish to have the students put their names on the papers, and study the responses to help you get a feel for each student's frame of mind.

3 *How would you answer the student?*

■ *Perhaps the best answer to the question is to recount the story of Tommy. His problem was solved by opening his mind, heart, and soul.*

PRAYER TIME with the Lord

The author uses the *three* exercises under "Prayer Time" as written assignments (sometimes done outside of class, sometimes in class.) This is followed by sharing the responses and discussing them.

QUESTION ***Compose a similar prayer to God. Begin with this sentence: "Lord, there is a question I'd like to ask you."***

***HOMEWORK*—**The author comments in writing and briefly on all homework assignments. (It takes only a few minutes, if you instruct the students to write neatly and according to a standard format.) Typical brief comments are:

> *"Barb, this is a great prayer!"*
> *"Joe, you're really improving"*
> *"Matt, I really like these two lines of your prayer."*

The better responses are shared with the other students, providing the author of the response is agreeable.

Sometimes the author shares only a few lines that he thinks worth sharing. This gives him the opportunity to affirm more students, especially those who are not that skilled in expressing themselves. Usually, he can find "something" he can honestly affirm from their work.

It is amazing how the reflections improve with positive feedback. Even parents comment on this approach and what it means to the students.

***DISCUSS*—**Explain the last line: "For in searching, I am already there—as 'there' as any searcher can ever be."

■ *A searcher is like a traveler going from Chicago to New York. The traveler is not yet in New York, but as close to it as any traveler can be, at any given moment in the trip. In other words, life is a pilgrimage or a journey. It is not a destination.*

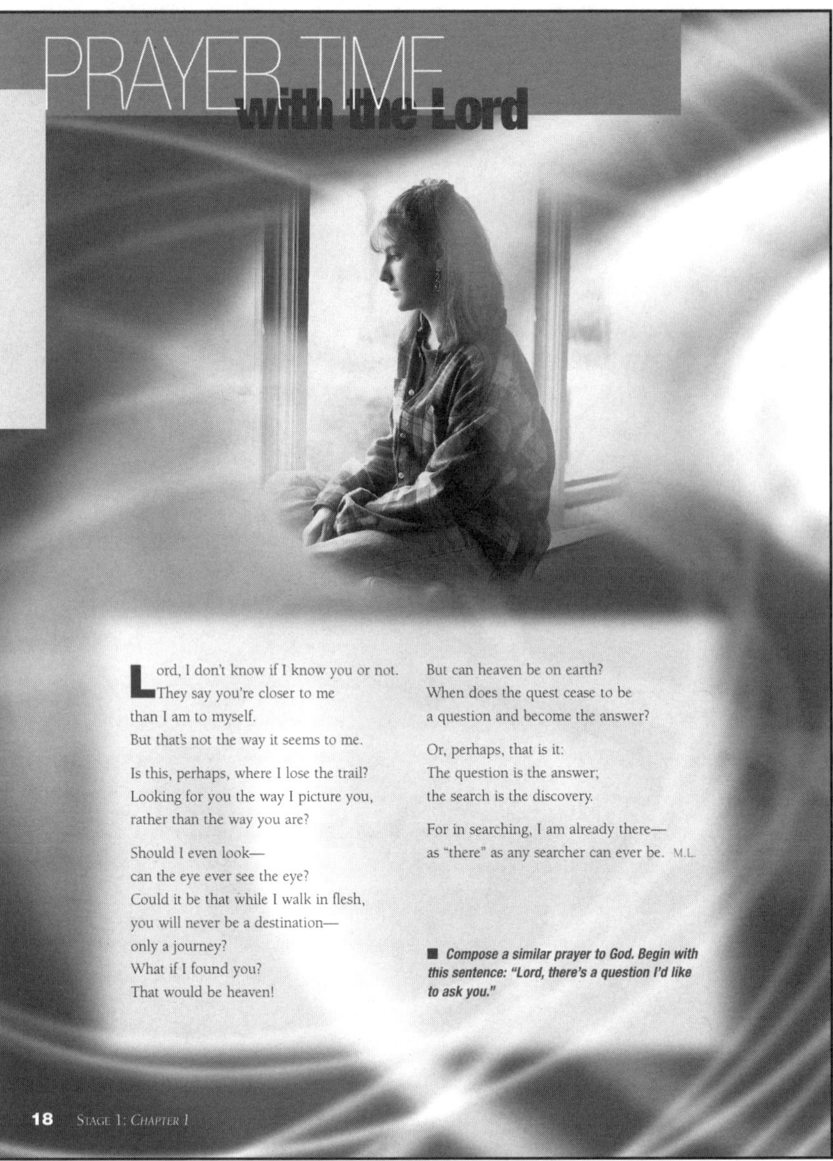

PRAYER TIME with the Lord

Lord, I don't know if I know you or not.
They say you're closer to me
than I am to myself.
But that's not the way it seems to me.

Is this, perhaps, where I lose the trail?
Looking for you the way I picture you,
rather than the way you are?

Should I even look—
can the eye ever see the eye?
Could it be that while I walk in flesh,
you will never be a destination—
only a journey?
What if I found you?
That would be heaven!

But can heaven be on earth?
When does the quest cease to be
a question and become the answer?

Or, perhaps, that is it:
The question is the answer;
the search is the discovery.

For in searching, I am already there—
as "there" as any searcher can ever be. M.L.

■ ***Compose a similar prayer to God. Begin with this sentence: "Lord, there's a question I'd like to ask you."***

18 STAGE 1: *CHAPTER 1*

PRAYER Journal

QUESTION ***Compose a prayer to God about some problem you are experiencing with, for example, faith, family, failure, or the future.***

***CLARIFY*—**Have the students reserve a special section of their notebooks for the exercises under this section.

***SHARE*—**The questions in this section can be done right in class in the student notebooks and shared later with a small group or the class.

NOTES

PRAYER Journal

Each year nearly 50,000 homeless teenagers show up at some 20 Covenant Houses seeking housing, counseling, medicine, or food. Frequently, they leave prayers in the house chapel. Here is an example of one of the prayers found there:

Help me, Dear Lord,
as I travel towards You.
There are many detours
which will try to distract me from you. . . .

Help me, though I may fall,
to continue my journey towards You.
Help me, Dear Lord.
I want so much to be with You.
PLEASE HELP ME, GOD, SISTER MARY ROSE MCGREADY

■ ***Compose a prayer to God about some problem you are experiencing with, for example, faith, family, failure, the future.***

SCRIPTURE Journal

1	**Opening to grace**	**John 1:35–51**
2	**Closing to grace**	**Matthew 19:16–26**
3	**Trusting in God**	**Genesis 22:1–19**
4	**Trusting in Jesus**	**Luke 5:1–11**
5	**Moments of darkness**	**Luke 24:13–35**

■ ***Pick one of the above passages. Read it prayerfully and write a short statement to Jesus expressing your feelings about it.***

STAGE 1: CHAPTER 1 **19**

SCRIPTURE Journal

QUESTION ***Pick one of the passages. Read it prayerfully and write a short statement to Jesus expressing your feelings about it.***

Treat the exercises in this section as you do those in the "Prayer Journal."

Again, have the students reserve a special section of their notebooks for these exercises.

Classroom Resources

CATECHISM

Catechism of the Catholic Church *Second Edition*

For further enrichment, you might refer to:

1. Faith	Index	pp. 791–92
	Glossary	p. 878
2. Trust	Index	p. 855

See also: God, Love, Abraham.

—AVAILABLE FROM THE UNITED STATES CATHOLIC CONFERENCE, WASHINGTON DC

VIDEO

Internalizing the Faith

William O'Malley, S.J.

Three 20-minute segments. Stimulating discussion of faith that includes knowing God, knowing about God, and putting it into practice. 1990.

—AVAILABLE FROM RCL, RESOURCES FOR CHRISTIAN LIVING, ALLEN, TX

What Makes Us Catholic:

Catholic Update Video

Thirty-minute multifaceted resource that highlights what Catholics believe and how they share their faith with others. 1998.

—AVAILABLE FROM ST. ANTHONY MESSENGER PRESS, CINCINNATI, OH

BOOK

The Challenge of Faith

John Powell, S.J.

Examines what authentic spirituality is from the viewpoint of ongoing interaction and dialogue with God. 1998.

—AVAILABLE FROM RCL, RESOURCES FOR CHRISTIAN LIVING, ALLEN, TX

NOTE

For a list of (1) General resources for professional background and (2) Addresses, phone/fax numbers of major publishing companies, see Appendix B of this Resource Manual.

CHAPTER 2
Divine Revelation

CHAPTER at a Glance

Chapter 1 dealt with the *nature* of faith. Chapter 2 deals with the twofold *object* of faith: (a) God and (b) God's Word.

DISCUSS—Have a student read aloud the four introductory paragraphs that begin with "Many people have done . . ." Reread paragraph four and ask:

In what sense did revelation begin with creation? In other words, how does it tell us something about God?

- *As a painting tells us something about the artist who painted it, so creation tells us something about God. Thus, Saint Paul writes: "Ever since God created the world, his invisible qualities . . . are perceived in the things that God has made."* ROMANS 1:20

DISCUSS—Ask: If we went to your room in your house, what are some of the things it might tell us about its occupant?

Have each student spend a few minutes listing five or six objects of interest in their own rooms. Tell them to be specific, like posters of *what* person, etc.

Next, have them share their responses in groups of three and four.

Finally, have them choose one set of responses to be read to the class, anonymously, to see if they can guess to which person in the group it belongs.

Caution the students to be respectful. Don't let the occasion be used to ridicule anyone for their tastes, etc.

Ways of knowing God

QUESTION **1 *What are three ways you could settle the argument?***

CHAPTER 2 Divine Revelation

Many people have done their best to write a report of the things that have taken place among us.

They wrote what we have been told
by those who saw these things
from the beginning
and who proclaimed the message. . . .

Because I have carefully studied
all these matters from their beginning,
I thought it would be good to write
an orderly account for you. LUKE 1:1–3

Divine revelation
is the Trinity's response
to the hunger in the human heart,
to know God and God's plan for us.
Revelation began with creation,
reached completion in Jesus,
and is passed on
by Tradition and Scripture.

CHAPTER at a Glance

Ways of knowing God
Experiencing God
Reasoning to God
Faith in God

Divine revelation
Handing on revelation
Sacred Tradition
Sacred Scripture

Divine inspiration
Inerrancy of Scripture
Interpretation of Scripture
Canon of Scripture

Ways of knowing God

A sailor was assigned to the gun crew on a small ship. He was given heat-resistant gloves and instructed to catch eighteen-inch shell casings as they ejected after each firing from the gun.

The reason for the gloves was that the casings were hot. The reason for catching them was to keep them from rolling around the gun pit and endangering the gun crew.

Suppose you were walking through a factory with a friend and you saw a workman wearing large gloves carrying a chunk of metal.

Your friend says, "I wonder why he's wearing such large gloves to carry such a small piece of metal." You explain to him that it's probably because the metal is hot. Your friend argues, "That metal certainly doesn't look hot. There must be another reason for the large gloves."

1 *What are three ways you could settle the argument?*

20

1	*Touch metal*	*Experience the heat*
2	*Spit on metal*	*Reason to the heat*
3	*Ask workman*	*Believe another's word*

NOTEBOOK—After discussing the three ways, list them on the chalkboard for entry into the students' notebooks.

By way of a reminder! Have the students do all work on 3-hole $8^1/_2$ x 11 paper. This permits them to insert written work in the proper section in their notebooks:

- *Section # 1* *Classwork*
- *Section # 2* *Homework*
- *Section # 3* *Prayer Journal*
- *Section # 4* *Scripture Journal*

Another teaching aid! Assign each student a number, depending on their seat assignment. (e.g., Mary Ellen, who sits in the third seat of the first row, is assigned #3.)

NOTES

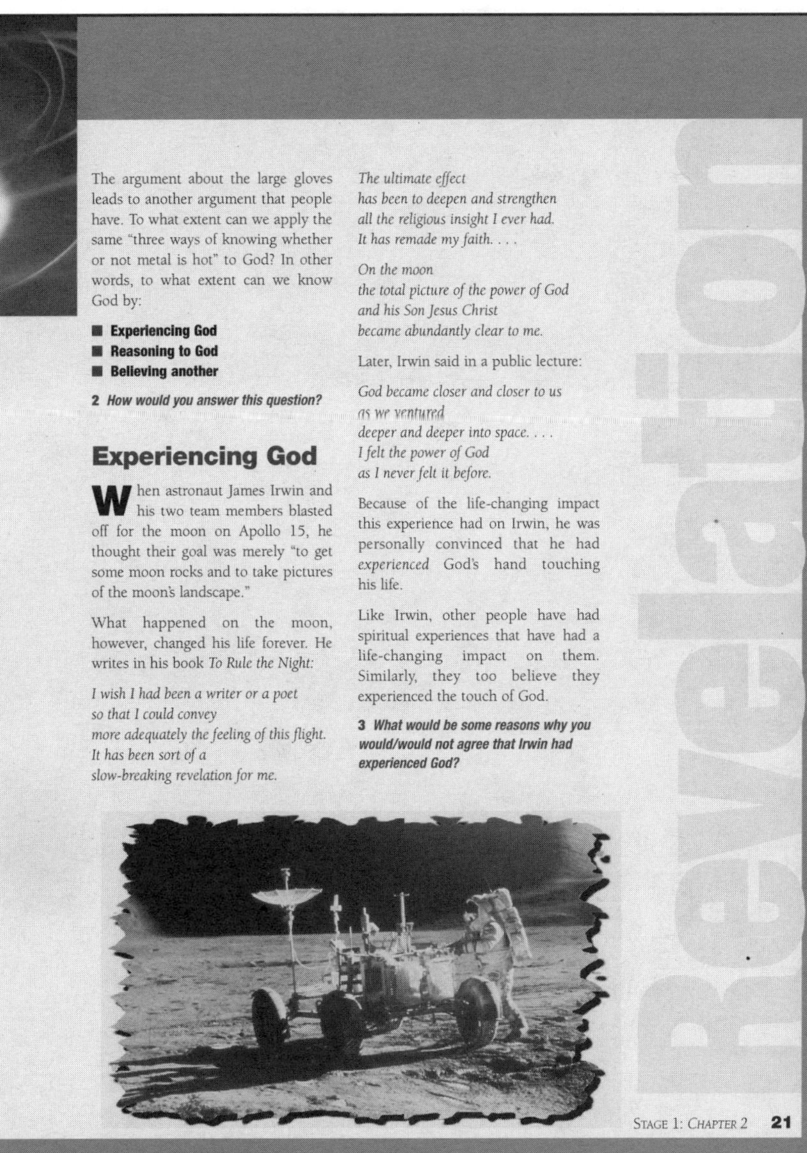

The argument about the large gloves leads to another argument that people have. To what extent can we apply the same "three ways of knowing whether or not metal is hot" to God? In other words, to what extent can we know God by:

- **Experiencing God**
- **Reasoning to God**
- **Believing another**

2 How would you answer this question?

Experiencing God

When astronaut James Irwin and his two team members blasted off for the moon on Apollo 15, he thought their goal was merely "to get some moon rocks and to take pictures of the moon's landscape."

What happened on the moon, however, changed his life forever. He writes in his book *To Rule the Night:*

I wish I had been a writer or a poet
so that I could convey
more adequately the feeling of this flight.
It has been sort of a
slow-breaking revelation for me.

The ultimate effect
has been to deepen and strengthen
all the religious insight I ever had.
It has remade my faith. . . .

On the moon
the total picture of the power of God
and his Son Jesus Christ
became abundantly clear to me.

Later, Irwin said in a public lecture:

God became closer and closer to us
as we ventured
deeper and deeper into space. . . .
I felt the power of God
as I never felt it before.

Because of the life-changing impact this experience had on Irwin, he was personally convinced that he had *experienced* God's hand touching his life.

Like Irwin, other people have had spiritual experiences that have had a life-changing impact on them. Similarly, they too believe they experienced the touch of God.

3 What would be some reasons why you would/would not agree that Irwin had experienced God?

Revelation

STAGE 1: CHAPTER 2 **21**

Have the students put their name and number in the upper right-hand corner of all written assignments (homework and classwork that is handed in before or after a class discussion). This facilitates sorting, grading, and returning assignments.

DISCUSS—Which of the three ways is the easiest way to learn? Why?

■ *Believing another. Experts say that 90% of our knowledge comes from reading (believing the word of another).*

QUESTION **2** ***How would you answer this question? (e.g., Can we learn about God by reasoning, experiencing, and believing?)***

The purpose of this question is to get the students thinking and to prepare them for what follows. Let the discussion continue as long as it seems productive.

Experiencing God

QUESTION **3** ***What would be some reasons why you would/would not agree that Irwin had experienced God?***

■ *Three tests help to shed light on whether it was a true experience. The tests are:*

1 *Faith* — *Did he grow more faith-filled?*
2 *Hope* — *Did he grow more hopeful?*
3 *Charity* — *Did he grow more loving?*

Faith, hope, and charity are called theological virtues because they come from God and lead to God. An increase in these virtues is a sign God has "graced" us. We can't increase them ourselves. We can only open our hearts to them.

CLARIFY—In his famous book, *Varieties of Religious Experience,* William James tells about a man who went for a walk one night across a field and ended up on a hilltop. As he stood there under the canopy of stars, something amazing took place within him.

The best he could describe it was this way:

■ *It was like orchestral music swelling and filling his soul until it seemed it would burst. All the while the "perfect stillness" held a presence that was all the more felt because it was not seen.*

I could not any more have doubted
that He was there than that I was.
Indeed, I felt myself to be,
if possible, the less real of the two.
My highest faith in God and truest idea
of God were then born in me.

Experiencing God is somewhat like experiencing the sun. We experience the sun not directly, but *indirectly* by its effects: heat, light, energy. Similarly, we experience God *indirectly* by increases in faith, hope, or love.

Share Your meditation

***CLARIFY*—**A. Cressy Morrison is a past president of the New York Academy of Science. His book, *Man Does Not Stand Alone,* lists seven reasons why he believes in God. One is the instinct of creatures.

Take the mother wasp. It stings a grasshopper in just the right place "so that it does not die but becomes unconscious and lives as a form of preserved meat." Then it digs a hole, puts the grasshopper in it, and lays its eggs there so that after they hatch her young can feed on the grasshopper. The mother wasp flies away after laying her eggs and never sees her young.

***DISCUSS*—**How do people experience a longing for God?

■ *Teenagers have a longing to be with friends. They long to be with those with whom they form community in a unique way, with those they love and by whom they are loved. Some interpret this as a kind of longing for God. Thus, a Cincinnati high-school football star said of the last day of practice before the state championship:*

> *"When we hugged . . . I felt a third Presence. It was the most unbelievable experience. It was as if God were hugging us as well. God had been there with us for four years—at every lift, run, practice. . . . My thirst for God is very much a thirst for . . . God in my friends."* David Bareswilt, *Liguorian* 9/99

If the spirit among the students is good, have them share their meditations in groups of three or four. Otherwise, collect the responses, review them, and choose two or three to share with the students in the next class session.

Reasoning to God

***DISCUSS*—**To illustrate the points of Von Braun and Saint Paul, imagine 26 word processors are placed at the entrance of the school. The first is labeled A, the second B, the third C, and so on, down to Z. Now, imagine that for four years students randomly punch the keys of the word processors as they enter and leave school. Then at the end of this time, printouts are made of the results.

What are the odds that the printouts for the A to Z word processors will be a perfect duplication of the A to Z sections of *Webster's Unabridged Dictionary*? The odds are so ridiculous they defy the imagination.

In a similar way, the only reasonable explanation of our universe is that an infinite intelligence created it. A good way to dramatize the point is to ask students the classic question: "Which came first: the chicken or the egg?"

SHARE YOUR **meditation**

The human heart was born with a "longing" or "hunger" for God. How did this longing get into the heart?

In *Man Does Not Stand Alone,* A. Cressy Morrison cites an example that points to a possible answer.

He tells how eels swim thousands of miles from Europe and America to Bermuda. There they breed, give birth, and die. Then some instinct or "inner longing" prompts their offspring to swim back across the same ocean in search of the river or lake from which their parent came.

The eel's "inner longing" for its true "home" is not unlike the "inner longing" that leads the heart to search for God who created it and put the "inner longing" in it.

■ ***How do people experience a longing for God?***

THINK about it

Follow the longing in your heart. It will lead you to Jesus, just as the star led the Magi to Jesus.

Reasoning to God

Wernher von Braun has been dubbed "the twentieth-century Columbus" of space travel. More than any other scientist, he was responsible for putting us on the moon.

Born in Germany, he and his team of scientists surrendered to the Allies near the end of World War II. They were sent to the United States. There he became the director of Alabama's Marshall Space Flight Center. Before he died, he wrote:

> *The natural laws of the universe*
> *are so precise that we have no difficulty*
> *building a spaceship to fly to the moon,*
> *and we can time the flight*
> *with the precision*
> *of a fraction of a second. . . .*
> *Anything . . . so precisely balanced . . .*
> *can only be the product of a Divine Idea.*
> Unpublished Lecture

Von Braun's words echo the inspired words of Saint Paul in his letter to the Romans. He comes to a similar conclusion:

> *Ever since God created the world,*
> *his invisible qualities,*
> *both his external power*
> *and his divine nature,*
> *have been clearly seen;*
> *they are perceived in the things*
> *that God has made.* Romans 1:20

Faith in God

Many people believe that we can know God from experience and reason. Others are not so sure. Most, however, agree that the surest way to know God is through God's own revelation to the human race. CCC 31–38

Dr. Warren Weaver, the author of several books on mathematical science, says:

> *I think a scientist*
> *has a real advantage in any struggle*
> *to conceive and believe in God.*
> *For he is expert in seeing the unseeable*
> *and in believing in the essentially*
> *undefinable.*

Weaver gives this example to illustrate: No scientist has succeeded in seeing or really defining an electron. For a while they thought of it as a particle, and then as a wave. Now they think of it as both or either. "Electron," says Dr. Weaver, "is simply the name for a consistent set of things that happen in certain circumstances."

4 Do you tend to be more comfortable with experiencing God or reasoning to God? Why?

Divine revelation

The word *revelation* is derived from the Latin word meaning "to unveil." Divine revelation is the "unveiling" of God and God's plan to the human race. CCC 50–67

> *This plan, which God will complete*
> *when the time is right,*
> *is to bring all creation together,*
> *everything in heaven and earth*
> *with Christ as head.* Ephesians 1:10

Revelation began in Old Testament times through such figures as Abraham and Moses. It reached completion

---

NOTES

Margaret Mehren

Margaret Mehren was 15 when she joined the Nazi youth movement in Germany. After the war she learned of the Nazi atrocities and was shocked. She realized that Hitler was not the glorious leader she thought he was.

It was in this frame of mind that she also began having doubts about her atheism. One night she picked up a Bible to read. But it made no sense, so she put it down. Some time later, she picked it up again. This time she opened to the Gospels. She wrote:

Something happened to me
when I read the words of Jesus.
I knew he was alive. . . .
I knew he was there in the room
with me,
even though I couldn't hear
or see anything. Jesus was real,
more real than anything
around me—
the furniture, my books,
the potted plants.
I was no longer alone.

A few years later, at age 21, she became a Franciscan nun and missionary to Africa.

in New Testament times in the life and teaching of Jesus. Saint Paul summed up God's revelation to us this way:

God spoke to our ancestors many times
and in many ways through the prophets;
but in these last days,
he has spoken to us through his Son.
HEBREWS 1:1–2

Before ascending to heaven, Jesus gave this commission to his disciples:

"Go . . . to all peoples everywhere
and make them my disciples:
Baptize them in the name of
the Father, the Son, and the Holy Spirit,
and teach them everything
I have commanded you." MATTHEW 28:19–20

With the coming of the Holy Spirit, the life and teaching of Jesus became the foundation and norm for our own Catholic faith. It is this divine revelation that the apostles, guided by the Holy Spirit, passed on to their successors, the bishops of the Church. CCC 74–79

Handing on revelation

We may think of divine revelation as having two stages: immediate and mediate.

By immediate revelation we mean the unveiling or communication of God and God's plan to God's people in biblical times.

By mediate revelation we mean the transmission of divine revelation to future generations. This is done in two ways, by:

- **Sacred Tradition** **Oral word**
- **Sacred Scripture** **Written word**

Sacred Scripture and Sacred Tradition are like two rails of a railroad track. They are inseparable, working together at all times to transmit God's Word to all people of all ages. CCC 80–83

Let us now take a closer look at Sacred Tradition, the oral communication of divine revelation.

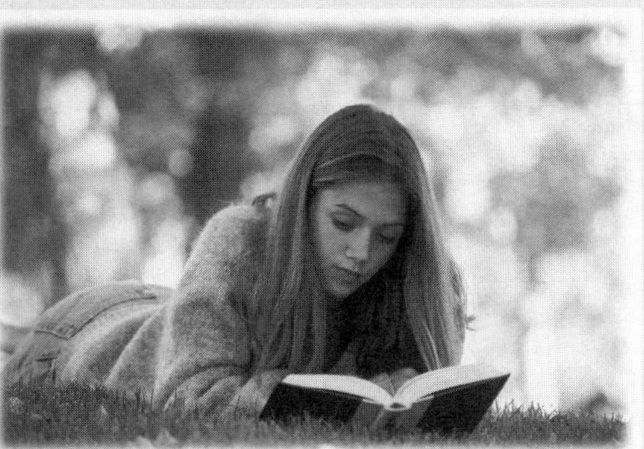

If we say the chicken, then we must ask, "Where did the egg from which the chicken was hatched come from?" And if we say the egg came first, then we must ask, "Where did the chicken come from that laid it?" Clearly, someone had to create one or the other to get the process started. That someone is God.

DISCUSS—Who created God?

- *God is uncreated. That's the point of the "chicken-egg" example. It illustrates that at some point we must come to an all-wise, all-powerful being who is uncreated: God.*

QUESTION **4** ***Do you tend to be more comfortable with experiencing God or reasoning to God? Why?***

We are very limited in what we can know about God from experience and reason. Only Jesus can give us a clear and certain knowledge of God. JOHN 1:18 Thus, we need divine revelation; without it, we are very much in the dark about God.

Divine revelation

CLARIFY—Divine revelation refers to *public* revelation (vs. *private* revelation). It ended with the last apostle's death. Even though public revelation has ended, we continue to uncover deeper meanings in it through study and prayer. CCC 66–67

What about "private revelations," like those at Fatima?

After investigation, the Church may rule that a specific "private revelation" is not in conflict with public revelation and may be believed; but it obliges no one to believe it.

Handing on Revelation

NOTEBOOK—Develop the following on the chalkboard for entry into notebooks:

Revelation — *Public (Bible/Tradition)*; *Private (e.g., visions)*

Immediate — *To prophets*; *To Apostles*

Mediate — *To future generations*; *Under Spirit's guidance*

CLARIFY—*Immediate* revelation takes place in various ways: ***deeds*** PSALMS 78:52, ***dreams*** MATTHEW 1:20, ***visions*** ISAIAH 6:1–8.

Stress that *mediate* revelation has to do with "handing on" *immediate* revelation.

DISCUSS—Use Mehren's experience to review:

1. *Three ways of knowing, page 20.*
2. *Three tests for discerning the authenticity of a reported experience of God, page 21.*

Share Your **meditation**

CLARIFY—Anderson was a correspondent for the Associated Press. He went through a conversion back to his faith in his captivity.

DISCUSS—What two points does Anderson make in the last paragraph?

■ *First, there can be no proof, in the sense of a scientific demonstration: like proving a liquid contains acid.*

Second, if we have faith in God, we can never be alone, even when our senses suggest we are.

SHARING—Again, if the class spirit is good, have the students share in groups of three or four. (They can form the groups by simply turning in their seats.) Otherwise, follow the second option: collect, read, and share the better ones in the next meeting.

Sacred Tradition

CLARIFY—Our Western culture finds it hard to see how teachings can be passed orally and unerringly from one generation to the next. Eastern cultures have no problem with this.

In his book, *Yoga and the Hindu Tradition*, Jean Varenne writes that Hindus who will be future leaders memorize hundreds of pages at an age when they do not understand what they are learning. They also perform such feats as reciting the text backward.

Sacred Scripture

QUESTION **5 *How does the final sentence indicate a significant time lapse between the event and the recording of it?***

■ *The expression "to this very day" indicates this. This same expression is found in Matthew 27:8.*

Concerning the field bought with the money Judas got for betraying Jesus, it says: "That is why it is called 'Field of Blood' to this very day."

CLARIFY—An oral tradition that was not recorded in Scripture is that Mary was a virgin all her life. Some suggest she was a virgin before Jesus' birth only. They base this on Luke 2:7, which says Mary gave birth to her *firstborn* son. *Firstborn,* however, is a *legal* title, entitling the first male to a special share in the family inheritance. DEUTERONOMY 21:17. It doesn't imply *more* children. For example, an ancient Egyptian tomb marker identifies a mother "who died giving birth to her firstborn."

Mark 6:3 refers to Jesus' "brothers." The classical Greek word for a blood brother (which Mark uses) is *adelphos.* But ancient documents show the term "brothers" was used in a wide sense.

SHARE YOUR **meditation**

Terry Anderson was kidnapped by Shiite Muslim extremists in 1985. He spent the next seven years in Lebanon in windowless cells, often in chains and in pain.

In December 1987, he nearly lost it, banging his head against a wall until blood oozed out. After his release in 1992, he remarked that some cynics deny God's existence, saying:

We made him up out of our need.
I only say that once in
my own need.
I felt a light and warm
and loving touch
that eased my soul
and banished doubt
and let me go on to the end.

It is not proof—there can be none.
Faith is what you have when
you're alone and find you're not.
Media interview

■ ***Explain the two points in the last paragraph.***
■ ***What is the closest thing to such an experience that you've had?***

Sacred Tradition

Toward the end of his gospel, Saint John refers to Sacred Tradition this way:

There are many other things that Jesus did.
If they were all written down one by one,
I suppose that the whole world
could not hold the books. JOHN 21:25

In other words, not everything that Jesus did or taught got written down. Saint Paul makes the same point about his own teaching. Some things he taught through word of mouth (preaching) and some things through writing (letters). He writes:

Hold on to those truths
which we taught you,
both in our preaching [Tradition]
and in our letter [Scripture].
2 THESSALONIANS 2:15

The first community of Christians began with no written gospels. They simply passed on God's Word orally.

This brings us to the written form of communication of divine revelation.

Sacred Scripture

At first, the things that Jesus said and did were passed on almost entirely by word of mouth. Only later were they written down. This is clear from the Gospels themselves.

For example, Saint Matthew says that after Jesus rose from the tomb on Easter morning, the guards were paid to say that the disciples stole his body while they were asleep. He then adds: "And so that is the report spread around by the Jews to this very day." MATTHEW 28:15

5 *How does the final sentence indicate a significant time lapse between the event and the recording of it?*

And so, the four Gospels passed through three stages in the process of

reaching the form they now have today. CCC 126 These stages are:

■ **Life**	**What Jesus said and did**
■ **Oral**	**What apostles preached**
■ **Written**	**What evangelists wrote**

NOTES

John refers explicitly to all three stages when he writes in his First Letter:

What we have seen [life stage] . . .
we announce to you [oral stage]. . . .
We write this in order [written stage]
that our joy may be complete.
1 John 1:3–4

An analogy might help to illustrate these three stages: life, oral, and written.

The ocean floor is littered with thousands of seashells. In time some of these *floor* shells wash up onto the beach.

One day an artist is out walking and sees the *beach* shells. She picks up the most beautiful ones, takes them home and shapes them into a lovely *vase*.

6 Which gospel stages do the following shells correspond to and why: floor, beach, vase? Explain.

Divine inspiration

The novel *The Last Temptation of Christ*, by Nikos Kazantzakis, portrays Matthew sitting at a table with an open notebook. Jesus enters. Matthew shows him the notebook, saying, "Rabbi, here I recount your works."

After reading a few lines, Jesus asks, "Who told you these things?" Matthew replies, "The angel." Jesus asks, "What angel?" Matthew replies, "The one who comes each night, as I take up my pen to write. He dictates what I should write."

This brings us to the question of divine inspiration. CCC 100–106 Saint Paul says, "All Scripture is inspired by God." 2 Timothy 3:16 When we think of divine inspiration, we have to avoid two extremes.

We should not imagine that the Holy Spirit dictated to the biblical writer as an executive might dictate an important letter. Nor should we imagine that the Holy Spirit has acted simply as a kind of "watchdog" keeping the biblical writers from making mistakes as they wrote.

Rather, we should envision inspiration as the Holy Spirit working in and through the personal talents of the biblical writers to communicate all and only what God wanted to say through them.

7 In what sense may we say Sacred Scripture is "the Word of God in the Words of Men"?

Inerrancy of Scripture

Although Sacred Scripture contains many accurate historical facts and descriptions that reflect the times and events of the day, this was not its goal.

Rather, guided by the Holy Spirit, its goal was to interpret the spiritual meaning of the events of the day. As a result, like Sacred Tradition, it is free from religious error, that is, *in matters related to salvation*. CCC 107–8

PRAYER hotline

God in heaven,
when the idea of you
awakes in my heart,
let it not awaken
like a frightened bird
that thrashes about in panic,
but like a child
waking from a nap—
its face aglow
with a trusting smile.

Soren Kierkegaard (free translation)

Stage 1: Chapter 2 **25**

For example, tribal members were referred to as brothers. Numbers 16:10 Citizens of the same nation were also referred to as brothers. Deuteronomy 23:7

Finally, on Calvary, Jesus gave Mary to John to be cared for after his death. John 19:27 Why do this if Mary had other children?

> *QUESTION* ***6 Which gospel stages do the following shells correspond to and why: floor, beach, vase? Explain.***

NOTEBOOK—With the help of the students, develop the following diagram for entry into the student notebooks:

Floor (Life stage)	*Jesus said and did*
Beach (Oral stage)	*Apostles preached*
Vase (Written stage)	*Evangelists wrote*

Divine inspiration

CLARIFY—With the help of students, develop the following two diagrams on the chalkboard for entry in student notebooks:

1 *Three references to inspiration:*

Spirit inspired David	*Mark 13:36*
Spirit moved prophets	*2 Peter 1:21*
God inspired Bible	*2 Timothy 3:16*

2 *Three theories of inspiration:*

Divine dictation	*Writer = robot*
Negative assistance	*Spirit = watchdog*
Positive assistance	*Both = team*

CLARIFY—*Divine dictation* fails to explain style differences, e.g., Isaiah is elegant; Amos crude. (Did God have a bad day when he "dictated" Amos?) *Negative assistance* fails because it reduces the Bible to a human work: the "word of men," not "word of God." The theory of *positive assistance* has the Holy Spirit and the human writer act as a team. (The Spirit acts through the talents of the writer.)

> *QUESTION* ***7 In what sense may we say Sacred Scripture is "the Word of God in the Words of Men?***

"Word of God"	*Spirit's role*
"Words of Men"	*Human writers' role*

Inerrancy of Scripture

CLARIFY—Stress that "inerrancy" means "free from religious error in matters related to salvation. Thus, the Spirit did not protect the biblical writers from scientific or historical error. God never intended to compose books on science and history.

Nor is the Bible free from *scientific* error. Deuteronomy 14:7 says hares chew cud, which isn't scientifically correct.

Nor is the Bible free from *historical* error. 1 Samuel 31:4 says Saul killed himself, while 2 Samuel 1:9–10 says someone else killed him.

Stress that God is an infinitely loving Father.

ART Connection

DISCUSS—Why the skull in the painting?

- *It reminded Jerome that he, too, would die—like the person whose skull it used to be. Jerome should, therefore, live accordingly attentive to this fact of life.*

CLARIFY—Jerome (A.D. 331–420) began life concerned mainly with the things of this world. One night he had a dream in which a voice reminded him that "your heart will always be where your treasure is." LUKE 12:34 Upon waking he was stricken with remorse and resolved to break with the world and devote the rest of his life to the study of God's Word.

CLARIFY—Caravaggio (1565–1609) was a disciple of the naturalistic school. In other words, contrary to later painters, like Van Gogh (1853–1890), his paintings were more "photographic" in style. (Direct the students to Van Gogh's "The Good Samaritan" on page 253.) Caravaggio's work is filled with dramatic interplays between light and darkness—highly in evidence in his painting of Saint Jerome.

BIBLE Connection

CLARIFY—It is believed that a religious group of "monks," called Essenes, hid the scrolls to protect them from invading Roman armies. They were put in large jars and sealed up to protect them from animals and insects.

Ancient peoples commonly put scrolls and important documents in jars. Jeremiah refers to this practice, saying, "Take these deeds and place them in a clay jar, so that they may be preserved for years to come." JEREMIAH 32:10

Interpretation of Scripture

CLARIFY—Pope Pius XII told biblical scholars:

THINK about it A thumbprint in the Bible is more important than a footprint on the moon.
E.C. McKenzie

ART Connection

This seventeenth-century painting was done by Italian painter Caravaggio. It portrays Saint Jerome translating the Bible into Latin.

BIBLE Connection

People ask, "Do we have the original biblical manuscripts?" The answer is no.

Remarkably, the oldest copies we have were found in caves near Qumran on the northwest corner of the Dead Sea. The discovery of these "Dead Sea Scrolls" reads like a novel.

While searching for a stray goat, a boy came upon a hole in a hillside. When he threw a stone through it, he heard something break. It turned out to be a tall jar containing an ancient scroll of the Book of Isaiah.

The boy's discovery touched off a hunt for more scrolls in more caves. Between 1947 and 1956, eleven caves yielded 800 documents (mostly fragments). Some 200 were documents of practically every book of the Hebrew Bible.

Interpretation of Scripture

Shortly before ascending to his Father in heaven, Jesus made a remarkable promise to his disciples. He said:

"When . . . the Spirit comes,
who reveals the truth about God,
he will lead you into all the truth."
JOHN 16:13

By these words, Jesus assured his disciples that the Holy Spirit would assist them in interpreting, recording, formulating, and transmitting divine revelation to future generations.

This brings us to the important task of interpreting God's Word.

The Church, or community of Jesus' followers, gave birth to Sacred Scripture, so to speak. Therefore, the awesome responsibility of preserving and interpreting Scripture falls to the Church, guided by the Holy Spirit. CCC 109–19

8 ***From a purely natural point of view, why is it logical that the Church be the interpreter of Sacred Scripture?***

Canon of Scripture

As used in the Bible, the word canon refers to the official list of books inspired by God. Therefore, these books are the "measuring stick," or norm, for our Christian faith.

26 STAGE 1: CHAPTER 2

You must go back, as it were, in spirit to those remote centuries of the East. With the aid of history, archaeology, ethnology, and other sciences, you must determine accurately what modes of writing the ancient writers would likely use, and in fact did use.

As a result remarkable advances in biblical interpretation have been made in recent years.

And new sciences, like biblical archaeology, have cast new light on passages and stories. Never, since the biblical time itself, has so much new information been available.

For example, in June 1961, a group of Israeli archaeologists unearthed a portion of a dedication stone while excavating an ancient amphitheater near Caesarea-on-the-Sea.

NOTES

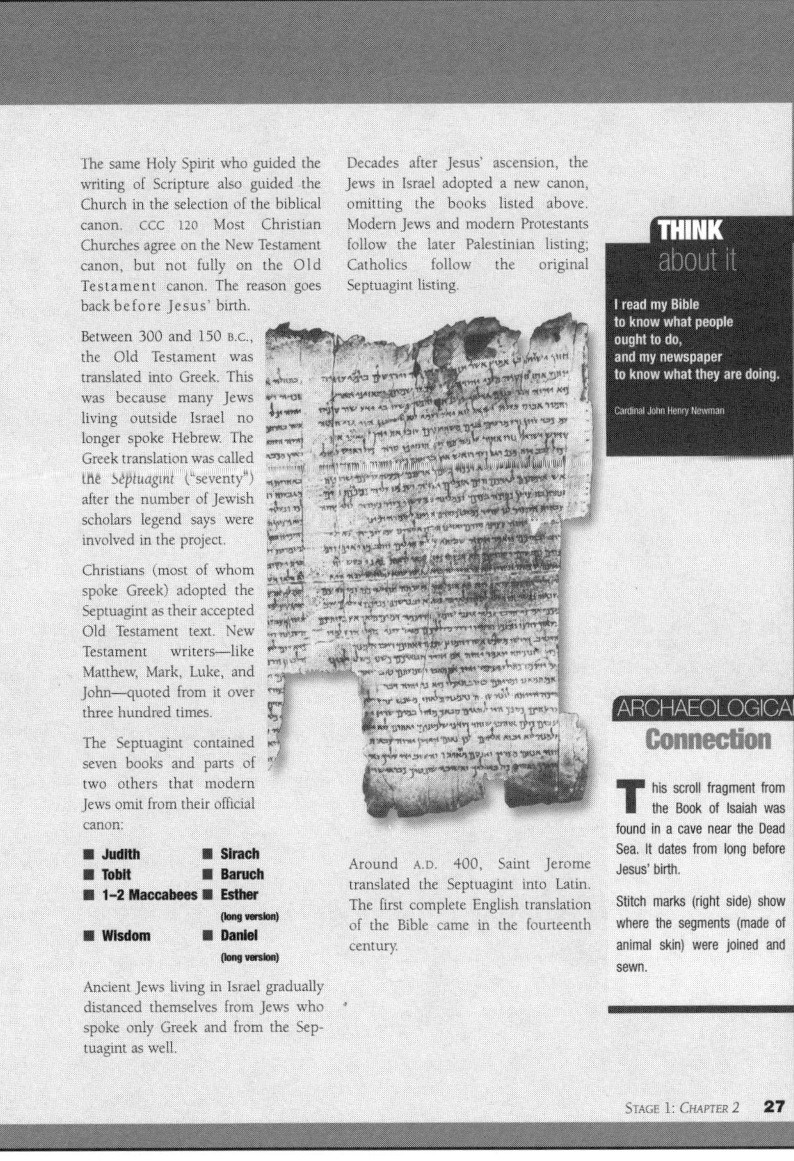

The same Holy Spirit who guided the writing of Scripture also guided the Church in the selection of the biblical canon. CCC 120 Most Christian Churches agree on the New Testament canon, but not fully on the Old Testament canon. The reason goes back before Jesus' birth.

Between 300 and 150 B.C., the Old Testament was translated into Greek. This was because many Jews living outside Israel no longer spoke Hebrew. The Greek translation was called the *Septuagint* ("seventy") after the number of Jewish scholars legend says were involved in the project.

Christians (most of whom spoke Greek) adopted the Septuagint as their accepted Old Testament text. New Testament writers—like Matthew, Mark, Luke, and John—quoted from it over three hundred times.

The Septuagint contained seven books and parts of two others that modern Jews omit from their official canon:

- **Judith**
- **Tobit**
- **1–2 Maccabees**
- **Wisdom**
- **Sirach**
- **Baruch**
- **Esther** (long version)
- **Daniel** (long version)

Ancient Jews living in Israel gradually distanced themselves from Jews who spoke only Greek and from the Septuagint as well.

Decades after Jesus' ascension, the Jews in Israel adopted a new canon, omitting the books listed above. Modern Jews and modern Protestants follow the later Palestinian listing; Catholics follow the original Septuagint listing.

THINK about it

I read my Bible to know what people ought to do, and my newspaper to know what they are doing.

Cardinal John Henry Newman

Around A.D. 400, Saint Jerome translated the Septuagint into Latin. The first complete English translation of the Bible came in the fourteenth century.

ARCHAEOLOGICAL Connection

This scroll fragment from the Book of Isaiah was found in a cave near the Dead Sea. It dates from long before Jesus' birth.

Stitch marks (right side) show where the segments (made of animal skin) were joined and sewn.

STAGE 1: CHAPTER 2 27

The first line read TIBERIEUM,
the second (PON)TIUS PILATUS,
the third (PRAE)FECTUS IUD(EAE).

The stone was part of a larger statement of dedication to Tiberius Caesar by Pontius Pilate, Prefect of Judea.

In ways like this, biblical archaeologists are confirming stories and passages in the Bible.

QUESTION 8 ***From a purely natural point of view, why is it logical that the Church be the interpreter of Scripture?***

■ *The Church is the mother of the New Testament. The New Testament was produced in the Church, by the Church, and for the Church. Therefore, the Church is the logical one to interpret the meaning of what it composed under the guidance of the Holy Spirit.*

Canon of Scripture

CLARIFY—The word *testament* comes from the Greek meaning a "sacred" agreement" (covenant). The Old Testament is God's covenant with Israel mediated by Moses. The New Testament is God's covenant with all people mediated by Jesus.

NOTEBOOK—With the help of the students, develop the following diagram for entry into their notebooks:

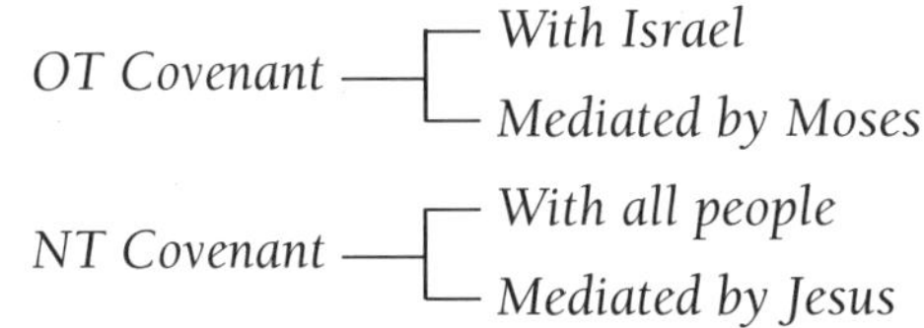

ARCHAEOLOGICAL Connection

CLARIFY—Dr. Willard Libby of the University of Chicago used a Geiger counter to date the Isaiah scroll (26 feet long when unrolled).

His conclusion? It dated back about 200 years before Jesus. Jesus, himself, could have read from it in the episode described in Luke 4:16.

Unlike English, which reads from left to right and front to back, Hebrew reads from right to left and back to front. The biblical authors did not divide their scrolls into chapters and verses.

Thirteenth-century scholars divided the Bible into verses; 16th-century scholars numbered the verses.

CLARIFY—The Dead Sea Scrolls are important for two reasons, especially.

1 *They are nearly 1,000 years older than the oldest* biblical *manuscripts known to us.*

2 *The* nonbiblical *scrolls (also found in the caves) not only fill in a gap of little-known Jewish history between 200* B.C. *and* A.D. *50, but also provide important new data to help clarify biblical writings from this period.*

Recap

This section summarizes the key points of the chapter. To repeat what was said in chapter 1, an easy way to construct a quick "daily quiz" is to convert the "summary diagrams" found here and in the text into "matching exercises" or "true-false" questions. Here's an example of "true-false" questions:

1. __F__ *By immediate* revelation, *we mean revelation to people of all times.*
2. __T__ Mediate *revelation involves "handing on" God's Word through Sacred Tradition or Sacred Scripture*
3. __T__ Inerrancy *means free from religious error in matters relating to salvation.*

You might give a total of ten "daily quiz" questions in the course of the week. Hold off the grade until the end of the week. Thus, a student who gets nine answers correct during the week is given a grade of 90% for the week. "Daily quiz" arrangements help to keep students alert and involved.

Review

DAILY QUIZ—The review questions may be assigned (one or two at a time) for homework or a part of the brief daily quiz described above. For example, the first review question reads: "List and briefly explain the three ways by which we can learn things." (This question could be worth six points: three points for "listing" and three points for "describing.")

CHAPTER TESTS—Reproducible chapter tests are found in Appendix A. For consistency and ease in grading, quizzes are restricted to (1) "Matching," (2) "True/False," and (3) "Fill in the Blanks."

TEST ANSWERS—The following are the answers to the test for Chapter 2." (See Appendix A, page 313.) All correct answers are worth four points.

Recap

Divine revelation is God's self-communication to the human race:

■ **Immediately**	**To people in biblical times**
■ **Mediately**	**To people of all times**

Mediate revelation involves the "handing on" of God's Word through:

■ **Sacred Tradition**	**Spoken word**
■ **Scripture**	**Written word**

Mediate and immediate revelation take place under the guidance of the Holy Spirit and, therefore, are:

■ **Inspired**	**The Word of God in the words of human beings**
■ **Inerrant**	**Free from religious error in matters relating to salvation**

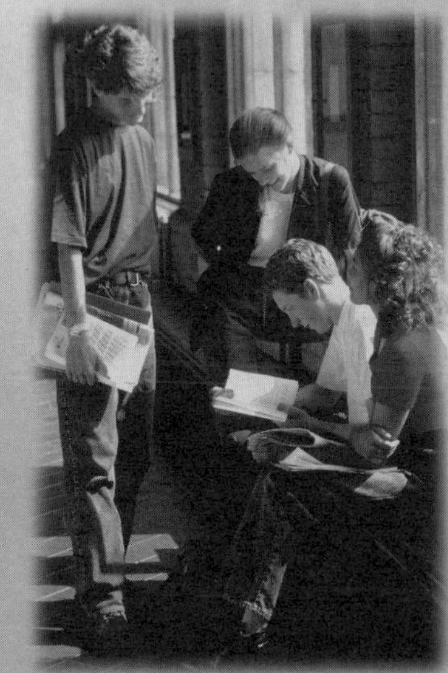

Review

1. List and briefly explain the three ways by which we can learn things.
2. What made astronaut James Irwin conclude that his spiritual experience on the Apollo 15 mission was truly an experience of God?
3. What convinced Werhner von Braun that the universe was created by God?
4. Explain (a) divine revelation, (b) immediate revelation, and (c) mediate revelation.
5. List and briefly explain the two ways divine revelation is transmitted to future generations.
6. How are (a) Sacred Tradition and (b) Sacred Scripture like the two rails of a train track, and how does Paul refer to each?
7. List and briefly explain (a) the three stages the four Gospels passed through to reach the form they now have today, and (b) how John refers to them.
8. List and briefly explain (a) the two extremes to avoid in how we envision divine inspiration, and (b) how we ought to envision it.
9. From what error is Scripture free?
10. What is the Septuagint, and how does it help to explain why the Catholic Bible differs from the Protestant Bible?

28 STAGE 1: CHAPTER 2

Matching

1 = f	2 = h	3 = c	4 = d
5 = a	6 = e	7 = b	8 = g

True/False

1 = F	2 = T	3 = T	4 = T
5 = F	6 = T	7 = F	8 = T
9 = T	10 = F		

Fill in the Blanks

1. (a) Experiencing
   (b) Reasoning
   (c) Believing
2. (a) Life
   (b) Oral
   (c) Written
3. Dead Sea Scrolls

NOTES

Reflect

1 *It was a peaceful evening.*
My mom and brother and sister and I
Were on our way
To a high school basketball game. . . .
It was quiet in the car. . . .
I was just looking out the window
at the still night, enjoying the stars . . .
happy to be on my way to the game.
The happiness that I was feeling
grew deeper and . . . I noticed that tears
were rolling down my cheeks.
This was really weird. . . . Then I understood.
This was how full joy could be . . .
a joy that comes only from God.

JACQUE BRAMAN, QUOTED IN *HOW CAN I FIND GOD?*

A study showed that certain situations were more likely than others to trigger a religious experience in us (e.g., awareness of God's presence). Four such situations were:

a. Reading the Bible
b. Contemplating nature
c. Meditating quietly
d. Listening to music

■ ***List the above four situations in the order that you have found they are more apt to trigger an awareness of God in you.***
■ ***List one or two other situations that tend to do it.***
■ ***Describe a situation when this happened.***

2 Father Francis F. Buckley, S.J., teaches theology at the University of San Francisco. He writes:

One of the ways
my students have surprised me
is that they find God in failure
more than in success or beauty.
The death of a parent or relative,
the breakup of a love affair,
the loss of a game or a job are
for them windows of discovery.

■ ***Why would failures lead students to God more than success or beauty?***
■ ***To what extent is this true of you? Explain.***
■ ***Describe a concrete time when a major failure or tragedy helped you to find God or led you to experience God in a special way.***

3 Suppose a TV camera crew got into a time machine and flew back into history to Jesus' time. Suppose the crew filmed Jesus' entire life, fed it into a computer, and programmed it. By keyboarding the name of any event, you could bring it up on a monitor and see and hear exactly what the Apostles saw and heard.

Now suppose you are given this choice. You can trade the four printed Gospels (as we now have them) for the computerized film. If you traded, however, the human race would lose the four printed Gospels forever. They would be totally destroyed and replaced by the film.

■ ***Why would/wouldn't you make that trade?***
■ ***List some of the advantages and disadvantages that a film of Jesus' life would have.***

Reflect

1 ***a) List the above four situations in the order that you have found they are more apt to trigger an awareness of God in you.***
b) List one or two other situations that tend to do it.
c) Describe a situation when this happened.

ACTIVITY—Have the students respond in writing. Tally and discuss the results. To help the students get started, share this response by a Chicago student:

■ *I was one of 70,000 people at a rock concert. There was a great sound system, so the music really energized me. . . . After one of the bands played a rock classic, I looked around me. Wow! What a sight! . . . As far as I could see everyone was standing up, clapping, and moving to the music. A fantastic feeling rushed over me. Then I thought . . . "God must be present. He has to be!"* MIKE GATTO

2 ***a) Why would failures lead students to God more than success or beauty?***
b) To what extent is this true of you? Explain.
c) Describe a concrete time when a major failure or tragedy helped you to find God or led you to experience God in a special way.

■ *Buckley says "failure made them realize they are not self-sufficient, not in control of life, so they look beyond themselves. They learn a lot from failure. It is one of the paradoxical secrets of Christian life."* GROWING IN THE CHURCH: FROM BIRTH TO DEATH

3 ***a) Why would/wouldn't you make that trade?***

■ *No biblical expert would make the trade. Reason? Jesus' disciples often did not understand something Jesus said or did* (MARK 9:9–10, JOHN 12:16). *It would be the same with the film. What happened to the disciples later to help them understand? Exactly what Jesus said would happen:*

"The Holy Spirit . . . will teach you everything and make you remember all that I have told you." The difference Pentecost made may be likened to developing film in a Polaroid camera. After you snap the picture, the film rolls out, but nothing seems to be on it. Then the "light" strikes it. Immediately, shapes and colors begin to appear.

The events of Jesus' life were like that. They didn't reveal their correct meaning until the "light of the Holy Spirit" struck them on Pentecost.

b) List some of the advantages and disadvantages that a film of Jesus' life would have.

■ *Advantage: You'd see exactly what happened. (But like the disciples, we'd probably not understand it.)*
Disadvantage: It would be in a strange language and take 33 years to view.

PRAYER TIME with the Lord

The author uses the three activities under "Prayer Time" as a written assignment (sometimes in class, sometimes outside of class). This is followed by sharing and discussing the responses.

QUESTION ***Compose a few paragraphs about what you would say to God in a situation like this.***

ACTIVITY—You might offer the students an alternate activity. Have them describe a "fantasy trip" of their own creation through the depths of the ocean.

The author comments briefly and in writing on all compositions. Always have the students do their writing on three-ring, lined, $8\frac{1}{2}$ x 11 binder paper. Encourage students to illustrate their compositions (photos from magazines or drawings or the Internet).

Reading and commenting on papers takes only a few minutes, if you instruct the students to write neatly and according to a standard format. As mentioned earlier, comments may be very brief. Here are some samples:

"Cindy, keep up the improvement!"

"Zack, I enjoyed reading this."

"Chris, I really like the part I underlined."

It's amazing what a few comments can do. You literally see the compositions improve from assignment to assignment.

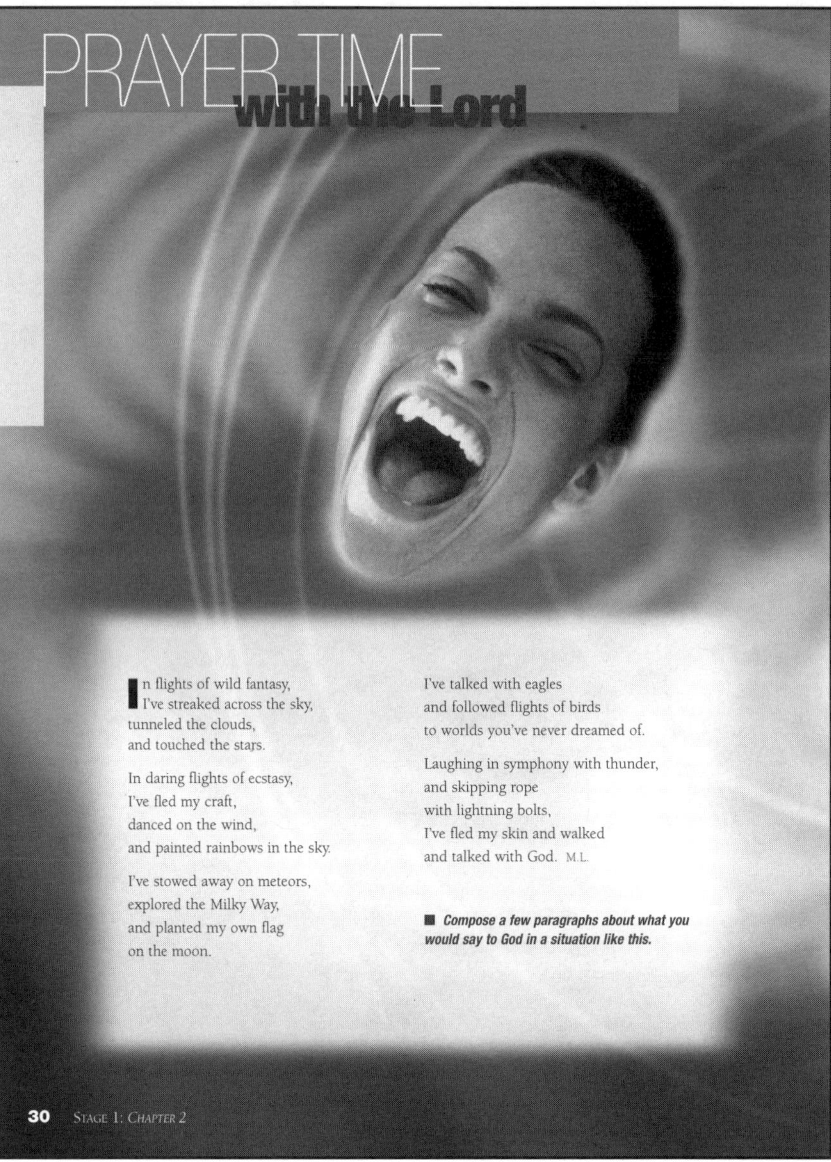

PRAYER TIME with the Lord

In flights of wild fantasy,
I've streaked across the sky,
tunneled the clouds,
and touched the stars.

In daring flights of ecstasy,
I've fled my craft,
danced on the wind,
and painted rainbows in the sky.

I've stowed away on meteors,
explored the Milky Way,
and planted my own flag
on the moon.

I've talked with eagles
and followed flights of birds
to worlds you've never dreamed of.

Laughing in symphony with thunder,
and skipping rope
with lightning bolts,
I've fled my skin and walked
and talked with God. M.L.

■ ***Compose a few paragraphs about what you would say to God in a situation like this.***

30 STAGE 1: CHAPTER 2

PRAYER Journal

QUESTION ***Write a similar prayer about God. Make it as practical and down-to-earth as you can.***

Have the students reserve a special section of their notebooks for the exercises under this section. Again, encourage them to illustrate their prayers with drawings or photos cut from magazines or newspapers.

The questions in this section can be answered right in class on three-ring paper and later inserted in their notebooks.

NOTES

PRAYER Journal

Cardinal John Henry Newman wrote a prayer that focused on God's intimacy in dealing with us:

God knows what is in me,
all my peculiar feelings and thoughts . . .

God sympathizes with me in my hopes
and temptations. . . .

God hears my voice,
the beating of my heart and my breathing.

I do not love myself
more than God loves me.

I cannot shrink from pain
more than God dislikes my bearing it.

SLIGHTLY ADAPTED AND TRANSPOSED INTO THE FIRST PERSON.

■ ***Write a similar prayer about God. Make it as practical and down-to-earth as you can.***

SCRIPTURE Journal

1	**Reasoning to God**	**Romans 1:20–25**
2	**Experiencing God**	**Genesis 3:1–17**
3	**Believing in God**	**John 20:24–29**
4	**Recording Scripture**	**Luke 1:1–4**
5	**Scripture is inspired**	**2 Timothy 3:14–4:5**

■ ***Pick one of the above passages. Read it prayerfully and write a short statement to Jesus expressing your feelings about it.***

STAGE 1: *CHAPTER 2* **31**

SCRIPTURE Journal

QUESTION ***Pick one of the passages. Read it prayerfully and write a short statement to Jesus expressing your feelings about it***

Treat the exercises in this section as you do those in the "Prayer Journal."

Again, have the students reserve a special section of their notebooks for these exercises—and have them use illustrations, if they wish.

Classroom Resources

CATECHISM

Catechism of the Catholic Church *Second Edition*

For further enrichment, you might refer to:

1. Revelation	Index	pp. 791–92
	Glossary	p. 878
2. Sacred Scripture	Index	p. 855
3. Tradition	Index	p. 855
	Glossary	p. 901

See also: Inspiration, Inerrancy, Interpretation.

—AVAILABLE FROM THE UNITED STATES CATHOLIC CONFERENCE, WASHINGTON DC

CD-ROMS

The Sources of Catholic Dogma

Denzinger

Scholarly, historical compendium of Church doctrine, councils, and documents.

—AVAILABLE ON THE *WELCOME TO THE CATHOLIC CHURCH* CD-ROM FROM HARMONY MEDIA INC., CERVAIS, OR

Catholic Encyclopedic Dictionary

—AVAILABLE ON THE *WELCOME TO THE CATHOLIC CHURCH* CD-ROM FROM HARMONY MEDIA, INC., CERVAIS, OR

Vatican II Documents

—AVAILABLE ON THE DESTINATION VATICAN II CD-ROM FROM RCL • RESOURCES FOR CHRISTIAN LIVING, ALLEN, TX

VIDEO

Meeting the Living God

William O'Malley, S.J.

Sixty minutes. Rich and engaging way to convey to high-school students what it means to encounter God.

—AVAILABLE FROM PAULIST PRESS, MAHWAH, NJ

NOTE

For a list of (1) General resources for professional background and (2) Addresses, phone/fax numbers of major publishing companies, see Appendix B of this Resource Manual.

CHAPTER 3
Old Testament

CHAPTER at a Glance

This chapter provides the student with an overview of the Old Testament and some basic guidelines for interpreting it.

DISCUSS—Have a student read aloud the three paragraphs beginning: "In the beginning . . ." Reread the last paragraph and ask: How is this paragraph a summary of the Old Testament?

The OT is like a three-act play:

Act 1	Creation	God creates
Act 2	De-creation	Sin destroys
Act 3	Re-creation	God saves us

Interpreting the Bible

CLARIFY—To set the stage for a discussion of biblical interpretation, have the students read down to QUESTION 1 on page 32 of the text. Then recall for the students the famous trial that took place in Dayton, Tennessee, in 1925.

It all began when the Tennessee legislature passed a law forbidding state schools to teach any theory that denies the biblical story of creation. To test the constitutionality of the law, the American Civil Liberties Union had a high-school biology teacher, John Scopes, break the law by teaching the theory of evolution to his students. Clarence Darrow, a prominent criminal lawyer, agreed to defend him.

To offset Darrow's fame and prestige, the prosecution enlisted the services of William Jennings Bryan, a former presidential candidate. On July 10, 1925, the courtroom in the city of Dayton, Tennessee, was packed. Darrow surprised everyone present by calling Bryan to the

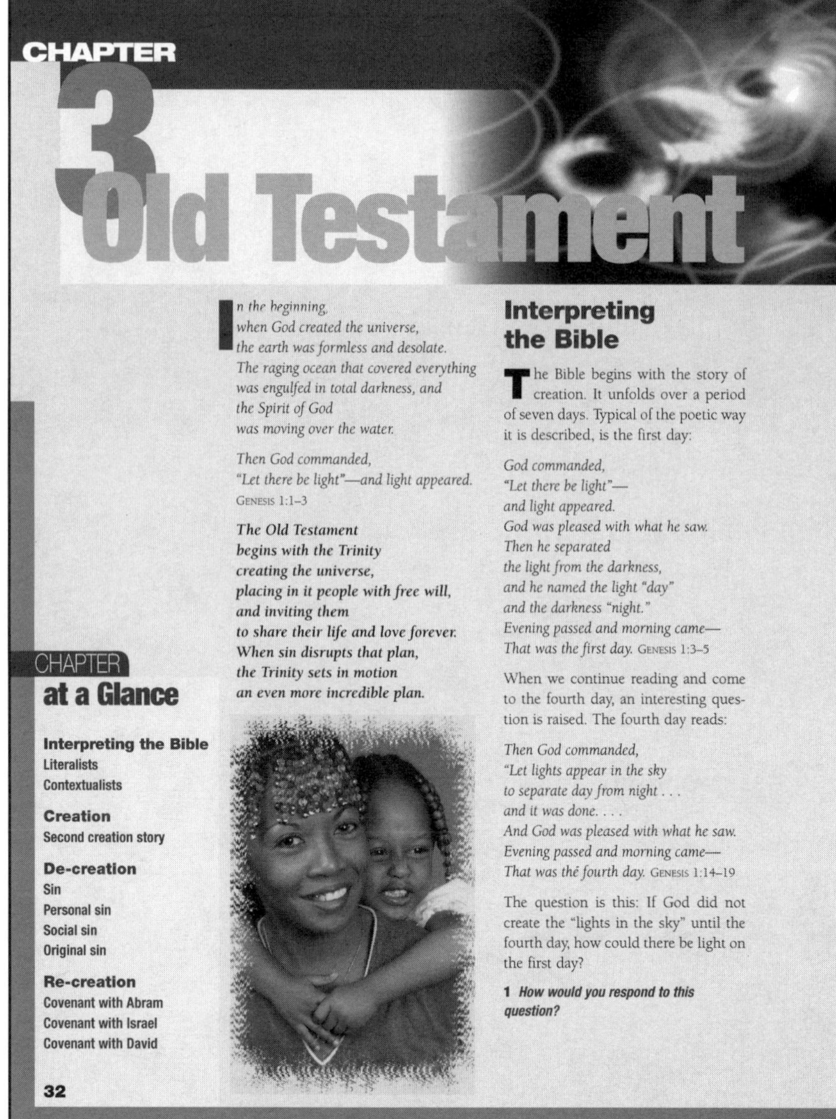

CHAPTER 3 Old Testament

In the beginning,
when God created the universe,
the earth was formless and desolate.
The raging ocean that covered everything
was engulfed in total darkness, and
the Spirit of God
was moving over the water.

Then God commanded,
"Let there be light"—and light appeared.
GENESIS 1:1–3

The Old Testament
begins with the Trinity
creating the universe,
placing in it people with free will,
and inviting them
to share their life and love forever.
When sin disrupts that plan,
the Trinity sets in motion
an even more incredible plan.

CHAPTER at a Glance

Interpreting the Bible
Literalists
Contextualists

Creation
Second creation story

De-creation
Sin
Personal sin
Social sin
Original sin

Re-creation
Covenant with Abram
Covenant with Israel
Covenant with David

Interpreting the Bible

The Bible begins with the story of creation. It unfolds over a period of seven days. Typical of the poetic way it is described, is the first day:

God commanded,
"Let there be light"—
and light appeared.
God was pleased with what he saw.
Then he separated
the light from the darkness,
and he named the light "day"
and the darkness "night."
Evening passed and morning came—
That was the first day. GENESIS 1:3–5

When we continue reading and come to the fourth day, an interesting question is raised. The fourth day reads:

Then God commanded,
"Let lights appear in the sky
to separate day from night . . .
and it was done. . . .
And God was pleased with what he saw.
Evening passed and morning came—
That was the fourth day. GENESIS 1:14–19

The question is this: If God did not create the "lights in the sky" until the fourth day, how could there be light on the first day?

1 ***How would you respond to this question?***

32

witness stand. Then he picked up the Bible and read: "Evening passed and morning came—that was the first day." GENESIS 1:5 Then he asked Bryan, "Do you believe that the sun was created on the fourth day—as the Bible says later on?"

When Bryan answered with a resounding "I do!" Darrow paused and asked Bryan, "Can you tell me how it was possible to have morning and evening on the first day if the sun wasn't created till the fourth day?" Snickers rippled across the courtroom.

Next, Darrow turned a few pages and said, "Do you believe God punished the snake by making it crawl—as the Bible says?" Bryan answered with another "I do!" Then Darrow asked, "Can you tell me how snakes moved about before that?"

NOTES

As we continue reading the creation story, we come to the sixth day. It portrays God creating people last, after having created all other things.

Moving on to the second chapter of the Book of Genesis, we run into another problem. The second chapter opens with a "second creation story." It portrays God creating people first, contradicting the "first creation story." The second story reads:

When the LORD God made the universe,
there were no plants on the earth
and no seeds

Then the LORD God took some soil
from the ground and formed a man. . . .
Then the LORD God planted a garden. . . .

Then the LORD God said,
"It is not good for the man to live alone.
I will make a suitable companion for him."

So he took some soil from the ground
and formed all the animals and birds.
Then he brought them to the man
to see what he would name them;
and that is how they all got their names.

So the man named all the birds
and all the animals; but not one of them
was a suitable companion to help him.
Then God formed the woman out of
[a rib taken from the man].
GENESIS 2:1–8, 18–21

This raises two questions: Which of the two creation stories is correct? Did God create people first or last?

2 *How would you answer this question?*

Apparent contradictions in the Bible, like the two mentioned above, led one woman to say, "The Bible is responsible for more atheism and agnosticism than any other book ever written."

The question of "apparent contradictions" raises the subject of biblical interpretation.

We may divide Bible readers into two main groups: *literalists* and *contextualists.*

Literalists

Literalists focus exclusively on the *text* of the Bible. They say the Bible "means exactly what it says." There is some disagreement, however, among these literalists.

For example, members of the Church of God say that we must interpret the word *day* to mean exactly twenty-four hours. Jehovah's Witnesses, on the other hand, say that we may interpret *day* to mean "era"—as in the *day* or *era* of Lincoln.

Thus, Church of God members, following a strict biblical timetable, hold that creation took place in the year 4004 B.C. People ask: "How can you hold this when science proves the earth is millions of years old?"

STAGE 1: *CHAPTER* 3 **33**

Laughter swept across the courtroom.

Bryan exploded! "Your Honor, this man, who doesn't believe in God, is using this court to ridicule him." Darrow shouted out, "I object! I'm simply questioning your fool ideas that no thinking Christian believes."

DISCUSS—This brings us to biblical interpretation. Ask the students: How would you answer the question on page 32?

QUESTION **1** ***How would you respond to this question? (How could you have light on the first day?)***

DISCUSS—Have the students record in their notebooks their answers to the question. Next, have volunteers share their responses with the class. Allow the discussion to continue as long as it seems to be productive.

Next, have students read down to QUESTION 2:

QUESTION **2** ***How would you answer this question?***

■ *Again, have students record and share their responses.*

This sets the stage for a discussion of the two main approaches to biblical interpretation. Introduce the subject this way.

Bible readers fall into two main groups: literalists (sometimes called fundamentalists) and contextualists. Literalists, like William Jennings Bryan, interpret the Bible literally, saying, "It means exactly what it says."

Literalists

Using biblical genealogies, Anglican archbishop Ussher (a 17th-century literalist) calculated that creation took place in 4004 B.C.

More recently, Jehovah's Witnesses calculated 4026 B.C. They used two genealogies (family trees), especially, for their calculations. The first is in chapter 5 of Genesis, the second in chapter 11.

The *first* begins with Adam and ends with Noah. Fantastic ages are assigned to the men:

Adam lived 930 years;
Seth lived 912 years;
Lamech lived 777 years.

The *second* begins with Shem, Noah's son, and ends with Terah, Abraham's father.

Shem lived 600 years;
Terah lived 205 years.

The genealogies were never intended to be taken literally (exact ages and sequences). They were simply literary devices:

1 *to build a literary bridge between Adam (father of all people) and Abraham (father of the Hebrews)*

2 *to show the effect of sin on the human family. (Declining age spans symbolize the tragic impact that sin is having on the human family.)*

To understand this symbolism, recall the film, *The Picture of Dorian Gray.* The thesis of the film is that sin impacts us not only spiritually, but also physically.

■ *The film concerns a youth who had his portrait painted. It was so lifelike and beautiful that he cried out, "I'd give my soul if the painted portrait would grow old and my own body would stay as the portrait is now." This happens. In time, Dorian slips into a life of sin. He is shocked to see how his sinfulness changes the portrait, causing it to grow old and hideous. Meanwhile, in real life, people praise Dorian and his youthful good looks.*

When Dorian can no longer endure the hypocrisy, he plunges a knife into the portrait. Instantly, the hideousness of the portrait passes into the real Dorian Gray.

QUESTION **3** ***How do you feel about all this (that the stories in the Book of Genesis were never intended to be taken literally)?***

Have the students record their responses in their notebooks. Have volunteers share their responses. Discuss them.

BIBLE Connection

NOTEBOOK—Both the OT (46 books) and NT (27 books) have four parts. Have students record them.

Pentateuch	*5 (3 sp)*	*Gospels*	*4*
Wisdom	*7*	*Acts*	*1*
Historical	*13*	*Letters*	*21*
Prophetic	*18*	*Revelation*	*1*

The Greek word *Pentateuch* means "five scrolls.") The Pentateuch is also called the *Books of Moses* and the *Torah*, a Hebrew word meaning "the law." (The word *Bible* comes from the Greek word *biblia*, meaning "books."

BIBLE Connection

Many books of the Old Testament are hard to classify. Nevertheless, using the classification of the New American Bible, we may list its 46 books (45, if we combine Jeremiah and Lamentations) as follows:

Pentateuch—5
(plus 3 special books)

Genesis	
Exodus	Special books
Leviticus	Joshua
Numbers	Judges
Deuteronomy	Ruth

Wisdom—7

Job	Song of Songs
Psalms	Wisdom
Proverbs	Sirach
Ecclesiastes	

Historical—13

1, 2 Samuel	Ezra
1, 2 Kings	Tobit
1, 2 Chronicles	Judith
1, 2 Maccabees	Esther
Nehemiah	

Prophetic—18

Isaiah	Habakkuk
Obadiah	Daniel
Jeremiah	Zephaniah
Jonah	Hosea
Lamentations	Haggai
Micah	Joel
Baruch	Zechariah
Nahum	Amos
Ezekiel	Malachi

Literal interpreters answer: "The very first paragraph of the creation story holds the key. It suggests that the heavens and the earth *already existed* before God began his six days of work. The six days, therefore, refer to the preparation of earth for human habitation."

Even if we grant this interpretation, which most scholars will not, this still leaves a problem. How do we explain the existence of fossils and bones that scientists say are millions of years old? Shouldn't they also be 6,000 years old, if God created them?

Literalists give various answers. Among them is the blunt statement: "The scientists are wrong!"

3 ***How do you feel about all this?***

This brings us to the second group of readers and how they interpret the Bible.

Contextualists

Contextualists say we must focus on both the text and the context of the Bible. For example, we must take into account the historical context in which a certain story or passage was written. This is especially true of the early chapters of the Book of Genesis. CCC 109–114

These early chapters deal with *prehistory,* that fuzzy era between the appearance of people and the recording of their stories.

Let us now take a closer look at how contextualists interpret the first creation story.

Creation

As we read the description of each day of creation, we find that each description follows relatively the same fourfold pattern:

- **Command** — **Let there be light**
- **Execution** — **Light appeared**
- **Reaction** — **God was pleased**
- **Conclusion** — **Evening passed**

4 ***What does this fourfold pattern suggest about the writing style used by the biblical author and how he intended us to interpret his account?***

What is true of each day is true also of each week of creation. It, too, follows a pattern:

- **Three days** — **Creation & Separation** (light/darkness, water/water, water/land)
- **Three days** — **Creation & Population** (sky, water, land)
- **One day** — **Celebration** (rest & blessing)

These literary patterns suggest that we are dealing with a special kind of writing. It is not the kind you will find in a science book or a newspaper report. CCC 337 Rather, it is the kind of *poetic* writing you will find in children's books. Poetic stories are enjoyable to listen to, easy to remember, and easy to repeat.

It is this kind of poetic writing that the Genesis writer used to teach people about God and creation. (Recall that most ancients could not read or write. They learned by listening.)

Contextualists

NOTEBOOK—Have the students record the two approaches to interpretation.

Literalists	*Text alone*
Contextualists	*Text and context*

CLARIFY—An example of how words and phrases change in meaning (depending on the context in which they appear) is CB (Citizen's Band) radio jargon used by truckers.

If your students are not familiar with CB jargon, have them try to guess the meaning of the CB terms in the left-hand column:

CB Jargon	*Meaning*
Pregnant roller skate	*Volkswagen*
Texas Chevy	*Cadillac*
Draggin' wagon	*Tow truck*

NOTES

Angels and Satan

Four religious truths

A study of the creation story reveals that it teaches four *religious* truths that would have been considered revolutionary at the time the Bible was composed:

- **God is one**
- **God planned creation**
- **God created everything good**
- **God made the Sabbath holy**

5 In what sense do you think these four truths were revolutionary at the time the Bible was composed?

God is one

Let us take a look at the *first* religious truth and why it was revolutionary. We need to consider not only the biblical *text*, but also the historical and cultural *context* in which it was written.

The first creation story was recorded at a time when people worshiped many gods. The Old Testament refers to this, saying:

"Do not sin by making for yourselves
an idol in any form at all—
whether man or woman,
animal or bird, reptile or fish.
Do not be tempted to worship and serve . . .
the sun, the moon, and the stars."
DEUTERONOMY 4:15–19

Tim Anderson and two friends were driving home from Connecticut to Chicago during one of the coldest winters on record.

Tim dropped off a friend in Fort Wayne and took a back road to the tollway. Miles from nowhere, his car died. No lights could be seen anywhere. As the cold invaded the car, the two boys began to pray. Suddenly, lights appeared: a tow truck. It took them back to Fort Wayne.

Tim ran in to get cash for the tow fee. When he came out, no tow truck was in sight—and only tire tracks in the snow were their own. To this day the boys believe an angel answered their prayer.

The Church teaches that angels are part of God's *unseen* creation. We pray at Mass: "We believe in one God . . . maker of heaven and earth, of all that is seen and unseen." Scripture portrays angels as God's *servants* and *messengers*. Thus, an angel stops Abraham from sacrificing Isaac. GENESIS 22:11 "What are angels, then? They are spirits who serve God and are sent by him to help those who are to receive salvation." HEBREWS 1:14

This brings us to Satan and "fallen" angels. They were created good, but became evil by choice. 2 PETER 2:4 They opposed Jesus throughout his ministry, trying to keep him from replacing "Satan's kingdom" with "God's Kingdom."
MARK 3: 20–27

STAGE 1: CHAPTER 3 **35**

Bear in the air — *Police aircraft*
Feed the bears — *Pay traffic fine*
Smokey's got ears — *Police have CB*

Creation

QUESTION 4 *What does this fourfold pattern suggest about the writing style used by the biblical author and how he intended us to interpret his account?*

■ *It's not a scientific writing style, but a poetic one. Its purpose is not to communicate* scientific facts, *but* religious truths. *We might compare it to Jesus' parable of the Prodigal Son. He used the parable to communicate a* religious truth *(God's readiness to forgive), not a* historical fact *(a boy left home and returned).*

Have the students enter into notebooks the key idea behind the creation story:

Creation Story — *Like Jesus' parables* / *Convey religious truths* / *Not historical facts*

Four religious truths

Stress that the four religious truths were revolutionary, given the historical and religious context of the times.

QUESTION 5 *In what sense do you think these four truths were revolutionary at the time the Bible was composed?*

■ *This question is asked here to get the students to start thinking. The answers will be forthcoming. Stop the discussion when it is ceases to be helpful and productive.*

God is one

CLARIFY—The Deuteronomy quote illustrates how revolutionary the idea of "one God" was at the time the Bible was written.

Angels and Satan

CLARIFY—The story is from Joan Webster Anderson's bestseller, *Where Angels Walk*. Tim was her son. After his experience, Joan began researching the topic of angels and wrote a *New York Times* bestseller.

For practical purposes, the words "Satan" and "devil" are interchangeable. Satan is a "tempter" who:

a) Approaches Jesus LUKE 4:2
b) Enters into Judas LUKE 22:3
c) Tests the disciples LUKE 22:31
d) Poses as an angel 2 CORINTHIANS 11:14

Jewish nonbiblical literature portrays Satan and his rebel army of evil spirits being expelled from heaven by Michael and his army of good spirits.

Revelation 12:7 alludes to a "war" in "heaven" in which Michael and good angels defeat Satan and evil angels. Jude 9 calls Michael an archangel.

Share Your meditation

An interesting book on where people find "God's face" easiest is *How Can I Find God*? edited by James Martin, S.J., Liguori, Missouri, 1997.

ACTIVITY—Have the students write their response to the meditation question in their notebooks. Next, have them share their response in groups of three and four. Let each group vote on which meditation in the group should be shared with the entire class.

DISCUSS—Lincoln's observation about "stars" recalls Oscar Wilde's line from "Reading Gaol." It reads: "Two men looked out through prison bars. / One saw mud; the other stars."

Ask the students: What's the difference between a pessimist and an optimist?

Pessimist	*Sees thorns on roses*
Optimist	*Sees roses on thorns*

Mark Twain had a *pessimistic* streak. Concerning humans beings, he said:

1 *Man was made at the end of the week's work when God was tired.*

2 *I don't know if there are men on the moon but, if there are, they must be using the earth as their lunatic asylum.*

LITERARY Connection

A major source of negative attitudes is a lack of a faith vision. Proverbs 29:18 says, "Where there is no vision, the people perish."

SHARE YOUR meditation

One summer night Abraham Lincoln and Gilbert Greene were out walking. Greene later wrote: "As we walked along, Lincoln turned his eyes to the sky full of stars and told me their names." Lincoln ended up saying:

I never behold them
that I do not feel
that I am looking
in the face of God.
I can see
how it might be possible
to look down upon earth
and be an atheist,
but I cannot conceive
how he could
look up into the heavens
and say there is no God.

■ ***Where do you see God's "face" easiest in our world? Explain.***

LITERARY Connection

Earth's crammed with heaven,
And every common bush
aflame with God;
And only he who sees
takes off his shoes—
The rest sit round it
and pluck blackberries.

E. B. Browning, Aurora Leigh

The biblical writer portrays the one true God creating the false "gods" that ancients worshiped.

His point is clear. If God created them, they cannot be God. Rather, there is only one God, the one who created them. CCC 293, 338 We may sum up the first biblical teaching this way:

■ **Old teaching** **Many gods**
■ **New teaching** **One God**
■ **How taught** **God creates gods**

God planned creation

This brings us to the *second* religious truth and why it was so revolutionary. To appreciate this, we need to recall that the creation story was written at a time when people believed the world happened by chance. (Some people still believe this.)

Against this background the biblical writer portrays God creating the world in an orderly way. CCC 295, 299

The writer's point, again, is clear. God created the world by plan, not by chance. We may sum up the second teaching this way:

■ **Old teaching** **Creation by chance**
■ **New teaching** **Creation by plan**
■ **How taught** **God follows plan**

6 ***From a practical viewpoint, what convinces you most that the world is not the product of chance?***

God created everything good

To understand the *third* truth, we need, again, to consider its *context*. It was recorded at a time when many people believed parts of creation were evil.

For example, they believed the human body was evil because it seemed to war against the human spirit.

Against this background, the biblical writer has God affirm the goodness of all things, including the human body. CCC 299, 339 We may sum up the third truth this way:

■ **Old teaching** **Creation part good**
■ **New teaching** **Creation is all good**
■ **How taught** **God says it is good**

7 ***In what sense does the human body seem to war against the human spirit?***

God blessed the Sabbath

Finally, the story was written at a time when the Sabbath was treated as any other day. Against this background, the biblical writer portrays God as blessing the Sabbath and resting on this day. CCC 345–49

His point is this: God fashioned the Sabbath to be a day of rest and prayer:

■ **Old teaching** **Sabbath is ordinary**
■ **New teaching** **Sabbath is special**
■ **How taught** **God blesses it**

36 Stage 1: Chapter 3

God planned creation

QUESTION **6** ***From a practical viewpoint, what convinces you most that the world is not the product of chance?***

■ *Recall the example of the 26 computers outside school.*

Someone came up with a similar example. To say the universe is the product of chance is like saying that the unabridged dictionary is the product of an explosion in a printing factory—all the type came down miraculously to define and spell every definition of every known word in perfect A to Z order.

NOTES

Second creation story

This brings us back to the second creation story and the questions it raises concerning the order in which God created people: first or last.

The key lies in how the Bible came to be recorded. From the Bible itself we learned that parts of it were passed on orally long before they were written down.

Clearly, there were two creation stories that were handed down orally. When the time came to record them, the biblical writer simply recorded both.

A closer study of the two creation stories shows that the biblical writer preserved both stories for a very good reason. They complement each other. They do this, especially, in two ways.

The second story, as we saw earlier, portrays God creating man much as a potter goes about making a vase. We read: "The LORD God took some soil from the ground and formed a man."

When God succeeded in forming the body exactly the way he wanted it, God breathed into it "life-giving breath." GENESIS 2:7

This image stresses the intimate relationship between God and humans. CCC 299 It is a relationship that is more intimate than the relationship of a mother to a child. The LORD says:

"Even if a mother should forget her child, I will never forget you! I have written your name on the palms of my hands." ISAIAH 49:15–16

The second story ends portraying God making woman from the side of man. Like many ancient societies, Hebrew society was dominated by men. Women were valued primarily as bearers of children (especially males: workers and warriors).

Many contextualists read the second story as a correction of the ancient social structure. CCC 383 It affirms the equality of men and women. They share the same flesh and bone. GENESIS 2:23

Thus, the second creation story complements the first story in two ways. It affirms:

- **The intimacy of God and people**
- **The equality of the sexes**

An anonymous poet cries out mournfully:

In the beginning was the earth,
and the earth was beautiful.
But the people living on it said,
"Let us build skyscrapers
and expressways." So they paved
the earth with concrete and said,
"It is good!"

On the second day, the people
looked at the rivers and said,
"Let us dump our sewage
into the waters."
So they filled the waters
with sludge and said, "It is good!"

On the third day, the people
looked at the forest and said,
"Let us cut down the trees
and build things." So they leveled
the forests and said, "It is good!"

On the fourth day, the people
saw the animals and said,
"Let us kill them for sport
and money." So they destroyed
the animals and said, "It is good!"

On the fifth day, the people
felt the cool breeze and said,
"Let us burn our garbage
and let the breeze blow it away."
So they filled the air with carbon
and said, "It is good!"

On the sixth day, the people
saw other nations on earth
and said, "Let us build missiles
in case misunderstandings arise."
So they filled the land
with missile sites and said,
"It is good!"

On the seventh day, the earth
was quiet and deathly silent,
for the people were no more.
And it was good!

God created everything good

QUESTION **7** ***In what sense does the human body seem to war against the human spirit?***

■ *Saint Paul expressed it this way: "I do not understand what I do; for I don't do what I would like to do, but instead I do what I hate. . . . What an unhappy man I am! Who will rescue me from this body that is taking me to death?*

"Thanks be to God who does this through our Lord Jesus Christ." ROMANS 7:15, 24–25

Note that there is a big difference between saying we are "totally evil" (Satan) and saying we are only "wounded" by original sin. "With God's grace we can be healed."

God blessed the Sabbath

DISCUSS—From a purely natural point of view, why is it good to have a "day of rest"?

■ *Henry Ford said that when he began running his automobile assembly line seven days a week in his factory, it took all day Monday to correct the mistakes made on Sunday.*

To what extent would you say Ford's point also applies to school seven days a week?

Second creation story

CLARIFY—Some experts suggest the image of God "breathing" life into clay was inspired by mouth-to-mouth resuscitation. It appears that the ancients were familiar with it. The Bible says:

■ *When Elisha arrived,*
he . . . lay down on the boy,
placing his mouth, eyes, and hands
on the boy's mouth, eyes, and hands.
As he lay stretched out over the boy,
the boy's body started to get warm.
2 KINGS 4:32–34

DISCUSS—Ask the students: Do you think this poem is pessimistic, or realistic?

■ *Be sure the students give a reason for their response.*

Share Your meditation

***DISCUSS*—List on the chalkboard and discuss the responses to the meditation question (use, misuse, or abuse of God's gifts).**

THINK about it

***DISCUSS*—How does the same idea behind this statement apply to:**

(a) *Contemporary music*
(b) *People*
(c) *Certain types of sports*

De-creation

QUESTION **8** ***What do you think Thoreau had in mind?***

■ *The same point the poet was making in "And It Was Good."*

***NOTEBOOK*—Environmental pollution occurs when we add substances to our environment that it can't recycle or handle. Have the students list them in their notebooks.**

Four kinds of environmental pollution:

1 *Particulate*	*Particles added*
2 *Chemical*	*Chemicals added*
3 *Thermal*	*Heat added*
4 *Sound*	*Noise added*

1 Particulate pollution *in some cities is so bad that it is the equivalent of smoking two packs of cigarettes a day. The impact of particulate pollution, according to Greenpeace magazine (July/August 1990), is the depletion of the earth's ozone layer. NASA Antarctic flights show a hole in the earth's ozone layer as big as the United States and as high as Mount Everest (29,000 feet). The EPA (Environmental Protection Agency) reports that a dramatic rise in skin cancer is due to ozone depletion.*

2 Chemical pollution *can occur when pesticides run off into streams.*

SHARE YOUR meditation

Years ago there was a popular TV program called Mork and Mindy. Mork, played by Robin Williams, was an alien who had remarkable power.

One day he shared some of this power with a few of his friends on earth. Touching his fingertips to theirs, he transferred just a little bit to them. Right away they began using it to make people do ridiculous things, like turn cartwheels and leap up and down.

Mork was horrified and shouted, "Stop! You're misusing the power. Give it back!" That episode is a good illustration of what sin is—misusing the power and talents that God has shared with us.

■ ***List some ways you see your friends misuse their talents or abuse God's gifts. What are some ways you yourself do this?***

THINK about it

To get a taste for the Old Testament, you must do more than sample it.

Anonymous

De-creation

The famous naturalist Henry David Thoreau was watching loggers level a forest of beautiful trees. He later wrote: "Thank God, they cannot cut down the clouds."

8 ***What do you think Thoreau had in mind?***

In many parts of our world, commercial interests are threatening our environment. For example, in certain areas, industrial wastes are pouring into the earth's atmosphere to the point that clouds are producing acid rain.

Similar wastes are pouring into the earth's upper atmosphere at such a rate that its ozone layer is eroding. This erosion has reached such an extent that it could become a threat to the future of our planet. CCC 2414–18

This devastation of our planet has been referred to as "de-creation," the physical destruction of God's creation. But tragic as it is, there is an even worse de-creation taking place: a spiritual one.

This "de-creation" has its origin in the human heart. It consists in misusing the free will that God gave us. Traditionally, we refer to spiritual de-creation as sin.

Sin

People are reluctant to talk about sin today. They are even more reluctant to admit that they sin. This reluctance has a lot of people concerned.

9 ***Why would so many people today be reluctant to talk about sin? To admit sin?***

We will discuss sin in more detail later. For the present, it will help to make some preliminary observations. We may describe sin as a fracture or a total break in our love relationship with God and God's people. CCC 1849–52 We may think of sin as falling into two general categories: personal and social.

Personal sin

In John Steinbeck's novel *East of Eden*, one of his characters says:

A man, after he has brushed off
the dusts and chips of life,
will have left only one hard clean question:
Was it good or was it evil?
Have I done well or ill?

38 STAGE 1: CHAPTER 3

3 Thermal pollution *can occur when power plants and dams shoot hot water into streams, upsetting spawning and the migration cycles of fish.*

4 Sound pollution *can occur in work areas causing raw nerves leading to accidents and the like.*

***NOTEBOOK*—Have the students record the two kinds of de-creation:**

De-creation — *Misuse of environment* / *Misuse of free will*

Sin

QUESTION **9** ***Why would so many people today be reluctant to talk about sin? To admit sin?***

NOTES

Steinbeck is talking about *personal* sin: the free act of a single individual. CCC 1868 This act takes two forms:

- **Commission** **Doing bad**
- **Omission** **Not doing good**

10 Do you think people sin more through omission than through commission? Why?

Social sin

The second category of sin is called social sin because it involves the collective behavior of a group of people, like a nation. CCC 1869 It also takes two forms: commission and omission.

A social sin of commission occurs when a group of people discriminates against a minority group in its midst. A social sin of omission occurs when a nation ignores its poor and homeless or lets industry pollute the environment.

Social sin is especially destructive because no one person feels responsible for it. Social sin is something "society" does, not something "I" do. Touching on this attitude, Dr. Martin Luther King said: "Whoever accepts evil without protesting against it is really cooperating with it."

Social evil is tolerated for many reasons. For example, people excuse themselves from responsibility, saying that their isolated opposition is too tiny to make a difference.

11 How would you respond to this excuse?

Regardless of the excuse, the bottom line on social sin is this: The responsibility to oppose it rests with individuals. Whoever shirks this responsibility is guilty of a *personal* sin of omission.

Origin of sin

Lance Morrow of *Time* magazine suggests there should be a TV character called "Dark Willard." This "sick" newscaster would begin each morning reciting the morning "evil" report. On the wall behind Willard would be a big map with ugly blotches. These blotches would indicate the places where "evil" defeated "good" during the night: crime in America, floods in India, war in the East.

The widespread presence of evil in our world poses a vexing question: If God created everything good, where did evil come from?

12 What answer would you give to this question?

The Bible answers the question with a series of "sin stories." We may call them the "de-creation" stories—stories of the victory of evil over good.

The biblical writer begins these sin stories with the account of a snake tempting Adam and Eve. The snake talks them into "eating" a fruit that God forbade them to eat, explaining:

"When you eat it, you will be like God
and know what is good
and what is bad . . ."
As soon as they had eaten it,
they were given understanding and
realized that they were naked. . . .

So the LORD God
sent them out of the Garden of Eden
and made them cultivate the soil
from which they had been formed.
GENESIS 3:5, 7, 23

LIFE Connection

I t isn't the thing you do, dear,
It's the thing you
leave undone
that gives you a bit of a
heartache
at the setting of the sun.

The tender word forgotten,
The letter you did not write,
The flowers
you did not send, dear,
are your haunting ghosts
at night.

Author unknown

PRAYER hotline

Can't you hear us cryin', Lord,
Can't you see our pain,
Are you gonna leave us here,
Just voices in the rain?

Cathy Bucci

■ *Point out that when they do talk about it, it is always in a sugar-coated way. List the sins in the left-hand column on the chalkboard. Have students fill in the right-hand column.*

	Sin	Sugar-coating
1	*Stealing*	*"Lifting" or "ripping off"*
2	*Lying*	*Misrepresenting facts*
3	*Adultery*	*Fooling around*
4	*Perversion*	*Sexual preferences*
5	*Kill unborn*	*Terminating a pregnancy*
6	*Porn*	*Adult entertainment*

Personal sin

DISCUSS—Refer the students to "Life connection" (margin of page 39) and ask them: (a) What kind of sin is the poem referring to? (b) What 'sin of omission' do teens commit most?

QUESTION **10** ***Do you think people sin more through omission than through commission? Why?***

■ *Interestingly, Jesus highlighted "sins of omission" in his parable of the Last Judgment, e.g., "I was hungry, homeless, etc."* MATTHEW 25

Social sin

QUESTION **11** ***How would you respond to this excuse? (My tiny opposition or contribution can't change things.)***

■ *To dramatize the importance of little things, Benjamin Franklin wrote the following "poem":*

"For want of a nail the shoe was lost.
For want of a shoe, the horse was lost.
For want of a horse the rider was lost.
For want of a rider the battle was lost."

Origin of sin

QUESTION **12** ***What answer would you give to this question (Evil's origin)?***

The purpose of the biblical response to this question that has plagued thinking people since the dawn of creation.

■ *Greek mythology explains it this way. Prometheus stole fire from the gods to improve the lot of humans. The gods grew angry because fire made humans more god-like. Zeus punished him by chaining him to a mountain. Vultures attacked him constantly, inflicting pain on him.*

One day, Hercules freed him. The gods grew more angry and sent Pandora to earth with a box of "gifts." In reality, it was a box filled with evil: sin, sickness, and death.

When the box was opened, these evils spread across the world.

DISCUSS—Ask students: If you were God, how would you respond to this prayer?

Share Your meditation

DISCUSS—Do you think MacDonald is pessimistic or realistic in his view of humans? Explain.

DISCUSS—Do you feel people are basically good or basically evil?

■ *William Golding's* Lord of the Flies *is the story of a group of good English schoolboys, most under 14. They become marooned on a deserted island during World War II when a plane evacuating them from bombings in England crash-lands at sea. The pilot and copilot are killed, but all the boys emerge unharmed.*

Gradually, they turn into savages. Golding's point seems to be that people are born basically evil. When the laws of society are removed, evil reigns.

J.D. Salinger's Catcher in the Rye, *seems to take the opposite viewpoint. Holden Caulfield is an innocent, pleasant youth. In time, however, his contact with adult society destroys his idealism and innocence.*

Ask the students: Imagine that this class was marooned on a desert island, with barely enough water and food to survive. Why do/don't you think it could succeed in setting up a peaceful society? How would you handle the first case of stealing food? Why this way?

Symbolic story

CLARIFY—Recall the three ways of learning (a) experience, (b) reason, (c) believing. The first couple learned about sin by experience.

A literalist approach to this story fails. It leads to such bizarre questions as:

1 *How did snakes move about before God condemned them to crawl?"*

2 *Was there a time when snakes talked?*

Recall how Pope Pius XII told Catholic biblical scholars (page 26):

SHARE YOUR meditation

Years ago, Dr. Norman MacDonald addressed a group of anthropologists gathered in Chicago from around the world. In the course of his address, he gave this gloomy assessment of human nature:

Man has been violent
since his remote ape-like
ancestors descended from trees
and there is little prospect
that his innate desire to kill
for dominance
will ever change. . . .

We have to face the truth
and accept one basic,
unpleasant fact. . . .
Biologically, man is a killer. . . .

From the time he fashioned
a club as his first weapon,
man has insisted on developing
more powerful weapons. . . .
that now, instead of killing
individuals or groups,
he can annihilate a planet.

■ ***To what extent do you agree or disagree with MacDonald's assessment?***

■ ***Which of the following statements best expresses your feelings about people and why? They are:***
(a) basically evil, but society civilizes them;
(b) basically good; society corrupts them.

Symbolic story

Contextualists interpret this story the same way they interpret the creation story. Like the parables that Jesus told, it is a *symbol* story.

This particular story was created by the biblical writer to answer the question "How did evil enter the world?" The key to the story lies in understanding two major symbols:

- **The snake**
- **Eating of the forbidden fruit**

The key symbol is the snake. To understand it we must keep in mind the context in which it was written.

Symbolic meaning

Archaeology reveals that snakes played a bizarre role in the worship ceremony of the Canaanites. Thus, the snake became a symbol of evil to the Hebrews, who looked upon Canaanite worship as an abomination. And so the snake symbolizes the *devil.*

To understand the second symbol, recall that the snake told the woman that if she *ate* the fruit, she would *know* good from bad. The snake makes a connection between *eating* and *knowing.*

Because most ancient peoples could not read, *experience* became a major source of *knowledge* for them. This explains the connection between *eating* and *knowing.*

"To eat" means "to know by experience." It is a symbolic way of saying that the first couple *learned* about evil by *experiencing* it. They "tasted" evil. They became evil. They sinned.

The biblical writer's answer to the question about how evil entered the world is this: It entered the world through the first sin of the first human couple. CCC 397–98

Sin dooms us

After the first couple sinned, the Bible says they were *aware* that they were naked. GENESIS 3:7 To understand this statement, we need to go back to the creation story. There we read, "The man and the woman were both naked, but they were not embarrassed." GENESIS 2:25

The couple's *awareness* of nakedness *after* they sinned symbolizes that sin did something to them. They were no longer at ease with themselves. Something went wrong inside them. Sin "flawed" them.

40 STAGE 1: CHAPTER 3

You must go back, as it were, in spirit to those remote centuries of the East. With the aid of history, archaeology, ethnology, and other sciences, you must determine accurately what modes of writing the ancient writers would likely use, and in fact did use.

NOTEBOOK—Have the students record a summary of the first sin story:

Symbols — *Snake = devil* / *Eating = sinful act*

Teaching — *evil enters the world through the sin of the first couple*

NOTEBOOK—Stress the three major tragic effects of the first sin. Develop

NOTES

The symbolic sin story ends with the first couple being expelled from the Garden of Eden. The point of the expulsion is obvious. The first couple is now separated from God.

The first sin not only introduced evil into the world but also "flawed" the first couple and "separated" them from God. The first sin did even more. CCC 399–405 It opened the floodgates of sin. CCC 401 Soon sin engulfed the world. GENESIS 11:1–9 The human race was *doomed.* The tragic condition that the first sin produced in the world is referred to as the *state of original sin.* The first sin.

- **Introduced evil into the world**
- **Flawed the human race**
- **Doomed it to destruction**

Ray of hope

The story of the first sin ends with God confronting the three guilty parties: the woman, the man, and the snake.

To the *woman,* God says, "I will increase . . . your pain in giving birth." GENESIS 3:16

To the *man,* God says, "You will have to work hard all your life to make [the ground] produce food." GENESIS 3:17

To the *snake,* God says: "You will crawl on your belly. . . . I will make you and the woman hate each other; her offspring and yours will always be enemies. Her offspring will crush your head, and you will bite her offspring's heel." GENESIS 3:14–15

13 In what sense might you interpret the final sentence God addresses to the snake as a ray of hope?

New Testament writers viewed God's remarks to the snake as a ray of hope. They viewed them as a "prophecy" that God would rescue the human race from its sinful condition. CCC 410–12

These writers interpreted the expression "hate each other" to refer to an ongoing state of "spiritual warfare" between the devil and the human race. They interpreted the expression "her offspring will crush your head" as a "prophecy" that the human race will win.

It is in this sense that God's remarks to the snake are viewed as a ray of hope. CCC 410–11 Jesus, the noblest offspring of the human race, will eventually defeat the devil. 1 JOHN 3:8

Re-creation

Mark Twain once wrote a story about a group of people who get trapped in a hopeless situation. It was like having them on a plane ten feet away from crashing into a cliff. He didn't want these people to die, but he didn't know how to save them in a credible way.

So he ended his story, writing, "I don't know how to save these people; if you think you do, you are welcome to try."

Thousands of years ago the world was in a similar hopeless situation. Sin was like a tidal wave threatening to destroy everyone in its path. But God had a plan to save the world. This brings us to the "re-creation story."

We may think of God's plan as a stage play in three acts:

■ Creation	**God creates**
■ De-creation	**Sin destroys**
■ Re-creation	**God saves us**

ART Connection

The three panels of this stained-glass window sum up the re-creation story. How does the first symbolize "re-creation promised"? The second, "re-creation begun"? The third "re-creation being extended to all nations"?

STAGE 1: *CHAPTER* 3 **41**

them on the chalkboard for entry into the students' notebooks:

1. *Introduced evil into world*
2. *Flawed human race*
3. *Doomed human race*

DISCUSS—What does it mean to be "flawed" and "doomed"?

■ *Once we are born into this world, it's just a matter of time before we take on its mentality and values. Our "flawed" or "sin-prone" human nature "dooms" us.*

The only way we can win is by being baptized into the body of Christ, who graces and saves us.

Ray of Hope

CLARIFY—God's response to the three guilty parties gave ancients their answer to the "origin" of such disturbing realities as:

1. *The pain involved in childbirth*
2. *The pain involved in hard labor*
3. *The ongoing struggle between good and evil in the world*

QUESTION **13** ***In what sense might you interpret the final sentence that God addresses to the snake as a ray of hope?***

■ *The purpose of this question is to get the students thinking.*

The answer is contained in the text that follows it. Briefly, it comes down to this:

"Her offspring (Jesus)
will crush your head (devil).
In the process, however,
Jesus will suffer (snake will bite his heel)."

Re-creation

CLARIFY—Stress the idea of the "stage play" in three acts:

Act 1	*God creates us*
Act 2	*Sin destroys us*
Act 3	*God re-creates us*

ART Connection

Panel 1:	*God's promise that "her (Mary's) offspring (Jesus) will crush your (devil's) head."*
Panel 2:	*Cross with the white cloth symbolizes Jesus' resurrection.*
Panel 3:	*The resurrection gives rise to the Church (Peter's boat). "You will become fishers of people." (all races: black, brown, yellow, white.)* MARK 1:17

HISTORICAL Connection

CLARIFY—The holy day for Islam is Friday; for Jews, Saturday; for Christians, Sunday. In one place in the city of Hebron, all three religions use the same hall on different days.

The *Azam* ("Call to Prayer") sounds five times daily at (1) sunrise, (2) midday, (3) afternoon, (4) sunset, (5) nightfall. In Saudi Arabia, even TV programs come to a halt during these brief periods of prayer.

The Muslim equivalent of a church is the mosque. Mosques face Mecca, the birthplace of Mohammed. It is a holy city for Islam, somewhat like Vatican City is to Roman Catholics. The *imam* (prayer leader) leads worship, reading from the Muslim "Bible" *(Qur'an)* and giving a brief address.

The *Qur'an* consists of 114 chapters in the Arabic language. Muslim school children repeat it so often that by the time they reach adulthood, some know it by heart.

Covenant with Abram

QUESTION **14** ***Can you give some examples of this practice even today? (Name changes)***

- *Women frequently take or add the last name of their spouse. The pope takes a new name. A king takes a new name.*

CLARIFY—When Joseph arrived in Egypt after being sold into slavery, he stared in disbelief at the great pyramids in Egypt. They were already 1,000 years old in his day.

- *The famous Pyramid of Cheops covered 13 acres of land and stood 480 feet high (about the height of a modern 30-story building). It housed the remains of Pharaoh Cheops.*

Medieval pilgrims called the pyramid "Joseph barns," believing them to be the storehouses for the grain collected by Joseph to prepare for the great famine. GENESIS 41:8–42:9 *Recall that the famine eventually brought the Israelites to Egypt to buy grain.*

The seven-story human head of the Sphinx was also over 1,000 years old in David's time. In 1926, archaeologists discovered that a body of a lion was attached to the head of the Sphinx. It covered the length of a football field. The face of the sphinx was damaged by soldiers of Napoleon's army, who used it for target practice.

Covenant with Israel

CLARIFY—A covenant is a solemn pact, sealed with a solemn ritual. It is similar to the way we "seal" a pact with a ritual (handshake). Moses and the Israelites "sealed" the Sinai covenant with

---

HISTORICAL Connection

Egypt's President Anwar Sadat did something on November 27, 1977, that no previous Arab leader had dared do. He risked the friendship of many Arabs by going to Israel and addressing the Kenesset, the Israeli parliament.

In his address, Sadat noted that the day was Id al-Adha, an Islamic holy day that celebrated Abraham's readiness to sacrifice his son Isaac.

That day inspired in him a readiness to risk all for peace between Arabs and Jews.

Sadat's words surprised many Christians. They didn't realize that Muslims, like Jews and Christians, have Abraham as their faith-father.

Muslims trace their lineage through Ishmael, Abraham's son by the slave girl Hagar. GENESIS 16 Jews and Christians trace it through Isaac, Abraham's son by his wife Sarah.

Covenant with Abram

God's plan to save the world begins with a man named Abram. One day God says to him:

"Leave your country, your relatives, and your father's home, and go to a land that I am going to show you. . . .

"I make this covenant with you: I promise that you will be the ancestor of many nations. Your name will no longer be Abram, but Abraham, because I am making you the ancestor of many nations. . . .

"You must no longer call your wife Sarai; from now on her name is Sarah. I will bless her, and I will give you a son by her. . . . You will name him Isaac.
GENESIS 12:1, 17:4–5, 15–16, 19

In biblical times, names were more than arbitrary identification tags. They said something significant about the person. Thus, a name change often accompanied a destiny change.

14 ***Can you give some examples of this practice even today?***

A covenant is a sacred pact between two parties. God's covenant with Abram changed his life in a remarkable way. It gave him:

- **New identity** **God's chosen person**
- **New destiny** **Father of nations**

Eventually, Sarah gave birth to Isaac. He grew up, married Rebecca, and they had two sons: Esau and Jacob. After Isaac's death, God said to Jacob: "Your name is Jacob, but from now on it will be *Israel*." GENESIS 35:10

Israel became the father of twelve sons, forerunners of the twelve tribes of Israel, who became known as *Israelites*. Jacob's favorite son was Joseph. GENESIS 37:3

One day Joseph's jealous brothers sold him into slavery in Egypt. There he rose to prominence by foretelling a famine and preparing Egypt for it.

Joseph invited his family to come to Egypt. They came, prospered, and grew into a great people. After Joseph died, however, they fell into disfavor and were enslaved by the Egyptians. Eventually, a leader named Moses arose to lead them out of Egypt to freedom.

Covenant with Israel

Moses led the Israelites out of Egypt to the foot of Mount Sinai. There God made a covenant with them, giving them:

- **New identity** **Chosen people**
- **New destiny** **Priestly people**

42 STAGE 1: CHAPTER 3

NOTES

The Israelites became God's Chosen People in the sense that God chose them to prepare all the nations of the world for the re-creation of the human race. CCC 1961–64

After making a covenant with the Israelites, God schooled them in the desert and, eventually, led them into the land promised to Abraham.

After preparing the people for entry into the land, Moses died. Joshua succeeded him, led the people into the land, and divided the land among the twelve tribes of Israel.

15 Moses is the first in a long line of great people who fathered a great cause but died without seeing it realized. Who were some others?

When Joshua died, leaving the Israelites without a strong leader, the tribes periodically drifted from the covenant. To deal with these situations, God used popular leaders, called judges, to bring them back to their senses.

In time, a holy man named Samuel anointed Saul to be Israel's first king. Saul began well but ended badly.

After Saul became king of Israel,
he fought all his enemies everywhere . . .
He fought heroically . . .
He saved the Israelites from all attacks.
1 SAMUEL 10:1; 14:47–48

But success has a way of turning a person's head. Soon Saul began to follow his own mind; he grew insensitive to the spirit of Yahweh.

The LORD said to Samuel,
"I am sorry that I made Saul king;
he has turned away from me
and disobeyed my commands."
1 SAMUEL 15:10–11

Covenant with David

When Saul died in battle, a young shepherd named David was anointed king. Under his brilliant leadership, Israel began its "glory years." David made Jerusalem the center of government and worship.

Then came a remarkable moment. One night while David was praying in the sacred tent (the forerunner of the Temple), God made a covenant with David. CCC 709–16 Through the prophet Nathan, God promised David.

"You will always have descendants,
and I will make your kingdom last forever.
Your dynasty will never end."
2 SAMUEL 7:16

This prophecy is the most important in the Bible. It begins a series of prophecies called the "messianic prophecies." They point to the coming of a king (Messiah) from David's line, whose kingdom (God's Kingdom) will last forever.

At Mount Sinai the covenant was set up in a general way between God and the people. Now it is linked specifically with the Davidic kings, who represent the kingdom and are responsible for its welfare.

New Testament writers saw God's promise of a Messiah fulfilled in Jesus. CCC 436–40 In announcing Jesus' birth to Mary, an angel says of Jesus:

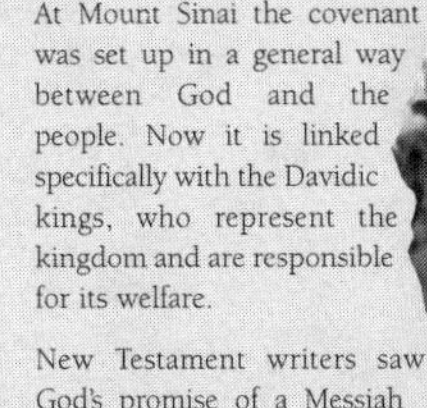

ART **Connection**

Michelangelo (1475–1564) created this masterpiece of David from a flawed block of marble abandoned by another artist. It was completed in 1504.

sacrificial animal blood, sprinkling half on an altar (symbol of God) and half on the people. EXODUS 24:5–8

QUESTION ***15 Moses is the first in a long line of great people who fathered a great cause but died without seeing it realized. Who were some others?***

■ *Susan B. Anthony and Julia Ward Howe died without seeing the vote given to women, something they both labored for vigorously.*

Martin Luther King died without seeing the fruits of the civil rights movement.

John F. Kennedy died without seeing a man walk on the moon (his dream, which few believed could become a reality for decades to come).

Covenant with David

CLARIFY—David possessed a remarkable charism (gift) that could lift the souls of men. Here's how Robert Wallace describes it in *Kingly Glory and Ordeal:*

■ *David's ability to inspire love and loyalty was remarkable; no other biblical figure, until the appearance of Christ, approaches it.*

During one battle in which he was severely pressed, David expressed a longing for a drink of cool water from a well in Bethlehem, apparently several miles distant. Without hesitation three of his men broke through the enemy lines to gratify his whim.

NOTEBOOK—Develop the following diagram for entry into the students' notebooks. It sums up the two key points of God's "messianic promise." From David's line will come the eternal:

1	*King*	*Jesus*
2	*Kingdom*	*Kingdom of God*

DISCUSS—Ask the students: As we study the three major covenants (Abraham, Israel, and David), how do you see telescoping or focus occurring?

■ *The covenant with Abraham involves many (all peoples).The covenant with Israel involves fewer (Israelites).*
The covenant with David focuses in on one person (Messiah).
Finally, in the angel's greeting to Mary, the telescoping and focus is complete.
The spotlight falls on Jesus.
The angel says:

"You will . . . give birth to a son,
and you will name him Jesus . . .
He will be great and will be called
the Son of the Most High God.
The Lord God will make him a king,
as his ancestor David was, and . . .
his kingdom will never end!" LUKE 1:32–33

ART **Connection**

CLARIFY—Michelangelo began the statue of "David" in 1501 and finished it in 1504—a three-year undertaking.

***DISCUSS*—Because David was the youngest son, his father Jesse thought it unlikely that God would choose him to succeed Saul.

***DISCUSS*—Ask the students, How do you explain the fact that God chose the son Jesse thought least qualified?

■ *The LORD, himself, answered that question, saying to Samuel:*
"I do not judge as people judge.
They look at the outward appearance,
but I look at the heart." 1 SAMUEL 16:7

Ask the students: What do you think God looks for in the human heart?

■ *A variety of answers are possible. (These include humility, love, generosity, courage, sincerity)*
List the responses on the chalkboard and let the students vote on what they consider the top three things God looks for in the human heart.

God's people sin

QUESTION **16** ***How do you account for the fact that so many people seem to follow the pattern of beginning nobly and ending tragically? Can you think of any examples?***

Saul began well, but ended badly. Many film stars and sports figures begin and end this way. Prosperity and fame tend to turn us away from spiritual things to worldly things. Recall Jesus' warning:

■ *"How hard it is for rich people*
to enter the Kingdom of God!
It is much harder for a rich person
to enter the Kingdom of God
than for a camel to go through
the eye of a needle." LUKE 18:25

When asked about this, Jesus said:
"What is humanly impossible
is possible for God." LUKE 18:27

Up Close & Personal

David

In the streams of Israel, you can still spot water-smooth stones, like the fabled disk that David used to kill Goliath. Fingering one of these stones helps to bridge the 3,000 years since King David lived.

As a youth, David was a shepherd. While his flocks munched grass, he practiced the shepherd's defense against unwelcomed intruders: the slingshot. Little did he realize that this skill would catapult him into the limelight of history.

The moment came when Philistine armies invaded Israel and prepared for attack. A giant warrior named Goliath issued a pre-battle challenge to duel any Israelite. David, a teenager, at the time, accepted the challenge.

Goliath was no match for the agile youth with his deadly sling. David's shepherding days were over, and his career as a warrior and king launched. Under the magic of David's leadership, Israel began her "glory years."

He will be great and will be called
the Son of the Most High God.
The Lord God will make him a king,
as his ancestor David was, and . . .
his kingdom will never end!
LUKE 1:32–33

As God's covenant moved from Abraham to Israel, it now moved to David. CCC 702–709 We may sum up the moves this way:

Abraham is given:

■ **New identity** **Chosen person**
■ **New destiny** **Father of many**

Israel is given:

■ **New identity** **Chosen people**
■ **New destiny** **Priestly people**

David is given:

■ **New identity** **Chosen king**
■ **New destiny** **Ancestor of Messiah**

God's people sin

After David's death, his son Solomon took over as king. Under his rule, Israel became a great world power.

But his most important achievement was fulfilling his father's dream and building a great Temple in Jerusalem.

Unfortunately, however, like Saul, he began nobly but ended tragically (turning from God and worshiping foreign gods).

16 ***How do you account for the fact that so many people seem to follow the pattern of beginning nobly and ending tragically? Can you think of any examples?***

After Solomon died, civil war broke out. The nation split in two: Israel (north) and Judah (south). This tragic split began a flood of personal and social sins against God and the covenant.

In the face of these sins, God raised up prophets like Elijah, Amos, and Hosea to warn the nation of Israel (north) to reform. But their words fell on deaf ears. In 722 B.C. Assyria invaded and destroyed Israel.

Ironically, the southern kingdom (Judah) did not learn from the tragedy. It soon drifted into some of the very same evils that doomed the north: idolatry, religious formalism, exploitation of the poor and the powerless.

17 ***Give an example from modern life of each of the following sins: idolatry, religious formalism, exploitation of the poor.***

Prophets like Isaiah and Jeremiah warned the people, but to no avail. Finally, their "days of glory" ended in a "day of drums." Babylonian armies destroyed Jerusalem and the Temple and led the people away into slavery. CCC 710

God's people suffer

For decades the people lived in exile in a foreign land. Their faith flickered and, at times, nearly went out. Among the prophets God sent them were Ezekiel and another spiritual giant called Second Isaiah. Scholars give him this name because his writings are appended to those of the earlier "great Isaiah."

44 STAGE 1: CHAPTER 3

QUESTION **17** ***Give an example from modern life of each of the following sins: (1) idolatry, (2) religious formalism, (3) exploitation of the poor.***

1 *Idolatry: making money, fame, power our "gods."*
2 *Religious formalism: praying without attending to what we are saying, making the sign of the cross out of habit rather than devotion.*
3 *Exploitation of the poor: wealthy companies paying meager wages to Third-World workers to fashion shoes and clothes for us.*

NOTES

Finally, the day came when Babylon fell to the armies of Cyrus of Persia. He freed Judah and allowed the Jews to return to Jerusalem. In time, under leaders like Nehemiah and Ezra, they rebuilt the city and the Temple. But further difficulties lay ahead.

Around 313 B.C. Alexander the Great conquered Judah. In the centuries that followed, the people isolated themselves from the world. In the process of doing so, they began to lose their spiritual focus. They began to make the creator of the universe into a national God who cared only about them.

Into this critical situation stepped prophets like Malachi and the unknown author of the Book of Jonah. These prophets helped the people regain their focus.

But another great challenge lay ahead. Around 200 B.C. a Syrian king conquered Judah and tried to destroy its ancient faith. Years of persecution followed. Into this crisis stepped the prophet called Daniel. Like prophets before him, he faced the problem of communicating a message of hope to a simple people. To do this, he used two literary devices: folktales and visions.

Typical of the visions is one in which Daniel saw a mysterious figure in the clouds. Jesus would refer to it when asked if he were the Messiah.

"I am," answered Jesus,
"and you will all see the Son of Man
seated at the right side of the Almighty
and coming with the clouds of heaven!"
MARK 14:62

Typical of the folktales is God's protection of Daniel in the lions' den. If God could save Daniel, God could save Judah.

God's people wait

The religious inspiration of Daniel and the political leadership of the Maccabees pulled the people through this threatening period. But Judah's joy was short-lived. In 63 B.C. the Romans conquered Judah.

The people cried out in profound anguish: "What happened to God's covenant with us? What happened to the promised Messiah? What happened to the promised kingdom?"

These questions are reflected in books like Ecclesiastes and Job. Together with the Book of Psalms, they act as a window through which we glimpse the anguished hearts and souls of Jews waiting for further revelation from God.

So, by their own admission, the Hebrew Scriptures end "unfinished." They end with faithful Jews, especially "the poor," waiting for the Messiah—praying for God to complete the work of re-creating the world. CCC 716

ART Connection

The four Old Testament persons shown here adorn the 700-year-old Cathedral of Chartres, France.

Explain why the artists chose the following symbols for the following persons and how each symbol points to Jesus.

Abraham, with Isaac GENESIS 22:1-12; Moses, with a seraph serpent mounted on a pole NUMBERS 21:9; Samuel, with a lamb 1 SAMUEL 7:9; David, with a crown 2 SAMUEL 5:4.

God's people suffer

CLARIFY—During Judah's times of suffering, it was the prophets like Ezekiel who kept their faith alive. Commenting on their importance, Emil Kraeling writes in his book, *The Prophets:*

■ *Without the prophets*
there would have been
no apostles and martyrs;
Jesus of Nazareth would have remained
at his carpenter's bench,
unheard of and unsung;
there would have been no Judaism;
Mohammed would have stayed
an unknown camel driver.

In other words, the prophets kept faith alive in Israel when it flickered and almost died.

God's people wait

After the Romans conquered Judah in 63 B.C., they installed Herod the Great as king. Instead of easing the suffering of his people, he added to it. He catered to the Romans and used brutality to control his own people. Here's how one author described him:

He murdered members of his own family—yet . . . would not eat pork. This provoked his Roman master Augustus into jesting, "I would rather be Herod's pig than Herod's son.
HOWARD LAFAY

ART Connection

ACTIVITY—First, have the students try to answer the question without a Bible. Then check the Bible for the symbols they can't explain from their own knowledge.

1 *Abraham: Offered a ram, when an angel stopped him from sacrificing his son Isaac.*

2 *Moses: Put a metal snake on a pole. People looked at it and were healed.*

3 *Samuel: Sacrificed a lamb to God, and the Philistines mysteriously fled.*

4 *David was crowned King of Judah.*

Recap

This section summarizes the key points of the chapter. To repeat what was said earlier, an easy way to construct a quick "daily quiz" is to convert the "summary diagrams" found here and in the text into "matching " or "true-false" questions. Here's a "true-false" example:

1 __F__ By immediate *revelation, we mean revelation to people of all times.*

2 __T__ Mediate *revelation involves "handing on" God's Word through Sacred Tradition or Sacred Scripture*

3 __T__ Inerrancy *means free from religious error in matters relating to salvation.*

You might give a total of ten "daily quiz" questions in the course of the week. Hold off the grade until the end of the week. Thus, a student who gets nine answers correct during the week is given a grade of 90%.

Review

DAILY QUIZ—The review questions may be assigned (one or two at a time) for homework or a daily quiz.

CHAPTER TESTS—Reproducible chapter tests are found in Appendix A. For consistency and ease in grading, quizzes are restricted to (1) "Matching," (2) "True/False," and (3) "Fill in the Blanks."

TEST ANSWERS—The following are the answers to the test for Chapter 3. (See Appendix A, page 314.) Each correct answer is worth 4 points.

Matching

1 = k	2 = a	3 = e	4 = g
5 = d	6 = h	7 = l	8 = c
9 = f	10 = b	11 = i	12 = j

Recap

To interpret the Old Testament correctly, we need to consider both:

- **Text** — **What it says**
- **Context** — **Literary, cultural, historical**

The *content* of the Old Testament may be divided into the following three themes:

- **Creation** — **God makes us**
- **De-creation** — **We sin**
- **Re-creation** — **God saves us**

The creation stories teach four *religious* truths that were revolutionary in the biblical era:

- **God is one**
- **God planned creation**
- **God created everything good**
- **God made the Sabbath holy**

The de-creation stories begin with the first sin by the first couple. It opened the floodgates of evil. The tragic condition that the first sin produced in the world is referred to as the *state of original sin.* The first sin:

- **Introduced evil into the world**
- **Flawed the human race**
- **Doomed it to destruction**

The *re-creation* story involves three important covenants with the following:

- **Abraham** — **Father of nations**
- **Israel** — **Chosen people**
- **David** — **Promise of a Messiah**

God's covenant with David began a series of prophecies called the *messianic* prophecies. They point to a king (Messiah) from David's line.

The Hebrew Scriptures end with faithful Jews waiting and praying for the Messiah to come and complete the work of "re-creation."

Review

1 List and briefly explain: (a) the two major groups into which Bible readers split, (b) two contradictory details in the two creation stories.

2 List and briefly explain: (a) the pattern used to describe each day of creation in the first creation story, (b) the pattern used to describe the week of creation, (c) what these patterns suggest about the kind of writing we have in the story.

3 List and briefly explain (a) each of the four new teachings contained in the first creation story, (b) what old teaching each new teaching replaced, and (c) how the new teaching was communicated.

4 Briefly explain and give an example of the following sins: (a) personal, (b) social, (c) commission, and (d) omission.

5 Explain the following points concerning social sins: (a) why it is especially bad, (b) one reason why we tolerate it, (c) the bottomline on where the responsibility to oppose it rests.

6 Explain the following symbols in the de-creation story: (a) snake, (b) eating the fruit, (c) awareness of nakedness.

7 Describe what we mean by original sin. List (a) the threefold impact it had on the human race, and (b) how God's remarks to the three guilty parties (woman, man, and devil) served as a "prophecy" that God would rescue the human race.

8 Explain the new identity and destiny conferred by the following covenants: (a) Abram, (b) Sinai, (c) messianic.

9 Briefly identify: Solomon, Judah, Israel, Elijah, Amos and Hosea, Isaiah and Jeremiah, Cyrus of Persia, Nehemiah and Ezra, Alexander the Great, Daniel.

46 STAGE 1: CHAPTER 3

True/False

1 = F	2 = T	3 = T	4 = T
5 = F	6 = T	7 = F	8 = T
9 = F	10 = T		

Fill in the Blanks

(a) Introduced evil into the world

(b) Flawed the human race

(c) Doomed the human race

NOTES

Reflect

1 The movie *Lili* is a delightful fantasy about a girl who is a member of a traveling carnival in France. She becomes depressed one day because she thinks no one cares about her, especially the carnival's bashful puppeteer. Her only friends are the puppets of the young puppeteer. She decides to run away. Before leaving, however, Lili says good-bye to the puppets. As they hug her and weep, Lili suddenly feels them trembling. Only then does she make the connection between the puppets and the puppeteer.

- ***How is this sequence in the movie a kind of parable of God and the human race? In other words, whom do the following stand for: Lili, the puppeteer, the puppets?***
- ***Describe a time when you felt like leaving home.***

2 In Avery Corman's book, *Oh God!* someone rebukes God for not lifting a finger to destroy the evil in the world, saying, "So you've decided to just let us stumble along and never do a thing to help?" God replies:

Such a smart fella and you missed the point. . . .
I set all this up for you and made it so it can work.
Only the deal is you have to work at it.

- ***Explain God's point.***
- ***What evil in the world are you most concerned about and why?***

3 When Joseph's father arrived in Egypt, Joseph threw his arms around him and "cried for a long time." GENESIS 46:29 This moving scene stands in contrast to the way many modern parents and children greet one another. For example, a parent wrote Ann Landers:

The greatest regret of my life
is that I kept my son at arm's length.
I believed it was unmanly for males
to show affection for one another.
I treated my son the way my father treated me,
and I realize what a terrible mistake it was.

- ***On an unsigned sheet of paper, answer these questions:***
(a) When was the last time your father and you hugged one another? Your mother?
(b) Would you like to have a more openly affectionate relationship with your parents?
(c) On a scale of one to ten, how would you rate your relationship, in general, with your father? Your mother?
- ***What do you think is the biggest obstacle to a better relationship?***

STAGE 1: CHAPTER 3 47

Reflect

1 a) *How is this sequence in the movie a kind of parable of God and the human race? In other words, who do the following stand for: Lili, the puppeteer, the puppets?*

■ *Lili is like the human race; the puppeteer, like God; and the puppets, like the material things God created. Like Lili, we some times think that God doesn't care about us. The only things that bring us happiness are the material things of creation. Just as Lili missed the point (the puppets were vehicles of the puppeteer's love), we miss the point (creation is a vehicle of God)*

b) *Describe a time when you felt like leaving home.*

This makes a good written homework assignment. If the spirit of the class is good, have them break into groups of three or four and share their stories.

Have each group pick the best story to share with the class.

2 a) *Explain God's point.*

Jesus taught us what to do and how to do it. If we do what he taught us, it'll work. Ask students: Why don't we do what Jesus taught us to do?

b) *What evil in the world are you most concerned about and why?*

Have the class list evils on the chalkboard, select the top three, and discuss them.

3 a) *When was the last time your father and you hugged one another? Your mother?*

b) *Would you like to have a more openly affectionate relationship with your parents?*

c) *On a scale of one to ten, how would you rate your relationship, in general, with your father? Your mother?*

d) *What do you think is the biggest obstacle to a better relationship?*

Have students answer these questions anonymously. Collect, shuffle, tally on the chalkboard, and discuss.

PRAYER TIME with the Lord

QUESTION ***Some modern songs have spiritual messages, just as the psalms do. Identify one. Explain its message.***

This exercise can be done in groups.

Each group will pool their conclusions and report to the class.

Or the exercise can be done as a homework assignment, shared, and discussed.

SHARE—An adaptation of Psalm 22 was found on a suicide victim in North Carolina:

■ *King Heroin is my shepherd,*
I shall always want.
He maketh me to lie down in gutters.
He leadeth me
beside the troubled waters.
He destroyeth my soul.
He leadeth me in paths of wickedness
for the effort's sake.

Yea, I shall walk through the valley
of poverty and will fear all evil
for thou, Heroin, art with me.
Thy Needle and capsule
try to comfort me.
Thou strippest the table of groceries
in the presence of my family.
Thou robbest my head of reason.

My cup of sorrow runneth over.
Surely heroin addiction shall stalk me
all the days of my life and I will dwell
in the House of the Damned forever.
AUTHOR UNKNOWN

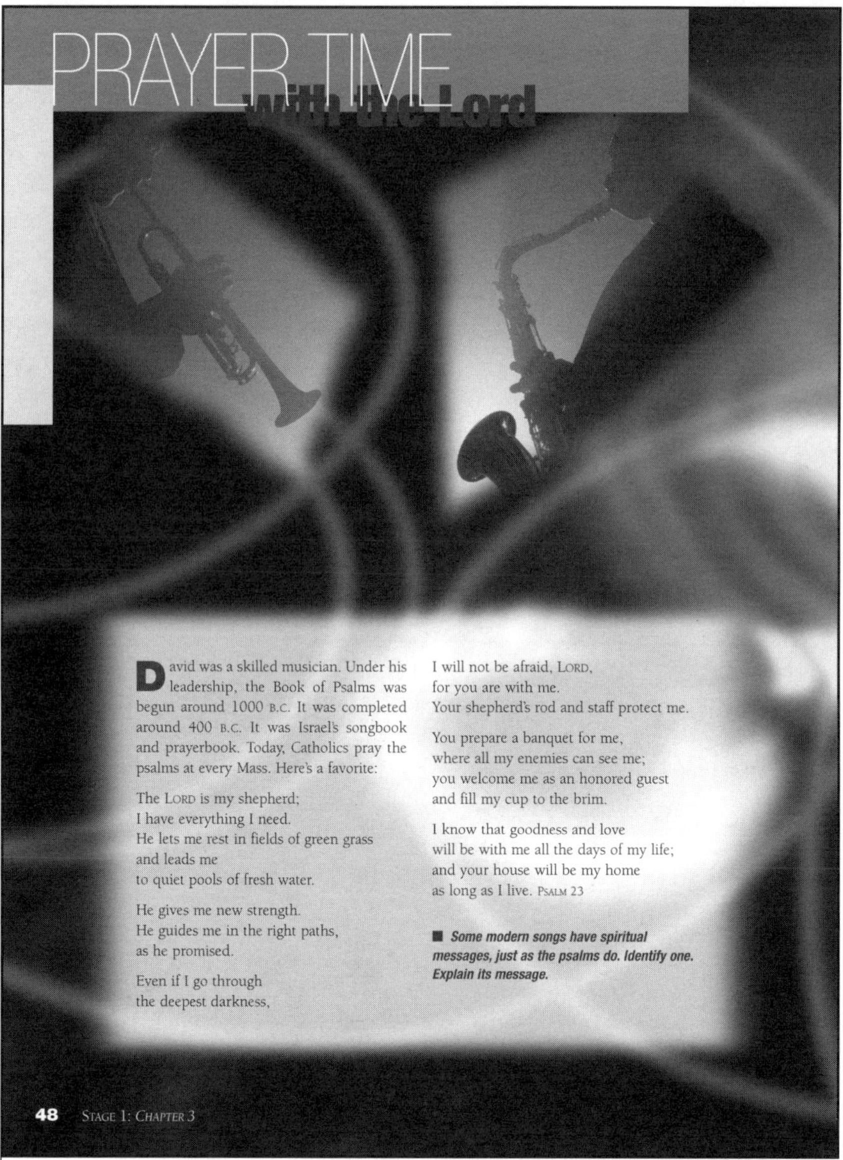

PRAYER TIME with the Lord

David was a skilled musician. Under his leadership, the Book of Psalms was begun around 1000 B.C. It was completed around 400 B.C. It was Israel's songbook and prayerbook. Today, Catholics pray the psalms at every Mass. Here's a favorite:

The LORD is my shepherd;
I have everything I need.
He lets me rest in fields of green grass
and leads me
to quiet pools of fresh water.

He gives me new strength.
He guides me in the right paths,
as he promised.

Even if I go through
the deepest darkness,
I will not be afraid, LORD,
for you are with me.
Your shepherd's rod and staff protect me.

You prepare a banquet for me,
where all my enemies can see me;
you welcome me as an honored guest
and fill my cup to the brim.

I know that goodness and love
will be with me all the days of my life;
and your house will be my home
as long as I live. PSALM 23

■ ***Some modern songs have spiritual messages, just as the psalms do. Identify one. Explain its message.***

48 STAGE 1: CHAPTER 3

PRAYER Journal

QUESTION ***Pick out some problem from your life or from our world. Compose a prayer to God about it. Speak from the heart as Jeremiah did. Here are suggestions for opening lines:***

(a) Lord, life is really unfair.

(b) Lord, why did you make growing up a hassle?

(c) Lord, why do you let drug pushers wreck people's lives?

ACTIVITY—Divide the class into groups of three or four. Have them share prayers and select the best ones to be read to the class.

NOTES

PRAYER Journal

One form of prayer is to speak to God from the heart, holding nothing back. It is telling it like it is. Here is an excerpt from such a prayer by the prophet Jeremiah:

LORD, everyone makes fun of me;
they laugh at me all day long. . . .
I am ridiculed and scorned all the time
because I proclaim your message. . . .

I hear everybody whispering. . . .
Even my close friends
wait for my downfall. . . .

Why was I born?
Was it only to have trouble and sorrow,
to end my life in disgrace? JEREMIAH 20:7–8, 10, 18

■ ***Pick out some problem from your life or from our world. Compose a prayer to God about it. Speak from the heart as Jeremiah did. Here are some suggestions for opening lines: (a) Lord, life is really unfair. (b) Lord, why did you make growing up a hassle? (c) Lord, why do you let drug pushers wreck people's lives?***

SCRIPTURE Journal

1	In praise of the Creator	Psalm 104
2	Covenant with Abram	Genesis 15
3	Sinai Covenant	Exodus 19–20
4	Davidic Covenant	2 Samuel 7
5	Re-creation	Revelation 21:1–8

■ ***Pick one of the above passages. Read it prayerfully and write a short statement to Jesus expressing your feelings about it.***

STAGE 1: CHAPTER 3 **49**

SCRIPTURE Journal

QUESTION ***Pick one of the passages. Read it prayerfully and write a short statement to Jesus expressing your feelings about it.***

ACTIVITY—Read aloud this excerpt from the fifth reading. Repeat it. Then have the students write a brief prayer to Jesus expressing their feelings about it:

I saw a new heaven and a new earth. The first heaven and the first earth disappeared . . . I heard a loud voice speaking . . . "Now God's home is with his people! He will live with them, and . . . wipe away all tears from their eyes. There will be no more death, no more grief or crying or pain. The old things have disappeared. REVELATION 21:1–4

Have volunteers share their prayer.

Classroom Resources

CATECHISM

Catechism of the Catholic Church *Second Edition*

For further enrichment, you might refer to:

1. Old Testament	Index	p. 829
	Glossary	p. 890
2. Creation	Index	pp. 779–80
	Glossary	p. 873
3. Covenant	Index	p. 779
	Glossary	p. 873

See also: Angel(s), Sin, Israel.
—AVAILABLE FROM THE UNITED STATES CATHOLIC CONFERENCE, WASHINGTON DC

VIDEO

Come Journey with Me

Six segments, 30–60 minutes each. A thematic approach to the Old Testament from the viewpoint of the prophets.
—AVAILABLE FROM BROWN-ROA, DUBUQUE, IA

BOOKS

The New Jerome Biblical Commentary

Editors: Raymond Brown, Joseph Fitzmyer, Roland Murphy

Chapters 1–39 contain a concise scholarly overview of the Old Testament books. Chapters 64–73 contain concise general articles on the Old Testament. 1992
—AVAILABLE FROM LITURGICAL PRESS, COLLEGEVILLE, MN

Psalms Beyond 2000

Twenty-two weeks of brief, daily meditations on each of the 150 psalms. Each week begins with a practical instruction on how to meditate (e.g. posture, journaling, God's presence, distractions, dryness). 1996
—AVAILABLE FROM THOMAS MORE PUBLISHING, ALLEN, TX

NOTE

For a list of (1) General resources for professional background and (2) Addresses, phone/fax numbers of major publishing companies, see Appendix B of this Resource Manual.

CHAPTER 4
New Testament

CHAPTER at a Glance

This chapter provides the student with an overview of the ministry and teaching of Jesus and how it applies to our lives today.

NOTEBOOK—Have a student read aloud the four paragraphs beginning: "In the beginning the Word already existed; . . ." Reread the last paragraph and have students summarize it in their notebooks:

OT = Radio	*We hear God's Word.*
NT = TV	*We also see God's Word*

Birth of Jesus

QUESTION **1** ***Some people observe that there is a close resemblance between this story and the Christmas story. What do you think they have in mind?***

■ *This story shows Dore waiting and praying for rescue, beginning to wonder if it will come.*

Then a "star" of light appears in the murky darkness of the water to give him hope.

The Christmas story shows the Jews waiting and praying for rescue by the promised Messiah. They, too, were beginning to wonder if he would ever come.

Then the "star" of Bethlehem appeared in the night sky to give them hope.

DISCUSS—Have the students recall a time when they were in a "praying-waiting" situation—wondering what would happen. To get them started, share with them such a situation from your own life.

In the beginning the Word already existed;
the Word was with God,
and the Word was God. . . .
The Word was the source of life. . . .

The Word became a human being, and . . .
lived among us. We saw his glory . . .
as the Father's only Son. . . .

No one has ever seen God.
The only Son, who is the same as God . . .
has made him known.
JOHN 1:1, 4; 14, 18

The Old Testament is like the radio;
you hear God's Word.
The New Testament is like television;
you not only hear God's Word
but also see it come alive in Jesus.

CHAPTER **at a Glance**

Birth of Jesus
Birth narratives
Ministry preview

Baptism of Jesus
New era
New creation
New Adam

Miracles of Jesus
Signs of the Messiah
Signs of the Kingdom
Signs inviting faith

Death of Jesus

Resurrection of Jesus

Spirit of Jesus

Birth of Jesus

Darrel Dore was inside a room in the platform of an oil rig in the Gulf of Mexico. Suddenly, the rig and its platform capsized. It began to sink into the sea. The lights of the room flickered and went out. Soon the room Dore was in began to fill with water—except for a big air bubble in the corner of the ceiling.

Dore plunged his head inside the air bubble. For twenty hours, he shivered and prayed inside it. Then when he had just about lost hope, a tiny glow of light appeared in the murky darkness of the water. It was a light on a diver's helmet. Rescue had arrived.

1 ***Some people observe that there is a close resemblance between this story and the Christmas story. What do you think they have in mind?***

50

The situation need not have been a life-changing one. For example, the author went through a "waiting-praying" situation years ago when he sent out his first article to a magazine for publication. He was waiting—and praying—hoping it would be accepted.

NOTEBOOK—Give the students time to think and record their thoughts. Have them share their experience in groups of three or four, choosing the most interesting experience to share with the entire class.

Birth narratives

QUESTION **2** ***How do the Gospels of Mark and John begin?***

NOTES

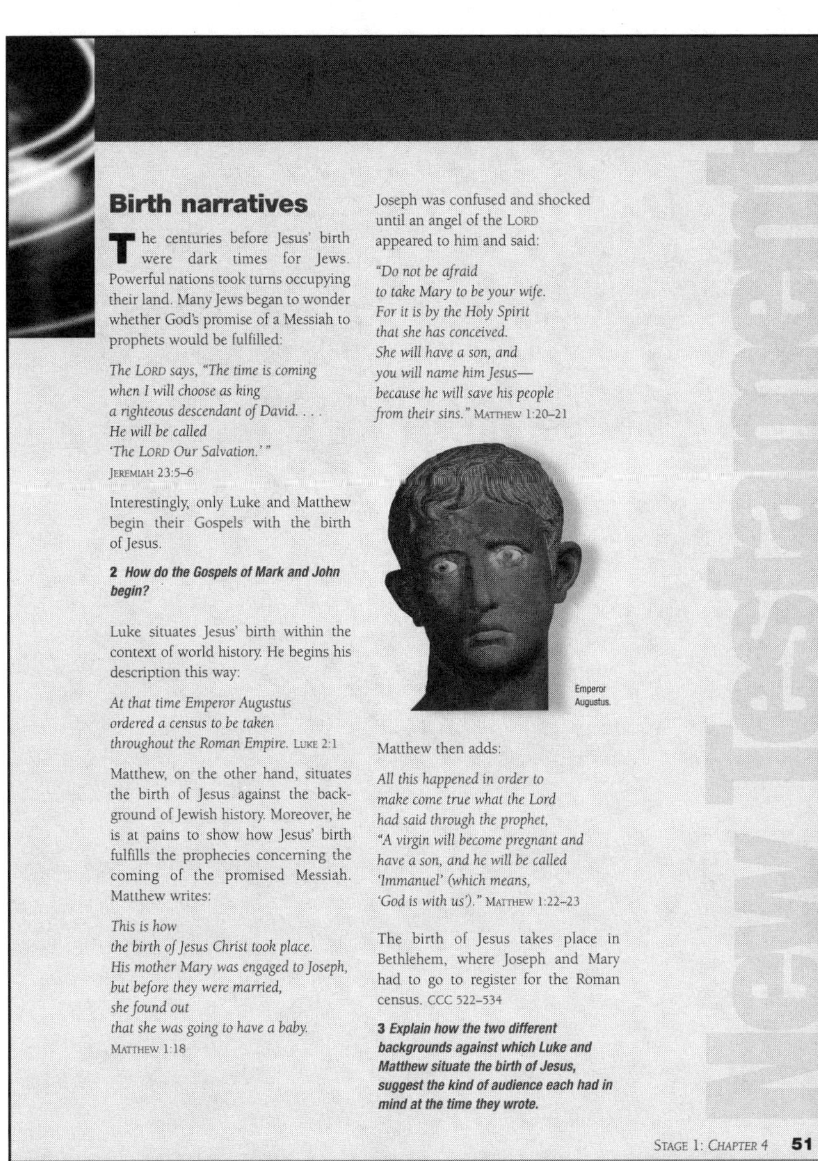

Birth narratives

The centuries before Jesus' birth were dark times for Jews. Powerful nations took turns occupying their land. Many Jews began to wonder whether God's promise of a Messiah to prophets would be fulfilled:

The LORD says, "The time is coming
when I will choose as king
a righteous descendant of David. . . .
He will be called
'The LORD Our Salvation.'"
JEREMIAH 23:5–6

Interestingly, only Luke and Matthew begin their Gospels with the birth of Jesus.

2 How do the Gospels of Mark and John begin?

Luke situates Jesus' birth within the context of world history. He begins his description this way:

At that time Emperor Augustus
ordered a census to be taken
throughout the Roman Empire. LUKE 2:1

Matthew, on the other hand, situates the birth of Jesus against the background of Jewish history. Moreover, he is at pains to show how Jesus' birth fulfills the prophecies concerning the coming of the promised Messiah. Matthew writes:

This is how
the birth of Jesus Christ took place.
His mother Mary was engaged to Joseph,
but before they were married,
she found out
that she was going to have a baby.
MATTHEW 1:18

Joseph was confused and shocked until an angel of the LORD appeared to him and said:

"Do not be afraid
to take Mary to be your wife.
For it is by the Holy Spirit
that she has conceived.
She will have a son, and
you will name him Jesus—
because he will save his people
from their sins." MATTHEW 1:20–21

Emperor Augustus.

Matthew then adds:

All this happened in order to
make come true what the Lord
had said through the prophet,
"A virgin will become pregnant and
have a son, and he will be called
'Immanuel' (which means,
'God is with us')." MATTHEW 1:22–23

The birth of Jesus takes place in Bethlehem, where Joseph and Mary had to go to register for the Roman census. CCC 522–534

3 Explain how the two different backgrounds against which Luke and Matthew situate the birth of Jesus, suggest the kind of audience each had in mind at the time they wrote.

New Testament

STAGE 1: CHAPTER 4 **51**

■ *Mark begins with a "one-sentence" outline of the "two-part" structure of his Gospel:*

This is the Good News about
Jesus Christ, the Son of God.

1 *Jesus is the Christ (Messiah).*
It ends with Peter saying to Jesus,
"You are the Messiah." MARK 8:29
2 *Jesus is the Son of God.*
It ends with a soldier on Calvary saying,
"Surely, this man was the Son of God."
MARK 15:39

John begins the way a composer begins a symphony: with an overture (preview of what is to come.) See the four-paragraph introduction on the previous page.

CLARIFY—Ancient Jews married very early. Rabbis held 13 to be a suitable age for women and 18 for men. Mary and Joseph were probably within this age range, even though classical paintings portray them as being much older, especially Joseph.

Jewish marriages began with a "betrothal" (similar to an engagement). It probably stemmed from the ancient custom of having parents pick marriage partners. Sometimes the partners barely knew one another.

The betrothal gave them a chance to get acquainted. Lasting about a year, it had all the legal force of a marriage. A betrothed man could not renounce his betrothed partner, except by divorce. If he died during the betrothal period, she became his legal widow.

In his book *Beyond East and West*, John Wu, a Chinese Christian, says that he didn't meet his wife until their wedding. When a Western friend was amazed at this, Wu said:

> *I was amazed at his amazement and said to him, "Did you choose your parents, your brothers and your sisters? You love them all the same."*

CLARIFY—Jesus was not born on December 25. Early Christians picked this day to celebrate Jesus' birthday because it was the pagan Roman feast of the "Unconquerable Sun."

The feast fell on the "winter solstice" (when nights grew shorter and days longer). Christians saw Jesus as the one and only "unconquerable sun" and true "light of the world."

QUESTION ***3 Explain how the two different backgrounds against which Luke and Matthew situate the birth of Jesus suggest the kind of audience each had in mind at the time they wrote.***

■ *Luke's world-history background suggests a non-Jewish audience.*

Matthew's Jewish history background suggests a Jewish audience. Thus, he peppers his Gospel with frequent references to the OT prophecies.

Share Your meditation

NOTEBOOK—To prepare students for their "pencil meditation," recall Simeon and Anna. They were aged Jews who were waiting for the Messiah and facing death without any sign of his coming. Luke says of the widow Anna:

> *She was now 84 years old.*
> *She never left the Temple;*
> *day and night she worshiped God,*
> *fasting and praying.* LUKE 2:36–37

ACTIVITY—Have students share their "pencil meditations" in groups. Share the best ones with the entire class.

PRAYER hotline

DISCUSS—What point is being made in the "Prayer hotline"?

> *Once the Bible touches your heart,*
> *you can never be the same.*

> *Martin Luther said of the Bible:*
> *"It is alive;*
> *it speaks to me;*
> *it has feet, it runs after me;*
> *it has hands, it lays hold of me."*

Ministry preview

NOTEBOOK—Develop on the chalkboard the following two diagrams for entry into the students' notebooks. The first diagram sums up the "gift" symbolism:

Gold	*Kingship*	*Son of David*
Myrrh	*Humanity*	*Son of Mary*
Incense	*Divinity*	*Son of God*

The second previews the Gentile/Jewish response to Jesus' message:

Magi	*Many Gentiles will accept it.*
Herod	*Many Jews will reject it.*

Four Gospels

QUESTION **4 *How would each approach and view be different from the other three? Why?***

SHARE YOUR meditation

Nathaniel Hawthorne was dead. On his desk lay the outline to a story he never got a chance to write.

It concerned an important person who was coming to a certain place. People dreamed about his coming. They prepared for it; they waited for it, but he never came.

Nathaniel Hawthorne's unfinished story is like the Old Testament. It centered around a promised Messiah for whom everyone was preparing and waiting. But he never came.

■ ***I imagine I am an old Jew, living a few months before Jesus' birth. All my life I've waited for the Messiah. What are my thoughts as I prepare to die without any sign of his coming?***

PRAYER hotline

Lord, help me lay hold of the Bible until it lays hold of me.

William H. Houghton (adapted)

Ministry preview

Shortly after Jesus' birth, Magi show up in Jerusalem and ask, "Where is the baby born to be king of the Jews?" King Herod calls his advisers and asks: "Where will the Messiah be born?" The advisers say:

> *In the town of Bethlehem. . . .*
> *For this is what the prophets wrote:*
> *"Bethlehem, . . .*
> *from you will come a leader*
> *who will guide my people Israel."*
> MATTHEW 2:5–6

The Magi go on to Bethlehem. When they see Jesus, they kneel down and present him with gifts of gold, frankincense, and myrrh. Early Christian writers saw these gifts as being prophetic and symbolic:

■ **Gold**	**"King" of metals** (Points to Jesus' *kingship*)
■ **Frankincense**	**used in worship** (Points to Jesus' *divinity*)
■ **Myrrh**	**used for burial** (Points to Jesus' *humanity*)

After the Magi depart, an angel appears to Joseph in a dream and warns him that Herod is plotting to kill Jesus.

> *Joseph got up,*
> *took the child and his mother,*
> *and left during the night for Egypt,*
> *where they stayed until Herod died.*
> *This was done to make come true*
> *what the Lord had said through the prophet,*
> *"I called my Son out of Egypt."*
> MATTHEW 2:14–15

Herod's hostile reaction to Jesus stands in contrast to the Magi's reverent reaction. It previews how people will react to Jesus in the days ahead. Many Jews will reject him; many Gentiles will accept him.

Four Gospels

A TV director was planning a series called *San Francisco: A Tourist's View.* He decided to present the city through the eyes of four tourists, as they approached it for the first time by:

■ **Rail**	**Train**
■ **Road**	**Car**
■ **Water**	**Boat**
■ **Air**	**Plane**

Thus, viewers would get four different views of San Francisco.

4 *How would each approach and view be different from the other three? Why?*

Similarly, the New Testament writers provide their readers with four views of Jesus. CCC 514–15 Three (Mark, Matthew, Luke) are quite similar, while John's view is quite different.

One reason for the difference is that John writes at a later date for a more mature Christian audience. Thus, John presumes some knowledge of Jesus.

52 STAGE 1: CHAPTER 4

■ *Each would give us a special view and insight into the city.*

The air approach would give us an overview, while the other approaches would give us close-up views.

Thus, three approaches to San Francisco (rail, road, water) are quite similar, while the fourth (air) is quite different.

In fact, Mark, Matthew, and Luke are so similar that we refer to them as the synoptic Gospels.

The word "synoptic"—syn ("together"), optic ("seen")—indicates that when "seen together," the similarities of these three Gospels are striking. Take the following example:

NOTES

For example, he identifies Jesus immediately as the Messiah and goes on from there. JOHN 1:41 John also substitutes the expression "eternal life" for the expression "Kingdom of God."

Because each evangelist wrote for a different audience, each stresses a different facet of Jesus:

- **Mark** — **Suffering Messiah**
- **Matthew** — **Teaching Messiah**
- **Luke** — **Compassionate Messiah**
- **John** — **Life-giving Messiah**

5 Why might Matthew, writing primarily for Jews, stress the "teaching Messiah"?

Baptism of Jesus

Matthew does a "fast forward" from the story of the Magi to the baptism of Jesus. CCC 535–37 Without any introduction, he writes:

At that time, John the Baptist came to the desert of Judea and started preaching. "Turn away from sins," he said, "because the Kingdom of heaven is near!" MATTHEW 3:1–2

Matthew then adds:

John was the man the prophet Isaiah was talking about when he said . . . "Someone is shouting in the desert, Prepare the road for the Lord. . . ." People came to him from . . . all over. . . . They confessed their sins, and he baptized them in the Jordan. MATTHEW 3:3, 5–6

One day, to John's surprise, Jesus waded into the Jordan to be baptized. John said to Jesus:

"I ought to be baptized by you. . . ." But Jesus answered him, "Let it be so for now." MATTHEW 3:13–15

After Jesus was baptized, a remarkable thing happened.

While he was praying, heaven was opened, and the Holy Spirit came down upon him in bodily form like a dove. And a voice came from heaven, "You are my own dear Son. I am pleased with you." LUKE 3:21–22

Three striking images stand out in this brief description:

- **The sky opens above Jesus**
- **A dovelike form descends upon Jesus**
- **A heavenly voice identifies Jesus**

To understand these images, we need to consider them within their historical and cultural context.

6 What is meant by a historical context? A cultural context?

BIBLE Connection

The 27 books of the New Testament are traditionally grouped as follows:

Gospels—4

Matthew	Luke
Mark	John

Acts of the Apostles—1

Letters—21

1–2 Thessalonians	1–2 Timothy
Galatians	Titus
1–2 Corinthians	Hebrews
Romans	1–2–3 John
Philippians	1–2 Peter
Colossians	James
Ephesians	Jude
Philemon	

Revelation—1

ART Connection

This fifteenth-century Italian wood carving portrays Saint Luke composing his Gospel. Unaware that books did not appear until 150 years after Luke lived, the artist portrays the evangelist writing in a book, not a scroll.

STAGE 1: CHAPTER 4 **53**

MARK 9:2–3	MATTHEW 7:1–2
Six days later Jesus took with him Peter, James and John, and led them up a high mountain where they were alone.	*Six days later Jesus took with him Peter and the brothers James and John and led them up a high mountain where they were alone.*
As they looked on, a change came over Jesus, and his clothes became shining white— whiter than anyone in the world could wash them.	*As they looked on, a change came over Jesus: his face was shining like the sun and his clothes were dazzling white.*

ACTIVITY—You may wish to have a student copy the above parallel on the chalkboard to illustrate the striking similarities.

Experts do not fully agree on the times, places, and audiences for whom the evangelists wrote, but the following is probable:

Mark	*70–*	*Rome*	*Persecuted Romans*
Matthew	*70+*	*Syria*	*Converted Jews*
Luke	*70+*	*Greece*	*Lower-class Greeks*
John	*90+*	*Ephesus*	*All Christians*

QUESTION **5** ***Why might Matthew, writing primarily for Jews, stress the "teaching Messiah"?***

- *Jews wanted to know how Jesus' teaching jived with Moses' teaching and how Jesus' life jived with what the prophets foretold concerning the Messiah. Commenting on this question, Jesus himself said:*

*"Do not think that I have come
to do away with the Law of Moses
and the teachings of the prophets.
I have not come to do away with them,
but to make their teachings come true.*
MATTHEW 5:17

Baptism of Jesus

QUESTION **6** ***What is meant by a historical context? A cultural context?***

- ***Historical** context: the time frame in which an event took place: pre-civil war, post-civil war.*

  ***Cultural** context: the moral, faith, social, artistic values of a people.*

ART Connection

What is unusual about the carving?

- *Bull under the desk. Drawing on Revelation 4:7, artists symbolized the four evangelists as:*

a man (Matthew)	*a lion (Mark)*
an ox (Luke)	*an eagle (John)*

Note that three are similar (walkers), the third quite different (a flyer).

Up Close & Personal

CLARIFY—In spite of his spiritual experiences, Merton was still a long way from conversion and becoming Catholic. This didn't happen until he was 23 years old.

At the age of 26, he put all he owned in a duffel bag and entered the Trappist monastery in Kentucky. There he became an influential author and international figure.

A freak accident (electrocution from faulty wiring) took his life in 1968 at the age of 53, while he was attending a world conference of monks in Bangkok.

ART Connection

The "tree of forbidden fruit" was the "tree that brought spiritual death" to Adam and Eve after they disobeyed God. It stood in the Garden of Eden. GENESIS 2:9, 3:2

New era

CLARIFY—The creation story says: "God made a dome" to separate the water under it from the water above it. GENESIS 1:6–7

1	*Waters under*	*Oceans, lakes, rivers*
2	*Waters above*	*Reservoirs of "rain" water*

The *World of God* is cited in Psalm 104:2: "You built your home on the waters above."

The *World of Dead* is cited in Psalm 139:7: "If I lay down in the world of the dead, you would be there."

New creation

CLARIFY—Recall the "three-act play" image of the Bible:

Act 1	*Creation*	*God creates us*
Act 2	*De-creation*	*Sin destroys us*
Act 3	*Re-creation*	*God saves us*

The "third act" deals with the "new creation" or "re-creation" of the world.

Up Close & Personal

Thomas Merton

Thomas Merton was orphaned at 16. The summer after graduating from high school, he backpacked his way across Europe. What happened that summer eventually led him to become a Catholic and a priest. In *The Seven Storey Mountain* he writes:

I don't know how it began—
I found myself looking into
churches. . . .

For the first time in my life
I began to find out
something of . . . this Person . . .
called Christ.
The saints of those forgotten
days had left upon the walls
of their churches
a word [I could understand]. . . .

But above all, the most real
and most immediate source . . .
was Christ himself
present in those churches.
It was he
who was teaching me . . .
more directly
than I was capable of realizing.

ART Connection

This church door contrasts the "tree of forbidden fruit" (de-creation) with the "tree of the cross" (re-creation). The first Adam and the first Eve are contrasted with Jesus (the new Adam) and Mary (the new Eve).

New era

First, let us consider the image of the sky opening above Jesus. Ancient Jews viewed the universe as being made up of three worlds stacked one upon the other, like pancakes:

- **World of God** — **Top world**
- **World of the Living** — **Middle world**
- **World of the Dead** — **Bottom world**

After Adam sinned, a tidal wave of sin flooded the "world of the living" (middle world). People prayed to God to come down and set things right. Thus, the psalmist prayed, "O LORD, tear the sky open and come down." PSALM 144:5

It is within this context that we must interpret the image of the sky opening above Jesus. God has heard the prayer of the people and is coming down, in the person of Jesus, to set things right.

The opening of the sky symbolizes that a *new era* in history is beginning.

New creation

The context for the "dove" image is the Book of Genesis. There it describes the "power of God . . . moving over the water" just prior to the creation of the universe. GENESIS 1:2

Ancient rabbis compared God's power moving over the water to the image of a dove hovering over its newborn. CCC 695, 701 Thus, the dove hovering over Jesus signifies that a *new creation* is about to take place. This fulfills what Isaiah foretold:

The Lord says,
"I am making a new earth. . . .
Be glad and rejoice forever
in what I create." ISAIAH 65:17–18

New Adam

This brings us to the final image: the voice from heaven saying to Jesus, "You are my own dear Son."

The Book of Genesis portrays God creating Adam as the "firstborn" of the human family. Thus, the voice identifies Jesus as the *new Adam*. He is the "firstborn" of the *new creation* (re-creation).

Saint Paul draws this comparison between the first Adam and "last Adam" (Jesus):

The first man, Adam,
was created a living being;
but the last Adam [Jesus]
is the life-giving Spirit. . . .

The first Adam,
made of earth, came from the earth;
the last Adam came from heaven. . . .
Just as we wear the likeness
of the man made of earth, so we will wear
the likeness of the Man from heaven.
1 CORINTHIANS 15:45, 47, 49

54 STAGE 1: *CHAPTER 4*

New Adam

NOTEBOOK—Have students sum up Paul's famous passage comparing Adam with Jesus:

Adam —— Man from earth / Firstborn of old creation

Jesus —— Man from heaven / Firstborn of new creation

We bear the image of the "earthly Adam" (flesh) and the "heavenly Adam" (spirit). This produces a "tension" in our lives. Paul describes it this way: "I don't do what I would like to do, but instead I do what I hate" ROMANS 7:15.

QUESTION **7** ***Besides revealing the "new creation," how do the three events at Jesus' baptism act as a revelation of the Trinity?***

NOTES

THINK about it Why not let Jesus take over my life? He can do more with it than I can.
Anonymous

LIFE Connection

Paul Stookey was in a popular singing group, "Peter, Paul, and Mary." In spite of his success, he was not at peace with himself.

One day he told singer Bob Dylan about it. Dylan told Stookey to go back to his old high school for a visit and start reading the Bible. Later, Stookey wrote:

All the truths I sought
were contained
in the life of this man. . . .
It was fantastic. . . .
He set a good example,
but it never occurred to me
that he could really be
the Son of God.

Then one night during a concert in Austin, Texas, he met a young man. Stookey writes:

Somehow this guy
made all the reading
in Scripture make sense . . .
and I asked Jesus to come in
and take over my life.

That was the start of a new life for Paul Stookey.

And so the three events that take place at Jesus' baptism signify the following:

- **Sky opens** — **New era**
- **Dove comes down** — **New creation**
- **Voice speaks** — **New Adam**

7 Besides revealing the "new creation," how do the three events at Jesus' baptism act as a revelation of the Trinity?

Let us now turn to the life and teaching of Jesus in the four Gospels.

Miracles of Jesus

A speaker on a Miami radio station startled a lot of listeners. He said that if he had the power to work miracles, he would use it far differently than Jesus did:

I would not cure one person of blindness;
I would make blindness impossible.
I would not cure one person of leprosy;
I would abolish leprosy.

The speaker's remarks raise an important question. What was the purpose of Jesus' miracles? Did he heal the blind and the lepers because he pitied them? Did he heal them because they asked him to? MARK 1:40–41 Or was there another reason?

8 What is your reaction to the speaker's remarks? What was the purpose of Jesus' miracles? For example, why do you think he healed people?

Miracles are signs

To understand the purpose of Jesus' miracles, we need to understand that Jesus' baptism sets in motion the "re-creation" of the world.

The *first step* in this "re-creation" process is the coming of the Messiah and the Kingdom of God. This is where the miracles of Jesus enter the picture. They are signs announcing the arrival of these two great events.

STAGE 1: *CHAPTER 4* **55**

Voice	*Father*
Jesus	*Son*
Dove	*Holy Spirit*

Miracles of Jesus

QUESTION **8** ***What is your reaction to the speaker's remarks? What was the purpose of Jesus' miracles? For example, why do you think he healed people?***

■ *The Miami speaker misses the point of Jesus' miracles—just as many people did in Jesus' day. We need to remind the speaker that:*

(a) Jesus fed the people (JOHN 6:26), *but they got hungry again.*
(b) Jesus raised Lazarus (JOHN 11:44), *but he died again.*
(c) Jesus healed Peter's mother-in-law (MARK 1:31), *but she got ill again.*

Obviously, therefore, there was deeper reason for Jesus' miracles. What was it?

Miracles were signs. Jesus himself referred to this. The day after feeding 5,000, many people came looking for him. Jesus said: "You are looking for me because you ate the bread and had all you wanted, not because you understood my miracles." JOHN 6:26

How, then, should we understand Jesus' signs? They were signs announcing two long-awaited events:

(1) the Kingdom of God
(2) the Messiah of God

LIFE Connection

Bob Dylan's career has spanned nearly forty years from 1961 to 2000—and still counting. Emerging from the small mining town of Hibbing, Minnesota, with just a guitar and the clothes on his back, he found his way to Greenwich Village, New York, where he became an immediate folk-singing hero. His protest songs, like "Blowin' in the Wind" and "The Times They Are A-Changin'," became rallying cries against injustice.

In telling Paul Stookey to go back to his high school, he was telling him to go back and get in touch again with his *physical roots*—from which he had apparently become disconnected.

In telling him to start reading the Bible, he was telling him to go back and get in touch again with his *spiritual roots*—from which he had also become disconnected. There he would find not only the peace he sought, but also the "giver" of that peace, Jesus Christ.

LIFE Connection

We all know people whose lives were changed by faith. Merton and Stookey are two examples.

LIFE Connection

Recall Jesus' words:

Everything is possible, for the person who has faith. MARK 9:23

THINK about it

Buechner's point is an important one. Miracles can strengthen faith, but they cannot produce faith (as we shall see). On the contrary, it is faith that produces the miracle.

Signs of the Messiah

The point of this section may be summed up in one sentence:

"What the prophets foretold
about the Messiah, Jesus fulfilled."

Signs of the Kingdom

A second way that miracles served as signs of the arrival of God's Kingdom is the manifestation of Jesus' power over demons (evil spirits). When Jesus began to manifest this power, people began to ask, "What does this mean?" MARK 1:27

Jesus, himself, answered that question. One day, when he was expelling evil spirits, he was accused of doing so by means of Satan's power. Jesus responded:

"No, it is rather by means of God's power
that I drive out demons,
and this proves the Kingdom of God
has already come to you." LUKE 11:20

QUESTION **9** ***If the Kingdom of God has arrived, why is there still so much evil in the world? Why do we still pray in the Lord's Prayer, "Thy Kingdom come"?***

The response to this question cannot be stressed enough. It needs to be repeated again and again:

a) God's Kingdom is like a seed. It is planted and growing, but it has not yet borne its intended fruit.

The four evangelists, who wrote in Greek, used three different Greek words in referring to the miracles of Jesus:

- **Teras** — **Something marvelous**
- **Dynamis** — **Something powerful**
- **Semeion** — **Important sign**

The favorite word for "miracle" in John's Gospel is *semeion.* John favored this word because it underscored the most important point about Jesus' miracles. They were signs announcing the arrival of the:

- **Messiah of God**
- **Kingdom of God**

LIFE Connection

When asked, "Why do you believe in miracles?" Henry Drummond replied: "Because I see them every day in the changed lives of men and women . . . through faith in the power of the living Christ."

Signs of the Messiah

To understand how miracles announced the Messiah, we need to keep in mind that the prophet Isaiah had foretold that certain events would signal the arrival of the Messiah:

The blind will be able to see,
and the deaf will hear.
The lame will leap and dance. ISAIAH 35:5–6

One day some people asked Jesus, "Are you the one John said was going to come, or should we expect someone else?" Jesus said:

"The blind can see,
the lame can walk . . .
the deaf can hear." LUKE 7:22

By his reply, Jesus makes it clear that the signs foretold by Isaiah are now taking place. Jesus is the promised Messiah.

This brings us to the second main purpose of Jesus' miracles. CCC 541–50

THINK about it

A miracle is an event that strengthens faith. But faith in God is less apt to proceed from miracles than miracles from faith in God.

Fredrick Buechner

Signs of the Kingdom

Before Adam and Eve turned their backs on God, there was no sin, sickness, or death in the world. All of this changed with their sin. It ushered in the "Kingdom of Satan" and from that moment on, those three evils held the human race in slavery.

It is against this background that we must read the Gospel accounts of Jesus' power over each of these three evils. Jesus:

- **Forgives sin** — **Luke 5:17–26**
- **Heals the sick** — **Mark 1:29–31**
- **Raises the dead** — **Luke 7:12–16**

Jesus' mastery over sin, sickness, and death is a dramatic sign pointing to the beginning of the demise of the "Kingdom of Satan" and the rise of the "Kingdom of God."

9 ***If the Kingdom of God has arrived, why is there still so much evil in the world? Why do we still pray in the Lord's Prayer, "Thy Kingdom come"?***

Jesus compared the coming of God's Kingdom to the planting of a seed. It takes time to grow and bear fruit. MARK 4:26–29 Jesus' point is that the coming of God's Kingdom isn't going to be an instant occurrence, but a gradual and painful process.

This is why there is still so much evil in the world. This is why we still pray in the Lord's Prayer, "Thy Kingdom come!" Meanwhile, the "Kingdom of Satan" continues to wreak havoc in the world. It has not yet been destroyed. It is only under the sentence of death, and it will not die without a fight.

56 STAGE 1: CHAPTER 4

---

b) Satan's Kingdom is doomed. It is like a flower severed from its roots. It still looks as though it has life, but its days are numbered.

Signs inviting faith

NOTEBOOK—With the help of students develop on the chalkboard how the following miracles of Jesus served as *signs* of faith and *invitations* to faith:

Have the students enter the following diagram into their notebooks:

Blind — *open your eyes* / *see what Jesus does*

Deaf — *open your ears* / *hear what Jesus says*

Raising — *open your hearts* / *begin a new life*

NOTES

LITERARY Connection

The novel *Father Malachy's Miracle* was made into a Hollywood movie. It is a fanciful story of a priest in Scotland who gets the idea of praying for a miracle so powerful that it will leave no doubt about the truthfulness of God and religion.

"One spectacular miracle," he tells a friend, "and we shall prove to the world . . . that we have the Light and the truth."

And so he prays that on a certain night an evil nightclub will take flight and be carried off to a barren island off Scotland's coast.

The miracle takes place. But it backfires. Instead of convincing people of the truth, it is turned into a big publicity stunt by the nightclub's owner.

The story ends with a wiser Father Malachy realizing that you can't make people believe. You can only invite them to open their hearts to the gift of faith.

Signs inviting faith

But the miracles of Jesus do more than merely announce the coming of the Messiah and the Kingdom. They invite us to faith and action. CCC 543–46 How so?

The healing of the blind beggar invites us to *open our eyes* to what Jesus does. The healing of the deaf man invites us to *open our ears* to what Jesus says. The raising of the dead man invites us to *open our hearts* to Jesus and begin a new life in God's Kingdom.

People responded to Jesus' invitation in four ways. Jesus used this parable to illustrate each of these ways:

A farmer sowed seed in his field. (Ancient farmers sowed seed atop the soil and then plowed it under.)

Some seed fell on a path by the field. Birds stole it and ate it instantly.

Some fell on soil-covered rocks. It sprouted quickly but died when the sun baked the layer of soil.

Some blew into thorn bushes that fenced in the field to keep out animals. It sprouted but was choked to death by the thick thorns.

Finally, some seed fell on good soil and bore abundant fruit.

Jesus compared the four fates of seed to the four ways that people respond to his invitation:

Seed's fate	People's response
Fails to sprout	Reject
Sprouts but withers	Accept but falter
Sprouts but chokes	Accept but forget
Sprouts and grows	Accept and grows

10 ***What is your response to Jesus' invitation? Explain.***

DISCUSS—Use the following exercise to give students a chance to apply the Parable of the Sower to everyday life. Four students were discussing a guidance counselor:

- *Mike went to him and admitted that he was half-hearted in his approach to study. He agreed to study a half-hour longer each day.*

  Jordan approached him about his inability to read with speed and comprehension. The counselor arranged for a reading program designed to help just such students.

  Amy mustered up courage to tell him about her mother's alcohol problem. With the help of Amy's father, the counselor arranged for professional help for her mother.

  Jan was moved by their stories and decided to talk with the counselor about a problem she was having with another teacher.

Two month's later the four friends met again, and shared the results of their efforts:

- *Mike had kept his agreement to study more for about three weeks. Then he gradually drifted into his old ways.*

  Jordan was doing fine with his reading program, but found it a lot harder than he had anticipated. So he quit after the fifth session.

  Amy was ecstatic. Professional help was just what her mother needed. She joined an AA group and was a new person.

  Jan found the counselor old-fashioned and out of touch with kid's problems. By dismissing the counselor outright, she allowed the seed to be picked off before it could take root, just like in the parable.

List on the chalkboard the following "fates" of the seed in the Parable of the Sower. Ask them how they would match them up with Mike, Jordan, Amy, and Jan.

1	*Seed falls on path*	*Jan*
2	*Seed falls on rocks*	*Jordan*
3	*Seed falls among thorns*	*Mike*
4	*See falls on good soil*	*Amy*

QUESTION **10** ***What is your response to Jesus' invitation (to open your eyes, ears, and heart to Jesus)? Explain.***

ACTIVITY—Have the students answer this question in writing and anonymously.

Collect the assignments, review them, pick out some of the better responses. Share and discuss them with the students at the next class session.

LITERARY Connection

A much wiser Father Malachy realizes that miracles can't produce faith.

Recall that this was the same point Buechner made in the "Think about it." Refer the students back to page 56.

Share Your meditation

CLARIFY—The young man is a kind of "Christ figure": unjustly condemned and executed, but forgiving.

Again, have students share their "pencil meditation" in groups. Have each group pick out the best one to be shared with the entire class.

Arrest and Trial

CLARIFY—Stress the reasons for:

1 *the sharp conflict between Jesus and the religious leaders*
2 *the decision to destroy Jesus*

Conflict: *They see Jesus as a threat to their authority, beliefs, and teaching.*

Decision: *They fear "everyone will believe in him," and the Romans will take action to destroy their Temple and nation.*

Death of Jesus

DISCUSS—Have students cite some modern examples of the unexpected, for example, the sudden deaths of famous personalities that shocked their fans or followers.

Political figures: *Assassinations of JFK, RFK, Martin Luther King.*

Popular figures: *Deaths of John Kennedy, Jr., his wife Carolyn Bessette Kennedy, and her sister, Lauren; and Princess Diana.*

Rock stars: *Plane-crash deaths of Buddy Holly, Richie Valens, "The Big Bopper" (The song "The Day the Music Died" spoke people's feelings about this triple tragedy).*

Film stars: *James Dean, River Phoenix.*

Way of the Cross

ACTIVITY—Have students choose a station and do a "pencil meditation" following the three points suggested in the introduction. Have volunteers share their meditations.

SHARE YOUR meditation

The film *The Ox Bow Incident* concerns town leaders who bypass the law and hang three people without a trial. Later they learn the terrible truth. The three people were innocent.

Before being hanged, one young man asks to write a letter to his wife. After he is hanged, someone reads it. A part of it reads:

I suppose there's
some good men here,
only they don't realize
what they're doing.
They're the ones
I feel sorry for,
'cause it'll be over for me
in a little while, but they'll
have to go on remembering
the rest of their lives.

■ ***How do you account for the young man's lack of anger and calmness?***

Arrest and Trial

Jesus' claim to be the Messiah and to inaugurate God's Kingdom brings him into sharp conflict with the Jewish religious leaders of his time. More and more, they see Jesus as a threat to their authority and their own beliefs and teachings.

As a result, the gap between Jesus and the leaders widens day by day and week by week.

Finally, it reaches the breaking point, when Jesus raises Lazarus from the dead. The news of this miracle spreads everywhere. The religious leaders panic and say:

What shall we do?
Look at all the miracles
this man is performing!
If we let him go on this way,
everyone will believe in him,
and the Roman authorities will take action
and destroy our Temple and our nation!
JOHN 11:47–48

From that fateful day, the religious leaders plot to do away with Jesus. JOHN 11:53 The day arrives when Jesus is arrested, tried, and sentenced to crucifixion.

THINK about it

It wasn't the nails that held Jesus on the cross but his love for us.

Anonymous

Death of Jesus

An Associated Press news release might have described Jesus' crucifixion on Good Friday something like this:

JERUSALEM (AP)—
Jesus of Nazareth was executed today
outside the walls of this ancient city.
Death came at about three o'clock.

A freak thunderstorm
scattered the crowd of curious onlookers
and served as a fitting climax
to the brief but stormy career
of the controversial preacher
from the hill country of Galilee.

Burial took place immediately.
A police guard was posted at the grave site
as a precautionary measure.
The Galilean is survived by his mother.

The events of Good Friday left Jesus' followers in a state of shock. Their faith was shaken to the foundation.

Weren't Jesus' miracles *signs* that he was the Messiah? Weren't they *signs* that he was inaugurating God's Kingdom? How, then, could all this be reconciled with his death on the cross? CCC 599–630

Suddenly, all their dreams seemed buried with Jesus.

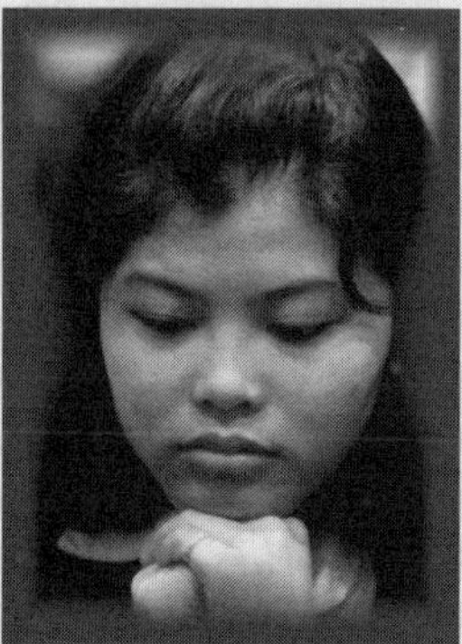

58 STAGE 1: CHAPTER 4

NOTEBOOK—With the help of the students, develop the following diagram of the four kinds of pain Jesus endured during his passion:

Mind	*Mental* / *Pain of anticipation*
Heart	*Emotional* / *Pain of desertion by apostles*
Body	*Physical* / *Pain of crucifixion*
Soul	*Spiritual* / *"Forsaken" by God*

CLARIFY—Explain how the crucifixion acts as a sign, an invitation, and a revelation.

Sign	*"No greater love"*
Invitation	*"Love as I love"*
Revelation	*"Love entails pain"*

NOTES

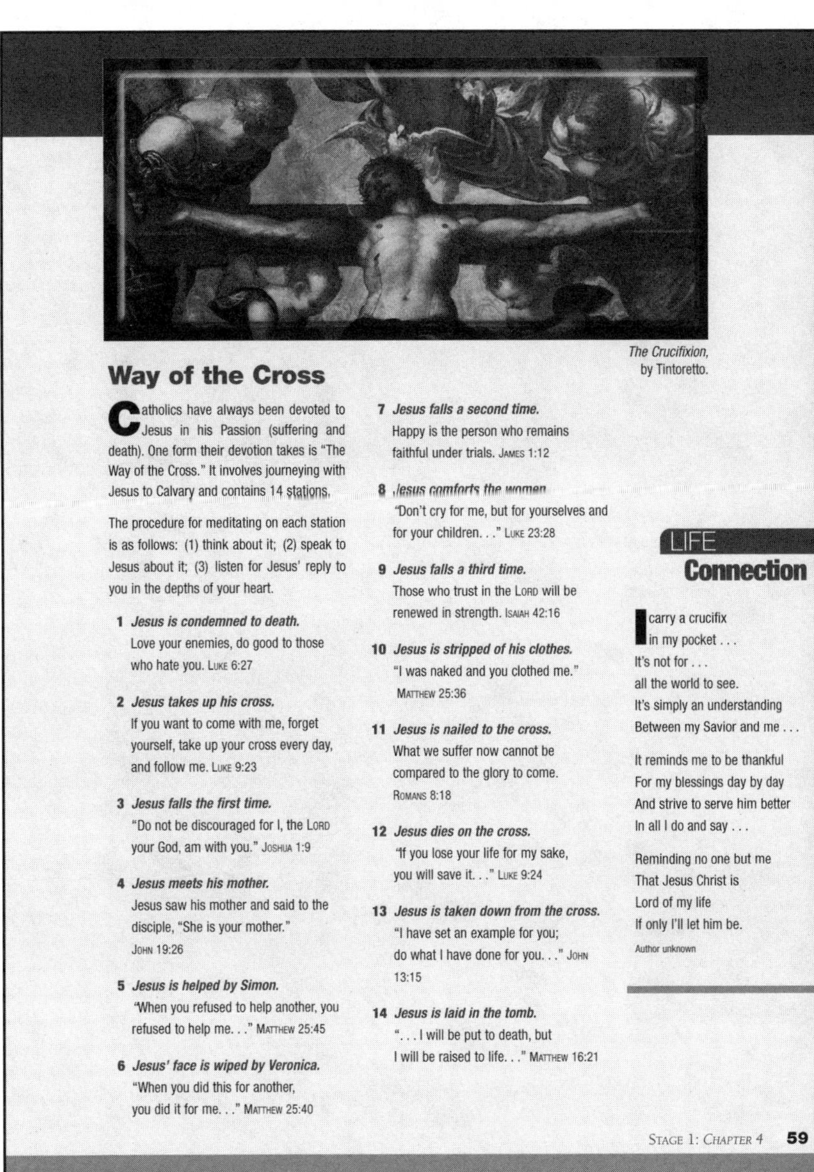

The Crucifixion, by Tintoretto.

Way of the Cross

Catholics have always been devoted to Jesus in his Passion (suffering and death). One form their devotion takes is "The Way of the Cross." It involves journeying with Jesus to Calvary and contains 14 stations.

The procedure for meditating on each station is as follows: (1) think about it; (2) speak to Jesus about it; (3) listen for Jesus' reply to you in the depths of your heart.

1 ***Jesus is condemned to death.***
Love your enemies, do good to those who hate you. LUKE 6:27

2 ***Jesus takes up his cross.***
If you want to come with me, forget yourself, take up your cross every day, and follow me. LUKE 9:23

3 ***Jesus falls the first time.***
"Do not be discouraged for I, the LORD your God, am with you." JOSHUA 1:9

4 ***Jesus meets his mother.***
Jesus saw his mother and said to the disciple, "She is your mother." JOHN 19:26

5 ***Jesus is helped by Simon.***
"When you refused to help another, you refused to help me. . ." MATTHEW 25:45

6 ***Jesus' face is wiped by Veronica.***
"When you did this for another, you did it for me. . ." MATTHEW 25:40

7 ***Jesus falls a second time.***
Happy is the person who remains faithful under trials. JAMES 1:12

8 ***Jesus comforts the women.***
"Don't cry for me, but for yourselves and for your children. . ." LUKE 23:28

9 ***Jesus falls a third time.***
Those who trust in the LORD will be renewed in strength. ISAIAH 42:16

10 ***Jesus is stripped of his clothes.***
"I was naked and you clothed me." MATTHEW 25:36

11 ***Jesus is nailed to the cross.***
What we suffer now cannot be compared to the glory to come. ROMANS 8:18

12 ***Jesus dies on the cross.***
"If you lose your life for my sake, you will save it. . ." LUKE 9:24

13 ***Jesus is taken down from the cross.***
"I have set an example for you; do what I have done for you. . ." JOHN 13:15

14 ***Jesus is laid in the tomb.***
". . . I will be put to death, but I will be raised to life. . ." MATTHEW 16:21

LIFE Connection

I carry a crucifix
in my pocket . . .
It's not for . . .
all the world to see.
It's simply an understanding
Between my Savior and me . . .

It reminds me to be thankful
For my blessings day by day
And strive to serve him better
In all I do and say . . .

Reminding no one but me
That Jesus Christ is
Lord of my life
If only I'll let him be.

Author unknown

STAGE 1: CHAPTER 4 59

ACTIVITY—The following is an excellent written assignment. Have the students answer these two questions:

1 *Describe a time when you suffered mentally, emotionally, physically, or spiritually.*

2 *Which of the above four sufferings do you think is the hardest to endure and why?*

Students seem to enjoy this kind of assignment. The assignment also gives the teacher an insight into the students. Here is a response by one of the author's students. You may wish to read it to your own students to get them started.

A high-school senior wrote:

Father, you may share this with the rest of the class, if you think it is worth reading.

You may also use my name if you wish. It's not that personal.

I have suffered tremendous physical pain at different times in my seventeen-year life. But the worst was when I broke my leg. I had broken five other bones before this, but this was the biggie. I can't begin to describe what the pain felt like.

Even though the physical pain connected with breaking a bone can be agonizing, I think emotional pain is even worse yet. Breaks can heal, but if you are betrayed by a loved one, it cuts into your heart in a way that is almost impossible to heal. Sure, you can get over things like that, but the betrayal always remains there in the back of your mind, ready to resurface.

The author always commented on student responses. On this paper, he made two brief comments:

1 *He circled the phrase "five other bones" and wrote in the margin, "You're a dangerous man, Brian!"*

2 *After the final comment, the author wrote, "Agreed!"*

These are not profound comments, but they do tell the student you care.

Be sure to have the students mark on their papers some kind of okay to share it with the class anonymously—or to use their name if they are agreeable.

Share Your meditation

SHARE—The canoeist in this story was the famous film director, Cecil B. DeMille. At the time the incident occurred he was drifting in a canoe on a lake in Maine, reading a book. Four similarities:

1 *Jesus died nailed to the wood of the cross, just as the beetle died fastened to the wood of the canoe.*

2 *Jesus underwent an amazing bodily transformation three days after his death, as did the beetle three hours after its death.*

3 *Jesus was not recognized by his followers, just as the beetle was not recognized.*

4 *Jesus' transformed body enjoyed new powers to move about, as did the transformed body of the beetle.*

Think about it

The "fall of the first Adam" was the end of the "beginning."
(First Act: Creation of the World)

The "rise of the second Adam" was the beginning of the "end."
(Third Act: Re-creation of the World)

Resurrection of Jesus

QUESTION **11** ***Didn't Lazarus and Jairus's daughter die and come back to life?***

■ *Stress the difference between resuscitation and resurrection.*

With the help of the students develop the following diagram on the chalkboard for entry into notebooks:

SHARE YOUR meditation

A canoeist saw a water beetle crawl up the side of his canoe, hook its talons in the wood, and die.

Three hours later he glanced down again. The beetle had dried in the sun, and the shell was cracking open. From it emerged a lovely dragonfly. The canoeist nudged the shell; it was like an empty tomb.

The dragonfly fluttered above the other beetles in the water. They saw it but didn't recognize it.

■ ***List several similarities between the beetle's transformation and Jesus' transformation.***

THINK about it

The fall of the first Adam was the end of the beginning.

The rise of the second Adam was the beginning of the end.

S. W. Duffield

Resurrection of Jesus

Some women went to visit the tomb on the Sunday after Good Friday. They were not prepared for what they found. It was empty! As they stood there totally bewildered, two men in white appeared and said:

Why are you looking among the dead
for one who is alive? He is not here;
he has been raised. LUKE 24:5–6

The women did not know what to make of their discovery. They ran back to tell the apostles what they had found.

Peter got up and ran to the tomb;
he bent down and saw the grave cloths
but nothing else. Then he went back home
amazed at what had happened. LUKE 24:12

Jesus was alive! He had risen from the dead.

11 ***Didn't Lazarus and Jairus' daughter die and come back to life? Explain.***

The word *resurrection* does not mean resuscitation. It is not a restoration to one's previous life, such as what happened to Lazarus and the daughter of Jairus. It involves far more. Resurrection involves complete transformation. It involves a quantum leap forward into a totally new life. It is something that no human being before Jesus had yet experienced.

To put it another way: The body of Jesus that rose on Easter Sunday was totally different from the body that was buried on Good Friday. CCC 631–66

Paul compares the body *before* resurrection to a seed planted in the soil and then compares the body *after* resurrection to the plant that emerges from the dead seed plant. He writes:

Someone will ask,
"How can the dead be raised to life?
What kind of body will they have?" . . .
When you plant a seed in the ground,
it does not sprout to life unless it dies.

60 STAGE 1: CHAPTER 4

Resuscitation — *Lazarus* / *Return to old life*

Resurrection — *Jesus* / *Leap to new life*

Stress the point that a resurrected body is one that has made a quantum leap forward into a higher life.

Promise of the Resurrection

CLARIFY—Jesus' resurrection from the dead is a promise that we too shall rise to new life after death. We know this by faith, but we also know it by a kind of deep-down intuition.

There is a memorable scene in Thornton Wilder's Pulitzer Prize-winning play, *Our*

NOTES

And what you plant is a bare seed . . .
not the full-bodied plant
that will grow up. . . .
That is how it will be
when the dead are raised to life.

When the body is buried, it is mortal;
when raised, it will be immortal.
When buried, it is ugly and weak;
when raised, it will be beautiful and strong.
When buried, it is a physical body;
when raised, it will be a spiritual body.
1 CORINTHIANS 15:42–44

Promise of the resurrection

The resurrection of Jesus is a promise that if we follow Jesus' teaching, we too will be raised to life on the last day. Jesus himself promised this:

"Those who eat my flesh and
drink my blood have eternal life, and
I will raise them to life on the last day."
JOHN 6:54

The resurrection of Jesus invites us to open our hearts to his presence among us. It invites us to let Jesus do for us what he has done for so many.

It invites us to love again after our love has been rejected and we are tempted to hate; to hope again after our hopes have been dashed and we are tempted to despair; and to believe again after our belief has been shaken and we are tempted to doubt.

The resurrection of Jesus is the good news that he has defeated death and wants to give us the power to do the same. The resurrection is the promise that nothing can destroy us: not pain, not rejection, not sin, not even death.

Spirit of Jesus

After the resurrection, Jesus enjoyed a totally new relationship with his brothers and sisters on earth. He was now glorified. He was now able to carry out his promise to send upon them the Holy Spirit. Luke describes the coming of the Holy Spirit this way in the Acts of the Apostles:

When the day of Pentecost came,
all the believers
were gathered together in one place.

Suddenly,
there was a noise from the sky. . . .
Then they saw what looked like
tongues of fire which spread out
and touched each person there.
They were all filled with the Holy Spirit.
ACTS 2:1–4

The sound of the noise was so loud that a huge crowd gathered outside to find out what was going on. Peter addressed them, saying:

Fellow Israelites!
Let me tell you what this means. . . .
This is what the prophet Joel spoke about:

"This is what I will do in the last days,"
God says: "I will pour out
my spirit on everyone."

"Turn away from his sins and
be baptized in the name of Jesus Christ . . .
and you will receive . . . the Holy Spirit."
ACTS 2:14; 16–17, 38

The coming of the Holy Spirit formed the disciples of Jesus into the Church, the "body of Christ." It empowered them to bring to completion God's Kingdom on earth, the re-creation of the world. 1 CORINTHIANS 12:1–29

THINK about it

One day he will come.
Once in the stillness . . .
you will know who he is . . .
not from a book
or the word of someone else,
but through him.

Romano Guardini

LIFE Connection

May the Babe
of Bethlehem
be yours to tend;
May the Boy of Nazareth,
be yours for a friend;

May the Man of Galilee
his healing send.
May the Christ of Calvary
his courage lend;

May the Risen Lord
his presence send;
And his holy angels
defend you to the end.

Author unknown

STAGE 1: CHAPTER 4 61

Town. At the start of the third act, the stage manager turns to the audience and says:

Everybody knows in their bones
that something is eternal,
and that something
has to do with human beings. . . .

There's something way down deep
that's eternal
about every human being. . . .

They're waitin'.
They're waitin' for something
that they feel is comin'.
Something important, and great.
Aren't they waitin' for the eternal part
in them to come out clear?

Spirit of Jesus

NOTEBOOK—The coming of the Holy Spirit changed everything. Have the students copy the following in their notebooks. It spells out the difference the Holy Spirit makes:

■ *Without the Spirit, God is far away.*
The cosmos is steeped in mystery;
Jesus is only a teacher;
Scripture is just a book;
The Church is only a club.

In the Spirit,
the cosmos is steeped in labor,
giving birth to the Kingdom.
Jesus is risen,
drawing all things to himself.
Scripture is God's Word,
revealing all truth.
The Church is God's People,
alive in the Spirit. M.L.

THINK about it

CLARIFY—Guardini is talking about the "gift of faith." Recall the solemn occasion when Jesus asked Peter:

"Who do you say that I am?"
Peter responded,
"You are the Messiah,
the Son of the living God."

Jesus said to Peter,
"This truth did not come to you
from any human being,
but it was given to you
directly by my Father in heaven."
MATTHEW 16:16–17

LIFE Connection

CLARIFY—This blessing makes a fitting conclusion to the New Testament message of the Gospels.

It makes a great toast at a wedding. It is wishing a couple everything another human can wish, but only God can fulfill.

Recap

This section summarizes the key points of the chapter.

To repeat what was said earlier, an easy way to construct a quick "daily quiz" is to convert the "summary diagrams" found here and in the text into "matching" or "true-false" questions.

You might give a total of ten "daily quiz" questions in the course of the week. Hold off the grade until the end of the week. Thus, a student who gets nine answers correct during the week is given a grade of 90%.

Review

DAILY QUIZ—The review questions may be assigned (one or two at a time) for homework or a daily quiz.

CHAPTER TESTS—Reproducible chapter tests are found in Appendix A. For consistency and ease in grading, quizzes are restricted to (1) "Matching," (2) "True/False," and (3) "Fill in the Blanks."

TEST ANSWERS—The following are the answers to the test for Chapter 4. (See Appendix A, page 315.) All correct answers worth four points.

Matching

1 = c	2 = a	3 = e	4 = b
5 = i	6 = g	7 = h	8 = d
9 = j	10 = f		

True/False

1 = T	2 = F	3 = T	4 = F
5 = F	6 = T	7 = F	

Fill In the Blanks

1. (a) Gold (b) Frankincense (c) Myrrh — (b) Kingship (d) Divinity (e) Humanity
2. (a) God's Messiah (b) God's Kingdom

Recap

The coming of Jesus and the Magi fulfill the Old Testament prophecies.

The baptism of Jesus marks the beginning of a new era, new creation, and new Adam. Jesus' miracles point to:

God's Messiah	**They fulfill prophecies: blind see and deaf hear.**
God's Kingdom	**They show power over sin, sickness, and death.**

Jesus' miracles invite us to:

Open our eyes	**Healing the blind**
Open our ears	**Healing the deaf**
Begin a new life	**Raising the dead**

Jesus compared the four ways people respond to his invitation of faith to the four fates of a seed that a farmer planted in his field.

Seed's fate	People's response
Fails to sprout	Reject
Sprouts but withers	Accept but fall
Sprouts but chokes	Accept but forget
Sprouts and grows	Accept and bear fruit

Jesus' resurrection is a promise that we will also be raised to life on the last day, if we walk with him in this life. It is also an invitation to open our hearts to Jesus' presence among us to let him do for us what he's done for so many.

The coming of the Holy Spirit formed Jesus' followers into the Church, Christ's body, and empowered them to complete his work on earth.

Review

1 The Gospels give us four approaches to Jesus. List (a) which Gospel was different from the other three, (c) why it was different, and (d) one example of how it differs from the others.

2 Against which background does Matthew situate Jesus' birth?

3 Who was responsible for giving Jesus his name, and what does the name *Jesus* mean?

4 List the three gifts the Magi presented to Jesus, and explain the symbolism of each.

5 List (a) the three events that take place at Jesus' baptism, and (b) what each signified.

6 What was John's favorite word for a miracle and why?

7 Explain how miracles announced the arrival of (a) the Messiah of God, and (b) the Kingdom of God.

8 Explain how the following miracles acted as an invitation to faith and action: (a) healing of the blind, (b) healing of the deaf, and (c) raising of the dead.

9 Briefly explain (a) the four different fates of the seed in Jesus' Parable of the Sower, and (b) how these fates correspond to the four different responses of people to Jesus' teaching.

10 Explain (a) the difference between resurrection and resuscitation, (b) in what sense the resurrection of Jesus is a promise to those who follow him faithfully, and (c) Paul's comparison to death and resurrection to a seed planted in the earth.

11 List the twofold effect the coming of the Holy Spirit had on Jesus' disciples.

62 STAGE 1: CHAPTER 4

Reflect

1 *Who/what do the following stand for: (a) king, (b) prince, (c) crooked back, (d) statue, and (e) studying the statue?*

■ *There are a variety of interpretations. One of the more acceptable ones follows:*

King	*God the Father*
Prince	*Humanity (you and I) flawed by original sin.*
Bad back	*Some defect in us that keeps us from being what we could be.*
Statue	*Jesus. In his humanity he is a model of what, by God's grace, we can become.*
Studying	*Meditating on Jesus.*

NOTES

Reflect

1 There was once a handsome prince who had a crooked back. It kept him from being the kind of prince he was meant to be. One day the king had a sculptor make a statue of the prince, portraying him with a straight back. The king put the statue in the prince's private garden.

In the days ahead, the prince found himself sitting in front of the statue daily, studying it and desiring to be like it. Months passed, and the people began to say, "The prince's back isn't as crooked as it once was." When the prince heard this, he grew excited. Now he began spending more time studying the statue.

One day a remarkable thing happened. The prince stood as straight as the statue.

- ***Who/what do the following stand for: (a) king, (b) prince, (c) crooked back, (d) statue, and (e) studying the statue?***

2 A London newspaper carried this ad in the early 1900s: "Wanted: Persons for dangerous journey. Small wages, bitter cold, long months of complete darkness, constant danger, safe return doubtful, honor and recognition if successful."

Over 5,000 applicants answered. From these Sir Ernest Shakleton chose twenty-eight for his polar expedition. All returned safely to honor and recognition.

Today, there is a great need for courageous, dedicated people in Christian ministry: priests, nuns, brothers, lay ministers.

Why do/don't you think more young people would address this need if they were approached frankly and straightforwardly, as Shakleton did in his ad?

- ***Have you ever thought of dedicating your life to Christian ministry? Explain.***
- ***List the pros and cons to Christian ministry as you see them.***

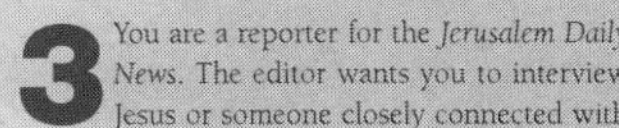

3 You are a reporter for the *Jerusalem Daily News*. The editor wants you to interview Jesus or someone closely connected with him. Select one of the following for the interview. List the questions you asked and the responses to them.

- ***A Magi on his visit to Jesus***
- ***Peter on Jesus' calming of the sea***
- ***A soldier on his crucifixion of Jesus***

Stage 1: Chapter 4 **63**

2 ***a) Why do/don't you think more young people would address this need if approached frankly and straightforwardly, as Shackleton did in his ad?***

b) Have you ever thought of dedicating your life to Christian ministry? Explain.

c) List the pros and cons to Christian ministry as you see them.

NOTEBOOK—Have the students write out their responses for the above questions in preparation for sharing them with the class. The responses tend to be more honest if written out. (The student is not influenced by what someone else has just said.)

3 ***Select one of the following for the interview. List the questions you asked and the responses to them.***

a) One of the Magi on his visit to Jesus

b) Peter on Jesus' calming the sea

c) A soldier on his crucifixion of Jesus

ACTIVITY—Allow the students to team up for this exercise. One acts as the reporter, asking the questions; the other plays the role of the Magi (or Peter or the soldier) responding to the questions.

PRAYER TIME with the Lord

QUESTION *Compose a similar "pencil meditation" on the crucifixion of Jesus.*

***ACTIVITY*—To help the students get started, read to them these excerpts from Psalm 22. Jesus recited them on the cross.** MARK 15:34 **Have the students keep their eyes on the photo of Jesus on page 64 as you read the psalm slowly, pausing between paragraphs.**

■ *My God, my God,*
why have you abandoned me?
I cried desperately for help,
but still it does not come. . . .

All who see me make fun of me;
they stick out their tongues
and shake their heads.

"You relied on the LORD," they say.
"Why doesn't he save you?
If the LORD likes you,
why doesn't he help you?"

My strength is gone,
gone like water spilled on the ground.
All my bones are out of joint;
my heart is like melted wax.
My throat is as dry as dust. . . .

My enemies look at me and stare.
They gamble for my clothes
and divide them among themselves.
O LORD, don't stay away from me!
Come quickly to my rescue!

Now have them do their own "pencil meditation" right in class. Collect and review them, sharing the better ones anonymously in the next class.

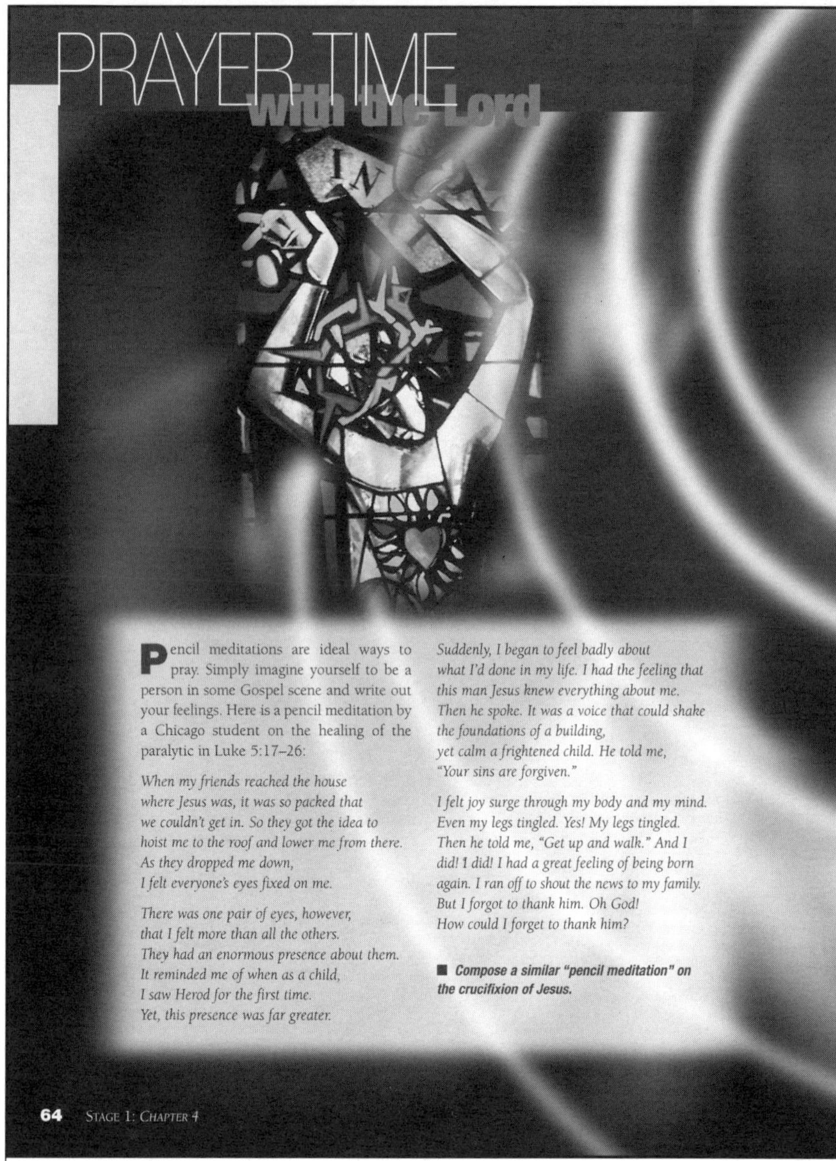

PRAYER TIME with the Lord

Pencil meditations are ideal ways to pray. Simply imagine yourself to be a person in some Gospel scene and write out your feelings. Here is a pencil meditation by a Chicago student on the healing of the paralytic in Luke 5:17–26:

When my friends reached the house
where Jesus was, it was so packed that
we couldn't get in. So they got the idea to
hoist me to the roof and lower me from there.
As they dropped me down,
I felt everyone's eyes fixed on me.

There was one pair of eyes, however,
that I felt more than all the others.
They had an enormous presence about them.
It reminded me of when as a child,
I saw Herod for the first time.
Yet, this presence was far greater.

Suddenly, I began to feel badly about
what I'd done in my life. I had the feeling that
this man Jesus knew everything about me.
Then he spoke. It was a voice that could shake
the foundations of a building,
yet calm a frightened child. He told me,
"Your sins are forgiven."

I felt joy surge through my body and my mind.
Even my legs tingled. Yes! My legs tingled.
Then he told me, "Get up and walk." And I
did! I did! I had a great feeling of being born
again. I ran off to shout the news to my family.
But I forgot to thank him. Oh God!
How could I forget to thank him?

■ ***Compose a similar "pencil meditation" on the crucifixion of Jesus.***

64 STAGE 1: CHAPTER 4

PRAYER Journal

QUESTION *Compose a similar prayer of your own. Or write a response to Jesus explaining why you find it hard to do these things.*

Be sure to have the students reserve a special section of their notebooks for the exercises under this section. Again, encourage them to illustrate their prayers with drawings or photos cut from magazines or newspapers.

The questions in this section can be done right in class on three-ring paper and later inserted in their notebooks.

NOTES

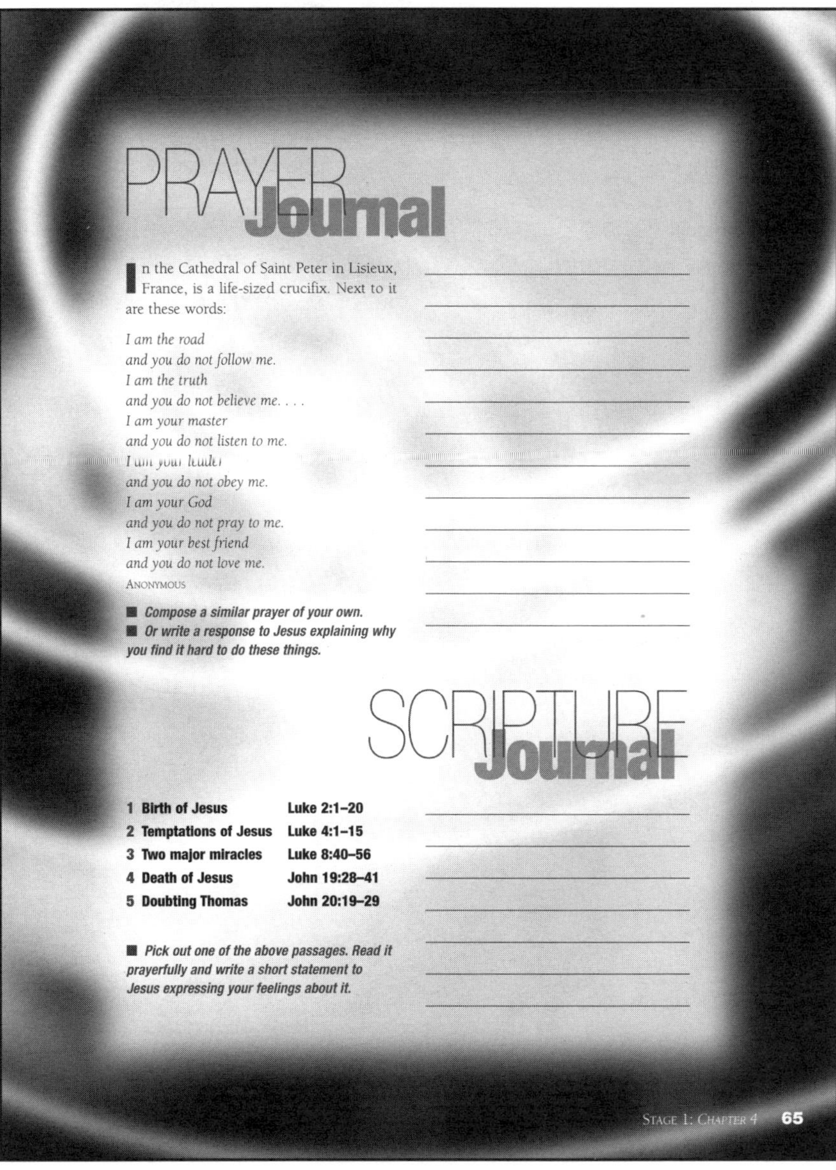

PRAYER Journal

In the Cathedral of Saint Peter in Lisieux, France, is a life-sized crucifix. Next to it are these words:

I am the road
and you do not follow me.
I am the truth
and you do not believe me. . . .
I am your master
and you do not listen to me.
I am your leader
and you do not obey me.
I am your God
and you do not pray to me.
I am your best friend
and you do not love me.
ANONYMOUS

- ***Compose a similar prayer of your own.***
- ***Or write a response to Jesus explaining why you find it hard to do these things.***

SCRIPTURE Journal

1	**Birth of Jesus**	**Luke 2:1–20**
2	**Temptations of Jesus**	**Luke 4:1–15**
3	**Two major miracles**	**Luke 8:40–56**
4	**Death of Jesus**	**John 19:28–41**
5	**Doubting Thomas**	**John 20:19–29**

- ***Pick out one of the above passages. Read it prayerfully and write a short statement to Jesus expressing your feelings about it.***

STAGE 1: CHAPTER 4 65

SCRIPTURE Journal

QUESTION ***Pick one of the passages. Read it prayerfully and write a short statement to Jesus expressing your feelings about it.***

An appropriate reading would be #4, Death of Jesus. Young people are deeply moved by the crucifixion of Jesus. It would be good to use this additional opportunity to appeal to this dimension in them.

ACTIVITY—Divide the class into groups of three or four. Have them share prayers and select the best one to be read to the class.

Classroom Resources

CATECHISM

Catechism of the Catholic Church *Second Edition*

For further enrichment, you might refer to:

1. New Testament	Index	p. 827
	Glossary	p. 889
2. Gospel(s)	Index	p. 801
	Glossary	p. 880
3. Kingdom of God	Index	p. 813
	Glossary	p. 885

See also: Christ, Messiah, Cross.
—AVAILABLE FROM THE UNITED STATES CATHOLIC CONFERENCE, WASHINGTON DC

CD-ROM

Hundreds of color illustrations

J. Tissot plus photographs of other works of art.
—WELCOME TO THE CATHOLIC CHURCH—CD-ROM FROM HARMONY MEDIA, INC., CERVAIS, OR

BOOKS

The Bible Jesus Read

Philip Yancey

Excellent introduction to the Jesus story. Shows us how the prophets help us to understand Jesus. 1999
—AVAILABLE FROM ZONDERVAN PUBLISHING HOUSE, GRAND RAPIDS, MI

The New Jerome Biblical Commentary

Editors: Raymond Brown, Joseph Fitzmyer, Roland Murphy

Chapters 40–63 contain a concise scholarly overview of the New Testament books. 1992 —AVAILABLE FROM LITURGICAL PRESS, COLLEGEVILLE, MN

NOTE

For a list of (1) General resources for professional background and (2) Addresses, phone/fax numbers of major publishing companies, see Appendix B of this Resource Manual.

CHAPTER 5
God the Father

CHAPTER at a Glance

The chapter walks students through the three fundamental scriptural images of God and probes their meaning and implications.

DISCUSS—Have a student read aloud the three paragraphs beginning: "Philip said to Jesus, 'Lord, show us the Father' . . ."

Reread the first paragraph and ask: How do you explain Jesus' answer to Philip: "Whoever has seen me has seen the Father?"

■ *The love and mercy Jesus showed toward people is a reflection of the Father's love and mercy. The Letter to the Hebrews answers the question this way:*

Jesus reflects
the brightness of God's glory
and is the exact likeness
of God's own being. HEBREWS 1:3

Parable of God

Laura is a film classic (1944). It still shows with regularity on network and cable TV.

QUESTION **1** ***Can you guess what could have happened?***

■ *The answer is given in the next paragraph. The purpose of the question is to give the students a "shot" at it before spelling it out for them. (Some students may have read ahead. Good! That's the kind of initiative we should encourage!)*

CHAPTER 5 God the Father

Philip said to Jesus,
"Lord, show us the Father . . ."
Jesus answered . . .
"Whoever has seen me
has seen the Father . . .
Do you not believe, Philip, that
I am in the Father
and the Father is in me? . . .

"Those who love me will obey my teaching.
My Father will love them, and
my Father and I will come to them
and live in them.
JOHN 14:8–10, 23–24

Scripture contains
many portraits of God.
Three stand out, like stars in the night.
God is a Trinity of persons:
Father, Son, and Holy Spirit.
God is our Creator,
who called us into being.
God is our Father,
who loves us more than
we love ourselves.

CHAPTER at a Glance

Parable of God

The movie *Laura* is about a young woman who is mysteriously killed in her apartment. A young detective named Mark MacPherson is assigned to the case. He spends hours in Laura's apartment looking for clues. He leaves no stone unturned, even reading her diary.

The more Mark learns about Laura, the more he finds himself attracted to her. He finds himself falling in love with her. Then, late one night, Mark is seated in Laura's apartment thinking about her. Soon he nods and falls asleep.

Suddenly, something awakens him. He opens his eyes; and there, standing in the doorway, is a lovely young woman. It's Laura! Then an amazing story unfolds.

1 ***Can you guess what could have happened?***

Laura had gone to the country for a weekend to rest. In all that time, she was out of contact with any news. The murder victim was an acquaintance, who had asked Laura to use her apartment that weekend.

The movie ends with Laura and Mark falling in love, marrying, and living happily ever after.

66

QUESTION **2** ***Can you explain what this person probably had in mind? (the movie critic who called*** **Laura** ***a "modern parable of God's plan")***

The explanation follows below.
Again, the purpose of the question is to give the students a "shot" at it before spelling it out.

Plan of God

CLARIFY—A parable may be described as a fictional short story used by Jesus to teach people.

The parables are constructed in a way that the characters or images in them mirror characters in real life (e.g., the parables of the Sower, Prodigal Son, Good Shepherd).

NOTES

Commenting on the movie, one critic observed that it could be used as a kind of "modern parable of God's plan for us."

2 ***Can you explain what this person probably had in mind?***

Plan of God

The movie mirrors the situation of all of us. Like Mark, we find ourselves in God's "apartment"—the universe. From its order and beauty, we get a clue of God's greatness.

Moreover, as Mark learned about Laura by studying her apartment, so we learn about God by studying the universe. Finally, as Mark's study attracted him to Laura, even though he'd never seen her; so our study of creation attracts us to the invisible God.

Hopefully, our story will also end happily, as did that of Mark and Laura.

Portraits of God

Ever since God created the world,
his invisible qualities,
both his eternal power
and his divine nature,
have been clearly seen. Romans 1:20

But the beauty and order of the universe is only a glimmer of God's glory and greatness. Reason cannot "paint a portrait" of God. Only Scripture can do that.

And so we turn to Scripture for a "word portrait" of God. First, we go to the Old Testament.

The Old Testament was written at a time when people lived close to nature. Thus, it uses many images from nature to speak about God. Consider a few of these images.

God is a mother eagle. She nourishes her young and teaches them how to fly. Deuteronomy 32:11

God is a shepherd. He protects his flock for wild animals, cares for the sick, and goes in search of the stray. Ezekiel 34:16

God is the creator. He "set the earth firmly on its foundations" and decorated it with seas, and mountains. Psalm 104: 5–8

This brings us to the New Testament.

Here we find Jesus speaking of God in a variety of images also.

God is a loving Father. He knows our needs and takes care of them without our asking. Luke 12:30

NOTEBOOK—Develop the "cast of characters" in *Laura* for entry into the students' notebooks:

Mark	*Us*
Laura	*God*
Laura's apartment	*World*
Marriage	*God's plan*

Portraits of God

CLARIFY—Reasoning from qualities in the universe to qualities in its creator can give us only a general idea of God. It can't paint a detailed portrait of God.

Dr. Mortimer Adler stressed this point in an interview with TV's Bill Moyers, saying:

■ *If reason enabled me*
to know everything about God,
he would not have to reveal himself.

Reason alone can't bridge the gap
from an infinite supreme being
to a being who is just, merciful,
and caring.

Adler taught Catholic philosophy at the University of Chicago, originally a Baptist-affiliated university. He was Jewish, and many of the school's students were nonbelievers. This led a wag to say of the university:

■ *"It's a Baptist school where a Jew*
teaches Catholic philosophy
to a bunch of atheists."

NOTEBOOK—Develop the following diagram of Old Testament images of God for entry into notebooks:

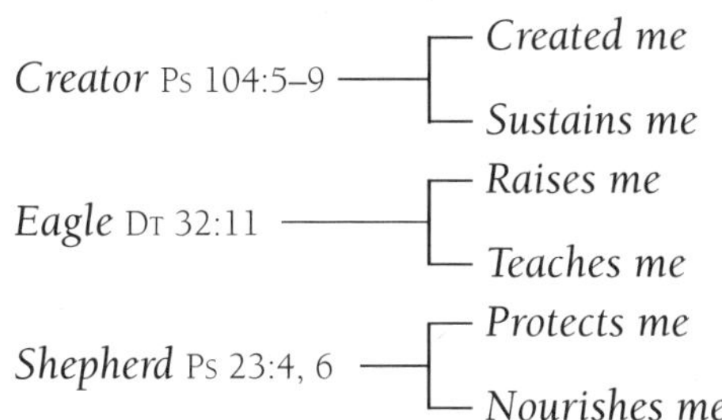

New Testament images of God include the following:

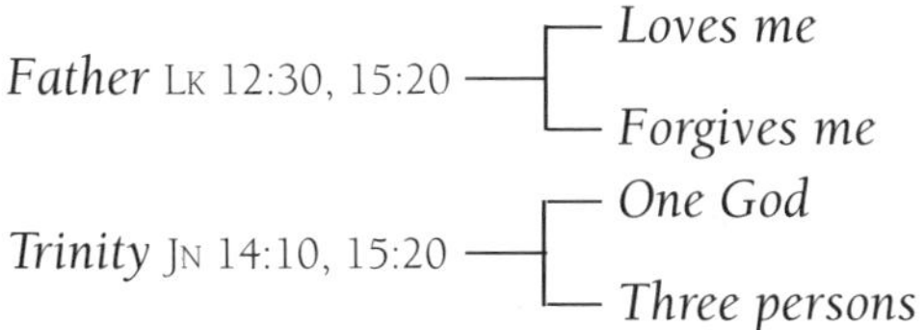

QUESTION **3** ***Which of these images do I find most appealing and why?***

Have students respond privately and in writing before sharing and discussing. (This usually ensures a more objective response.)

Share Your meditation

DISCUSS—What do we mean by the expression "give glory to God"?

■ *"For people in biblical times, glory meant the visible manifestation of God's presence and power."* DENNIS HAMM, "THE WORD," *AMERICA MAGAZINE*, 5/8/99

We give glory to God when we mirror and celebrate God's presence and power—as the cornet player did.

DISCUSS—List some ways you can give "glory" to God in your situation.

■ *Saint Irenaeus (A.D. 130–200), French bishop, said, "God's glory is a human being fully alive."*

We give glory to God when we use our time, talent, and treasure freely, fully, and joyfully for the greater honor and glory of God.

God as Creator

SHARE—The amazing facts below were gleaned from an article in the *Chicago Sun-Times* (12/25/68).

Depending on the interest and ability of your students, share and discuss the facts with them.

Jules Verne was a French science-fiction writer with incredible gifts of imagination and vision. He wrote a novel in 1865 called *From Earth to the Moon.* It dealt with a space trip:

Launched from Florida on Dec. 1.
Three men aboard
Twelve feet tall and 12,230 lbs.
Traveled about 25,000 mph
on its 238,000-mile journey
Splashed down: Pacific, Dec. 11.

Compare Verne's fictional projectile with Apollo 8 in 1968:

Launched from Florida on Dec. 22.
Three men aboard,
Twelve feet tall and 12,392 lbs.
(minus 36-story Saturn rocket).
Traveled 24,200 mph
on its 225,000-mile journey.
Splashed down: Pacific, Dec. 27

You may wish to have a pair of students research the *Sun-Times* article for other interesting points.

God sustains all

NOTEBOOK—Summarize the comparison of God to a projector:

God	*Projector*
Creates all	*Produces image*
Sustains all	*Preserves image*
Present in all	*Puts self on screen*

NOTES

SHARE YOUR meditation

One afternoon a musician was standing on the tower that marks the highest peak of the Mohawk Trail in the Berkshire Mountains.

Three great states—New York, Connecticut, and Massachusetts—lay before him with their lakes, forests, and valleys. He was so moved by the grandeur of it all that he ran to his car, grabbed his cornet, and climbed back up the tower.

There he played with all his heart—for his joy, the joy of the tourists, and the glory of God.

Retold from Ardis Whitman

■ ***What do we mean by the expression "give glory to God"? List some ways that you can give "glory" to God in your situation.***

God is a forgiving Father. He runs out to meet his repentant son and smothers him with a hugs and kisses. LUKE 15:20

Finally, God is a mystery of Unity and Trinity: Father, Son, and Holy Spirit. JOHN 14:10, 15:26

3 ***Which of these images do you find most appealing and why?***

Let's take a closer look at three of these images of God: Creator, Father, and Trinity.

God created all

Recall that in 1968, four days before Christmas, Apollo lifted off with astronauts Frank Borman, Bill Anders, and Jim Lovell aboard.

As they rounded the moon on Christmas Eve, they sent greetings to earth, taking turns reading the story of creation from the Bible. The story portrays God creating the universe over a six-day period, much as an artisan works.

The point of this quaint imagery is to teach us that creation did not occur by chance or accident. It came into being by the creative act of a loving God.

God sustains all

God's work did not stop with creating the universe and everything in it. God also continues to hold it in existence. CCC 301 An example will illustrate.

Think of the things God created as being like images on a movie screen.

Think of God as being like the movie projector that put them there.

Just as the images owe their existence to the projector, so creation owes its existence to God.

Furthermore, just as the images on the movie screen would vanish into nothingness if the projector withdrew its light from them, so creation would vanish into nothingness if God withdrew his power from it.

But this is not all.

68 STAGE 1: CHAPTER 5

God is present in all

Late one hot afternoon, archaeologist Gene Savoy became lost in a jungle in Peru. A sickening feeling came over him. In panic, he began to run around feverishly, searching for the trail he had used to enter the jungle.

Suddenly, he realized that this frantic running was only making matters worse. Then he stopped and stood perfectly still. As he did, a strange thought flashed across his mind. God was in this jungle. It is God's house.

Gene had been introduced to the beauties of nature when he was a boy in Oregon. His parents taught him that God had created the universe, sustains it, and resides in it.

Why had he closed his eyes to God's presence in the jungles of Peru?

Didn't God create them also? Doesn't God sustain them also? Doesn't God reside in them also?

Instantly, Gene relaxed and put all his trust in God, in whose house he was. He said later:

I looked up
into the beautiful emerald world
of wild orchids and fragrant blossoms
where hummingbirds hovered.
Yes, God was there, too.
My heart quieted.

At that moment, something deep within him seemed to say, "Walk a few paces to the left." He did. And there was the tiny trail! He said later:

I am proud
of my archaeological discoveries.
But my greatest discovery, I believe, was
in recognizing God's presence everywhere.

4 How might we explain the "voice" Gene heard deep within him? Which explanation fits best?

THINK about it

Our hearts have a God-shaped hole in them that only God can fill.

Author Unknown

God's presence

Let us go back to the example of the movie projector. Its light gives the images a real presence on the movie screen. So, too, the projector's light gives the projector a real presence on the screen.

In a similar way, God's creation gives God a real presence on earth. CCC 300 Saint Paul refers to this when he says of us, "In God we live and move and have our being." Acts 17:28

THINK about it

If God seems far away, guess who moved.

Anonymous

STAGE 1: CHAPTER 5 69

God is present in all

QUESTION **4** ***How might we explain the "voice" Gene heard deep within him? Which explanation fits best?***

■ *Prayer is also "listening" to God, not with the ears of our body, but with the "ears of the soul." Consider this example:*

British playwright George Bernard Shaw wrote a play, *St. Joan,* based on the life of Saint Joan of Arc (1412–1431), a French peasant.

She heard "inner voices" telling her to liberate Orleans from the British, who were brutally oppressing its citizenry.

She went to King Charles VII. When she arrived at the king's palace, Charles tested her by switching places with a courtier. She not only located him in the crowd but also told him what he had been praying about earlier. She was also tested by priests, passing the tests brilliantly. Joan got her army and freed the city.

In his play, Shaw has an interrogator ask Joan: "How do you mean, voices?" Joan says, "I hear voices telling me what to do. They come from God." The interrogator says, "They come from your imagination." Joan replies, "Of course. That is how the messages of God come to us."

Later, She was captured by the British, condemned unjustly as a witch, and burned. She was canonized in 1920.

THINK about it

CLARIFY—Recall Saint Augustine's words, "Our hearts were made for you, O Lord, and they will not rest until they rest in you."

THINK about it

CLARIFY—A convict put the idea this way: "God is always with us; it's just that we're not always with God."

God's presence

CLARIFY—Stress the point that the light from the projector gives the images a real presence on the screen.

In a similar way, God's creation gives God a real presence in our world.

Conclude by stressing that God is present in different ways and different degrees: Creation, Bible, Jesus.

Other ways and degrees by which God is present among us include:

1. *the Church*
2. *the Eucharist*
3. *indwelling each Christian, etc.*

QUESTION **5** ***What are some other different ways and degrees the boy can be present to his mother?***

■ *E-mail, television, telephone, photo, a few flowers he picked for her.*

Share Your meditation

A variety of responses will probably be forthcoming. The question of prayer in general will be handled later in chapter 17.

THINK about it

Saint Augustine (A.D. 354–430) expressed the same idea this way: "If you pray and do what you can do, God will hear you and help you do what you can't do alone."

God as Father

CLARIFY—While walking along the Sea of Galilee, author Dorothy Dawes came upon children playing on a beach. A little boy ran up, introduced himself, and ran off again.

A minute later he was standing on top of a makeshift highdive, calling out to his father to watch: "Abba! Abba!" ("Daddy! Daddy").

Palestinian children still use the word *Abba* to address their father. This is the same word Jesus used to address his Father.

QUESTION **6** ***Can you recall the first and last recorded words of Jesus in Scripture? (They refer to his heavenly Father.)***

■ *At age 12 Jesus said to Mary: "Didn't you know I had to be in my Father's house?"* LUKE 2:49

Before dying on the cross, Jesus prayed, "Father, in your hands I place my spirit." LUKE 23:46

CLARIFY—Stress the two important facts in this section:

1 *Our love is finite: we love.*
2 *God's love is infinite: God is love.*

SHARE YOUR meditation

A small boy was trying to lift a rock, but with no success. His father, who was watching nearby, asked: "Todd, are you sure that you're using all the strength you have?" The boy began to cry.

His father said gently, "Todd, you haven't asked me to help you. And I want to help you more than you could ever guess."

■ ***What keeps me from asking my heavenly Father for help when I can't do something alone?***

This brings us to a very important point. God is present to us in different ways and degrees. For example, God is present through:

■ **Creation** — **Which God made**
■ **Scripture** — **Which God inspired**
■ **Jesus** — **Who is God's Son**

An example may help to clarify these different kinds of presence.

A little boy can be present to his mother in different ways and degrees. For example, he can be present through:

■ **A drawing** — **Which he made**
■ **A letter** — **Which he sent**
■ **In person** — **Visiting his mother**

In a similar way, God can be present to us in different ways and degrees.

5 ***What are some other ways and degrees the boy can become present to his mother?***

God's presence in different ways and degrees inspired the Hebrew psalmist to sing:

Where could I go to escape from you?
Where could I get away
from your presence? . . .

If I flew away beyond the east
or lived in the farthest place in the west,
you would be there to lead me,
you would be there to help me.
PSALM 139:7, 9–10

THINK about it

Like a human parent, God will help us when we ask for help, but in a way that will make us more mature, more real, not in a way that will diminish us.

Madeleine L'Engle

God as Father

The entire lower half of Lois Olson's body was in a cast. She lay in a bed unable to move. One night a tornado struck, and Lois began to panic. Just then her father appeared and carried her to safety. As he struggled under the weight of the cast, Lois could see sweat breaking out on

70 STAGE 1: CHAPTER 5

Bishop Fulton Sheen summed up the biblical story in terms of love this way:

Creation	*God gives life*
Redemption	*God's love forgives*
Eucharist	*God's love unites*
Heaven	*God's love is eternal*

Stress, also, that God's love is often mediated through people. This is especially true in the case of children, whose concept of God is derived from their parents. John Drescher makes this point in his book *If I Were Starting My Family Again.* He tells this delightful story:

I remember a little fellow,
frightened by lightning and thunder,
who called out in the dark,
"Daddy, come. I'm scared."
"Son," the father said, "God loves you,
and he'll take care of you."

NOTES

Spriggs

A man named Spriggs recalls his first night as a homeless person. Someone directed him to a shelter. There he found "a lot of rough-looking men waiting in line."

Finally, the door opened, and they all got beds—about a hundred men in all. Minutes later, they turned out the lights. Spriggs writes:

I was terrified. . . .
Then out of the darkness
a voice said, "Our Father,
who art in heaven . . ."
and the entire dormitory
joined in.
At that moment
I could feel God's presence
in the shelter. My fears
were replaced by peace.

The Catholic Standard, Washington D.C.

his forehead and blood vessels bulging from his temples. This unforgettable experience gave Lois Olson a deep appreciation of God as Father.

Jesus used this image "Father" of God over 170 times. The Gospel According to Luke portrays Jesus addressing God as Father in his first and his last recorded words.

6 *Can you recall the first and the last recorded words of Jesus in Scripture?*

The word for "Father" that Jesus used in his own prayer was *Abba.* MARK 14:36 Literally, it means "Daddy."

Early Christians imitated Jesus and used the word *Abba,* also, in praying to God. ROMANS 8:15, GALATIANS 4:6

This means they addressed the infinite and all-powerful creator of the universe with the tender love and trust of a child, addressing a parent as "Mommy" or "Daddy." Thus, God says through the prophet Isaiah:

"Can a woman forget her own baby
and not love the child she bore?
Even if a mother should forget her child,
I will never forget you." ISAIAH 49:15

But God's love is infinitely different and greater than human love. Peter van Breeman explains the difference this way:

We are divided in our love.
We like a person very much (90%)
or in an ordinary way (50%). . . .

God does not measure love. . . .
If we think God is a person
who can divide love,
then we are thinking not of God
but ourselves. . . .
We have love, but God is love.
AS BREAD THAT IS BROKEN

Some people ask, "How can we reconcile the statement 'God is love' 1 JOHN 4:16 with Jesus' statement that God is to be 'feared'?" LUKE 12:5

7 *How would you answer this question?*

Poet Rod McKuen reconciled the paradox of love and fear with this analogy: "I love the sea, but that doesn't make me less afraid of it." In other words, the sea's beauty attracts him; but, at the same time, its awesome power makes him afraid of it.

8 *How validly might this analogy be applied to God also? Explain.*

PRAYER hotline

God,
do take care of yourself,
because
if anything happens to you,
we're all sunk.

Adlai Stevenson, speech at Harvard Business School, June 6, 1959

STAGE 1: *CHAPTER 5* **71**

"I know God loves me," the boy replied, "but right now I want somebody who has skin on."

QUESTION **7** ***How would you answer this question: How can we reconcile the statement that "God is love"*** 1 JOHN 4:6 ***with Jesus' statement that God is to be "feared"?*** LUKE 12:5

■ *The next paragraph answers in an excellent way with Rod McKuen's analogy to loving and fearing the sea.*

QUESTION **8** ***How validly might this analogy be applied to God also? Explain.***

■ *Very! Moreover, it is an analogy that students will have no trouble grasping.*

Thomas Browne observes that fear and being afraid are not always synonymous in the Bible. Fear arises out of an awareness that I am at another's mercy. He ends by saying, "I fear God, but I'm not afraid." In other words, even if I am at God's mercy, I am not afraid, because "God is love."

Up Close & Personal

***CLARIFY*—**Describing his feelings when the lights were turned out, Spriggs writes:

> *I was shaking in my boots. . . . I was in this room with a hundred other guys. You could hear them coughing and turning as they tried to get comfortable in the night.*

***CLARIFY*—**Tom Schuman was a successful general counsel for a Fortune 500 company in Chicago. He had a six-figure salary and all the perks that go with such a job. One Sunday morning at Mass his pastor said that unless a volunteer director could be found, they might have to close their homeless shelter. After praying over it, Tom retired from his job and volunteered.

He says that in the first year alone, he learned more about life than in all the previous years put together. Before volunteering, he was barely aware of the homeless problem. When he did see a homeless person, he was critical of why someone would choose to live in such a humiliating fashion. Tom soon learned they did not choose to live that way. It's often the result of mental illness or substance abuse, which render them virtually unemployable.

PRAYER hotline

***ACTIVITY*—**Have the students compose and share a similar prayer. To get them started, read these prayers from the Book of Psalms:

1 *Save me, O God! The water is up to my neck.* 69:1
2 *My heart is pounding, my strength is gone. Help me now.* 38:10, 22
3 *My God, why have you left me for dead in the dust?* 21:1, 15

Share Your meditation

***DISCUSS*—To whom might we compare Daddy Long Legs? For what gifts am I especially grateful? Explain.**

■ *We might compare him to God.*

Give the students a little time to reflect on what gifts from God they are especially grateful for and proud of. To get them started, share with them this passage from the autobiography of the famous black athlete and activist Dick Gregory:

■ *I kept running*
all that fall and all that winter,
sometimes through the snow. . . .
I don't think I ever would have finished
high school without running. . . .

I felt so good when I ran. . . .
Nobody could point to me and say
I was poor or crazy; they'd just look at me
with admiration and say: "He's training." . . .
I was proud of my body that kept me going.

THINK about it

***DISCUSS*—Give some examples to illustrate the difference between someone who is a "religious nut" and someone who bears "spiritual fruit."**

■ *Religious nuts "talk the talk" only; bearers of spiritual fruit "walk the walk."*

God as Trinity

***CLARIFY*—Jesus mentions or refers to the Father or the Spirit over a hundred times in John's Gospel.**

***NOTEBOOK*—A study of the Gospel According to Luke and his Acts of the Apostles shows he has a Trinitarian perspective of history.**

Have the students copy the following diagram in their notebooks and explain the focus of three Trinitarian divisions of the Bible:

SHARE YOUR meditation

Jean Webster's story "Daddy Long Legs" concerns an orphan girl who received many gifts from a person she never knew or met.

As a result she grew up blessed with remarkable opportunities that she would otherwise never have had. Often she would try to imagine what her benefactor was like, but she had no way of knowing if her image was correct.

Then one day the magic moment came: she met her benefactor. He exceeded her wildest dreams.

■ ***To whom might we compare Daddy Long Legs? For what gifts from God am I especially grateful? Explain.***

God as Trinity

This brings us to the most incredible image of God that emerged from the life and teaching of Jesus: the mystery of God as Trinity.

It is the central mystery of our Christian faith. In the one, true God, there are three distinct persons: Father, Son, and Holy Spirit. CCC 266

Had God not revealed this mystery to us in Scripture, we could never have dreamed it. CCC 237

John's Gospel, especially, refers to God as Trinity: Father, Son, and Spirit. For example, Jesus tells his disciples:

"Whoever
has seen me has seen the Father. . . .
I will ask the Father,
and he will give you the Spirit."
JOHN 14:9, 16–17

The best-known reference to the Trinity is found in Matthew's Gospel. There Jesus tells his disciples:

"Go, then, to all peoples everywhere,
and make them my disciples,
baptizing them in the name of the Father,
the Son, and the Holy Spirit."
MATTHEW 28:19

The most graphic reference occurs in Luke's Gospel, as we saw, at the baptism of Jesus:

■ **Son** **Jesus stands in the water.**
■ **Spirit** **A dove hovers over Jesus.**
■ **Father** **A voice says, "My Son."**

A beautiful reference to the Trinity is found at the end of Paul's Second Letter to the Corinthians. Paul uses it as a blessing upon his readers:

The grace of the Lord Jesus Christ,
the love of God,
and the fellowship of the Holy Spirit
be with you. 2 CORINTHIANS 13:13

9 ***Which of the above Scripture references to the Holy Trinity do you find the clearest and the most helpful? Explain.***

THINK about it

God wants spiritual fruit, not religious nuts.
E.C. McKenzie

72 STAGE 1: CHAPTER 5

Old Testament	*Father*
Gospel	*Son*
Acts/Letters/Revelation	*Spirit*

The Father (focus of the OT) sent the Son (focus of the Gospel). The Father and the Son sent the Spirit (focus of the rest of the NT books).

QUESTION **9** ***Which of the above Scripture references to the Holy Trinity do you find the clearest and the most helpful? Explain.***

Have students make their choices privately and in writing. When they have finished, have them reveal their choice, as a secretary tallies them on the chalkboard. Invite discussion on the results.

NOTES

Image of the Trinity

Some years ago, environmentalist Denis Hayes wrote a book entitled *Ray of Hope: The Transition to a Post-Petroleum World.*

The *Ray of Hope* is the sun. Its rays already light and heat our planet. Hayes writes that it is now time to let the sun's rays energize our planet even more than they currently do. He is referring to a more efficient use of solar energy.

Hayes's observation inspired some people to see the sun as an image of the Trinity:

Its *light* is an image of the Father who created the world, saying, "Let there be light!" And there was light.

Its *heat* is an image of Jesus, who saved us by the warmth of his love.

Its *energy* is an image of the Holy Spirit, who energizes us with grace.

And so the rays of the *one* sun bless us in *three* ways—lighting our planet, heating our planet, and energizing our planet—and in the process, serve as an image of the Trinity.

10 ***Can you recall other images of the Trinity? Which image do you find most helpful and why?***

Saint Augustine was walking along a beach and meditating on the Trinity. "How can God be three and one at the same time?" he kept saying over and over to himself.

Suddenly, his attention was drawn to a little girl carrying a small container of water from the sea to a hole she had dug on the beach. "What are you doing?" he asked her. With childlike simplicity, she replied: "I'm emptying the sea into this hole."

Saint Augustine stopped dead in his tracks and thought: "I am trying to do what that little girl is doing. I'm trying to crowd the infinite God into the finite structure of my mind."

11 ***To which member of the Holy Trinity can you relate and pray most easily? Which one is hardest to pray to? Why?***

HISTORICAL Connection

Father Paul Schulte offered Mass on the giant dirigible Hindenburg on its sixty-two-hour maiden voyage from Germany to Lakehurst, New Jersey, May 18, 1936. In his homily, he said:

Glory to God the Father
who created the earth;
and to God the Son
who redeemed the earth;
and to God the Holy Spirit
who hallowed the earth.

Let the "Amen" be pronounced
by the skies and the marvelous
clouds which surround us,
by the ocean over which we are
hovering, by the sun, the
breeze, and the stars.

Let the "Amen"
be spoken by the motors,
the wonderful airship,
the crew, the passengers.
Glory be to thee today,
tomorrow,
and in all eternity. Amen.

Quoted by John M Scott, S.J., in *Journeys Into Space: Scientific and Spiritual Events;* Liguorian, July–August 1999

STAGE 1: *CHAPTER* 5 **73**

Image of the Trinity

NOTEBOOK—Sum up on the chalkboard Denis Hayes's image of the Trinity for entry in notebooks:

Light	*Father*	*(Creator)*
Heat	*Son*	*(Redeemer)*
Energy	*Spirit*	*(Sanctifier)*

QUESTION **10** ***Can you recall other images of the Trinity? Which do you find most helpful and why?***

■ *St. Ignatius* *audial image*	*3 notes / 1 sound*
St. Patrick *visual image*	*3 petals / 1 leaf*
John Wesley *visual image*	*3 candles / 1 light*
H_2O *functional image*	*3 forms / 1 substance* *solid/gas/liquid*
Mother *relational image*	*3 roles / 1 person* *wife/mother/friend*

ACTIVITY—Have students vote (privately and in writing) on the image they find most helpful. Tally the results on the chalkboard and discuss them.

QUESTION **11** ***To which member of the Holy Trinity can you relate and pray most easily? Which one is hardest to pray to? Why?***

Kevin Axe wrote an article entitled "How Fathers Might Pray the Our Father." He said he prefers to pray to God "father to Father" instead of "child to Father."

The reason? They both have the same problem. He explains the problem this way: "God the Father has a few billion people who are forever behaving like children. God can identify with me, and I with him."

You might suggest that those students who have problems with their fathers at times write a brief note to God the Father and ask his "fatherly" help and advice in dealing with the situation.

HISTORICAL Connection

CLARIFY—Less than a year later, May 6, 1937, the dirigible caught fire and exploded while landing at Lakehurst.

Thirty of its 97 passengers and crew were killed. The toll would have been higher but for the heroic efforts of the crew and Navy personnel.

One theory is that a spark from static electricity ignited the hydrogen gas that was being released preparatory to landing.

The tragedy ended passenger travel by dirigible.

The "Goodyear" blimps and others used by the advertising industry are a throwback to the dirigible era.

Recap

"Ever since God created the world, his invisible qualities, both his eternal power and his divine nature have been clearly seen." ROMANS 1:20

But the beauty and order of the universe is only a glimmer of God's glory and greatness. Reason cannot "paint a portrait" of God. Only Scripture can do that.

Scripture gives us many images of God. Three, however, stand out: (1) Creator, (2) Father, (3) Trinity: the mystery of one loving God in whom there are three distinct persons—Father, Son, and Holy Spirit.

A modern parable of God's plan for the world of people is the film *Laura*. With the help of God's revelation in Scripture, especially through Jesus, the eternal Son of God, we are called to learn about God, fall in love with God, and live with God forever.

Review

DAILY QUIZ—The review questions may be assigned (one or two at a time) for homework or a daily quiz.

CHAPTER TESTS—Reproducible chapter tests are found in Appendix A. For consistency and ease in grading, quizzes are restricted to (1) "Matching," (2) "True/False," and (3) "Fill in the Blanks."

TEST ANSWERS—The following are the answers to the test for Chapter 5. (See Appendix A, page 316.) All correct answers are worth four points.

Matching

1 = b	2 = c	3 = a	4 = g
5 = d	6 = e	7 = f	

True/False

1 = T	2 = F	3 = T	4 = T
5 = F	6 = F	7 = T	8 = T
9 = F	10 = T	11 = T	12 = T

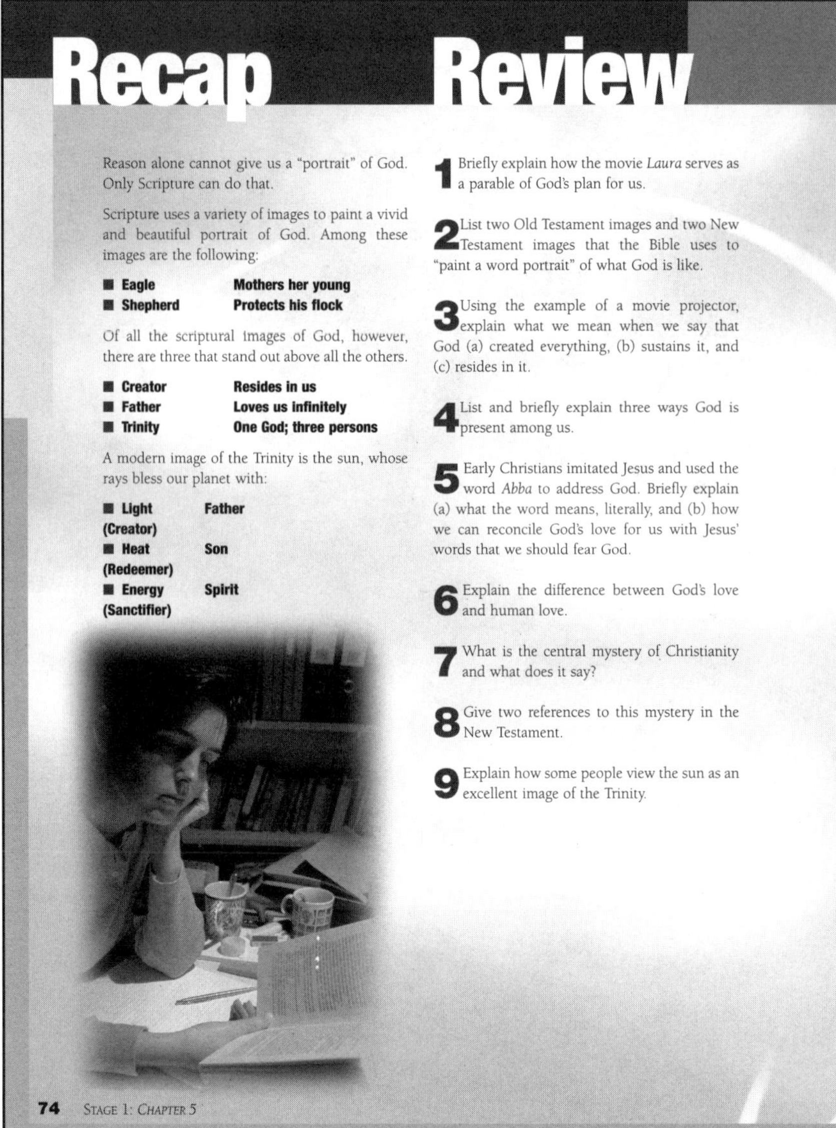

Recap Review

Reason alone cannot give us a "portrait" of God. Only Scripture can do that.

Scripture uses a variety of images to paint a vivid and beautiful portrait of God. Among these images are the following:

- **Eagle** — **Mothers her young**
- **Shepherd** — **Protects his flock**

Of all the scriptural images of God, however, there are three that stand out above all the others.

- **Creator** — **Resides in us**
- **Father** — **Loves us infinitely**
- **Trinity** — **One God; three persons**

A modern image of the Trinity is the sun, whose rays bless our planet with:

- **Light (Creator)** — **Father**
- **Heat (Redeemer)** — **Son**
- **Energy (Sanctifier)** — **Spirit**

1 Briefly explain how the movie *Laura* serves as a parable of God's plan for us.

2 List two Old Testament images and two New Testament images that the Bible uses to "paint a word portrait" of what God is like.

3 Using the example of a movie projector, explain what we mean when we say that God (a) created everything, (b) sustains it, and (c) resides in it.

4 List and briefly explain three ways God is present among us.

5 Early Christians imitated Jesus and used the word *Abba* to address God. Briefly explain (a) what the word means, literally, and (b) how we can reconcile God's love for us with Jesus' words that we should fear God.

6 Explain the difference between God's love and human love.

7 What is the central mystery of Christianity and what does it say?

8 Give two references to this mystery in the New Testament.

9 Explain how some people view the sun as an excellent image of the Trinity.

74 STAGE 1: CHAPTER 5

Fill in the Blanks

1. (a) Creation	2. (a) Son
(b) Scripture	(b) Spirit
(c) Jesus	(c) Father

Reflect

1 a) *Why should only a few people be blessed with such a spiritual presence?*

Unfortunately, many people—through a lack of faith, lack of effort, ignorance, or whatever reason—do not open themselves to such a presence.

NOTES

Reflect

1 Estlin Carpenter served as a chaplain at Harvard University. The surprising thing about him was that during his school days he was apathetic about God and religion. What happened to change him?

One afternoon, while out for a walk, he felt an incredible presence of God all around him. It was as if God suddenly began walking along with him just as Jesus did with the disciples returning to Emmaus.

That experience impacted him dramatically. His attitude toward God and religion did an about face. He said, "I could now not only believe in God with my mind, but also love him with my heart." Carpenter was never the same again after that afternoon.

- ***Why should only a few people be blessed with such a spiritual presence?***
- ***What is the nearest thing you have had to Carpenter's experience? Be as detailed as you can be.***

2 For years, a small statue of Cupid stood in the entrance hall of an old New York City mansion. Its arms and face were badly damaged; but the statue had a charm about it that made it a good conversation piece.

One day it caught the attention of Professor Brandt of New York University. It matched the description of a lost work of Michelangelo. Sure enough, it was. The story of the statue makes a good parable of God.

Like the statue, God is present in our midst, but unrecognized by the majority of people. But every once in a while, someone claims to recognize God's presence with the same surprise and certitude that Professor Brandt experienced when she recognized Cupid.

- ***How can we distinguish between a graced experience of God and an imaginary one?***

3 Sunday morning, May 18, 1980, the volcano Mount Saint Helens exploded. Photographer David Crocket of KOMO-TV, Seattle, was caught at the foot of the volcano when it blew. He was nearly buried by the flying debris and tons of suffocating volcanic ash.

David remained motionless for the next several hours to conserve air amidst the dust and ash that engulfed the site like a huge cloud.

Then a miraculous thing happened. A Coast Guard helicopter spotted David and rescued him. After his ordeal, he wrote in *Guideposts* magazine:

During those ten hours
I saw a mountain fall apart.
I saw a forest disappear. . . .
I saw that God is the only one
who is unmovable, unshakable, infallible.

I feel somehow
that I'm being allowed to start over
whatever is in his master plan for me.

- ***To what extent do you agree that God has a master plan for the human race and each of us has a part to play in it?***
- ***Describe your closest brush with death and how it affected you as it did David.***

Stage 1: Chapter 5 **75**

b) *What is the nearest thing you have had to Carpenter's experience? Be as detailed as you can be.*

To start the students thinking, recall the Cincinnati high-school football star's description of practice before the state championship game (Chapter 2 of this manual):

- *"When we hugged . . . I felt a third Presence. It was the most unbelievable experience. It was as if God were hugging us as well. God had been there with us for four years—at every lift, run, practice.*

Recall, also, the Chicago high-school student's rock concert experience:

- *As far as I could see, everyone was standing up, clapping and moving to the music. A fantastic feeling rushed over me. Then I thought . . . "God must be present. He has to be!"*

2 *How can we distinguish between a graced experience of God and an imaginary one?*

Recall three tests mentioned in chapter 2 this manual. Did the person experience an increase (a) in faith, (b) in hope, (c) in love, as a result of it?

3 a) *To what extent do you agree that God has a master plan for the human race and each of us has a part to play in it?*

This question sets up the "Prayer Journal" exercise on page 77. You may wish to conclude this exercise by having the students do the letter recommended there.

b) *Describe your closest brush with death and how it affected you as it did David.*

Have students share in small groups first and then pick out one of the more dramatic responses to share with the class.

PRAYER TIME with the Lord

Write out a three-minute replay of your own.

***ACTIVITY*—**Give the students about five minutes to reflect seriously on each one of these three points before writing them down. Also, have them be more detailed than the examples in the text. They were deliberately kept short to conserve space.

***DISCUSS*—**In Question 11 (final question in the text) the students were asked, "To which member of the Holy Trinity can you relate and pray most easily? Which one is the hardest to pray to?"

Without mentioning this question, ask the students which of the three persons they find easiest to pray to in this exercise. Hardest?

Did this agree with the way they answered Question 11? If not, how do they explain the difference?

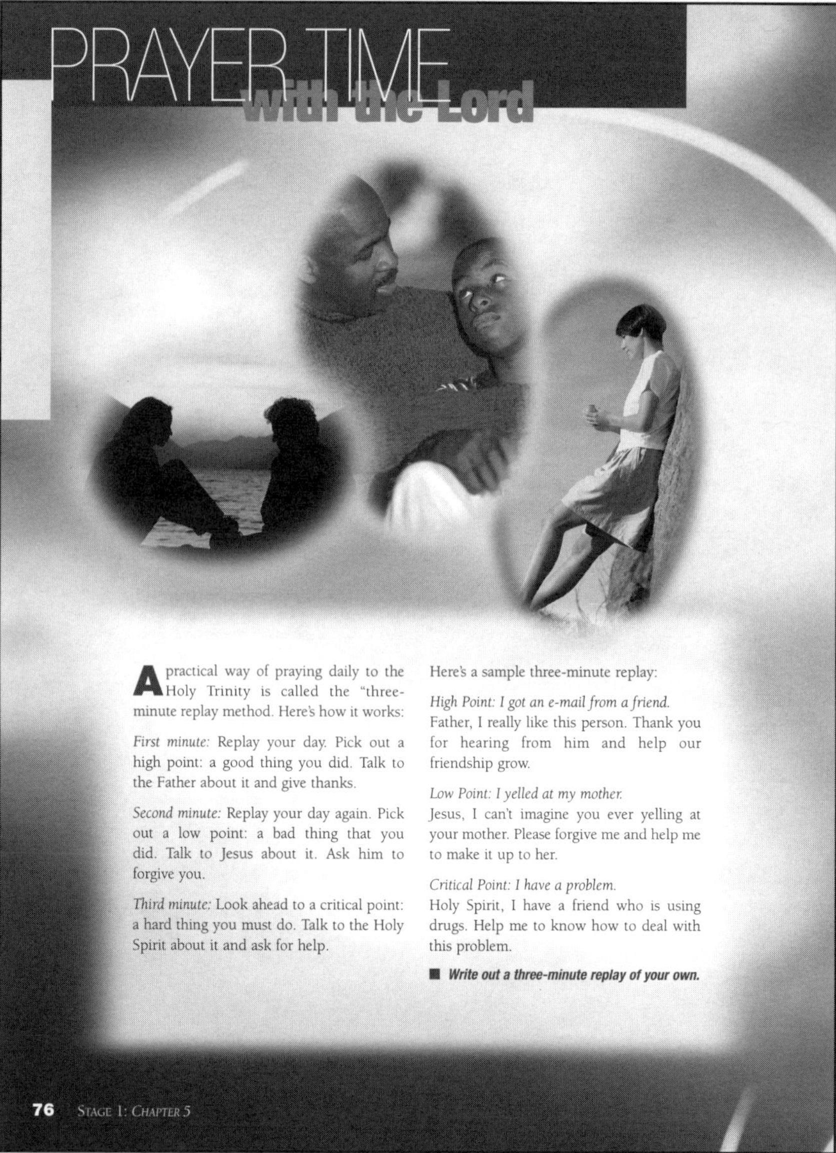

PRAYER TIME with the Lord

A practical way of praying daily to the Holy Trinity is called the "three-minute replay method. Here's how it works:

First minute: Replay your day. Pick out a high point: a good thing you did. Talk to the Father about it and give thanks.

Second minute: Replay your day again. Pick out a low point: a bad thing that you did. Talk to Jesus about it. Ask him to forgive you.

Third minute: Look ahead to a critical point: a hard thing you must do. Talk to the Holy Spirit about it and ask for help.

Here's a sample three-minute replay:

High Point: I got an e-mail from a friend. Father, I really like this person. Thank you for hearing from him and help our friendship grow.

Low Point: I yelled at my mother. Jesus, I can't imagine you ever yelling at your mother. Please forgive me and help me to make it up to her.

Critical Point: I have a problem. Holy Spirit, I have a friend who is using drugs. Help me to know how to deal with this problem.

■ ***Write out a three-minute replay of your own.***

76 STAGE 1: CHAPTER 5

PRAYER Journal

Compose a brief letter to God the Father concerning his purpose in creating you.

You might want to have the students hand in their letters, so that you can check them and select two or three to read and discuss.

NOTES

PRAYER Journal

An excellent way to begin your "Prayer Time with the Lord" is by beginning with the following prayer to the Trinity.

Father, you created me
and put me on earth for a purpose.
Jesus, you died for me
and called me to complete your work.
Holy Spirit, you help me
to carry out the work
for which I was created and called.

In your presence and name—
Father, Son, and Spirit—
I begin my meditation.
May all my thoughts and inspirations
have their origin in you
and be directed to your glory.

■ ***Compose a brief letter to God the Father concerning his purpose in creating you.***

SCRIPTURE Journal

1	**Loving Father**	**Hosea 11:1–4**
2	**Loving host**	**Psalm 23**
3	**Loving creator**	**Psalm 8**
4	**Forgiving Father**	**Luke 15:11–32**
5	**Forgiving Jesus**	**John 8:1–11**

■ ***Pick one of the above passages. Read it prayerfully and write a short statement to Jesus expressing your feelings about it.***

STAGE 1: CHAPTER 5 **77**

SCRIPTURE Journal

You might recommend that the students select the first reading: Hosea 11:1–4.

Another good reading for students is the fifth one: John 8:1–11.

Classroom Resources

CATECHISM

Catechism of the Catholic Church *Second Edition*

For further enrichment, you might refer to:

1.	Father (God, The)	Index	p. 793
		Glossary	p. 879
2.	Trinity	Index	pp. 854–55
		Glossary	p. 902

—AVAILABLE FROM THE UNITED STATES CATHOLIC CONFERENCE, WASHINGTON DC

VIDEOS

Mystery of God: Father, Son, and Spirit

Three thirty-minute segments. A contemporary approach to the story of creation, salvation, and God's abiding presence in our lives.
—AVAILABLE FROM THOMAS MORE PUBLISHING, ALLEN, TX

Meeting the Living God

William O'Malley, S.J.

Sixty minutes. Rich and engaging way to convey to high-school students what it means to encounter God.
—AVAILABLE FROM PAULIST PRESS, MAHWAH, NJ

BOOK

God the Father: Meditations for the Millennium

Mark Link, S.J.

Twenty-two weeks of brief, practical daily meditations. Each week is introduced with a basic theme related to God the Father (e.g., Search for the Father, Touch of the Father, Word of the Father, Prayer of the Father).
—AVAILABLE FROM THOMAS MORE PUBLISHING, ALLEN, TX

NOTE

For a list of (1) General resources for professional background and (2) Addresses, phone/fax numbers of major publishing companies, see Appendix B of this Resource Manual.

CHAPTER 6
God the Son

CHAPTER at a Glance

God has spoken to the human family through three words:

Cosmic word	*Creation*
Inspired word	*Scripture*
Incarnate word	*Jesus*

We've seen how God spoke to us through the first two. Now we take a look at the third one.

DISCUSS—A *Peanuts* cartoon shows Schroeder holding a sign saying, "Jesus is the answer!"

Next to him is Snoopy holding a sign saying, "What is the question?"

Ask the students: How would you answer Snoopy's question?

Some examples might be:

1. *How can we find happiness?*
2. *How can we change ourselves?*
3. *How can we change the world?*

End the discussion by having a student read aloud the three opening paragraphs that begin: "We write to you . . ."

Ask: How do the paragraphs answer Snoopy's two questions?

■ *Jesus is the answer to many questions; but the two most important questions are:*

(1) What is God like?
(2) What did God make me to be like?

Image of God the Son

ACTIVITY—Have a student artist illustrate on the chalkboard the fish-shaped lettering on the car.

CHAPTER 6 God the Son

We write to you about the Word of Life, which has existed from the beginning. We have heard it, and we have seen it, and our hands have touched it . . .

What we have seen and heard we announce to you, also, so that you will join us in the fellowship that we have with the Father and with his Son, Jesus Christ. We write this in order that your joy may be complete. 1 John 1:1–4

Jesus is Son of God, both human and divine. He is also the Word of God. He reveals God to us; and he reveals what we can become, if we open ourselves to the Spirit, which he sent upon us.

CHAPTER at a Glance

Image of God the Son

Titles of God the Son
Jesus
Christ
Son of God
Savior
Lord
Word of God

Image of God the Son

A young man pulled into a parking lot. Above the rear bumper of his car were the letters I CH TH Y S, shaped like a fish. Someone asked, "What's the meaning of the fish-shaped word?"

The young man explained that they were the first letters of the Greek expression that is translated "Jesus, Christ, Son of God, Savior."

In Greek the letters spell "fish." This explains why the image of a fish became the secret sign for Jesus during times of persecution in early Christianity.

The words "Jesus," "Christ," "Son of God," and "Savior" sum up four titles we give to the second person of the Trinity.

- Jesus
- Son of God
- Christ
- Savior

Jesus

The most personal thing we own is our name. It identifies us as a member of the human family. It is the way our friends address us; and it is the way that people speak about us. The name "Jesus" did the same thing for the Son of God.

78

I C H T H Y S

NOTEBOOK—The Greek word *ICHTHYS* is formed from the first letter/letters of the five Greek words *Iesous Christos Yios Theou Soter* ("Jesus Christ, Son of God, Savior").

We call a word formed in this manner an "acronym."

After having the students record the following table, have them give an example of an English "acronym."

Greek	English
Iesous	*Jesus*
Christos	*Christ*
Theou	*God's*
Yios	*Son*
Soter	*Savior*

NOTES

In biblical times, names often did more than just identify a person. They also revealed something about the person. Jesus' name did that also.

Jesus received his name from an angel, who said to Joseph, "You will name him Jesus—because he will save his people from their sins."
MATTHEW 1:21

The name "Jesus" not only identifies him as a member of the human family, but also as having a saving mission from God. CCC 430–35

Trapped

Three high school boys set out on a four-day climb up Mount Hood in Oregon. They were fairly experienced climbers, but they were not prepared for what happened about 9,000 feet up the mountain.

A giant blizzard struck. Unable to move up or down the mountain, they tunneled into a snowbank to make a snow cave in which to wait out the storm.

A week passed and the blizzard still raged on. The three were now growing frightened. Fortunately, there was just enough light in the snow cave to read by, so they took turns reading aloud from a pocket Bible, which one of the boys happened to have in his pack.

As the blizzard raged into the second week, their food supply ran out. Now they began to lose hope that they'd survive or be rescued. As they read the Bible and prayed, they began to see a parallel between their situation and that of the Jewish people before the birth of Jesus. They, too, were beginning to lose hope as they waited and waited for the Messiah.

On the sixteenth day, the weather cleared. The students crawled out of the cave, barely able to stand up. As they looked around, one of them saw a rescue team coming up the mountain. The glorious feeling that the students felt as they saw the rescuers was overwhelming.

1 What parallel might we draw between the students waiting for rescue and faithful Jews waiting for the Messiah?

STAGE 1: CHAPTER 6 **79**

■ *Two examples of an English acrostic are:*

1 ***Radar:*** ***ra****dio* ***d****etecting* ***a****nd* ***r****anging*

2 ***NASA:*** ***N****ational* ***A****eronautic* ***S****pace* ***A****dministration*

Jesus

CLARIFY—Native Americans gave descriptive names to their children: "Sure Foot," "Running Deer."

We do the same thing. The "hang-time" of Michael Jordan's basketball leaps won him the title "Air Jordan." Similarly, his former teammate, the great rebounder Dennis Rodman, was given the dubious name "The Worm."

DISCUSS—Ask the students to give other examples of names/nicknames that say something about the person.

NOTEBOOK—This brings us to the name "Jesus." It, too, is a descriptive name. It does two things. Sum them up as follows for entry in notebooks:

Jesus —
- *Points to the Son of Man— as being a member of mankind*
- *Points to the Son of God— as being the Savior of mankind*

Trapped

Philip Yancey tells this remarkable story in an article entitled "Ordeal on Mt. Hood." The author lost the reference to it, but it probably appeared in *Campus Life*. Commenting on the reading of the Bible, Yancey says of the boys:

> *They read aloud, taking turns, eight hours a day. It was an eerie scene—three bodies propped up on their elbows inside a five-foot square, the Bible lit by a spooky, reflected light from the tunnel.*
>
> *Psalms seemed to fit best—David wrote many of them while trapped in situations not unlike theirs—hungry, lonely, sometimes even in a cave. . . . "Wait on the Lord," he said. "Trust him." It was hard.*

QUESTION **1** ***What parallel might we draw between students waiting for rescue and faithful Jews waiting for the Messiah?***

1 *Neither could save themselves.*
2 *Both were waiting for a "rescuer."*
3 *Both were losing hope.*
4 *Both drew strength from God's Word: Jews read it in the synagogue; the three boys read it in the eerie half-light of their snow cave.*

DISCUSS—Ask the students: What detail tips us off that this event took place in the early 1990s, not the late 1990s?

Brown says, "You may hit three-fifty for a lifetime and get $5 million a year. If you did that today, you'd probably get $10 and $15 million a year."

Christ

CLARIFY—After David succeeded Solomon as King, God covenanted with him, saying through the prophet Nathan: *"Your kingdom will last forever."* 2 Samuel 7:16

This covenant begins a series of promises known as the "messianic prophecies." They point to the Messiah, who would come from David's line.

Jesus identifies himself as that Messiah. John 10:24 His kingdom (the Kingdom of God) will last forever.

NOTEBOOK—List the Hebrew, Greek, and English words for "the anointed" on the board:

	Messiah	*(Hebrew)*
The Anointed:	*Christos*	*(Greek)*
	Christ	*(English)*

Cold and Confused

QUESTION **2** ***How does the woman's experience shed light on what Christmas is all about?***

■ *Christmas is about God becoming one of us to save us and teach us what is for our good, both:*

1 *In this life and*
2 *In the life to come*

CLARIFY—Use this opportunity to share with the students what a prominent non-Christian had to say about Jesus.

H.G. Wells (1866–1946) was a science-fiction writer. His novels include *The Time Machine, The Island of Dr. Moreau, The War of the Worlds*—to name only a few.

Wells was also a great historian. He was commissioned to pick the "three greatest men of history." He placed Jesus first (Buddha, second; Aristotle, third).

Explaining his choice of Jesus, he began by saying that millions of people regard Jesus as being more than a man. But a historian must disregard that fact. He must treat Jesus as a man, just as a painter must paint him as a man.

In other words, he must stick to the evidence that would be accepted by everyone. He goes on to say:

■ *Now it is interesting and significant that a historian . . . like myself,*
who does not even call himself a Christian,

Up Close & Personal

Cordell Brown

Cordell Brown was a cerebral palsy victim. He was invited to speak at a pre-game chapel service in the clubhouse of the Philadelphia Phillies. Why? What did he, living in a world of pain and deformity, have to say to athletes?

He began by putting the players at ease. He said: "I know I'm different; but by the grace of God I am what I am." Then for the next twenty minutes he talked of God's goodness to him.

He concluded by answering the question: "What could he say to a group to superstars?" He said in a loving way:

You may hit three-fifty
for a lifetime
and get $5 million a year,
but when the day comes
that they close
the lid on that box,
you won't be any different
than I am.
That's one time when
we'll all be the same.
I don't need what you have,
but one thing is for sure:
You need what I have:
Jesus Christ.

Retold from Pat Williamson (slightly adapted)

Christ

This brings us to the second title of the second person of the Holy Trinity. One day Jesus asked Peter, "Who do you say I am?" Peter replied, "You are the Messiah, the Son of the living God." Matthew 16:15, 16

The Hebrew word *Messiah* means "the anointed." It is translated into Greek as *Christos*—from which we get our English "Christ." The title "Christ" identifies Jesus as the long-awaited Messiah. CCC 436–40, 711–16

Thus, the words *Messiah* (Hebrew), *Christos* (Greek), and *Christ* (English) are simply different ways to refer to the same person: the descendent of David, promised by God through the prophets.

Old Testament kings, priests, and, in some cases, prophets were anointed—consecrating and empowering them to carry out their mission from God. CCC 436

How much more appropriate was it then that the promised Messiah be anointed king, priest, and prophet. And this is precisely how Jesus identified himself in the synagogue in Nazareth, saying:

"The Spirit of the Lord is upon me,
because he has chosen [anointed] me
to bring good news to the poor . . .
to proclaim liberty to the captives
and recovery of sight to the blind . . .
and [to] announce that the time has come
when the Lord will save his people."
Luke 4:18–19

And so the title "Christ" identifies Jesus as the long-promised Messiah, whose reign will extend to all peoples of all times. CCC 727–30

Cold and Confused

One Christmas day, a woman was seated in front of her fireplace thinking about the birth of Jesus. She asked herself, "Why would the Creator of the world choose to be born on earth and live among us as a man?" The whole thing seemed absurd.

Just then she heard a strange sound outside. Going to the window, she saw a half-dozen geese staggering about in the snow. They had apparently wandered off from a warm barn and were now cold and confused.

She went outside, opened the door to her warm garage, and tried to get the geese to go in. But the more she tried, the more frightened they became—and the more they scattered. Finally, she gave up. She realized that the geese had no idea that she was trying to help them.

At that moment, a strange thought crossed her mind: "If for one minute I could become a goose, I could explain to them that what I was trying to do was for their good!" Then it struck her. That's what Christmas is all about!

2 ***How does the woman's experience shed light on what Christmas is all about?***

80 Stage 1: Chapter 6

NOTES

Son of God

This brings us to the most important title that is given to Jesus: "Son of God." CCC 441–45

In the Old Testament, the title "Son of God" is applied to a wide range of people. For example, it is given to Israel's kings (2 Samuel 7:14). It is also given to Israel as a whole (Exodus 4:22). In this case, it signifies God's "adoption" of Israel as the "Chosen People."

In other words, the title is used in the Old Testament not in the *literal* sense of the words, but in a kind of *figurative* sense, much as we might refer to a good person as an "angel."

In the New Testament, we find the title "Son of God" used of Jesus over a hundred times. More importantly, we find it used of Jesus in the *literal* sense of the words. Thus, John writes near the end of his Gospel:

These [things] have been written in order that you may believe that Jesus is the Messiah, the Son of God, and that through your faith in him you may have life. John 20:31

Similarly, Matthew has Peter use the title in the full *literal* sense when he says of Jesus, "You are the Messiah, the Son of the Living God." Jesus acknowledges the literal use of the title, saying to Peter:

"This truth did not come to you
from any human being,
but it was given to you directly
by my Father in heaven." Matthew 16:17

There are two solemn moments, especially, when the title applied to Jesus in the literal sense. In both cases, the title comes from God the Father. The first is at Jesus' baptism. Matthew writes:

As soon as Jesus was baptized,
he came up out of the water.

THINK
about it
When Jesus teaches us his song, how can we keep from singing it.
Author Unknown

ART
Connection

This painting of the *Baptism of Jesus*, by the Italian painter Paolo Cagliari, was completed about 1570.

finds the picture centering irresistibly around the life and character of this most significant man.

The historian's test of an individual's greatness is "What did he leave to grow?" Did he start men thinking along fresh lines with a vigor that persisted after him? By this test Jesus stands first.
Readers Digest, May 1935

What did Jesus leave to grow? It was the concept of the Fatherhood of God. Commenting on this concept in the first volume of his *Outline of History,* Wells says:

■ *It is one of the most revolutionary changes of outlook that has ever stirred and changed human thought. No age has even yet understood fully the tremendous challenge it carries.*

But the world began to be a different world from the day that doctrine was preached and every step toward wider understanding and tolerance and good will is a step in the direction of that universal brotherhood that Christ proclaimed.

This brings us back to the Jesus of faith.

Son of God

CLARIFY—John writes in his Gospel:

It was winter, and the Festival of the Dedication of the Temple was being celebrated in Jerusalem. John 10:22

This festival of *Hanukkah* always falls around Christmas time. The rededication took place in 164 B.C. after the Maccabees retook it from the Syrians.

During this *Hanukkah* festival, some people asked Jesus if he was the Messiah. He said, "I have already told you, but you would not believe me."

Jesus went on, saying, "The Father and I are one!" The people clearly took this literally (not figuratively) and tried to stone him, saying, "You are trying to make yourself God!" John 10:25–33

NOTEBOOK—Put the following on the board for entry into notebooks:

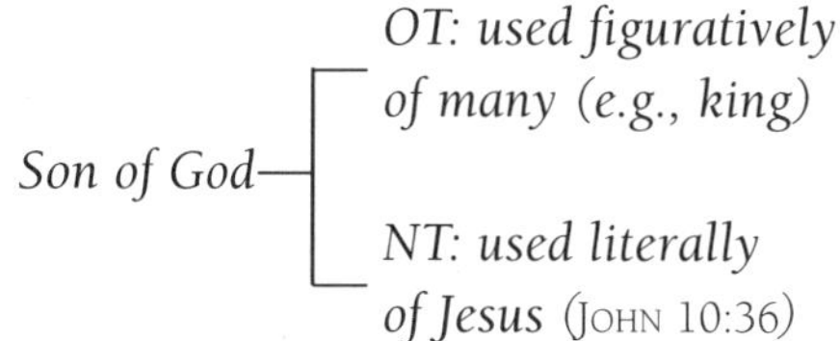

OT: used figuratively of many (e.g., king)
NT: used literally of Jesus (John 10:36)

ART
Connection

DISCUSS—Cagliari, also known as Paulo Veronese, added five figures to the scene. Two are humans with angel "wings."

Later, he created an uproar when he put similar decorative figures in his painting of the *Last Supper*. He was ordered by religious authorities to remove them, on the basis that they were both irrelevant and irreverent.

NOTEBOOK—List the two solemn moments (when Jesus is identified as "my own dear Son") on the board for entry into the students' notebooks:

My Son — *Baptism: voice from heaven* / *Mountain: voice from cloud*

Years later Peter would write of the "mountain" episode:

> *With our own eyes we saw his greatness.*
> *We were there when . . .*
> *the voice came to him, saying,*
> *"This is my own dear Son. . . ."*
>
> *We ourselves heard his voice coming from heaven, when we were with him on the holy mountain.* 2 PETER 1;17–18

CLARIFY—On *Mount* Tabor three apostles (Peter, James, and John) saw Jesus in a *moment of ecstasy*—when his *divine nature* shone through in a way it never had before. MATTHEW 17:2–6

On the *Mount* of Olives the same three disciples saw Jesus in a *moment of agony*—when his *human nature* shone through him in a way that it never had before. LUKE 22:39, 42

NOTEBOOK—Develop on the board and list in notebooks:

Mt. Tabor — *Moment of ecstasy* / *Divinity shines through*

Mt. Olives — *Moment of agony* / *Humanity shines through*

QUESTION **3 *Why is/isn't it easier for you to think of Jesus as "true God" or "true man"?***

DISCUSS—Have the students share their responses orally.

Share Your meditation

Have students answer the three questions (Jesus' impact on their lives) privately. Then have them share their responses in groups of three or four. Finally, have them select the best response in their group and share it with the entire class.

SHARE YOUR meditation

Mike Moran was a Navy helicopter pilot. One day, while explaining his "chopper" to his parents, he said, "As complex as those machines are, their whirling rotors are held in place by one simple hexagonal nut." Then turning to his mother he said, "Guess what that nut is called, Mom?" She shrugged. He smiled and said, "It's called a 'Jesus Nut.'"

■ ***To what extent does Jesus hold my life together?***

■ ***What is one area of my life that is still not under his control?***

■ ***What is one step I might take to change this?***

Then heaven was opened to him, and
he saw the Spirit of God coming down
like a dove and lighting on him.

Then a voice said from heaven,
"This is my own dear Son,
with whom I am pleased.
MATTHEW 3:16–17

The second of these solemn moments occurred at the transfiguration of Jesus on the mountain, in the presence of Peter, James, and John. Matthew writes:

As they looked on,
a change came over Jesus:
his face was shining like the sun,
and his clothes were dazzling white.
Then the three disciples
saw Moses and Elijah talking with Jesus.

So Peter spoke up and said to Jesus,
"Lord, how good it is that we are here! . . .
While he was talking,
a shining cloud came over them,
and a voice from the cloud said,
"This is my own dear Son,
with whom I am pleased—listen to him!"

When the disciples heard the voice,
they were so terrified
that they threw themselves
face downward on the ground.
MATTHEW 17:2–6

So Jesus the Son of man is also the Son of God. Within his person he harmonizes two natures: our *human* nature and God's *divine* nature. Jesus is true God and true man. CCC 442–45, 479–83

3 *Why is/isn't it easier for you to think of Jesus as "true God" or "true man"?*

PRAYER hotline

O Lord, help me understand that nothing can come my way that you and I together can't handle.

Author unknown

Rescued

There's a story about a man who dove into a raging river to save a ten-year-old from drowning. A few days later, the ten-year-old and his mother went to see the man.

The child said to the man, "How can I thank you for what you did for me?" The man put his arm around the ten-year-old and said, "Son, the best thanks you can give me is to live your life in a way that will have made it worth saving."

4 *If you asked Jesus, your Savior, what this means in terms of living your life, what might he say?*

Savior

This brings us to the fourth title of the second person of the Holy Trinity.

One day, Jesus met a woman at a well outside a village. She was so impressed with Jesus that she hurried back to her village. Describing Jesus to the villagers, she said, "Could he be the Messiah?" JOHN 4:29

The villagers went to Jesus and invited him to teach them. After listening to him for two days, they said to one another, "He really is the Savior of the world." JOHN 4:42, CCC 457

Jesus impacted other people in the same way. For example, Saint John writes:

What we have seen and heard
we announce to you also . . .
that the Father sent his Son
to be the Savior of the world.
1 JOHN 1:3, 4:14

82 STAGE 1: CHAPTER 6

Rescued

DISCUSS—Ask the students, How might the story of the man who dove into the raging river to save the ten-year-old boy serve as a parable of Jesus?

■ *Jesus is the man who, poetically, dove into a "raging river of sin" and saved the human family (symbolized by the boy).*

QUESTION **4 *If you asked Jesus, your Savior, what this means in terms of living your life, what might he say?***

Have the students answer this question privately in writing. Have them share in groups of three or four and pick out the best responses to share with the class.

NOTES

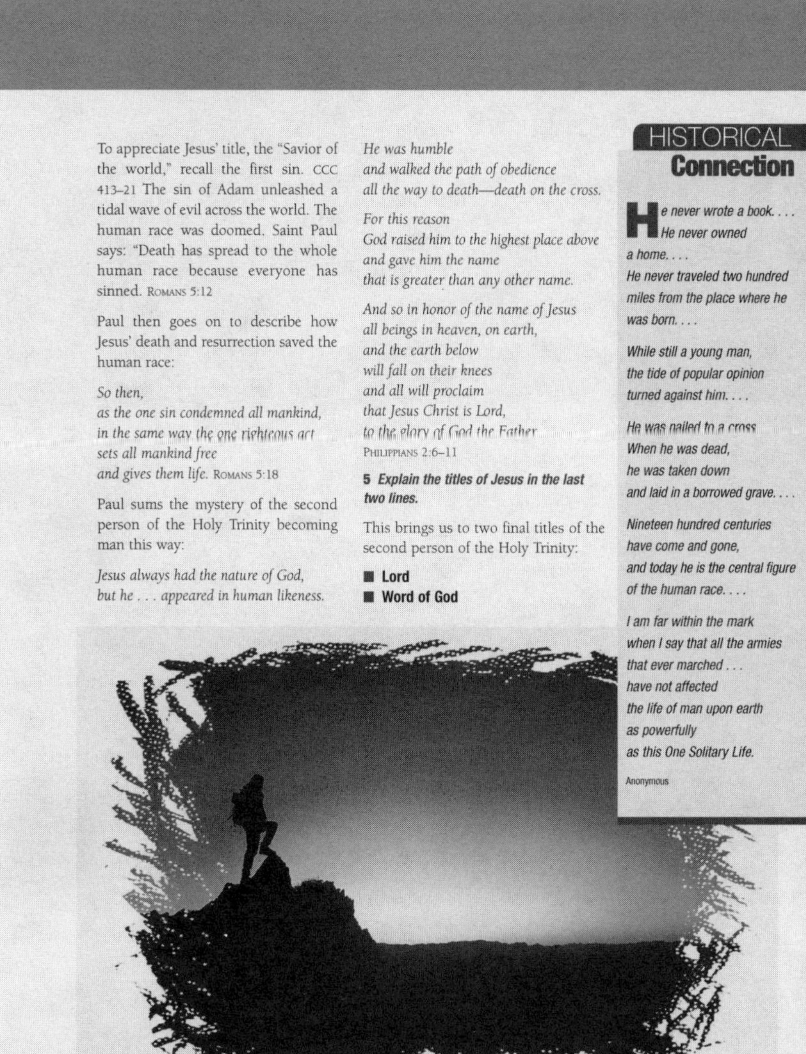

To appreciate Jesus' title, the "Savior of the world," recall the first sin. CCC 413–21 The sin of Adam unleashed a tidal wave of evil across the world. The human race was doomed. Saint Paul says: "Death has spread to the whole human race because everyone has sinned. ROMANS 5:12

Paul then goes on to describe how Jesus' death and resurrection saved the human race:

So then,
as the one sin condemned all mankind,
in the same way the one righteous act
sets all mankind free
and gives them life. ROMANS 5:18

Paul sums the mystery of the second person of the Holy Trinity becoming man this way:

Jesus always had the nature of God,
but he . . . appeared in human likeness.
He was humble
and walked the path of obedience
all the way to death—death on the cross.

For this reason
God raised him to the highest place above
and gave him the name
that is greater than any other name.

And so in honor of the name of Jesus
all beings in heaven, on earth,
and the earth below
will fall on their knees
and all will proclaim
that Jesus Christ is Lord,
to the glory of God the Father.
PHILIPPIANS 2:6–11

5 *Explain the titles of Jesus in the last two lines.*

This brings us to two final titles of the second person of the Holy Trinity:

- **Lord**
- **Word of God**

HISTORICAL **Connection**

He never wrote a book. . . .
He never owned
a home. . . .
He never traveled two hundred
miles from the place where he
was born. . . .

While still a young man,
the tide of popular opinion
turned against him. . . .

He was nailed to a cross.
When he was dead,
he was taken down
and laid in a borrowed grave. . . .

Nineteen hundred centuries
have come and gone,
and today he is the central figure
of the human race. . . .

I am far within the mark
when I say that all the armies
that ever marched . . .
have not affected
the life of man upon earth
as powerfully
as this One Solitary Life.

Anonymous

STAGE 1: CHAPTER 6 **83**

Savior

***DISCUSS*—Point out that Jesus "saved" us in a twofold sense: (1) "from" something, and (2) "for" something. Ask the students:**

(1) What did Jesus save us "from"?
(2) What did Jesus save us "for"?

■ *The sin of Adam unleashed a tidal wave of evil across the world. The human race was doomed.*

Or to put it in another way, after the sin of Adam, the "Kingdom of Satan" doomed the human family to spiritual slavery. Satan and sin held sway over the human family. Jesus came into the world and saved us "from" this doomed situation.

Besides saving us "from" spiritual slavery and death, Jesus saved us "for" something. He saved us "for" the task of bringing to completion the saving work he began: replacing the "Kingdom of Satan" with the "Kingdom of God."

QUESTION **5 *Explain the titles of Jesus in the last two lines.***

Jesus	*The Son of man (human)*
Lord	*The Son of God (divine)*
Christ	*The promised Messiah*

HISTORICAL **Connection**

***CLARIFY*—We saw how historian H.G. Wells looked at Jesus from a purely human perspective and concluded that he ranked as history's greatest man. Using this same human perspective only, Napoleon reasoned that Jesus was more than a man. He said:**

I know men and
I tell you that Jesus is not a man . . .
I have so inspired multitudes
that they would die for me . . .
a word from me, then the sacred fire
was kindled in their hearts. I do indeed
possess the secret of this magical power
which lifts the soul, but I could never
impart it to anyone (as Jesus did and
continues to do across the ages).

THE HISTORY OF NAPOLEON BONAPARTE, VOL. II
BY J. S. ABBOT

Share Your meditation

ACTIVITY—Have the students answer the three questions privately, share them in groups of three or four, and select the best responses to share with the entire class.

Lord

CLARIFY—The name for God, YHWH, is translated into the Greek as Kyrios and into English as Lord.

The NT uses this full sense of the title 'Lord' both for the Father and . . . for Jesus, who is thereby recognized as God Himself. CCC 449

NOTEBOOK—Have the students enter the following two summaries in student notebooks:

God Names	*YHWH*	*(Hebrew)*
	Kyrios	*(Greek)*
	Lord	*(English)*

QUESTION **6** ***Why do/don't you think it is significant that John used a number of "I am" titles of Jesus in his Gospel: I am the Good Shepherd, I am the Light of the World, I am the Bread of Life?***

■ *It is significant! Think of it this way: "I am who I am" (the God who can't be named or defined) now begins to be named and defined in the person of Jesus:*

"I am the Good Shepherd,"
"I am the Light of the World,"
"I am the Bread of Life."

Word of God

DISCUSS—Charles Schulz (1922–2000) was the author of the *Peanuts* cartoon and a person of deep faith. An interviewer once asked him what the focus of his faith was. He said:

Always Jesus . . .
What Jesus means to me is this:
"In him we are able to see God, and understand his feelings toward us."

SHARE YOUR meditation

Paul Waldeman was a Jew. He fled from Nazi Germany, settled in Chicago, and married a Catholic girl. The two talked a lot about religion. Then, one day, a startling question popped into Paul's mind: Could Jesus really be the Son of God? He writes:

My first reaction
was to dismiss it. . . .
But it kept coming back. . . .
I had to investigate. . . .
But the more I read, the more
confused . . . I became. . . .
For weeks on end . . .
I pleaded with God,
"Please show me
what you want me to do." . . .
But he remained silent. . . .
[Then one evening God spoke.]
I was filled with a peace and
lightheartedness
I had never known before.

Richer Than a Millionaire: One Man's Journey to God (Liguori, Mo.: Liguori Publications, 1992), pp. 98–99, 104.

■ ***Why does God let some of us struggle long and hard for the faith?***
■ ***What is one thing about the faith that I am struggling with? What should I do about resolving it?***

Lord

One day, Moses was grazing his sheep. Suddenly, he saw a nearby bush on fire. There wasn't anything alarming about that. Occasionally, a dried sagebrush caught fire in the hot sun, blazed up for a moment, and went out. But this time the fire didn't go out. Moses went over to see why.

GOD *Do not come any closer.*
Take off your sandals,
because you are standing
on holy ground.
I am the God of your
ancestors. . . .

MOSES *When I go to the Israelites*
and say to them,
"The God of your ancestors
sent me to you," they will ask me,
"What is his name?"
So what can I tell them?

GOD *I am who I am.*
You must tell them:
"The one who is called I AM
has sent me . . .
this is my name forever;
this is what all future
generations are to call me."
EXODUS 3:5–6, 13–15

The expression "I am who I am" introduces us to the Hebrew proper name for God. It is designated by the four Hebrew letters YHWH.

The original meaning of YHWH is uncertain, but scholars suggest the translation "I am who I am," that is, "I cannot be named or defined." CCC 206

6 ***Why do/don't you think it is significant that John used a number of "I am" titles of Jesus in his Gospel: I am the Good Shepherd, I am the Light of the World, I am the Bread of Life?***

Since New Testament times, YHWH has been translated into Greek as *Kyrios*, which means "Lord" in English. New Testament writers used this title to refer both to Jesus and the Father. By giving the name "LORD" to Jesus, early Christians made it clear that the same "power, honor, and glory" due to the Father was due also to Jesus. CCC 446–51 They made it clear that Jesus is divine: one with the Father and the Holy Spirit. And this is how Peter used the title in his speech to the people on Pentecost. He said, "This Jesus, whom you crucified, is the one that God has made Lord and Messiah!" ACTS 2:36 This is also the same way that Paul used the title in his letter to the Romans, saying:

If you confess Jesus is Lord
and believe that God raised him from
death, you will be saved. ROMANS 10:9

This brings us to the final title of the second person of the Holy Trinity.

Word of God

John begins his Gospel somewhat as a musical composer begins a symphony: with a beautiful overture that previews what is to follow. He writes:

In the beginning the Word already existed;
the Word was with God,
and the Word was God. . . .
The Word was the source of life,
and this life brought light to people.
JOHN 1:1, 4

John is speaking, of course, of Jesus, the "Word of God" made flesh. This is what we mean when we speak of Jesus as the "Incarnate Word" of God. CCC 461–63

We may think of Jesus as being the Word of God in a twofold sense. He tells us:

One of Schulz's strips was a kind of cartoon *parable*, illustrating the above point. Read it to the students.

1st frame: Linus says to Charlie Brown, "That's ridiculous!"

2nd frame: Charlie Brown says, "Maybe so! But come and see for yourself!"

3rd frame: He leads Linus into a room where Snoopy is sitting atop a TV set, his ears out like a TV antenna. Charlie Brown says, "See!"

4th frame: Linus says, "You're right, it does make the picture better!"

Ask the students: Who/what do the following stand for in Schulz's "cartoon parable":

(1) Snoopy (Jesus); (2) TV image (God); (3) Linus and Charlie Brown (us).

NOTES

- **About the Father**
- **About ourselves**

Let's take a look at each. We begin with Jesus, the Word of God, who tells us about God the Father.

One day Jesus was speaking to his apostles about his Father in heaven. At a certain point in the discussion, Philip said:

"Lord, show us the Father . . ."
Jesus answered . . . "Whoever has seen me
has seen the Father. . . .
Believe me when I say
that I am in the Father and
the Father is in me.
If not, believe because
of the things I do." JOHN 14:8, 9, 11

Jesus is the "Word of God" in the sense that he reveals God to us. He does this not only by what he says about the Father, but also in what he is—compassionate, merciful, loving. CCC 238–42 The Letter to the Hebrews does not hesitate to say of Jesus:

He reflects
the brightness of God's glory and
is the exact likeness of God's own being.
HEBREWS 1:31

Besides telling us about God the Father, Jesus also tells us about ourselves. He reveals to us what God intended for us to become when he created us.

One day a missionary began her class on Jesus, saying to the children:

Today I want to tell you
about someone you must meet.
He is a person who loves you and
cares for you even more
than your own family and friends.
He is a person who is kinder
than the kindest person you know.

The missionary noticed that a little boy was getting more and more excited as she talked. Suddenly, the boy blurted out, "I know that man! He lives on our street."

The second way Jesus is the Word of God is that he reveals to us what every Christian can become, if we open

ourselves to the Holy Spirit. CCC 459–60, 520 Each of us can become a living image of the Word of God. Jesus says the way for us to live in order that we be worth saving is to imitate him.

Jesus sums it up in one sentence: "Love one another, just as I love you." JOHN 15:12 In other words, we are called to:

- **Love our enemies**
- **Forgive those who persecute us**
- **Befriend outcasts of our society**
- **Be a "light" to our world**

7 Which of these would you find the most difficult to do? Why?

FAITH
Connection

Jesus and I were riding
a tandem bicycle.
At first, I sat in front;
Jesus in the rear.
I couldn't see him,
but I knew he was there.
I could feel his help
when the road got steep.

Then, one day,
Jesus and I changed seats.
Suddenly,
everything went topsy-turvy.
When I was in control,
the ride was predictable,
even boring.

But when Jesus took over,
it got wild!
I could hardly hold on.
"This is madness!" I cried.
But Jesus just smiled
and said, "Pedal!"

And so I learned to shut up
and pedal—and
trust my bike companion.
Oh, there are still times
when I get scared
and I'm ready to quit.
But Jesus turns around,
touches my hand, smiles,
and says, "Pedal!" M.L.

Inspired by and
modeled after an unknown author

Schulz continued his interview, saying:

I refuse to go out and speak to groups
as a so-called celebrity, because I think
anyone who becomes religious
because somebody else is religious
is already on the wrong track.

Ask the students, Where was this same point made in the textbook?

See Think about it (page 14). It reads:

Faith is like a toothbrush.
Everyone should have one
and use it regularly,
but he should not
try to use someone else's.

There comes a time in our spiritual life when we must be able to say what the Samaritan townspeople said to the woman at the well:

We believe now
not because of what you said,
but because we ourselves
have heard Jesus, and we know
that he is really the Savior
of the world. JOHN 4:39–42

Schulz ended his interview, saying:

A person should be converted
because he has seen . . . Jesus
and has been inspired by him.

Refer students back to the "Up Close & Personal" featuring Thomas Merton on page 54. It recounts how his conversion began when he began to "see Jesus" for the first time.

ACTIVITY—The chapter on Jesus ends saying that followers of Jesus are called to:

1 Love our enemies
2 Forgive those who persecute us
3 Befriend outcasts of our society
4 Be a "light" to our world

QUESTION ***7 Which of these would you find the most difficult to do? Why?***

After the students have recorded in their notebooks Jesus' "most difficult" command and given their reason for saying so, tally the results on the chalkboard and discuss them.

FAITH
Connection

DISCUSS—Read the poem out loud. Ask: How does the poem imply that following Jesus entails: (1) risk, (2) courage, (3) trust, (4) commitment? (List words on board.) Conclude by sharing these words of Jesus:

"If you want to come with me, you must
forget yourself, take up your cross
every day. . . . For if you want to save
your own life, you will lose it,
but if you lose your life for my sake
you will save it. Will you gain anything
if you win the whole world but are
yourself lost or defeated? LUKE 9:23–25

Recap

Putting his signature to a massive study of history the great scholar, A. J. Toynbee said of Jesus:

■ *When we set out on this quest,*
we found ourselves
moving in the midst of a mighty host,
but, as we pressed forward,
the marchers, company by company,
have all fallen out of the race. . . .

And now, as we stand and gaze
with our eyes on the farther shore,
a single figure raises from the flood
and straightway fills the whole horizon.

Review

DAILY QUIZ—The review questions may be assigned (one or two at a time) for homework or a daily quiz.

CHAPTER TESTS—Reproducible chapter tests are found in Appendix A. For consistency and ease in grading, quizzes are restricted to (1) "Matching," (2) "True/False," and (3) "Fill in the Blanks."

TEST ANSWERS—The following are the answers to the test for Chapter 6. (See Appendix A, page 317.) All correct answers worth four points.

Matching

1 = b 2 = e 3 = a 4 = d
5 = c

True/False

1 = T 2 = T 3 = F 4 = F
5 = F 6 = T 7 = T 8 = F
9 = T 10 = F

Fill In the Blanks

1. (a) baptism
   (b) transfiguration
2. (a) God
   (b) ourselves
3. (a) Jesus
   (b) Christ
   (c) Son of God
   (d) Savior
4. (a) divine
   (b) human

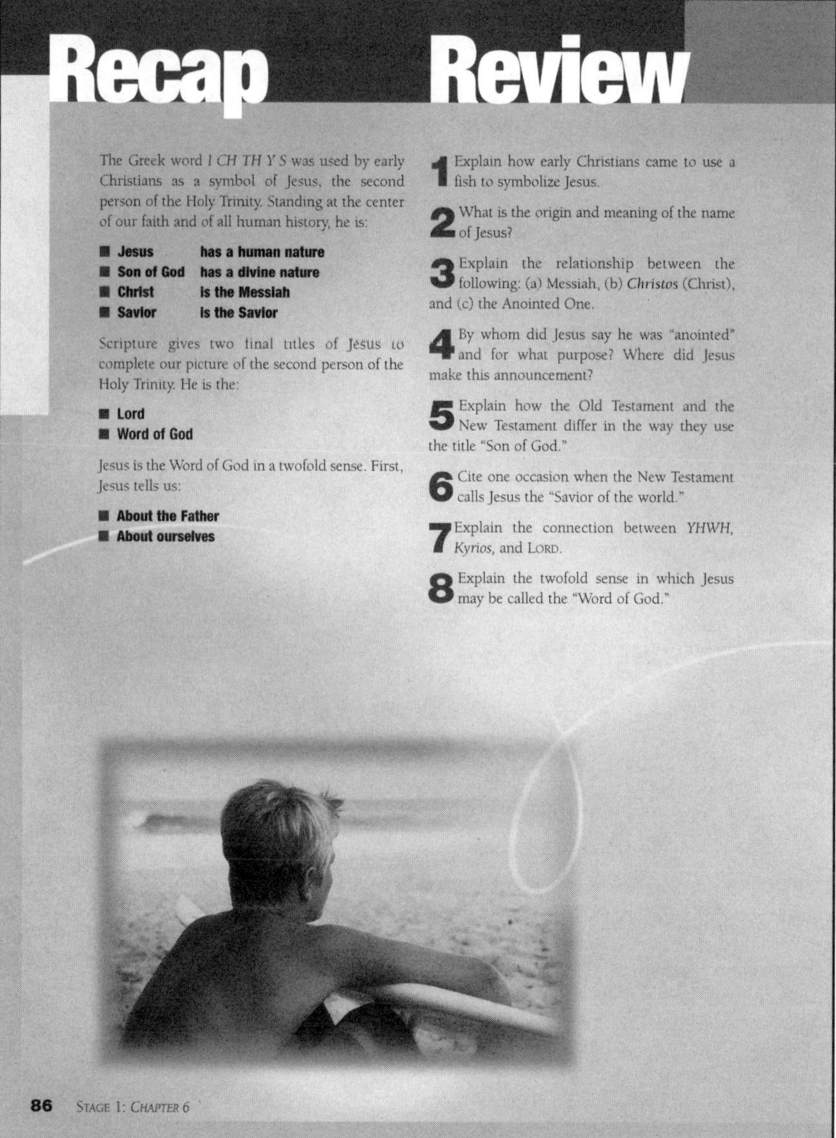

Recap Review

The Greek word *I CH TH Y S* was used by early Christians as a symbol of Jesus, the second person of the Holy Trinity. Standing at the center of our faith and of all human history, he is:

■ **Jesus** **has a human nature**
■ **Son of God** **has a divine nature**
■ **Christ** **is the Messiah**
■ **Savior** **is the Savior**

Scripture gives two final titles of Jesus to complete our picture of the second person of the Holy Trinity. He is the:

■ **Lord**
■ **Word of God**

Jesus is the Word of God in a twofold sense. First, Jesus tells us:

■ **About the Father**
■ **About ourselves**

1 Explain how early Christians came to use a fish to symbolize Jesus.

2 What is the origin and meaning of the name of Jesus?

3 Explain the relationship between the following: (a) Messiah, (b) *Christos* (Christ), and (c) the Anointed One.

4 By whom did Jesus say he was "anointed" and for what purpose? Where did Jesus make this announcement?

5 Explain how the Old Testament and the New Testament differ in the way they use the title "Son of God."

6 Cite one occasion when the New Testament calls Jesus the "Savior of the world."

7 Explain the connection between *YHWH*, *Kyrios*, and LORD.

8 Explain the twofold sense in which Jesus may be called the "Word of God."

86 STAGE 1: CHAPTER 6

Reflect

1 a) *How is this story a parable of every person?*

■ *Each one of us was saved by Jesus. The greatest "thanks" we can give him is to live our lives as he taught us.*

b) List three things you're considering doing with your life. After each one write one reason for and one reason against doing it.

Here's an example:

BUSINESS ADMINISTRATION:

FOR—My dad wants me to take over the family business.

AGAINST—I feel I want to do more with my life than just make a good living.

NOTES

Reflect

1 Recall the story in the text about the boy who was saved from drowning. After the boy recovered from shock, he threw his arms around the man and thanked him. The man said, "That's okay, son! Just make sure your life was worth saving."

- ***How is this story a parable of every person?***
- ***List three things you're considering doing with your life. After each one write one reason for and one reason against doing it.***
- ***Which possibility attracts you most and why?***

2 A woman said that if we accept the Gospels as being faithful to Jesus' claim, the following three options are open to us:

Jesus was a liar. He knew that he was not one with God the Father and deceived the people into thinking that he was.

Jesus was a lunatic. He was a sick person who was under the illusion that he was God's Son and one with the Father.

Jesus was the Lord. He was God's Son, of whom John said, "God loved the world so much that he gave his only Son, so that everyone who believes in him may not die but have eternal life." John 3:16

- ***Explain to what extent you agree or disagree with Jesus Christ being (a) a liar, (b) a lunatic, (c) the Lord.***

3 Leonard Le Sourd wrote an article called "The Five Christs I Have Known." It describes how his personal relationship with Jesus developed as he grew up.

First, there was the *fanciful* Christ. This was the Christ of his childhood. This Christ was like Santa Claus or the Easter Bunny—pretty much a figment of his immature imagination.

Second, there was the *historical* Christ of his student years. This Christ was like Abraham Lincoln or George Washington: an admirable person, but someone who did not make any concrete demands on his personal life.

Third, there was the *teacher* Christ of his early adult life. This Christ was like Aristotle: a wise person whose teaching is still valid today.

Fourth, there was the *savior* Christ. This Christ was different from any other person who ever lived. He was the Son of God, the Savior of the world. After discovering this Christ, LeSourd committed his life to Jesus.

Finally, there was the *indwelling* Christ. This Christ formed Jesus' followers into one body and empowered them to go forth and transform their world. It was this same Jesus who now took control of Le Sourd's life.

- ***Briefly describe how your relationship with Jesus has changed over the years.***
- ***How would you describe it at this point in your life: growing, in a holding pattern, declining? Explain.***

Stage 1: Chapter 6 87

c) *Which possibility attracts you most? why?*

TEACHING HIGH SCHOOL
You can have an impact on kids' lives.

2 *Explain to what extent you agree or disagree with Jesus Christ being (a) a liar, (b) a lunatic, (c) the Lord.*

(a) LIAR? Jesus' courage, selflessness, and heroic death are hardly the earmarks of a liar.

(b) LUNATIC? How could the world's greatest teacher be right about everything but his own identity?

(c) LORD? No one can force another to accept this claim, nor can anyone ignore it.

3 a) *Briefly describe how your relationship with Jesus has changed over the years.*

b) *How would you describe it at this point in your life: growing, in a holding pattern, declining? Explain.*

To get the students started, share with them this response by a college girl:

In grade school, Jesus was kind of just there. It wasn't until high school and my sophomore retreat that Jesus became real for me—a friend, as it were.

From that day on, he became the one who listened to me, understood me, and guided me through some rough years. He was there for me, even when I failed—which was more often than I care to remember.

My present relationship with Jesus is growing, largely because I've found a daily meditation book and have set aside ten minutes a day to meditate.

If you want to get to know someone, you hang out with them. That's the way I look at meditation: hanging out with Jesus on a daily basis.

PRAYER TIME with the Lord

QUESTION ***Write out your meditation on one of the above five verses.***

To get the students started, share with them this meditation by a Chicago student. He was meditating on this passage from a daily meditation book:

■ *A coach stood before a team*
at halftime of a tough game.
He shouted, "Did Tiger Woods ever quit?"
"No!" yelled the team.
"Did Sammy Sosa ever quit?"
"No!" yelled the team.
"Did Derek Jeter ever quit?"
"No!" yelled the team.
"Did Elmer McKay ever quit?"

This time,
there was an awkward pause.
Then the team captain said.
"Coach, we never heard of him!"
"Of course you haven't," shouted the coach.
"He quit!"

The Chicago student wrote:

■ *Reading that passage made me realize*
that being a star athlete
is a lot like being a true Christian.

Just today, someone was leaning on me
to do something I knew was wrong.
When I refused, he said,
"When are you going to start living
in the real world,
instead of your little dream world?"

The Chicago student concluded
speaking to Jesus by repeating these words
from the above poem:

Give us your strength, Lord.
For sometimes things get tough,
and we are ready to quit.

PRAYER Journal

QUESTION ***Compose a similar, brief dialogue with Jesus on trying to be his follower today.***

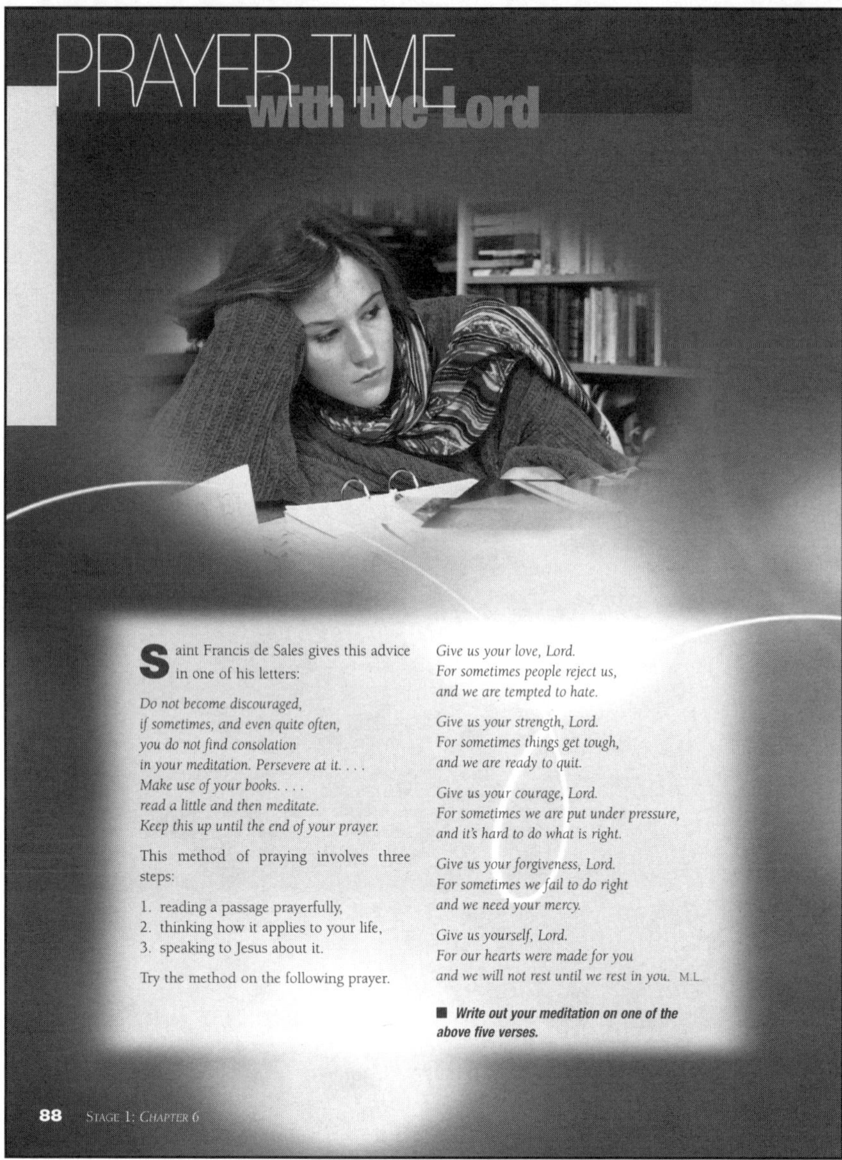

PRAYER TIME with the Lord

Saint Francis de Sales gives this advice in one of his letters:

Do not become discouraged,
if sometimes, and even quite often,
you do not find consolation
in your meditation. Persevere at it. . . .
Make use of your books. . . .
read a little and then meditate.
Keep this up until the end of your prayer.

This method of praying involves three steps:

1. reading a passage prayerfully,
2. thinking how it applies to your life,
3. speaking to Jesus about it.

Try the method on the following prayer.

Give us your love, Lord.
For sometimes people reject us,
and we are tempted to hate.

Give us your strength, Lord.
For sometimes things get tough,
and we are ready to quit.

Give us your courage, Lord.
For sometimes we are put under pressure,
and it's hard to do what is right.

Give us your forgiveness, Lord.
For sometimes we fail to do right
and we need your mercy.

Give us yourself, Lord.
For our hearts were made for you
and we will not rest until we rest in you. M.L.

■ ***Write out your meditation on one of the above five verses.***

88 STAGE 1: CHAPTER 6

Another approach to this exercise is to read the following to the students. Then have them write out how Jesus might answer them.

Student *Jesus,*
when the winds of temptation
are blowing like crazy,
I feel like the apostles
during the storm at sea.
I start to panic, just as they did.
I call out to you,
but you don't always answer!
Sometimes you seem to desert
me. Why?

Jesus *(Response to student)*

The questions in this section can be done right in class on three-ring paper and later inserted in section #3 of their notebooks.

NOTES

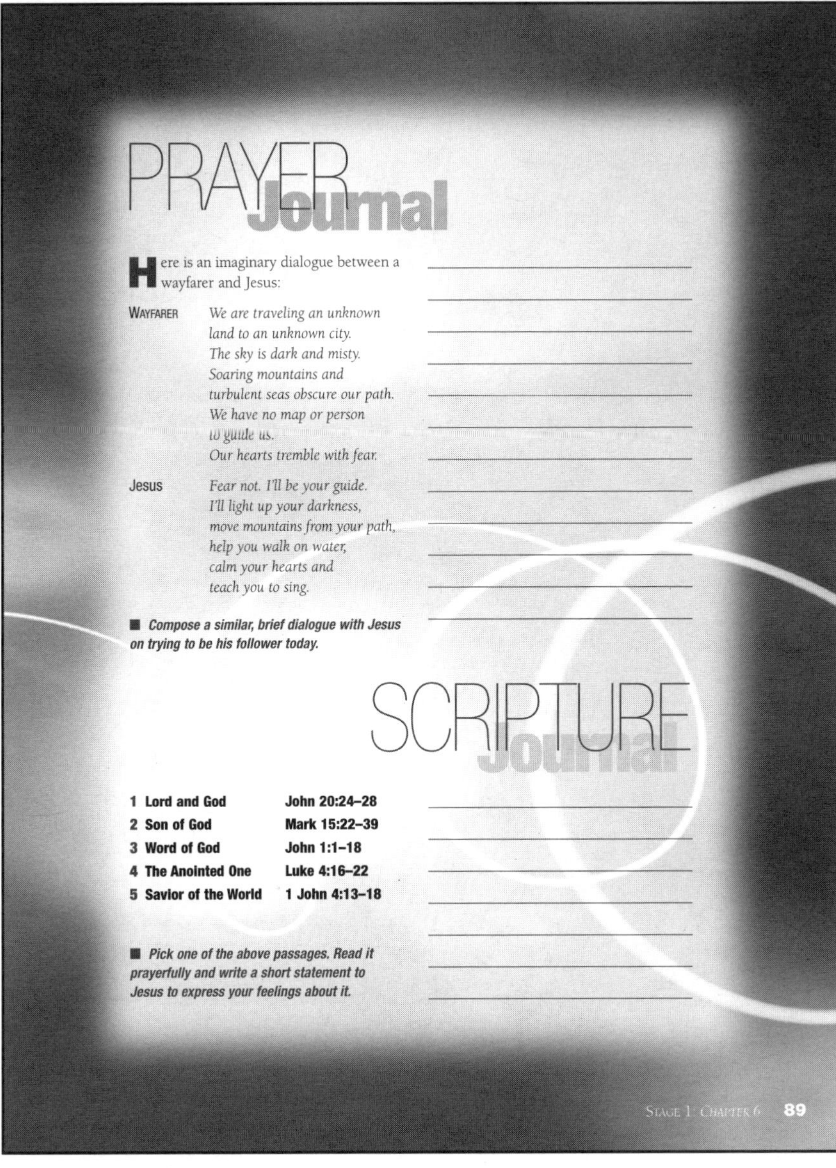

PRAYER Journal

Here is an imaginary dialogue between a wayfarer and Jesus:

WAYFARER *We are traveling an unknown land to an unknown city. The sky is dark and misty. Soaring mountains and turbulent seas obscure our path. We have no map or person to guide us. Our hearts tremble with fear.*

JESUS *Fear not. I'll be your guide. I'll light up your darkness, move mountains from your path, help you walk on water, calm your hearts and teach you to sing.*

■ ***Compose a similar, brief dialogue with Jesus on trying to be his follower today.***

SCRIPTURE Journal

1	Lord and God	John 20:24–28
2	Son of God	Mark 15:22–39
3	Word of God	John 1:1–18
4	The Anointed One	Luke 4:16–22
5	Savior of the World	1 John 4:13–18

■ ***Pick one of the above passages. Read it prayerfully and write a short statement to Jesus to express your feelings about it.***

STAGE 1: CHAPTER 6 89

SCRIPTURE Journal

QUESTION ***Pick one of the above passages. Read it prayerfully and write a short statement to Jesus expressing your feelings about it.***

■ *A good reading is the first one on the list. You might read aloud to the students this line from it and have them write their response in section #4 of their notebooks:*

"Jesus said to Thomas . . .
'Reach out your hand
and put it in my side.
Stop your doubting, and believe.' "

If time permits, have them share their responses in groups of three or four and select the best ones to be read to the group.

Classroom Resources

CATECHISM

Catechism of the Catholic Church *Second Edition*

For further enrichment, you might refer to:

1. Christ	Index	p. 766–70
	Glossary	p. 870
2. Son of God	Index	p. 851
	Glossary	p. 900
3. Savior	Index	p. 847
	Glossary	p. 899
4. Lord	Index	p. 818
	Glossary	p. 886

See also: Son of Man, Messiah, Word of God.

—AVAILABLE FROM THE UNITED STATES CATHOLIC CONFERENCE, WASHINGTON DC

VIDEOS

Jesus in My Life Today

Thirty-minute segment. Two young people examine what they really believe about Jesus and their personal relationship with him.

—AVAILABLE FROM BROWN-ROA, DUBUQUE, IA

Mystery of God: Father, Son, and Spirit

Three thirty-minute segments. A contemporary approach to the story of creation, salvation, and God's abiding presence in our lives.

—AVAILABLE FROM THOMAS MORE PUBLISHING, ALLEN, TX

MOVIE

Jesus of Nazareth

Three two-hour segments. A vivid, accurate portrayal of the life of Jesus.

—AVAILABLE FROM OBLATE MEDIA, 1977, ST. LOUIS, MO

NOTE

For a list of (1) General resources for professional background and (2) Addresses, phone/fax numbers of major publishing companies, see Appendix B of this Resource Manual.

CHAPTER 7
God the Holy Spirit

CHAPTER at a Glance

The goal of this chapter is to give students an understanding and an appreciation of the Spirit's role in the transformation of:

1 *Our world*
2 *Our personal lives*

DISCUSS—Have one student read the scriptural part of the introduction, which begins "For forty days after his death . . ." and concludes ". . . ends of the earth."

Have a second student read the concluding paragraph of commentary, which begins "On Pentecost the Holy Spirit . . ." and ends ". . . God's Kingdom."

Review what was said in chapter 2 about the difference Pentecost made. The coming of the Holy Spirit not only formed Jesus' followers into the Church, but also clarified for them the meaning of Jesus and his teachings.

Ask the students: "Do you recall the example we used to illustrate in what sense the coming of the Holy Spirit gave his followers a better understanding of the life and teachings of Jesus?

■ *On page 29 of this manual, we used the example of a self-developing camera. After you snap the picture with the camera, the film rolls out. At first, it seems to be totally blank. Then the "light of the sun" strikes the blank film and a beautiful picture emerges.*
Many teachings and events of Jesus' life were like that. At first, they seemed "totally blank." They didn't seem to have any really profound meaning. Then the "light of the Spirit" on Pentecost struck them. Suddenly, those same teachings and events of Jesus' life came alive with profound meaning and beauty.

CHAPTER 7 God the Holy Spirit

For forty days after his death,
Jesus appeared to his disciples many times
in ways that proved beyond doubt
that he was alive. . . .
He gave them this order:

"Do not leave Jerusalem,
but wait for the gift I told you about. . . .
In a few days you will be baptized
with the Holy Spirit. . . .
You will be filled with power,
and you will be witnesses for me . . .
to the ends of the earth." Acts 1:4–5, 8

On Pentecost the Holy Spirit came and filled the disciples with amazing power. Collectively, they became temples of the Holy Spirit, Christ's Body, the Church. Individually, they were graced with remarkable virtues, gifts, and fruits to be used for the building up of God's Kingdom.

CHAPTER at a Glance

The maestro

A mother took her very young son, Jason, to a matinee concert by the famous pianist Ignace Paderewski. She hoped the experience would encourage his own musical efforts.

She was delighted to see how close to the stage their seats were. Then she saw an old friend sitting nearby. She got so involved talking with her that she didn't notice her son leaving to do some exploring.

Shortly, the auditorium lights dimmed, the audience hushed, and a spotlight fell on the piano on stage. Only then did the audience notice a tiny boy sitting on the piano bench, innocently picking out "Twinkle, Twinkle, Little Star." The five-year-old's mother gasped in total disbelief.

But before she could do anything, Paderewski emerged from the wings, walked over to Jason, and whispered, "Son, keep playing!"

Then, leaning over the boy, he reached out his left hand and began filling in the bass. A few seconds later, he

90

The maestro

CLARIFY—Ignace Paderewski (1860–1941) was not only a remarkable composer and pianist, but also a great statesman. He served a brief term as Premier of Poland after World War I, in 1919.

One critic wrote of one of his concerts in New York's Carnegie Hall: "The audience was clearly moved by his superb art, his feeling and enthusiasm."

DISCUSS—The text says that Paderewski "reached around the other side of the boy, encircling him, and added a running obbligato." Ask: What's an obbligato?

■ *It's a secondary melody that enhances the primary melody. In this case the*

NOTES

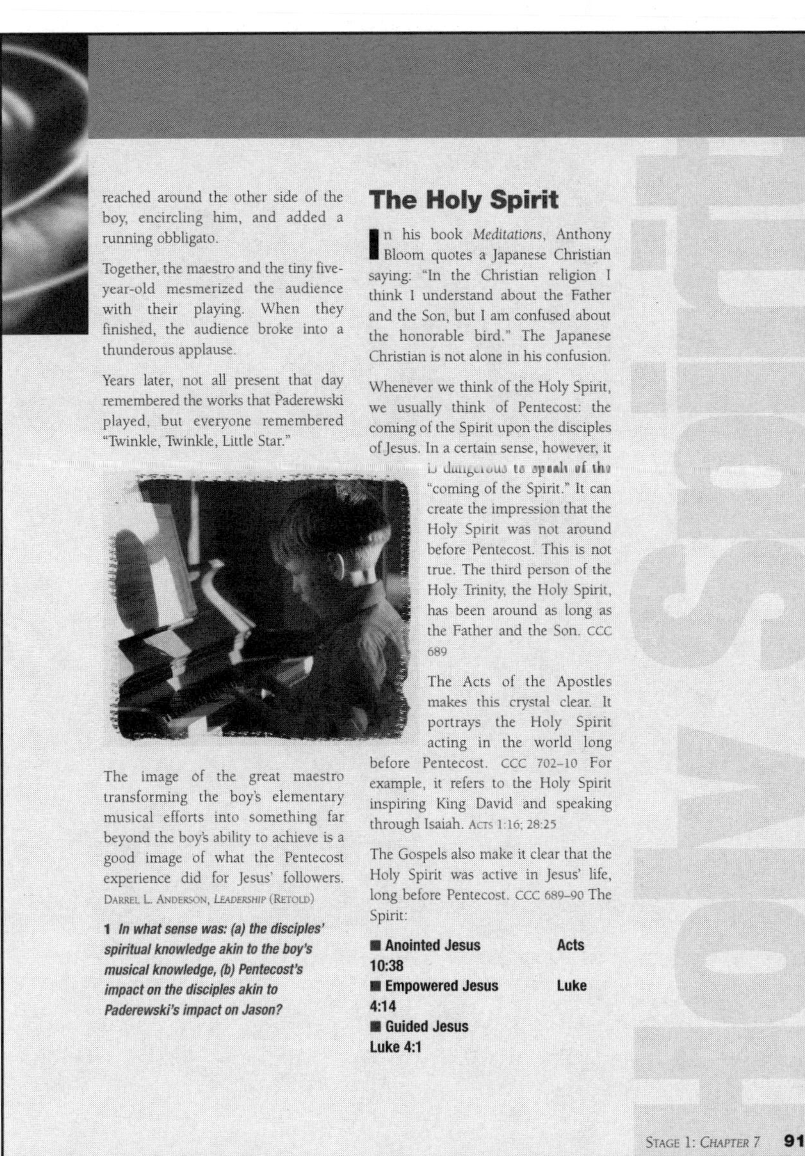

reached around the other side of the boy, encircling him, and added a running obbligato.

Together, the maestro and the tiny five-year-old mesmerized the audience with their playing. When they finished, the audience broke into a thunderous applause.

Years later, not all present that day remembered the works that Paderewski played, but everyone remembered "Twinkle, Twinkle, Little Star."

The image of the great maestro transforming the boy's elementary musical efforts into something far beyond the boy's ability to achieve is a good image of what the Pentecost experience did for Jesus' followers. DARREL L. ANDERSON, *LEADERSHIP* (RETOLD)

1 ***In what sense was: (a) the disciples' spiritual knowledge akin to the boy's musical knowledge, (b) Pentecost's impact on the disciples akin to Paderewski's impact on Jason?***

The Holy Spirit

In his book *Meditations*, Anthony Bloom quotes a Japanese Christian saying: "In the Christian religion I think I understand about the Father and the Son, but I am confused about the honorable bird." The Japanese Christian is not alone in his confusion.

Whenever we think of the Holy Spirit, we usually think of Pentecost: the coming of the Spirit upon the disciples of Jesus. In a certain sense, however, it is dangerous to speak of the "coming of the Spirit." It can create the impression that the Holy Spirit was not around before Pentecost. This is not true. The third person of the Holy Trinity, the Holy Spirit, has been around as long as the Father and the Son. CCC 689

The Acts of the Apostles makes this crystal clear. It portrays the Holy Spirit acting in the world long before Pentecost. CCC 702–10 For example, it refers to the Holy Spirit inspiring King David and speaking through Isaiah. ACTS 1:16; 28:25

The Gospels also make it clear that the Holy Spirit was active in Jesus' life, long before Pentecost. CCC 689–90 The Spirit:

- **Anointed Jesus** Acts 10:38
- **Empowered Jesus** Luke 4:14
- **Guided Jesus** Luke 4:1

STAGE 1: CHAPTER 7 **91**

primary melody was that of "Twinkle, Twinkle, Little Star."

QUESTION **1** ***In what sense was: (a) the disciples' spiritual knowledge akin to the boy's musical knowledge, (b) Pentecost's impact on the disciples akin to Paderewski's impact on Jason?***

■ *The disciple's spiritual knowledge was akin to Jason's musical knowledge in the sense that both were minimal.*

Then Paderewski entered the picture. His amazing impact on Jason was to transform his minimal playing skill into something beautiful and exciting. The Holy Spirit had a similar impact on the apostolic and pastoral skills of Jesus' disciples.

Here's still another example. It illustrates even more clearly how the coming of the Holy Spirit impacted the apostolic and pastoral skills of Jesus' followers.

■ *A children's TV show featured a cartoonist who would invite children to take a pen and make a couple of scribbles on a clean sheet of paper.*

Then, against a background of spritely music, the cartoonist transformed the childish scribbles into a beautiful drawing. One scribble became a girl's ponytail; another became the branch of a tree, and so on.

ACTIVITY—If you have an artist in the class, you might demonstrate this by having a student make a scribble on the board and have the student artist endeavor to transform it into something meaningful.

The Holy Spirit

CLARIFY—An example of the Spirit's activity in Old Testament times is cited by Paul and quoted by Luke in the Acts of the Apostles.

One day, some of his listeners responded with such a closed mind that Paul exclaimed:

> *"How well the Holy Spirit spoke through the prophet Isaiah to your ancestors! . . .*
> *'This people's minds are dull,*
> *and they have stopped their ears. . . .*
> *Otherwise . . . they would turn to me . . .*
> *and I would heal them.'"* ACTS 28:27

A good example of the Holy Spirit's activity in Jesus' own life is cited several times in Luke's Gospel. There we read:

> *Jesus returned*
> *from the Jordan (his baptism)*
> *full of the Holy Spirit*
> *and was led by the Spirit*
> *into the desert. . . .*
> *Jesus returned to Galilee,*
> *and the power of the Holy Spirit*
> *was with him.* LUKE 4:1, 14

ART Connection

***CLARIFY*—Ask the students: Where did we see a painting by Caravaggio earlier?**

■ *The painting of Saint Jerome translating the Bible from Hebrew into Latin around* A.D. *400. See page 26 of the text.*

Ask the students: Do you remember how his style of painting differed from someone like Van Gogh? (See the painting of the "Good Samaritan" on page 253 of the textbook.)

■ *Caravaggio was a disciple of the naturalistic school. His paintings were more "photographic" in style than impressionistic, like Van Gogh's.*

Recall, also, Caravaggio's style of using dramatic interplays of light and darkness in his paintings. Again, this is clearly in evidence in his painting of the "Descent of the Holy Spirit."

Promise of the Spirit

***NOTEBOOK*—The following summary diagram shows why wind and fire are fitting symbols of the Holy Spirit.**

- *Wind*
  - *Its whisper touch* 1 Kings 19:12
  - *Its hurricane power* Acts 2:2
- *Fire*
  - *Burning bush* Exodus 3:3
  - *Burning mountain* Exodus 19:18

***NOTEBOOK*—The following sums up the symbolic role that "speech" played at Babel and Pentecost**

- *Speech*
  - *Babel* — *Sin divides*
  - *Pentecost* — *Spirit reunites*

QUESTION **2** ***Why is the world still divided into hostile factions centuries after the Spirit's coming?***

■ *Years ago the famous Broadway musical,* Man of La Mancha, *posed this same vexing question.*

The play was inspired by the tragic life of the 17th-century author, Cervantes. He came from a poor Spanish family and, as a young soldier, he was wounded and captured in battle. He spent five years in brutal slavery in Africa. In 1616 he died broken in body and spirit.

A moving scene from the musical occurs shortly after the stopping song, "The Impossible Dream." Cervantes cries out in agony at all the hostility between nations and races, saying:

"I have seen life as it is. Pain, misery . . .
cruelty beyond belief. I have . . .
seen my comrades fall in battle . . .
or die slowly under the lash in Africa. . . .
their eyes filled with confusion,
whimpering the question: "Why?"

This raises a question. If Jesus has inaugurated the Kingdom of God and the Holy Spirit came to re-create and

NOTES

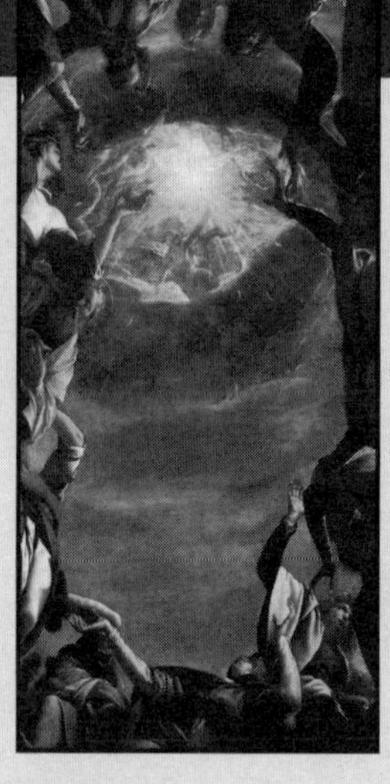

ART **Connection**

Italian painter Michelangelo Amerighi Caravaggio (1563–1510) was known for dramatic realism. Here he portrays the descent of the Holy Spirit upon his disciples.

Promise of the Spirit

Even though the Holy Spirit acted long before Pentecost, something unique and monumental did happen on Pentecost. Toward the end of his earthly life, while celebrating the Passover supper, Jesus said to his disciples:

"I shall not be with you
very much longer. . . .
I will ask the Father,
and he will give you another Helper. . . .
He is the Spirit. John 13:33; 14:16–17

Then, just before ascending to heaven, Jesus gave his disciples this instruction:

"Do not leave Jerusalem,
but wait for the gift I told you about. . . .
John baptized with water, but in a few days
you will be baptized with the Holy Spirit."
Acts 1:4–5

The stage was set for one of the most important events in history: the coming of the Holy Spirit on the followers of Jesus. It changed their lives forever.

When the day of Pentecost came,
all the believers
were gathered together in one place.
Suddenly, there was a noise from the sky,
which sounded like a strong wind
blowing. . . .

Then they saw what looked like
tongues of fire which spread out
and touched each person there.
They were all filled with the Holy Spirit
and began to talk in other languages,
as the Spirit enabled them to speak.
Acts 2:1–4

The "noise from the sky" was so loud that it attracted a huge crowd to the house. The apostles went out to tell them what happened. Peter explained that it was what God had foretold through Joel the prophet:

"I will pour out my Spirit on everyone.
Your sons and daughters
will proclaim my message." Acts 2:17

The people in the crowd had come from many different nations to celebrate the feast of Pentecost. They were amazed to hear the apostles speaking in their native tongues. They asked one another: "How is it . . . that all of us hear them speaking in our own native languages?" Acts 2:8 Then it dawned on them. The answer lay in the Old Testament story of the Tower of Babel. It begins:

At first, the people of the whole world
had only one language
and used the same words.

92 Stage 1: Chapter 7

As they wandered about in the East,
they came to a plain in Babylonia
and settled there.
They said to one another . . .
"Let's build a city with a tower
that reaches the sky, so that we can
make a name for ourselves." GENESIS 11:1–3, 4

But the LORD did not approve. He mixed up their language and "scattered them all over the earth."

The city was called Babylon because
there the LORD mixed up the languages
of all the people, and from there he
scattered them all over the earth.
GENESIS 11:9

Hearing the apostles speak in their own native tongue was a sign that what happened at the Tower of Babel is now being reversed.

The Holy Spirit will unite the peoples of the world, who split into hostile factions and whose sin had scattered across the earth. It is a giant leap forward in God's plan to re-create the world.

2 Why is the world still divided into hostile factions centuries after the Spirit's coming?

Pieter Brueghel (1525–1569)
Tower of Babel

Birth of the Church

Peter then went on to explain to the crowd that what had just taken place was what God had foretold through the prophet Joel:

"I will pour out my Spirit on everyone.
Your sons and daughters
will proclaim my message." ACTS 2:17

Peter's words moved the people profoundly. Nearly three thousand were baptized that very day. From that moment, the followers of Jesus shared not only the same belief, but also the same life of the Holy Spirit. CCC 694

The monumental event that took place on Pentecost is this: The Holy Spirit, the third person of the Holy Trinity, came upon those who believed in him, forming them into the Church: the Body of Christ and the Temple of the Holy Spirit.

Jesus and his followers now form one body, as Jesus had foretold, saying:

I will ask the Father,
and he will give you another Helper. . . .
He is the Spirit. . . .
When that day comes, you will know that
I am in the Father and you are in me,
just as I am in you. JOHN 14:16–17, 20

Paul experienced this amazing mystery firsthand before his conversion. He was on his way to Damascus to arrest Christians and return them to Jerusalem for punishment.

Suddenly, a light from the sky flashed
around him. He fell to the ground and
heard a voice saying to him,
"Saul, Saul! Why do you persecute me?"

Up Close & Personal

Kathryn Koob

Kathryn Koob was one of the fifty-two Americans held hostage in the 1980s for 444 days by Iranian extremists and terrorists. Angry mobs shouted outside her room almost around the clock. One night she woke up with a start. She says: "I turned quickly, expecting to see a guard. But no one was there."

Kathryn then said that, for some reason, she was reminded of the Holy Spirit. From that scary moment on, the Holy Spirit seemed to be with her in a special way. Her attitude toward her situation and her guards changed markedly. She says: "The Holy Spirit was teaching me love . . . and new understanding."

STAGE 1: CHAPTER 7 93

transform our world, why is there still so much hostility and evil in the world?

We will discuss this more in detail in the next chapter. For the time being, suffice it to say that the Kingdom of God is like a plant. It is growing, but not yet fully grown. The coming of the kingdom is not an instant event, but a gradual process.

From the opposite viewpoint, we may say that the "Kingdom of Satan" (sin, sickness, and death) is not yet at an end. It is only under sentence of death.

Birth of the Church

NOTEBOOK—The following diagram sums up how the "coming of Jesus" and the "coming of the Spirit" are uniquely parallel.

Christmas
- *Jesus becomes the sign of God's presence in his world*
- *Jesus becomes the instrument of God's activity in his world*

Pentecost
- *Church becomes the instrument of God's presence in our world*
- *Church becomes the sign of God's presence in our world*

DISCUSS—An old legend says that when Jesus ascended to heaven, he still bore the wounds of the crucifixion:

When the angel Gabriel saw him, he said, "Lord, how greatly you suffered! Do all the people on earth know how much you loved them?" Jesus replied, "Oh, no! Only a few do."

Gabriel was even more shocked and said, "How will the rest find out?" Jesus said, "I told Peter, James, John, and their friends to tell them."

Gabriel said, "Lord, what if they fail to do so? What if they let you down? Don't you have a backup plan—just in case?"

Jesus said, "No, I'm counting on them not to let me down. And I'm counting on the people they tell not to let me down."

Ask the students: What assures you that people like yourself will not let Jesus down?

Up Close & Personal

CLARIFY—Kathryn said a great source of strength in dealing with her 444-day ordeal is summed up by the words of an old hymn:

Have thine own way, Lord!
Have thine own way!
Thou are the potter; I am the clay.
Mold me and make me after thy will.

These words gave Kathryn not only the strength to resign herself to God's will, but they also gave her a deep peace.

QUESTION 3 Explain the similarity between the "body of Christ" image and the "vine and branches" image.

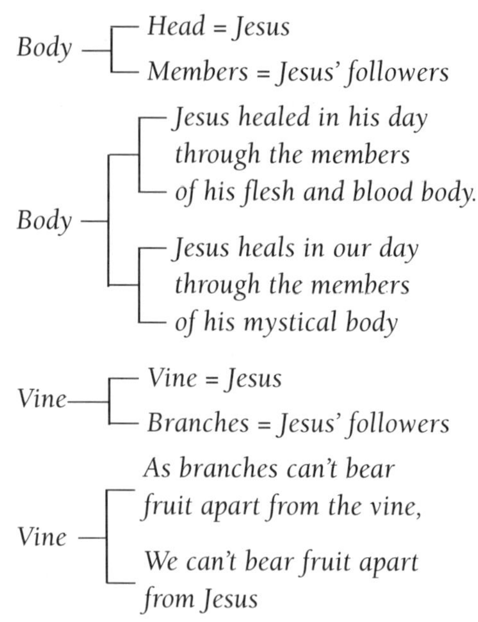

Body
Head = Jesus
Members = Jesus' followers
Jesus healed in his day through the members of his flesh and blood body.
Body
Jesus heals in our day through the members of his mystical body
Vine
Vine = Jesus
Branches = Jesus' followers
As branches can't bear fruit apart from the vine,
Vine
We can't bear fruit apart from Jesus

THINK about it

A woman was an alcoholic, but refused to admit it. Then she ran across a poem that gave her the courage to admit her problem and seek help in AA. She added, "I can't begin to tell you how many of us this poem has helped." An excerpt reads:

> *To reach out to another . . . expose your feelings . . . going forward in the face of overwhelming odds is to risk . . . The person who risks nothing, does nothing, has nothing, is nothing . . . Chained to his certitudes, he is a slave. . . . Only a person who dares to risk is free.*

That poem introduces us to the Holy Spirit's "gift of fortitude." It empowers us to risk . . . to dream, to love. It empowers us to "plunge into the deep without fear, with the gladness of April in our heart."
RABINDRANATH TAGORE

Images of the Spirit

QUESTION 4 What other "natural" connection do you see between God and fire?

■ *Recall how the sun acts as an image of the Trinity.*

ART Connection

Italian painter Michelangelo Amerighi Caravaggio (1563–1510) portrays Paul's Damascus experience. Paul was never the same after it.

"Who are you, LORD?" he asked.
"I am Jesus, whom you persecute,"
the voice said. ACTS 9:3–5

This mysterious experience changed Paul from a persecutor of Jesus to an evangelist of Jesus. He later wrote:

We are one body in union with Christ . . .
[We] have been baptized
into the one body by the same Spirit. . . .
Christ is the head of his body, the church;
he is the source of the body's life.
ROMANS 12:5, CORINTHIANS 12:13, COLOSSIANS 1:18

3 Explain the similarity between the "body of Christ" image and Jesus' "vine and branches" image.

THINK about it

Where the human spirit fails, the Holy Spirit fills.

Anonymous

Images of the Spirit

A small boy got a toy sailboat for his birthday. He was so excited he ran to the window, looked up at the sky, and shouted, "O God! Have you seen my boat?" A long pause followed, as if the boy were waiting for God to answer. Then the boy turned to his mother and asked, "What is God like?" But before she could answer, he said, "I know! God's like the wind!"

Ancient Jews also linked God and the wind. The unseen wind's feather-like touch and its storm-like power spoke to the Jews of God's own unseen gentleness and power. It is interesting that the Hebrew word *RUAH* is used to designate both "wind" and the "Spirit" of God. CCC 691

Ancient Jews also linked God and fire. God appeared in a burning bush to Moses. And God came down in fire on Mount Sinai. EXODUS 3:3–6, 19:16–18

4 What other "natural" connection do you see between God and fire?

Finally, Jews connected the Holy Spirit and water. Jesus himself said to his disciples:

"Whoever believes in me . . .
'Streams of life-giving water will pour out from his side.'" Jesus said this about the Spirit, which those who believed in him were going to receive. JOHN 7:38–39

5 Can you think of a "natural" connection the Spirit and water have in common?

94 STAGE 1: CHAPTER 7

Its light is an image of the Father, the Creator, who said, "Let there be light."
Its heat is an image of Jesus, who saved us by the warmth of his love.
Its energy is an image of the Spirit, who enlivens and energizes us with grace

Fire produces these same three effects. It lights, heats, and produces energy. In that sense, it exhibits a natural connection to God.

QUESTION 5 Can you think of a "natural" connection the Spirit and water have in common?

■ *With the help of the students, develop the following diagram on the board. It sums up the natural connection between water and the Spirit.*

NOTES

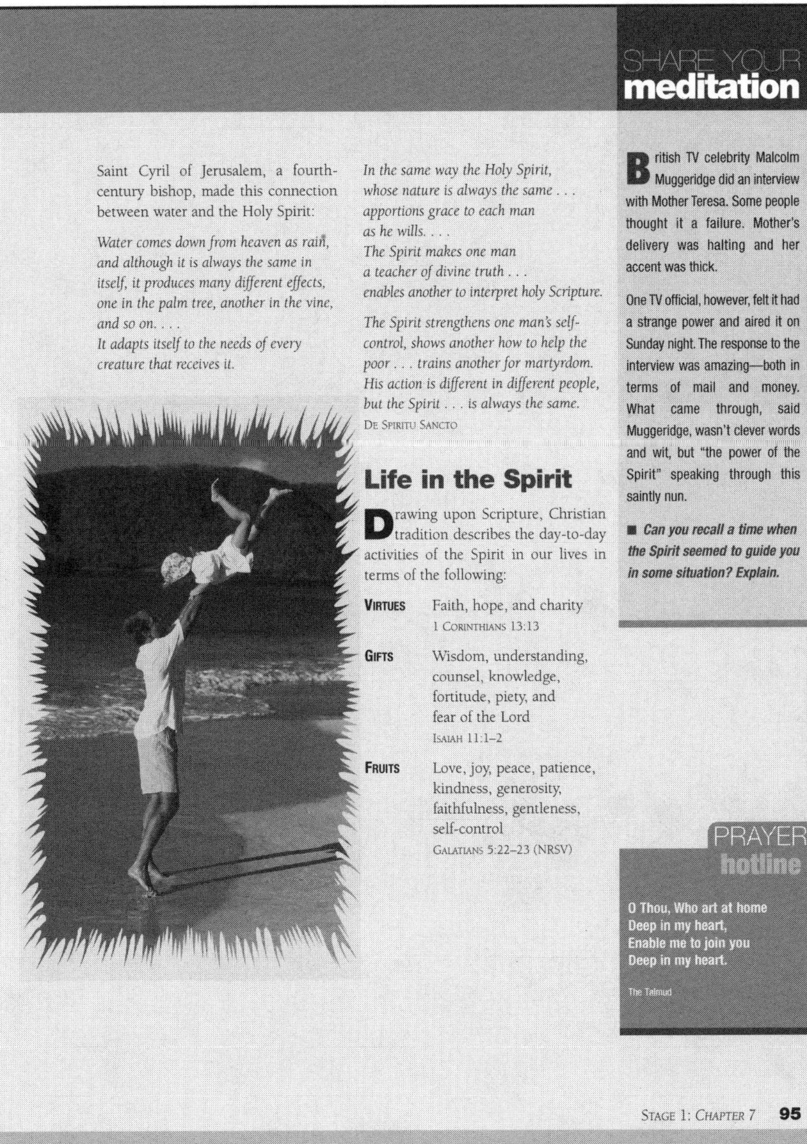

SHARE YOUR **meditation**

Saint Cyril of Jerusalem, a fourth-century bishop, made this connection between water and the Holy Spirit:

Water comes down from heaven as rain,
and although it is always the same in itself, it produces many different effects,
one in the palm tree, another in the vine, and so on. . . .
It adapts itself to the needs of every creature that receives it.

In the same way the Holy Spirit,
whose nature is always the same . . .
apportions grace to each man
as he wills. . . .
The Spirit makes one man
a teacher of divine truth . . .
enables another to interpret holy Scripture.

The Spirit strengthens one man's self-control, shows another how to help the poor . . . trains another for martyrdom.
His action is different in different people,
but the Spirit . . . is always the same.
De Spiritu Sancto

British TV celebrity Malcolm Muggeridge did an interview with Mother Teresa. Some people thought it a failure. Mother's delivery was halting and her accent was thick.

One TV official, however, felt it had a strange power and aired it on Sunday night. The response to the interview was amazing—both in terms of mail and money. What came through, said Muggeridge, wasn't clever words and wit, but "the power of the Spirit" speaking through this saintly nun.

■ ***Can you recall a time when the Spirit seemed to guide you in some situation? Explain.***

Life in the Spirit

Drawing upon Scripture, Christian tradition describes the day-to-day activities of the Spirit in our lives in terms of the following:

Virtues	Faith, hope, and charity 1 Corinthians 13:13
Gifts	Wisdom, understanding, counsel, knowledge, fortitude, piety, and fear of the Lord Isaiah 11:1–2
Fruits	Love, joy, peace, patience, kindness, generosity, faithfulness, gentleness, self-control Galatians 5:22–23 (NRSV)

PRAYER **hotline**

O Thou, Who art at home
Deep in my heart,
Enable me to join you
Deep in my heart.

The Talmud

Stage 1: *Chapter 7* **95**

Water — *Is life-giving to every plant according to its own needs*

Spirit — *Is life-giving to every person according to their own needs*

Life in the Spirit

CLARIFY—Since the first Pentecost, every person who has turned from sin and been baptized has experienced the "touch of the Spirit" in a special way. Paul writes:

God poured out
his Holy Spirit abundantly on us
through Jesus Christ our Savior,
so that we might be put right with God
and come into possession
of the eternal life we hope for. Titus 3:6–7

A dramatic illustration of the "touch of the Spirit" occurs in *The Cross and the Switchblade* by David Wilkerson.

Wilkerson worked with gang members and other delinquents in New York City.

Here's a firsthand account in the book. It's by a young heroin addict named Joe. He writes:

The Holy Spirit
is called the Comforter, they told me.
When I thought of comfort
I thought of a bottle of wine and
a dozen goof balls.

But these guys
were talking about comfort from heaven
where I could feel clean later.
I got to wanting this. . . .

I cried to God for help and that's when
the Holy Spirit came. . . .
I didn't want any more drugs.
I loved everybody.
For the first time in my life I felt clean.

Share Your **meditation**

CLARIFY—Before having the students share their responses in small groups of three or four, give them this additional background on Malcolm Muggeridge.

At the end of his life, he confessed in an interview that he'd just done something he swore he'd never do. He became a Catholic. He attributed his conversion to Mother Teresa of Calcutta, saying:

Words cannot express how much I owe her.
She showed me Christianity in action.
She showed me the power of love.
She showed me how one loving person
can start a tidal wave of love
that can spread across the entire world.

Concerning the TV interview referred to in the meditation, he said the numerous letters he received all said pretty much the same thing: "This woman spoke to me like no other ever has, and I feel I must help her."

HISTORICAL Connection

QUESTION Why do you think the Holy Spirit frequently works through very unlikely people, like Saint Joseph of Cupertino?

■ *Saint Paul explains it this way in his first Letter to the Corinthians:*

What seems to be God's foolishness
is wiser than human wisdom,
and what seems to be God's weakness
is stronger than human strength. . . .

God purposely chose
what the world considers nonsense
in order to shame the wise,
and he chose what the world considers weak
in order to shame the powerful.

He chose what the world looks down on
and despised and thinks is nothing,
in order to destroy
what the world considers important.
1 CORINTHIANS 1:25–28

Virtues

QUESTION 6 Which of the virtues do you feel most in need of at this time in your life? Explain.

Have the students record their responses in the notebooks, share them in small groups, and then choose one to share with the entire class.

Gifts of the Spirit

CLARIFY—Stress three things concerning the gifts:

1 Their *end purpose* is to "build up the body of Christ." EPHESIANS 4:12

2 *The gifts form a ladder going step by step from a fear of God to resting peacefully in the presence of God.*

3 *The gifts make us more sensitive to the "movement of the Spirit" in our daily lives.*

QUESTION 7 Which of the above gifts do you feel most in need of at this time in your life? Explain.

HISTORICAL Connection

Young Joseph of Cupertino labored under a learning disability and was considered dull and clumsy. When he tried to enter the religious life, he was turned down by one monastery after another.

Finally, guided by the Holy Spirit, a Franciscan group agreed to accept him. Joseph acquired enough knowledge to be ordained a priest. Eventually, many miracles were attributed to him.

■ ***Why do you think the Holy Spirit frequently works through very unlikely people, like Saint Joseph of Cupertino?***

Virtues

Faith, hope, and charity are called the theological virtues. CCC 1812–13 Given to us through baptism, they relate us in a personal way to the Trinity—Father, Son, and Spirit— and are the foundation of our spiritual life.

FAITH	Empowers us to receive and accept God's revelation CCC 1814–16
HOPE	Empowers us to trust that God's plan for us will be realized CCC 1817–21
CHARITY	Empowers us to love God above all else and our neighbor as ourselves CCC 1827–29

6 Which of the virtues do you feel most in need of at this time in your life? Explain.

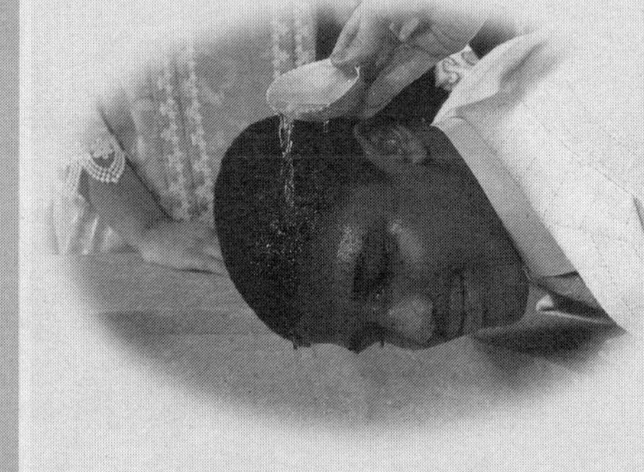

Gifts of the Spirit

The prophet Isaiah lists seven gifts of the Spirit. CCC 1830–31 Christian traditions describe them as dispositions that make us more sensitive to the touch of the Spirit. Saint Augustine points out that Isaiah lists the gifts in reverse order:

The prophet begins with wisdom and ends with fear of the Lord. . . .
He begins, therefore, by identifying the goal we are striving for and ends with the starting point where we must begin.

Thus, the Book of Proverbs repeats over a dozen different times that "fear of the Lord" is the beginning of "wisdom." Beginning with the fear of the Lord, the gifts of the Holy Spirit mount up the spiritual ladder in the following way:

FEAR OF GOD	Draws us from sin to God
PIETY	Awakens us to God's love
KNOWLEDGE	Helps us to see how all things come from God and lead back to God
FORTITUDE	Strengthens us to pursue our journey to God with joy and courage
COUNSEL	Helps us discern the right path of action, especially in difficult situations

96 STAGE 1: CHAPTER 7

Have the students record their responses in the notebooks, share them in small groups, and then choose one to share with the entire class.

Fruits of the Spirit

CLARIFY—Point out that the fruits act as a kind of foretaste of heaven.

Also stress that they are simpy colors in the "rainbow of love."

QUESTION 8 Which of the above fruits do you feel most in need of at this time in your life?

Have students record their response in the notebooks, share them in small groups, and then choose one to share with the entire class.

NOTES

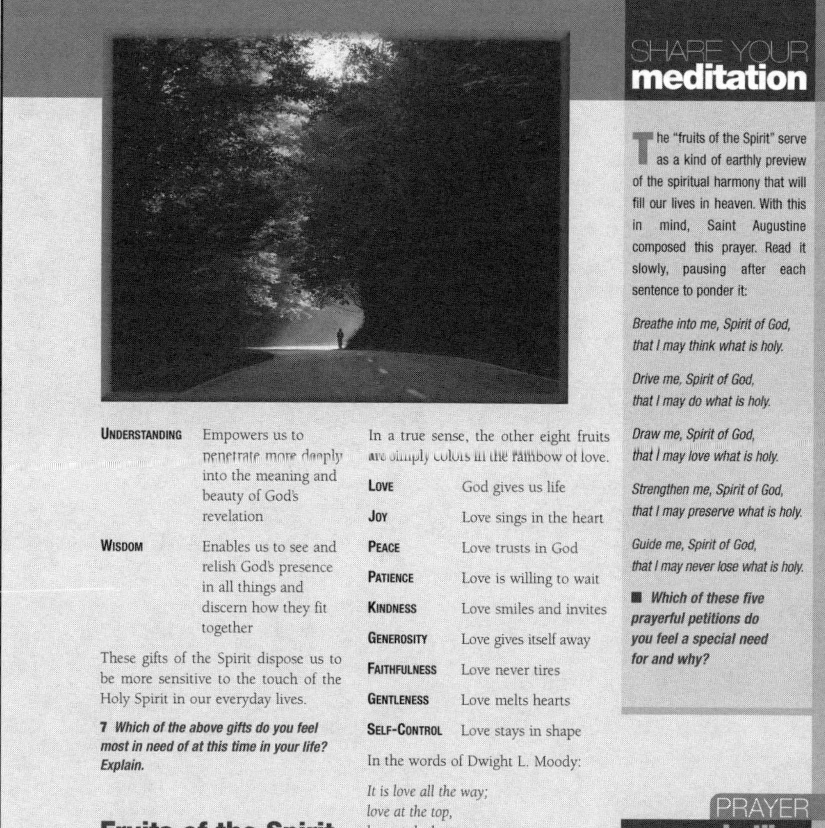

SHARE YOUR meditation

The "fruits of the Spirit" serve as a kind of earthly preview of the spiritual harmony that will fill our lives in heaven. With this in mind, Saint Augustine composed this prayer. Read it slowly, pausing after each sentence to ponder it:

Breathe into me, Spirit of God,
that I may think what is holy.

Drive me, Spirit of God,
that I may do what is holy.

Draw me, Spirit of God,
that I may love what is holy.

Strengthen me, Spirit of God,
that I may preserve what is holy.

Guide me, Spirit of God,
that I may never lose what is holy.

■ ***Which of these five prayerful petitions do you feel a special need for and why?***

Understanding	Empowers us to penetrate more deeply into the meaning and beauty of God's revelation
Wisdom	Enables us to see and relish God's presence in all things and discern how they fit together

These gifts of the Spirit dispose us to be more sensitive to the touch of the Holy Spirit in our everyday lives.

7 Which of the above gifts do you feel most in need of at this time in your life? Explain.

Fruits of the Spirit

Christian tradition teaches us that when we live in harmony with the virtues and the gifts of the Spirit, we are blessed with a variety of fruits.

Saint Paul lists nine fruits of the Spirit. CCC 1832 He puts love at the top of the list. He puts it there for a good reason.

In a true sense, the other eight fruits are simply colors in the rainbow of love.

Love	God gives us life
Joy	Love sings in the heart
Peace	Love trusts in God
Patience	Love is willing to wait
Kindness	Love smiles and invites
Generosity	Love gives itself away
Faithfulness	Love never tires
Gentleness	Love melts hearts
Self-Control	Love stays in shape

In the words of Dwight L. Moody:

It is love all the way;
love at the top,
love at the bottom,
and love all the way along
down this list of graces.

If we only just brought forth
the fruit of the Spirit,
what a world we would have!

8 Which of the above fruits do you feel most in need of at this time in your life? Explain.

PRAYER hotline

Lord,
"Don't walk in front of me,
I may not follow.
Don't walk behind me,
I may not lead.
Walk beside me,
and just be my friend."
Albert Camus

Stage 1: *Chapter 7* **97**

CLARIFY—Here are some one-word summaries of the "fruits."

Love	*Life-giving*
Joy	*Sings*
Peace	*Trusts*
Patience	*Waits*
Kindness	*Invites*
Generosity	*Self-giving*
Faithfulness	*Loyal*
Gentleness	*Mild-mannered*
Self-control	*Disciplined*

CLARIFY—Here are some insights on the Fruits of the Spirit. Besides giving us an insight into the fruit, they invite discussion.

LOVE—The touch of a loving hand can release more healing than a bucket of pills. Anonymous

JOY—To get the full value from joy you must have someone to divide it with. Mark Twain

PEACE—Happy are those who work for peace. God will call them his children. Matthew 5:9

PATIENCE—If you are patient in one moment of anger, you will escape a hundred days of sorrow. Chinese Proverb

KINDNESS—Treat people the way they ought to be treated and you will help them become what they are capable of being. Johnan von Goethe

GENEROSITY—It is possible to give without loving, but it is impossible to love without giving. Richard Brounstein

FAITHFULNESS—Never let go of loyalty and faithfulness. Tie them around your neck; write them on your heart. Proverbs 3:3

GENTLENESS—Feelings are everywhere—be gentle. J. Masai

SELF-CONTROL—We first make our habits, and then our habits make us. E.C. McKenzie

Share Your meditation

Have the students record their responses in the notebooks, share them in small groups, and then choose one to share with the entire class.

PRAYER hotline

CLARIFY—Here are some insights on leadership that lend themselves to discussion:

1 *You can't lead anyone any further than you have gone yourself.* Gene Mauch

2 *Our chief want in life is somebody who shall make us do what we can.* Emerson

3 *The nation will find it very hard to look up to the leaders who keep their ears to the ground.* Winston Churchill

4 *Good leaders inspire us to put confidence in them. Great leaders inspire us to put confidence in ourselves.* Author unknown

Recap

Without the Spirit:
God is far away.
The cosmos is steeped in mystery.
Jesus is only a teacher;
Scripture is just a book;
the Church is only a community club.

In the Spirit:
The cosmos is steeped in labor,
giving birth to the Kingdom.
Jesus is risen.
Scripture is God's Word revealing all truth.
The Church is God's people on earth.

Review

DAILY QUIZ—The review questions may be assigned (one or two at a time) for homework or a daily quiz.

CHAPTER TESTS—*Reproducible chapter tests are found in Appendix A. For consistency and ease in grading, quizzes are usually restricted to (1) "Matching," (2) "True/False," and (3) "Fill in the Blanks."*

TEST ANSWERS—*The following are the answers to the test for Chapter 7." (See Appendix A, page 318.) All correct answers worth four points.*

Matching

1 = h	2 = b	3 = c	4 = g
5 = j	6 = i	7 = d	8 = a
9 = f	10 = e		

True/False

1 = T	2 = T	3 = F	4 = F
5 = F	6 = T	7 = F	8 = T
9 = F	10 = F		

Fill In the Blanks

1. Charity
2. Hope
3. Fear of God
4. Paul
5. Isaiah

Recap

The central mystery of Christianity is the revelation of God as Trinity. The third person of the Trinity is the Holy Spirit. With the Father and the Son, the Spirit is eternal: without beginning or end.

On Pentecost the Holy Spirit came upon the disciples, fulfilling Jesus' promise to them and filling them with amazing power. On this day, the re-creation of the world took a quantum leap forward.

Collectively, the disciples became temples of the Holy Spirit and members of Christ's body, the Church. Individually, they were graced with special:

Virtues	Faith, hope, and charity
Gifts	Fear of the Lord, piety, knowledge, fortitude, counsel, understanding, and wisdom
Fruits	Love, joy, peace, patience, kindness, generosity, faithfulness, gentleness, self-control

These virtues, gifts, and fruits were to be used not just for the disciples' own personal good, but for the good of all and for the building up and spreading of God's Kingdom on earth.

Review

1 Give two examples from Scripture that describe the Holy Spirit at work in Old Testament times.

2 Give two examples from the Gospels that describe the Holy Spirit at work in Jesus' life.

3 What two instructions by Jesus to his disciples set the stage for the Spirit's coming on Pentecost?

4 Explain the relationship between Pentecost and (a) the prophecy of Joel and (b) the Tower of Babel story.

5 Explain why and how ancient Jews connected (a) the wind with God, (b) fire with God, (c) water with the Holy Spirit.

6 How did the crowd react to Peter's words?

7 Briefly describe (a) the monumental event that took place on Pentecost, (b) how Paul experienced this event firsthand before his conversion.

8 Explain (a) why the theological virtues are so called, (b) how they are given to us, (c) for what purpose they are given to us.

9 List and briefly describe (a) three of the seven *gifts* of the Spirit, (b) three of the nine *fruits* of the Spirit.

NOTES

Reflect

1 Karen Karper rarely saw deer near her house during the day. But at night, she heard them prowling about and, in the morning, saw their footprints in her lawn. She writes:

If you are in the right place
at the right moment, you will see deer,
perhaps even very close at hand.
But once you try to touch them, they flee.

It is kind of like this
with the comings and goings
of the Spirit of God.

If I wait quietly going about the tasks
of my day, I might glimpse a trace
of his activity in my life, a subtle sign
that he is just beyond the edge of my vision.

WHERE GOD BEGINS TO BE

- ***Recall a time when you felt the urge to help someone or do something that resulted in something beautiful for one or both of you. In other words, recall a time when the Holy Spirit touched your life.***
- ***Describe what kind of an effect this had on you and/or the other person.***

2 A farmer had a large rock located in the center of his field. It was troublesome plowing around it each year. Worse yet, he sometimes forgot it and damaged his plow on it. He wanted to dig it out. But he kept putting it off.

Finally, he acted. To his surprise, it was totally on the surface and easily removed. He thought to himself: "Why did it take me so long to dig it up? How much grief I could have saved myself had I removed it right away!"

- ***What "fruit" of the Spirit does this story illustrate?***
- ***Describe a "rock" in your life causing you grief.***
- ***What keeps you from digging it up?***

3 Take two paper cups. Fill one with water; leave the other empty. Now take a cigarette lighter and hold it under the empty cup so that the flame from the lighter touches it. Next hold the lighter under the cup filled with water so that the flame touches it also.

- ***What happened in the case of the empty cup? Filled cup?***
- ***How might this experiment be used to illustrate the change that took place in disciples as a result of Pentecost?***

STAGE 1: CHAPTER 7 **99**

Reflect

1 ***a) Recall a time when you felt the urge to help someone or do something that resulted in something beautiful for one or both of you. In other words, recall a time when the Holy Spirit touched your life.***
b) Describe what kind of an effect this had on you and/or the other person.

***DISCUSS*—Open the discussion by reading this student's answer:**

An experience like this that I had was on a student work trip to Appalacchia. We lived and worked with each other twenty-four hours a day. For ten days we did jobs working together. We cooked meals together and slept together in the same room. But most important, we talked about everything. We weren't afraid to tell our innermost feelings. We hid nothing from each other. What a great experience this was! I really felt that the Holy Spirit touched all our lives on that trip.

***DISCUSS*—Have the students share in small groups a time when they experienced something similar.**

2 ***a) What fruit of the Spirit does this story illustrate?***
b) Describe a "rock" in your life causing you grief.
c) What keeps you from digging it up?

You might wish to share this student's response to get them started:

The fruit is the "joy" or the "peace" that comes from doing something you've been putting off. A "rock" in my own life was not talking to my dad about my mom's recent death. It wasn't until I read a piece by a Terry Kettering that gave me the courage to do it. An excerpt reads:

"There's an elephant in the room. . . .
We talk about everything else—
except the elephant in the room.
We all know it is there. . . .
It is constantly on our minds. . . .
Oh, please, let's talk about the elephant
in the room. . . .
For if I cannot, you are leaving me
alone . . . in a room with an elephant."

3 ***a) What happened in the case of the empty cup? Filled cup?***
b) How might this experiment illustrate the change that took place in the disciples as a result of Pentecost?

- *The empty wax paper cup burns. But the cup filled with water does not. The heat of the flame is transferred into the water.*

The water in the cup is like the Holy Spirit in us. The presence of the Holy Spirit in them strengthens them to bear trials and problems that would normally have destroyed them.

PRAYER TIME with the Lord

QUESTION ***Compose your own prayer to the Holy Spirit and share it with the class.***

***CLARIFY*—**Suggest that the students base the prayer on their answers to Questions 6, 7, 8 (pages 96–97). These three questions referred to "virtues," "gifts," and "fruits" that they feel most in need of at this time in their lives.

Here's a sample prayer that you may read to them to get them started.

Holy Spirit, you came upon me in
Confirmation in a special way,
just as you came upon the Apostles
on the day of Pentecost.

Suddenly, I feel a great need for you.
I am going through some faith problems.
As a result, I really need an increase
of faith.

I'd also ask you to give an increase of the
gift of counsel to my older brother.
He's trying to discern how he should
handle a problem that has developed with
his wife.

Finally, help our whole family experience
the fruit of peace and patience. For some
reason there is a lot of turmoil in our
home and everybody is snapping at the
other person.

I ask all of these things in the name
of Jesus, our Lord and Savior.

PRAYER Journal

QUESTION ***Write out a few of the thoughts that came to you during your meditation.***

Here's an example that you might read to the students to get them started:

While meditating on the first line,
the thought occurred to me that before
I can change the world, I'd better start
changing myself.

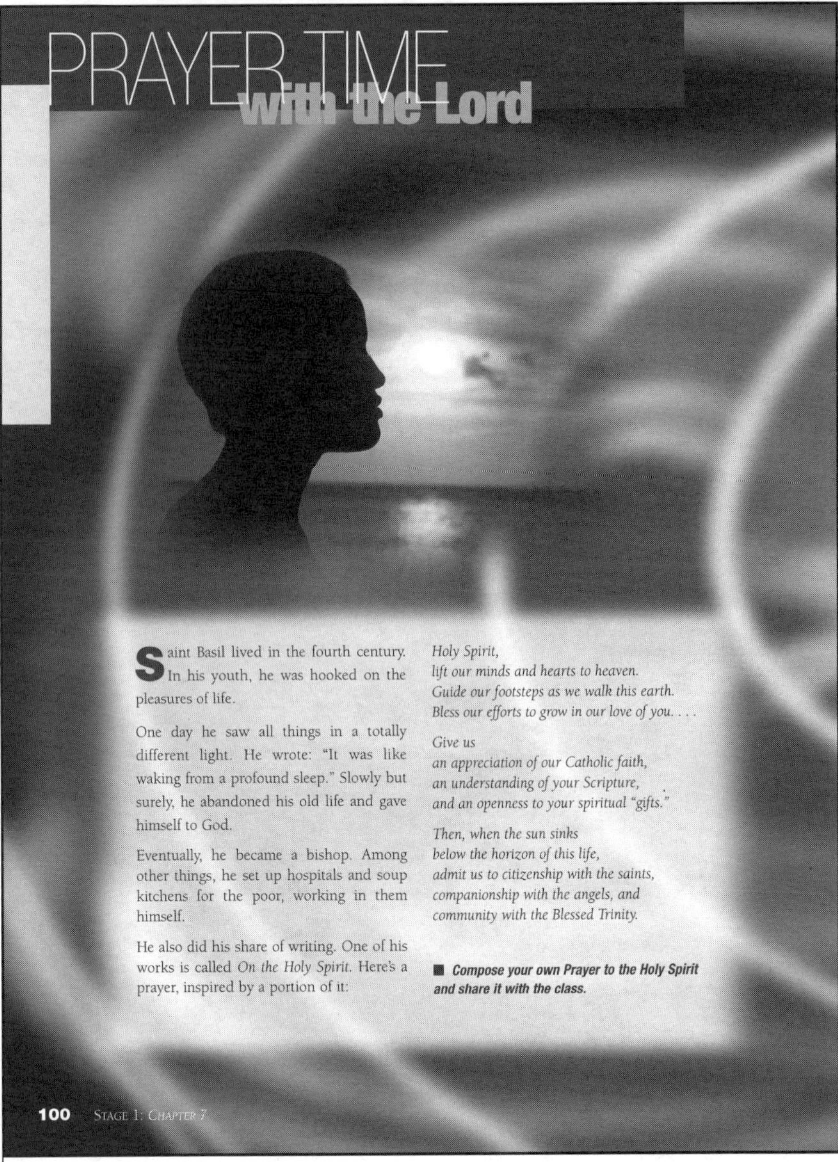

PRAYER TIME with the Lord

Saint Basil lived in the fourth century. In his youth, he was hooked on the pleasures of life.

One day he saw all things in a totally different light. He wrote: "It was like waking from a profound sleep." Slowly but surely, he abandoned his old life and gave himself to God.

Eventually, he became a bishop. Among other things, he set up hospitals and soup kitchens for the poor, working in them himself.

He also did his share of writing. One of his works is called *On the Holy Spirit*. Here's a prayer, inspired by a portion of it:

Holy Spirit,
lift our minds and hearts to heaven.
Guide our footsteps as we walk this earth.
Bless our efforts to grow in our love of you. . . .

Give us
an appreciation of our Catholic faith,
an understanding of your Scripture,
and an openness to your spiritual "gifts."

Then, when the sun sinks
below the horizon of this life,
admit us to citizenship with the saints,
companionship with the angels, and
community with the Blessed Trinity.

■ ***Compose your own Prayer to the Holy Spirit and share it with the class.***

100 STAGE 1: CHAPTER 7

I could have spent ten minutes meditating on the second line. I'm embarrassed to say why. It's because I've been tearing down a few people recently. I tried to figure out if it was because I'm crabby because I'm not getting enough sleep. I'll have to think more about that. It also occurred to me that I'd much rather sit in a comfortable nest not far from the sturdy trunk of the tree, rather than venture out on the limb.

The third line raised a big question for me. What "one candle" might I light to remove the "darkness" and "depression" that descends upon my mother every so often?

NOTES

PRAYER Journal

Read the prayer below one line at a time. Pause after each line to meditate for ten seconds or so on its meaning:

Lord God, strengthen me by your Holy Spirit, to carry out my mission of changing the world or some definite part of it, for the better. . . .

Nourish in me a practical desire to build up rather than tear down, to go out on a limb rather than crave security.

Never let me forget that it is far better to light one candle than to curse the darkness.

EXCERPTED AND SLIGHTLY ADAPTED FROM THE "CHRISTOPHER PRAYER"

■ ***Write out a few of the thoughts that came to you during your meditation.***

SCRIPTURE Journal

1	Jesus and the Spirit	Luke 4:14–22
2	Waiting for the Spirit	Acts 1:1–8
3	Coming of the Spirit	Acts 2:14–18
4	Fruits of the Spirit	Galatians 5:16–26
5	Life in the Spirit	Romans 8:1–17

■ ***Pick one of the above passages. Read it prayerfully and write a short statement to Jesus, expressing your feelings about it.***

STAGE 1: *CHAPTER 7* **101**

SCRIPTURE Journal

QUESTION ***Pick one of the above passages. Read it prayerfully and write a short statement to Jesus expressing your feelings about it.***

Read "verse 6" from the fifth reading and have the students comment on it: "To be controlled by human nature results in death; to be controlled by the Spirit results in life and peace."

Jesus, I'm glad you were born in a stable, because I sometimes give in to my human nature; and I feel more like a stable than a temple of the Holy Spirit. Knowing that you didn't avoid contact with stables, gives me the courage to invite you into my heart, even when it feels like a stable.

Classroom Resources

CATECHISM

Catechism of the Catholic Church *Second Edition*

For further enrichment, you might refer to:

1.	Holy Spirit	Index	pp. 805–807
		Glossary	p. 882
2.	Virtue	Index	p. 857
		Glossary	p. 903

See also: Fruits, Gifts of the Holy Spirit.
—AVAILABLE FROM THE UNITED STATES CATHOLIC CONFERENCE, WASHINGTON DC

VIDEO

Mystery of God: Father, Son, and Spirit

Three thirty-minute segments. A contemporary approach to the story of creation, salvation, and God's abiding presence in our lives.
—AVAILABLE FROM THOMAS MORE PUBLISHING, ALLEN, TX

BOOK

Holy Spirit: Meditations for the Millennium

Mark Link, S.J.

Nineteen weeks of daily meditations on the Holy Spirit, based on the virtues, gifts, and fruits of the Spirit. Each week begins with an introduction and explanation of the virtue, gift, or fruit on which the meditations of that week are based.
—AVAILABLE FROM THOMAS MORE PUBLISHING, ALLEN, TX

NOTE

For a list of (1) General resources for professional background and (2) Addresses, phone/fax numbers of major publishing companies, see Appendix B of this Resource Manual.

CHAPTER 8
The Church

CHAPTER at a Glance

The purpose of this chapter is to explore the origin, growth, and nature of the Church according to its:

1. *Five scriptural stages*
2. *Four identifying marks*
3. *Three fundamental models*
4. *Two paradoxical dimensions*

DISCUSS—Have one student read the scriptural part of the introduction, which begins: "Saint Paul writes . . ."

Have a second student read the commentary which follows it and begins: "God's plan from all eternity . . ."

Ask the students: Identify the five stages by which the Church—the heart of God's plan—developed and is moving toward completion.

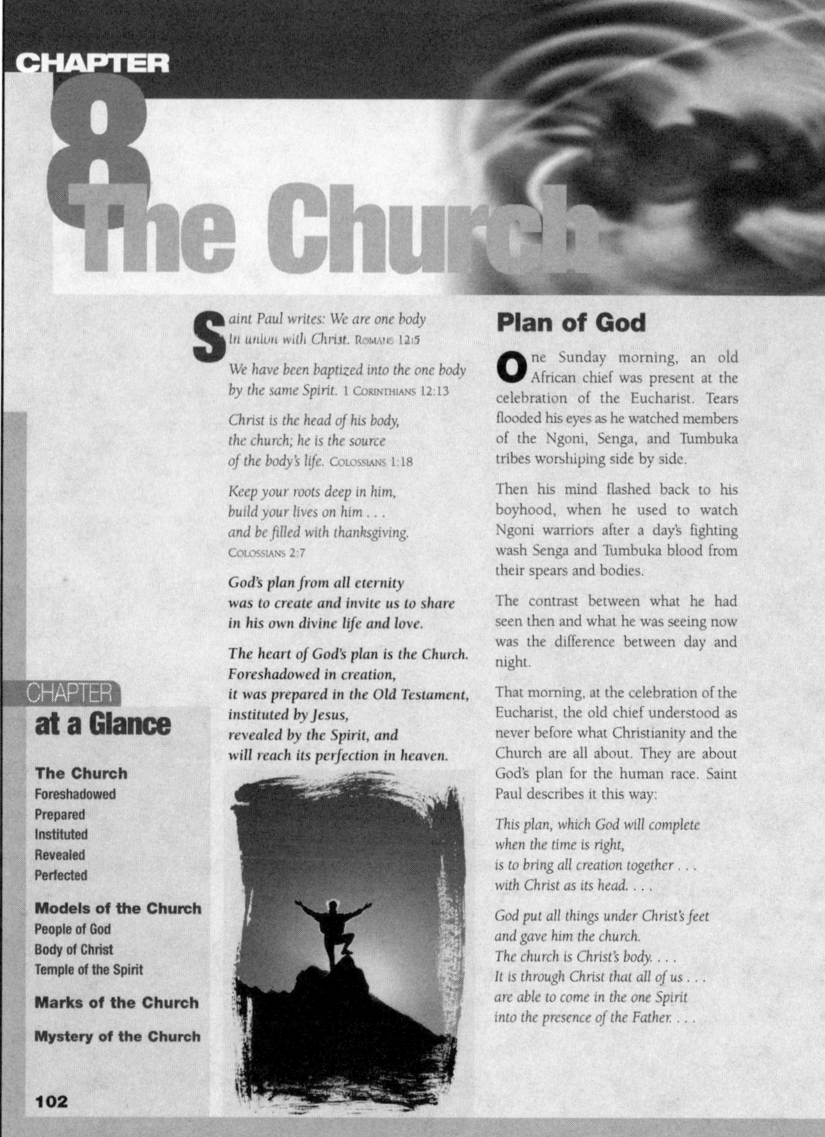

CHAPTER 8 The Church

Saint Paul writes: We are one body in union with Christ. ROMANS 12:5

We have been baptized into the one body by the same Spirit. 1 CORINTHIANS 12:13

Christ is the head of his body,
the church; he is the source
of the body's life. COLOSSIANS 1:18

Keep your roots deep in him,
build your lives on him . . .
and be filled with thanksgiving.
COLOSSIANS 2:7

God's plan from all eternity was to create and invite us to share in his own divine life and love.

The heart of God's plan is the Church.
Foreshadowed in creation,
it was prepared in the Old Testament,
instituted by Jesus,
revealed by the Spirit, and
will reach its perfection in heaven.

CHAPTER **at a Glance**

The Church
Foreshadowed
Prepared
Instituted
Revealed
Perfected

Models of the Church
People of God
Body of Christ
Temple of the Spirit

Marks of the Church

Mystery of the Church

Plan of God

One Sunday morning, an old African chief was present at the celebration of the Eucharist. Tears flooded his eyes as he watched members of the Ngoni, Senga, and Tumbuka tribes worshiping side by side.

Then his mind flashed back to his boyhood, when he used to watch Ngoni warriors after a day's fighting wash Senga and Tumbuka blood from their spears and bodies.

The contrast between what he had seen then and what he was seeing now was the difference between day and night.

That morning, at the celebration of the Eucharist, the old chief understood as never before what Christianity and the Church are all about. They are about God's plan for the human race. Saint Paul describes it this way:

This plan, which God will complete
when the time is right,
is to bring all creation together . . .
with Christ as its head. . . .

God put all things under Christ's feet
and gave him the church.
The church is Christ's body. . . .
It is through Christ that all of us . . .
are able to come in the one Spirit
into the presence of the Father. . . .

102

Plan of God

CLARIFY—The students may recall the popular Hollywood films *Zulu* and *Chaka Zulu*. Both rerun regularly on TV.

The Ngoni tribe split with the Zulus in the late 19th century at the time of King Chaka's wars with the British.

The Ngoni then went on a thousand-mile migration north as far as Lake Victoria, leaving a trail of wreckage and bloodshed as they went.

Eventually, they split up into a number of subgroups.

CLARIFY—Concerning the goal of God's plan, Saint Paul wrote:

> *This plan, which God will complete*
> *when the time is right,*
> *is to bring all creation together. . . .*
> *It is through Christ that all of us,*
> *Jews and Gentiles, are able to come*
> *in one Spirit into the presence of the*
> *Father.* EPHESIANS 1:10–11, 22–23

Note the Trinitarian dimension of the plan.

The Church

CLARIFY—The high point of Old Testament history was the "sacred assembly" of Israelites at the foot of Mount Sinai. The "sacred moment" came when God covenanted them and made them his "chosen people."

The Hebrew word given to this "sacred assembly" was *kahal*.

Centuries later, the Old Testament was translated into Greek. The translators

NOTES

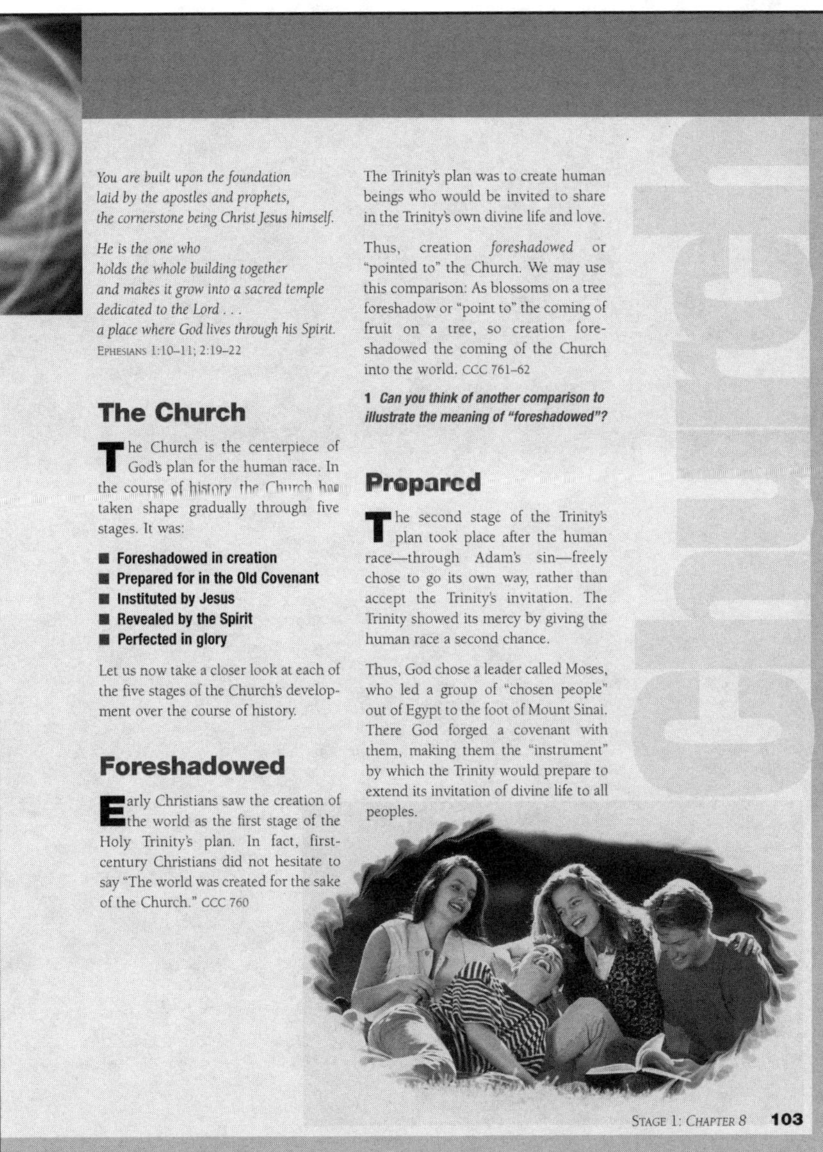

You are built upon the foundation
laid by the apostles and prophets,
the cornerstone being Christ Jesus himself.

He is the one who
holds the whole building together
and makes it grow into a sacred temple
dedicated to the Lord . . .
a place where God lives through his Spirit.
EPHESIANS 1:10–11; 2:19–22

The Church

The Church is the centerpiece of God's plan for the human race. In the course of history the Church has taken shape gradually through five stages. It was:

- **Foreshadowed in creation**
- **Prepared for in the Old Covenant**
- **Instituted by Jesus**
- **Revealed by the Spirit**
- **Perfected in glory**

Let us now take a closer look at each of the five stages of the Church's development over the course of history.

Foreshadowed

Early Christians saw the creation of the world as the first stage of the Holy Trinity's plan. In fact, first-century Christians did not hesitate to say "The world was created for the sake of the Church." CCC 760

The Trinity's plan was to create human beings who would be invited to share in the Trinity's own divine life and love.

Thus, creation *foreshadowed* or "pointed to" the Church. We may use this comparison: As blossoms on a tree foreshadow or "point to" the coming of fruit on a tree, so creation foreshadowed the coming of the Church into the world. CCC 761–62

1 Can you think of another comparison to illustrate the meaning of "foreshadowed"?

Prepared

The second stage of the Trinity's plan took place after the human race—through Adam's sin—freely chose to go its own way, rather than accept the Trinity's invitation. The Trinity showed its mercy by giving the human race a second chance.

Thus, God chose a leader called Moses, who led a group of "chosen people" out of Egypt to the foot of Mount Sinai. There God forged a covenant with them, making them the "instrument" by which the Trinity would prepare to extend its invitation of divine life to all peoples.

STAGE 1: CHAPTER 8 **103**

chose the Greek word *Kyriake* to refer to the "sacred assembly" of Israelites.

Later, the Old Testament was translated into German. The translators chose the word *Kirche* to refer to the "sacred assembly."

Finally, when the Old Testament was translated into English, the word *Church* was chosen to designate the "sacred assembly."

And so the Church, which was instituted by Jesus, traces its ancestry, in a sense, back to the "sacred assembly" at the foot of Mount Sinai.

NOTEBOOK—Have the students copy the following summary into their notebooks:

Sacred assembly		
	Hebrew	*Kahal*
	Greek	*Kyriake*
	German	*Kirche*
	English	*Church*

Foreshadowed

QUESTION **1** ***Can you think of another comparison to illustrate the meaning of "foreshadowed"?***

- *The married love of a man and a woman "foreshadow" a child.*

Prepared

CLARIFY—Use this section to stress the remarkable transformation that took place in the Israelite community at the foot of Mt Sinai in the desert. We get so used to hearing the story that we forget what a remarkable phenomena it was.

- *The historian shakes his head when he looks back at that "sacred moment." He asks himself:*

"How did a mob of ex-slaves from Egypt, with no organization, no education, and no apparent way to survive, eventually change the entire course of human history?"

The biblical writer's own explanation is simple. At the foot of a mountain in the Sinai desert the Israelite community encountered God and were transformed utterly by it.

That encounter gave them a new identity (God's chosen people) and a new destiny (God's chosen instrument to re-create the world).

CLARIFY—Apart from Christianity and Islam—which both owe their origin, in part, to Israel—no other religion came about as did Israel's. Other religions sprang from nature. Israel's sprang from history; that is, at a specific moment in time, at a specific place on this planet, they encountered the awesome Creator of the universe and were totally transformed by the encounter.

REALITY Connection

***DISCUSS*—The Jesus who walked the roads of Galilee was both God and man. That is, he had both a *human* dimension and a *divine* dimension.**

In a similar way, the Church that Jesus instituted has both a human dimension and a divine dimension. Jesus—the head of his body, the Church—is the source of its divine dimension; we—the members of his body, the Church—constitute the human dimension.

Just as the human dimension of the person Jesus made him vulnerable to sickness, weariness, and depression, in a similar way, the human dimension of of the Church makes it vulnerable to various evils. Consider this statement referring to the human dimension of the Church:

> *The Church is not a collection of saints,*
> *but a collection of sinners,*
> *desperately seeking to become saints.*
>
> *Jesus himself said, "I have not come to call respectable people, but outcasts."* MARK 2:17
>
> *To those who insist upon complaining about the "flaws" in the Church, Billy Graham said in a tongue-in-cheek mood:*
>
> *"If you find a perfect church,*
> *by all means join it!*
> *Then it will no longer be perfect."*

Instituted

QUESTION **2 *In what sense did the "Kingdom of Satan" hold the human race "in slavery"?***

■ *It unleashed into the world the three ancient evils of the human family: sin, sickness, and death. Once they entered the world, there was no human defense against them. All the human race could do was pray for a rescuer.*

That rescuer came in the person of Jesus. He inaugurated the Kingdom of God. It is now in the process of destroying the Kingdom of Satan: We say that it is "in the process," because the "coming" of the Kingdom of God is a process, not an instant event.

Thus, the Kingdom of Satan is not yet dead. It is in the process of dying; its days are numbered. Like a prisoner on death row, it is under sentence of death, awaiting execution. So, each time we say the Lord's Prayer, we pray, "Thy Kingdom come."

Meanwhile, we might compare the institution of the Church to the conception of a child in the womb. It is in its embryonic state. Its goal is to become the seed, sign, and instrument that will effect the "coming" Kingdom of God on earth.

We may describe the Kingdom of God in its present state as God's presence among us, gradually and invisibly re-creating us and our world.

Instituted

The third stage took place when, in a mystery of love, the second person of the Trinity became a human being. He was named *Jesus* (which means "he will save his people from their sins"). He was also given the title *Immanuel* (which means he is "God is with us"). MATTHEW 1:21

To carry out the Trinity's plan, Jesus established the Kingdom of God. We may describe the Kingdom of God as *the power of God at work in the world.* It is the power of God gradually destroying the "Kingdom of Satan," which held the human race in slavery since the first sin.

2 *In what sense did the "Kingdom of Satan" hold the human race "in slavery"?*

This explains why we still pray "Thy Kingdom come" in the Lord's Prayer. It is because the "Kingdom of Satan" will not die without a struggle. In other words, the coming of the Kingdom of God is not an instant happening but a gradual process. It will reach completion only in heaven.

Here, it is important to note that the Kingdom of God is not something visible. Jesus said to a group of Pharisees:

> *"The Kingdom of God*
> *does not come in such a way as to be seen.*
> *No one can say, 'Look, here it is!' or*
> *'There it is!' because the Kingdom of God*
> *is within you."* LUKE 17:20–21

In other words, the Kingdom of God is a thing of the heart. It is present wherever God's will reigns.

This brings us back to the Church. Jesus instituted the Church to be the *seed, sign,* and the *instrument* of God's Kingdom on earth. Toward that end, Jesus chose twelve apostles, under the headship of Peter, to continue to spread and bring forth God's Kingdom on earth. CCC 763–66, 880–96

3 *In what sense is the Church the seed, sign, and instrument of God's Kingdom?*

Revealed

Jesus completed his mission on earth and ascended to heaven, but not before promising to send the Holy Spirit. With the coming of the Spirit on Pentecost, the plan of the Holy Trinity entered its final phase, namely, to:

- **Reveal the Church to the nations**
- **Empower it to disciple all nations**

To help the Church fulfill its mission to the world, the Holy Spirit endowed it with special gifts and powers.

Perfected

The Church will reach perfection in heaven when the "Kingdom of God" will be fully established. CCC 769

We might compare the five stages of the Church to the five stages of a plant's growth:

- **Seed** **Church foreshadowed**
- **Stem** **Church prepared**
- **Bud** **Church instituted**
- **Bloom** **Church revealed**
- **Fruit** **Church perfected**

REALITY Connection

I think I shall never see
a Church
that's all it ought
to be:

A Church
whose members never stray
beyond the straight
and narrow way.
A Church
that has no empty pews,
whose pastor
never has the blues. . . .

Such perfect Churches
there may be,
but none of them
are known to me.
But still,
we'll work and pray and plan
to make our own
the best we can.

Author Unknown

104 STAGE 1: CHAPTER 8

NOTES

Up Close & Personal

Unfinished work

Composer Giacomo Puccini wrote a number of operas. His last one, *Turandot* (Tour-en-doe) is regarded by many to be his best.

While working on it, he discovered he had a rapidly growing cancer. One day he said to his students, "If I am not able to finish this opera, I want you to finish it for me."

Shortly afterward, Puccini went to Brussels for an operation. He died two days after surgery. In the months that followed, his students completed his final opera. The world premiere was performed in Milan and directed by Puccini's favorite student, Toscanini.

Everything went well until the opera reached the place where Puccini stopped writing. Tears ran down Toscanini's cheeks. He stopped the music, put down his baton, turned to the audience, and cried out, "Thus far the Master wrote, but he died."

Then there was silence throughout the Milan opera house. No one moved; no one spoke.

After a minute, Toscanini picked up the baton, smiled through his tears, and cried out, "But the disciples finished his work." When the opera ended, the audience broke into a long and thunderous applause.

The story of the completion of *Turandot* bears a similarity to the story of the completion of the Church.

Jesus laid the foundation. But, like Puccini, Jesus died before its completion, leaving that important work to his disciples.

4 What have you done to work for the Church's completion? What are you doing now? What ought you do in the future?

Models of the Church

There's a well-known poem by John Godfrey Saxe. It describes six blind men from Indostan. They are standing around an elephant, trying to figure out what it's like.

One blind man feels its side and says the elephant looks like a wall. Another feels its tail and says it looks like a rope. A third feels its trunk and says it looks like a snake. A fourth feels its ear and says it looks like a fan. A fifth feels

Alexis de Tocqueville

A nineteenth-century French statesman, Alexis de Tocqueville came to America to learn the secret of its genius and greatness. After a careful study of the country, he wrote:

I sought for
the genius and greatness
of America . . .
in her fertile fields
and boundless forests—
and it was not there. . . .

[I sought for it] in her rich mines
and her vast world commerce—
and it was not there. . . .

[I sought for it]
in her democratic Congress
and matchless Constitution—
and it was not there."

Not until I went
into the churches of America
and heard her pulpits
flame with righteousness
did I understand the secret
of her genius and power.

America is great
because she is good,
and if America
ever ceases to be good,
America
will cease to be great.

Attributed to de Tocqueville by Dwight D. Eisenhower in his final campaign address in Boston, Mass., Nov. 3, 1952.

It manifests God's invisible "presence of God among us" by certain signs; for example, wherever people:

1. *love one another*
2. *forgive one another*
3. *carry one another's burdens*
4. *work together for peace on earth*

It manifests its presence whenever and wherever people proclaim the Good News and—with the help of God's grace—live their lives according to God's will. It is a thing of the heart.

Revealed

CLARIFY—The Church was revealed to the world on Pentecost. We might compare that incredible moment as the emerging of the embryonic child (embryonic Church) from the womb. Pentecost is the "birthday" of the Church. With the coming of the Spirit on Pentecost, the Church becomes the seed, sign, and the instrument which will effect the "ultimate coming" of God's Kingdom on earth.

Perfected

The Church and the Kingdom of God will reach perfection when Jesus returns to lead into the presence of the Father in heaven.

Unfinished Work

QUESTION **4** ***What have you done to work for the Church's completion? What are you doing now? What ought you do in the future?***

■ *Two points that should be covered in the discussion are: (1) live according to Jesus' teaching, and (2) discern your gifts and ask the Holy Spirit's guiding as to how to use them for the benefit of the Kingdom.*

Up Close & Personal

CLARIFY—Alexis de Tocqueville was amazed to see how American people helped one another and organized all kinds of volunteer organizations to meet social needs. He said he "did not know ten men in all of France who would do what ordinary Americans do daily, as a matter of course."

Models of the Church

Ask the students: Explain the last line of Saxe's poem about the blind men:

Though each was partly in the right,
They all were in the wrong.

■ *Each man was in the right about the part of the elephant they observed. But they were all wrong about the whole of the elephant. Only by dialoguing with one another could the blind men get a better idea of what an elephant is like. But even then, given their blindness, their view will leave a lot to be desired.*

SHARE YOUR **meditation**

A girl said,
I find it hard to believe
that the Church is Christ's Body
when I see
how some Christians act.

A friend said,
I felt the same way
until I recalled that
I shouldn't blame Beethoven
because of how some musicians
play his music.

■ ***What is the friend's point?***

its tusk and says it looks like a sword. A sixth feels its leg and says it looks like a tree trunk. The poem ends:

And so these men of Indostan
Disputed loud and long.
Each in his own opinion
Exceedingly stiff and strong.
Though each was partly in the right,
They all were in the wrong.

5 ***How are the blind men trying to describe the elephant like people in the world trying to describe the Church?***

Because the Church is a many-sided reality, it can't be described in simple terms. This explains why theologians use models to describe the Church. A *model* is an image that helps us to better understand a complex reality.

Theologians are not the only ones who use models. Scientists also use them. For example, no scientist has ever seen the complex reality known as the electron.

The word "electron" is simply a name scientists give to a consistent set of events that happen in certain circumstances.

In dealing with the electron, scientists sometimes use a *wave* as their model and sometimes a particle. What they can't explain by one model, they can usually explain by the other.

Traditionally, Christians have used three models to help us get a better understanding of the Church. Drawn from Scripture, and mirroring the Trinity, they are:

- ***People of God***
- ***Body of Christ***
- ***Temple of the Spirit***

Let us take a closer look at each one of these three models:

People of God

A persecution left a large area of Guatemala without priests in 1980. The Catholics in this area, however, continued to gather in their village churches to pray, read Scripture, and share their faith.

Once a month they sent someone to a distant part of Guatemala (where priests still functioned) to bring back the Eucharist.

Saint Peter's Basilica, Rome, Italy.

106 STAGE 1: CHAPTER 8

QUESTION **5** ***How are the blind men trying to describe the elephant like people in the world trying to describe the Church?***

■ *We get it from our experiences with the leaders and members of the local Church. If our experiences are good, our view will be good. Thus, our limited view of the Church is like each blind man's limited view of the elephant.*

***DISCUSS*—Ask the students: How can we keep from making the mistake that the blind men made?"**

■ *First of all, we should realize that our viewpoint of the Church is terribly limited. Prejudging the Church on the basis of such a limited view is folly.*

Second, we should go to Scripture to see what it says about the Church. There we find a variety of models. Three essential models stand out:

1 *People of God*
2 *Body of Christ*
3 *Temple of the Spirit*

Here we need to keep in mind that Jesus used many models or images to describe the Kingdom of God: a tiny seed that grows into a great tree. MATTHEW 13:31–32, *a tiny bit of yeast that makes a large batch of dough rise* MATTHEW 13:3, *a pearl that a merchant finds and sells all to purchase.* MATTHEW 13:45–46

Jesus' use of many images to describe the Kingdom illustrates an important point about models. They must be used in clusters, never alone. Models are like viewpoints. If you rely on just one, it could be limiting or misleading (blind men and elephant). Here are two examples of misleading viewpoints (by experts):

Before 1960 there were virtually no "blocked shots" in basketball. When Bill Russell first started "blocking shots," his coach said his defensive style was "fundamentally unsound." Today, the blocked shot is universally accepted as a defensive move.

The Chicago Sun-Times *commented on Lincoln's* Gettysburg Address *as follows: "The cheek of every American must tingle with shame as he reads the silly, flat, and dishwatery utterance." Today, the* Gettysburg Address *is considered one of the greatest speeches in history.*

Share Your **meditation**

QUESTION ***What is the friend's point?***

■ *Beethoven's Ninth Symphony is one of the greatest pieces of music. Yet if we heard it played by a bunch of amateurs with squeaky violins and out-of-tune horns, we would probably say it was awful. Applying this to the Church, it is folly to condemn the Church because of "amateur" Christians who wreck it.*

NOTES

The Guatemalan communities illustrate the most basic model of the Church: the "People of God." It is an "assembly" of Jesus' followers who gather in Jesus' name to witness to their common faith that "Christ has died, Christ is risen, Christ will come again."

The Guatemalan communities recall the very early Christian community described in the Acts of the Apostles. ACTS 2:44–47 Christians become members of the "People of God," not by physical birth, but by spiritual birth—faith in Christ and baptism into his Body. CCC 781–86

Peter addresses a community of the "People of God" in these exciting words:

You are the chosen race,
the King's priests, the holy nation,
God's own people, chosen to proclaim
the wonderful acts of God,
who called you out of darkness
into his own marvelous light.
At one time you were not God's people,
but now you are. 1 PETER 2:9–10

This brings us to a second biblical image of the Church:

Body of Christ

Saint Paul had come from Tarsus to Jerusalem to study under the great Jewish rabbi Gamaliel. Shortly after his arrival, he witnessed the stoning of Stephen, the first Christian martyr. ACTS 7:57–58

This episode fueled his opposition to Christianity. He sought and got authority from Jewish leaders to track down and arrest Christians.

Going from house to house,
he dragged out the believers, both men
and women, and threw them in jail.
ACTS 8:3

One day, Paul was riding to Damascus to arrest Christians. Suddenly, a light flashed and he fell to the road unable to see. A voice said:

"Saul, Saul! Why do you persecute me?"
"Who are you, Lord?" he asked.
"I am Jesus, whom you persecute. . . .

"Get up and go into the city,
where you will be told what you
must do . . ."

Saul got up from the ground
And opened his eyes,
but he could not see a thing.

So they took him by the hand
and led him into Damascus. ACTS 9:4–8

As Saul groped along in total darkness, he was confused. What did the voice mean? He and his companions were not persecuting Jesus, only his followers. Slowly, the meaning of Jesus' words dawned upon him. After his conversion to Christianity, Paul wrote:

We are one body in union with Christ. . . .
He is the head of his body, the church;
he is the source of the body's life.
ROMANS 12:5, COLOSSIANS 1:8

All of us . . . have been baptized
into the one body by the same Spirit.
1 CORINTHIANS 12:13

The Church as the body of Christ focuses on this great mystery: Christ and his followers form one body. His followers are the members of the body and Christ himself is their head and source of life.

PRAYER hotline

LORD, teach us that we need the Church, the Church needs us, and the world needs both of us.

STAGE 1: *CHAPTER 8* **107**

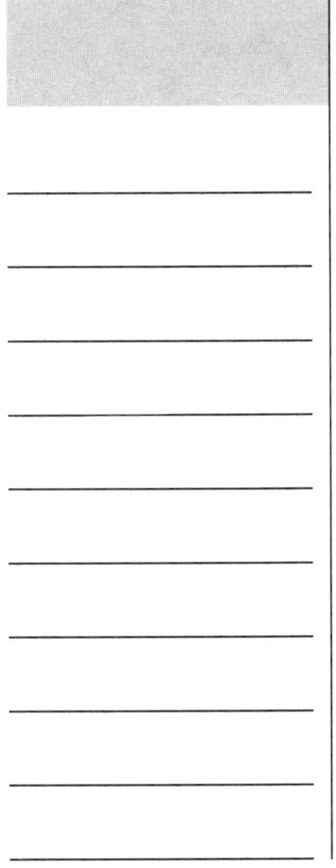

Use this question as an opportunity to say a few words about the brilliant composer. Ludwig van Beethoven (1770–1827. The son of an alcoholic father, he lost his hearing at age twenty-eight. When he conducted the first performance of his Ninth Symphony, he could not actually hear the music as it was played. He could only hear it in his imagination.

People of God

CLARIFY—If you wish to know the heart and soul of another, you must either become his close friend or trust someone who is. So it is in knowing Jesus.

The New Testament was written by a community of a "People of God" who knew Jesus intimately. Jesus revealed himself to them in a deeply personal way. He made them his witnesses: "You are to bear witness because from the beginning you are with me." JOHN 15:27

The inner secrets of Jesus' heart and soul were entrusted to the early Christian community. We must either trust them or have Jesus lost forever.

To accept Jesus in isolation from his followers, the early "People of God," would be unthinkable. It would be to isolate yourself from the source of knowledge about Jesus. It would be to do something that Jesus never intended.

There can be no true portrait of Jesus except that based on the witness of his early followers. Faith in Jesus involves faith in the early Christian community, who walked with him, listened to him, and knew him as no one ever did.

We sometimes forget that the Christian community that knew Jesus authored the New Testament. It is our continuity with them that we can never forget or sever.

From this point of view, it is folly for people to say, "I follow Jesus in my own way. I don't need a Church (the People of God) to tell me what to do or to interpret the Scriptures for me."

PRAYER hotline

DISCUSS—Ask the students: In what sense: (a) do we need the Church? (b) does the Church need us? (c) does the world need both of us?

Body of Christ

NOTEBOOK—With help from the students, develop the following diagram on the chalkboard entry in their notebooks:

Church —
- *Is a living organism: Body of the Risen Christ*
- *As Jesus shared the Father's life, we share Jesus' life*

NOTEBOOK—With the help of students, develop the following parallel between the way Jesus preached, healed, and forgave in Gospel times and how he continues to do those same things today.

Gospel times — *Jesus acted through the physical actions of his historical body.*

Today — *Jesus continues to act through liturgical actions*[1] *of his mystical body.*

[1] The word *liturgical* refers to the Church *praying* and *worshiping*. For all practical purposes, the words *liturgical* and *sacramental* are interchangeable here.

Temple of the Spirit

NOTEBOOK—A comparison that the students would easily understand is Saint Augustine's. Put the following diagram on the chalkboard for entry into notebooks.

Soul / *Human Body* = *Holy Spirit* / *Body of Christ*

Soul/Holy Spirit —
- *Permeate the body*
- *Unify the body*
- *Enliven the body*

QUESTION **6 *Which of the three images of the Church—People of God, Body of Christ, or Temple of the Holy Spirit—appeals to you most and why?***

DISCUSS*—This is the kind of question that could be handled out loud in the group. Or it can be written out and discussed in groups of three or four. The better choice and explanation of the group discussion could then be shared with the entire class.*

Marks of the Church

DISCUSS—Ask the students: If CNN took one of its two-minute breaks during its "Headline News" and a friend asked you to use the break to summarize what Catholics believe, could you do it?"

■ *The fact of the matter is, you could do it. Moreover, you'd have time enough left to get a soft drink from the refrigerator. How so? Simply recite the* Apostles' Creed.

It is made up of 12 articles (statements), that outline and summarize faith of the twelve Apostles. It did not originate—as some have suggested—with each Apostle contributing one article. Rather, it originated in the early centuries of Christianity in Rome as a profession of faith by converts about to receive Baptism.

A longer and more detailed creed is the Nicene Creed.

DISCUSS—Ask the students when and where it is usually recited.

■ *Each Sunday at Mass by the community right after the homily. More detailed than the Apostles' Creed, it dates back to* A.D. *325 and the ecumenical Council of Nicaea (Asia Minor). It is*

NOTES

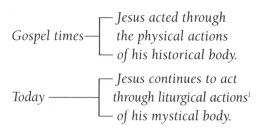

Organizational Connection

Vatican City is a tiny, independent state located inside the city of Rome. It has the status of a nation and a full diplomatic corps. Headed up by the pope, the "Vatican" is the seat of the world Catholic community.

Like other leaders, the pope has a "cabinet" to assist him. Called the Curia, its departments are usually headed by a bishop or cardinal. "Cardinal" is an honorary title given to a bishop who has distinguished himself.

A duty of the "College of Cardinals" is to elect the pope.

Another honorary title is that of "Monsignor," usually given to a priest who has distinguished himself.

A simplified organizational chart of the Church might look like this:

Parish—served by a pastor and a staff of ordained and lay associates.

Diocese—cluster of parishes, served by a bishop and a staff of ordained and lay associates.

Archdiocese—cluster of dioceses, overseen by an archbishop.

The Church, under the image of the body of Christ, underscores this incredible reality: As Jesus shared his Father's life, the Church shares Jesus' life. Jesus said:

"I am the vine, and you are the branches.
Those who remain in me, and I in them
will bear much fruit;
for you can do nothing without me."
JOHN 15:5

This brings us to a final biblical image of the Church, which rounds out its trinitarian dimension.

Temple of the Spirit

In one of his homilies, Saint Augustine, the bishop of Hippo in Africa, said:

What the soul is to the human body,
the Holy Spirit is to the Body of Christ,
which is the Church.

The soul permeates, unites, and enlivens every part of the human body. In the same way the Holy Spirit permeates, unites, and enlivens every part of the Body of Christ, forming it into the Spirit's own Temple. CCC 797–801

Paul wrote to the Church at Corinth, "You are God's temple." 1 CORINTHIANS 3:16 He spelled out this image more completely in his letter to the Church at Ephesus, saying:

You are . . . built upon the foundation
laid by the apostles and prophets,
the cornerstone being Christ Jesus himself.
He is the one
who holds the whole building together
and makes it grow into a sacred temple
dedicated to the Lord.
EPHESIANS 2:19–21

6 *Which of the three images of the Church—People of God, Body of Christ, or Temple of the Holy Spirit—appeals to you most and why?*

Marks of the Church

Father Walter Cizsek was arrested in Russia during World War II. He spent twenty-three years in prison. After his release, he wrote a book entitled *He Leadeth Me*.

In it he describes how a tiny community of Catholic prisoners used to gather in secret to celebrate the Eucharist "in drafty storage shacks, or huddled together in mud and slush in the corner of a building."

At this Mass, they prayed the same Creed that we pray at each Sunday Mass. We pray: "We believe in *one, holy, catholic*, and *apostolic* Church." These four marks describe the Church's calling.

First, it is to be *one*. It is called to "unity." CCC 813–22 Jesus prayed for us to his Father, saying: "May they be in us, just as you are in me and I am in you. May they be one, so that the world will believe that you sent me." JOHN 17:21

7 *What keeps you from feeling a greater unity with the Church?*

Second, the Church is called to be *holy* because its head is "the Holy One." But its members are still struggling to become holy, including its ministers. CCC 823–29 All must admit they are sinners. 1 JOHN 1:8–10

8 *Can you recall a parable that Jesus used to illustrate the point that the Church will be a mixture of good and bad people until the end of the world?*

Third, the Church is *catholic* in the sense of being *total and universal*. It is *total* in that Jesus gave it the total means of salvation. It is universal in the sense that it carries these means to all nations. CCC 830–36

Finally, the Church is *apostolic*. It traces its origin to the apostles. The bishops are the successors of the apostles; and the bishop of Rome (pope) is Peter's successor. Under the Spirit's guidance, the bishops preserve and proclaim the teachings given them. CCC 857–62

Mystery of the Church

The Church is a mystery of the Trinity's love. Unlike any other community on earth, the Church, mirroring Christ (whose body is the Church), has two dimensions:

- ***A divine dimension***
- ***A human dimension***

The divine dimension is invisible. It is none other than Christ himself, who is the head and the life of his body, the Church.

The human dimension is visible. It is the members of the Church. By our witness and worship, we make Christ visibly present and active in the world.

The human dimension of the Church is like everything human: flawed. This includes not only its membership, but also its leadership. Because of this, it does not always show the "face of Christ" to the world as it should.

In other words, the Church is not unlike each one of us. It, too, is vulnerable to sin and still struggling to be what God called it to be.

As a result, the Church in its pilgrimage on earth will always be a mixture of light and darkness. There will always be enough light for those who wish to see and enough darkness for those whose disposition is otherwise. This is how it should be. The light should never overpower us. It should only invite us. That is, it should never take away our freedom.

Or to put it another way: When it comes to Jesus' presence in the Church, it will never be revealed so clearly as to leave us without questions. Nor will it be concealed so completely as to mislead the sincere searcher. It leaves open both possibilities. Jesus respects our freedom to accept or reject him.

9 *Explain why it is fitting that the light should not overpower us, but leave us with a certain number of questions.*

THINK about it

It is impossible for the Church to remain on its feet if it doesn't get on its knees.

E.C. McKenzie

STAGE 1: *CHAPTER 8* **109**

accepted by all Catholics and many Protestant churches.

***NOTEBOOK*—List the following on the chalkboard for entry into the students' notebooks. The four marks are:**

One	*We are one body for we share one loaf.* 1 CORINTHIANS 10:17
Holy	*Keep yourselves holy, for I am holy.* LEVITICUS 11:44
Catholic	*Go to all peoples; teach and baptize them.* MATTHEW 28:19
Apostolic	*Your faith rests on the Apostles' faith.* EPHESIANS 2:20

Paul alludes to the marks of the Church when he writes to Church members at Ephesus:

You, too, are built upon the foundation laid by the apostles [apostolic] and prophets, the cornerstone being Christ Jesus himself. He is the one who holds the whole building together and makes it grow into a sacred [holy] temple dedicated to the Lord. In union [one] with him you too are being built together with all [catholic] the others into a place where God lives through his Spirit. EPH. 2:20–22

QUESTION **7 *What keeps you from feeling a greater unity with the Church?***

As a "birth family" grows in "unity" by working, playing, praying together, so does a "faith family." Involvement is the key to building and experiencing unity.

QUESTION **8 *Can you recall a parable Jesus used to illustrate the point that the Church will be a mixture of good and bad people until the end of the world?***

1 *Weeds and wheat* *Mt. 13:24–30, 36–43*
2 *Net* *Mt. 13:47–50*

Mystery of the Church

***NOTEBOOK*—Develop the following on the chalkboard for entry into notebooks:**

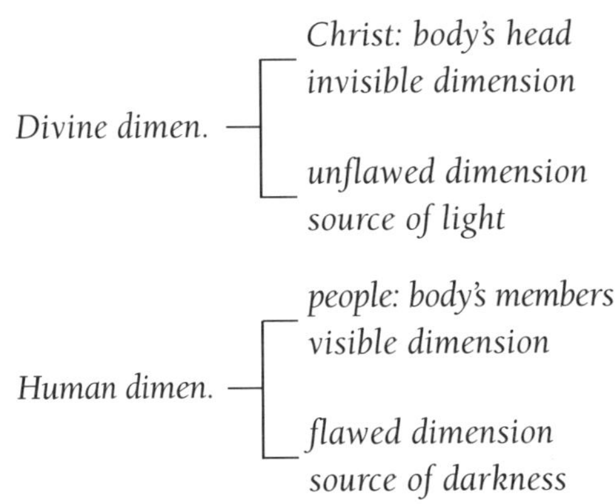

QUESTION **9 *Explain why it is fitting that the light should not overpower us, but leave us with a certain number of questions.***

The greatest respect I can tender another is to respect their freedom and not lean on them or coerce them in any way.

Recap

It is absolutely essential that the students see the parallel between Jesus and the Church:

Just as Jesus acted in Gospel times through the *physical* actions of his *historical* body, so the Church acts in our time through the *liturgical* actions of his *mystical* body.

It is absolutely essential also that the students realize that, just as Jesus had a *human* dimension and a *divine* dimension, so the Church is composed of these same two dimensions.

Jesus, in his *human* dimension, got cold, hungry, and weary. He also got discouraged and physically sick. In a similar way, the human dimension of the Church goes through the same trials.

Concerning the *divine* dimension of the Church, there will always be enough light for those who wish to see and enough darkness for those whose disposition is otherwise.

Recap

The Trinity's plan for the Church unfolded in five stages. It was:

- ***Foreshadowed in creation***
  Seed
- ***Prepared for by the Old Covenant***
  Stem
- ***Instituted by Jesus***
  Bud
- ***Revealed by the Spirit***
  Flower
- ***Perfected in Glory***
  Fruit

Three biblical images help to give us a clear picture of the Church's trinitarian, orientation, nature, and mission:

- ***People of God***
- ***Body of Christ***
- ***Temple of the Spirit***

The Church bears four distinguishing marks of identity. It is:

- **One**
- **Holy**
- **Catholic**
- **Apostolic**

Finally, the Church is different from every other community on earth. It has both:

- **A divine dimension**
- **A human dimension**

Because of its human dimension, the Church is not unlike each one of us. It, too, is vulnerable to sin and still struggling to be what God called it to be.

As a result, the Church in its pilgrimage on earth will always be a mixture of:

- **Light**
- **Darkness**

There will always be enough light for those who wish to see and enough darkness for those whose disposition is otherwise.

Review

1 List and briefly explain (a) the five stages of the Trinity's plan for the Church, (b) how the five stages of the Trinity's plan parallel the five stages of a plant's growth.

2 List and briefly explain three biblical images of the Church that highlight its Trinitarian dimension.

3 List and briefly explain the four marks of the Church.

4 Explain in what sense the Church (a) mirrors Christ, whose body it is, (b) will always be a mixture of light and darkness.

5 Identify: (a) Vatican City, (b) Curia, (c) Cardinal, (d) bishop, (e) monsignor, (f) priest, (g) diocese, and (h) archdiocese.

110 STAGE 1: CHAPTER 8

Review

DAILY QUIZ—Just a reminder: review questions may be assigned (one or two at a time) for homework or a daily quiz.

CHAPTER TESTS—Reproducible chapter tests are found in Appendix A. For consistency and ease in grading, quizzes are restricted to (1) "Matching," (2) "True/False," and (3) "Fill in the Blanks."

TEST ANSWERS—The following are the answers to the test for Chapter 8. (See Appendix A, page 319.) Each correct answer worth 4 points.

Matching

1 = j	2 = i	3 = c	4 = f
5 = h	6 = d	7 = a	8 = e
9 = b	10 = g		

True/False

1 = T	2 = F	3 = T	4 = T	5 = T

Fill in the Blanks

1. (a) Soul
   (b) Holy Spirit
2. (a) People of God
   (b) Body of Christ
   (c) Temple of Spirit
3. (a) Prepared for
   (b) Instituted
   (c) Spirit
   (d) Human
   (e) Divine

NOTES

Reflect

1 When eighty-four-year-old Dorothy Day died in 1980, the *New York Times* praised her as one of the truly great Christians of our time. She became a Catholic in her adult years and worked among New York's poor.

In her autobiography, *The Long Loneliness*, Dorothy said that the "human" dimension of the Church was often a scandal to her. Yet she loved the Church's "human" dimension because it made Christ visible to her. She compared the "human" dimension of the Church to the cross on which Christ was crucified, saying, "You can never separate Christ from his cross."

- ***Why do you agree/disagree with her on the two points relating to the Church's human dimension?***
- ***How does Jesus' Parable of the Weeds and the Wheat** Matthew 13:24–30 **help us understand why there is scandal in the Church and always will be?***
- ***What is one thing about the Church you find to be a scandal? How do you cope with it?***

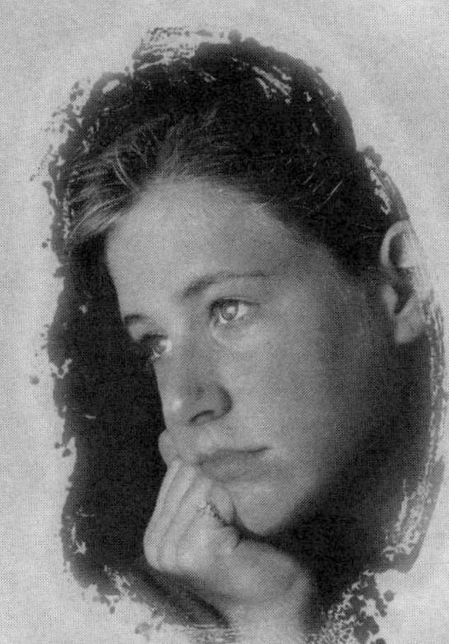

2 Martin Luther King Jr. wrote a famous letter while confined in the Birmingham City Jail. Referring to the early Church, he said:

In those days, the Church was not merely
a thermometer that recorded ideas
and principles of popular belief;
it was a thermostat that transformed
the mores of society.

If the Church of today does not recapture
the sacrificial spirit of the early Church,
it will lose its authentic ring,
forfeit the loyalty of millions,
and be dismissed
as an irrelevant social fan club
with no meaning for the twentieth century.

- ***Explain (a) thermostat, (b) thermometer.***
- ***In what sense did Jesus intend his Church to be a thermostat?***
- ***What is one thing the Church might do to regain its sacrificial spirit and authentic ring?***

3 A survey shows that forty percent of Catholics between the ages of 15 and 29 stop practicing their faith for a period of two years or more. Seventy percent of these return to the Church. Sixty percent of those who return do so because of the positive influence of a friend, relative, or neighbor.

- ***On a scale of one (rarely) to ten (regularly), grade the frequency of your participation in the celebration of Sunday Mass. Explain.***
- ***On a scale of one to ten, grade and explain your involvement in youth activities in your parish.***

Reflect

1 a) ***Why do you agree/disagree with her on the two points relating to the Church's human dimension?***

b) ***How does Jesus' Parable of the Weeds and the Wheat** MATTHEW 13:24–30 **help us to understand why there is scandal in the Church and always will be?***

Ask: Where did we meet Dorothy Day before? ("Up Close & Personal" page 11.)

- *Dorothy Day's point is that, in spite of its bad points, the Church is the way Jesus makes himself present in the world.*
- *Jesus' Parable of the Weeds and the Wheat tells us that "good" and "bad" will be found side by side in the Church right up until the end of the world.*

c) ***What is one thing about the Church you find to be a scandal? How do you cope with it?***

Have the students respond in writing. Collect the responses, check them, and present the better ones for discussion in the next class session.

2 a) ***Explain (a) thermostat, (b) thermometer.***

b) ***In what sense did Jesus intend his Church to be a thermostat?***

A thermostat controls temperature, while temperature controls a thermometer.

Ask the students: Was Jesus a thermostat or a thermometer? Explain how does this shed light on what Jesus intended his Church to be? Give examples.

c) ***What is one thing the Church might do to regain its sacrificial spirit and authentic ring?***

When a reporter asked Mother Teresa, "What's wrong with the Church?" she said, "You and I, sir? We're the Church."
(SEE "THINK ABOUT IT," PAGE 109)

3 a) ***On a scale of one (rarely) to ten (regularly), grade your frequency of participation in the celebration of Sunday Mass. Explain.***

A student wrote: *I'd give myself a 7. When I was younger, my family went to church every week. As I got older, we stopped going—except on special days. Lately, I've been going much more often. My faith has always been in the searching phase. Recently, I've come to the conclusion that many of my questions can't be answered. So, I must put more trust in God. If I do, I have a feeling that my questions will be answered someday.*

The author wrote on the paper, "I wish everyone could say what you did. Your heart and instinct are good; it says a lot about you."

b) ***On a scale of one to ten, grade and explain your involvement in youth activities in your parish.***

PRAYER TIME with the Lord

QUESTION **_Send an e-mail to Jesus. Share with him three or four ideas that you think could help people better appreciate the Church today._**

ACTIVITY—*Before doing the e-mail, have the students review the "four marks" of the Church and have them say which mark applies to each of the five paragraphs of the prayer. (The categories are not air tight so allow for some differences of opinion.)*

One application is as follows:

> *Par.* **1**—*Church built on Peter the rock. The Church traces its origin to the apostles.*
> Mark = **Apostolic**
>
> *Par.* **2**—*Church is a community of many. Jesus said: "May they be one, so that the world will believe that you sent me.*
> Mark = **One**
>
> *Par.* **3**—*The Church proclaims the message of Jesus handed on to it by the Apostles.*
> Mark = **Apostolic**
>
> *Par.* **4**—*"All of us, though many, are one body, for we all share the same loaf."*
> Mark = **One**
>
> *Also, "Those who eat my flesh and drink my blood live in me, and I in them."* John 6:56
> Mark = **Holy**
>
> *Par.* **5**—*Church has as its mission to "Go to all peoples and make them disciples of Jesus; that is, bring them salvation.*
> Mark = **Catholic**

Just a reminder: **Have the students respond to the exercise at the end of the prayer on an 8 ½ x 11 sheet of punched paper. This will allow them to file it in their notebooks. Comment on the responses when you return them. Select and share the better ones with the class.**

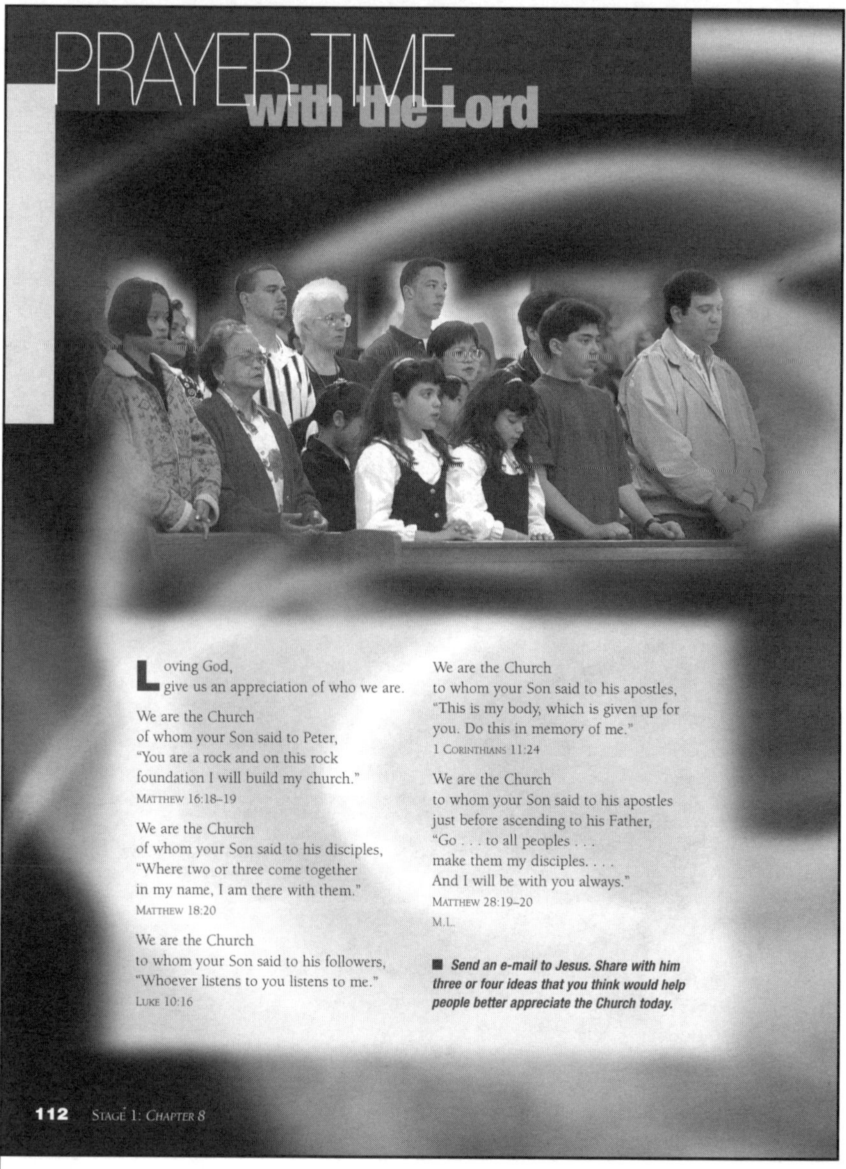

PRAYER TIME with the Lord

Loving God,
give us an appreciation of who we are.

We are the Church
of whom your Son said to Peter,
"You are a rock and on this rock
foundation I will build my church."
Matthew 16:18–19

We are the Church
of whom your Son said to his disciples,
"Where two or three come together
in my name, I am there with them."
Matthew 18:20

We are the Church
to whom your Son said to his followers,
"Whoever listens to you listens to me."
Luke 10:16

We are the Church
to whom your Son said to his apostles,
"This is my body, which is given up for
you. Do this in memory of me."
1 Corinthians 11:24

We are the Church
to whom your Son said to his apostles
just before ascending to his Father,
"Go . . . to all peoples . . .
make them my disciples. . . .
And I will be with you always."
Matthew 28:19–20
M.L.

■ ***Send an e-mail to Jesus. Share with him three or four ideas that you think would help people better appreciate the Church today.***

112 Stage 1: Chapter 8

PRAYER Journal

QUESTION **_Imagine that the Holy Father visited your city and you acted as spokesperson for its youth. Using the above statement as a model, write out what you would say._**

To get the students started you might share with them this response by a Chicago student.

> *Before I respond let me say something about the example of the spokesperson in Peru. I think the person was saying that even though the world may not care about them, God does. And the day will end—perhaps in eternity—when God will comfort them.*
>
> *I would make the following comments to the Holy Father:*

NOTES

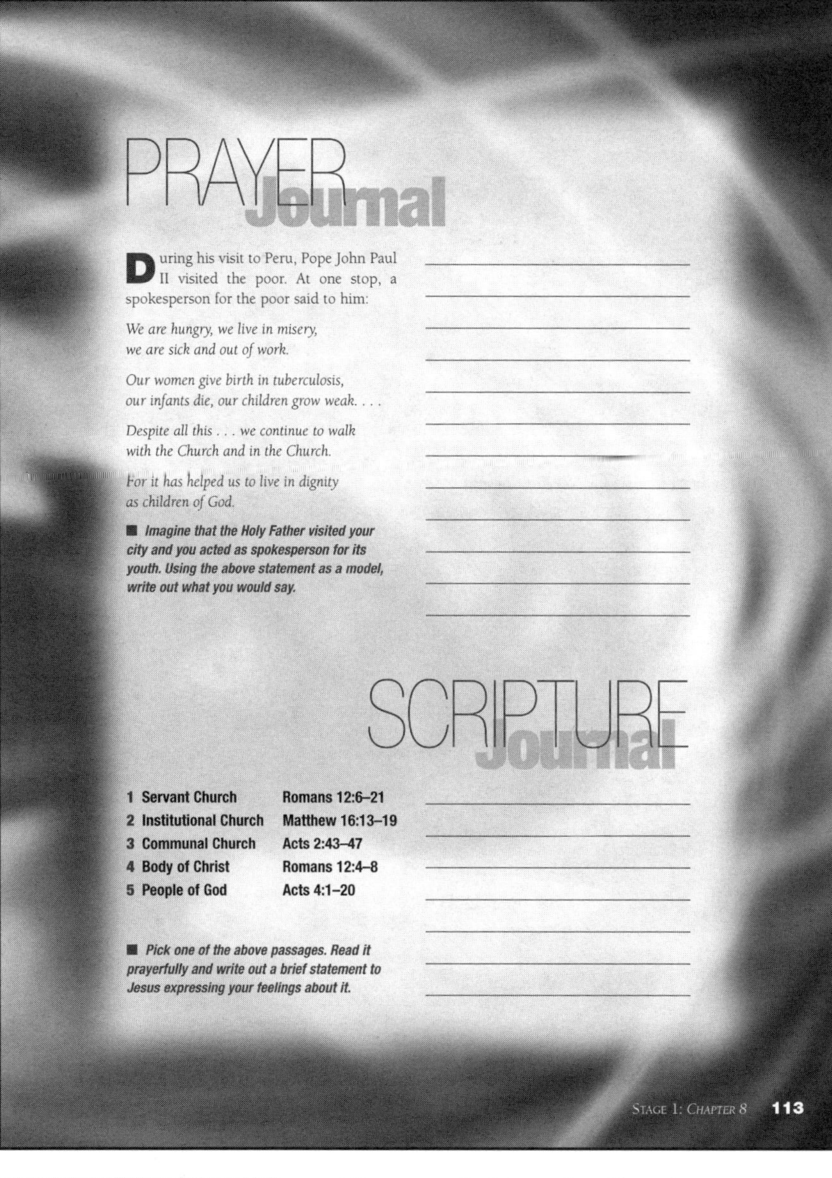

PRAYER Journal

During his visit to Peru, Pope John Paul II visited the poor. At one stop, a spokesperson for the poor said to him:

We are hungry, we live in misery,
we are sick and out of work.

Our women give birth in tuberculosis,
our infants die, our children grow weak. . . .

Despite all this . . . we continue to walk
with the Church and in the Church.

For it has helped us to live in dignity
as children of God.

■ ***Imagine that the Holy Father visited your city and you acted as spokesperson for its youth. Using the above statement as a model, write out what you would say.***

SCRIPTURE Journal

1 Servant Church	**Romans 12:6–21**
2 Institutional Church	**Matthew 16:13–19**
3 Communal Church	**Acts 2:43–47**
4 Body of Christ	**Romans 12:4–8**
5 People of God	**Acts 4:1–20**

■ ***Pick one of the above passages. Read it prayerfully and write out a brief statement to Jesus expressing your feelings about it.***

STAGE 1: CHAPTER 8 **113**

We are pulled into the Church,
but are, also, often pushed away.
Our elders want us to follow them,
but are often unwilling to lead.

We are a part of the Church,
but are often treated like outsiders.

We need to be listened to.
We need to be understood.
We have a lot to offer. We love Jesus too.

SCRIPTURE Journal

QUESTION ***Pick one of the passages. Read it prayerfully and write a short statement to Jesus expressing your feelings about it.***

Treat the exercises in this section as you do those in the "Prayer Journal."

Classroom Resources

CATECHISM

Catechism of the Catholic Church *Second Edition*

For further enrichment, you might refer to:

1. Church	Index	pp. 770–73
	Glossary	p. 871
2. People of God	Index	p. 833
	Glossary	p. 893
3. Body of Christ	Index	p. 833
	Glossary	p. 893

—Available from the United States Catholic Conference, Washington DC

CD-ROM

Dogmatic Constitution on the Church *(Lumen gentium)*

Pastoral Constitution on the Church in the Modern World *(Gaudium et spes)*

Constitution on the Sacred Liturgy

Chart of Church Structures

—Available on the *Welcome to the Catholic Church* CD-ROM from Harmony Media Inc., Cervails, OR

VIDEO

The Faithful Revolution

Five 60-minute videos and blackline masters. Beautifully and meaningfully captures the spirit and vision of Vatican II and what it means to be Church.
—Available from Thomas More Publishing, 1997, Allen, TX

BOOK

Catholic Customs and Traditions

Greg Dues

Engaging overview of how Catholics practice their faith.
—Available from Twenty-Third Publications, Rev. ed. 1993, Mystic, CT

NOTE

For a list of (1) General resources for professional background and (2) Addresses, phone/fax numbers of major publishing companies, see Appendix B of this Resource Manual.

STAGE 2 WORSHIP

We reach out to God

DISCUSS—Begin with the photo on page 115. Ask: Are the students "looking back" or "looking ahead"?

■ *Looking back: yearbooks.*

Ask: Why is it good to look back occasionally—especially on good times?

1 *It's enjoyable—Novelist James Matthew Barrie says: "God gives us memory so that we can have roses in December."*
2 *We learn from the past—Philosopher George Santyana says, "He who forgets the past is condemned to repeat it."*

LOOKING**Back**

DISCUSS—Have a student read the direction on page 114: "One time in my life when words couldn't express how I felt was . . ." To give them a start, share with them this answer Jimmy Cagney gave. (Who was he?)

When Jimmy's mother had a stroke, she lost the use of her left arm and speech, and was going downhill fast. She gathered her four sons and daughter Jeannie around her. After hugging each one separately, Jimmy writes:

■ *Mom indicated Harry*
with the index finger of her useless hand,
she indicated me with her second finger,
she indicated Eddie with the third,
and the fourth finger indicated Bill.

Then she took the thumb,
moved it to the middle of her palm,
and clasped the thumb tightly
under the other four fingers.
Then she patted this fist
with her good hand.

Ask the students: What was Jimmy's mother trying to say? Why was her wordless way of saying it more moving than had she written a note and had her children read it?

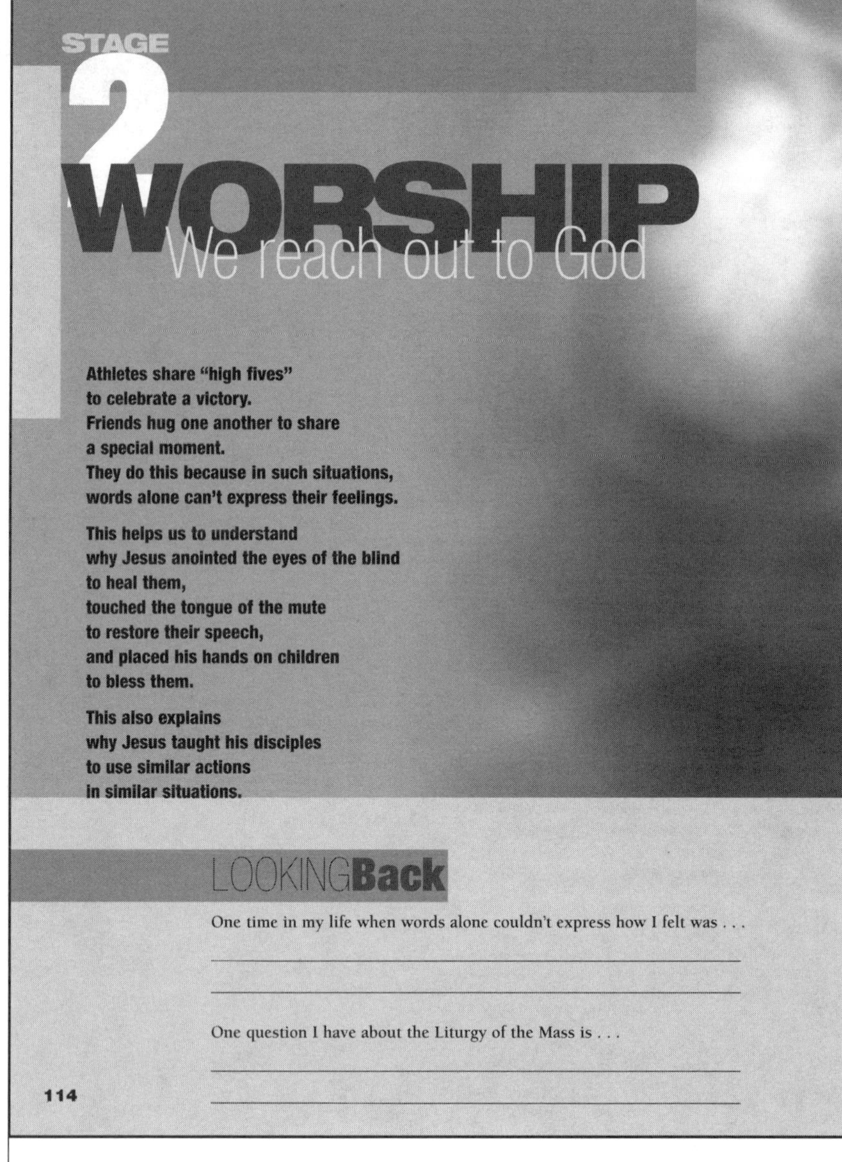

STAGE
2
WORSHIP
We reach out to God
Athletes share "high fives"
to celebrate a victory.
Friends hug one another to share
a special moment.
They do this because in such situations,
words alone can't express their feelings.
This helps us to understand
why Jesus anointed the eyes of the blind
to heal them,
touched the tongue of the mute
to restore their speech,
and placed his hands on children
to bless them.
This also explains
why Jesus taught his disciples
to use similar actions
in similar situations.
LOOKINGBack
One time in my life when words alone couldn't express how I felt was . . .
One question I have about the Liturgy of the Mass is . . .
114

■ *What?—She was saying to the boys, "Take care of Jeannie!"*
Why?—Her gesture showed her great heart and touched their hearts.

ACTIVITY—Give the students quiet time to let the story sink in and to prepare their own answers to the question. After they finish, have them share their responses in small groups and pick the best to share with the class.

DISCUSS—Take up the next direction: "One question I have about the liturgy of the Mass is . . ." To give the students a start, share with them this question:

Apart from the advantage of moving about, why do we sit at Mass sometimes, kneel at others, and stand at others?

NOTES

STAGE 1

WORD

1 Light of Faith
2 Divine Revelation
3 New Testament
4 Old Testament
5 God the Father
6 God the Son
7 God the Holy Spirit
8 The Church

STAGE 2

WORSHIP

9 Liturgy
10 Baptism
11 Confirmation
12 Eucharist
13 Reconciliation
14 Anointing of the Sick
15 Marriage
16 Holy Orders

STAGE 3

WITNESS

17 Praying
18 Choosing Love
19 Loving God
20 Loving Neighbor
21 Discerning Love
22 Witnessing to Love
23 Rejoicing in Love

LOOKING**Ahead**

Recall that our faith journey is divided into the following three stages:

- WORD — God reaches out to us. (Revelation)
- WORSHIP — We reach out to God. (Sacraments)
- WITNESS — We journey together. (Commandments)

In the first stage, we saw how the Holy Spirit formed Jesus' followers into the Body of Christ, the Church.

In this second stage, we will see how Jesus continues to heal, to forgive, and to teach people in our times just as he did in Gospel times.

115

Ask: How would you answer this question?

■ **1** *We sit (e.g, during the first two readings) to help us listen more carefully and reflect more deeply on God's Word.*
2 *We stand (e.g., for the Gospel and the Creed) to remind ourselves that this is what we Christians "stand for" and, if necessary, are willing to die for. ("If we don't stand for something, we end up falling for everything.")*
3 *We kneel (e.g, after returning from receiving the Body of Christ) to show special reverence and to facilitate prayer.*

LOOKING**Ahead**

CLARIFY—We've just finished "Stage 1," in which we explored the eight topics listed in the top right-hand corner of page 115. Stage 1 was titled: "Word: God reaches out to us" (Revelation). This title sums up the content of the stages: (1) God's revelation of himself and (2) God's plan for the world. Review the three words by which God revealed these great truths to us:

1	*Cosmic Word*	*Creation*
2	*Inspired Word*	*Scripture*
3	*Incarnate Word*	*Jesus*

First, the cosmic word (creation). *Just as the beauty of a song reveals something of its composer, so the beauty of creation reveals something of its Creator.*

Second, the inspired word (Scripture). *God spoke mainly though deeds. He didn't merely say, "Israel, I love you." God showed it through loving actions:*

The LORD says, "I was the one
who taught Israel to walk.
I took my people in my arms. . . .
I picked them up
and held them to my cheek;
I bent down to them and fed them."
HOSEA 11:3–4

Third, the Incarnate Word (Jesus).

He was the "Word of God made flesh." Jesus said, "Whoever has seen me has seen the Father." JOHN 14:9 *"He reflects the brightness of God's glory."* HEBREWS 1:3

We begin "Stage 2." It is entitled "Worship: We reach out to God" (Sacraments). The eight topics of this stage are listed in the middle of the right-hand column of page 115.

DISCUSS—Ask: In what sense do we reach out to God in "worship" and the "sacraments"?

■ *In the same sense that people in biblical times reached out to Jesus.*

1 *They came to listen to him and to learn about God and God's plan for us.*
2 *They came to receive forgiveness, healing, and nourishment.*
3 *They came to thank God for sending his Son into the world to teach us what is for our happiness.*

(Recall the story of the woman and the cold, confused geese in the snow, page 80.)

CHAPTER 9
Liturgy

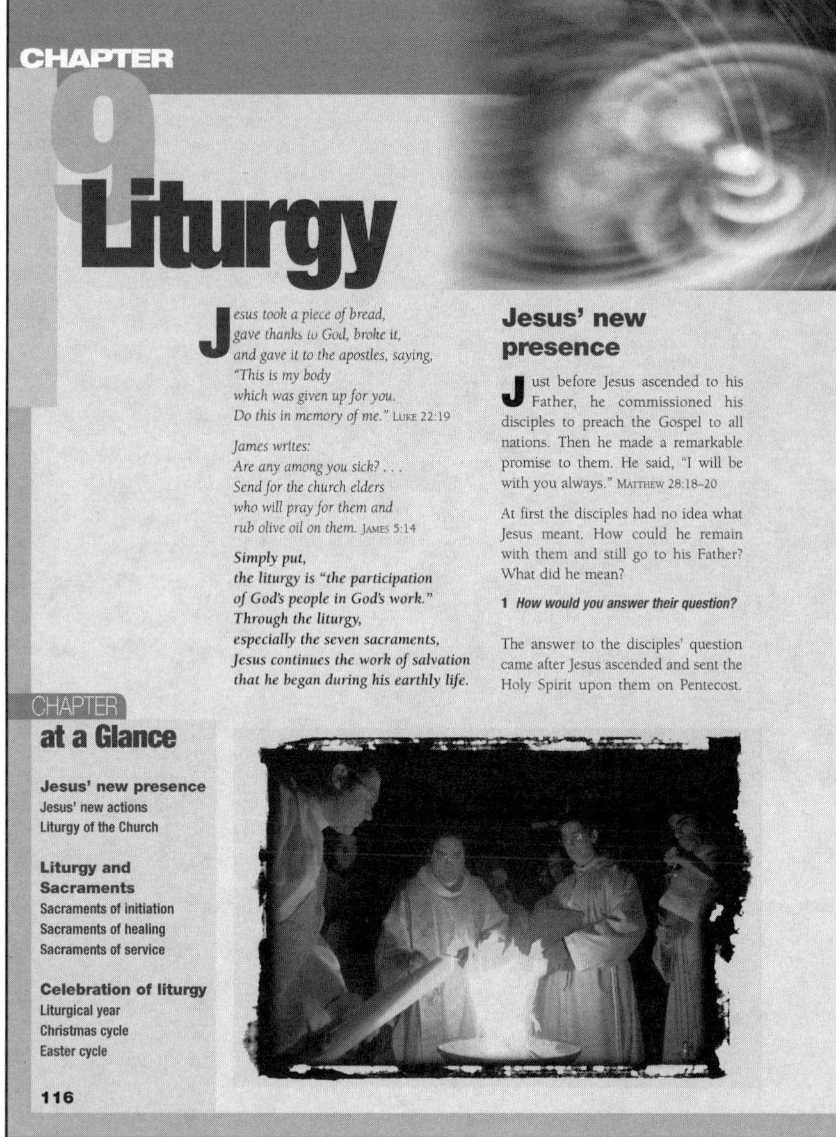

CHAPTER 9

Liturgy

Jesus took a piece of bread,
gave thanks to God, broke it,
and gave it to the apostles, saying,
"This is my body
which was given up for you.
Do this in memory of me." LUKE 22:19

James writes:
Are any among you sick? . . .
Send for the church elders
who will pray for them and
rub olive oil on them. JAMES 5:14

Simply put,
the liturgy is "the participation
of God's people in God's work."
Through the liturgy,
especially the seven sacraments,
Jesus continues the work of salvation
that he began during his earthly life.

Jesus' new presence

Just before Jesus ascended to his Father, he commissioned his disciples to preach the Gospel to all nations. Then he made a remarkable promise to them. He said, "I will be with you always." MATTHEW 28:18–20

At first the disciples had no idea what Jesus meant. How could he remain with them and still go to his Father? What did he mean?

1 ***How would you answer their question?***

The answer to the disciples' question came after Jesus ascended and sent the Holy Spirit upon them on Pentecost.

CHAPTER **at a Glance**

Jesus' new presence
Jesus' new actions
Liturgy of the Church

Liturgy and Sacraments
Sacraments of initiation
Sacraments of healing
Sacraments of service

Celebration of liturgy
Liturgical year
Christmas cycle
Easter cycle

116

CHAPTER at a Glance

The purpose of this chapter is to explain the "liturgy" in a personal, prayerful way. It is Jesus continuing to heal, forgive, and teach in our times, through the members of his "Church (mystical) Body."

DISCUSS—Have one student read the scriptural introduction, which begins: "Jesus took a piece of bread." Have a second student read the commentary, which begins: "Simply put, the liturgy is . . ."

Ask: In the first two paragraphs, (1) what two sacraments are referred to, and (2) how do you know it is these two sacraments?

1 *What?—The Eucharist and the Anointing of the Sick.*
2 *How?—They describe the "sacred action" (liturgy) of the sacrament.*

Jesus' new presence

DISCUSS—In his spiritual autobiography, ***How Christ Came to Church***, A. J. Gordon recounts a dream that affected his life deeply. Read it to the students.

■ *It was Sunday.*
Just as Gordon was starting to preach,
a stranger entered the Church.
All during the homily Gordon's eyes
kept drifting to the stranger.
He thought, "I must meet this person
after the service."

But after the service,
Gordon lost sight of him in the crowd.
He did, however, see the person
who sat next to him.
He said to the person,

"I'm sorry I missed the stranger
sitting next to you.
Do you know who it was?"
"Why yes," said the person.
"Didn't you recognize him? It was Jesus."

"Why didn't you detain him,"
said Gordon, "so I could speak with
him?" "Don't worry," said the person.
"He comes every Sunday; he'll be back."
RETOLD FROM A REFERENCE TO THIS EPISODE BY MORTON KELSEY IN *DREAMS*

Ask the students: Why do you think this dream had such an impact on the rest of Gordon's life?

■ *It dramatized in a vivid way*
what Jesus said in Matthew's Gospel:
"Where two or three come together
in my name, I am there with them." (16:20)

Ask the students: Is Jesus' presence as a member of the congregation (in Gordon's

NOTES

Some time after Pentecost, a persecution of Christians broke out.

One day, one of the leaders, Saul of Tarsus—also known as Paul—was traveling to Damascus to arrest some Christians.

Suddenly a light from the sky
flashed around him.
He fell to the ground and
heard a voice saying to him,
"Saul, Saul!
Why do you persecute me?"
"Who are you, Lord?" he asked.
"I am Jesus, whom you persecute,"
the voice said. ACTS 9:3–5

This experience converted Paul and made him a follower of Jesus. Later Paul wrote to other Christians:

We are one body
in union with Christ. . . .
He is the head
of his body the church;
he is the source of the body's life.
ROMANS 12:5, COLOSSIANS 1:18

Jesus' new actions

As the Christian community reflected upon this remarkable mystery, they began to realize something even more remarkable.

Jesus not only formed one body with them, but also began acting through them. The members of his Church body became his new arms and new voice, so to speak.

In other words, as Jesus once healed people through the members of his earthly body, he heals them now through the members of his Church body (*mystical* body). Through them he continues his work on earth.

Jesus' disciples now understood what Jesus meant when he said to them while still on earth, "Whoever listens to you listens to me." LUKE 10:16

2 In what sense do we listen to Jesus when we listen to his disciples?

Jesus' disciples now understood that when they teach in his name, it is not they who teach, but Jesus who teaches through them. When they heal in his name, it is not they who heal, but Jesus who heals through them.

An example of this mystery took place one day when a crippled beggar asked Peter and John for money. Peter said to him:

"I have no money at all,
but I give you what I have:
in the name of Jesus Christ . . .
I order you to get up and walk. . . ."
At once the man . . . started walking.
ACTS 3:6, 8

When the people saw this they stared in amazement at Peter. Peter said to them:

"Why do you stare at us?
Do you think that it was by means
of our own power . . . that we made
this man walk?" ACTS 3:12

Rather, said Peter, it was by the power of Jesus that this man is able to walk again.

And so, we come to this very remarkable conclusion. Beginning with Pentecost, Jesus not only becomes *present* in the world through his

dream) an accurate image of how Jesus is really present?

Technically, "No!" Jesus is present not as a "member" of the body, but as its "head."

QUESTION **1** ***How would you answer their question? (How Jesus could remain with us, and still return to the Father.)***

■ *This is a difficult question, even though it is an application of what was learned in chapter 8.*

The text following the question spells out the application. It recalls the story of Paul's Damascus experience.

This amazing experience revealed this great mystery: the Risen Jesus (in heaven) forms one body with his Church (on earth).

In this sense, Jesus "has gone to the Father in heaven," but " still remains on earth with us."

Jesus' new actions

QUESTION **2** ***In what sense do we listen to Jesus when we listen to his disciples?***

■ *This question takes the mystery of the Church a step further. It stresses that Jesus is not just "present" on earth through his body the Church, but also "acts" through its members.*

The text following question 2 drives home this point. It cites the episode of the healing of the beggar at the Temple door.

Peter and John were going to the Temple at "three o'clock in the afternoon, the hour of prayer. . . . A man who had been lame all his life . . . saw them . . . [and] begged them to give him something. ACTS 3:1–3

Then the beggar held out his cupped hands, "expecting to get something."

A long minute of silence ensued. Then Peter placed in the beggar's hands not a few coins, but a whole "new life from God."

The point of the healing of the beggar is that Jesus is not only *present* in his Church, but also *acts through its members*. Peter reinforces this point when people stare at him in disbelief after he heals the beggar. Peter says:

"Why do you stare at us?
Do you think that it was by means
of our own power . . .
that we made this man walk?" ACTS 3:12

Like so many people who ask God for something, God ends up giving the beggar something better than what he asked for.

Liturgy of the Church

CLARIFY—Stress this great mystery (It can't be stressed enough):

■ *Through the Church's liturgy, Christ continues the work of our salvation, which he began during his earthly ministry.*

NOTEBOOK—Recall this diagram from the last chapter. With the help of the students, reconstruct it again on the chalkboard. Have them re-enter it in their notebooks.

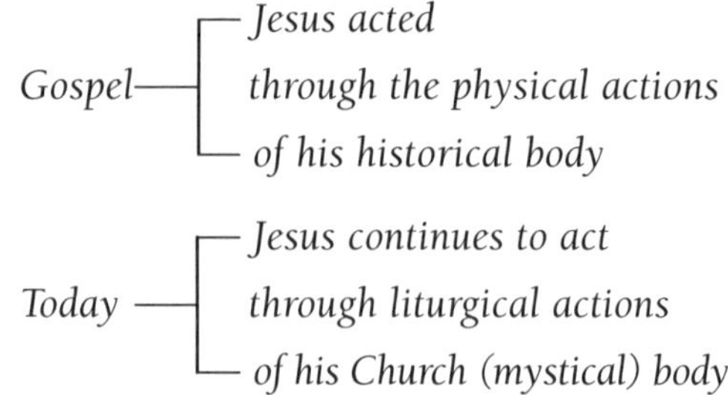
Gospel
Jesus acted
through the physical actions
of his historical body
Today
Jesus continues to act
through liturgical actions
of his Church (mystical) body

QUESTION **3** ***Why is the liturgy the most sacred action in the Church?***

■ *It is Christ himself acting through the members of his Church body, continuing the work of our salvation. Recall Saint Augustine's words a few paragraphs earlier, "When the Church baptizes, it is Christ himself who baptizes."*

FAITH
Connection

People look at us the rest of the week to see what we really meant by our worship together on Sunday.

Anonymous

Church body (mystical body) but also *acts* through it. Thus, Saint Augustine could say, "When the Church baptizes, it is Christ himself who baptizes."

Liturgy of the Church

In time, Christians gave a special name to the actions of Jesus' Church body. They called them *liturgical* actions.

Technically, the word *liturgy* means "the participation of God's People in God's work." Through the Church's *liturgy*, Christ continues the work of our salvation, begun during his earthly life. CCC 1069

No action of the Church is more sacred than the liturgy. CCC 1070

3 ***Why is the liturgy the most sacred action of the Church?***

And so on Pentecost, Jesus not only became *present* in the world in a new way (through his Church) but also began to *act* in the world in a new way (through its *liturgy*).

Liturgy and sacraments

Over the centuries the Church gradually discerned that *seven actions* of its liturgy surpassed all others.

It gave them the name *sacraments*. They may be grouped under the following three headings:

- **Sacraments of Initiation**
- **Sacraments of Healing**
- **Sacraments of Service**

The sacraments of initiation include Baptism, Confirmation, and the Holy Eucharist.

The sacraments of healing include Reconciliation and the Anointing of the Sick.

The sacraments of service include Marriage and Holy Orders.

4 ***In what sense do the sacraments under each group involve initiation, healing and service?***

118 STAGE 2: CHAPTER 9

Liturgy and Sacraments

CLARIFY—Over the centuries, the Church discerned that certain actions—baptizing, anointing the sick, and celebrating the Eucharist—are "special."

Jesus is present in these actions in a uniquely privileged way. And so his followers gave these actions a special name: *sacraments.*

Early Christians compared Baptism to the *sacramentum* (ritual by which recruits were initiated into the Roman army). Baptism (with Confirmation and the Eucharist) initiates us into Christ's body.

Early Christians also used the word *sacrament* in a "wide" sense; namely in anything that revealed God's presence in the world in a *tangible* way: a beautiful sunset, a loving parent. Eventually, however, the Church reserved the word exclusively for the "seven sacraments."

And so the word *sacrament* is not a word that Jesus used. It does not appear in the Bible. The word *Trinity* does not appear in the Bible either. These words simply evolved among Jesus' followers as a way to express certain mysterious realities and truths of their faith.

QUESTION **4** ***In what sense do the sacraments under each group involve initiation, healing, and service?***

■ *Skip this question, if you wish. Its purpose is simply to challenge the students to probe for the answers, which now follow under the next three headings.*

NOTES

Sacraments of initiation

The "sacraments of initiation" relate us to the Trinity in a remarkable new way. CCC 1123, 1212

Baptism gives the Trinity's divine life to us. Jesus said, "No one can enter the Kingdom of God without being born again of water and the Spirit. JOHN 3:5 Confirmation deepens the life of the Trinity within us.

Finally, the Eucharist nourishes the divine life. Jesus said, "If you do not eat the flesh of the Son of Man and drink his blood, you will not have life in yourselves." JOHN 6:53

Sacraments of healing

The "sacraments of healing" are exactly what they say. They restore, repair, and fortify divine life.

Reconciliation restores divine life when we have weakened or lost it through sin. CCC 1420–21

The Anointing of the Sick fortifies and strengthens our divine life against the vulnerabilities linked with illness or old age. CCC 1511, 1527

5 Give an example to illustrate how bodily illness or old age could leave us spiritually vulnerable.

Sacraments of service

The "sacraments of service" have as their purpose the growth and well-being of the Body of Christ and the spread of the Kingdom of God.

Marriage unites husband and wife in a union that mirrors the relationship of Christ with his Church. EPHESIANS 5:25, 32 It calls them and graces them to build up Christ's Body, the Church. CCC 1534

Holy Orders consecrates special members to serve the Church by teaching it, leading it in worship, and guiding it pastorally. CCC 1592

Definition of sacraments

We may define sacraments in the following fourfold manner. CCC 1131 They are:

- **Efficacious signs of grace**
- **Instituted by Christ**
- **Entrusted to his Church**
- **To give divine life to us**

First, they are *efficacious signs of grace* in that it is Christ himself who is present in them and acting through them.

THINK about it

Our redeemer's visible presence has passed into the sacraments.

Pope Saint Leo the Great

STAGE 2: CHAPTER 9 119

Sacraments of initiation

NOTEBOOK—Sum up how each sacrament initiates a Christian person into *spiritual* life:

Initiation — *Baptism* — *Communicates life*
Initiation — *Confirmation* — *Enriches life*
Initiation — *Eucharist* — *Nourishes life*

Sacraments of healing

NOTEBOOK—The following diagram sums up how each sacrament heals when spiritual life is lost or threatened. Have the students enter it in their notebooks.

Healing — *Reconciliation* — *Restores life*
Healing — *Anointing* — *Fortifies life*

QUESTION ***5 Give an example to illustrate how bodily illness or old age could leave us physically vulnerable.***

■ *Joseph Cardinal Bernardin of Chicago died on November 14, 1996, after a long bout with cancer. Describing his final days in* The Gift of Peace, *he said: "I was a bit taken aback when I realized that immediately after surgery I really didn't have the desire or strength to pray."*

Sacraments of service

NOTEBOOK—Sum up how each sacrament contributes to the spiritual life of Christ and the spread of God's Kingdom.

Service — *Marriage* — *Builds up and Spreads*
Service — *Orders* — *Ministers to pastorally*

THINK about it

DISCUSS—What point is Pope Saint Leo the Great making?

■ *The "visibility" of the person Jesus, who anointed the eyes of the blind and healed them, has now "passed into the sacraments." In other words, the sacramental "signs" are faith-evidence of the presence of Jesus acting through the sacraments in a sensible, symbolic way, as he did in Gospel times.*

Definition of sacraments

CLARIFY—Sacraments are "efficacious signs of grace."

1 Sacraments are "efficacious." They accomplish what they signify. Consider an example. A blinking light on the left rear of a car "signifies" that the car is going to turn left. The blinking light, however, does not turn the car. It is not "efficacious." The sacraments, on the other hand, accomplish what they signify. They are "efficacious." They really heal and forgive spiritually.

2 Sacraments are "signs" in a twofold sense. They have a "sensible" dimension and a "symbolic" dimension.

Take the use of water in Baptism. It has a "sensible" dimension (you can see it and feel it). It also has a "symbolic" dimension. It is life-giving and cleansing. (We need water to survive; it also washes and cleans things.) Thus, it is "symbolic" of the nature of Baptism, which is life-giving and cleansing spiritually. (It "communicates divine life" to us and "cleanses us from sin."

***NOTEBOOK*—**Have the students enter the following summary of the twofold nature of the sacramental sign in their notebooks:

Sign	*Sensible*	*Perceptible to senses*
	Symbolic	*Suggestive of nature of the sacrament*

3 Sacraments involve the communication of "grace." In the case of the sacraments, the grace (gift of God) involves the "life of God" in one form or another.

In conclusion, it is Christ himself who is present in the sacraments and acts through them in a *sensible, symbolic* way.

Or to put it in another way, the sacraments make present in a *sensible, symbolic* way the:

Life-giving power of God	*Baptism*
Forgiving power of God	*Reconciliation*
Healing power of God	*Anointing*

FAITH Connection

***CLARIFY*—**Recall the Letter of James, which says bluntly:

■ *What good is it for one of you*
to say that you have faith
if your actions do not prove it. . . .
Faith, if it is alone and
includes not actions is dead. 2:14, 17

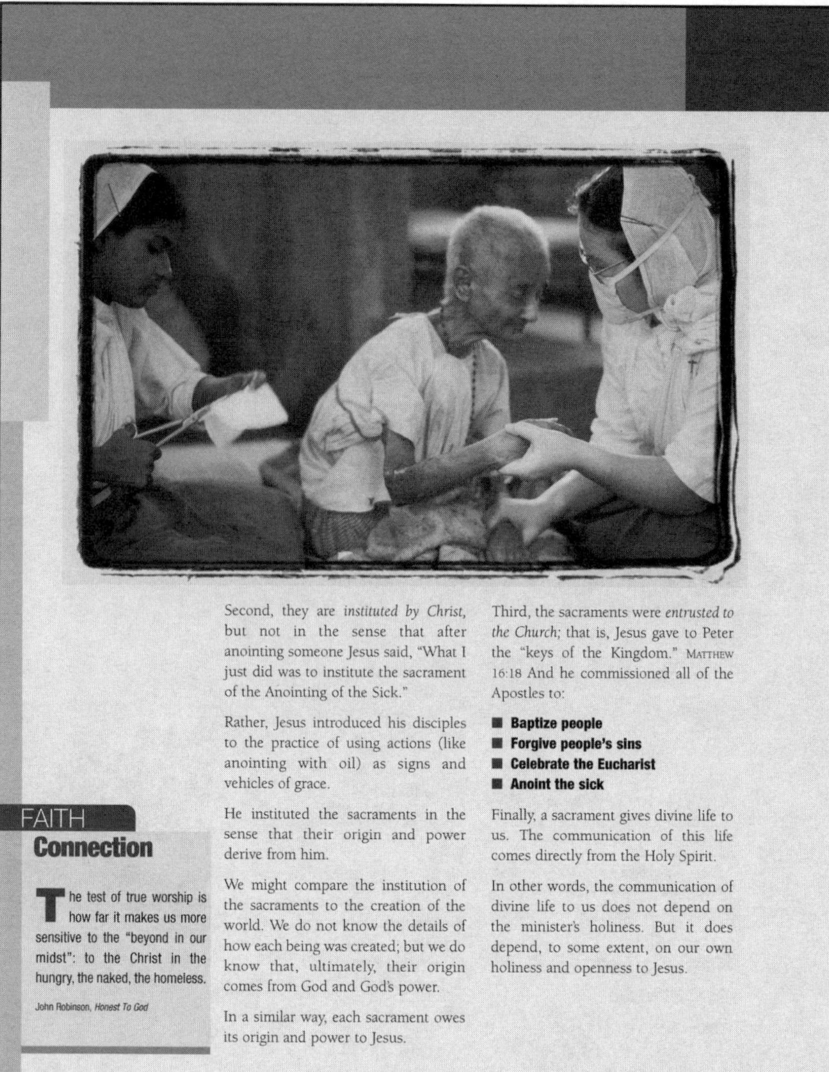

Second, they are *instituted by Christ,* but not in the sense that after anointing someone Jesus said, "What I just did was to institute the sacrament of the Anointing of the Sick."

Rather, Jesus introduced his disciples to the practice of using actions (like anointing with oil) as signs and vehicles of grace.

He instituted the sacraments in the sense that their origin and power derive from him.

We might compare the institution of the sacraments to the creation of the world. We do not know the details of how each being was created; but we do know that, ultimately, their origin comes from God and God's power.

In a similar way, each sacrament owes its origin and power to Jesus.

Third, the sacraments were *entrusted to the Church;* that is, Jesus gave to Peter the "keys of the Kingdom." MATTHEW 16:18 And he commissioned all of the Apostles to:

- **Baptize people**
- **Forgive people's sins**
- **Celebrate the Eucharist**
- **Anoint the sick**

Finally, a sacrament gives divine life to us. The communication of this life comes directly from the Holy Spirit.

In other words, the communication of divine life to us does not depend on the minister's holiness. But it does depend, to some extent, on our own holiness and openness to Jesus.

FAITH Connection

The test of true worship is how far it makes us more sensitive to the "beyond in our midst": to the Christ in the hungry, the naked, the homeless.

John Robinson, *Honest To God*

120 STAGE 2: CHAPTER 9

***CLARIFY*—**The sacraments were "instituted by Christ."

Stress the point that at the Last Supper, Jesus did not conclude by saying, "What I have just done here tonight is to institute the most important sacrament of all, the Eucharist." Rather, Jesus did and said the following:

■ *He took a piece of bread,*
gave thanks to God, broke it,
and gave it to his disciples, saying,
"This is my body
which will be given up for you.
Do this in memory of me."

In the same way,
he gave them the cup after supper, saying,
"This cup is God's new covenant
sealed with my blood,
which is poured out for you." LUKE 22:19–21

NOTES

Up Close & Personal

Celebration of liturgy

Elie Wiesel's story *The Town Beyond the Wall* deals with the power of friendship. In one episode Michael survives a period of torture because Pedro, his absent friend, lives on in his memory.

The power of the friendship flows not from Pedro directly, but from Michael's memory of him. This touches on a profound biblical truth. Henri Nouwen expresses it this way in his book *The Living Memory:*

Memory not only connects us
with our past, but also
keeps us alive in the present. . . .

To remember is not simply
to look back at past events:
more importantly
it is to bring these events into
the present and celebrate them
in the here and now.
For Israel, remembrance
meant participation.

Thus, when Jews celebrated the Passover, they did more than recall the event that freed them from Egyptian slavery.

By faith, they brought the event into the present, relived it, and received from it the same blessing their ancestors did.

6 ***How does this shed light on what happens in our celebration of the liturgy and sacraments?***

It is with the above understanding of "memory" that Jesus said to his disciples at the Last Supper, "Do this in memory of me." When we celebrate the Eucharist, therefore, we do far more than recall what Jesus did at the Last Supper.

In some mysterious way, we bring this awesome event into the present and share in it just as really as the Apostle did. CCC 1104 The same is true for all the other sacraments.

Liturgical year

The liturgical year celebrates the great events of Christ's life. Pope Pius XII said:

The liturgical year . . .
is not a cold, lifeless representation
of the events of the past. . . .
It is rather Christ himself . . .
ever living in his Church. MEDIATOR DEI

And so the liturgical year is a *living* reality, not a dead ritual. The novelist John Steinbeck expressed the idea beautifully in his story, *The Winter of Our Discontent*. He wrote:

Aunt Deborah
read the Scripture to me
like a daily newspaper and I suppose
that's the way she thought of it,
as something going on,
happening eternally
but always exciting and new.

William Simon

William Simon was the Secretary of the Treasury under President Nixon and Ford. He was also a eucharistic minister in his own Catholic parish.

This means he brought the Eucharist to hospital patients and infirm people. While doing this, something happened to him that he hadn't anticipated. He says:

Many times I have come away
from the hospital wondering if
I have given the sick and infirm
half of what they've given me.
I feel profoundly grateful
to them for helping me
to strengthen my faith.

He concludes saying that when people ask, *"Where can we find God in today's world?"* one answer is: *"Almost anywhere—in fact, many times right in front of us, if we just open our eyes and hearts."*

Quotes from *How Can I Find God?*: James Martin, editor

STAGE 2: CHAPTER 9 **121**

In other words, when we say that Jesus instituted the sacraments, we mean we owe their origin and power to Jesus himself.

CLARIFY—The sacraments were "entrusted to the Church."

Stress two important facts. First, Jesus entrusted the "keys of the kingdom" to Peter, saying, "What you prohibit on earth will be prohibited in heaven, and what you permit on earth will be permitted in heaven." MATTHEW 16:19

Second, Jesus commissioned all of the Apostles to baptize, forgive, celebrate, and anoint (see text).

CLARIFY—The purpose of the sacraments is "to give divine life to us."

Stress that the ultimate purpose of the sacraments is not just to symbolize divine life in a sensible way, but to "communicate it to us." This is their bottom-line purpose.

Celebration of liturgy

CLARIFY—Stress this point: "Christian liturgy not only recalls the events that save us but actualizes them, makes them present." CCC 1104 In other words, through faith, it is making real contact with these events and drawing from them spiritual nourishment and life.

> QUESTION **6** ***How does this shed light on what happens in our celebration of the liturgy and sacraments?***

■ *In some mysterious way, we bring this awesome event into the present and share in it as really as did the Apostles.*

Up Close & Personal

CLARIFY—Simon makes a great point. One of the places where we find God is in the process of serving others. Recall Jesus' words at the Last Judgment: "What you did for these, you did for me." MATTHEW 25:40

Liturgical year

CLARIFY—Stress the two quotes (1) Pius XII and (2) John Steinbeck. They say it all; and they say it well.

DISCUSS—Ask the students: When does the liturgical year begin?

■ *On the first Sunday of Advent, which is usually the last Sunday of November.*

> QUESTION **7** ***Why should Easter, not Christmas, be the high point of the liturgical year?***

Christmas celebrates the "birth of Jesus," who has come to reconcile the world to the Father. The actual reconciliation, the most important event in human history, takes place on Easter: our passage with Christ from spiritual death to spiritual life.

Share Your **meditation**

QUESTION ***How does the liturgical year provide a framework to remind us of who we are and what we are about?***

Each liturgical year recalls and relives the reality of our relationship with God. It walks us through the "three-act play" of salvation history:

Act 1 Creation
Act 2 De-creation
Act 3 Re-creation

In other words, each liturgical year puts us in recall and relives:

1 *Our identity* *Who we are*
2 *Our destiny* *What we are about*

Prayer **hotline**

This prayer stresses the kind of reverence and humility necessary for entry into true prayer.

Christmas cycle

CLARIFY—In the strict sense of the word, Advent is a preparation for two comings of Jesus: in *history* 2,000 years ago, and in *majesty* or glory at the end of the world.

Saint Bernard observed, however, that, in a wider sense, Advent is a preparation for three comings of Jesus: LITURGY OF THE HOURS, V. 1, P. 169

1 *History* *Christmas*
2 *Mystery* *Daily*
3 *Majesty* *End of the World*

Jesus' first coming in *history* and his final coming in *majesty* are *visible* comings. Mary, Joseph, and the shepherds saw the first coming. Every person who ever lived will see the final coming.

SHARE YOUR meditation

Alvin Toffler's book *Future Shock* deals with the impact of rapid change on modern society. This change often leaves us uprooted and disorientated.

Today more than ever, says Toffler, we need a framework for our lives. We need a pattern of holidays and rotating seasonal events to remind us who we are and what we are about.

Without this pattern, we are like castaways, adrift in a boat on a trackless sea. We have no reference point to indicate where we are or the direction in which we are headed.

■ ***How does the liturgical year provide a framework to remind us of who we are and what we are about?***

Every Easter,
Jesus really rose from the dead,
an explosion, expected
but nonetheless new.
It wasn't 2000 years ago to her;
it was now.

This is what the liturgical year is. It is not something that happened two thousand years ago. It is something "going on now, happening eternally, but always exciting and new."

The liturgical year is made up of two liturgical seasons. The focus of the minor one is the feast of Christmas. The focus of the major one is the feast of Easter. Each season has two periods relating to the feast:

■ **Preparation** **Anticipating it**
■ **Celebration** **Reliving it**

7 Why should Easter, not Christmas, be the highpoint of the liturgical year?

PRAYER hotline

When I fall on my knees
with my face
to the rising sun,
O Lord, have mercy on me.

Negro Spiritual

Christmas cycle

The Church's *preparation* for Christmas is called *Advent* (which means "coming"). The *coming* for which we prepare is twofold: Jesus':

■ **1st coming** **in history**
■ **2nd coming** **in glory**

The *celebration* of Christmas focuses on the incredible mystery that God, in the person of Jesus, entered human history and lived among us.

The celebration of the Christmas season ends on Epiphany (coming of the Magi and, through them, Jesus' *manifestation* of himself to the non-Jewish world).

The Christmas season is followed by "Ordinary Time after Christmas." It is usually six to seven weeks long and sets the stage for the high point of the liturgical year: the celebration of Easter and the Easter season.

Saint Bernard went on to say that Jesus also comes in an *invisible* way in *mystery*. Jesus' *invisible* coming in *mystery* takes place in three ways, especially in:

1 *Word* *Reading Scripture*
2 *Worship* *Celebrating the liturgy*
3 *Witness* *Living out Jesus' teaching*

Concerning Jesus' coming in "witness," Jesus said to his disciples:

■ *Those who love me*
will obey my teaching.
My Father will love them,
and my Father and I will come to them
and live with them. JOHN 14:23

NOTEBOOK—By way of conclusion, have the students list the two above summaries (three comings and three comings in mystery) in their notebooks.

NOTES

Easter cycle

Just as the Eucharist is the "sacrament of sacraments" of the Church's liturgy, Easter is the "feast of feasts" of the Church's liturgical year. CCC, 1169

Easter makes present and celebrates the great mystery of our faith. By Jesus' death and resurrection we "pass over" from slavery to sin to freedom as God's adopted children.

Sometimes referred to as the *passover* or *paschal mystery*, Easter celebrates our passage in Christ from spiritual death to spiritual life.

The *preparation* for Easter is called Lent ("spring"). This word underscores the fact that Easter coincides in the western world with the "resurrection" of all nature.

Lent begins with Ash Wednesday and the marking of our foreheads with ashes.

8 *What is the symbolic meaning of this action?*

Marking our foreheads reminds us that, like Jesus who died on Good Friday and rose on Easter Sunday, we must die to sin, if we are to rise to new life with Jesus.

Lent ends with Holy Week. It celebrates the final week of Jesus' life on earth, especially his Last Supper on Holy Thursday and his crucifixion on Good Friday.

The *celebration* of Easter begins with the Holy Saturday Easter Vigil service. At this time, adult converts are baptized and received into the Church.

The season ends 50 days later on Pentecost. This feast celebrates the coming of the Holy Spirit, which is the birthday of the Church.

The Easter season is followed by "Ordinary Time after Easter." About 25 weeks long, it ends with the feast of Christ the King.

This feast reminds us of our responsibility to bring to completion the Kingdom of God which Jesus inaugurated during his lifetime.

LITERARY Connection

The readings of the liturgical year are found in a book called the Lectionary. It contains all the most important readings of the Bible.

The Lectionary is arranged so that these important readings are covered every three years. The Sunday readings of the first year are called Year A; the second year, Year B; the third year, Year C.

Three readings from the Lectionary are read each Sunday. The first is from the Old Testament (Acts during the Easter season); the second is from the Letters or Revelation; the third from one of the four Gospels.

The first and the third readings at each Mass are matched and set forth the theme of the Mass. The second reading is taken consecutively from the Letters or Revelation and, thus, doesn't necessarily match the theme.

STAGE 2: CHAPTER 9 **123**

Easter cycle

***CLARIFY*—**Stress the meaning of the term "paschal mystery." Paschal and "pass-over" are often used interchangeably.

The word "passover" derives from the Book of Exodus, which reads:

> ■ *The LORD said: "On that night*
> *I will go through the land of Egypt,*
> *killing every firstborn male. . . .*
> *The blood on the doorposts will be a sign*
> *to mark the houses in which you live.*
> *When I see the blood,*
> *I will pass over you and will not harm you*
> *when I punish the Egyptians.*
> *You must celebrate this day*
> *as a religious festival . . . for all time.*
> 12:12–14

QUESTION **8 *What is the symbolic meaning of this action? (marking the forehead with ashes)***

This question is answered in the following paragraph. It is posed here to give the students a shot at answering it. This procedure usually results in stimulating curiosity and better preparing students for the explanation of the meaning.

LITERARY Connection

***CLARIFY*—**Stress the point that the first reading and the Gospel reading at each Sunday Mass set the theme for the Mass. The Responsorial Psalm follows the first reading and continues the theme.

Illustrate this for the students by sharing with them these excerpts from the Sunday Mass for the 16th Sunday of Ordinary Time, Year B. Read aloud to the class the following:

The *First Reading* is from the Book of Jeremiah. It condemns the leaders in Israel for ignoring the people and looking after their own selfish interests. An excerpt reads:

> *The LORD God of Israel says,*
> *"Woe to you shepherds. . . ."*
> *You have scattered my sheep and . . .*
> *not taken care of them, . . .*
> *I myself will . . . bring them back.* 23:1–3

The *Responsorial Psalm* picks up on the theme. The psalmist speaks for the sheep, saying:

> *The LORD is my shepherd;*
> *there is nothing I shall want.* 23:1

The *Gospel Reading* describes Jesus doing what God would do in the first reading:

> *Jesus . . . saw a vast crowd.*
> *He pitied them, for they were like sheep*
> *without a shepherd; and he began*
> *to teach them at great length.* 6:34

Recap

In his book *God of the Oppressed*, James H. Cone describes a "liturgy" that reflects the great "mystery of faith" that Jesus is *present* and *active* in every liturgy. It makes an excellent "recap" of the chapter. Read it to the students:

■ *On Sunday morning,*
after spending six days of struggling
to create meaning out of life,
the people of Bearden would go to church
because they knew
Jesus was going to be there. . . .

Through song, prayer, and sermon
the community affirmed Jesus' presence
and their willingness to
make it through their troubled
situation. . . .

How could black slaves know . . .
that they were somebody
when everything . . . said
that they were nobody?
How could they know
that they had value . . . ?

Only because they knew
that Christ was present with them and
that presence included
the divine promise to come again
and take them to the "New Jerusalem."

DISCUSS—Ask the students: "What keeps the average Sunday congregation from this kind of experience in its worship?

■ *Recall Fr. Ciszek's Masses in Siberia. Are we so comfortable and conditioned by this world that we need some kind of a tragedy or period of difficulty to make us aware of how much we need God's help?*

Review

DAILY QUIZ—Just a reminder: Review questions may be assigned (one or two at a time) for homework or a daily quiz.

CHAPTER TESTS—Reproducible chapter tests are found in Appendix A.

Recap

On Pentecost the Holy Spirit came upon the disciples and formed them into one body:

■ **Jesus**	**Head of the body**
■ **Disciples**	**Members of the body**

From that moment on, the risen Jesus not only became present in the Church but also acted through it, in the liturgy, especially the seven sacraments:

■ **Initiation**	**Baptism, Confirmation, Eucharist**
■ **Healing**	**Reconciliation Anointing of sick**
■ **Service**	**Marriage Holy Orders**

We may define sacraments as:

- **Efficacious signs of grace**
- **Instituted by Christ**
- **Entrusted to his Church**
- **To give divine life to us**

No action of the Church is more sacred than the *liturgy.* We may describe the liturgy as the participation of the people of God in the work of God.

The "liturgical year" is a 12-month reliving of Jesus' work of salvation. It centers around two focal points or great mysteries:

■ **Christmas**	**Birth of Jesus**
■ **Easter**	**Resurrection of Jesus**

The celebration of each of these two mysteries involves a period of:

■ **Preparation**	**Anticipating it**
■ **Celebration**	**Reliving it**

Review

1 Explain the difference between Jesus' presence among his followers in biblical times and his presence among them in our times.

2 Explain the difference between the way Jesus healed and blessed in biblical times and the way he heals and blesses people today.

3 List (a) the three groups of sacraments, (b) the sacraments under each, and (c) the four elements that make up the definition of sacraments.

4 List and briefly explain: (a) the liturgical year, (b) the two major seasons of the liturgical year, (c) the main focus of each major season, (d) the three periods of each major season.

5 List the three biblical sources (books) from which the three Sunday readings are taken.

6 Identify: (a) liturgy, (b) Church body (mystical body), (c) birthday of the Church body, (d) biblical meaning of "to remember," (e) lectionary, (f) paschal mystery.

7 In which two readings is the theme of each Sunday Mass set forth?

124 STAGE 2: CHAPTER 9

For consistency and ease in grading, quizzes are restricted to (1) "Matching," (2) "True/False," and (3) "Fill in the Blanks."

TEST ANSWERS—The following are the answers to the test for Chapter 9. (See Appendix A, page 320.) Each correct answer is worth 4 points.

Matching

1 = e	2 = g	3 = i	4 = c
5 = a	6 = f	7 = b	8 = h
9 = d			

True/False

1 = T	2 = F	3 = T	4 = F
5 = T			

NOTES

Reflect

1 A woman had a strange dream. An angel took her to a church to worship. The woman was startled by what she saw.

The organist played; the organ's keys went up and down, but no music came from the organ. The choir sang; the singers' mouths opened and closed, but no song came from their lips. The congregation prayed; their lips moved, but no sound could be heard.

The woman turned to the angel and said, "Why don't I hear anything?"

■ ***How do you think the angel answered the woman? Explain.***

2 Some members of the French underground were arrested by the German army and sentenced to death by a firing squad. On the eve of their execution, the prisoners, mostly Catholic, asked to celebrate the Eucharist.

The Germans explained that the only priest available was German. After discussing the matter, the prisoners agreed to accept the priest. Now, one of the German guards happened to be Catholic also. He asked to join the French prisoners at Mass.

■ ***How would you respond to the guard's request and why?***

3 A little girl came home from religion class with a puzzled look on her face. She said to her mother:

"Today our teacher talked about the importance and responsibility of celebrating the Liturgy of the Mass with the Christian community at least every Sunday. Then she told us a story that didn't seem to have anything to do with celebrating the Eucharist on Sunday. She said:

A monk went to market with seven coins.
Seeing a poor beggar,
he gave him six of his coins.
The beggar thanked the monk over and over.
Then he followed the monk
until he got the chance
to steal the monk's last coin.

■ ***How would you explain the teacher's story to the little girl?***

Fill In the Blanks

1. (a) First Reading
   (b) Gospel Reading
2. (a) Baptism
   (b) Confirmation
   (c) Eucharist
3. (a) Earthly (or equivalent)
   (b) Mystical
4. (a) Efficacious sign of grace
   (b) Instituted by Christ
   (c) Entrusted to the Church
   (d) To give divine life to us

Reflect

1 How do you think the angel answered the woman? Explain.

■ *There was nothing to hear. The congregation was merely going through the formality of worship. All show! No soul!*

Many people fall into a kind of cold formality in their worship. They don't do this out of hypocrisy or anything like that. They just drift into it, without realizing it. Ask for some examples; e.g,. genuflecting upon entering a church (sign of reverence to Blessed Sacrament), blessing ourselves with holy water (renewal of baptismal vows), reciting the Creed or Lord's Prayer without averting to what you are saying.

2 How would you respond to the guard's request and why?

■ *This is a difficult question in the sense that it is hard for us to put ourselves in the position of the French resistance forces. Many of them suffered greatly at the hands of the Nazis.*

In point of fact, the French accepted the German guard, on the condition that he leave his rifle with one of the other guards.

One must commend the French for bearing witness to the fact that the Eucharist is, among other things, a symbol of the banquet of heaven when all will be one in symbol and in fact.

3 How would you explain the teacher's story to the little girl?

■ *This is also a difficult question, but for a different reason than the one above. It is a parable. The monk stands for God; the beggar for us; and the seven coins the seven days of the week.*

God gave us six days (six coins) to use as we wish, when it comes to how we worship. Now we are demanding the seventh coin (Sunday) to do with it as we wish when it comes to worship, also—rather than as God has asked.

PRAYER TIME with the Lord

QUESTION ***Pick out a couple of lines from a song you like and apply them to Jesus or his teaching, the way the pope did with Dylan's song.***

***DISCUSS*—What do you think the pope had in mind when he said that Jesus would come to them "on the road to music"?**

■ *Music has a way of touching the heart and the soul in a way that few other things do. Recall the example of the Chicago student, Mike Gatto. He wrote:*

"I was one of 70,000 people at a rock concert. There was a great sound system, so the music really energized me. . . . After one of the bands played a rock classic, I looked around me. Wow! What a sight! . . . As far as I could see everyone was standing up, clapping and moving to the music. A fantastic feeling rushed over me. Then I thought . . . "God must be present. He has to be!"

PRAYER Journal

QUESTION ***Write a similar prayer to Jesus, asking him to help you on your faith journey.***

Here's a simpler model for the students to imitate. You might copy it on the board and let them take off from there.

Come, Lord, come!
Come as a guide to show me the way.
Come as a friend in whom I can confide.
Some as a singer and teach me your song.
Come, Lord, come! M.L.

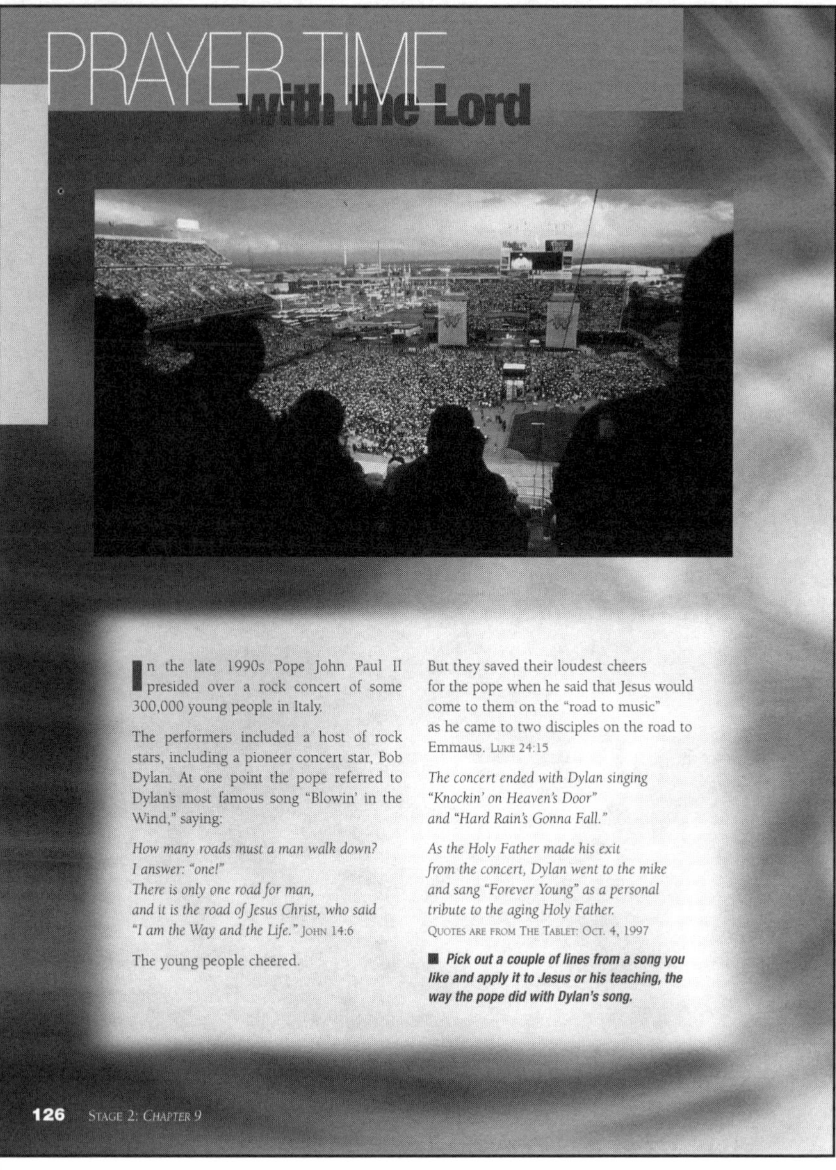

PRAYER TIME with the Lord

In the late 1990s Pope John Paul II presided over a rock concert of some 300,000 young people in Italy.

The performers included a host of rock stars, including a pioneer concert star, Bob Dylan. At one point the pope referred to Dylan's most famous song "Blowin' in the Wind," saying:

How many roads must a man walk down?
I answer: "one!"
There is only one road for man,
and it is the road of Jesus Christ, who said
"I am the Way and the Life." JOHN 14:6

The young people cheered.

But they saved their loudest cheers
for the pope when he said that Jesus would
come to them on the "road to music"
as he came to two disciples on the road to
Emmaus. LUKE 24:15

The concert ended with Dylan singing
"Knockin' on Heaven's Door"
and "Hard Rain's Gonna Fall."

As the Holy Father made his exit
from the concert, Dylan went to the mike
and sang "Forever Young" as a personal
tribute to the aging Holy Father.
QUOTES ARE FROM THE TABLET: OCT. 4, 1997

■ ***Pick out a couple of lines from a song you like and apply it to Jesus or his teaching, the way the pope did with Dylan's song.***

SCRIPTURE Journal

QUESTION ***Pick one of the above passages. Read it prayerfully and write a short statement to Jesus expressing your feelings about it***

You may wish to read to the students the following excerpt from the 4th reading. Have them copy it in their notebooks, and write a short statement to Jesus expressing their feeling about it:

■ *When the hour came,*
Jesus took his place at table
with his apostles. . . .
Then he took a piece of bread,
gave thanks to God, broke it,
and gave it to them, saying,

NOTES

PRAYER Journal

Lord Jesus,
look with love upon the human race
especially those of us who have left you
behind in a Good Friday tomb.

Surprise us on the road and
walk along with us as you did with
the two disciples going to Emmaus.
Break open the Scriptures for us
as you did for them.

Come into our house; and sit at the table
with us, as you did with them.
Take into your hands our bread;
bless it, break it, and share it.

Heal us of our spiritual blindness, as you
healed their blindness, that we, too, might
recognize you in all your risen glory. M.L.

■ ***Write a similar prayer to Jesus, asking him to help you on your faith journey.***

SCRIPTURE Journal

1	Passover liturgy	Exodus 12:15–28
2	Atonement liturgy	Leviticus 16:29–34
3	Harvest liturgy	Leviticus 23:15–22
4	Liturgy of Eucharist	Luke 22:14–20
5	Liturgy of Word	Luke 4:16–22

■ ***Pick one of the above passages. Read it prayerfully and write a brief statement to Jesus expressing your feelings about it.***

Stage 2: Chapter 9 **127**

"This is my body
which is given for you.
Do this in memory of me."
In the same way
he gave them the cup after supper.
Luke 22:14–19

Classroom Resources

CATECHISM

Catechism of the Catholic Church *Second Edition*

For further enrichment, you might refer to:

1. Worship	Index	p. 860
	Glossary	p. 904
2. Liturgy	Index	pp. 817–18
	Glossary	p. 886
3. Sacrament	Index	p. 844
	Glossary	p. 898

See also: Initiation, Healing, Service.
—Available from the United States Catholic Conference, Washington DC

CD-ROMS

Liturgical Musical Clips

—Available on *The Illustrated Catholic Bible* CD-ROM from Harmony Media Inc., Cervais, OR

Constitution on the Sacred Liturgy and All Vatican II Documents

—Available on the *Welcome to the Catholic Church* CD-ROM from Harmony Media Inc., Cervais, OR

VIDEO

This Is the Night

Thirty minutes. Examines the richness and highpoint of the liturgical year, the Easter Vigil.
—Available from Liturgy Training Publications, 1992, Chicago, IL

BOOK

Vision 2000: Year A, Mission 2000: Year B, Action 2000: Year C

Mark Link, S.J.
Inspirational story meditations on the daily and Sunday readings of the liturgical year.
—Available from Thomas More Publishing, 1991, 1992, 1993, Allen, TX

NOTE

For a list of (1) General resources for professional background and (2) Addresses, phone/fax numbers of major publishing companies, see Appendix B of this Resource Manual.

CHAPTER 10
Baptism

CHAPTER at a Glance

The aim of this chapter is to give the students an appreciation of the nature and purpose of the:

1. *Sacraments of Initiation, in general*
2. *Sacrament, liturgy, and grace of Baptism, in particular*

READ—Have one student read the scriptural introduction, which begins: "When we were baptized . . ." Have a second student read the commentary which begins: "Through the sacrament of Baptism . . ."

DISCUSS—In his Letter to the Romans, Saint Paul writes:

> *You Gentiles*
> *are like the branch of a wild olive tree*
> *that is, . . . joined to a cultivated olive*
> *tree. The Jews are the cultivated tree.* 11:24

Ask: What name do farmers give to the process described by Paul?

- *They refer to it as grafting. It is something like skin grafting.*

Ask: In what sense does the image of grafting apply to what is referred to in the first sentence of the commentary?

- *In Baptism we are "grafted" into the Body of Christ and draw new life from him just as the wild olive branch draws new life from a cultivated olive tree.*

Ask: In what sense does the second sentence of the commentary reflect the new situation (1) the wild olive branch and (2) a newly baptized person?

- *It dies to its "wild life" and begins living a new "cultivated" life. It is reborn. In a similar way, a newly baptized person dies to an old life and is reborn to a new one.*

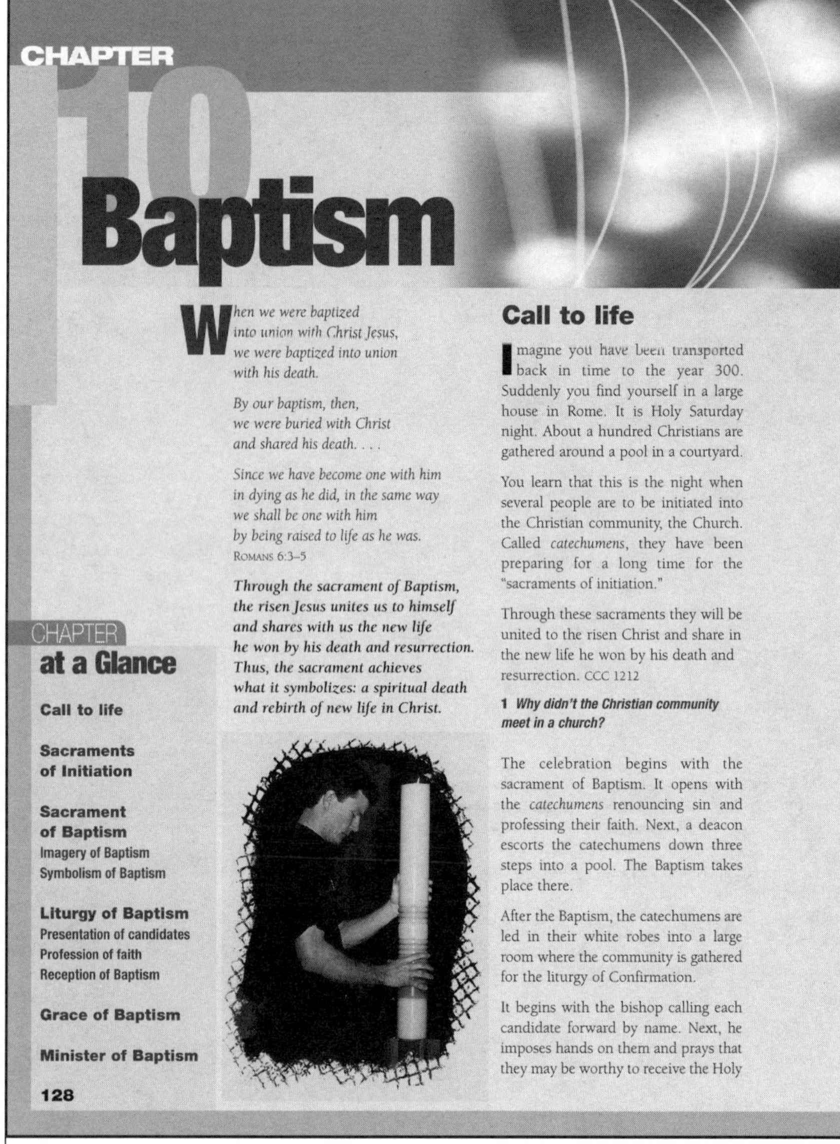

CHAPTER 10

Baptism

When we were baptized
into union with Christ Jesus,
we were baptized into union
with his death.

By our baptism, then,
we were buried with Christ
and shared his death. . . .

Since we have become one with him
in dying as he did, in the same way
we shall be one with him
by being raised to life as he was.
ROMANS 6:3–5

Through the sacrament of Baptism, the risen Jesus unites us to himself and shares with us the new life he won by his death and resurrection. Thus, the sacrament achieves what it symbolizes: a spiritual death and rebirth of new life in Christ.

CHAPTER **at a Glance**

Call to life

Imagine you have been transported back in time to the year 300. Suddenly you find yourself in a large house in Rome. It is Holy Saturday night. About a hundred Christians are gathered around a pool in a courtyard.

You learn that this is the night when several people are to be initiated into the Christian community, the Church. Called *catechumens*, they have been preparing for a long time for the "sacraments of initiation."

Through these sacraments they will be united to the risen Christ and share in the new life he won by his death and resurrection. CCC 1212

1 *Why didn't the Christian community meet in a church?*

The celebration begins with the sacrament of Baptism. It opens with the *catechumens* renouncing sin and professing their faith. Next, a deacon escorts the catechumens down three steps into a pool. The Baptism takes place there.

After the Baptism, the catechumens are led in their white robes into a large room where the community is gathered for the liturgy of Confirmation.

It begins with the bishop calling each candidate forward by name. Next, he imposes hands on them and prays that they may be worthy to receive the Holy

Ask: What is the name of the large candle in the photo below the commentary?

It is referred to as the "Easter" or "Paschal" candle. The "paschal mystery" refers to our passage with, in, and through Christ from spiritual death to spiritual life.

Call to life

NOTEBOOK—Review the sacraments of Initiation on the chalkboard.

Initiation	*Baptism*	*Gives life*
	Confirmation	*Enriches life*
	Eucharist	*Nourishes life*

NOTES

Spirit. Finally, he anoints them with oil, embraces them, and welcomes them into the community.

The final sacrament is the Eucharist. The liturgy begins with singing and a procession of people carrying loaves of bread and cups of wine. The bread and wine are placed on a table in the center of the room.

The bishop then prays over them, just as Jesus did at the Last Supper. The loaves and the wine (now the Body and Blood of Christ) are shared by the entire community, including the new members.

Sacraments of Initiation

This imaginary scenario illustrates how the early Christian community celebrated the sacraments of initiation in a single ceremony.

As Christian communities began to multiply rapidly, the bishops could no longer preside over every ceremony. To stay personally involved in the initiation of each Christian, the bishops reserved to themselves the celebration of Confirmation. Thus, it became detached from Baptism and was celebrated when the bishop was available.

Similarly, as the community grew, the question of initiating infants arose. This led to the practice of initiating infants into the first stage (Baptism), but postponing the latter two stages (Confirmation and Holy Communion) until the infants reached the age of reason and could participate more personally in the liturgy. CCC 1250–1252

Thus, gradually, adult Confirmations and First Communions were separated from Baptism.

This situation lasted until modern times, when the Church restored the *Rite of the Initiation of Christian Adults* to its original form. CCC 1247–49 Now adults are normally incorporated into the Christian community at a single ceremony at the Easter Vigil.

This brings us to a closer look at the first sacrament of the initiation process.

Sacrament of Baptism

The famous anthropologist Thor Heyerdahl once had a deathly fear of water. Then something happened to change that.

One day while on military maneuvers on the Oxtongue river in Canada, his canoe capsized near a waterfall. The roaring waters pulled his body down into the murky depths of the river and carried him rapidly toward the falls. Filled with fear, he began to pray the Lord's Prayer.

Baptism

QUESTION 1 *Why didn't the Christian community meet in a church?*

■ *There were no Christian churches. At first they continued to go to the Temple to pray. Recall that Peter and John were on their way "to the Temple at three o'clock" when they encountered and healed the crippled beggar.* ACTS 3:1–10

Soon, however, Christians stopped going to the Temple and began meeting in homes. Saint Paul refers to these "house meetings" in his letters. He writes to Philemon:

"To our friend and fellow worker Philemon, and the church that meets in your house." PHILEMON 1:2

And to the Romans, Paul writes:

My host Gaius, in whose house the church meets, sends you his greetings. 16:23

Sacraments of Initiation

CLARIFY—In the early days of space exploration, a rocket was boosted into orbit in three stages. Each stage made an important contribution to the orbiting process.

This space-age image might be used to illustrate the rite of becoming a Christian. Three stages are also involved: Baptism, Confirmation, and the Eucharist. These three stages are called the sacraments of Initiation.

Stress that we should not think of them as three separate ceremonies, but as *three stages in one ceremony.* In this sense they act as an image of the Trinity—as *three persons in one God.*

Sacrament of Baptism

DISCUSS—Norwegian Thor Heyerdahl won international fame in 1947, just a few years after his "rebirth" in Canada.

■ *At age 33, he built a tiny raft (according to ancient specifications) and floated it from South America to Polynesia. As a result, he proved his theory that it was possible that South Americans could have migrated to Polynesia centuries ago.*

Thor says when he felt himself going under in Canada, a strange thought came to him. He said, "I thought I would soon learn which of my parents was right: my father (who believed in afterlife) or my mother (who did not)."

Ask the students: How many of you have fathers and mothers who have different religious views?

If it seems appropriate, you may wish to pursue the question by discussing how this impacts their family.

QUESTION 2 *In what sense were the river waters an "agent of death"? "Agent of life"?*

■ *The following diagram summarizes the response to this question:*

River — Death — Old life: fear of water
River — Birth — New life: no fear

Imagery of Baptism

CLARIFY—The story of the flood is found in chapters 6 to 8 of Genesis. The story of the crossing of the Red Sea is found in chapter 14 of Exodus.

Flood — Death — Old world of sin
Flood — Birth — New world of grace

Red Sea — Death — Old life of slavery
Red Sea — Birth — New life of freedom

Symbolism of Baptism

CLARIFY—Since Vatican II, the Catholic Church actively encourages Baptism by immersion. The reason? It better symbolizes the theological reality of Baptism: dying and rising with Jesus. Recall COLOSSIANS 2:12:

> *When you were baptized,*
> *you were buried with Christ,*
> *and in baptism*
> *you were also raised with Christ.*

Early Christians dramatized this dimension of Baptism in a spectacular way. They constructed their baptistries in the floors of their churches, so that they resembled tombs.

They even built three steps going down into the pool of water to symbolize the three days that Jesus was buried in the tomb. Going down into the water (as into a tomb) symbolized dying with Jesus. Coming out of the water (as from a womb) symbolized rising with Jesus.

NOTEBOOK—Have a student with some artistic ability place the following diagram on the chalkboard. Have all the students enter it into their notebooks.

Suddenly he felt a burst of energy surge through his body. Fighting his way up through the strong undertow of the river, he barely reached safety just before being carried over the falls.

That experience transformed him. Somewhere in the watery depths of the river, the old, fearful Thor died and a new, courageous Thor was born. The waters of that river were for Thor both an agent of death and an agent of rebirth.

2 *In what sense were the river waters an "agent of death"? An "agent of life"?*

Imagery of Baptism

Thor's death-life experience introduces us to an important theme that weaves its way through Scripture: Water is both a symbol and an agent of death and rebirth.

For example, the Book of Genesis portrays a great flood destroying all human life except for Noah's family. Thus, the flood waters act as a symbol and agent of death and rebirth—death to an "old world of sin" and rebirth to a "new world of grace."

In a similar way, the Book of Exodus portrays the Israelites fleeing Egypt through the waters of the Red Sea. Thus, water again acts as a symbol and agent of death and rebirth—death to an "old world of slavery" and rebirth to a "new world of freedom."

This brings us to the symbolism of Baptism.

Symbolism of Baptism

Water is used in baptism much as it is used in Scripture: as a *death-birth* symbol and agent. It symbolizes and achieves our passage from spiritual *death* to spiritual *life*.

Recall that the first sin doomed the human race. Paul writes:

> *Sin came into the world through one man,*
> *and his sin brought death with it.*
> *As a result, death has spread*
> *to the whole human race*
> *because everyone has sinned.* ROMANS 5:12

This "original" sin doomed the human race. Our only hope was that God would have mercy on us and save us. And that is just what God did.

God sent Jesus into the world to save us. The second person of the Trinity shared our humanity, died for our sins, and rose to new life. Referring to the saving act of Jesus, Paul writes:

> *As the one sin condemned all mankind,*
> *in the same way the one righteous act*
> *sets all mankind free and gives them life.*
> ROMANS 5:18

130 STAGE 2: CHAPTER 10

The diagram helps to dramatize the fact that we enter the water of Baptism as one person and emerge from it a totally new person. We die with Christ and rise to new life with Christ. An example will illustrate.

> *Federico Fellini's film* La Strada *portrays a circus strong man named Zampano, who awes audiences by breaking chains.*
>
> *One day Zampano acquires a half-witted peasant girl, named Gelsomina, to be part of his act. He treats her insensitively and cruelly and, eventually, abandons her.*

NOTES

Through the sacrament of Baptism, the risen Jesus unites us to himself and shares with us the new life he won by his death and resurrection. Thus, the sacrament achieves what it symbolizes: a spiritual death and rebirth in Christ.

In other words, as the old Thor died and was buried in the Oxtongue river, and a new Thor was reborn, so too we are buried and reborn in the waters of Baptism.

We may sum up the sacramental and scriptural images of water this way. They both act as agents of *death* and *birth*.

- **Scriptural** **Physical death/birth**
- **Sacramental** **Spiritual death/birth**

Let us now look more closely at how the sacrament of Baptism symbolizes this spiritual death and rebirth.

The early Christians used to baptize new members by immersing them in a large pool of water—a practice the Catholic Church recommends today.

This way of baptizing better symbolizes our participation in Jesus' death and resurrection. An ancient Christian writing describes the symbolism this way:

You were led down
to the font of holy Baptism
just as Christ was taken down
from the cross and placed in the tomb. . . .
You were plunged in the water. . . .
It was night for you
and you could not see.

But when you rose again,
it was like coming into broad
daylight.
In the same instant
you died and were born again;
the saving water
was both a tomb and a womb.
JERUSALEM CATECHESIS: 3RD CENTURY

In brief, then, Baptism symbolizes our sacramental dying and rising in and with Christ:

- **Dying** **Tomb image (death)**
- **Rising** **Womb image (birth)**

Liturgy of Baptism

We may divide the liturgy of Baptism into the following three sacramental stages:

- **Presentation of the candidates**
- **Profession of faith**
- **Reception of Baptism**

Presentation of candidates

The first stage begins with the candidates being called forward with their godparents and being presented to the community. This highly personal moment recalls God's call to Jeremiah to be a prophet. God said:

I chose you before I gave you life,
and before you were born I selected you
to be a prophet to the nations.
JEREMIAH 1:5

PRAYER hotline

Lord,
help us to realize
that all human life is sacred
from the moment
of conception and
through all
subsequent stages,
because human life is created
in the image and likeness
of God.

Nothing surpasses the
greatness or dignity
of a human person.

Pope John Paul II
Adapted

Later, Zampano learns the girl has died. This news fills him with remorse at the way he had treated her. Zampano goes down to the sea, wades into the water, and sobs bitterly. As the waves crash against his muscular body, he senses something amazing happening.

His tears and the sea are washing away his guilt. He experiences a spiritual rebirth. He entered the water a sinner and emerged a new person. He was reborn.

What happened to Zampano is an image of what happens to us in Baptism.

CLARIFY—People sometimes wonder about Jesus' words to Nicodemus:

"No one can see the Kingdom of God
without being born again. . . .
No one can enter the Kingdom of God
without being born of water and the
Spirit" JOHN 3:3, 5

People ask, "Does this mean that an unbaptized person will not enter heaven? Would God deprive someone of heaven simply because she or he was not baptized?"

The simplest way to read Jesus' instructions to Nicodemus is to keep in mind their context. Jesus addressed his remarks to an adult, who believed in him. Recall the words of Nicodemus to Jesus:

"Rabbi, we know that
you are a teacher sent by God.
No one could perform the miracles
you are doing unless
God were with him." JOHN 3:2

Nicodemus was, in effect, inquiring into what he (a believer) should do next.

In other words, Jesus did not give his instructions (about the need to be baptized) to people who had never heard of him or to people who lived hundreds of years before him. Therefore, these instructions would not appear to be directed to their situations.

God will have his own way of dealing with the unbaptized (infants or adults). What it is, we do not know. It will be one of heaven's joys to learn what it is.

Liturgy of Baptism

CLARIFY—Some parishes baptize infants in groups at Sunday Mass. This helps to highlight the communal aspect of Baptism. The Christ in whom we now live is Christ's Church (mystical) Body.

Presentation of candidates

CLARIFY—Because Baptism makes us brothers and sisters, the reception and presentation of candidates involves the total community. The poet John Donne spelled out the implications of this as follows:

CONTINUED ON NEXT PAGE

When the Church baptizes a child,
that action concerns me,
for the child is thereby ingraphted
into that body whereof I am a member.

Thus, when a child is baptized into the Body of Christ, the other members of the Body incur a responsibility. It is to provide the faith environment in which the "seed of faith" planted in the child may grow to maturity.

This responsibility explains the Church's refusal to baptize an infant whose parents do not practice their faith and do not intend to practice it. There is no reasonable assurance that their child will be instructed in the faith and brought up in a faith environment.

CLARIFY—The community's responsibility to the newly baptized is beautifully expressed in an article entitled "Our Whole Church Baptized our Son," by William Kane.

He tells how, after his son's Baptism at Sunday Mass, he addressed the community briefly, saying:

Gina and I have always been
accepted and loved by you
since we came to this community.
So, too, Matthew will grow and learn
by what he sees and hears.

Kane concluded with a plea to all present to pray for Matthew and to help him grow in his faith by their Christian example.

CLARIFY—Sometimes, people ask why Catholics baptize infants when some Protestants do not.

Both Catholic scholars and prestigious Protestant scholars, like Joachim Jeremias and Oscar Cullman, have shown that Christians have baptized their infants from earliest Christian times.

The New Testament refers to this practice implicitly, saying that entire households were baptized. Acts 16:15, 16:33, 18:8, 1 Corinthians 1:16

Solidarity of the family in faith matters was taken for granted in ancient times. In other words, when parents were baptized, so were their children.

SHARE YOUR
meditation

A native in a village refused baptism, even though his friends asked for it. The surprised missionary asked, "Is there something in your instruction that bothers or confuses you?" "No!" said the native. "The thing I want to discover now is if baptism will make a difference in the lives of my friends."

After a month of careful observation, the native returned to the missionary and said, "I am now ready to be baptized. Baptism does, indeed, make a difference. I want Jesus Christ to do for me what he has done for my friends."

■ ***Why doesn't baptism seem to make a difference in the life of some people? How about my own life?***

As God called Jeremiah into existence, so God called each one of us. It is this mysterious calling that we celebrate in this opening moment of the baptismal liturgy.

The call and the presentation are followed by the praying of the Litany of the Saints over the candidates.

It is a beautiful prayer that goes back to the early days of Christianity.

It concludes by asking God to "give new life to these chosen ones" about to be baptized.

3 ***Why involve prayers to the saints in the baptismal liturgy?***

Profession of faith

After the Litany of the Saints, the celebrant blesses the water to be used in baptizing the catechumens. A portion of the blessing rite reads:

We ask you, Father, with your Son
to send the Holy Spirit
upon the water of this font.
May all who are buried with Christ
in the death of Baptism
rise also with him to newness of life.

Then the celebrant charges the candidates to profess the faith into which they are about to be baptized.

They affirm their pledge to "refuse to be mastered by sin" and to "reject Satan, father of sin and prince of darkness."

The profession continues with an affirmation of faith in the Trinity: the Father, the Son, and Spirit.

The most sacred moment of the liturgy of Baptism now arrives.

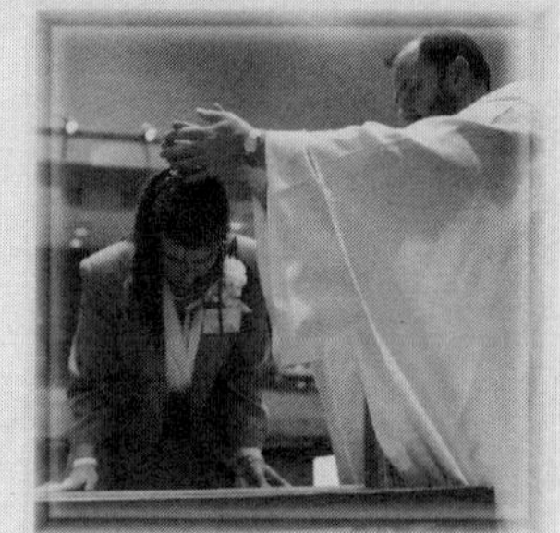

Reception of Baptism

Each candidate approaches the baptismal font individually. The celebrant bathes each one in water three times, either by immersing them completely or pouring water over them. CCC 694 He uses this baptismal formula:

I baptize you
in the name of the Father [first bath],
and of the Son [second bath],
and of the Holy Spirit [third bath].

Next, the presider anoints the newly baptized with holy oil (chrism). This symbolizes and communicates to the newly baptized a share in the priestly, prophetic, and kingly missions of Jesus. (Ancient priests, prophets, and kings were anointed.) The presider prays:

[God] now anoints you
with the chrism of salvation,
so that, united with his people,
you may remain forever
a member of Christ
who is Priest, Prophet, and King.

Share Your
meditation

CLARIFY—Recall the role the community plays in baptism. It is to provide the climate of "good example" and Christian witness for the young.

Sadly, one reason why Baptism doesn't seem to make a difference is the failure of the adult community to provide the climate of faith that the young need: "The worst danger that confronts the younger generation is the example set by the older generation." E. C. McKenzie

NOTES

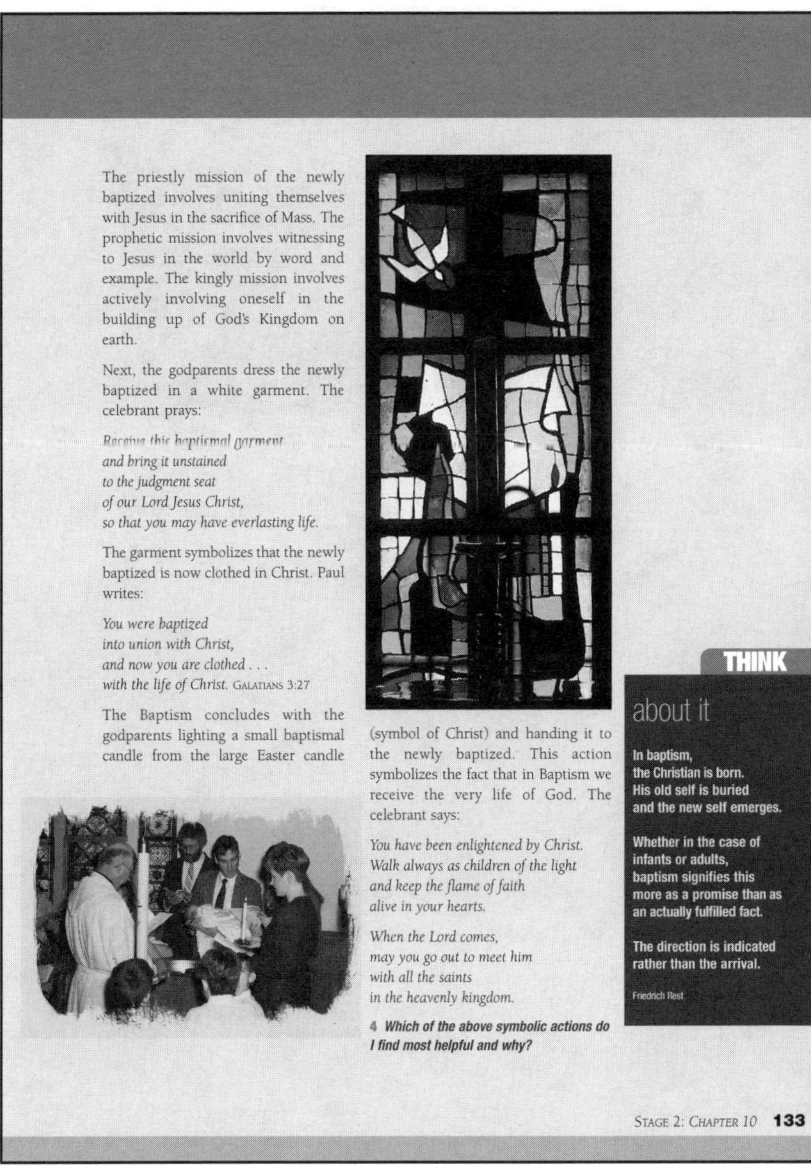

The priestly mission of the newly baptized involves uniting themselves with Jesus in the sacrifice of Mass. The prophetic mission involves witnessing to Jesus in the world by word and example. The kingly mission involves actively involving oneself in the building up of God's Kingdom on earth.

Next, the godparents dress the newly baptized in a white garment. The celebrant prays:

Receive this baptismal garment
and bring it unstained
to the judgment seat
of our Lord Jesus Christ,
so that you may have everlasting life.

The garment symbolizes that the newly baptized is now clothed in Christ. Paul writes:

You were baptized
into union with Christ,
and now you are clothed . . .
with the life of Christ. GALATIANS 3:27

The Baptism concludes with the godparents lighting a small baptismal candle from the large Easter candle (symbol of Christ) and handing it to the newly baptized. This action symbolizes the fact that in Baptism we receive the very life of God. The celebrant says:

You have been enlightened by Christ.
Walk always as children of the light
and keep the flame of faith
alive in your hearts.

When the Lord comes,
may you go out to meet him
with all the saints
in the heavenly kingdom.

4 *Which of the above symbolic actions do I find most helpful and why?*

THINK about it

In baptism, the Christian is born. His old self is buried and the new self emerges.

Whether in the case of infants or adults, baptism signifies this more as a promise than as an actually fulfilled fact.

The direction is indicated rather than the arrival.

Friedrich Rest

STAGE 2: CHAPTER 10 **133**

QUESTION **3 *Why involve prayers to the saints in the baptismal liturgy?***

■ ***NOTEBOOK****—Baptism involves the whole Church, which is made up of three groups: Have the students list them in their notebooks:*

1	*Church on earth*	*In pilgrimage*
2	*Church in purgatory*	*In purification*
3	*Church in heaven*	*In perfection*

Profession of faith

CLARIFY—Recall that the "Apostles' Creed" was used from earliest times as a "profession of faith" in the Baptism of new Christians.

Reception of Baptism

NOTEBOOK—Summarize the four "sacramental actions" of the "reception liturgy" for entry into the students' notebooks:

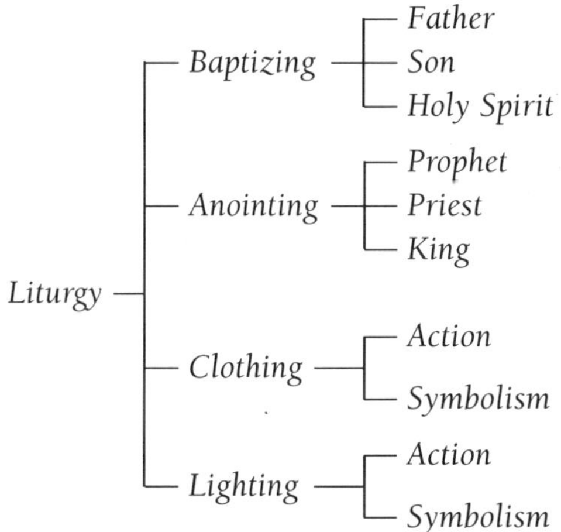

QUESTION **4 *Which of the above symbolic actions do you find most helpful and why?***

ACTIVITY*—Have the students explain the baptismal symbols in the stained glass window photo:*

1 *Dove (Graced by Holy Spirit)*
2 *Water (New life and cleansing)*
3 *White cloth (Clothed in Christ)*
4 *Oil (Gold streak—Chrism anointing)*
5 *Candle (Enlightened by Christ)*

THINK about it

CLARIFY—This is an important point. Baptism may be compared to a seed. It is not the full-grown plant. In that sense the direction is indicated, rather than the arrival.

Grace of Baptism

CLARIFY—Stress the importance of the idea that in Baptism the *direction* is indicated rather than the arrival. A story will illustrate.

A farm boy had a fear of the dark.
One night his father told him
to go out to the barn to feed the horses.
The boy turned pale.
When his father saw this,
he stepped out into the darkness
lit a lantern, held it up, and said,
"How far can you see?" The boy said,
"I can see halfway to the barn." The
father said, "Good! Go halfway."

When the boy reached the halfway point,
the father shouted, "Now how far can you
see?" The boy called back,
"I can see the barn." The father said,
"Good! Walk to the barn door,
open it, and tell me what you see."
The boy shouted back,
"I see the horses."
The father said, "Good! Now feed them."
RETOLD FROM *IN HIS LIGHT* BY WILLIAM ANDERSON

DISCUSS—Ask the students: How does this story relate to baptism?

The lantern did not light up the whole barnyard. It lit only a part of the path leading to the barn. But this was enough to get the boy started. It's the same with Baptism. It doesn't light up the whole faith journey, but enough to get started.

CLARIFY—Getting started on our faith journey and continuing it are works of "grace." The third stanza of "Amazing Grace" puts it this way:

'Tis grace hath bro't me safe thus far,
and grace will lead me home.

CLARIFY—Grace is indeed amazing. Saint Paul's letters stress two important points about grace. It communicates to us:

1 *God's life* — *Sanctifying grace*
2 *God's help* — *Actual grace*

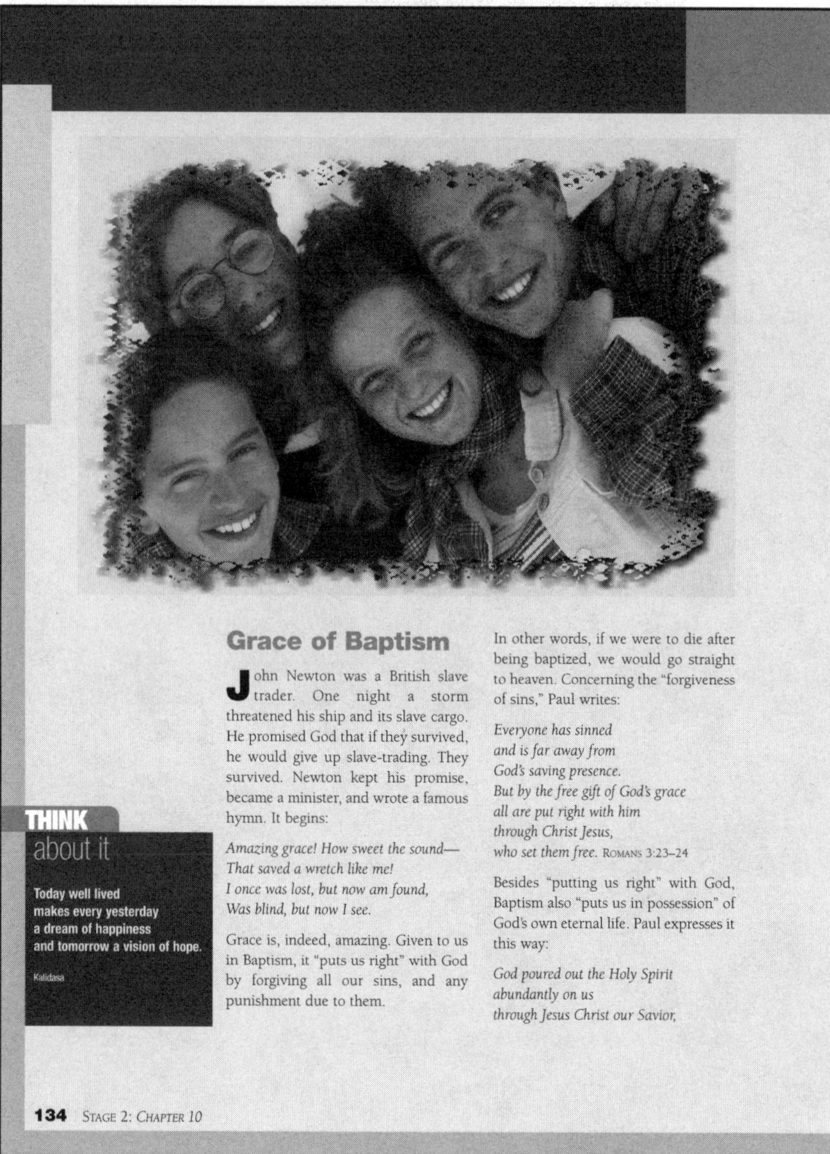

Grace of Baptism

John Newton was a British slave trader. One night a storm threatened his ship and its slave cargo. He promised God that if they survived, he would give up slave-trading. They survived. Newton kept his promise, became a minister, and wrote a famous hymn. It begins:

Amazing grace! How sweet the sound—
That saved a wretch like me!
I once was lost, but now am found,
Was blind, but now I see.

Grace is, indeed, amazing. Given to us in Baptism, it "puts us right" with God by forgiving all our sins, and any punishment due to them.

In other words, if we were to die after being baptized, we would go straight to heaven. Concerning the "forgiveness of sins," Paul writes:

Everyone has sinned
and is far away from
God's saving presence.
But by the free gift of God's grace
all are put right with him
through Christ Jesus,
who set them free. ROMANS 3:23–24

Besides "putting us right" with God, Baptism also "puts us in possession" of God's own eternal life. Paul expresses it this way:

God poured out the Holy Spirit
abundantly on us
through Jesus Christ our Savior,

THINK about it

Today well lived makes every yesterday a dream of happiness and tomorrow a vision of hope.

Kalidasa

134 STAGE 2: *CHAPTER 10*

Let's take a closer look at each one of those two points. We begin with the first.

Concerning this "sanctifying grace," the *Catechism of the Catholic Church* says:

This "grace of Christ" is "God's own life.
It is" infused by the Holy Spirit
to heal our soul "of sin and to sanctify it.
It is the sanctifying or deifying grace
received in Baptism." CCC 1999

This brings us to "actual grace." God does not just give us a share of his divine life and leave it at that. God helps us to preserve and nourish. This is what Newton has in mind when he says:

Thru many dangers, toils, and snares
I have already come;
'Tis grace hath bro't me safe thus far,
And grace will lead me home.

NOTES

so that by his grace we might . . .
come into possession of . . . eternal life.
TITUS 3:6–7

Finally, besides putting us "right with God" and "in possession of God's life," Baptism relates us to the Holy Trinity in a deeply intimate way. CCC 1997 We become:

- **Adopted children of God**
- **Members of Christ's body**
- **Temples of the Spirit**

We become adopted children of God in this sense. Having been united with Christ by Baptism, we are now empowered to call God (through Christ) "Our Father." GALATIANS 4:5–7

Our membership in Christ's body empowers and missions us to share in and continue Christ's work of bringing forth God's Kingdom on earth. 1 CORINTHIANS 12:28

Finally, our transformation into Temples of the Holy Spirit places at our disposal the gifts and fruits of the Holy Spirit. 1 CORINTHIANS 6:4

And so we may sum up the amazing grace of Baptism as follows. It is a gift that:

- **Puts us right with God**
- **Gives us a share in God's life**
- **Relates us intimately to the Trinity**

Minister of Baptism

Ordinarily, the minister of Baptism is either a bishop, a priest, or a deacon. In an emergency, however, any person—even an unbaptized person—can baptize. This option is rooted in the "universal saving will of God." CCC 1256–61 Paul writes:

Christ Jesus . . . gave himself
to redeem the whole human race.
That was the proof at the right time
that God wants everyone to be saved.
1 TIMOTHY 2:6

The minister of Baptism must intend to do what the Church does as he pours water over the person while reciting:

I baptize you
in the name of the Father,
and of the Son,
and of the Holy Spirit.

We may sum up the heart of the liturgy of Baptism in terms of the:

- **Water ritual** **Pouring/immersing**
- **Word ritual** **Saying "I baptize . . ."**

Linda Marshall

One day Linda Marshall was about to take a shower. She had one foot in the shower stall and the other foot on the bathroom rug. As she stood in this awkward position, it suddenly occurred to her that this was a good picture of her life.

Linda wanted to commit her life to God, but she never quite could do it. She always kept one foot in and one foot out. Now, it seemed that the moment had finally come when she must decide for God or against God.

Standing there, Linda thought about what choosing the Lord would cost. The price was high, but she was tired of living in two worlds and enjoying neither.

She paused for a long time, took a deep breath, and said aloud, "Lord, I choose you!" With that she stepped into the shower. It was a kind of renewal of her baptism.

Retold from Catherine Marshall in Something More

STAGE 2: CHAPTER 10 135

In other words, God gives us not only *divine life* (sanctifying grace) but also *divine help* (actual grace) to preserve and nourish it. The Letter to the Hebrews refers to this *divine help* (actual grace) when it says:

Let us have confidence, then,
and approach God's throne. . . .
There we will . . . find grace to help us
just when we need it. 4:16

The Catechism of the Catholic Church contrasts the two graces this way:

Sanctifying grace is a habitual gift,
a stable and supernatural disposition . . .
to enable it to live with God,
to act by his love.
It is distinguished from actual graces,
which refer to God's interventions,
whether at the beginning of conversion or
in the course of the work of sanctification.
CCC 2000

We may sum up the "amazing grace" of Baptism the way the text does. It is a gift that:

1. *Puts us right with God*
2. *Gives us a share in God's life*
3. *Relates us intimately to the Trinity*

Concerning this third point, we may spell out the intimate relationship with the Trinity as the text does. By virtue of Baptism, we become

1. *Adopted children of God*
2. *Members of Christ's body*
3. *Temples of the Holy Spirit*

Minister of Baptism

DISCUSS—Stress the following two points:

1. Who may baptize "in an emergency" *Even an unbaptized person can baptize in an emergency.*
2. The three minimal requirements that must be observed by the one baptizing are:
   a) Intending to do what the Church does
   b) Reciting the baptismal formula
   c) While pouring water over the person being baptized.

To test the students' comprehension of this section, you may wish to turn to Exercise 3 on page 137 and have the students answer the two questions posed.

Marshall's story stresses that Baptism is the beginning of the faith journey, not the end.

Recap

Stress that Baptism is a *sacrament*. It *achieves* what it *signifies*: a spiritual death and rebirth of new life in Christ.

1 *Review the four elements that comprise a sacrament.*

2 *Review the mystery that Jesus is not only present in the Church, his Body, but also acts through its liturgy, especially in the seven sacraments. He teaches and forgives through his Church (mystical) Body today, as truly as he taught and healed through his flesh-and-blood body in Gospel times.*

Stress that Baptism is the first sacrament of the *Sacraments of Initiation*. Along with Confirmation and the Eucharist, these sacraments are ideally—and whenever feasible—administered in a single ceremony.

1 *Review the three categories or groups into which we divide the sacraments.*

2 *Review the graces of Baptism, especially the intimate relationship it sets up between us and the Trinity.*

Review

DAILY QUIZ—The review questions may be assigned (one or two at a time) for homework or a daily quiz.

CHAPTER TESTS—Reproducible chapter tests are found in Appendix A. For consistency and ease in grading, quizzes are restricted to (1) "Matching," (2) "True/False," and (3) "Fill in the Blanks."

TEST ANSWERS—The following are the answers to the test for Chapter 10. (See Appendix A, page 321.) Each correct answer worth 4 points.

Matching

1 = e	2 = f	3 = c	4 = d
5 = b	6 = a		

Recap

On Pentecost the Holy Spirit came upon the disciples and formed them into one body:

- **Jesus** — **Head of the body**
- **Disciples** — **Members of the body**

From that moment on, the risen Jesus not only became present in the Church but also acted through it, in the liturgy, especially the seven sacraments. We may define a sacrament as:

- **An efficacious sign of grace**
- **Instituted by Christ**
- **Entrusted to his Church**
- **To give divine life to us**

We may divide the sacraments into the following three categories or groups:

- **Initiation**
- **Healing**
- **Service**

The sacraments of initiation include Baptism, Confirmation, and the Eucharist. Baptism:

- **Puts us right with God**
- **Gives us a share in God's life**
- **Relates us intimately to the Trinity**

Our new relationship to the Trinity makes us:

- **Adopted children of God**
- **Members of Christ's body**
- **Temples of the Spirit**

Review

1 Pick one biblical example involving water and explain how the water acted as a symbol and agent of death and rebirth.

2 Explain why baptism by immersion better symbolizes our participation in Jesus' death and resurrection.

3 Briefly explain (a) how Baptism came to be separated from the other two sacraments of initiation and (b) when and under what circumstances they have now been restored to a single ceremony.

4 List and briefly explain (a) the three stages of the baptismal liturgy; (b) the symbolism of the following: anointing, clothing with a white garment, handing of a lighted candle to the newly baptized; (c) the threefold grace of Baptism.

5 List (a) the three ordinary ministers of Baptism, (b) who may baptize in an emergency, (c) the three minimal requirements that need to be observed by one baptizing in an emergency.

True/False

1 = T	2 = F	3 = F	4 = T
5 = T	6 = T		

Fill in the Blanks

1. (a) Bishop, (b) priest, (c) deacon
2. (a) Intention to do what Church does
   (b) Recite baptismal formula
   (c) Pour water on person while reciting the formula
3. (a) Efficacious sign of grace
   (b) Instituted by Christ
   (c) Entrusted to the Church
   (d) To give divine life to us
4. (a) People of God
   (b) Body of Christ
   (c) Temple of the Spirit

NOTES

Reflect

1 Fifty-two Americans were held hostage by Iran for 444 days during 1980 and 1981. On Christmas, three American ministers were permitted to enter Iran, hold services, and give the hostages messages from loved ones.

One message to hostage Barry Rosen was especially moving. The minister began by saying to Barry, "I saw your wife, Barbara, and your son, Alexander, in New York. Alexander is a lovely boy; he told me to give you this." Then he kissed Barry on the cheek. Barry had all he could do to fight back the tears.

- **Why do you think kissing the boy's father was more effective than saying, "Your son sends his love"?**
- **How was the real kiss (relayed through the minister) somewhat like a sacrament?**
- **Why do people often become less affectionate (outwardly) as we grow older, and is this good or bad?**

2 Upon entering a church, Catholics frequently dip their hand in holy water and bless themselves. A girl said recently:

I just learned that taking holy water and signing ourselves "In the name of the Father, and of the Son, and of the Holy Spirit" is intended to be a renewal of our Baptism. That makes this practice so much more meaningful. But I'll bet most Catholics don't know the meaning of it.

- **To test the girl's thesis, ask three Catholics if they know the meaning of taking holy water and blessing themselves upon entering a church. Write out a brief report on the response each of the three gave.**

3 The following is an excerpt from a letter from a Chicago father to his son in college:

I had breakfast with Joe, my friend,
the elderly Jewish doctor.
He was reminiscing
about his days as a young resident
at Alexian Brothers Hospital
on Chicago's southwest side.
He was there in the 30s
when the neighborhood was mostly composed
of immigrants from middle Europe.

Often he would receive a call at an odd hour
and would hurry through a cold winter night
to deliver a baby in some old two-flat.
Most of these buildings
had just a single coal-fired stove in the kitchen.
It provided heat for the entire flat.

And so, more often than not,
the mother would give birth in the kitchen
near the stove.
Joe said about half a dozen times
during those years
the child would be stillborn.
There he would be next to all that heat and pain
holding a dead baby
while trying to comfort a grieving mother.

He said that on each of these occasions
he put the child in the mother's arms,
went to the sink for a cup of water,
dipped his finger into it,
and traced on the child's forehead
the sign of the cross, saying,
"I baptize you in the name of the Father,
the Son, and the Holy Spirit."
He asked me
if I thought these baptisms were valid.

George Pence

- **How would you answer the old Jewish doctor's question?**
- **What struck you most about the above letter? Explain.**

Stage 2: Chapter 10 137

Reflect

1 a) Why do you think kissing the boy's father was more effective than saying, "Your son sends his love"?
b) How was the real kiss (relayed through the minister) somewhat like a sacrament?

A kiss is far more personal and moving. The minister's kiss is somewhat like a sacrament in that Alexander could not kiss his father with his own flesh-and-blood lips, but only through the lips of a mediator (the minister). In a similar way, Jesus can no longer touch us with his own flesh-and-blood hands. He can only do so through the hands of a mediator, the Church.

c) Why do people often become less affectionate outwardly as we grow older, and is this good or bad?

Alexander was 10 years old and uninhibited. Unfortunately, age often (though not always) inhibits people in showing affection. Recall the comments of Mark Chapman. *(See page 9 of this manual.)*

2 To test the girl's thesis, ask three Catholics if they know the meaning of taking holy water and blessing themselves upon entering a church. Write out a brief report on the response of each.

Most students are interested in the reasons behind Church practices, e.g., (a) genuflecting before the Blessed Sacrament, (b) keeping a candle burning before the tabernacle, (c) receiving ashes.

(a) Genuflecting is related to Moses' removing his sandals before approaching the burning bush. Exodus 3:5 *It's a sign of reverence.*

(b) Keeping a candle burning near the tabernacle stems from fire being the traditional symbol of God's presence, e.g., burning bush. Exodus 3:2–6; *fire and smoke on Mount Sinai.* Exodus 19:18; *tongues of fire on Pentecost.* Acts 2:3

(c) Receiving ashes at the start of Lent is discussed on page 123.

3 a) How would you answer the old doctor's question?

If there is a possibility that the baby is still alive, Baptism should take place. In the 30s, it was not always clear when life ceased. So the doctor baptized the stillborns. Tracing the forehead with water was sufficient to qualify as pouring.

b) What struck you most about the letter? Explain.

This could lead to an interesting discussion about father-son relationships.

PRAYER TIME with the Lord

***ACTIVITY*—Compose a similar prayer that begins, "Build me a parent, O Lord. . . ."**

■ *You might offer the students an option—to describe the kind of parent they will try to be toward their son or daughter.*

To get them started (for either option), you might wish to share with them the following:

Lee Salk's book, My Father, My Son, *contains an interview with Mark Chapman, convicted slayer of Beatle John Lennon.*

After describing how his father failed him, Chapman describes the kind of father he'd try to be, saying:

I'd be very compassionate and loving,
and I'd give him as much love as my wife,
maybe more so. . . .
I'd hug him . . . and I'd kiss him
until he was a certain age and . . .
let him know that . . .
he could trust me and come to me . . .
and get advice, and . . .
when I made a mistake in front of him,
I'd tell him,
"Son, I'm sorry, I know . . .
you think a lot of me
but I am a human being also . . .
If you'll forgive me,
we'll just go on from here."
Those are the things I'd tell my son.
PAGE 218

Chapman's description of how he would treat a son is especially tragic, since he will probably never get out of prison to have a family of his own.

PRAYER Journal

QUESTION ***Compose a similar prayer to Jesus about one sacrament in particular, explaining how you feel about it; why you don't receive it more often; how you might make the reception of it more meaningful.***

PRAYER TIME with the Lord

The following prayer was written by General MacArthur in the Philippines in the opening days of the Pacific War. Made public after the general's death in 1964, it was left as a spiritual legacy to his son.

Build me a son, O Lord,
who will be strong enough
to know when he is weak,
brave enough
to face himself when he is afraid . . .

Build me a son whose wishes
will not take the place of deeds.
Lead him, I pray,
not in the path of ease and comfort,
but under the stress and spur
of difficulties and challenge.
Let him learn to stand up in the storm;
let him learn compassion for those who fall.

Build me a son
whose heart will be clear,
whose goals will be high;
a son who will master himself
before he seeks to master other men;
one who will reach into the future,
yet never forget the past.

And after all these things are his,
add, I pray, enough of a sense of humor
so that he may always be serious
yet never take himself seriously. . . .
Then, I his father, will dare to whisper,
'I have not lived in vain.'

■ ***Compose a similar prayer that begins, "Build me into a parent, O Lord. . . ."***

138 STAGE 2: CHAPTER 10

To get the students started you might share with them this prayer composed by Jack Joe Holland, prisoner #30067 in the Kentucky State Penitentiary in Eddyville. It relates to the sacrament of Reconciliation:

■ *I come to you a bent and broken man,*
and humble myself before you,
with no strength left to stand. . . .
I come to you from prison,
from a place that's called death row,
and ask you to take pity, Lord,
on this convict's wretched soul. . . .
Replace his hate with blessed love
and dry these tear-stained eyes;
have mercy on this awful man;
please hear his mournful cries.
I'm sorry for all the grief
I've caused you and everyone . . .
So wash me, Lord, with your loving blood
that was spilled so long ago.

NOTES

PRAYER Journal

The following prayer is a reflection on the sacraments by a twentieth-century theologian.

Lord, your salvation
is bound up with a visible Church. . . .
Your grace comes to us in ways
that we can see, hear, and feel. . . .
It warms my heart
to know that I can be sure
of your powerful life-giving presence
in the water of Baptism,
in the word of Reconciliation,
and in the bread of the Eucharist.
KARL RAHNER (SLIGHTLY ADAPTED)

■ ***Compose a similar prayer to Jesus about one sacrament in particular, explaining how you feel about it; why you don't receive it more often; how you might make the reception of it more meaningful.***

SCRIPTURE Journal

1	**Baptism**	**Acts 8:26–40**
2	**Baptism mandate**	**Matthew 28:16–20**
3	**Baptism into Christ**	**Romans 6:3–11**
4	**Baptism is a rebirth**	**John 3:1–6**
5	**Baptism unites us all**	**Galatians 3:26–29**

■ ***Pick one of the above passages. Read it prayerfully and write a short statement to Jesus expressing your feelings about it.***

STAGE 2: CHAPTER 10 **139**

SCRIPTURE Journal

QUESTION ***Pick one of the passages. Read it prayerfully and write a short statement to Jesus expressing your feelings about it.***

You may wish to read to the students the following excerpt from the 4th reading.

Have them copy it in their notebooks, and write a short statement to Jesus expressing their feeling about it:

You were baptized into union with Christ . . .
So there's no difference
between Jews and Gentiles,
between slaves and free people,
between men and women;
you are all one in union with Christ Jesus.
GALATIANS 3:27–28

Classroom Resources

CATECHISM

Catechism of the Catholic Church *Second Edition*

For further enrichment, you might refer to:

1. Baptism	Index	pp. 759–60
	Glossary	p. 867
2. Grace	Index	pp. 801–02
	Glossary	p. 881
3. Faith,	Index	p. 838
Profession of	Glossary	p. 895

See also: Initiation, Creed/Symbols of Faith.
—AVAILABLE FROM THE UNITED STATES CATHOLIC CONFERENCE, WASHINGTON DC

VIDEOS

This Is the Night

Examines the richness and highpoint of the liturgical year, the Easter Vigil. 30 min.
—AVAILABLE FROM LITURGY TRAINING PUBLICATIONS, 1992, CHICAGO, IL

Baptism: Sacrament of Belonging

Classic story about the meaning of Baptism as a sacrament of welcome into God's family. 15 min.
—AVAILABLE FROM ST. ANTHONY MESSENGER PRESS, CINCINNATI, OH

New Life: A Parish Celebrates Infant Baptism

Highlights the celebration of Baptism within the Sunday Eucharist. 30 min.
—AVAILABLE FROM LITURGY TRAINING PUBLICATIONS, 1997, CHICAGO, IL

BOOK

Catholic Customs and Traditions *Greg Dues*

Engaging overview of how Catholics practice their faith.
—AVAILABLE FROM TWENTY-THIRD PUBLICATIONS, REV. ED. 1993, MYSTIC, CT

NOTE

For a list of (1) General resources for professional background and (2) Addresses, phone/fax numbers of major publishing companies, see Appendix B of this Resource Manual.

CHAPTER 11
Confirmation

CHAPTER at a Glance

The aim of this chapter is to give students an appreciation of Confirmation, especially a "personal Pentecost" in their lives.

READ—Have one student read the scriptural introduction, which begins: "Philip went to the principal city. . . ." Have another read the commentary following the scriptural introduction. It begins: "Confirmation communicates to us. . . ."

DISCUSS—Ask: Explain in what sense Confirmation acts as a "personal Pentecost" in the life of each Christian.

- *It confers on us the same fullness of the Spirit that the disciples received on the first Pentecost.*

Ask: If Confirmation confers on us the same fullness of the Spirit as it did on the disciples, why doesn't it "seem" to have the same dramatic effect on us as it did on them?

- *The key in this question is the word "seems." Confirmation may be likened to a seed planted in the ground. Some seeds take a long time to mature. An example is the Chinese bamboo seed."*

  Joel Weldon put together a seminar to help people activate their human potential. One of the talks in the seminar was entitled "The Chinese Bamboo Tree." It explained how, once planted, the bamboo seed takes five years to mature. Meanwhile, the farmer must water and cultivate it.

  Once it sprouts, however, it literally explodes—growing 90 feet tall in 6 weeks. Weldon explains that all the while the seed "seems" to be asleep in the ground, it is actually working hard. It is putting down an elaborate system of roots. It is this system of roots that gives it the potential to "explode" so quickly.

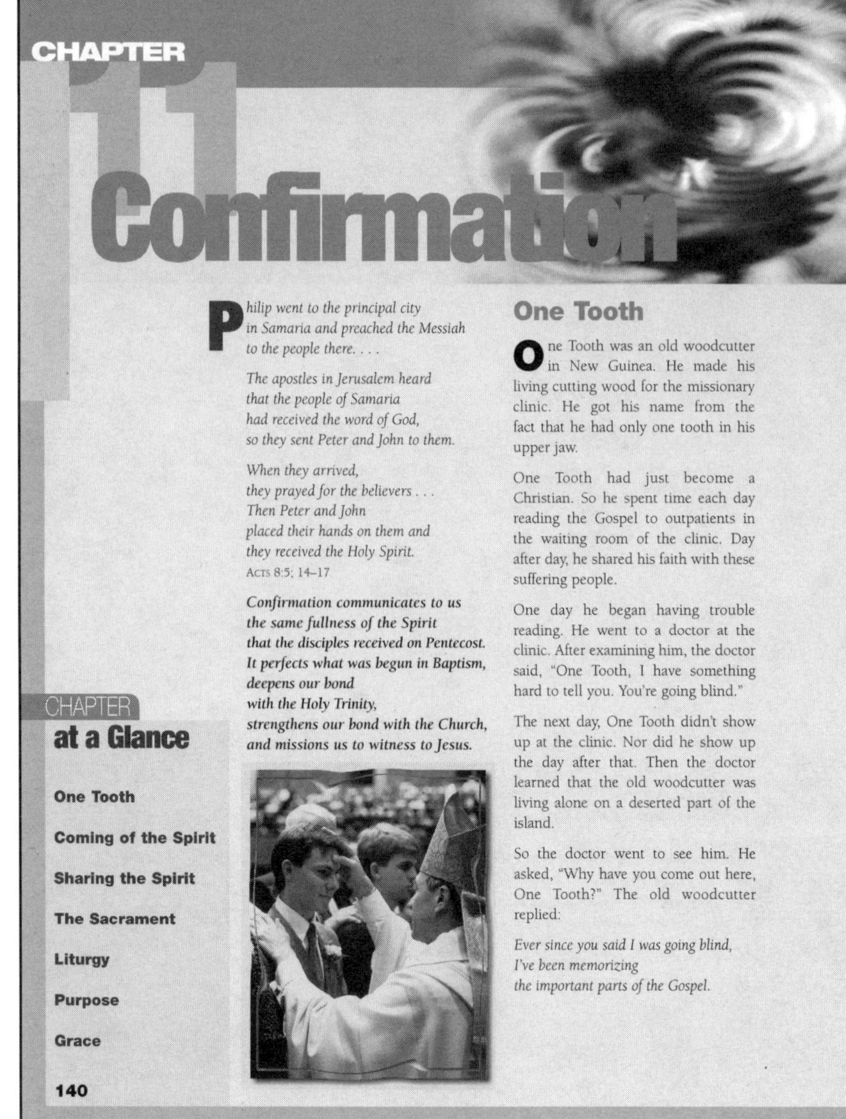

CHAPTER 11 Confirmation

Philip went to the principal city in Samaria and preached the Messiah to the people there. . . .

The apostles in Jerusalem heard that the people of Samaria had received the word of God, so they sent Peter and John to them.

When they arrived, they prayed for the believers . . . Then Peter and John placed their hands on them and they received the Holy Spirit.

ACTS 8:5; 14–17

Confirmation communicates to us the same fullness of the Spirit that the disciples received on Pentecost. It perfects what was begun in Baptism, deepens our bond with the Holy Trinity, strengthens our bond with the Church, and missions us to witness to Jesus.

CHAPTER at a Glance

One Tooth

One Tooth was an old woodcutter in New Guinea. He made his living cutting wood for the missionary clinic. He got his name from the fact that he had only one tooth in his upper jaw.

One Tooth had just become a Christian. So he spent time each day reading the Gospel to outpatients in the waiting room of the clinic. Day after day, he shared his faith with these suffering people.

One day he began having trouble reading. He went to a doctor at the clinic. After examining him, the doctor said, "One Tooth, I have something hard to tell you. You're going blind."

The next day, One Tooth didn't show up at the clinic. Nor did he show up the day after that. Then the doctor learned that the old woodcutter was living alone on a deserted part of the island.

So the doctor went to see him. He asked, "Why have you come out here, One Tooth?" The old woodcutter replied:

Ever since you said I was going blind, I've been memorizing the important parts of the Gospel.

140

Confirmation is much like the Chinese bamboo seed. It may "seem" not to have had an impact on us. But if we water and cultivate it (through prayer and works) the day will come when it, too, will have the potential to "explode."

Recall that for 30 years Jesus didn't preach or work miracles. Then, suddenly, this part of his life "exploded." In other words, like the bamboo seed, he was hard at work putting down an elaborate "spiritual" root system.

To sum up! Confirmation may "seem" not to have an effect on us. It may "feel like" nothing is happening. In reality, a great deal may be happening beneath the surface—if we are watering and cultivating through prayer and works.

NOTES

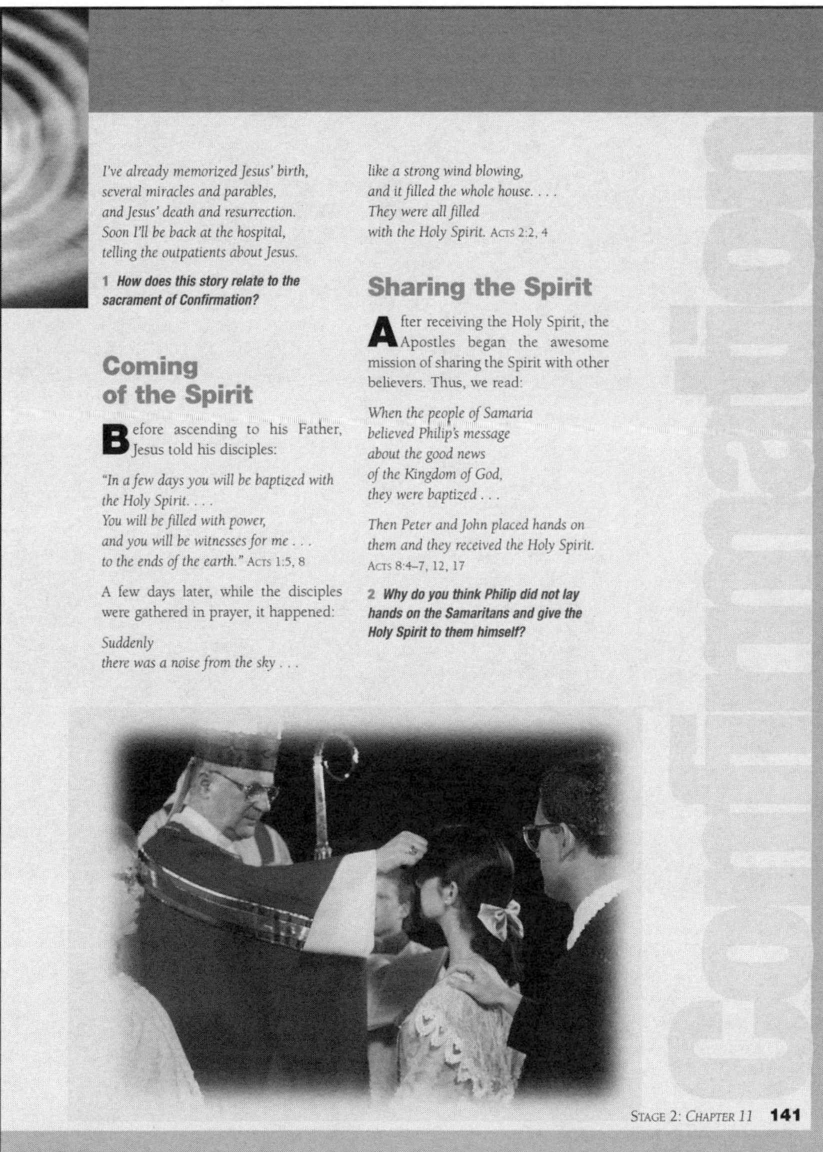

I've already memorized Jesus' birth,
several miracles and parables,
and Jesus' death and resurrection.
Soon I'll be back at the hospital,
telling the outpatients about Jesus.

1 *How does this story relate to the sacrament of Confirmation?*

Coming of the Spirit

Before ascending to his Father, Jesus told his disciples:

"In a few days you will be baptized with
the Holy Spirit. . . .
You will be filled with power,
and you will be witnesses for me . . .
to the ends of the earth." Acts 1:5, 8

A few days later, while the disciples were gathered in prayer, it happened:

Suddenly
there was a noise from the sky . . .
like a strong wind blowing,
and it filled the whole house. . . .
They were all filled
with the Holy Spirit. Acts 2:2, 4

Sharing the Spirit

After receiving the Holy Spirit, the Apostles began the awesome mission of sharing the Spirit with other believers. Thus, we read:

When the people of Samaria
believed Philip's message
about the good news
of the Kingdom of God,
they were baptized . . .

Then Peter and John placed hands on them and they received the Holy Spirit. Acts 8:4–7, 12, 17

2 *Why do you think Philip did not lay hands on the Samaritans and give the Holy Spirit to them himself?*

CLARIFY—Concerning the disciples, one thing that may have contributed to the *immediate* effect the coming of the Spirit had on them was the preparation that preceded it. For three years they were with Jesus daily, learning from him. Then, after he ascended to the Father, they made a "long retreat" to prepare for the Spirit's coming. Acts says: "They entered the city and . . . gathered frequently to pray as a group." Acts 1:12–14

One Tooth

DISCUSS—After reviewing One Tooth's story, ask the students: Why does tragedy leave some people bitter, and others better?

■ *A dramatic example is Helen Keller. When she was 19 months old, scarlet fever left her blind and deaf. As a result, she never learned to speak. Therefore, she grew up dumb, also. Yet, before she died, she wrote 10 books, lectured widely, and met a half-dozen U.S. presidents. In* The Story of My Life *she describes how Miss Fuller taught her how to speak:*

> *She passed my hand lightly over her face, and let me feel the position of her tongue and lips when she made a sound. . . . I labored night and day. My work was practice, practice, practice*
>
> *I thank God for my handicaps,*
> *for through them, I have found myself,*
> *my work, and my God.*

Keller offered this insight on one of the reasons why tragedy leaves some people bitter, while making others better:

> *When one door of happiness closes, another one opens; but we look so long at the closed door that we do not see the one which has been opened for us.*

QUESTION **1 *How does this story [of "One Tooth"] relate to the sacrament of Confirmation?***

■ *One of the purposes of the descent of the Spirit upon us in Confirmation is to mission and empower us to spread the Gospel by word and example. This is what "One Tooth" did so beautifully.*

Coming of the Spirit

CLARIFY—Review the contrast and the symbolic link between Pentecost and Babel. See pages 92 and 93.

Sharing the Spirit

QUESTION **2 *Why do you think Philip did not lay hands on the Samaritans and give the Holy Spirit to them himself?***

■ *He was a deacon.* Acts 6:5 *The laying on of hands, at least at first, seems to have been restricted to the Apostles, especially Peter and John.* Acts 6:6 *In point of fact, they were the first bishops.*

Share Your **meditation**

CLARIFY—Before having the students begin their meditation, share with them this further background information on Mother Clara Hale.

At one time "Mother" Hale had over 20 babies in her home simultaneously. At another time, she ran out of money buying food and clothing for the babies. But she managed to scrape by.

According to Mother Hale, it takes four to six weeks for babies to withdraw from their drug addiction. Meanwhile, she says, "They reach to you in pain and cry, and all you can do is hold them and love them."

Mother Hale's work "exploded," like the Chinese bamboo seed, when someone happened to mention it to President Reagan. He was so deeply moved that he mentioned it in his State of the Union address to Congress in 1985. Instantly, the camera cut away to Mother Hale in the White House gallery.

There was the 81-year-old grandmother. Tears were running down her cheeks. She became an overnight celebrity. Newspaper reporters interviewed her and talk-show hosts invited her to be on their programs.

Money poured in, and her work grew into a fully equipped center with a full-time staff. Soon, other cities were contacting her for information on how to set up similar centers for drug-addicted babies.

Have the students share their thoughts in groups of three or four (simply turning in their seats). Have them select the best response to share with the entire class.

Sacrament of Confirmation

QUESTION **3** ***Where and at what age were you confirmed? What do you remember most about the occasion?***

SHARE YOUR meditation

In the last 20 years of her life, Clara Hale has served as foster mother to over 500 babies born of drug-addicted mothers.

These babies enter life with a drug dependency themselves. When a baby is crying from the pain of withdrawal, Clara says:

All you can do is hold it close
and say to it,
"I love you, and God loves you,
and your mama loves you.
Your mama just needs
more time."

■ *Give an example of an adult you know who performs some volunteer service.*

■ *What service are you performing or might you perform?*

Sacrament of Confirmation

This brings us to the sacrament of Confirmation. Through it, we receive the same full outpouring of the Holy Spirit that the disciples themselves received when the Holy Spirit descended upon them on Pentecost. CCC 1302

The purpose of the outpouring is to do for us what it did for the disciples: to mission and empower us to assume an active role in the work of the Church by:

- **Witnessing to the faith**
- **Spreading the faith**

3 ***Where and at what age were you confirmed? What do you remember most about the occasion?***

Liturgy of Confirmation

The sacrament of Confirmation is celebrated for new adult Catholics at the Easter Vigil Service.

It follows immediately after Baptism to underscore the close unity between these two sacraments.

The liturgy of Confirmation involves three stages:

- **Invitation**
- **Laying on of hands**
- **Anointing with Chrism**

Invitation

The presiding minister begins by saying to the candidates and their godparents and sponsors these or similar words:

Born again in Christ by baptism,
you have become members of Christ
and of his priestly people.

Now you are to share in the outpouring
of the Holy Spirit . . .
sent by the Lord upon his apostles . . .

It will make you more like Christ,
help you to witness to him,
and take an active role
in building up the Body of Christ.

The presiding minister then invites the entire congregation to pray, saying:

Let us pray to God our Father,
that he will pour out the Holy Spirit
on these newly baptized
to strengthen them with his gifts
and anoint them to be more like Christ,
the Son of God.

Laying on of hands

The second stage of the liturgy begins with the presiding minister extending his hands over the entire group to be confirmed. CCC 1299

The rite of extending hands over another, or laying hands on them, dates back to Old Testament times. Thus, when Moses was old, God instructed him to communicate to Joshua a share in his own authority, saying:

■ *Point out that the confirmation photos on pages 140, 141, and 144 show young people in their teens being confirmed. Ask: Why do/don't you think this is a good age for Confirmation to take place?*

Liturgy of Confirmation

CLARIFY—Use this as an opportunity to review the way Jesus healed and forgave in Gospel times and the way he continues to heal and forgive today:

Gospel — *Jesus acted / through the physical actions / of his historical body*

Today — *Jesus continues to act / through liturgical actions / of his Church (mystical) body*

NOTES

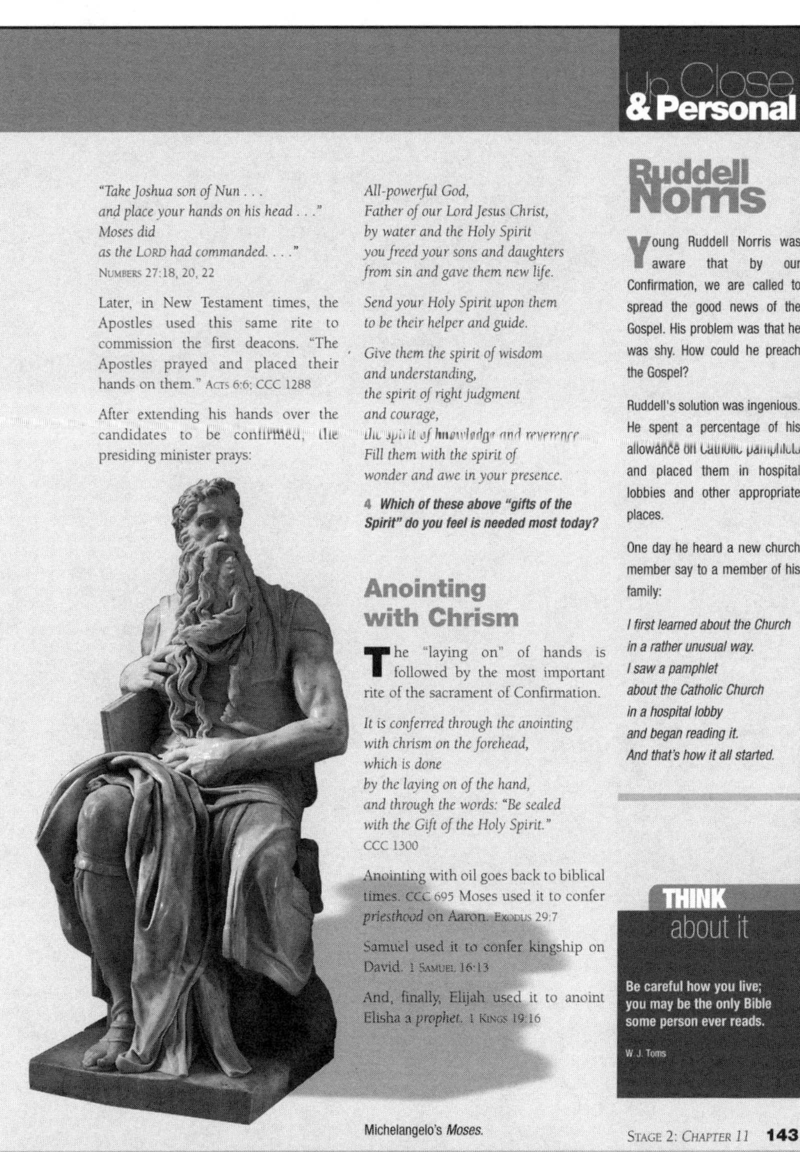

"*Take Joshua son of Nun . . .*
and place your hands on his head . . ."
Moses did
as the L*ORD had commanded. . . .*"
NUMBERS 27:18, 20, 22

Later, in New Testament times, the Apostles used this same rite to commission the first deacons. "The Apostles prayed and placed their hands on them." ACTS 6:6; CCC 1288

After extending his hands over the candidates to be confirmed, the presiding minister prays:

All-powerful God,
Father of our Lord Jesus Christ,
by water and the Holy Spirit
you freed your sons and daughters
from sin and gave them new life.

Send your Holy Spirit upon them
to be their helper and guide.

Give them the spirit of wisdom
and understanding,
the spirit of right judgment
and courage,
the spirit of knowledge and reverence.
Fill them with the spirit of
wonder and awe in your presence.

4 ***Which of these above "gifts of the Spirit" do you feel is needed most today?***

Anointing with Chrism

The "laying on" of hands is followed by the most important rite of the sacrament of Confirmation.

It is conferred through the anointing
with chrism on the forehead,
which is done
by the laying on of the hand,
and through the words: "Be sealed
with the Gift of the Holy Spirit."
CCC 1300

Anointing with oil goes back to biblical times. CCC 695 Moses used it to confer *priesthood* on Aaron. EXODUS 29:7

Samuel used it to confer kingship on David. 1 SAMUEL 16:13

And, finally, Elijah used it to anoint Elisha a *prophet*. 1 KINGS 19:16

Michelangelo's *Moses*.

Up Close & Personal

Ruddell Norris

Young Ruddell Norris was aware that by our Confirmation, we are called to spread the good news of the Gospel. His problem was that he was shy. How could he preach the Gospel?

Ruddell's solution was ingenious. He spent a percentage of his allowance on Catholic pamphlets and placed them in hospital lobbies and other appropriate places.

One day he heard a new church member say to a member of his family:

I first learned about the Church
in a rather unusual way.
I saw a pamphlet
about the Catholic Church
in a hospital lobby
and began reading it.
And that's how it all started.

THINK about it

Be careful how you live; you may be the only Bible some person ever reads.

W. J. Toms

STAGE 2: CHAPTER 11 **143**

Invitation

DISCUSS—After noting that the liturgy of Confirmation differs slightly when adults are baptized and confirmed in one ceremony at the Easter Vigil, ask the students: "What phrase in the prayer, cited in the text, tips us off to which liturgy (ceremony) it is from?

■ *The phrase "Born again by baptism" in the first paragraph is inconclusive as to the time of baptism. The phrase "newly baptized" in the final paragraph makes it clear the prayer is from the Easter Vigil liturgy.*

Laying on of hands

DISCUSS—After rereading the final paragraph of the prayer recited during the "laying on of hands," ask: Can you recall the "seven gifts" of the Holy Spirit?

■ *Wisdom, Understanding, Counsel, Fortitude, Knowledge, Piety, Fear of God.*

Have someone list the "seven gifts" on the chalkboard as students call them out. When the "gifts" are listed, ask: Can you arrange them in the order that Isaiah lists them?

■ *See above or page 95 of manual or text.*

Ask: "Do you recall Saint Augustine's explanation for putting the "seven gifts of the Spirit" in this order?

■ *See page 96 of manual or text.*

Next: Identify the seven gifts and the order they follow in the last paragraph of the prayer said during the laying on of hands.

■ *They follow Isaiah's order, but a different translation from the one on page 95. (Which translation is best?)*

QUESTION **4 *Which of the above "gifts of the Spirit" do we feel is needed most today?***

(NOTE: THIS IS NOT THE SAME AS QUESTION 7 ON PAGE 97).

Have the students write down two gifts in their notebooks, along with their reason. Next have them share their response in small groups. Finally, have the group pick one gift and its reason to share with the class.

Anointing with Chrism

NOTEBOOK—In Old Testament times, three special groups of people were anointed with oil. Have students list the following in notebooks for quick visual reference:

Prophets (Elisha)	*1 Kings 19:16*
Priests (Aaron)	*Exodus 29:7*
King (David)	*1 Samuel 16:13*

Read the following passage to the students in connection with each anointing:

1) **Prophets: Elisha** 1 KINGS 19:6
The LORD said to Elijah, "Return to the wilderness near Damascus, then enter the city . . . and anoint Elisha son of Shaphat . . . to succeed you as prophet."

2) **Priests: Aaron** EXODUS 29:5–9
The LORD said to Moses: EXODUS 25:1
"Dress Aaron in priestly garments . . .
Put the turban on him . . . Then take the anointing oil, pour it on his head and anoint him. . . . This is how you are to ordain Aaron and his sons. They and their descendants are to serve me as priests forever."

3) **Kings: David** 1 SAMUEL 16:13
The LORD said to Samuel, "This is the one—anoint him!" Samuel took the olive oil and anointed David in front of his brothers. Immediately the spirit of the LORD took control of David and was with him from that day on.

Sharing in the missions of Jesus

CLARIFY—Stress that Confirmation calls, empowers, and perfects in a share in the three missions of Jesus. See page 80.

NOTEBOOK—Have students enter the following diagram in their notebooks, showing in what sense we share in these same three missions:

Prophet	*Teach and witness to Christ*
Priest	*Offer selves with Christ*
King	*Build up Body of Christ*

CLARIFY—Ancient soldiers were sealed with a tattoo. It showed that they belonged to a certain king. Ancient Christians were "sealed" with the "Gift of the Holy Spirit." It showed that they belonged to Jesus.

The "Gift of the Holy Spirit" was just as visible as a tattoo. After receiving the Holy Spirit, Jesus' followers became

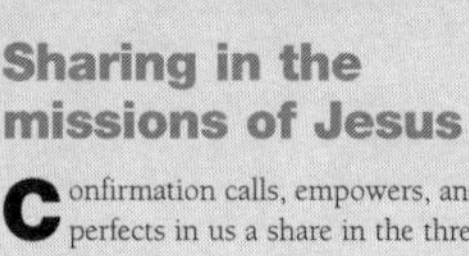

Sharing in the missions of Jesus

Confirmation calls, empowers, and perfects in us a share in the three missions of Jesus:

- **Prophet**
- **Priest**
- **King**

The *prophetic* mission commissions us to teach and to witness to the Gospel. CCC 904–907

THINK about it

John Ruskin lived before the age of electricity. City streets were lit by gas lamps. Lamplighters went from lamp to lamp lighting them with a flaming torch.

One night, Ruskin was sitting by a window in his house. Across the valley was a street on a hillside. There Ruskin could see the torch of a lamplighter lighting lamps as he went.

Because of the darkness, he could not see the lamplighter. He could see only the torch and the trail of lights it left behind him.

After a few minutes, he turned to a friend and said:

That's a good illustration
of a Christian.
People may have never
known him.
They may have never met him.
They may have never
even seen him.
But they know he passed
through their world
by the trail of lights
he left behind him.

Anointing with oil played an important role in Old Testament times in creating *prophets, priests,* and *kings*. Understandably, it plays a similar role in New Testament times. CCC 783–86

This brings us to an important moment in the liturgy of anointing. It is called "sealing." CCC 698 An ancient Christian writing explains it this way:

The soldier chosen for service . . .
receives on his hand the seal
showing what king he will serve.

So it is with you.
You were chosen
to serve the king of heaven,
and will henceforth bear his seal.

Saint Paul writes:

The Spirit is God's mark of ownership [seal] on you, a guarantee that the day will come when God will set you free. EPHESIANS 4:30

And so the anointing ends with these words: "Be sealed with the Gift of the Holy Spirit."

The *priestly* mission commissions us to offer ourselves with Christ to the Father in the Eucharist. CCC 900–903

The *kingly* mission commissions us to continue Christ's work of building up God's kingdom on earth. CCC 908–913

144 STAGE 2: CHAPTER 11

living witnesses to the Spirit's presence within them. Consider this example.

At one point, the Sanhedrin (High Jewish Council) ordered Peter and John never to speak or teach again in the name of Jesus. Peter and John answered,
"We cannot stop speaking of what we ourselves have seen and heard." ACTS 4:20

On another occasion, a group of disciples were praying together.

When they finished praying,
the place where they were meeting
was shaken.
They were all filled with the Holy Spirit
and began to proclaim God's message
with boldness. ACTS 4:31

NOTES

THINK about it

Xvxn though my typxwritxr's old, it works wxll xxcxpt for onx kxy. Sincx all the othxr kxys work wxll, thx fact that mxrxly onx kxy isn't working doxsn't really causx that much of a problxm.

Anonymous

Four graces of Confirmation

Confirmation communicates to us the same Holy Spirit that the disciples received on Pentecost. Through Confirmation, the Holy Spirit confers on us a fourfold grace.

It *perfects* what was begun in Baptism, *deepens* our union with the Trinity, *strengthens* our bond with the Church, and *missions* us to witness and work for the spread of God's Kingdom.

5 ***List some situations where young people can be more effective witnesses and workers in God's Kingdom.***

The Confirmation liturgy of the Easter Vigil Service ends with the whole community welcoming the new Christians. Then comes a dramatic moment.

Everyone present stands in solidarity with the new Christians. Holding lighted candles, they renew their baptismal commitment, saying "I do" to these questions:

Do you believe in God,
the Father Almighty,
creator of heaven and earth?

Do you believe in Jesus Christ,
his only Son, our Lord,
who was born of the Virgin Mary,
was crucified, died, and was buried,
rose from the dead, and now is seated
at the right hand of the Father?

Do you believe in the Holy Spirit,
the holy Catholic Church,
the communion of saints,
the forgiveness of sins,
the resurrection of the body,
and the life everlasting?

A fitting way to conclude our study of the sacrament of Confirmation is to reflect on these words of Saint Anselm:

Recall that you have received
the spiritual seal . . .
Guard what you have received.

God the Father
has marked you with his sign;
Christ the Lord has confirmed you
and placed his pledge,
the Holy Spirit, in your hearts.
DE MYSTERIIS

PRAYER hotline

During the desert campaign in Africa during World War II, a British soldier spotted a scrap of paper in a trench.

Seeing handwriting on it, he stooped down, picked it up, and read it. It was a prayer-poem, which appeared later in *Poems from the Desert* by the British army:

Stay with me, God.
The night is dark,
The night is cold:
My little spark
of courage dies.
The night is long;
Be with me God,
and make me strong.

STAGE 2: CHAPTER 11 145

Four graces of Confirmation

NOTEBOOK—Stress that being "sealed with the Spirit" does not witness to Jesus, automatically, any more than being "sealed with a tattoo" automatically made ancient men loyal soldiers to the king. In other words, Confirmation does not destroy human freedom. Ultimately, we must decide to exercise the grace it confers on us.

End by listing the following four graces on the board for entry into the students' notebooks:

1 *Perfects what was begun in Baptism*
2 *Deepens our relationship with the Trinity*
3 *Strengthens our bond with the Church*
4 *Missions us to spread the Gospel*

DISCUSS—Share the following story with the students and ask them if they feel the same way about his decision, as many of his friends and relatives did, thinking it to be foolish.

■ *A prestigious international group voted Dr. Albert Schwietzer (1875–1965) the "Man of the 20th Century." His life story read like a Hollywood movie.*

At the age of 21, he promised himself that he would enjoy art and science until he was 30. Then he would devote the rest of his life to working among the needy in some direct form of service. In the years ahead, he became a concert pianist.

On his 30th birthday, he sent letters to his parents and closest friends, telling them that he was going to college to get a degree in medicine in preparation for becoming a missionary doctor in Africa. The letters created a big stir. Many people felt that he was foolishly burying his talents. He could do far more for the missions by the publicity and money he could give to them.

At the age of 38, Schweitzer became a medical doctor. In 1917, at the age of 43, he left for Africa, where he opened a hospital on the edge of the jungle. He died there in 1965 at the age of 90.

THINK about it

Recall Benjamin Franklin's poem. How does it make the same point?

For want of a nail the shoe was lost.
For want of a shoe the horse was lost.
For want of a horse the rider was lost.
For want of a rider the battle was lost.

Ralph Waldo Emerson (1803–1882), poet and essayist, put the same idea this way: "The creation of a thousand forests is in one acorn."

Recap

By way of recap, share this story of a Catholic who lived out his Confirmation in a wonderful way and bore beautiful witness to his faith to millions.

In 1998, on the 30th anniversary of Robert Kennedy's assassination, both Time *and* Newsweek *magazines retold the story of Juan Romero. They also reprinted the photograph of this 17-year-old busboy in a white coat kneeling on the floor cushioning the head of Robert Kennedy, just after his assassination in 1968 (on the eve of RFK's winning the California democratic primary).*

Juan had heard that when the presidential rally at the hotel was over, Kennedy, his wife, close friends, and body guards would be leaving by the hotel's kitchen exit. Hoping to shake the hand of RFK (whom he idolized and whose picture he had in his room next to a crucifix), Juan positioned himself along the exit route in the kitchen.

As Juan shook RFK's hand, he felt a hot flash near his own head. It was from the gun that killed Kennedy. The next day the photo appeared on TV news clips and in practically every major newspaper in the country.

Reporters tracked Juan down to let them tell his story. One offered him college tuition in exchange for the story. But Juan refused. (His stepfather told him that no honorable man profits from another's tragedy.)

Today Juan has four children and four grandchildren. He and his family share their home with immigrant families from Mexico who need help getting a start.

Review

DAILY QUIZ—The review questions may be assigned (one or two at a time) for homework or a daily quiz.

CHAPTER TESTS—Reproducible chapter tests are found in Appendix A. For consistency and ease in grading, quizzes are restricted to (1) "Matching," (2) "True/False," and (3) "Fill in the Blanks."

Recap

On Pentecost the Spirit came upon the disciples and formed them into one body, with Jesus as head of the body. Colossians 1:18

From that moment on, the risen Jesus not only became present in the Church but also began to act through it, especially in the sacraments. The first of these seven sacraments is Baptism.

The second sacrament is Confirmation. Its overall purpose is to mission and empower us to assume a more active role in the work of the Church by:

- **Witnessing to the faith**
- **Spreading the faith**

Toward this end, it empowers us to share in the threefold mission of Jesus as:

- **Prophet**
- **Priest**
- **King**

The liturgy of Confirmation involves three stages:

- **Invitation**
- **Laying on of hands**
- **Anointing with Chrism**

The fourfold grace of the sacrament of Confirmation includes the following:

perfects what was begun in us in Baptism,
deepens our relationship with the Trinity,
strengthens our bond with the Church, and
missions us to spread the Gospel.

Review

1. What is the name of the day on which we celebrate the Holy Spirit descending upon the disciples?
2. Who (a) converted and baptized many in Samaria, (b) came from Jerusalem to communicate the Holy Spirit to them?
3. List and briefly explain the three stages of the liturgy of Confirmation.
4. Briefly explain how the "laying on of hands" is deeply rooted in the Old Testament.
5. List and briefly explain the three missions of Jesus that Confirmation calls and empowers us to continue.
6. Briefly explain how "anointing" is deeply rooted in the Old Testament.
7. List the four main graces of the sacrament of Confirmation.

146 Stage 2: Chapter 11

TEST ANSWERS—The following are the answers to the test for Chapter 9. (See Appendix A, page 322.) Each correct answer is worth 4 points.

Matching

1 = c	2 = f	3 = a	4 = d
5 = e	6 = b		

True/False

1 = F	2 = T	3 = F	4 = F
5 = T	6 = T		

Fill in the Blanks

1. (a) Prophet
   (b) Teach and witness to Christ's Divinity
   (c) Priest
   (d) Offer selves with Christ
   (e) King
   (f) Build up Body of Christ

NOTES

Reflect

1 October 23, 1945, was the day Jackie Robinson became baseball's first black athlete. Jackie's entry into baseball was not easy. Racial slurs and insults were a common occurrence.

One day in Boston's Fenway Park, the situation got especially bad. At one point the all-star shortstop, Pee Wee Reese, a Southerner, called time, walked over to second base, put his arm around Jackie, and just stood there looking at the fans.

■ ***On a scale of one (low) to ten (high), how strong is prejudice in your school; and how do you account for the amount of prejudice that is there?***

■ ***Describe a time when, like Pee Wee Reese, you took a stand against some prejudice (racial or otherwise).***

2 Imagine, for the moment, that you are financially secure and could spend the rest of your life doing whatever you wished for the spreading of the Gospel.

■ ***What are one or two things that you would seriously consider doing and why?***

3 Robert was one of Esther Thompson's favorite young people. After her husband died, Robert did all her odd jobs, like mowing the lawn and shoveling snow. A real friendship developed between them.

Thus, Esther faced an embarrassing situation when Robert invited her to his Confirmation. All her life she had mistrusted Catholic "magical" rituals. After agonizing over the invitation, she finally pushed aside her distrust and went. Esther was unprepared for what happened. She wrote later:

The Confirmation service dissolved
my years of ignorant distrust. . . .
The Catholic faith was beautiful.
Three years have passed and
I'm a Catholic now.
I thank God every day that Robert invited me
to attend the sacrament of Confirmation.

■ ***That beautiful story raises a question. If someone like Esther asks you, "What are these magical rituals that you Catholics have?" how would you go about answering the question in a way they might understand and find helpful?***

2. (a) Perfects what was begun in Baptism
   (b) Deepens our relationship with Trinity
   (c) Strengthens our bond with Church
   (d) Missions us to spread Gospel (Build up Body of Christ—or equivalent)
3. (a) Invitation
   (b) Laying on of Hands
   (c) Anointing with Chrism

Reflect

1 **a)** ***On a scale of one (low) to ten (high), how strong is prejudice in your school; and how do you account for the amount of prejudice that is there?***

CLARIFY—Before taking up the first half of the question, you might give some background to the group on Jackie Robinson. He was National League rookie of the year in 1947, won the National League batting title in 1949, and was elected to the Hall of Fame in 1961.

ACTIVITY—Have the students vote anonymously. After collecting, shuffling, and tallying the results on the chalkboard, discuss the second half of the question.

b) ***Describe a time when, like Pee Wee Reese, you took a stand against some prejudice (racial or otherwise).***

■ *Have students discuss this question in small groups.*

2 ***What are one or two things that you would seriously consider doing and why?***

■ *Give students time to think about this question. After they have written out their responses on a sheet of homework paper, have them share them in small groups.*

Be sure to have them turn in their responses. It will give you some valuable information about each student.

3 ***That beautiful story (Robert and Esther) raises a question. If someone like Esther asks you, "What are these magical rituals that you Catholics have?" how would you go about answering the question in a way they might understand and find helpful?***

■ *Perhaps the simplest answer is to say we are simply following the example of Jesus. Take Mark 7:32–34:*

Some people brought Jesus a man who was deaf and could hardly speak . . . Jesus . . . put his fingers in the man's ears, spat, and touched the man's tongue.

Then Jesus looked up to heaven, gave a deep groan and said to the man, "Ephphatha," which means "Open up!"

Or take John 9:6–9:

Jesus spat on the ground and made some mud with spittle; he rubbed the mud on the man's eyes and told him, "Go and wash your face in the Pool of Siloam. . . ." So the man went, washed his face, and came back seeing.

PRAYER TIME with the Lord

QUESTION ***One spiritual writer suggests that God may actually speak to us in prayer through our distractions. How might God do this?***

■ *Keith Miller, author of* A Taste of New Wine, *was plagued by distractions. His mind would flit from a phone call he should make to a letter he should write.*

A friend suggested he keep a notepad next to his "prayer chair." Whenever a distraction came, he should simply jot it down and go on praying. He did this.

It not only rid him of the distractions, but when he read over the notes later, he discovered that a number of them were things he should do. In that sense, God had spoken to him through his distractions.

Saint Francis de Sales stressed that we should not be discouraged by distractions. When they occur, he says,

"Bring your wayward heart
back home quietly.
If you did nothing else during prayer
but return your heart continually and
patiently to the Master's side,
your time of prayer would be well spent."

ACTIVITY—**Compose a prayer to Jesus, similar to the one above, about the distractions you encounter in praying.**

■ *To get the students started,*
you might share this meditation
from the Book of Job.
It's an example of praying distraction:

"If only my life could once again
be as it was when God watched over me.
God was always with me then
and gave me light
as I walked through the darkness.
Those were the days. . . .

"Now I am suffering . . . I call to you,
O God, but you never answer . . .
when I pray, you pay no attention. . . .

"I am torn apart by worry and pain . . .
I go about . . . without any sunshine . . .
Where once I heard joyful music,
Now I hear only mourning and weeping.
30:2–3, 16, 20, 27–28, 31

PRAYER TIME with the Lord

One of the problems people encounter in praying is distractions. Here's one person's prayer about the problem:

God, help my thoughts!
They stray from me,
setting off on the wildest journeys.
When I am at prayer, they run off
like naughty children, making trouble. . . .

My thoughts can cross an ocean
with a single leap.
They can fly from earth to heaven,
and back again, in a single second.

They come to me for a fleeting moment,
and then away they flee.
No chains, no locks can hold them back. . . .

They slip from my grasp like tails of eels;
they swoop hither and thither
like swallows in flight. . . .

Christ, who can see into every heart, and
read every mind,
take hold of my thoughts.
Bring my thoughts back to me,
and clasp me to yourself. AUTHOR UNKNOWN

■ ***One spiritual writer suggests that God may actually speak to us in prayer through our distractions. How might God do this?***
■ ***Compose a prayer to Jesus, similar to the one above, about the distractions you encounter in praying.***

PRAYER Journal

QUESTION ***Now pray one of the next six lines.***

Reading a prayer slowly and reflectively can act as an excellent guide to prayer. Commenting on this way of praying, Saint Francis de Sales wrote in a letter to a friend:

Do not become discouraged,
if sometimes, and even quite often,
you do not find consolation
in your meditation.
Persevere at it with patience
and humility. . . .
Make use of your books,
when you grow weary.
That is, read a little and then meditate.
Keep this up until the end of your prayer.

NOTES

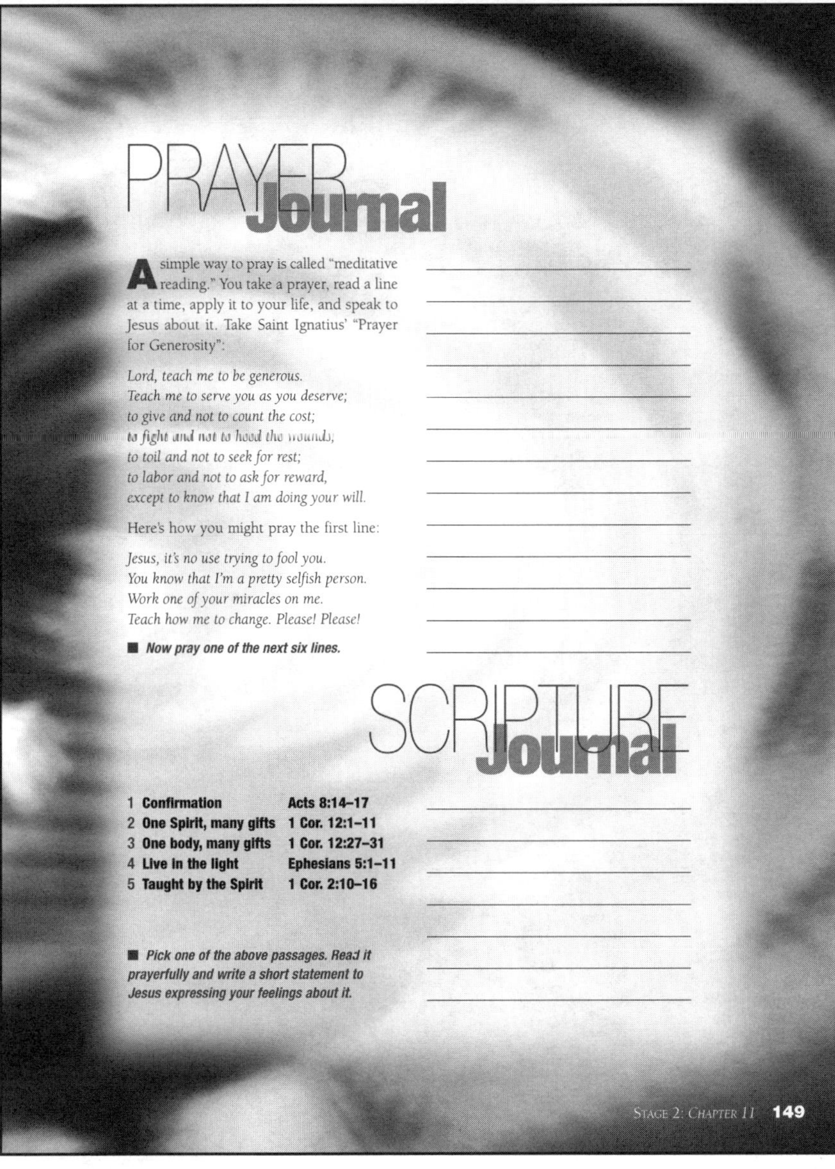

PRAYER Journal

A simple way to pray is called "meditative reading." You take a prayer, read a line at a time, apply it to your life, and speak to Jesus about it. Take Saint Ignatius' "Prayer for Generosity":

Lord, teach me to be generous.
Teach me to serve you as you deserve;
to give and not to count the cost;
to fight and not to heed the wounds;
to toil and not to seek for rest;
to labor and not to ask for reward,
except to know that I am doing your will.

Here's how you might pray the first line:

Jesus, it's no use trying to fool you.
You know that I'm a pretty selfish person.
Work one of your miracles on me.
Teach how me to change. Please! Please!

■ ***Now pray one of the next six lines.***

SCRIPTURE Journal

1	**Confirmation**	**Acts 8:14–17**
2	**One Spirit, many gifts**	**1 Cor. 12:1–11**
3	**One body, many gifts**	**1 Cor. 12:27–31**
4	**Live in the light**	**Ephesians 5:1–11**
5	**Taught by the Spirit**	**1 Cor. 2:10–16**

■ ***Pick one of the above passages. Read it prayerfully and write a short statement to Jesus expressing your feelings about it.***

STAGE 2: CHAPTER 11 **149**

Have the students write out their reflections and turn them in. You can collect them, pick out the better ones, and share them with the class anonymously.

SCRIPTURE Journal

QUESTION ***Pick one of the passages. Read it prayerfully and write a short statement to Jesus expressing your feelings about it.***

You may wish to read to the students the excerpt below from the 2nd reading. Have them write a short statement to Jesus expressing their feeling about it:

> *The Spirit's presence*
> *is shown in some way*
> *in each person for the good of all.*
> 1 CORINTHIANS 12:4, 7

Classroom Resources

CATECHISM

Catechism of the Catholic Church *Second Edition*

For further enrichment, you might refer to:

1. Confirmation	Index	pp. 776–77
	Glossary	p. 872
2. Anointing of the Sick	Index	p. 756
	Glossary	p. 866
3. Holy Spirit	Index	pp. 805–07
	Glossary	p. 882

See also: Healing, Chrism, Mission.
—AVAILABLE FROM THE UNITED STATES CATHOLIC CONFERENCE, WASHINGTON DC

VIDEOS

This Is the Night

Thirty minutes. Examines the richness and highpoint of the liturgical year, the Easter Vigil.
—AVAILABLE FROM LITURGY TRAINING PUBLICATIONS, 1992, CHICAGO, IL

Confirmation: Commitment to Life

Joseph Kempf

Sixty minutes. Focuses on a group of high-school students who discover how God and the sacrament of Confirmation fit into the real world.
—AVAILABLE FROM OBLATE MEDIA, ST. LOUIS, MO

BOOK

Spirit 2000: Daily Meditations on Discipleship

Mark Link, S.J.

A 7-week program on following Jesus, intended for Confirmation candidates.
—AVAILABLE FROM THOMAS MORE PUBLISHING, 1993, ALLEN, TX

NOTE

For a list of (1) General resources for professional background and (2) Addresses, phone/fax numbers of major publishing companies, see Appendix B of this Resource Manual.

CHAPTER 12
Eucharist

CHAPTER at a Glance

The aim of this chapter is to give the students an appreciation of the origin, meaning, and practical living out of the Eucharist.

READ—Have a student read aloud the scriptural introduction, which begins: "When the hour came. . . ." Have another student read the commentary following the scriptural introduction. It begins: "In the Mass. . . ."

DISCUSS—Mary Reilly's father was leaving for work. As usual, he was about a half-hour early. Mary said, "Dad, why don't you relax at home for an extra half-hour, rather than go right to work." Her dad said, "Actually, Mary, I don't go right to work. I usually try to catch the 8 o'clock Mass at Holy Trinity."

Mary was stunned. She said later, "I was really impressed. Sometimes I used to complain because Dad insisted we attend Sunday Mass together as a family. But he never once said to me, 'Hey, Mary, I go every day; the least you can do is to join us on Sunday.'"

■ *Have the students respond anonymously to the following three questions:*

1 *On an average, how many times a month do you attend Sunday Mass? Explain.*

2 *How do your parents feel about your Mass attendance and why?*

3 *How do you feel about it and why?*

Have the students turn in their responses, leaving them unsigned. Review them before the next class to "feel" for where your class is in worship. Share the better responses in class and discuss.

Call to worship

CLARIFY—Father Ciszek is very honest in his book. At one point during the 23

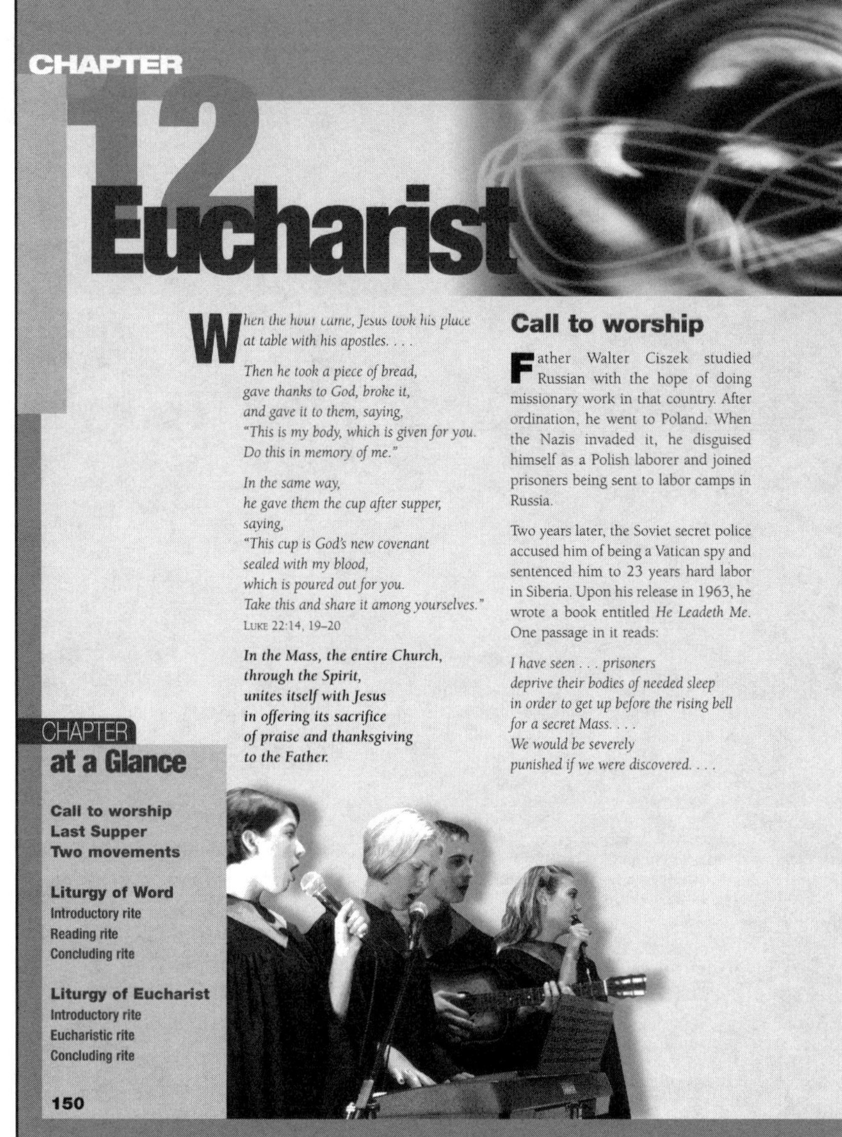

CHAPTER 12

Eucharist

When the hour came, Jesus took his place
at table with his apostles. . . .

Then he took a piece of bread,
gave thanks to God, broke it,
and gave it to them, saying,
"This is my body, which is given for you.
Do this in memory of me."

In the same way,
he gave them the cup after supper,
saying,
"This cup is God's new covenant
sealed with my blood,
which is poured out for you.
Take this and share it among yourselves."
LUKE 22:14, 19–20

In the Mass, the entire Church,
through the Spirit,
unites itself with Jesus
in offering its sacrifice
of praise and thanksgiving
to the Father.

Call to worship

Father Walter Ciszek studied Russian with the hope of doing missionary work in that country. After ordination, he went to Poland. When the Nazis invaded it, he disguised himself as a Polish laborer and joined prisoners being sent to labor camps in Russia.

Two years later, the Soviet secret police accused him of being a Vatican spy and sentenced him to 23 years hard labor in Siberia. Upon his release in 1963, he wrote a book entitled *He Leadeth Me*. One passage in it reads:

I have seen . . . prisoners
deprive their bodies of needed sleep
in order to get up before the rising bell
for a secret Mass. . . .
We would be severely
punished if we were discovered. . . .

CHAPTER at a Glance

Call to worship
Last Supper
Two movements

Liturgy of Word
Introductory rite
Reading rite
Concluding rite

Liturgy of Eucharist
Introductory rite
Eucharistic rite
Concluding rite

150

years, he fell into a pit of deep "spiritual blackness." He writes:

I began to tremble. . . . I had lost not only
hope but the last shreds of my faith.
I knew immediately what I must do. . . .
I must abandon myself
entirely to the will of the Father. . . .
That one decision has since affected
every subsequent moment of my life.

Describing life in the prison camps, he said:

For stretches of a month or more,
prison authorities would keep us at work
without a single day off.
Awakened by an iron gong at 5 a.m.,
marched out to work for 12 to 14 hours,
marched back to the camp
for a meager meal . . .
dropped exhausted on plank bunks—
such was our routine as one day

NOTES

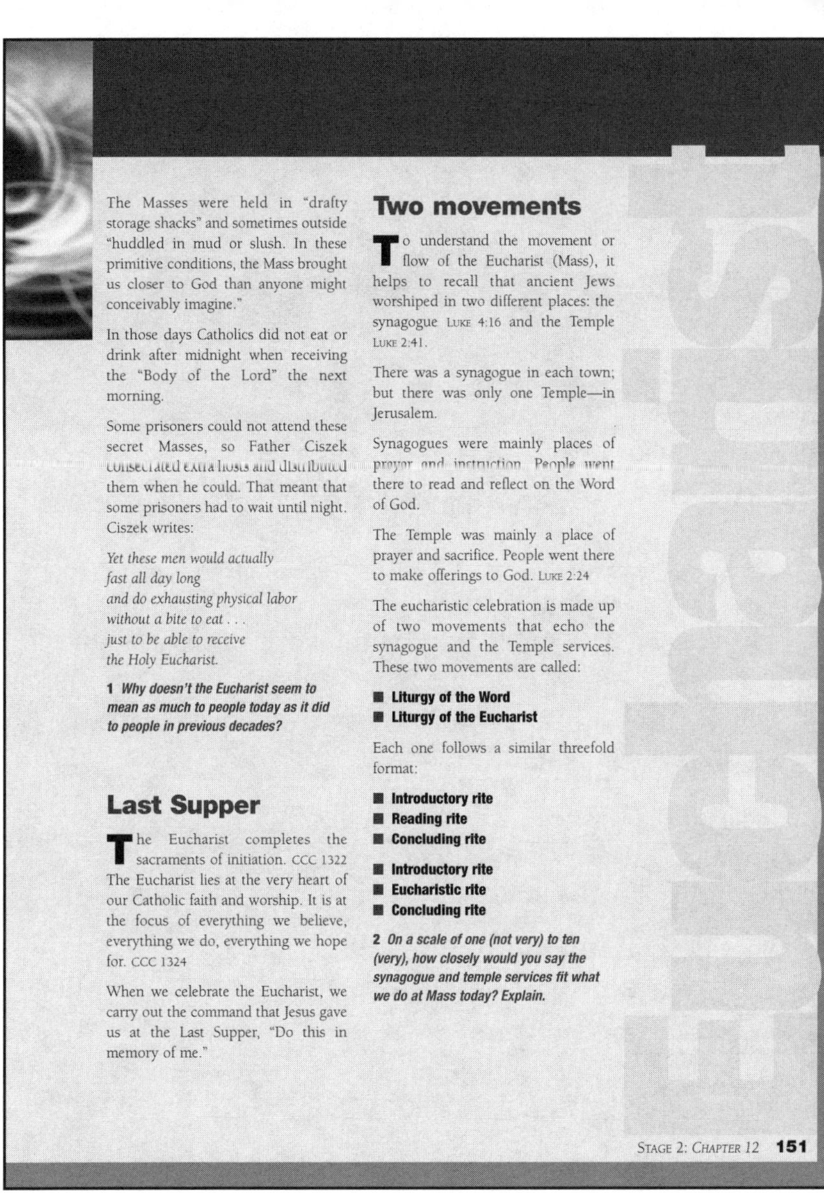

The Masses were held in "drafty storage shacks" and sometimes outside "huddled in mud or slush. In these primitive conditions, the Mass brought us closer to God than anyone might conceivably imagine."

In those days Catholics did not eat or drink after midnight when receiving the "Body of the Lord" the next morning.

Some prisoners could not attend these secret Masses, so Father Ciszek consecrated extra hosts and distributed them when he could. That meant that some prisoners had to wait until night. Ciszek writes:

Yet these men would actually
fast all day long
and do exhausting physical labor
without a bite to eat . . .
just to be able to receive
the Holy Eucharist.

1 Why doesn't the Eucharist seem to mean as much to people today as it did to people in previous decades?

Last Supper

The Eucharist completes the sacraments of initiation. CCC 1322 The Eucharist lies at the very heart of our Catholic faith and worship. It is at the focus of everything we believe, everything we do, everything we hope for. CCC 1324

When we celebrate the Eucharist, we carry out the command that Jesus gave us at the Last Supper, "Do this in memory of me."

Two movements

To understand the movement or flow of the Eucharist (Mass), it helps to recall that ancient Jews worshiped in two different places: the synagogue LUKE 4:16 and the Temple LUKE 2:41.

There was a synagogue in each town; but there was only one Temple—in Jerusalem.

Synagogues were mainly places of prayer and instruction. People went there to read and reflect on the Word of God.

The Temple was mainly a place of prayer and sacrifice. People went there to make offerings to God. LUKE 2:24

The eucharistic celebration is made up of two movements that echo the synagogue and the Temple services. These two movements are called:

- **Liturgy of the Word**
- **Liturgy of the Eucharist**

Each one follows a similar threefold format:

- **Introductory rite**
- **Reading rite**
- **Concluding rite**

- **Introductory rite**
- **Eucharistic rite**
- **Concluding rite**

2 On a scale of one (not very) to ten (very), how closely would you say the synagogue and temple services fit what we do at Mass today? Explain.

STAGE 2: CHAPTER 12 151

blurred monotonously into the next.
To survive in this situation,
a man needed more than food . . .
he needed spiritual strength.

QUESTION **1** ***Why doesn't the Eucharist seem to mean as much to people today as it did to people in previous decades?***

Have the students list reasons in notebooks, discuss them in small groups, and pick out one to share with the class.

Last Supper

CLARIFY—English poet Rudyard Kipling wrote a poem called "Cold Iron." It's about a baron who rebels against a king, tries to overthrow him, is defeated, and is led in chains to the king. Instead of punishing him, the king treats him kindly and sets before him a meal of bread and wine.

DISCUSS—Ask: How is this poem an image of our experience with Jesus?

- *We rebel against Jesus by sinning. He forgives us by spreading before us the Lord's Supper.*

Two movements

DISCUSS—Ask: Why do you think there was only one Temple in all of Israel?

- *In a world of polytheism (many gods), it proclaimed the revolutionary truth that there was only one God. It also served as a unifying force.*

CLARIFY—The Jerusalem Temple was destroyed by the Romans in A.D. 70—as Jesus foretold. MATTHEW 24:2 All that remains is the Western Wall, part of the plaza upon which it stood.

When Israeli tanks rumbled into Jerusalem's old city in 1969, it was the first time since A.D. 70, except for a brief period in A.D. 135, that Jews controlled the site. Although they now control the site, they would not dare remove the Dome of the Rock, a mosque, which now occupies the exact spot where the Temple stood.

Since the site was also sacred to Muslims (via Abraham, page 42), they built a mosque there in the seventh century. Beneath it lies a 40-by-60-foot rock, said to be the site where Abraham led Isaac to be sacrificed. David chose this spot for the Jerusalem Temple.

CLARIFY—A description of the Liturgy of the Word is found in Luke 4:16–21, the Liturgy of the Eucharist in Luke 22:19–20.

QUESTION **2** ***On a scale of one (not very) to ten (very), how closely would you say the synagogue and temple services fit what we do at Mass today? Explain.***

Structurally, the Liturgy of the Word matches the synagogue service. The Liturgy of the Eucharist matches the Temple service. As for content, they are totally different, especially the Eucharist.

THINK about it

This statement by Mohandas Gandhi is typical of his spiritual wisdom and insight.

Tony de Mello wrote a book called *Taking Flight*. He quotes Gandhi as saying that while studying in South Africa, he was drawn by the life and teaching of Jesus. One Sunday he went to a church to attend Mass and get instructions. He was stopped at the door and told that if he desired to attend services, he was welcome to do so in a church reserved for black people. Gandhi did not pursue the matter.

The spiritual leader of Indian independence, the 78-year-old Gandhi was killed in 1948 by a Hindu extremist. The assassin was waiting with his hands folded before him, palms together in the Hindu gesture of a friendly greeting. Hidden in his hands was a small, low-caliber revolver.

As Gandhi passed, the man fired three shots at close range. Gandhi crumpled to the ground, putting his hand to his forehead in the Hindu gesture of forgiveness.

Liturgy of the Word

CLARIFY—It is customary to think of modern Judaism in terms of three major groups: Reform, Conservative, Orthodox.

In his book *Judaism,* Rabbi Stuart Rosenberg stresses that all three believe in (1) the unity of God and (2) their desire to witness to the Word given them at Mt. Sinai.

"Orthodox Jews still pray for the coming of the Messiah" whom they believe will "cleanse the world of evil. . . . He will serve as the 'anointed one,' who will lead his people as the 'light of the nations.'"

"Conservative and Reform Jews, by and large, do not accept the idea of a personal Messiah." They see Jewish messianism as the provider of a religious vision that will lead mankind into a truly "Golden Age."

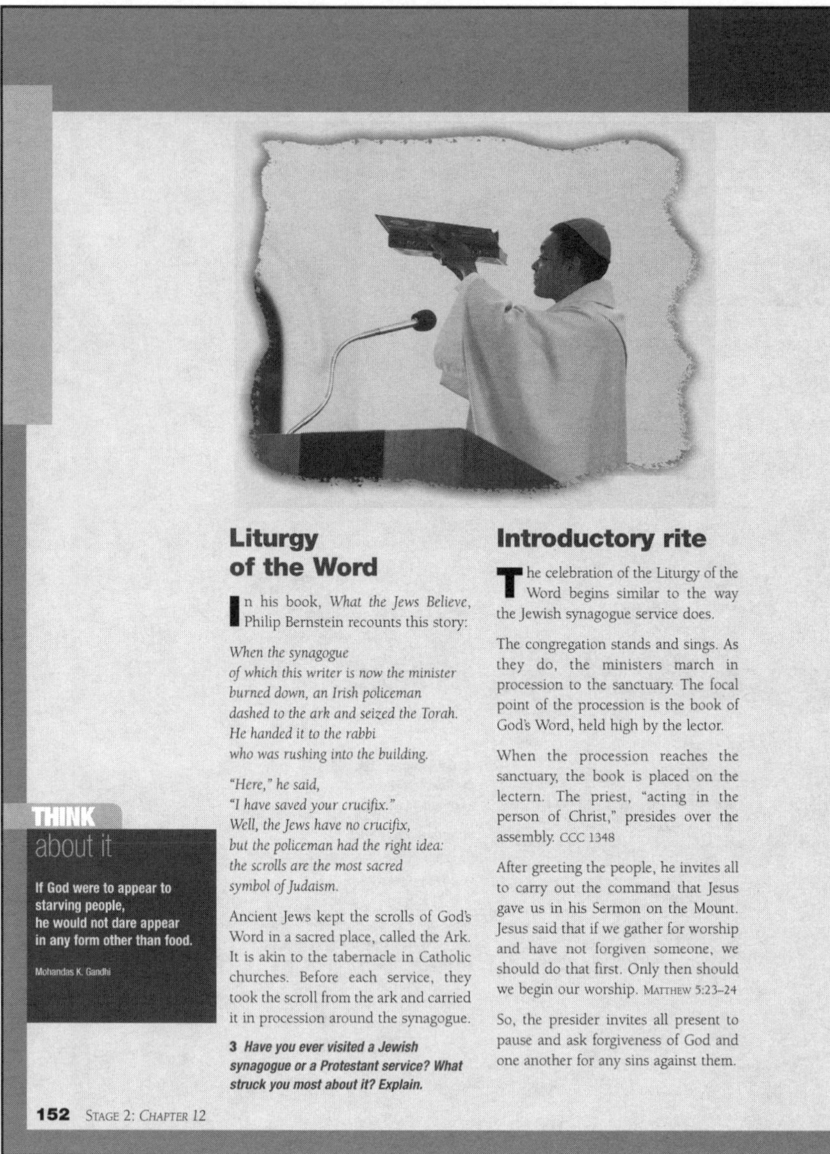

Liturgy of the Word

In his book, *What the Jews Believe*, Philip Bernstein recounts this story:

When the synagogue
of which this writer is now the minister
burned down, an Irish policeman
dashed to the ark and seized the Torah.
He handed it to the rabbi
who was rushing into the building.

"Here," he said,
"I have saved your crucifix."
Well, the Jews have no crucifix,
but the policeman had the right idea:
the scrolls are the most sacred
symbol of Judaism.

Ancient Jews kept the scrolls of God's Word in a sacred place, called the Ark. It is akin to the tabernacle in Catholic churches. Before each service, they took the scroll from the ark and carried it in procession around the synagogue.

3 Have you ever visited a Jewish synagogue or a Protestant service? What struck you most about it? Explain.

THINK about it

If God were to appear to starving people, he would not dare appear in any form other than food.

Mohandas K. Gandhi

Introductory rite

The celebration of the Liturgy of the Word begins similar to the way the Jewish synagogue service does.

The congregation stands and sings. As they do, the ministers march in procession to the sanctuary. The focal point of the procession is the book of God's Word, held high by the lector.

When the procession reaches the sanctuary, the book is placed on the lectern. The priest, "acting in the person of Christ," presides over the assembly. CCC 1348

After greeting the people, he invites all to carry out the command that Jesus gave us in his Sermon on the Mount. Jesus said that if we gather for worship and have not forgiven someone, we should do that first. Only then should we begin our worship. MATTHEW 5:23–24

So, the presider invites all present to pause and ask forgiveness of God and one another for any sins against them.

QUESTION **3** ***Have you ever visited a Jewish synagogue [often referred to by modern Conservative and Reform Jews as a "temple"] or a Protestant service? What struck you most about it? Explain.***

Have the students share their experiences with the entire class.

In biblical times, synagogue services were conducted by congregation members LUKE 4:16–17 or invited guests. ACTS 13:13–16 Today, a rabbi, assisted by a cantor, leads the synagogue service.

In ancient times, the title "rabbi" was given to any learned person in the community. Today, the "rabbi" is reserved for those educated in rabbinical schools.

NOTES

4 What do you do when you find it hard to forgive someone for something they've done to you?

At some celebrations, this "penitential rite" is followed by a hymn of thanks and adoration (praise). Called the *Gloria*, it begins:

Glory to God in the highest,
and peace to his people on earth.
Lord God, heavenly King,
almighty God and Father,
we worship you, we give you thanks,
we praise you for your glory. . . .

The presider then leads the assembly in prayer. Here is a typical prayer:

Almighty God, ever-loving Father,
your care extends
beyond the boundaries of race and nation
to the hearts of all who live.
May the walls,
which prejudice raises between us,
crumble beneath the shadow
of your outstretched arm.
We ask this through Christ our Lord.
Twentieth Sunday of the Year

And so the Introductory Rite prepares us for the heart of the Liturgy of the Word, which now follows.

Reading rite

Saint Luke gives us a beautiful description of how the reading of God's Word was celebrated in ancient synagogues. He writes:

Jesus went to Nazareth,
where he was brought up,
and on the Sabbath,
he went as usual to the synagogue.
He stood up to read the Scriptures and
was handed the book
of the prophet Isaiah.
He unrolled the scroll
and found the place where it is written,

"The Spirit of the Lord is upon me,
because he has chosen me
to bring good news to the poor.

"He has sent me
to proclaim liberty to the captives
and recovery of sight to the blind,
to set free the oppressed and
announce that the time has come
when the Lord will save his people."

Jesus rolled up the scroll,
gave it back to the attendant,
and sat down.
All the people in the synagogue
had their eyes fixed on him,
as he said to them,

"This passage of scripture
has come true today,
as you heard it being read."
They were all well impressed with him
and marveled at the eloquent words
that he spoke. Luke 4:16–22

At Sunday celebrations of the Eucharist, the proclamation of the Word consists of three readings.

SHARE YOUR **meditation**

A young Protestant said:

I admire Catholics a lot,
but I must admit
that they also puzzle me a lot.
For example,
they say Jesus is really
present at the Mass,
just as truly as he was
at the Last Supper.
If they believe this,
why don't they go more
frequently and participate
more devoutly?

■ **How would you respond to that question?**

Introductory rite

NOTEBOOK—Before discussing the "Introductory rite," have students enter the following parallel structure between the Mass and the synagogue and the Temple services into their notebooks.

Prayers of faithful

1st part of Mass	2nd part of Mass
Liturgy of Word	Liturgy of Eucharist
Luke 4:16–21	Luke 22:19–20
Synagogue Service	Temple Service
Instruction	Sacrifice

QUESTION **4 What do you do when you find it hard to forgive someone for something they've done to you?**

■ *A sign of authentic Christianity is our readiness to forgive—"Not seven times but seventy times seven."* Matthew 18:22 *How do we forgive when we find it hard? Consider an example:*

Corrie ten Boom was a survivor of a Nazi concentration camp. After the war, she toured Europe giving talks, urging rival nations to forgive one another.

One night, in Munich, a man came up after her talk and extended his hand in a gesture of reconciliation. Corrie froze. It was one of the most hated guards of the camp she'd been in. She couldn't take his hand. She prayed: "Jesus, help me! I can't forgive him!" Instantly, some higher power helped her to take his hand in forgiveness.

That night Corrie learned a great truth. The same Jesus who taught us to love our enemies empowers us to do so. All we need to do is ask for the power.

CLARIFY—The *Gloria* is a 1500-year-old hymn. It recalls the angel's words at Jesus' birth: "Glory to God in the highest." Luke 2:14 When the shepherds heard this, they left their flocks, hurried through the night, and put themselves in the presence of the infant Jesus. The *Gloria* invites us to do the same: to leave behind our earthly cares and put ourselves, consciously, in God's presence.

Reading rite

CLARIFY—Stress that the heart of the Liturgy of the Word is the Reading rite. It is the key to "setting the mood of faith in which we celebrate the mystery of faith."

Share Your **meditation**

Acting on what we know to be true is not always easy. Example: We know we should exercise; we know we should study; we know we should treat others as we would want them to treat us—why don't we do it?

It's part of the territory of being human. As Jesus put it, "The spirit is willing, but the flesh is weak." Matthew 26:41 Our goal is to open ourselves to God's grace and meet the challenge.

Listening to the Word

NOTEBOOK—Develop on the chalkboard the following summary for entry into the students' notebooks:

Body:	*with attention*	*Heart:*	*with love*
Mind:	*with imagination*	*Soul:*	*with faith*

The "pencil meditation" on page 64 is a good example of listening with imagination.

First reading

QUESTION **5** ***During what season of the year is the first reading taken not from the Old Testament, but from the Acts of the Apostles? Why the Acts?***

- *During the "seven weeks" of the Easter Season: from the Holy Saturday Easter Vigil through Pentecost Sunday.*

CLARIFY—Ancient writers used the word "Acts" to refer to the feats of great leaders, like Alexander the Great. Written by Luke (Acts 1:1–2) the Acts of the Apostles models itself after such writings. It gives us this picture of the Apostles:

- *Off they went with burning urgency*
  to tell the news to all the world.
  The Messiah had come.
  Truly the Kingdom of God was at hand.
  Many were to find crosses of their own
  on which to hang. F.B. Rhein

  Their witness never wavered.
  Rather, they experienced an amazing
  power that even enabled them
  to work miracles. The lives and message
  of these men changed the course of human
  history. Robert L. Cleath

Responsorial psalm

CLARIFY—If the Old Testament got lost, except for the Book of Psalms, we could recover much of its spirit from that book alone. It is the hymnbook and the prayer book of the Bible.

Listening to the Word

A Broadway play, *The Royal Hunt of the Sun,* dealt with Spain's conquest of Peru. In one scene a Spaniard gives an Inca leader a Bible, saying that it is God's Word.

Filled with curiosity, the leader raises the Bible to his ear and listens. When he hears nothing, he slams the Bible to the ground, feeling that he has been deceived.

This raises the question: How do we go about listening to God's word?

First we listen with our *body;* that is, we listen with reverent attention.

Second, we listen with our *mind;* that is, we try to make the passage come alive in our imagination. We try to visualize the scene and feel the excitement Jesus' disciples felt as they watched and listened to it unfold.

Third, we listen with our *heart;* that is, we "take it to heart."

Finally, we listen with our soul. This means that we listen with faith. We believe God's Word has the power to touch us and transform us. So we listen with confidence, knowing that if we persevere, the day will come when it will touch us profoundly.

- ***Which of the four ways to listen do you find most difficult: body, mind, heart, or soul? Explain.***

First reading

This reading is usually from the Old Testament, the same collection of readings from which Jesus read in the synagogue at Nazareth.

5 ***During what season of the year is the first reading taken not from the Old Testament, but from the Acts of the Apostles? Why the Acts?***

Responsorial psalm

The first reading is followed by a *Responsorial Psalm.* Selected from the Book of Psalms, it serves as a prayerful meditation on the first reading.

Second reading

The next reading is taken from the New Testament, usually one of Paul's letters. These letters deal with early Christian problems. Surprisingly, they often deal with problems that are similar to our own problems.

Third reading

The final reading is the most important one. It is taken from one of the four Gospels. Normally, we show the importance of this reading in a fourfold way:

- **Introducing it with an acclamation**
- **Standing for the reading of it**
- **Signing ourselves when it begins**
- **Having it read by presider or deacon**

The "signing" of ourselves goes back to early Christian times. It consists in tracing a small cross on the forehead, lips, and heart. While doing so, many people pray silently:

May God's Word
be in my mind, on my lips, and in my
heart that I may worthily proclaim it
by word and by example.

After the reading of the Gospel, the presider usually kisses the text, elevates the book, and says, "The Gospel of the Lord." All respond, "Praise to you, Lord Jesus Christ."

154 Stage 2: Chapter 12

Second reading

CLARIFY—Stress that the Letters that make up the second reading do not necessarily match the theme of the *Mass during Ordinary Time.* (see page 123)

Third reading

CLARIFY—The Gospel reading is the key reading. Review how the Gospels went through three stages in their development (page 24) and recall the "seashell" analogy (page 25).

Life	*What Jesus said and did*
Oral	*What the apostles preached*
Written	*What the evangelists wrote*

The Gospel divides neatly into "reading packages." This is because the first

NOTES

SHARE YOUR meditation

A pastor began his homily by holding up a huge triangle. He said:

*My homily is like this triangle.
It has three points.
The first point is
that millions of people
are starving and homeless.*

*The second point is
that most people
don't give a damn.*

*The third point is
that some of you
are probably more disturbed
by the fact that
I just said "damn"
than you are by the fact
that millions are starving
and homeless.*

■ ***How would you evaluate the pastor's homily and why?***
■ ***If you could preach one homily on national TV, what would you preach about? Why?***
■ ***What visual aid/aids might you use?***

Homily

The Gospel reading is followed by the homily. It is given either by the presider or a deacon. The homilist does what Jesus did in the synagogue in Nazareth. He explains and applies the Word to the congregation.

Homilists have a difficult assignment. First, most congregations are made up of people of different ages and backgrounds. This makes it hard to appeal to everyone. Second, not all homilists are gifted communicators.

And so the homily may not always be as inspiring as we'd like it to be. But we should not forget Jesus' words to his disciples: "Whoever listens to you listens to me." LUKE 10:16

6 Describe a recent homily that you found to be better than ordinary.

Concluding rite

The Liturgy of the Word concludes in a twofold way: with the Creed and the General Intercessions.

The Creed is a summary of what we Catholics believe. The General Intercessions are an expression to God of our needs and the needs of our world.

And so the first movement of the Mass sets the *mood of faith* in which we can celebrate the *mystery of faith*. This brings us to the second movement of the Mass.

Christians "packaged" the events of the Gospel this way for handy use in worship and catechesis (teaching).

Homily

DISCUSS—Ask: The homilist stands to deliver the homily. How is this different from what Jesus did in the synagogue at Nazareth?

■ *Jesus sat to explain the reading. Sitting was the ancient posture for teaching. We still speak of a professor as occupying the "chair of theology" or the "chair of philosophy." The Latin word for the teacher's chair is "cathedra." This word gave rise to the bishop's church being called the* cathedral.

QUESTION **6 *Describe a recent homily that you found to be better than ordinary.***

Allow the students a bit of time to reflect. When they have been given a chance to respond, you might share with them the following example:

■ *The homilist began by holding a large host in his hand. He said that it was next in line (in the container) to be used at Mass. He said the host's destiny is the highest one any created thing could dream of: becoming the Body of Christ. He dramatized how the grains of wheat in the host were probably one in a billion.*

Then the homilist paused for several seconds. When everybody was completely silent, he crushed the host with his hand.

The point was that we Christians are like the host. We, too, have been called to the highest destiny anyone can be called to: to be followers of Jesus. The crushing of the host stands for sin. It is the one thing that can keep us from our destiny.

DISCUSS—You might get an unconsecrated host and dramatize this example. In any event, have the students evaluate the effectiveness of the homily.

Concluding rite

CLARIFY—Legend says that before carrying the Gospel to the four corners of the earth, the 12 apostles outlined the message they would preach. The result was the 12 articles of the Apostles' Creed, each Apostle contributing an article. The story is sheer legend, but it does make an important point. Our faith comes to us from the Apostles.

DISCUSS—Have students write their responses to the questions. Discuss the first question in class. Delay the last two until you've had time to review them and then pick one or two to share with the class.

Up Close & Personal

Skeeter

Young Skeeter Rayburn could not speak or use his limbs. He lay on his back 24 hours a day. His only means of communication was an electric typewriter, which he pressed one key at a time by means of a stylus attached to his head. Using this method, he wrote an article on what the Eucharist meant to him. He writes:

One of my crosses . . .
is cerebral palsy's jerkiness. . . .
My muscles have spasms and
my arms and legs jerk wildly
until I think I will go mad.
At these moments,
I remember Jesus' torturous
writhings on the cross . . .
But he endured it silently.
Can I do less with my little
contortions with Jesus
living in me?

Another cross is
waiting for things.
I have to wait
to go to the bathroom;
wait to have my nose
cleaned out
when I can hardly breathe;
wait to be covered
when I am cold. . . .
In these periods I recall, again,
what Jesus did for me
on the cross.
Can I do less for him?

Eucharist magazine

Liturgy of the Eucharist

Charles Butler went to visit his son, who was working in the Amazon Basin in Brazil. When he arrived in Brazil, he took a small plane to a tiny town in the Basin. There, he and the pilot went to a local cafe for a meal.

An old-timer in the cafe began talking to the pilot. They soon discovered that they were both from the same province of Brazil. Next they discovered they were both from the same small town.

When Charles and the pilot finished their meal, the old-timer said to the pilot jokingly, "You know, if we keep talking, we might discover that we are from the same family."

That story makes a good bridge to the second movement of the Mass, the Liturgy of the Eucharist. Through it, we discover, in a special way, that we are family. We are much more. We are members of Christ's Body. Saint Paul says of the Eucharistic meal:

Because there is one loaf of bread,
all of us, though many, are one body,
for we all share the same loaf.
1 Corinthians 10:17

To understand the Liturgy of the Eucharist, we need to go back to the Jewish Passover meal.

In eating this meal together, Jews did far more than *remember* and celebrate the event that freed their ancestors from Egyptian slavery.

They believed that, through faith, they brought that event into present, so that they could participate in it as truly as if they had been present at the original event.

It was with this understanding that Jesus sat down with his disciples to eat the Passover meal. And it was during this meal that he instituted the Eucharist.

Jesus took his place at the table
with his apostles. . . .
Then he took a piece of bread,
gave thanks to God,
broke it, and gave it to them, saying:
"This is my body
which is given up for you.
Do this in memory of me."
Luke 22:14, 19

When Jesus said, "Do this in *memory* of me," he did more than give us a command to remember and reenact what he did. He gave us a way to be

156 Stage 2: Chapter 12

Up Close & Personal

CLARIFY—Share this story of a person who had an appreciation of the Eucharist similar to the appreciation Skeeter and Father Ciszek had.

■ *In 1985 millions of TV screens in the country showed footage of a woman pinned beneath a crane that had fallen in New York City. The TV cameras showed a team of medics fighting to keep her alive until a larger crane could be brought in to lift the fallen crane. They gave a blood transfusion, fluids, and massive doses of painkiller.*

Then came a dramatic moment. The woman had a special request. She asked for the Body of Christ in Holy Communion. This, too, the TV cameras caught in all of its moving drama. It was a beautiful witness to the woman's faith in the Eucharist. She was eventually freed and rushed to a hospital, where a team of medical people saved her life.

DISCUSS—Ask the students: How do you account for the love that Skeeter and the woman had for the Eucharist?

■ *Faith told them that Jesus was present in the Eucharist. When they experienced Jesus' help in Eucharist—especially in time of need—their faith and love of the Eucharist grew.*

Liturgy of the Eucharist

CLARIFY—To understand why Jesus chose the passover meal as the context for giving us the Eucharist, we need to understand the background of the meal. It has its origin in God's instructions to Moses to prepare the people for flight from Egypt after centuries of enslavement. God said:

"I will send only one more punishment on the king of Egypt and his people. After that . . . he will drive you out. . . . Every firstborn son
in Egypt will die." Exodus 11:1–5

"Give these instructions to the whole community of Israel. . . . Choose either a lamb or a young goat. . . .
Kill the animals. . . . Take some of the blood and put it on the doorposts . . .
of the houses in which the animals are to be eaten. . . .

"You are to eat it quickly . . .
dressed for travel. . . .
You are to celebrate this day . . .
for all time to come.

"When your children ask you,
'What does this ritual mean?'
you will answer, 'It is the sacrifice
of Passover to honor the Lord,
because he passed over the houses
of the Israelites in Egypt.

NOTES

present, in faith, to this great mystery just as truly as his apostles were 2000 years ago. CCC 1341, 1363

7 Why was it fitting for Jesus to choose the Jewish passover meal as the setting and the occasion for instituting the Eucharist?

Introductory rite

Just as the Liturgy of the Word began with a procession, so the Liturgy of the Eucharist begins with a procession. It begins with members of the congregation bringing the gifts of bread and wine to the Lord's Table (altar).

The presider takes them and prepares them. When he is finished preparing them, he invites the assembly to pray that they "may be acceptable to God, the almighty Father." The introductory rite ends with the presider praying in words like this:

Lord our God, may the bread and wine you give us for our nourishment on earth become the sacrament of our eternal life.
FIFTH SUNDAY OF THE YEAR

We are now ready for the most sacred moment of the entire eucharistic celebration.

Eucharistic prayer

This sacred prayer begins with a "dialogue" in which the presider exhorts the assembly: "Lift up your hearts" and "give thanks to the Lord."

The brief dialogue is followed by the preface. It begins with the presider giving thanks to God:

Father,
all-powerful and ever-living God,
we do well always and everywhere
to give you thanks.

The Preface concludes with the entire assembly saying or singing:

Holy, holy, holy Lord,
God of power and might.
Heaven and earth
are full of your glory.

Hosanna in the highest.
Blessed is he who comes
in the name of the Lord.
Hosanna in the highest.

The words "Holy, holy, holy" recall Isaiah's vision of heaven. The Lord was seated on a throne. "Around him flaming creatures . . . were calling out: 'Holy, holy, holy!'" ISAIAH 6:2–3

The words "Hosanna . . . Blessed is he who comes in the name of the Lord" recall the first Palm Sunday. The crowds called out to Jesus: "Hosanna . . . blessed is he who comes in the name of the Lord." MATTHEW 21:9 NAB

8 Why are the references to Isaiah and the Palm Sunday crowd appropriate at this point in the Mass?

FAITH Connection

INVITATION

Jesus of Nazareth
requests the honor of your
presence at a meal
to be given in his honor.
Attire informal.
RSVP

STAGE 2: CHAPTER 12 **157**

He killed the Egyptians,
but spared us.'" EXODUS 12:1–27 PASSIM

CLARIFY—Some people suggest that when Jesus said "This is my body," he meant it *metaphorically*, as when he said, "I am the vine, and you are the branches." JOHN 15:5 But Jesus meant these words in the *literal* sense and the people understood them that way. Listen to what Jesus said:

"I am the living bread that came down from heaven. If you eat this bread, you will live forever. The bread that I will give you is my flesh. . . ."

This started an angry argument among them. "How can this man give us his flesh to eat?" they asked. Jesus said to them, "I am telling you the truth: if you do not eat the flesh of the Son of Man and drink his blood, you will not have life. . . . Many of his followers heard this and said, "This teaching is too hard. Who can listen to it?" Because of this, many of Jesus' followers turned back and would not go with him any longer. So he said to the twelve disciples, "And you—would you also like to leave?" JOHN 6:51–53, 60, 66

QUESTION **7 *Why was it fitting for Jesus to choose the Jewish passover meal as the setting for instituting the Eucharist?***

NOTEBOOK—**Develop this diagram on the board for entry into the students' notebooks:**

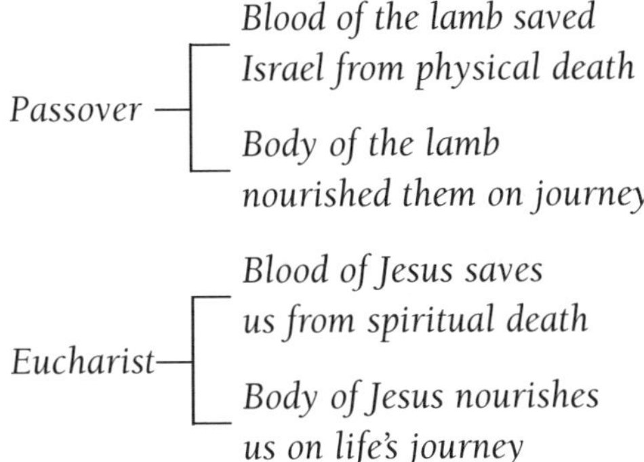

Passover
Blood of the lamb saved Israel from physical death
Body of the lamb nourished them on journey
Eucharist
Blood of Jesus saves us from spiritual death
Body of Jesus nourishes us on life's journey

Introductory rite

CLARIFY—**Stress that both the Liturgy of the Word and the Liturgy of the Eucharist begin with processions: Book and Gifts.**

Eucharistic prayer

QUESTION **8 *Why are the references to Isaiah and the Palm Sunday crowd appropriate at this point in the Mass?***

■ *The Isaiah reference prepares us for the most sacred moment of the Mass: our gifts of bread and wine will be transformed into the Body and Blood of Jesus, the Son of God.*

The Palm Sunday crowd models for us the reverence the people had for Jesus. They spread their cloaks and palm branches for him to ride across. Their reverence invites us to a similar reverence during this "most sacred moment of the Mass."

Invocation of the Spirit

Catholic teaching on the Eucharist used to be one of the things that kept people from the Church.

In recent years, however, it has become one of the things that draws people to the Church.

For example, literary critic Emilie Griffin writes in her book *Turning:*

A growing devotion to the Eucharist
and to my belief in the Real Presence
drew me to Roman Catholic Churches. . . .

As my devotion to the Eucharist grew,
so did my attraction to Roman
Catholicism.

Institution narrative

CLARIFY—The "Institutional narrative" makes it clear that the Eucharist is above all a meal.

But it is no ordinary meal. Like the Trinity, it is a mystery of unity (oneness) and trinity (threeness). It contains three distinct but inseparable dimensions. It is a: (1) Memorial meal, (2) Sacrificial meal, (3) Covenant meal.

It is a *memorial* meal in the mysterious sense described earlier under "Liturgy of the Eucharist":

When Jesus said,
"Do this in memory of me,"
he did more than give us a command
to remember and reenact what he did.
He gave us a way to be present in faith
to this great mystery just as truly
as his apostles were 2,000 years ago.

It is a *sacrificial* meal, closely linked to Jesus' sacrifice on the cross. This link is clear from Jesus' own words:

1 *My body: "Given up for you"*
2 *My blood: "Poured out for you."*

Eucharistic Prayer 1 reads:
"All of us . . . offer you this sacrifice."

Invocation of the Spirit

The Eucharistic Prayer continues with the presider asking the Father to send the Holy Spirit to make present the Body and Blood of Jesus under the signs of bread and wine. CCC 1353

Institution narrative

Next, the presider recalls the words of Jesus at the Last Supper, saying:

He took a piece of bread,
gave thanks to God, broke it,
and gave it to them, saying:

"This is my body,
which is given up for you.
Do this in memory of me."

These words recall the day when, on a hillside outside Capernaum, Jesus made this awesome promise to his followers:

"I am the living bread
that came down from heaven.
If anyone eats this bread,
he will live forever.
The bread that I will give . . .
is my flesh . . .
that the world may live." John 6:51

Then the presider does what Jesus did at the end of the Passover meal, saying:

In the same way
he gave them the cup after supper,
saying, "This cup is God's new covenant
sealed with my blood,
which is poured out for you."
Luke 22:19–20

Two points need to be stressed here. The *first point* is Jesus' words:

"This is my body,
which is given for you. . . .
This cup is . . . my blood
which is poured out for you"

They speak of *sacrifice* and indicate that the Last Supper is closely linked with Jesus' sacrifice on the cross. By sharing in the Eucharist we are sharing, also, in Jesus' sacrifice on the cross. Saint Paul writes:

The cup we use in the Lord's Supper . . .
when we drink from it,
we are sharing in the blood of Christ.
And the bread we break: when we eat it,
we are sharing in the body of Christ.
1 Corinthians 10:16

The *second point* is Jesus' words: "This cup is God's new covenant sealed with my blood." They recall the "new covenant" promised in Jeremiah 31:31 and indicate that it is being inaugurated by Jesus. The words "sealed with my blood" recall God's

THINK about it

Before Communion the Host does not look as if Christ is in it.
After Communion some Catholics do not look as if Christ is in them.

Frank Sheed (adapted)

Eucharistic Prayer III reads:
"Father . . . we offer you in thanksgiving
this holy and living sacrifice."

Finally, it is a *covenant* meal. This is made explicit by the two phrases: (1) "God's new covenant" (2) "Sealed with my blood."

The phrase "God's new covenant" recalls
Jeremiah 31:31–33:

The Lord *says, "The time is coming*
when I will make a new covenant
with the people of Israel
and the people of Judah.

"It will not be like the covenant
that I made with their ancestors
when I took them by the hand
and led them out of Egypt. . . .

NOTES

covenant with Israel at Mount Sinai, when Moses splashed blood on the people and said:

This is the blood that seals the covenant
which the Lord made with you.
Exodus 24:8

Memorial acclamation

The "Institutional narrative" is followed by the entire assembly proclaiming together the "mystery of faith," in words like this:

Christ has died,
Christ is risen,
Christ will come again.

9 Why is this particular acclamation appropriate for this moment in the Mass?

Memorial prayer

The Eucharistic Prayer continues with what is called the Memorial Prayer. The presider recalls Jesus' death and resurrection and offers them to the Father, in words like this:

In memory of his death and resurrection,
we offer you, Father,
this life-giving bread and this saving cup.

And so every Eucharist makes "sacramentally present under the species of bread and wine, Christ's body and blood, his sacrifice offered on the cross once for all." CCC 1353 In other words, "the sacrifice of Christ and the sacrifice of the Eucharist are one single sacrifice." CCC 1367

Moreover, the whole Church is united in the offering of the Mass: those still on earth, those already in heaven, and the faithful departed who have died in Christ. CCC 1370–71

Intercessions

The Memorial Prayer is followed by a series of intercessions, asking the Father's help in and through Jesus:

Grant that we, who are nourished
by his body and blood,
may be filled with the Holy Spirit,
and become one body,
one spirit in Christ.

May he make us an everlasting gift
to you and enable us to share
in the inheritance of the saints. . . .

We hope to enjoy forever
the visions of your glory
through Christ our Lord,
from whom all good things come.

PRAYER hotline

Jesus, give us new ears
to hear your cry in the cry of
those who call out in pain.

Give us new eyes
to see your face in the face
of those who look to us for
help.

Give us new tongues
to tell your story to those
who have never been told it.

Give us new hearts
to share your love with those
who have need of it most.

M.L.

The new covenant
that I will make with my people Israel
will be this:

"I will put my law within them
and write it on their hearts.
I will be their God,
and they will be my people."

The phrase "sealed with my blood" recalls God's covenant with Israel at Mount Sinai, when Moses collected the blood of sacrificed animals in bowls.

Half he threw against the altar.
Then he took the book of the covenant,
in which the Lord's commands were
written, and read it aloud to the people.
They said, "We will obey the Lord and
do everything that he has commanded."

Then Moses took the blood in the bowls
and threw it on the people. He said,
"This is the blood that seals the covenant
which the Lord made with you
when he gave all these commands."

"This is the blood that seals the covenant
which the Lord made with you."
Exodus 24:6–8

NOTEBOOK—**With the help of students, develop the following summary on the board for entry into student notebooks.**

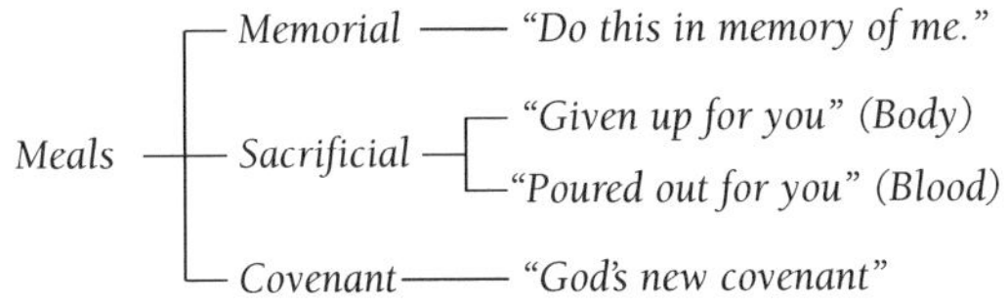

Memorial acclamation

QUESTION **9 *Why is this particular acclamation appropriate at this moment?***

- *It is a verbal summary and explanation of what we have just celebrated: the death of Jesus on the cross, his resurrection to new life, and his promise to return to take us with him into eternal life.*

Memorial prayer

Stress two things: (1) Jesus sacrificed himself on the cross but once. He does not sacrifice himself over and over at each Mass. What the Mass does is to make sacramentally present that one, single sacrifice. (2) The whole Church is united in the offering of the Mass: those on earth, in heaven, and in purgatory.

HISTORICAL Connection

Stress the remarkable similarity between how early Christians celebrated the Eucharist and how we celebrate it today.

■ *Christians in Saint Justin's time usually assembled for Sunday Mass before sunrise. The reason was that they lived in a culture that did not regard Sunday as the chief day of worship. Thus, since most Christians were workers, and quite a few were slaves, they had to gather before the day's work began.*

Sunrise was an ideal time to celebrate the Sunday Eucharist because Christians viewed the sun as a symbol of Christ, the true "light of the world." JOHN 8:12 *And they viewed the sunrise as a symbol of the resurrection.*

Concluding doxology

CLARIFY—A doxology is simply a brief prayer of praise, and/or thanksgiving to God.

Communion rite

Lord's Prayer

CLARIFY—Review what was said about God as "Father" on pages 70–71.

DISCUSS—Share this story. It captures the spirit of the Lord's Prayer.

Jesse, the son of a rich father, had everything he wanted, except a brother. He used to talk to his dad about it. One day his dad adopted Todd, a boy who was Jesse's age. They got along great.

One day they were tossing a football. Todd said to Jesse: "I wish my old friend Dan had a football like this, but his father can't afford it." Jesse said, "Ask dad to get him one." Todd said, "I couldn't do that. Your dad has given me so much. I couldn't ask him for more." Jesse said,

HISTORICAL Connection

Saint Justin was born around A.D. 100. In a letter to the pagan Roman emperor, Antoninus Pius, he described the Mass, as it was celebrated in his day:

On the day of the sun,
all who dwell
in the city or country
gather in the same place.

The memoirs of the apostles
and the writings of the prophets
are read. . . .

Then someone brings
bread and a cup of water
and wine mixed together
to him who presides. . . .
He takes them
and offers praise and glory
to the Father of the universe,
through the name of the Son
and of the Holy Spirit
and for a considerable time
he gives thanks. . . .

When he. . . .
has given thanks
and the people have responded,
those whom we call deacons
give to those present
the "eucharisted" [consecrated]
bread, wine, and water
and take them
to those who are absent.

Concluding doxology

The Eucharistic Prayer concludes with the presider saying or singing:

Through him, with him, and in him
in the unity of the Holy spirit,
all glory and honor
is yours almighty Father,
forever and ever. CCC 1354

The community responds with a resounding "Amen." From earliest times, this response has been called the "Great Amen." In some churches, it explodes to the accompaniment of musical instruments.

Communion rite

The presider then begins the communion rite. He introduces it by inviting everyone to pray in the words Jesus taught us.

Lord's Prayer

The words "give us this day our daily bread" take on special meaning at this moment. For in a few moments, we will receive the body of Christ, who is the "Bread of Life." JOHN 6:35

Sign of peace

The communion rite continues with the presider inviting the community to share a "sign of peace." This usually takes the form of a handshake or hug, with the words "The peace of Christ be with you."

The word "peace" translates the Hebrew word *shalom*, which has no English equivalent. Roughly, it means we wish one another the fullness of every good thing that Jesus came to bring: forgiveness, love, joy.

160 STAGE 2: CHAPTER 12

"'My father' is now 'your father.' He's 'our father'! You show your love and trust in him, when you share your desires with him. If he thinks it will be for your good, he'll give it to you. He gave me you!"

Suddenly, Todd realized what a wonderful father he had. At that moment, his relationship with his father took a giant leap forward.

ACTIVITY—Have the students write their answers to this question in their notebooks: What keeps me from approaching God as I would a parent whom I love deeply and trust totally?

DISCUSS—When they've finished, invite them to discuss their responses in small groups and pick one to share with the class.

NOTES

Communion

The eucharistic meal follows. It is a special moment for the entire community. A priest writes in his Journal:

People come up, hundreds of them. . . .
Suddenly, in the midst of it all,
a wave of gladness comes over me.
I'm so very glad to be here today. . . .
For a few moments I choke and can't say
the simplest words: "The Body of Christ."
JOHN EAGAN, S.J., *A TRAVELLER TOWARD THE DAWN*

Saint Paul said, "Because the loaf of bread is one, we, though many, are one body, for we all partake of the one loaf." 1 CORINTHIANS 10:17

Paul's words remind us that what we eat in ordinary meals becomes a part of us. In the eucharistic meal, however, we become a part of what we eat—the Body of Christ.

10 How do I spend the moments in line walking up to receive Holy Communion? Walking back after receiving it? How might I use them in the best possible way?

Concluding rite

The presider brings to a close the communion rite, praying in words like this:

Lord, you have nourished us
with bread from heaven.
Fill us with your Spirit and
make us one in peace and love.
We ask this through Christ our Lord.
SECOND SUNDAY OF THE YEAR

The Mass ends with the "dismissal rite." The presider blesses the assembly and charges all to "go in peace and love to serve the Lord."

Commenting on the dismissal rite someone said:

The holiest moment
in the church service
is the moment when God's people—
strengthened by preaching
and sacrament—
go out of the church door into the world
to be Church.
ERNEST SOUTHCOURT

11 How would you explain what he had in mind?

PRAYER hotline

Lord Jesus,
you are to me
medicine
when I am sick;
strength
when I need help;
life itself
when I fear death.

You are
the way
when I long for heaven;
light
when all is dark;
nourishment
when I need food.

Glory be to you
for ever and ever.

Saint Anselm

Sign of peace

***CLARIFY*—The purpose of the sign of peace is not only to extend it, but also to be it.**

Lord,
make me an instrument of your peace.

Where there is hatred,
we are to sow love;
where there is injury, pardon,
where there is doubt, faith;
where there is despair, hope;
where there is darkness, light;
and where there is sadness, joy.

Grant that we may not so much
seek to be consoled as to console;
to be understood as to understand;
to be loved as to love;
for it is in giving that we receive;
it is in pardoning
that we are pardoned;
and it is in dying
that we are born to eternal life.

Communion

***CLARIFY*—Here are a few practical points to share with the students:**

1 *Should fast from food and liquids (water excepted) for one hour before Communion (not, therefore, one hour before the Mass begins).*
2 *May receive Communion a second time on the same day if attending a second Mass, for example, a funeral.*
3 *Must celebrate Reconciliation before receiving Communion, if they have had the misfortune of falling into mortal sin.*

QUESTION **10** ***How do I spend the moments walking up to receive Communion? Walking back after receiving it? How might I use them in the best possible way?***

■ *Refer the students back to "Think about it" on page 158 to stress the point that the times before and after Communion are special and should be treated that way.*

Concluding rite

QUESTION **11** ***How would you explain what he had in mind?***

■ *We might compare the celebration of the Eucharist to the eye of a hurricane. As we gather each Sunday, the winds of war, social unrest, and racial tension roar and rage around us.*

Here inside the church, however, there is a different atmosphere. We are in the eye of the hurricane. We are in the presence of a loving Father, Son, and Spirit; and we see the world as they made it to be.

But Jesus never intended us to remain inside the eye of the hurricane. He intended for us to go out again into the winds and wars of the world, and what we experience now he intends us to be instruments of peace.

Recap

These words of the *Constitution on the Liturgy* of the Second Vatican Council form a fitting recap of the chapter:

> *Christ is always present in his Church . . .*
> *in the sacrifice of the Mass,*
> *in the person of the minister . . .*
> *and most of all*
> *under the eucharistic species. . . .*
>
> *He is present in his word,*
> *for it is he himself who speaks when*
> *the holy Scriptures are read in the Church.*
> *Finally, he is present when the Church*
> *prays and sings, for he himself promised:*
> *"When two or three are gathered in my*
> *name, I am there in their midst."*
>
> *Indeed, in this great work which brings*
> *perfect glory to God and holiness to men,*
> *Christ is always joining in partnership*
> *with . . . the Church. . . . It is therefore*
> *right to see the liturgy as an exercise*
> *of the priestly office of Jesus Christ,*
> *in which . . . public worship*
> *is celebrated in its fullness*
> *by the mystical body of Jesus Christ,*
> *that is, by the head and by its members.*
>
> *In the liturgy on earth*
> *we are given a foretaste and share*
> *in the liturgy of heaven.* NN. 7–8

Review

DAILY QUIZ—The review questions may be assigned (one or two at a time) for homework or a daily quiz.

CHAPTER TESTS—Reproducible chapter tests are found in Appendix A. For consistency and ease in grading, quizzes are restricted to (1) "Matching," (2) "True/False," and (3) "Fill in the Blanks."

TEST ANSWERS—The following are the answers to the test for Chapter 12. (See Appendix A, page 323.) Each correct answer is worth 4 points.

Recap

When we celebrate the Eucharist, we carry out the Lord's Last Supper command: "Do this in memory of me." It consists of "one single act of worship" with a twofold moment:

- **Liturgy of the Word**
- **Liturgy of the Eucharist**

Each begins with an Introductory Rite and ends with a Concluding Rite: CCC 1346

- **Introductory Rite**
- **Liturgy of the Word**
- **Concluding Rite**

- **Introductory Rite**
- **Liturgy of the Eucharist**
- **Concluding Rite**

The Liturgy of the Eucharist is the heart of celebration. In it, the presider calls upon the Father to send the Holy Spirit to transform the bread and wine into Jesus' body and blood.

The liturgy continues with the entire Church offering itself with Jesus in "his sacrifice of praise and thanksgiving offered once and for all on the cross to his Father." CCC 1407

It ends with the eucharistic meal, which proclaims the Lord's death until he comes in glory.

It transforms the members of the Church more fully into what they receive: the Body of Christ.

Review

1 List (a) the two worship places in Israel in Jesus' time, (b) the kind of service held in each, (c) to what movement of the Eucharist each service is related.

2 List (a) the source from which each of the three Sunday readings is usually taken, (b) what follows the first reading and the purpose it serves, (c) what follows the the third reading and it's purpose.

3 List and briefly explain (a) two reasons why the homily is a difficult assignment, (b) what we should keep in mind as we listen to it, (c) the four ways we should listen to God's Word, as it is proclaimed and explained, (d) the twofold way the Liturgy of the Word ends.

4 List (a) the Jewish meal during which Jesus instituted the Eucharist, (b) what this Jewish meal celebrated, (c) in what sense are Jesus' words, "Do this in memory of me," more than an invitation to remember some event that took place 2,000 years ago.

5 Explain how the words Jesus used to institute the Eucharist recall (a) God's old covenant with Israel, (b) God's promise to Jeremiah, (c) Jesus' promise to his followers on a hillside outside Capernaum.

6 List and briefly explain the two points in the "institutional narrative" that need to be stressed.

7 List and briefly explain (a) how the sacrifice of Christ on Calvary is related to the sacrifice of the Eucharist, (b) how the sacrifice of the Christ on Calvary is made present in the Eucharist (Mass).

8 Explain briefly (a) what the words "Holy, holy, holy" recall, (b) what event the word "Hosanna" recalls, (c) the meaning of the Hebrew word *shalom*, (d) how the effect of the food we eat at ordinary meals has a totally different effect from the food we eat in the eucharistic meal.

162 STAGE 2: CHAPTER 12

Matching

1 = c 2 = f 3 = d 4 = e
5 = b 6 = a

True/False

1 = T 2 = T 3 = F 4 = F
5 = T 6 = T

Fill in the Blanks

1. (a) Synagogue (b) Instruction
   (c) Jerusalem (d) Temple
   (e) sacrifice

2. (a) Liturgy of Word (b) Procession
   (c) Book (Lectionary)
   (d) Liturgy of Eucharist
   (e) Procession (f) Bread, wine

3. (a) Sacrificial (b) Covenant

NOTES

Reflect

1 Neil Armstrong and Ed Aldrin landed on the moon July 20, 1969. Aldrin writes:

I was able to serve myself communion
on the moon . . . My pastor gave me
a miniature chalice . . .
with a small amount of bread and wine.

Just after Mike Collins passed over
us one revolution after our landing . . .

I unstowed these elements . . . during my
requested air-to-ground silence.
I then read some passages from the Bible . . .
celebrated communion . . .
and offered some private prayers.

LIFE MAGAZINE 8/22/69

■ **Why do/don't you think it was appropriate for Aldrin to perform such a personal act of worship on the moon?**

■ **What private prayers do you offer before and after Communion? Explain.**

2 As a young man, Scott ripped apart a rosary, and gave out anti-Catholic literature. Later as a Protestant minister, he questioned what he'd been taught about the Eucharist, namely that it was a symbol. To make a long story short, he began to read up on Catholic belief in the Eucharist. The more he read, the more he was drawn to Catholicism. One day, he went to a Catholic church to see what went on at the celebration of the Eucharist. Deeply moved, he wrote:

After pronouncing the words of consecration,
the priest held up the Host. I felt as if the last drop
of doubt had been drained from me.
With all my heart, I whispered,
"My Lord and my God.". . .

I left the chapel not telling a soul
where I had been . . .
But the next day I was back,
and the next, and the next. . . .
I had fallen . . . in love
with our Lord in the Eucharist.
His presence to me . . .
was powerful and personal.

SCOTT HAHN: ONE COMES HOME TO ROME

■ **Why do "convert" Catholics often have a greater appreciation of the Mass than "cradle" Catholics do?**

3 Regina Riley prayed for years that her two sons would return to the practice of their faith. One Sunday she saw them across the aisle. Later she asked them what brought them back.

They said that while vacationing in Colorado, they picked up an old man one Sunday. It was pouring rain, and he was getting soaked. He said he was on his way to Mass three miles up the mountain road.

When they got to the church, they decided to attend the Mass and take the man home afterward. "You know," the younger brother told his mother, "it felt so right—like returning home after a long trip."

■ **What are some reasons young people stop practicing their faith? What are some of the reasons they begin again?**

Reflect

1 a) *Why do/don't you think it was appropriate for Aldrin to perform such a personal act of worship on the moon?*

■ *The Communion bread and wine were sealed in plastic packets (as all in-flight food is wrapped on space travel). He poured the Communion wine into a small silver chalice, which he stowed in his personal-preference kit. (All astronauts are permitted a few personal items on the flight.) Aldrin wrote later:*

"It was interesting to think that the very first liquid ever poured on the moon, and the first food eaten there, were Communion elements." One reason why Aldrin "sensed especially strong" his "unity with our church back home, and the Church everywhere" was that his own church (Webster Presbyterian, just outside of Houston) was holding a Communion service at the same time that he was receiving Communion on the moon.

FOR A COMPLETE ACCOUNT OF ALDRIN'S STORY, SEE "COMMUNION IN SPACE" BY BUZZ ALDRIN IN *THE GUIDEPOSTS TREASURY OF HOPE*, PAGES 286–89.

2 *Why do "convert" Catholics often have a greater appreciation of the Mass than "cradle" Catholics do?*

■ *You might have the students take up this question in small groups before opening the discussion up to the class. They could then share their conclusions with the class.*

3 *What are some reasons young people stop practicing their faith? What are some reasons why they begin again?*

Have a "class secretary" make two lists on the chalkboard: (1) Why stop? (2) Why start again? List student responses.

■ *A national survey reported that nearly half of Catholics between the ages of 15 and 29 stop practicing their faith for a period of two years or more. More than half of these eventually return—for various reasons:*

a) **Marriage**. *They meet a practicing Catholic who reconnects them.*

b) **Personal crisis**. *A family death, illness, or loss of employment makes them feel the need to return.*

c) **Feeling of emptiness**. *They achieve a measure of worldly success. But a spiritual void persists; something is still missing from their lives.*

d) **Regain control of lives**. *They become tired of moral disarray and sin. They long for self-control. They long to be the kind of person they want to be.*

PRAYER TIME with the Lord

QUESTION ***Can you recall a memorable Communion moment of your own? When? Where? With whom?***

■ *To get the students started, have them recall and recount some memorable Communions referred to in the text:*

African chief	*page 102*
Fr. Ciszek	*page 150*
Skeeter Rayburn	*page 156*
Aldrin on moon	*page 163*
N.Y. woman	*page 156 (Manual)*

You might wish to share this memorable Communion with the students. Father Joseph Hogan, S.J., describes it in *A Do-it-yourself Retreat*, Loyola Press, Chicago, 1961:

■ *I was a chaplain in Europe with the U.S. Third Army during World War II. One Sunday I felt the presence of God in a way that touched me deeply.*

I was saying Mass on top of a jeep. The men were standing there with their guns slung over their backs. . . . The ack-ack was pecking at the planes upstairs.

There was a torrent of rain coming down and a sea of mud to wallow in. So I said, "Don't bother to kneel down." And they didn't, until the Consecration. Then every man went down on his knees. . . .

When they sloshed up to receive Holy Communion, they again knelt in mud puddles. It was a memorable Communion scene I will never forget as long as I live.

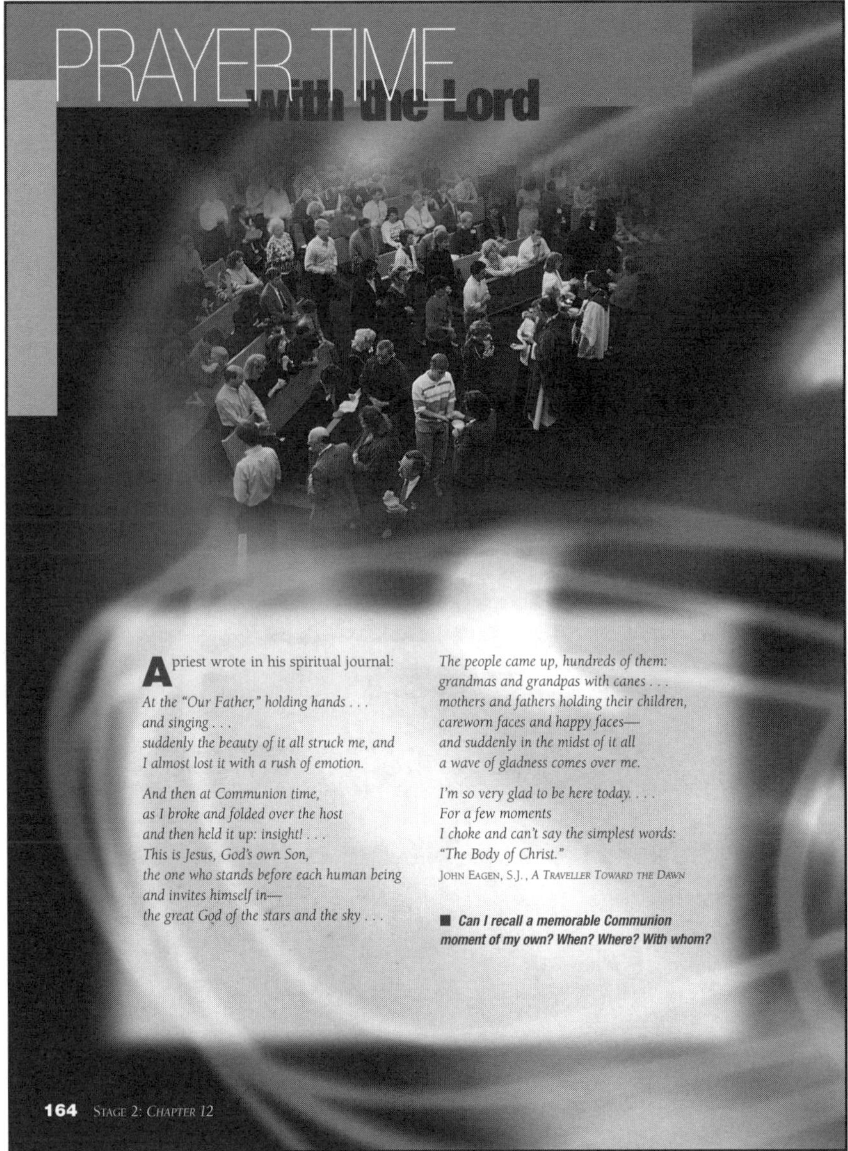

PRAYER TIME with the Lord

A priest wrote in his spiritual journal:

At the "Our Father," holding hands . . .
and singing . . .
suddenly the beauty of it all struck me, and
I almost lost it with a rush of emotion.

And then at Communion time,
as I broke and folded over the host
and then held it up: insight! . . .
This is Jesus, God's own Son,
the one who stands before each human being
and invites himself in—
the great God of the stars and the sky . . .

The people came up, hundreds of them:
grandmas and grandpas with canes . . .
mothers and fathers holding their children,
careworn faces and happy faces—
and suddenly in the midst of it all
a wave of gladness comes over me.

I'm so very glad to be here today. . . .
For a few moments
I choke and can't say the simplest words:
"The Body of Christ."

JOHN EAGEN, S.J., A TRAVELLER TOWARD THE DAWN

■ ***Can I recall a memorable Communion moment of my own? When? Where? With whom?***

164 STAGE 2: CHAPTER 12

The prayer refers to Jesus as the following: (1) Medicine, (2) Strength, (3) Life, (4) The Way, (5) Light, (6) Nourishment. You might suggest that the students use the first three dimensions of Jesus in their "Prayer before Communion."

■ *How are they spiritually sick and in need of a medicine? How are they spiritually weak and in need of strength? How are they spiritually dead and in need of life?*

Suggest that they use the last three dimensions in their "Prayer after Communion."

■ *How are they spiritually lost in a deep forest and need of someone like Jesus to show them the way back? How are they in the dark about something and in need of light? How are they spiritually run-down and in need of spiritual nourishment?*

PRAYER Journal

QUESTION ***Compose a prayer that you could put in your wallet and pray to prepare for Communion; another to pray after receiving Communion.***

Have the students turn to "Prayer hotline" on page 161 as an example of such a prayer. Ask: "Would it be more fitting for a prayer after Communion or before Communion?"

NOTES

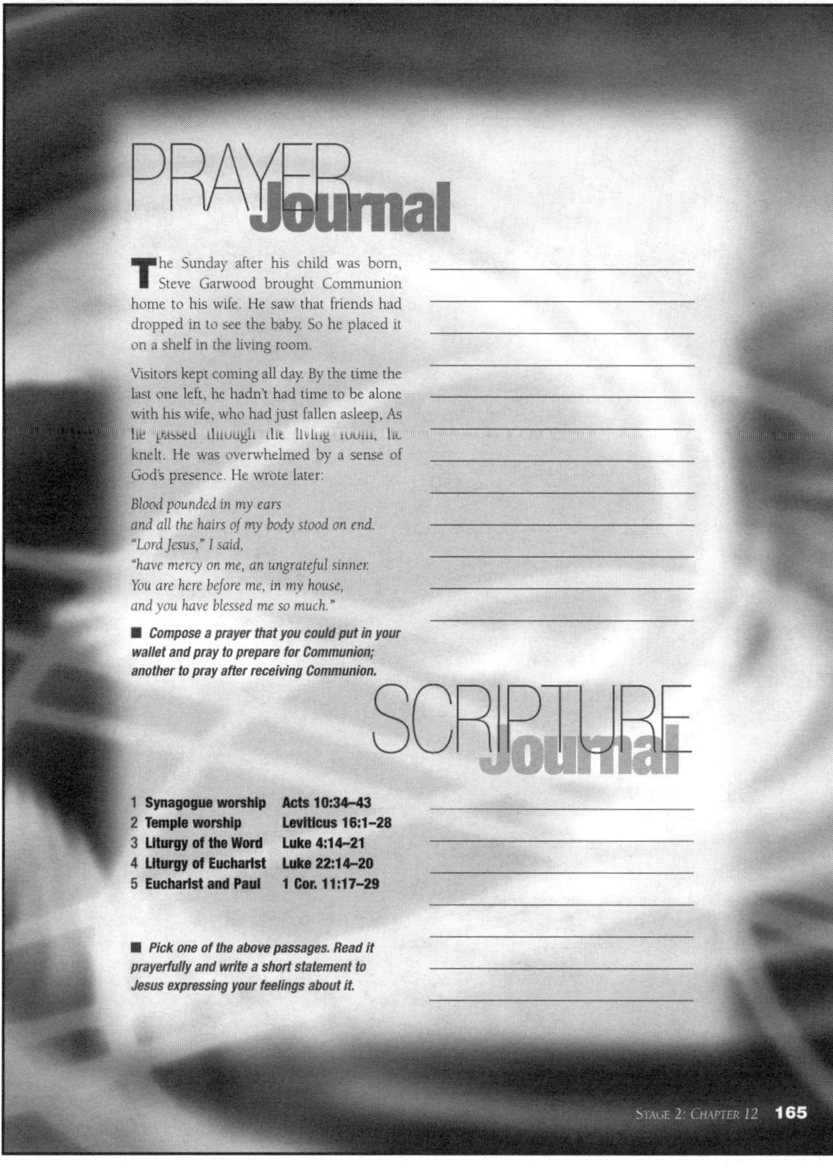

PRAYER Journal

The Sunday after his child was born, Steve Garwood brought Communion home to his wife. He saw that friends had dropped in to see the baby. So he placed it on a shelf in the living room.

Visitors kept coming all day. By the time the last one left, he hadn't had time to be alone with his wife, who had just fallen asleep. As he passed through the living room, he knelt. He was overwhelmed by a sense of God's presence. He wrote later:

Blood pounded in my ears
and all the hairs of my body stood on end.
"Lord Jesus," I said,
"have mercy on me, an ungrateful sinner.
You are here before me, in my house,
and you have blessed me so much."

■ ***Compose a prayer that you could put in your wallet and pray to prepare for Communion; another to pray after receiving Communion.***

SCRIPTURE Journal

1	Synagogue worship	Acts 10:34–43
2	Temple worship	Leviticus 16:1–28
3	Liturgy of the Word	Luke 4:14–21
4	Liturgy of Eucharist	Luke 22:14–20
5	Eucharist and Paul	1 Cor. 11:17–29

■ ***Pick one of the above passages. Read it prayerfully and write a short statement to Jesus expressing your feelings about it.***

STAGE 2: CHAPTER 12 165

SCRIPTURE Journal

QUESTION ***Pick one of the passages. Read it prayerfully and write a short statement to Jesus expressing your feelings about it.***

■ *Read the first line from the fourth reading: "When the hour came, Jesus took his place at the table with the apostles."*

Have the students imagine they are seated at the table across from Jesus. Suddenly, they realize that for Jews to drink from another's cup in such a setting is to share one another's fate and to eat their bread is to share one another's blessing.

Have them write a brief statement to Jesus expressing their feelings about forming such a solemn covenant with Jesus.

Classroom Resources

CATECHISM

Catechism of the Catholic Church *Second Edition*

For further enrichment, you might refer to:

1. Eucharist	Index	pp. 788–89
	Glossary	p. 877
2. Communion	Index	p. 775
	Glossary	p. 871
3. Word of God	Index	p. 859
	Glossary	p. 903

See also: Last Supper, Rite, Paschal Mystery.
—AVAILABLE FROM THE UNITED STATES CATHOLIC CONFERENCE, WASHINGTON DC

VIDEOS

Eucharist: A Taste of God

Joseph Kempf

114 minutes. This lively program explores the Eucharist as a source of spiritual growth. 1995.
—AVAILABLE FROM OBLATE MEDIA, ST. LOUIS, MO

The History and Meaning of the Eucharist

Forty minutes. Dialogue is used to explain the Mass in a way that helps teens relate to it more personally.
—AVAILABLE FROM BROWN-ROA, DUBUQUE, IA

A Teen's Guide to Living the Mass *Dale Fushek*

Forty-five minutes. Explains how teens can and should play a vital role in the Mass and in the life of the Church. 1995
—AVAILABLE FROM OBLATE MEDIA, ST. LOUIS, MO

BOOK

The Mystery and Meaning of the Mass *Joseph Champlin*

Fascinating historical and theological explanation of the Mass and the symbols surrounding it. 1999.
—AVAILABLE FROM CROSSROAD PUBLISHING COMPANY, NEW YORK

NOTE

For a list of (1) General resources for professional background and (2) Addresses, phone/fax numbers of major publishing companies, see Appendix B of this Resource Manual.

CHAPTER 13
Reconciliation

CHAPTER at a Glance

The aim of this chapter is to deepen the students' understanding of the:

1 *Nature of sin*
2 *Our reluctance to admit sin*
3 *Scriptural basis for Reconciliation*
4 *Liturgy and graces of the sacrament*

READ—Have a student read aloud the scriptural introduction, which begins: "Be merciful to me, O God . . ." Have another student read the commentary following the scriptural introduction. It begins: "Like the father of the prodigal son . . ."

CLARIFY—Richard Pindell wrote a short story called "Somebody's Son." It is a good modern adaptation of the Parable of the Prodigal Son. Adaptations have been made into song and a film. Share it with your students. It will set a good opening tone in which to approach the sacrament of Reconciliation:

■ *The story opens with a runaway boy writing a letter home to his mother. He expresses the hope that his old-fashioned father will forgive him and accept him again as his son. The boy writes: "In a few days I'll be passing our property. If Dad'll take me back, ask him to tie a white cloth on the apple tree in the field next to our house."*

Days later, the boy is seated on a train, rapidly approaching his house. Soon the tree will be visible around the next bend. But the boy can't bring himself to look at it. He's afraid the white cloth won't be there. Turning to the man sitting next to him, he says nervously, "Mister, will you do me a favor? Around the bend on the right, you'll see a tree. See if there's a white cloth tied to it."

As the train rumbles past the tree, the boy stares straight ahead. Then in a quaking voice he asks, "Mister, is there a white cloth tied to one of the branches of the tree?" The man answers in a surprised voice, "Why, son, there's a white cloth tied to practically every branch!"

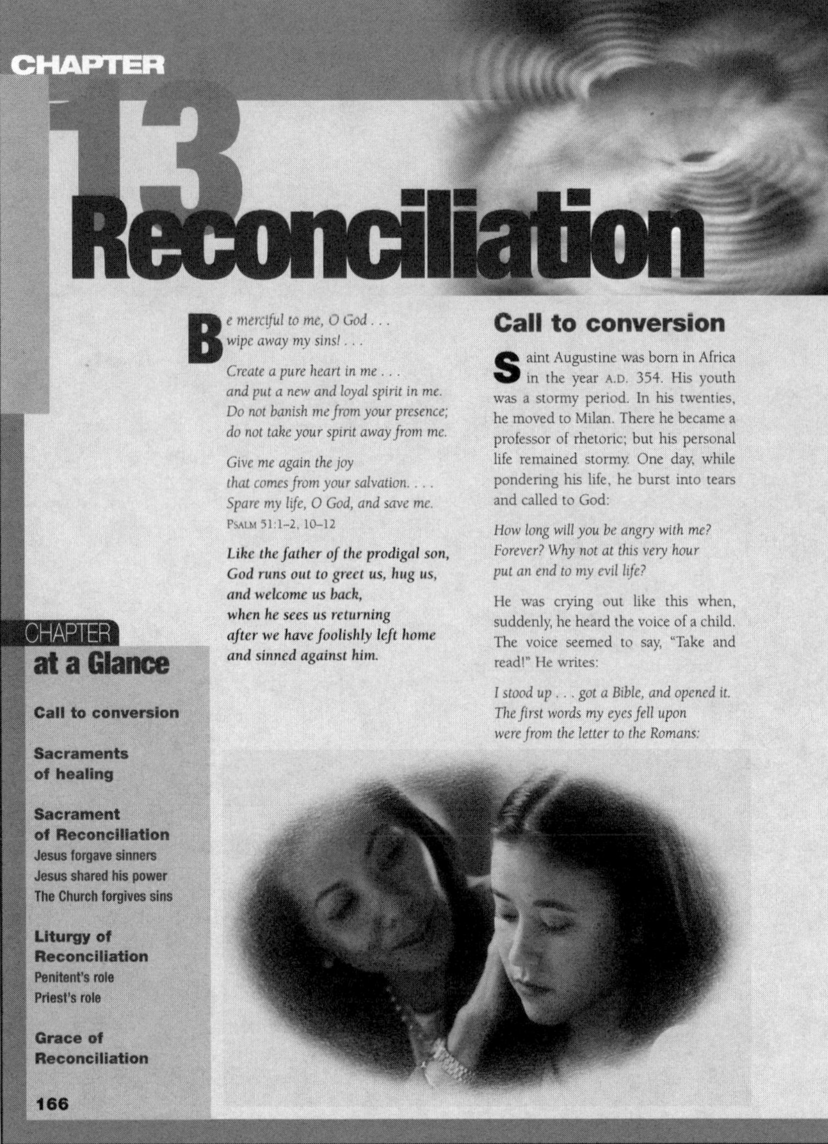

CHAPTER 13

Reconciliation

Be merciful to me, O God . . .
wipe away my sins! . . .

Create a pure heart in me . . .
and put a new and loyal spirit in me.
Do not banish me from your presence;
do not take your spirit away from me.

Give me again the joy
that comes from your salvation. . . .
Spare my life, O God, and save me.
PSALM 51:1–2, 10–12

Like the father of the prodigal son,
God runs out to greet us, hug us,
and welcome us back,
when he sees us returning
after we have foolishly left home
and sinned against him.

Call to conversion

Saint Augustine was born in Africa in the year A.D. 354. His youth was a stormy period. In his twenties, he moved to Milan. There he became a professor of rhetoric; but his personal life remained stormy. One day, while pondering his life, he burst into tears and called to God:

How long will you be angry with me?
Forever? Why not at this very hour
put an end to my evil life?

He was crying out like this when, suddenly, he heard the voice of a child. The voice seemed to say, "Take and read!" He writes:

I stood up . . . got a Bible, and opened it.
The first words my eyes fell upon
were from the letter to the Romans:

CHAPTER at a Glance

CLARIFY—Earlier on pages 68–69, we compared God to a movie projector. We compared the human images on the screen to ourselves. Suppose the images were to say to the projector, "We don't need you anymore. We declare our independence from you."

■ *In a sense this is what the prodigal son did with regard to his father and his family. In a sense this is what we do when we sin. We foolishly declare our independence from the Trinity:*

1 *God the Father, who created us*
2 *Jesus, who died for us*
3 *The Spirit, who graces and guides us*

NOTES

Reconciliation

"Throw off the words of darkness . . .
put on the Lord Jesus Christ,
and make no provision
for the desires of the flesh."
ROMANS 13:12–14

My heart was suddenly flooded
with a light that erased all my doubts.
My soul was filled with a deep peace.
THE CONFESSIONS OF SAINT AUGUSTINE, BOOK 8

1 Why do you think it took Augustine so many years and so much spiritual pain before he was able to turn his life around?

Augustine experienced what all of us must go through to some extent: conversion. By conversion we mean, with the help of God's grace, to turn away from sin and to turn back to God.

The first step in the conversion process is to admit that we have sinned. Commenting on the inability of many people to admit they have sinned, someone said: "The worst sin is not to sin, but to deny it." Scripture adds:

If we say that we have no sin,
we deceive ourselves, and . . .
make a liar out of God. 1 JOHN 1:8, 10

2 How do you account for the inability of a growing number of people today to admit they have sinned?

Sacraments of healing

Each of us has been incorporated into Christ's Body, the Church, by the "sacraments of Initiation." This transformed us into new beings. Saint Paul writes:

Anyone who is joined to Christ
is a new being;
the old is gone, the new has come.
1 CORINTHIANS 5:17

But even after our incorporation into Christ, we still remain fragile human beings both physically and spiritually. This brings us to the sacraments of healing: Reconciliation and Anointing of the Sick.

Reconciliation restores or repairs our divine life when it has been weakened or lost through sin. CCC 1420–21

The Anointing of the Sick strengthens our divine life against vulnerabilities linked with illness or old age. CCC 1511, 1527

Let us now take a closer look at the first of these two "healing" sacraments.

Sacrament of Reconciliation

Jesus, the Son of God . . .
is not one who cannot feel sympathy
for our weaknesses.

On the contrary . . .
[Jesus] was tempted in every way
that we are, but did not sin.

Let us have confidence, then,
and approach God's throne,
where there is grace.

There we will receive mercy
and find grace to to help us
just when we need it. HEBREWS 4:14–16

STAGE 2: CHAPTER 13 167

Call to conversion

QUESTION **1 *Why do you think it took Augustine so many years and so much spiritual pain before he was able to turn his life around?***

DISCUSS—In Book 7 of his *Confessions*, Augustine (354–430) prays to God: "The beauty you made . . . held me back from you." Ask students: What did he mean?

■ *One of Augustine's biographers describes his youth as "an anxious grasping after empty pleasure." This, he later believed, was the nature of all sin: a disorder in our desires, that leads us to seek pleasure, beauty, and truth in creatures rather than their Creator. . . . Although he was intellectually convinced of the truth of Christianity, Augustine . . . remained attached to his sins. . . .*
In the agony of his internal warfare he prayed to God, "Give me chastity and continence, but not yet." Finally, as his crisis became unbearable, he heard a voice speak to him, "Take and read."
ROBERT ELLSBERG: ALL SAINTS, PAGE 371

CLARIFY—Explain Augustine's use of the terms "continence" and "chastity." Continence refers to self-restraint in general; chastity is self-restraint from sexual activity.

QUESTION **2 *How do you account for the inability of a growing number of people today to admit they have sinned?***

■ *One of the big reasons is a loss of the sense of sin. Pope Pius XII called this loss "the sin of our century." John Paul II said, "The restoration of a sense of sin" is the first step in resolving the "spiritual crisis" our society is currently facing.*
RECONCILIATION ET PAENITENTIA (#18)

Sacraments of healing

CLARIFY—Review in what sense Anointing of the Sick and Reconciliation heal us.

Reconciliation — *Restores/repairs divine life when it is weakened or lost through sin*

Anointing — *Strengthens divine life against vulnerabilities of old age and illness*

Sacrament of Reconciliation

CLARIFY—Stress paragraph 2. "Jesus was tempted in every way that we are, but did not sin." Students will find it helpful to call to mind the next time the lightning of temptation strikes.

CLARIFY—Some years ago, columnist Abigail Van Buren described a program for removing "*gang-related*" tattoos. Over a thousand letters flooded in wanting more information on the program. This led to the making of a film, *Untattoo You*. The stars of the film were young people themselves and they dramatized why they now wanted the tattoos removed.

The story behind the film illustrates the point Somerset Maugham makes: We have all done things in our lives that we regret and want to erase. This is what the sacrament of Reconciliation is all about.

QUESTION **3 *Can you recall how Jesus showed that he had the power to forgive? Can you recall when and how he shared this power with his Church?***

■ *This question sets the next two topics: Jesus (1) had power; (2) shared power.*

Depending upon the discussion it generates, you may simply wish to use it as a bridge to the next two topics.

Jesus forgave sinners

ACTIVITY—To set the stage for the dialogue found here, have the students turn back to page 64 and the "pencil meditation" on this Gospel event. Have one of the students (preferably interested and skilled in drama) read it out loud in front of the class.

ACTIVITY—Return to the dialogue on page 168 and have two students (preferably interested in and skilled in drama) read it.

NOTEBOOK—Have the students enter the following in their notebooks:

Had power — *I will prove to you . . . that the Son of Man has authority . . . to forgive.* LUKE 5:24

QUESTION **4 *Had friends not brought the paralytic to Jesus, he may never have been healed physically and spiritually. Describe some way we bring others to Jesus.***

■ *Stress the idea that what often begins as a cross can turn into a beautiful blessing—as it did in the case of the paralytic.*

Recall these words of Helen Keller quoted on page 141 of the Resource Manual:

"I thank God for my handicaps,
for through them, I have found myself,
my work, and my God."

CLARIFY—A good example of how we bring others to Jesus—often without even knowing it—is the following:

■ *Dr. Robert Healy wrote a letter to* Psychology Today *magazine. In it he told about a young man who entered therapy after a brush with suicide.*

Jesus forgave sinners

A beautiful illustration of Jesus' power over sin occurs in Luke's Gospel. One day, some religious leaders were listening to Jesus teach. Suddenly, a group of people came forward carrying a paralyzed man.

When Jesus saw the man, he was moved with pity and said, "Your sins are forgiven." When the religious leaders heard this, they grew angry.

NARRATOR *Jesus knew their thoughts and said to them:*

JESUS *Why do you think such things? Is it easier to say, "Your sins are forgiven you," or to say, "Get up and walk"? I will prove to you, then, that the Son of Man has authority on earth to forgive sins.*

NARRATOR *So he said to the paralyzed man . . .*

JESUS *Get up, pick up your bed, and go home!*

NARRATOR *At once the man got up in front of them all, took the bed he had been lying on, and went home, praising God.*

They were all completely amazed! Full of fear, they praised God, saying, "What marvelous things we have seen today!" LUKE 5:22–25

4 *Had friends not brought the paralytic to Jesus, he may never have been healed physically and spiritually. Describe some way we bring others to Jesus.*

Jesus knew human nature and how fragile and vulnerable it is. This is why he instituted the sacrament of Reconciliation. It was to invite us to open our hearts to forgiveness "just when we need it." Novelist Somerset Maugham spoke for many when he wrote:

I have committed follies.
I have a sensitive conscience and
I have done certain things in my life
that I am unable to entirely forget.

If I had been fortunate enough
to be a Catholic, I could have delivered
myself of them at confession and
after performing the penance imposed,
received absolution
and put them out of my mind forever.

To get a better understanding of the sacrament of Reconciliation, we need to recall two important truths. Jesus:

- **Had the power to forgive sins**
- **Shared this power with his Church**

3 *Can you recall how Jesus showed that he had the power to forgive? Can you recall when and how he shared this power with his Church?*

THINK about it

When the soul has laid down its faults at the feet of God, it feels as though it had wings

Eugenie de Guerin

168 STAGE 2: CHAPTER 13

NOTES

SHARE YOUR **meditation**

Jesus shared his power

Jesus did more than forgive people. He shared with his Church his power to forgive sins. He did this in two stages. First, he shared his power, in a general way. CCC 551–53

NARRATOR *Jesus went to the territory near the town of Caesarea Philippi, where he asked his disciples:*

JESUS *Who do people say the Son of Man is?*

DISCIPLES *Some say John the Baptist. Others say Elijah, while others say Jeremiah or some other prophet.*

JESUS *What about you? Who do you say I am?*

PETER *You are the Messiah, the Son of the living God.*

JESUS *Good for you, Simon son of Jonah! For this truth did not come to you from any human being, but it was given to you directly by my Father in heaven.*

And so I tell you, Peter:
you are a rock,
and on this rock foundation
I will build my church. . . .

I will give you the keys
to the Kingdom of heaven;
what you prohibit on earth
will be prohibited in heaven,
and what you permit on earth
will be permitted in heaven.
MATTHEW 16:13–19

And so Jesus shared his power, *in general,* with his Church. He made Peter the rock of his Church and gave him the "keys of the Kingdom of heaven." CCC 1443–44

This brings us to the second stage, sharing with his Church in a specific way the power *to forgive sins.* It took place on Easter Sunday night, when the Apostles were gathered together in prayer. Suddenly, Jesus appeared to them. They were overjoyed. After greeting them, Jesus said:

"Peace be with you.
As the Father sent me, so I send you."
Then he breathed on them and said,

"Receive the Holy Spirit.
If you forgive people's sins,
they are forgiven;
if you do not forgive them,
they are not forgiven." JOHN 20:21–22

That first Easter night, Jesus shared with his Church, in an explicit way, the power to forgive.

At first, the power to forgive sins, sounds like a strange Easter gift. But a little thought shows that it is not. Rather, it is the perfect Easter gift. This is why Jesus came into the world: to free people from the tyranny of sin and to reconcile them with God and one another. CCC 1440–45, 1485

Thus, Jesus' Easter gift empowers his Apostles to communicate his saving power to all peoples of all times. CCC 1447

5 Scripture describes God "breathing" life into Adam. Why do you think Jesus chose to use this same "breathing" image to share his power with his Apostles?

The Man Who Lost Himself concerns a hero who trails a suspect to a Paris hotel. To learn the suspect's room number without arousing suspicion, the hero gives the clerk his own name and asks if a man by that name is registered.

While the clerk checks the room list, the hero plans to watch for the suspect's number.

To the hero's surprise, the clerk doesn't check the list. He simply says, "He's in room 40; he's expecting you." The hero follows the bellhop to room 40.

When the door opens, he sees a man who is his double, except that he's heavier and older. It is the hero himself, twenty years in the future.

The story is science fiction, but it contains an important truth: There's a person in everyone's future. It is the person we are becoming.

■ ***What kind of person am I becoming?***
■ ***How sure am I of this?***

STAGE 2: CHAPTER 13 **169**

The young man was on his way to a bridge to leap off to his death. He stopped for a traffic light and happened to glance toward the sidewalk. On the curb stood an elderly woman. She gave him the most beautiful smile he'd ever seen. Then the light changed.

He drove off, but the smile haunted him. He said later that he had no idea who that woman was. All he knows is that he owes his life to her. She was the source of a blessing to him at the most critical moment of his life.

John Henry Cardinal Newman composed a brief prayer that we all ought to pray each day of our lives. You may have the students copy it in their notebooks:

■ *Shine through me and be so in me that every soul I come in contact with may feel your presence in my spirit.*

Jesus shared his power

ACTIVITY—Have two students (preferably interested in and skilled in drama) read the dialogue (one student to take the part of Jesus; the second to take the other parts).

NOTEBOOK—Have the students copy the following into their notebooks:

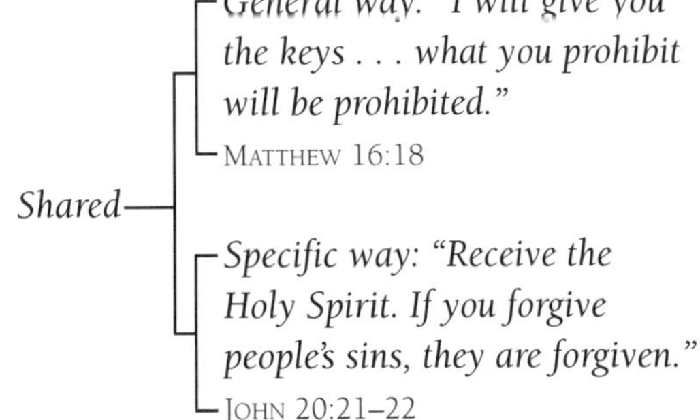

Shared
General way: "I will give you the keys . . . what you prohibit will be prohibited."
MATTHEW 16:18
Specific way: "Receive the Holy Spirit. If you forgive people's sins, they are forgiven."
JOHN 20:21–22

QUESTION ***5 Scripture describes God "breathing" life into Adam. Why do you think Jesus chose to use this same "breathing" image to share his power with his Apostles?***

■ *Scripture presents breath as a communication of life and/or power from God to people:*

1 *The LORD God took some soil from the ground and formed man out of it; he breathed life-giving breath into his nostrils and the man began to live.* GENESIS 2:7

2 *After three and a half days a life-giving breath came from God and entered them, and they stood up; and all who saw them were terrified.* REVELATION 11:11

CLARIFY—It is important to stress that the power to forgive was a perfect "Easter gift." Jesus became man primarily to forgive people and to reconcile them to the Father. This "Easter gift" empowers his Church to share it with all people of all time.

ACTIVITY—Have students think out and write out the answers. This will help give you an insight into individual students.

PRAYER hotline

In 1974 Charles Colson had "an office next to the President of the United States, a six-figure income, a yacht, a limousine, and a chauffeur." Then he lost it all. He was convicted and sentenced to prison for his role in the Watergate scandal that led to the resignation of President Nixon.

In prison, Colson went through a radical conversion to Christ—which had begun before his imprisonment. The more he read and reflected on the Gospel, the more he felt called to make Jesus' work a full-time work.

To make a long story short, he set aside his personal interests and began what is now known as Prison Fellowship. It is a Christian ministry to prisoners and their families.

He has over 150,000 volunteers in the Fellowship program. Forty thousand of these are actually preaching the Gospel in prisons. They provide outreach to over 25,000 prisoners in 500 prisons.

More importantly, in terms of material and spiritual help, this outreach extends to the families of prisoners. They are often the real victims when a parent or spouse is imprisoned.

The first stage of his conversion occurred one night when he was visiting the home of Tom Phillips, 40-year-old president of Raytheon, the largest company in the state of Massachusetts. They were talking about Phillips' own conversion a few years before. Colson wrote later:

The more I listened to Tom, the more I became convinced that he had put his finger on the unhappiness of my own life.

He left the Phillips' home that night knowing exactly what he must do.

He hadn't driven 100 yards from the house when he pulled up alongside the road and began to cry so loudly that he was afraid the Phillips' family might hear him.

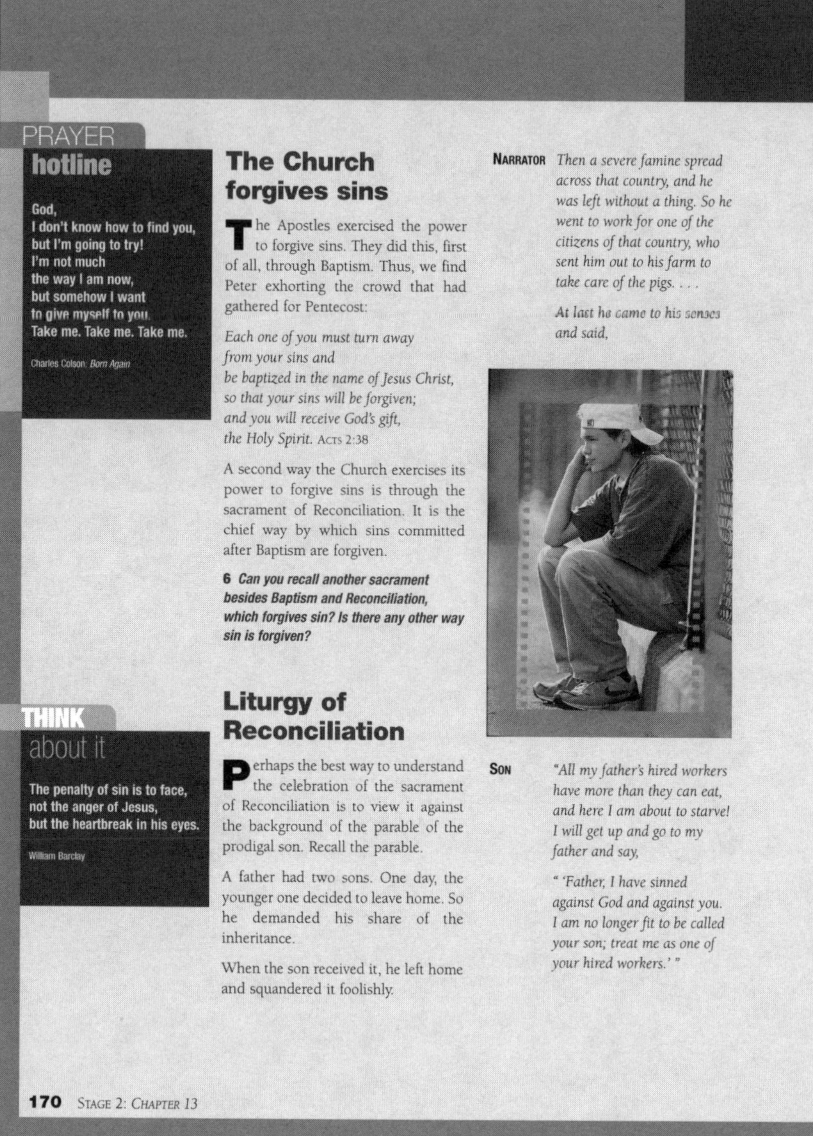

PRAYER hotline

God,
I don't know how to find you,
but I'm going to try!
I'm not much
the way I am now,
but somehow I want
to give myself to you.
Take me. Take me. Take me.

Charles Colson: *Born Again*

The Church forgives sins

The Apostles exercised the power to forgive sins. They did this, first of all, through Baptism. Thus, we find Peter exhorting the crowd that had gathered for Pentecost:

Each one of you must turn away
from your sins and
be baptized in the name of Jesus Christ,
so that your sins will be forgiven;
and you will receive God's gift,
the Holy Spirit. Acts 2:38

A second way the Church exercises its power to forgive sins is through the sacrament of Reconciliation. It is the chief way by which sins committed after Baptism are forgiven.

6 ***Can you recall another sacrament besides Baptism and Reconciliation, which forgives sin? Is there any other way sin is forgiven?***

Liturgy of Reconciliation

Perhaps the best way to understand the celebration of the sacrament of Reconciliation is to view it against the background of the parable of the prodigal son. Recall the parable.

A father had two sons. One day, the younger one decided to leave home. So he demanded his share of the inheritance.

When the son received it, he left home and squandered it foolishly.

THINK about it

The penalty of sin is to face,
not the anger of Jesus,
but the heartbreak in his eyes.

William Barclay

NARRATOR *Then a severe famine spread across that country, and he was left without a thing. So he went to work for one of the citizens of that country, who sent him out to his farm to take care of the pigs. . . .*

At last he came to his senses and said,

SON *"All my father's hired workers have more than they can eat, and here I am about to starve! I will get up and go to my father and say,*

" 'Father, I have sinned against God and against you. I am no longer fit to be called your son; treat me as one of your hired workers.' "

170 Stage 2: Chapter 13

Describing what happened next, Colson said he prayed the prayer quoted on page 170 of the text.

Today his work in prison reform extends into foreign countries as well.

THINK about it

CLARIFY—Suggest to the students that when temptation comes they recall this image. It has the potential to be a powerful deterrent.

NOTES

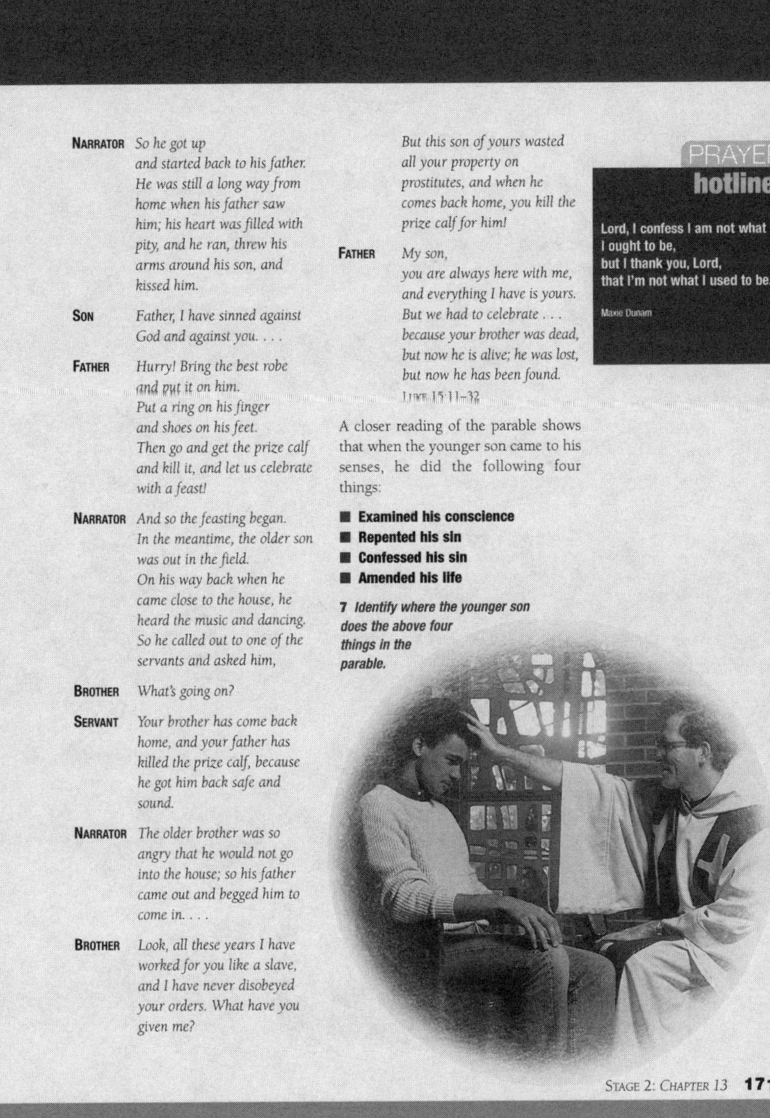

NARRATOR *So he got up and started back to his father. He was still a long way from home when his father saw him; his heart was filled with pity, and he ran, threw his arms around his son, and kissed him.*

SON *Father, I have sinned against God and against you. . . .*

FATHER *Hurry! Bring the best robe and put it on him. Put a ring on his finger and shoes on his feet. Then go and get the prize calf and kill it, and let us celebrate with a feast!*

NARRATOR *And so the feasting began. In the meantime, the older son was out in the field. On his way back when he came close to the house, he heard the music and dancing. So he called out to one of the servants and asked him,*

BROTHER *What's going on?*

SERVANT *Your brother has come back home, and your father has killed the prize calf, because he got him back safe and sound.*

NARRATOR *The older brother was so angry that he would not go into the house; so his father came out and begged him to come in. . . .*

BROTHER *Look, all these years I have worked for you like a slave, and I have never disobeyed your orders. What have you given me? But this son of yours wasted all your property on prostitutes, and when he comes back home, you kill the prize calf for him!*

FATHER *My son, you are always here with me, and everything I have is yours. But we had to celebrate . . . because your brother was dead, but now he is alive; he was lost, but now he has been found.*

LUKE 15:11–32

PRAYER **hotline**

Lord, I confess I am not what I ought to be,
but I thank you, Lord,
that I'm not what I used to be.

Maxie Dunam

A closer reading of the parable shows that when the younger son came to his senses, he did the following four things:

- **Examined his conscience**
- **Repented his sin**
- **Confessed his sin**
- **Amended his life**

7 Identify where the younger son does the above four things in the parable.

STAGE 2: CHAPTER 13 **171**

The Church forgives sins

QUESTION **6 *Can you recall another sacrament besides Baptism and Reconciliation, which forgives sin? Is there any other way sin is forgiven?***

■ *The sacrament of the Anointing of the Sick forgives a person's sins, if he is too sick to celebrate the sacrament of Penance.* CCC 1532

Perfect contrition (sorrow arising from a love of God above all else) forgives venial sins. It also forgives mortal sins, if it includes the resolution to celebrate Reconciliation as soon as reasonably possible. CCC 1452–53

Liturgy of Reconciliation

CLARIFY—Give the students the backdrop to the Parable of the Prodigal Son.

One day, when some Jewish religious leaders grew angry because Jesus welcomed sinners and even ate with them, Jesus told them this parable.

DISCUSS—After telling the students that this parable has "two acts," have them identify where the second "act" begins ("In the meantime").

Ask: Which of the two groups listening to Jesus is referred to in the "first act" (sinners) and in the "second act" (Jewish leaders)?

Ask: Why do you think Jesus left the "second act" unfinished? (Did the older brother join the party?)

■ *This half of the parable was directed to the religious leaders. Each one had to decide whether he would accept Jesus' invitation to enter the Kingdom.*

QUESTION **7 *Identify where the younger son does the above four things in the parable.***

1 Examined conscience
"At last he came to his senses and said, 'I am about to starve.'"

2 Repented sin
"I will go back to my father and say, 'I am no longer fit to be your son.'"

3 Confessed sin
"Father, I have sinned against God and against you."

4 Amended life
"Treat me as one of your hired workers."

PRAYER **hotline**

There's always room for improvement. The important thing is not so much where I am now, but in what direction I am moving.

PRACTICAL Connection

CLARIFY—The question of stealing will be handled more in detail on page 268.

CLARIFY—John Churton Collins has an excellent analogy for illustrating that "sinful" thoughts are usually involuntary in origin:

■ *We are no more responsible for the evil thoughts that pass through our minds than a scarecrow for the birds which fly over the seedplot he has to guard. The responsibility in each case is to prevent them from settling.*

Bishop Fulton Sheen said, "We are not tempted because we are evil; we are tempted because we are human." In other words, temptations go with the territory of being human. Ralph Waldo Emerson makes this motivational observation about temptation:

■ *As the Sandwich-Islander believes that the strength and the valor of the enemy he kills passes into himself, so we gain strength and valor from the temptations we resist.*

Penitent's role

QUESTION **8 *Which one of the above four things do you find most difficult in the sacrament of Reconciliation? Explain.***

■ *The fourth point might need a bit of an explanation before having the students respond. You might wish to have one of the students read aloud the four paragraphs under "Satisfaction" beginning on page 173 and extending over onto page 174.*

Examination

CLARIFY—Stress the following three things to keep in mind in examining our conscience:

1 *Three conditions must be present for a sin to be mortal.*

PRACTICAL Connection

Here are four steps involved in confessing our sins:

1. We introduce ourselves.
   Father, I am a 15-year-old high school student.
2. We state when we last celebrated the sacrament.
   It's been a year since my last confession.
3. We explain any long absence from the sacrament.
   The reason for my absence is fear or shame (or whatever).
4. We confess our sins.
   I don't think I committed any mortal sins. I did steal a $10 item from a large department store. I unintentionally drank too much one time. I had sinful thoughts frequently, but I tried to put them out of my mind as best I could. I'd appreciate any suggestions you might have on this latter problem. This is all, Father.

9 *Explain why the information under each step is important.*

Penitent's role

The parable of the prodigal son is a beautiful illustration of what we do in the sacrament of Reconciliation. CCC 1439, 1480–84 It is the same four things that the son did. We:

- **Examine our conscience**
- **Repent our sins (contrition)**
- **Confess our sins**
- **Amend our life (satisfaction)**

8 *Which one of the above four things do you find most difficult in the sacrament of Reconciliation? Explain.*

Let us now look at each one of these four points more closely.

Examination

In our daily lives, we sometimes fail, through our own fault, to live and love as Jesus taught us to do. We call these moral failures *sin.* We prepare for the sacrament of Reconciliation by examining our conscience. Catholic tradition distinguishes two kinds of sin: *mortal* (very serious) and *venial* (less serious). 1 JOHN 5:16–17

For a sin to be mortal, three conditions must be present: CCC 1857

- **Grave matter**
- **Full knowledge**
- **Full consent of the will**

Grave matter means that what we do is objectively grave; e.g., adultery. CCC 1858

Full knowledge means we are fully aware of the graveness of an act. In spite of this, we choose to do it anyway. CCC 1859

Full consent of the will means we act freely. We are not influenced or pressured in a way that diminishes our free will. CCC 1859

For a sin to be *venial*, we do something that does not involve serious matter (stealing a small article); or we do something without our full knowledge or consent (vandalize someone's property while intoxicated). CCC 1862–63

172 STAGE 2: CHAPTER 13

2 *Sufficient reflection does not mean that we "meditate" on what we are about to do. It is enough that our conscience tells us in a general way the action is gravely wrong.*

3 *Full consent of the will is impeded by such things as alcohol, drugs, great fear, great pressure.*

NOTEBOOK—Develop the following diagram on the chalkboard. It sums up the difference between mortal and venial sin:

Mortal — *Total rejection* / *Involves total self in total way*

Venial —— *Partial rejection*

NOTES

Contrition

Contrition consists of being sorry for our sins, along with the resolve—with the help of God's grace—not to sin again. Depending on whether our sorrow stems from a love of God or from a lesser motive, such as fear of punishment, it is:

- **Perfect** **Love of God**
- **Imperfect** **Lesser motive**

Perfect contrition forgives venial sins and mortal sins, providing it includes the resolve to celebrate the sacrament as soon as reasonable. CCC 1451–52

Imperfect contrition, of itself, does not forgive mortal sin, but prepares us to receive forgiveness in the sacrament of Reconciliation. CCC 1453

It is well to make our act of contrition before entering the confessional.

Confession

Mortal sins must be confessed according to kind (what we did) and number (how often we did it).

Strictly speaking, venial sins need not be confessed. Nevertheless, it is highly advisable, at least, in a general way. For example, we may say, "I am not always as patient as I should be, especially with my younger brothers and sisters."

Here is a thumbnail review of some sins of *commission* (doing something we shouldn't do) and *omission* (not doing something we should do):

Commission:
- **Damaging what is another's**
- **Misusing alcohol, drugs, or sex**
- **Stealing**
- **Other (jealousy, lying, cheating)**

10 ***Pick one of the above sins under "commission" and decide what would make it a mortal sin. Do the same with one of the sins listed under "omission."***

Omission: failing in:
- **Love of family or others**
- **Prayer or worship of God**
- **Kindness toward family or others**

Satisfaction

Many sins wrong others. So we must do what is reasonably possible to repair any harm. Sin, also, harms ourself, as well as our relationship with God and our brothers and sisters. CCC 1459

Satisfaction has to do with "making up for" or "making satisfaction for" the harmful effects of our sins, both to ourselves and to others.

STAGE 2: CHAPTER 13 **173**

Contrition

CLARIFY—Encourage the students to memorize an "Act of Contrition." We will return to this point under "Prayer Time with the Lord" on page 178.

Confession

CLARIFY—One reason for confessing mortal sins according to kind and number is to help the priest counsel the person.

ACTIVITY—You may wish to consider contacting Alcoholics Anonymous (see phone directory) about having someone (a recovering alcoholic) talk to the students about the twelve-step program, in general, and the fifth step, in particular. Read the first five steps to the students:

1 *We admitted we were powerless over alcohol, that our lives had become unmanageable.*
2 *Came to believe that a Power greater than ourselves could restore us to sanity.*
3 *Made a decision to turn our will and our lives over to the care of God as we understood him.*
4 *Made a searching and fearless moral inventory of ourselves.*
5 *Admitted to God, to ourselves, and to another human being the exact nature of our wrongs.*

Steps four and five fit in perfectly with what we find in the Parable of the Prodigal Son and the sacrament of Reconciliation.

QUESTION **10** ***Pick one of the above sins under "commission" and decide what would make it a mortal sin. Do the same with one of the sins listed under "omission."***

- *Commission: Deliberately take an old car and crash it into a new one. Omission: Deliberately stop going to Sunday Mass.*

Satisfaction

CLARIFY—An example of repairing the damage of one's sins is William F. Murray, son of atheist Madalyn Murray O'Hair.

- *As a child, he was the plaintiff in the lawsuit that resulted in the 1963 Supreme Court decision to ban Bible reading and prayer from all public schools. At age 33 he experienced a conversion. Afterward, he tried to repair the damage for which he considered himself to be partially responsible.*

He wrote two open letters. One was to a newspaper in Austin, Texas, apologizing for helping build the American Atheist Center in Austin. The other was to the Baltimore Sun, *apologizing for his part in the Baltimore lawsuit that led to the Supreme Court decision. Murray also embarked upon a personal crusade of spreading the Gospel.*

Up Close & Personal

***DISCUSS*—Write on the board:**

Forgiveness is the fragrance the violet sheds on the heel that crushed it.
MARK TWAIN

Ask the students: Explain Twain's point. How does it apply to Reconciliation? What is the heel in the story? The fragrance?

Priest's role

***CLARIFY*—"The father ran, threw his arms around his son, and kissed him."**

Dr. Smiley Blanton writes in "The Magic of Touch": "I once heard a family-court judge say that although hundreds of juveniles and their parents had been brought before him, he never once had seen a parent put an arm around the youngster's shoulder." GUIDEPOSTS, 1965

How differently the father in the parable treats his wayward son.

***CLARIFY*—The father said, "Put shoes (sandals) on his feet."**

- *In biblical times bare feet were often a sign of a slave. Putting shoes on his son's feet symbolizes that he is somebody's son, not somebody's slave. This was also true in American slave days. A Negro spiritual rejoices, saying that in heaven "All God's children got shoes": "When I get to heaven, I'm goin' put on my shoes and walk all over God's heaven."*

***CLARIFY*—"Bring the best robe and put it on him. Put a ring on his finger."**

- *Placing a robe on the boy's body and a ring on his finger recalls* 1 MACCABEES 6:14–15: *Before he died, Antiochus IV called a trusted friend, Philip, placed a crown on his head, a robe on his body, and a ring on his finger. He transferred to him his authority and power.*

The ring the father gave his son was probably a "signet" ring. It contained the family seal. To possess it was to have the power to act in the name of the family or person to whom the seal belonged. Thus, we find Pharaoh saying to Joseph: "You shall be in charge of my palace. . . ." With that, he took off his signet ring and put it on Joseph's finger. GENESIS 41:39–42

Up Close & Personal

John Eagen

John Eagen was a student at Campion High School in Wisconsin. One weekend he made a closed retreat. During the retreat, he made a decision to do something he'd been putting off. He decided to celebrate the sacrament of Reconciliation. He writes:

To my surprise the priest said
nothing about my sins.
He spoke only
of God's love for me.
I left the chapel and
walked out into the beauty
of the afternoon.
Joy began to well up
and run in my heart
different from anything I'd ever
experienced. I don't think I'd
ever been happier in my life.

At length, I found myself
out on the golf course.
I remember lying down
out of sheer joy
on a bunker with my eyes
to the blue sky
and my arms wide open
to the Lord. . . .
How long I lay there
I don't remember.
All I do remember
is that I felt
enormously close to God.

John Eagen: *A Traveler Toward the Dawn* (slightly adapted)

To help us begin our journey back to spiritual health, the priest assigns a penance. For example, he assigns prayers designed to help open our hearts to God's healing grace. CCC 1460

If a priest assigns a penance that would prove difficult to do, we should feel free to ask him to change it to something else.

Priest's role

The priest's role in the celebration of the sacrament follows the pattern of the father in the Parable of the Prodigal Son. CCC 1461–67

First, the father threw his arms around his son and kissed him. In other words, he welcomed him back as if he had never left home.

Next, he put shoes on his son's feet. This symbolized that he was forgiving him totally. In ancient times, slaves went barefoot; sons wore shoes. The shoes took away the sign that said the boy was somebody's slave and gave the sign that he was somebody's son.

Then the father gave his son a ring, symbolizing that he was restoring the son to the full status he had before he left home. Undoubtedly, the ring was a signet ring, containing the family seal. To possess it was to possess the power to act in the family's name.

Finally, the father held a feast in his son's honor. This celebration recalls Jesus' words:

"There will be more joy in heaven
over one sinner who repents
than over ninety-nine respectable people
who do not need to repent." LUKE 15:7

Thus, in the sacrament of Reconciliation, the priest does what the father in the parable did:

- **Welcomes us back**
- **Forgives us**
- **Restores us to full life**
- **Rejoices with us**

174 STAGE 2: CHAPTER 13

***CLARIFY*—"Go and get the prize calf and kill it, and let us celebrate with a feast!"**

- *The father's feast to celebrate his son's return recalls Jesus' words:*
"There will be more joy in heaven
over one sinner who repents than over
ninety-nine respectable people
who do not need to repent. LUKE 15:7

***NOTEBOOK*—The Parable of the Prodigal Son shows the father doing four beautiful things for his repentant son. Develop the following summary on the chalkboard for entry into the students'**

NOTES

Grace of Reconciliation

British violinist Peter Cropper was invited to Finland for a special concert. As a personal favor, the Royal Academy of Music lent Peter their priceless 285-year-old Stradivarius violin. That violin was known the world over for its incredible sound.

At the concert, a nightmare happened. Going on stage, Peter tripped and fell. The violin broke into several pieces. Peter flew home to England in a state of shock.

The Royal Academy of Music hired a master craftsperson, Charles Beare, to try to repair the priceless violin. He spent countless, tedious hours repairing the violin.

Then came the moment of truth. How would the violin sound? Those present couldn't believe their ears. The violin's sound was better than before.

This story makes a beautiful conclusion to our study of the sacrament of Reconciliation. Many people, including Saint Augustine, have personally experienced that the celebration of the sacrament often leaves them stronger and more committed to God than they were before they sinned.

We may summarize the graces of the sacrament as follows:

- **Reconciliation with God and Church**
- **Remission of punishment due to sin**
- **Healing to better follow Jesus**
- **Serenity of conscience** CCC 1496

PRACTICAL Connection

People ask, "How often should we celebrate Reconciliation?" The obvious answer is, "As often as the Spirit moves us to do so." Certainly, we will want to celebrate it after a serious break with God and God's family (mortal sin).

Normally, during certain periods of our life we will experience the need or desire to celebrate more often. CCC 1425–39 There are, however, spiritual benefits from celebrating it regularly (say every few months). It sharpens spiritual sensitivity, combats spiritual laziness, heals spiritual weakness, and deepens spiritual unity with God and God's people.

notebooks. The Father:

1. *Welcomed* — *Hugged and kissed his son*
2. *Forgave* — *Shod his son*
3. *Restored* — *Robed and ringed his son*
4. *Rejoiced* — *Feasted his son*

Grace of Reconciliation

CLARIFY—Just as a break in an arm or leg often grows back more strongly at the break, so does a person's break with the Church.

NOTEBOOK—Shorten and modify the diagram in the book for entry into the students' notebooks. It will serve as a better memory aid.

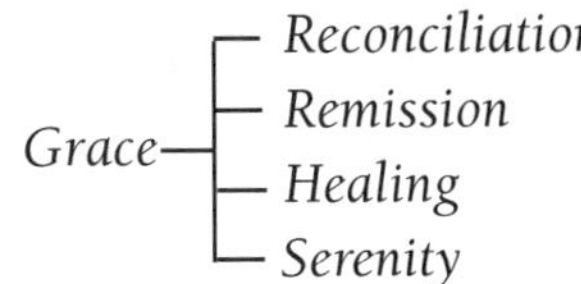

God and Church	
Punishment due to sin	
To better follow Jesus	
Peace of conscience	

PRACTICAL Connection

CLARIFY—The leader of the Protestant Reformation, Martin Luther, "went to confession every day, even after his breach with Rome." In his catechism, Luther urged the same practice for his followers.

AMERICA, AUGUST 27, 1966, PAGE 210

NOTEBOOK—Sum up the following benefits of frequent confession for entry into the students' notebooks.

1. *Sharpens sensitivity*
2. *Combats laziness*
3. *Heals weaknesses*
4. *Deepens unity with God/community*

When we speak of spiritual sensitivity, we mean awareness of spiritual things, like God and sin. Our spiritual sensitivity can be sharpened or dulled with the passage of time. Consider an analogy:

- *With the passage of time, the disease of leprosy can dull the body's physical sensitivity or awareness. In other words, after a while, the body feels little or no pain. The result can be tragic.*

A mother told this story about her infant, who had lost its physical sensitivity through disease:

Hearing the child cooing in the next room, the mother peeked in, expecting to see her baby playing contentedly with its toys. Instead, she was horrified to see the infant gnawing on its fingertip and drawing patterns on the wall with the blood coming out of it.

Just as the baby became physically insensitive, so we can become spiritually insensitive to things like God and sin. The result can be more tragic than the baby's physical insensitivity.

Recap

A fitting recap is an old ballad concerning Judas, who betrayed Jesus. After he committed suicide, MATTHEW 27:5 his soul searches for a place to put his body, but he is unsuccessful. Hell refuses his body, the sun won't shine on it, and the soil rejects it. So the soul keeps searching.

One night in the polar regions of the north, the soul happens upon a lighted hall. It lays the body down in the snow. Then, with weary feet, it runs up and down, "moaning like a wolf," trying to see inside the hall.

Finally, it finds a slit in the curtain and looks in. There, he sees a host seated at a banquet table, waiting for a guest. Just then, the host picks up a candelabra and goes to the door. The ballad concludes with the host saying to the soul of Judas:

The Holy Supper is spread within,
And the many candles shine,
And I have waited long for thee
Before I poured the wine!
ROBERT BUCHANAN (1841–1901)

DISCUSS—Ask: What is the point of the ballad? How does it serve as a "recap" of the sacrament of Reconciliation?

Review

DAILY QUIZ—The review questions may be assigned (one or two at a time) for homework or a daily quiz.

CHAPTER TESTS—Reproducible chapter tests are found in Appendix A. For consistency and ease in grading, quizzes are restricted to (1) "Matching," (2) "True/False," and (3) "Fill in the Blanks."

TEST ANSWERS—The following are the answers to the test for Chapter 13. (See Appendix A, page 324.) Each correct answer is worth 4 points.

Matching

1 = f	2 = d	3 = c	4 = a
5 = e	6 = b		

Recap

Jesus forgave sin and shared this power and ministry with his Church. The Church exercises this power and ministry in a special way in the sacrament of Reconciliation.

To understand Reconciliation it helps to view it against the backdrop of the parable of the prodigal son. What the son does in the parable, we do in Reconciliation:

- **Examine our conscience**
- **Repent our sins (contrition)**
- **Confess our sins**
- **Amend our lives (satisfaction)**

And what the father of the prodigal son does, the priest does:

- **Welcomes us back**
- **Forgives us our sins**
- **Restores us to full life**
- **Rejoices with us**

Sin divides into two groups: commission and omission. It also divides into:

- **Mortal** **grave**
- **Venial** **less grave**

For a sin to be mortal three conditions must be present:

- **Grave matter**
- **Full knowledge**
- **Full consent of the will**

Review

1 Explain (a) what we mean by conversion and (b) what is the first step in the conversion process.

2 Explain when and how Jesus (a) showed he had the power to forgive sins, (b) shared this power in a general way, (c) shared it in a specific way.

3 Why was the power to forgive sins a perfect Easter gift?

4 List and explain (a) the four things the prodigal son did when he came to his senses and (b) how the four things relate to what we do in the sacrament of Reconciliation.

5 List and briefly explain (a) the two kinds of sin and how each affects our relationship with God, (b) the three conditions that must be present for the most serious of these two sins, (c) what we mean by contrition, (d) the two kinds of contrition.

6 List and briefly explain (a) the four steps involved in confessing our sins, (b) what we mean by satisfaction, and (c) why the priest assigns a penance.

7 List and briefly explain (a) the four things the father of the prodigal son did upon his son's return, and how they relate to Reconciliation, (b) the symbolism of the kiss, shoes, ring, feast, (c) how often we should celebrate reconciliation, (d) the graces of the sacrament of Reconciliation.

True/False

1 = T	2 = F	3 = T	4 = F
5 = T	6 = T	7 = F	8 = T

Fill in the Blanks

1. (a) Examine conscience
   (b) Repent sins
   (c) Confess sins
   (d) Amend life
2. (a) Grave matter
   (b) Full knowledge
   (c) Full consent of will
3. (a) Welcomes back
   (b) Forgives us
   (c) Restores to life
   (d) Rejoices with us

NOTES

Reflect

1 In 1984 Velma Barfield became the first woman in 22 years to be executed in the United States. Convicted of killing four people in 1978, the Velma of 1984 was totally different from the Velma of 1978. She had undergone a deep conversion. A high point in her conversion came when she wrote on the flyleaf of her Bible:

Sin is being called all kinds
of fancy names nowadays
but it's time we came to grips with ourselves and
call sin what it really is—SIN.

It's the ancient enemy of the soul.
It has never changed.
Tonight . . . I'm going to start . . .
naming my sins before the Lord
and trust him for deliverance.

VELMA BARFIELD: WOMAN ON DEATH ROW

■ ***Why don't people today "call sin what it really is—SIN"?***
■ ***When was the last time you named your sins "before the Lord" in the sacrament of Reconciliation, and what led you celebrate it then?***
■ ***What are several things that tend to keep you from celebrating it more often?***

2 Lee Iacocca has been called an "American legend." He rescued the Chrysler corporation from bankruptcy. In his autobiography, he says of the sacrament of Reconciliation:

In my teens I began to appreciate
the importance of the most misunderstood rite
in the Catholic Church.
I not only had to think out
my transgressions . . .
I had to speak them . . .

The necessity of weighing right from wrong
on a regular basis
turned out to be the best therapy I ever had.

IACOCCA: AN AUTOBIOGRAPHY

■ ***Why do you think Iacocca "began to appreciate the importance" of the sacrament in his teens?***
■ ***Why would/wouldn't you agree that it's the Church's "most misunderstood rite"?***
■ ***What are some of the reasons you think "weighing right from wrong on a regular basis turned out to be the best therapy" Iacocca ever had?***

3 Greek Orthodox Catholics celebrate the sacrament of Reconciliation facing an icon of the risen Christ.

■ ***Why do you think they stand, rather than kneel or sit?***
■ ***Why do you think they face an icon, rather than face each other?***

STAGE 2: CHAPTER 13 **177**

Reflect

1 a) *Why don't people today "call sin what it really is—SIN"?*

■ *Velma Barfield's note on the flyleaf of her Bible underscores what was said at the start of this chapter. Many people deny or "candy-coat" the reality of sin.*

Have the students respond in small groups or directly to the entire class.

b) When was the last time you named your sins "before the Lord" in the sacrament of Reconciliation, and what led you to celebrate it then?
c) What are several things that tend to keep you from celebrating it more often?

■ *Have the students respond to these two questions anonymously and in detail. Collect the responses, select the better ones, and discuss them in the next class session.*

2 a) *Why do you think Iacocca "began to appreciate the importance" of the sacrament in his teens?*

■ *That's when he was in a transition stage of his life and really appreciated the need for forgiveness, healing, and guidance during this transition.*

b) Why would/wouldn't you agree that it's the Church's "most misunderstood" rite?

Set this question up by having a student reread aloud to the class "Up Close & Personal," page 174.

Ask the students: Why do people often fail to experience the kind of peace, joy, and closeness to God that John did after his celebration of Reconciliation?

c) What are some of the reasons you think "weighing right from wrong on a regular basis turned out to be the best therapy" Iacocca ever had?

■ *This exercise could be discussed right in class. Iacocca's final sentence touches on the first benefit of celebrating the sacrament of Reconciliation regularly. It maintains and sharpens our spiritual sensitivity.*

3 a) *Why do you think they stand, rather than kneel or sit?*
b) Why do you think they face an icon, rather than face each other?

■ *Standing is seen as a more responsible, active, and alert posture. (Recall that we stand to listen to the Gospel reading at Mass.) Facing the icon of Jesus stresses that the sacrament is an encounter with the Risen Christ. In other words, it focuses on Jesus' role in the sacrament rather than the role of his representative, the priest.*

PRAYER TIME with the Lord

A man once said that one of the best things he ever did was to memorize the "Act of Contrition."

Sin came into his life in later years, he said. It was the one prayer that gave him peace of mind and eventually changed his life.

The following "Act of Contrition" is one every Catholic should take time to memorize:

Merciful God,
like the prodigal son,
I come home in sorrow.
I have sinned against you
and your people.

With the help of your grace,
I promise to try to walk
in the light of your presence
and avoid whatever might lead me
back into the darkness. M.L.

■ ***Compose a similar "Act of Contrition." Make it come from the heart.***

178 STAGE 2: *CHAPTER 13*

PRAYER TIME with the Lord

QUESTION **Compose a similar "Act of Contrition." Make it come from the heart.**

To put the students in the mood, share with them David's "Act of Contrition" after his grave sin against both God and man. 2 SAMUEL 11:2–12:9

■ *Be merciful to me, O God . . .*
I have sinned against you—and . . .
you are justified in condemning me. . . .

Remove my sin . . .
wash me whiter than snow . . .
and wipe out all my evil.

Create a pure heart in me, O God,
and put a new and loyal spirit in me.
Do not banish me from your presence;
do not take your holy spirit
away from me.
Give me again the joy
that comes from your salvation. . . .

Then I will teach sinners your commands,
and they will turn back to you.
PSALM 51:1–13 PASSIM

PRAYER Journal

QUESTION **What is one page you'd like to tear out and throw away? Write a brief prayer to Jesus about it.**

To get the students in the mood and started, share with them an example from *Lord Jim*, the famous novel by Joseph Conrad (1857–1924).

Conrad lost both parents when he was 12, went to sea at 18, and made it his life's work before retiring, almost 40 years later. Here's the example from *Lord Jim*:

■ *As a boy Jim spent hours dreaming of doing brave things at sea. Eventually, he grew up and became the skipper of the Patna. One night the Patna struck something and began to sink. In a fit of unexplainable panic, Jim leaped into the sea to save himself. Although braver hands saved the ship and its passengers, Jim never forgave himself.*

The story does, however, have a happy ending. Years later, Jim redeemed himself by performing a splendid act of courage that exceeded his boyhood dreams.

After the students have completed this exercise *anonymously*, collect the papers, review, share, and discuss the better response.

SCRIPTURE Journal

QUESTION **Pick one of the above passages. Read it prayerfully and write out a brief statement to Jesus expressing your feelings about it.**

NOTES

PRAYER Journal

A Broadway play concerned a young drug addict who quit school and left home. In an unforgettable scene, the young person looks up to heaven and cries out in deep anguish:

How I wish life was like a notebook,
so I could tear out the pages where
I made mistakes and throw them away!

Thanks to Jesus, life is like a notebook. We can tear out the pages with the mistakes and throw them away.

■ ***What is one page I'd like to tear out and throw away? Write a brief prayer to Jesus about it.***

SCRIPTURE Journal

1 **Jesus came for sinners** **Luke 5:27–32**
2 **Jesus visits a sinner** **Luke 19:1–10**
3 **Jesus defends a sinner** **Luke 7:36–50**
4 **Jesus forgives a sinner** **Luke 5:17–26**
5 **Jesus says, "Forgive"** **Matthew 18:21–35**

■ ***Pick one of the above passages. Read it prayerfully and write out a brief statement to Jesus expressing your feelings about it.***

Stage 2: Chapter 13 **179**

You may simply wish to read this passage from the second reading and have the students express their feelings about it to Jesus. It begins:

■ *Zacchaeus*
was trying to see who Jesus was,
but he was a little man and
could not see Jesus because of the crowd.

So he ran ahead of the crowd
and climbed a sycamore tree to see Jesus,
who was going to pass that way.

When Jesus came to that place,
he looked up and said to Zacchaeus,
"Hurry down, Zacchaeus,
because I must stay in your house today."

Classroom Resources

CATECHISM

Catechism of the Catholic Church *Second Edition*

For further enrichment, you might refer to:

1. Penance	Index	pp. 831–33
	Glossary	p. 892
2. Conversion	Index	pp. 778–79
	Glossary	p. 873
3. Forgiveness	Index	pp. 795

See also: Reparation, Contrition, Healing.
—Available from the United States Catholic Conference, Washington DC

VIDEOS

The Church Celebrates the Reconciling God
27 minutes. Focuses on the history, theology, and practice of the sacrament of Reconciliation.
—Available from St. Anthony Messenger Press, Cincinnati, OH

Little Friend
43 minutes. A young boy betrays his Japanese-American friend, who is sent to a World War II internment camp.
—Available from St. Anthony Messenger Press, Cincinnati, OH

Pardon and Peace Remembered
15 Minutes. A marvelous story of reconciliation and healing between an old man and a troubled young woman. 1998
—Available from Oblate Media, St. Louis, MO

Walks with Jesus: Meditations for Quiet Moments—Reconciliation
Mark Link, S.J.
Three seven-minute meditations: Babe Ruth Story, Teenager's Story, Death Row Prisoner's Story. 1998.
—Available from Christian Classics, A Division of Thomas More Publishing, Allen, TX

NOTE

For a list of (1) General resources for professional background and (2) Addresses, phone/fax numbers of major publishing companies, see Appendix B of this Resource Manual.

CHAPTER 14
Anointing of the Sick

CHAPTER at a Glance

The aim of this chapter is to deepen the students' understanding of the:

1 *Reasons for the sacrament*
2 *Scriptural foundation for it*
3 *Liturgy and graces of the sacrament*

READ—Have a student read aloud the scriptural introduction which begins: "My friends, remember . . ." Have another student read the commentary following the scriptural introduction. It begins: "The sacrament of the Anointing . . ."

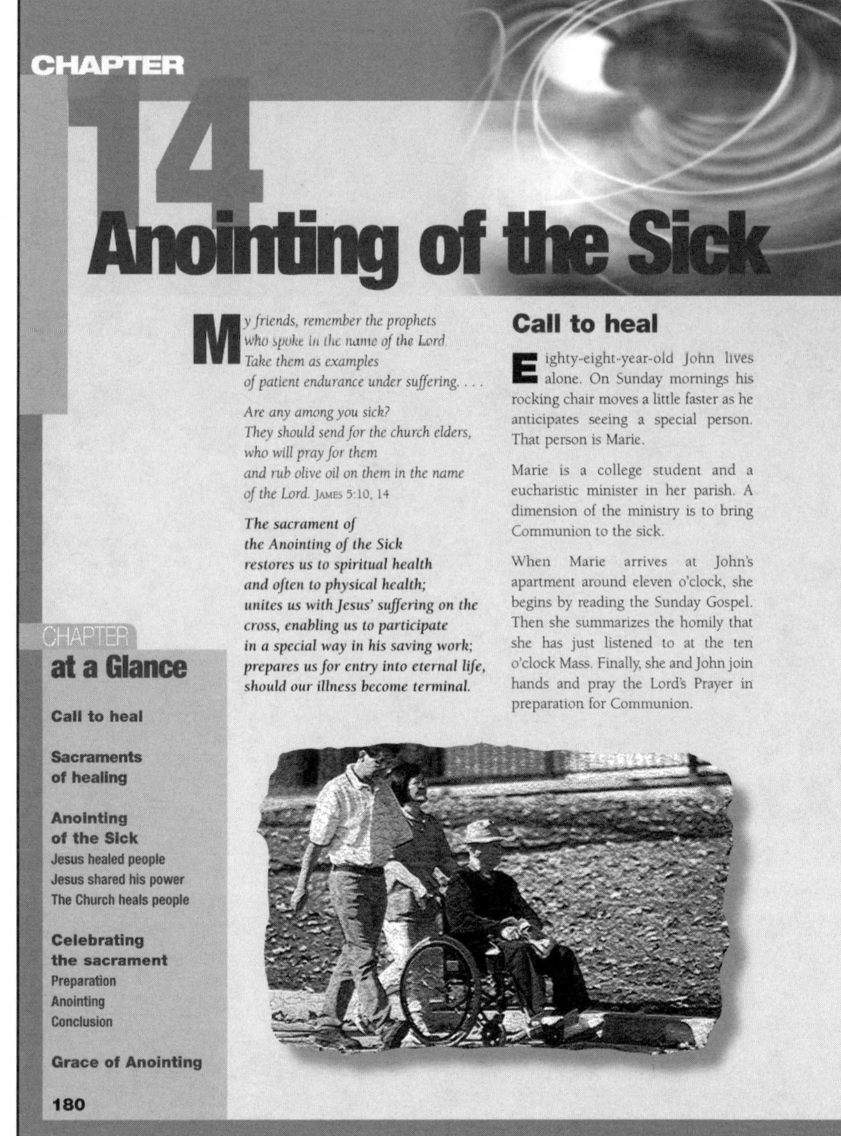

CHAPTER 14

Anointing of the Sick

My friends, remember the prophets
who spoke in the name of the Lord
Take them as examples
of patient endurance under suffering. . . .

Are any among you sick?
They should send for the church elders,
who will pray for them
and rub olive oil on them in the name
of the Lord. James 5:10, 14

The sacrament of
the Anointing of the Sick
restores us to spiritual health
and often to physical health;
unites us with Jesus' suffering on the
cross, enabling us to participate
in a special way in his saving work;
prepares us for entry into eternal life,
should our illness become terminal.

Call to heal

Eighty-eight-year-old John lives alone. On Sunday mornings his rocking chair moves a little faster as he anticipates seeing a special person. That person is Marie.

Marie is a college student and a eucharistic minister in her parish. A dimension of the ministry is to bring Communion to the sick.

When Marie arrives at John's apartment around eleven o'clock, she begins by reading the Sunday Gospel. Then she summarizes the homily that she has just listened to at the ten o'clock Mass. Finally, she and John join hands and pray the Lord's Prayer in preparation for Communion.

180

DISCUSS—The commentary says that the sacrament often restores the person to "physical" health. Ask: Apart from the healing grace of the sacrament, how might the reception of the sacrament from a purely "natural" viewpoint tend to do this?

■ *At an appropriate point in the discussion, have the students flip ahead to "Life Connection" (Babe Ruth) on page 187.*

DISCUSS—Have a student read it aloud. Ask: How does it provide a clue to why the sacrament from a purely natural viewpoint might tend to have a "healing" impact?

■ *The "peace of mind" that Babe Ruth felt from just receiving the sacrament would be conducive to healing on its own.*

Call to heal

CLARIFY—Review what a eucharistic minister is. In other words, the eucharistic minister does far more than help in the distribution of Communion at the Sunday Eucharist.

■ *Recall the impact their ministry has not only on those to whom they minister, but also on their own personal lives. Review the impact it had on the personal life of William Simon, Secretary of the Treasury under Presidents Nixon and Ford (See page 121). He said:*

"Many times I have come away from the hospital wondering if I have given the sick and infirm half of what they've given me. I feel profoundly grateful to them for helping me strengthen my faith."

CLARIFY—Stress the beautiful way Marie went about her ministry to John. Indeed, she not only brought John Holy Communion, but also a great deal of compassion, love, and support.

QUESTION **1** ***What are some ways you might reach out to the elderly and the very sick to make their lives less lonely and more pleasant?***

■ *You might get a show of hands to see if any of the students are involved in visiting or helping out in homes for the elderly.*

NOTES

After John receives Communion, Marie pauses briefly to give John a little time to pray silently. Then she reads slowly to John from a prayerbook. His favorite prayer is:

Lord, free your servant
from sickness, and restore him to health . . .
strengthen him by your power,
protect him by your might, and
give him all that is needed for his welfare.

Following the prayer, John and Marie spend a few minutes visiting with each other. Then she disappears down the steps, as John stands at the window and waves good-bye.

Marie leaves with the realization that she has not only brought John Communion but also assurance that the Christian community is concerned about his physical and spiritual well-being and healing.

1 *What are some ways I might reach out to the elderly and the very sick to make their lives less lonely and more pleasant?*

Sacraments of healing

Each of us has been incorporated into Christ's Body, the Church, by the "sacraments of initiation." This transformed us into new beings.

But even after our incorporation into Christ, we still remain fragile human beings, both physically and spiritually.

When our physical well-being is threatened, the second "healing" sacrament comes to our aid. Let's take a closer look at how it does this.

Anointing of the Sick

The true story of John and Marie dramatizes the Church's special concern for the elderly and the very sick. One of the reasons for this concern is that illness and old age—especially when prolonged—tend to adversely affect not only the body but, more importantly, the spirit.

For example, they can create in us a feeling of isolation and deep loneliness. They can plunge us into a state of mental depression that can threaten our very life of faith. CCC 1500–1501

It is for reasons like this that Jesus himself reached out in a special way, during his life on earth, to the sick and the infirm.

Stage 2: Chapter 14 181

If there are students doing so, you might ask them to share their experience briefly—and the impact it has had on their own personal lives.

Sacraments of healing

CLARIFY—Stress the point that we are fragile human beings both physically and spiritually.

Anointing of the Sick

DISCUSS—Before having a student read aloud this section, ask the students these two questions:

1 *Have you ever been disabled or confined for several days or more? Explain. What was hardest about the confinement?*

2 *How do confinement and/or mental depression tend to impact your faith or affect your attitude toward God and others?*

DISCUSS—After having a student read this section, point out that there are some elderly and chronically sick people who experience confinement and depression on a daily basis.

CLARIFY—Stress that sickness and the infirm can have a crippling effect and not just on the elderly. Consider a tragic example:

■ *A returning Vietnam vet telephoned his wealthy, socialite mother to let her know when he would be arriving home. Before going into the details, he asked her if he could bring home a badly injured buddy for a long stay—for months, perhaps even a year.*

She paused and asked, "How badly is he injured." He said, "Real bad! He has only one arm, one leg, and a messed-up face." She said, "Of course, honey! He can stay a day or so, but beyond that it is out of the question."

He persisted, saying his buddy had no where else he could go. He needed a family. His mother said, "I feel sorry for him, believe me! But my answer is final." The boy hung up.

A few hours later, police called the mother from California, saying they just found a boy with one arm, one leg, and a badly disfigured face. He'd shot himself. The identification papers on his body indicate he's your son."

DISCUSS—How does this story repeat itself every day—only on a lesser scale?

■ *There are a lot of sick people, elderly people, and young people—more than we would ever imagine—who need loving care and support but do not get it. In fact, they get just the opposite.*

PRAYER hotline

Here are four observations from Scripture that relate to this prayer. You may wish to share and discuss them with the students.

1 *When the face is sad*
the heart grows wiser.
ECCLESIASTES 7:3

2 *I have learned this secret . . .*
anywhere, at any time . . .
I have the strength
to face all conditions
by the power that Christ gives me.
PHILIPPIANS 4:13

3 *I consider*
that the sufferings of this present time
are not worth comparing with
the glory about to be revealed to us.
ROMANS 8:18 NRSV

4 *Do not be afraid or discouraged*
for I, the LORD your God,
am with you wherever you go.
JOSHUA 1:9

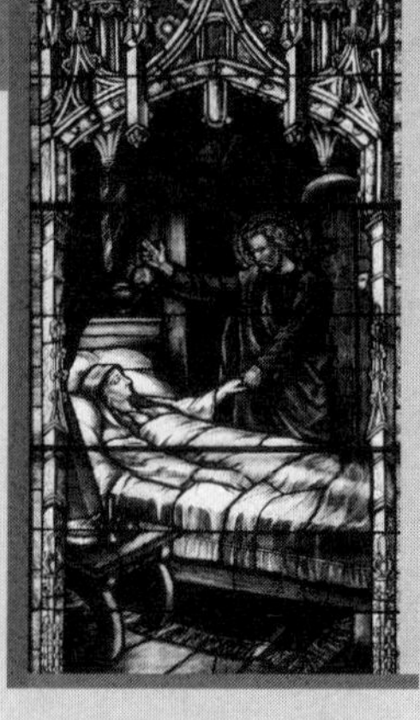

Jesus healed people

The Church's special concern for sick and infirm people, therefore, is an extension of Jesus' own concern for them. Consider this example of Jesus' concern:

Jesus and his disciples . . .
left the synagogue and went straight to the home of Simon and Andrew.

Simon's mother-in-law
was sick in bed with fever. . . .
Jesus took her by the hand,
and helped her up. The fever left her,
and she began to wait on them.

After the sun had set and evening had come, people brought to Jesus all the sick and those who had demons.

All the people of the town
gathered in front of the house.
Jesus healed many who were sick . . .
and drove out many demons.
MARK 1:29–34

PRAYER hotline

Lord, I do not ask
that I never be afflicted,
but only
that you never abandon me
in affliction.

Saint Bernadette Soubirous

From the beginning of his ministry, Jesus showed a special concern for people suffering from serious ailments. It led him to heal people, especially those whose ailments were longstanding. MATTHEW 9:2, 20, 27; JOHN 5:5

2 If Jesus had the power to heal people, why didn't he heal all people, and not just a few?

Jesus shared his power

Jesus did more than heal seriously ailing people. He also shared with his followers the power to heal them. CCC 1506–9

Jesus called the twelve disciples together
and gave them power and authority
to drive out demons and to cure diseases.
Then he sent them out to preach the
Kingdom of God and to heal diseases. . . .

The disciples
left and traveled through all the villages,
preaching the Good News
and healing people everywhere.
LUKE 9:1–2, 6

The impact that the healing of people had on the disciples made them acutely aware of the new power that Jesus had given them.

The Church heals people

The awareness of their healing power led the disciples to alert the Christian community to make use of this great gift. CCC 1510–11 Thus, we read in the Letter from James:

182 STAGE 2: CHAPTER 14

Jesus healed people

QUESTION **2** ***If Jesus had the power to heal people, why didn't he heal all people, and not just a few?***

Review the response to a similar question on page 55. It dealt with Jesus' miracles in general: Why didn't he feed all the hungry people, raise all the dead, heal all the sick?
We began by noting these three facts:

(a) Jesus fed the people, but
they got hungry again. JOHN 6:26
(b) Jesus raised Lazarus (JOHN 11:44),
but he died again.
(c) Jesus healed Peter's mother-in-law
(MARK 1:31), *but she got ill again.*

In addition to Jesus' special loving concern for the sick and suffering there was also another important reason why Jesus worked miracles. What was it?

Miracles were prophetic signs. Jesus himself referred to this. Recall that the day after feeding 5,000 people, many of them returned again, looking for Jesus. He said to them: "You are looking for me because you ate the bread and had all you wanted, not because you understood my miracles."
JOHN 6:26

How, then, should we understand Jesus' miracles? Of what were they signs? They were signs announcing two long-awaited events: (1) the Kingdom of God and (2) the Messiah of God.

Jesus shared his power

DISCUSS—Stress the twofold mandate Jesus gave his disciples:

NOTES

Are any among you sick?
They should send for the church elders,
who will pray for them
and rub olive oil on them
in the name of the Lord.

This prayer made in faith
will heal the sick . . .
and the sins they have committed
will be forgiven. JAMES 5:14–15

3 Why didn't early Christians simply rub olive oil on the sick themselves, rather than call church elders?

Sacramental healing

We saw how Jesus healed people by touching them, anointing them, and praying over them. In other words, he healed them through the *bodily* actions of his *earthly* body.

Today, Jesus continues to heal people by touching them, anointing them, and praying over them. Only now he does this through the *sacramental* (liturgical) actions of his *mystical* body. CCC 1070 Consider an example:

A Vietnam veteran was recuperating in Walter Reed Hospital in Washington, D.C. In a letter to a friend, he described his experience of the sacrament of the Anointing of the Sick. It took place shortly after he was hit by mortar fire in battle. He writes:

From the split second I was hit,
I was completely alone.
I've heard it said, but never realized it—
when you're dying there's no one but you.
You're all alone.

I was hurt bad, real bad;
a 4.2 mortar shell landed
about six feet behind me and took off my left leg, badly ripped up my left arm,
hit me in the back, head, hip, and ankle.

Shock was instantaneous, but I fought it—
knowing that if I went out
I'd never wake up again.

There were three or four medics
hovering over me, all shook up,
trying to help me. . . .
I tried to pray but couldn't. . . .
Well, with a hell of a lot of stubbornness
and luck (providence),
I lived to make it to the chopper
two hours after being hit.

After they carried me
into the first aid station,
I felt four or five people scrubbing my body
in different places.
This brought me to open my eyes,
and I could see about a foot
in front of me—
not too well at that.

LIFE Connection

A Hill with Three Crosses—
One cross
where a thief died *in* sin;
One cross
where a thief died *to* sin;
A center cross
where a Redeemer died *for* sin.

Author Unknown

STAGE 2: CHAPTER 14 **183**

1 *"Drive out demons" and "cure diseases."*
2 *Preach the Kingdom of God."*

Ask the students: Why this twofold instruction? What was so significant about it?

Recall what was said on page 55. Healing the sick and driving out demons were signs pointing to the arrival of the Kingdom of God.

In other words, healing the sick and driving out demons authenticated the preaching of Jesus' disciples.

The Church heals people

CLARIFY—The mandate Jesus passed on to his disciples is now passed on to their successors.

QUESTION **3 *Why didn't early Christians simply rub olive oil on the sick themselves, rather than call church elders?***

■ *The sacrament of the Anointing of the Sick forgives sin, even mortal sin, in the event we are too sick to celebrate the sacrament of Reconciliation.*

The power to forgive sins was reserved specifically to the Apostles. JOHN 20:22

Sacramental healing

QUESTION **4 *What part of the soldier's account did you find most inspiring and personally meaningful? Explain.***

CLARIFY—This moving letter holds a special personal interest for the author of this textbook.

■ *The young soldier wrote it from Walter Reed Hospital at the author's request. The vet not only wrote it out and gave permission to share it, but wrote it out in a way that it is truly moving and inspiring.*

The amount of good the letter has done is incalculable. In a sense, the vet has preached the "Good News" in a way that even he doesn't fully realize. He has used his tragedy to make it a blessing for thousands, maybe even millions.

LIFE Connection

CLARIFY—The "Hill with Three Crosses" serves as a symbol of:

1 *The awesome gift of forgiveness that Jesus holds out to each one of us.*
2 *The awesome decision Jesus leaves us free to make: to "die to sin" or to "die in sin."*

THINK about it

A good example to illustrate the wisdom of this statement is Eugene O'Neill.

Until the age of 25, his life was erratic and lacked purpose and direction. Then he took ill and ended up in a hospital for a prolonged stretch. There he had a chance to think. As a result, two things happened: (1) he reformed his life, and (2) he discovered that he could write.

To make a long story short, critics credit him as being the single most powerful influence in redeeming American drama from triviality and superficiality.

He went on to become a three-time winner of the Pulitzer Prize for Literature and winner of the Nobel Prize for Drama.

In 1947, in an interview before the Broadway opening of his play, *The Ice Man Cometh*, he replied to one of the questions with a burst of emotion, saying:

If the human race is so stupid that
in 2,000 years it hasn't had brains enough
to appreciate that the secret of happiness
is contained in one simple sentence
which you'd think any school kid
could understand and apply,
then it's time we dumped it
down the nearest drain
and let the ants have a chance.

That simple sentence is, "What shall it profit a man if he shall gain the whole world and lose his own soul?"

GREAT READING FROM LIFE, PAGE 179, 1960

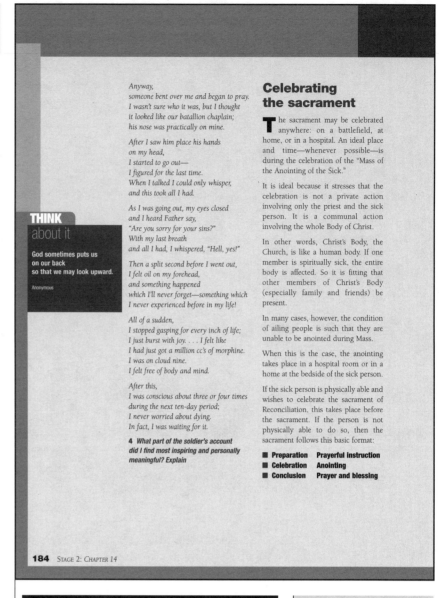

Anyway,
someone bent over me and began to pray.
I wasn't sure who it was, but I thought
it looked like our batallion chaplain;
his nose was practically on mine.

After I saw him place his hands
on my head,
I started to go out—
I figured for the last time.
When I talked I could only whisper,
and this took all I had.

As I was going out, my eyes closed
and I heard Father say,
"Are you sorry for your sins?"
With my last breath
and all I had, I whispered, "Hell, yes!"

Then a split second before I went out,
I felt oil on my forehead,
and something happened
which I'll never forget—something which
I never experienced before in my life!

All of a sudden,
I stopped gasping for every inch of life;
I just burst with joy. . . . I felt like
I had just got a million cc's of morphine.
I was on cloud nine.
I felt free of body and mind.

After this,
I was conscious about three or four times
during the next ten-day period;
I never worried about dying.
In fact, I was waiting for it.

4 What part of the soldier's account did I find most inspiring and personally meaningful? Explain

THINK about it

God sometimes puts us on our back so that we may look upward.

Anonymous

Celebrating the sacrament

The sacrament may be celebrated anywhere: on a battlefield, at home, or in a hospital. An ideal place and time—whenever possible—is during the celebration of the "Mass of the Anointing of the Sick."

It is ideal because it stresses that the celebration is not a private action involving only the priest and the sick person. It is a communal action involving the whole Body of Christ.

In other words, Christ's Body, the Church, is like a human body. If one member is spiritually sick, the entire body is affected. So it is fitting that other members of Christ's Body (especially family and friends) be present.

In many cases, however, the condition of ailing people is such that they are unable to be anointed during Mass.

When this is the case, the anointing takes place in a hospital room or in a home at the bedside of the sick person.

If the sick person is physically able and wishes to celebrate the sacrament of Reconciliation, this takes place before the sacrament. If the person is not physically able to do so, then the sacrament follows this basic format:

- **Preparation** **Prayerful instruction**
- **Celebration** **Anointing**
- **Conclusion** **Prayer and blessing**

184 STAGE 2: CHAPTER 14

Celebrating the Sacrament

CLARIFY—Stress two things in particular:

1 *The communal nature of the sacrament (It involves the whole body of Christ and should reflect this fact, thus the desirability of celebrating the sacrament at Mass when possible;*

2 *The practice of conditions governing the reception of the sacrament of Reconciliation along with the sacrament of the Anointing of the Sick.*

NOTES

Up Close & Personal

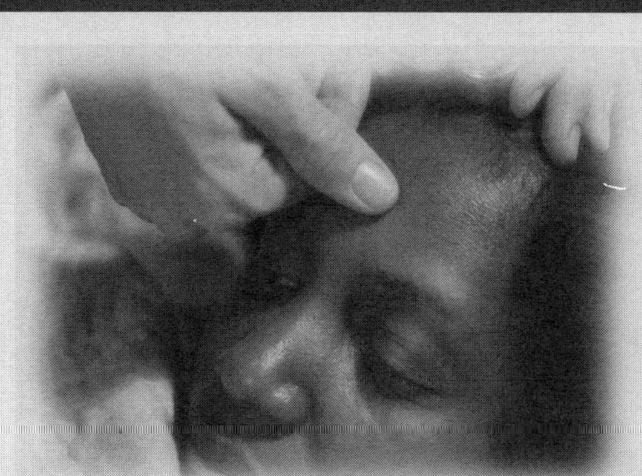

Francis Keller

In 1909 Father Francis Keller took a train to Gillette, Wyoming, to celebrate Mass and minister to settlers there. Many had not seen a priest in years.

After he was finished, a settler took him for a horseback ride into the hills. Suddenly, they saw a woman waving for help. As they approached and she saw Fr. Keller's Roman collar, an amazing expression came over her face.

"Father," she said, "my brother's dying." Father Keller went inside, heard the man's confession, and anointed him. No sooner had he done so, than the man died. Afterward, the woman said to Father Keller:

No one told me
you were saying Mass
in Gillette today. But all his life,
my brother has prayed
that a priest
would be present at his death
to give him the sacraments.
This morning, we both prayed
one last time for this grace.

Retold from *Friar* magazine, September 1957

Preparation

The liturgy begins with a greeting similar to the one used at Mass. The Instruction consists of recalling the words of the Letter from James (cited on p.184) followed by a brief prayer for the sick person.

The liturgy continues with the priest laying his hands on the ailing person, as Jesus often did when healing people. MARK 6:5, CCC 1513

If it is fitting, the priest may invite those present to lay hands on the sick person also. This reinforces the fact that the sacrament is an action of the whole Body of Christ. CCC 1516

Anointing

Next, the priest follows the instruction of Jesus to his disciples and the instruction of the Letter of James.

He anoints the sick person with oil. MARK 6:13, JAMES 5:14–15 He begins with the forehead, praying:

Through this holy anointing,
may the Lord in love and mercy help you
with the grace of the Holy Spirit. Amen.

Then the priest anoints the hands, praying:

May the Lord who frees you from sin
save you and raise you up. Amen.

STAGE 2: CHAPTER 14 185

Preparation

CLARIFY—The text says, "The liturgy begins with the priest laying his hands on the ailing person, as Jesus often did in healing people."

Review again the amazing poll conducted by columnist Ann Landers. She asked her women readers to respond by postcard or letter to the following question:

> *"Would you be content to be held close and treated tenderly and forget about 'the act' [intercourse]?"*

More than 90,000 women responded. Nearly three-fourths said yes to that question. Even more surprising is the fact that 40 percent of those who said yes were under 40 years old.

The poll was eloquent testimony to the power of touch to convey a sense of being wanted and loved.

For typical explanations of the responses given by women respondents, see Ann Lander's column for Tuesday, January 15, 1985.

CLARIFY—Point out the fact that it is fitting that those present at the anointing "lay hands on the sick person," along with the priest. This reinforces the communal dimension of the sacrament.

Anointing

CLARIFY—Point out the four key petitions contained in the anointing formula:

1. *Help by the grace of the Spirit*
2. *Forgiveness of sin*
3. *Eternal salvation*
4. *Resurrection from the dead*

Up Close & Personal

This story, along with the Babe Ruth story and the story of the soldier's story (page 183), form the trio of stories featured in the 21-minute meditation video "Walks with Jesus: Anointing of the Sick."

See details in "Classroom Resources."

Share Your meditation

Saint Francis de Sales (1567–1622) is the patron saint of authors. He wrote two famous books. The first, *Introduction to the Devout Life*, was for beginners in the spiritual life. The second was *Treatise on the Love of God*, for those more advanced in the spiritual life.

Who should be anointed?

CLARIFY—Stress the four groups who should receive the sacrament and the three conditions necessary before anointing someone not Catholic:

1. *Is baptized*
2. *Believes Jesus acts in the sacraments*
3. *Requests the sacrament*

Grace of Anointing

CLARIFY—The text describes another grace of the sacrament this way: "It unites us with the suffering of Jesus on the cross, enabling us to participate in a special way in his saving work." An excellent example of this is Gary Cooper.

> *Gary Cooper was a Hollywood superstar. He won two Oscars during his career—one for the title role in* Sergeant York; *the other for the high-drama role of the town sheriff in* High Noon.
>
> *Cooper's life seems to have fallen into two stages. The first stage was pretty much one of living, exclusively. The second stage was living in preparation for the life to come. That stage shifted into high gear when he entered the Catholic Church just a few years before dying from cancer in 1961.*

In the final days of his life, the pain from cancer became intense. Msgr. James Cunnigham, pastor of Good Shepherd Church in Beverly Hills, who ministered to Cooper in his final days gave him a small, steel crucifix, saying:

> *Gary, hang on to this tight.*
> *When the pain gets really bad,*
> *squeeze it and remind yourself to unite*
> *your pain with the pain of Jesus*
> *for the salvation of souls.*

After Cooper died, Mgsr. Cunningham saw an article in a popular magazine by a popular author. The author said that when he visited with Gary in his last days, he noticed that during their visit, Gary kept gripping and regripping a small, steel crucifix. Msgr. Cunningham wrote, later:

> *The author of that article had no idea*
> *of the significance of the crucifix,*
> *but Gary did, and so did I.*
>
> Retold from "The Last Days of Gary Cooper," by Monsignor James A. O'Callaghan, *Catholic Digest*, March 1997, pp 68–74

To recap, Gary Cooper is a beautiful, concrete example of someone who received the grace of uniting his own

---

SHARE YOUR meditation

Actress Ann Jillian found a growth on her body; she feared the worst. Before going to the doctor, she went to St. Francis de Sales Church. Over its entrance is an inscription she had often seen, but never read until now. It said:

The same everlasting Father
who cares for you today
will take care of you tomorrow
and every day.
Either he will shield you
from suffering, or he will give you
unfailing strength to bear it.
Be at peace then and put aside
all anxious thoughts and
imaginations.

Those words gave Ann hope just when she needed it most. Two weeks later, she successfully underwent a double mastectomy (removal of both breasts).

■ ***What keeps me from greater trust in God?***

Conclusion

The liturgy ends with everyone present reciting the Lord's Prayer. It is followed by a brief closing prayer and a blessing.

If the person is physically able and wishes to receive communion, that takes place at this point. If not, the celebration ends with a blessing similar to the one used at Mass.

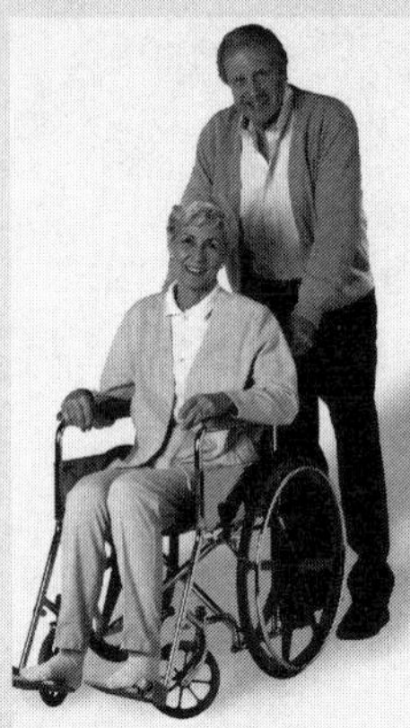

Who should be anointed?

A priest was called to a Los Angeles hospital to anoint an elderly woman named Gladys. She was not Catholic, but had asked to receive the sacrament. Just before the chaplain arrived, Gladys lapsed into a coma. He anointed her and she went on to recover.

It surprises some Catholics that the chaplain gave the sacrament to a person who was not Catholic. The Church permits this if the person has been baptized, believes Jesus acts through the sacrament, and requests to receive it.

It also surprises some Catholics that the sacrament was celebrated while Gladys was in a coma. The Church celebrates the sacrament in this situation (and similar situations such as unconsciousness or sedated patients) if they have requested it or would probably request it if they could.

Generally speaking, the sacrament of the Anointing of the Sick is for people who are seriously ill, or seriously weakened from advanced age.

It is important to note here that serious illness does not mean terminal illness. Nor does it mean an illness that puts a person in immediate danger of death. It simply means any illness that seriously impairs the health of a person. It also means the sacrament should be received before a serious operation. CCC 1514–15

If during the same illness the person's condition takes a turn for the worse or develops a new illness (e.g., pneumonia), the sacrament may be repeated. This holds true, also, for the elderly whose frailty becomes more pronounced.

LIFE Connection

An illness
is like a TV commercial—
even a short one is too long.

E. C. McKenzie

NOTES

In brief, then, the sacrament of the Anointing of the Sick may and should be celebrated by those who are:

- **Seriously ill**
- **Seriously weakened by advanced age**
- **Scheduled for serious surgery**
- **Suffering a relapse or new illness**

Grace of Anointing

People suffering from serious illness often suffer from anxiety. They may even be tempted to lose their trust in God. To these people the sacrament of the Anointing of the Sick is the occasion for special grace. We may sum this grace up as follows.

It restores us to health, if this be for our good. If not, it gives us the strength and the serenity to bear suffering, as Jesus did. CCC 1520, 1532

It forgives our sins if, for any reason, we are unable to celebrate the sacrament of Reconciliation. CCC 1532

It unites us with the suffering of Jesus on the cross, enabling us to participate in a special way in his saving work. CCC 1521

Finally, if our illness, in God's providence, is destined to become terminal, the sacrament of the Anointing of the Sick prepares us for entry into eternal life. CCC 1523

5 Reread the Vietnam soldier's account of his experience of the sacrament of the Anointing of the Sick and indicate where he seems to be alluding to one or several of the above graces.

Viaticum

With the sacrament of Anointing of the Sick, the Church offers those who are about to leave this life the Eucharist as *viaticum* (spiritual nourishment for the journey). CCC 1517, 1524

Received at this moment, the Eucharist acts as a kind of preparation for *eternal life* and the *resurrection*. Jesus said: "Those who eat my flesh and drink my blood have *eternal life*, and I will *raise them to life* on the last day." JOHN 6:54

So the sacraments of Baptism, Confirmation, and the Eucharist form a spiritual unity. They *begin* our earthly pilgrimage and serve as *sacraments of initiation*. CCC 1525

The sacraments of Reconciliation, Anointing of the Sick, and the Eucharist form a similar spiritual unity. They *end* our earthly pilgrimage and serve as *sacraments of completion*. CCC 1525

LIFE Connection

During his career, Babe Ruth drifted from his faith, but he didn't abandon it totally. He wrote in *Guideposts* magazine:

I did have my own altar,
a big window
in my New York apartment
overlooking the city lights.
Often I would kneel
before that window
and say my prayers.
I would feel quite humble then.
I'd ask God to help me.

At the end of his career, Ruth took seriously ill. Paul Carey, a close friend, said to him, "They're going to operate in the morning. Don't you think you should see a priest?" Babe agreed. After meeting with the priest, Babe wrote: "As I lay in bed that night, I thought . . . what a comfortable feeling to be free from fear and worries."

■ ***Did you ever advise a friend to seek spiritual help? Explain. Without using names, give an example of someone who needs spiritual help.***

suffering with the suffering of Jesus on the cross, enabling him to participate in a special way in Jesus' saving work."

QUESTION **5 *Reread the Vietnam soldier's account of his experience of the sacrament of the Anointing of the Sick and indicate where he seems to be alluding to one of several of the above graces.***

1 *"I felt free of my body and mind."*
LAST LINE OF THE SECOND LAST PARAGRAPH.
This seems to allude to "spiritual" and "physical" healing.

2 *"I never worried about dying. In fact I was waiting for it."*
LAST LINE OF LAST PARAGRAPH.
This seems to allude to "preparation to enter into eternal life."

Viaticum

CLARIFY—After Cooper's death from cancer, Monsignor Cunningham wrote:

■ *As a priest, I have prepared many people for death. But I have never met a person more resigned and disposed for death than Gary. Like Christ, he remained meek and humble of heart to the end.*

It is this kind of death that the sacrament of Anointing of the Sick and the Eucharist as viaticum (spiritual nourishment for the journey) make possible. They serve as "sacraments of completion" ending the pilgrimage on this earth, which began with the "sacraments of initiation."

LIFE Connection

CLARIFY—Babe Ruth (1895–1948) grew up in his parents' saloon in Baltimore. He writes: "Looking at my youth, I honestly don't think I knew the difference between right and wrong. . . . I hardly knew my parents." Eventually, he was sent to Saint Mary's Industrial School in Baltimore, a home for problem boys. It was there that Ruth met Brother Matthias, who introduced him to Catholicism and baseball. Ruth died of cancer. He held three remarkable records:

1 *Hit 714 career home runs, a record broken 39 years later in 1974 by Hank Aaron.*
2 *Hit 60 home runs in 1927, a record broken 71 years later by Mark Maguire in 1998;*
3 *Pitched 29 consecutive scoreless innings in a world series (with Boston) before being sold to the Yankees in 1920.*

Recap

A fitting recap is to end as we began, with:

(1) The core Scripture passage relating to the sacrament:

Are any among you sick?
They should send for the church elders,
who will pray for them
and rub olive oil on them in the name
of the Lord. James 5:14

(2) A summary of the graces of the sacrament.

Restores us to spiritual health and often physical health; Unites us with Jesus' suffering on the cross, enabling us to participate in a special way in his saving work, should our illness become terminal.

Review

DAILY QUIZ—The review questions may be assigned (one or two at a time) for homework or a daily quiz.

CHAPTER TESTS—Reproducible chapter tests are found in Appendix A. For consistency and ease in grading, quizzes are restricted to (1) "Matching," (2) "True/False," and (3) "Fill in the Blanks."

TEST ANSWERS—The following are the answers to the test for Chapter 14. (See Appendix A, page 325.) Each correct answer is worth 4 points.

True/False

1 = T	2 = F	3 = T	4 = T
5 = F	6 = T	7 = F	8 = F
9 = F	10 = T	11 = F	12 = T
13 = F	14 = F	15 = T	

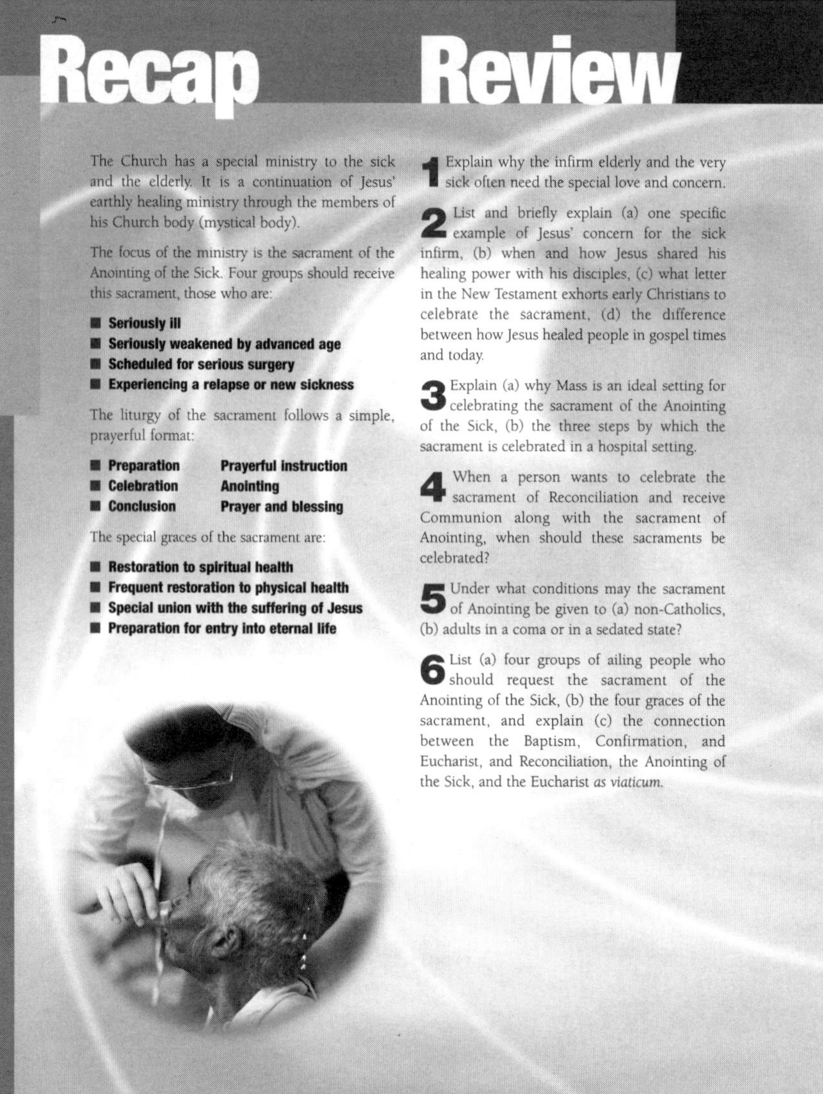

Recap Review

The Church has a special ministry to the sick and the elderly. It is a continuation of Jesus' earthly healing ministry through the members of his Church body (mystical body).

The focus of the ministry is the sacrament of the Anointing of the Sick. Four groups should receive this sacrament, those who are:

- **Seriously ill**
- **Seriously weakened by advanced age**
- **Scheduled for serious surgery**
- **Experiencing a relapse or new sickness**

The liturgy of the sacrament follows a simple, prayerful format:

- **Preparation** — **Prayerful instruction**
- **Celebration** — **Anointing**
- **Conclusion** — **Prayer and blessing**

The special graces of the sacrament are:

- **Restoration to spiritual health**
- **Frequent restoration to physical health**
- **Special union with the suffering of Jesus**
- **Preparation for entry into eternal life**

1 Explain why the infirm elderly and the very sick often need the special love and concern.

2 List and briefly explain (a) one specific example of Jesus' concern for the sick infirm, (b) when and how Jesus shared his healing power with his disciples, (c) what letter in the New Testament exhorts early Christians to celebrate the sacrament, (d) the difference between how Jesus healed people in gospel times and today.

3 Explain (a) why Mass is an ideal setting for celebrating the sacrament of the Anointing of the Sick, (b) the three steps by which the sacrament is celebrated in a hospital setting.

4 When a person wants to celebrate the sacrament of Reconciliation and receive Communion along with the sacrament of Anointing, when should these sacraments be celebrated?

5 Under what conditions may the sacrament of Anointing be given to (a) non-Catholics, (b) adults in a coma or in a sedated state?

6 List (a) four groups of ailing people who should request the sacrament of the Anointing of the Sick, (b) the four graces of the sacrament, and explain (c) the connection between the Baptism, Confirmation, and Eucharist, and Reconciliation, the Anointing of the Sick, and the Eucharist *as viaticum.*

188 Stage 2: *Chapter 14*

Fill in the Blanks

1. (a) Seriously ill
   (b) Seriously weakened by advanced age
   (c) Scheduled for serious surgery
   (d) Suffer a relapse or new illness
2. (a) Preparation
   (b) Prayerful instruction
   (c) Celebration
   (d) Anointing
   (e) Conclusion
   (f) Prayer and blessing

NOTES

Reflect

1 Advanced age can make people feel that they are useless and even a burden to others. This is tragic, because they can often give to others (especially the young) something no one else can give them. To illustrate, consider this excerpt from an essay by a third grader:

Grandmothers don't have to be smart,
only answer questions like,
"Why isn't God married?"
and "How come dogs chase cats?"
A grandmother is a lady
with no children of her own
She likes other people's little girls and boys.
Everyone should have a grandmother, especially if
they don't have TV. Quoted by Dr. James Dobson

■ ***Describe an experience that made you realize the important role (a) older people can play in the lives of younger people, (b) younger people can play in the lives of older people.***

2 Brother Mike Newman ministers to the sick, not only bodily but also spiritually. One day he prayed over a patient named Alice, who was in a coma. Three days later, she came out of the coma. She recalled his prayer and told him how much it meant to her. He gives these suggestions for dealing with people when they appear completely unconscious:

(a) Talk to them, because there is a good chance they can still hear you.
(b) Talk to them by name and in an adult way.
(c) Pray out loud and slowly, using familiar prayers like the Lord's Prayer.
(d) Suggest they pray with you in their minds.

■ ***Describe a time when you prayed for (or with) a very sick person. Did you feel comfortable doing this? Why would or wouldn't you like someone to do this for you when you were seriously sick?***

3 *The American Journal of Nursing* describes an experiment at a New York hospital, in which nurses placed hands on patients with the intention to heal them. The patients improved dramatically over a similar group not treated in this way. Francis MacNutt says:

These studies provide evidence
to show that, simply in the natural order,
the patients' power to recover
improves when the nurses lay on hands. . . .
The way they understand it is
that there is a natural power of life
in loving people
which is communicated in a special way through the
power of touch.

■ ***If "loving hands" can heal naturally, why do we need a sacrament for this?***
■ ***Can you think of an everyday example in which placing loving hands on someone can help them immensely?***
■ ***Describe a time when someone's love and concern produced an emotional or spiritual healing in you.***

Stage 2: Chapter 14 **189**

Reflect

1 ***Describe an experience that made you realize the important role (a) older people can play in the lives of younger people, (b) younger people can play in the lives of older people.***

■ *A senior citizen's complex in Minnesota combines a retirement home with a day-care center. They says it works. Why?*

2 ***Describe a time when you prayed for (or with) a very sick person. Did you feel comfortable doing this? Why would or wouldn't you like someone to do this for you when you were seriously ill?***

■ *Pianist Marta Korwin-Rhodes was in Warsaw when the city was besieged. She stayed on to help the wounded. One night she came upon a soldier with his face buried in a pillow, sobbing and moaning. She stopped, put her hands on his head, and prayed. He grabbed them with such force that she thought his nails would pierce her flesh. Then, she said: "His sobs quieted; his hands released their grip, and he fell asleep."*

3 **a)** ***If "loving hands" can heal naturally, why do we need a sacrament for this?***

■ *Sometimes a person is in a coma or too ill to be aware of the "loving" hands. Sometimes more than love is needed.*

b) ***Can you think of an everyday example in which placing loving hands on someone can help immensely?***

■ *Author Ardis Whitman was having trouble adjusting to her son's death. One night her young granddaughter and her granddaughter's boyfriend took her to a nightclub.*

When the orchestra played a song that reminded Ardis of her son, tears welled up in her eyes. Spontaneously, the young couple took her hands in theirs.
That beautiful gesture, said Ardis, "made God very close to me."

c) ***Describe a time when someone's love and concern produced an emotional or spiritual healing in you.***

■ *Years ago, Jo Jo Starbuck was a well-known American ice skater. She said that when she was a youngster, struggling to become a good skater, she often came home depressed because her coach had screamed at her. Jo Jo said:*

"I'd come home and cry and want to quit. But my mother would constantly build me up. . . . until my batteries were recharged."

PRAYER TIME with the Lord

QUESTION ***Recall an episode that gave you an insight into the faith of one or both of your parents.***

To get the students started, recount for them this true story that author Alan Loy McGinnis tells about Dr. Norman Lobsenz:

■ *Young Norman's wife was in the midst of a serious illness; and the ordeal was taking its toll on Norman. He was on the verge of collapse when he recalled an incident from his childhood.*

One night when his mother had taken ill, Norman got up around midnight to get a drink of water. As he passed his parents' bedroom, he saw his father sitting in a chair on his mother's side of the bed. She was fast asleep.

Norman tiptoed in. Fighting back tears, he asked, "Daddy, is Mom worse?" "No, Norman," his father said softly. "I'm just sitting here watching over her, in case she wakes up and needs something."

That long-forgotten incident from his childhood gave Norman all the strength he needed to carry on.

PRAYER Journal

QUESTION ***Reflect on the final sentence of the prayer and recall an example (preferably from your own life) to illustrate it.***

Recall Helen Keller's famous words on page 141 of this Resource Manual:

■ *I thank God for my handicaps,*
for through them I have found myself,
my work, and my God.

QUESTION ***Imagine you are alone and have only minutes to live. Compose a prayer you would like to make to God at that critical moment of your life.***

A 13-year-old girl was dead of leukemia. While going through her belongings, her

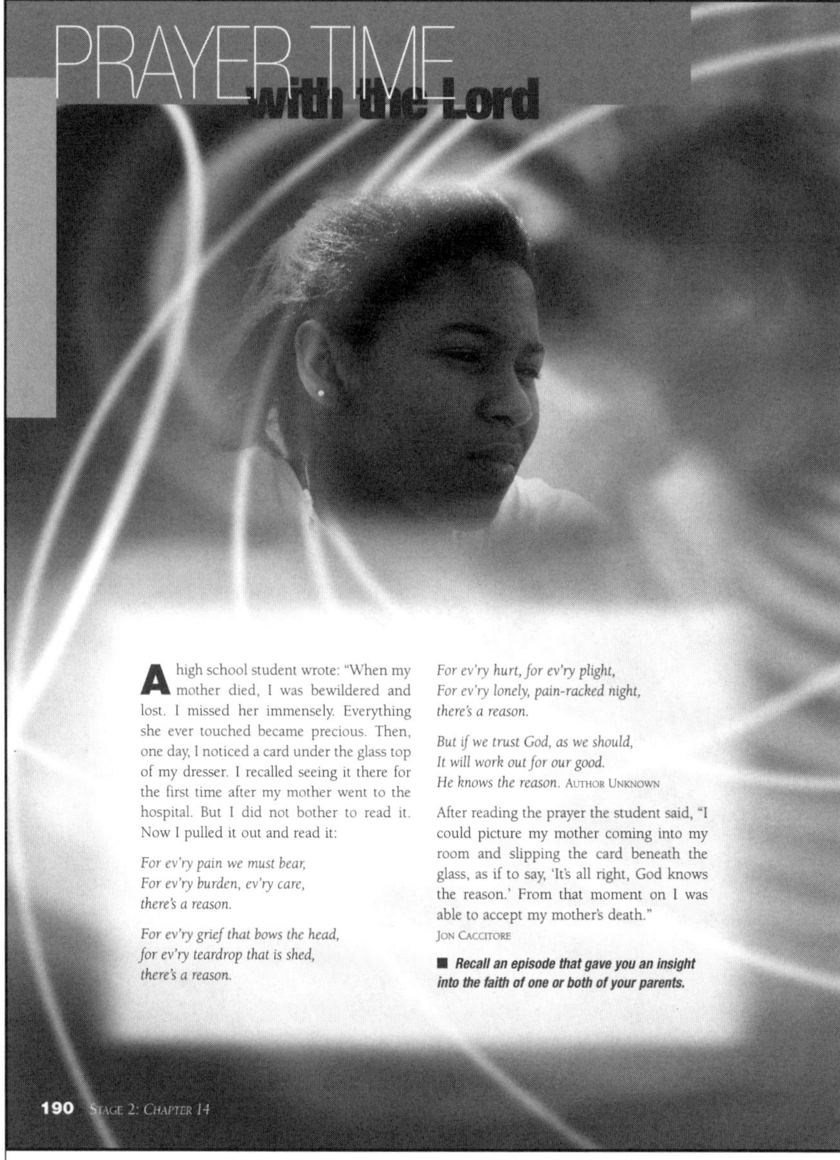
PRAYER TIME with the Lord

A high school student wrote: "When my mother died, I was bewildered and lost. I missed her immensely. Everything she ever touched became precious. Then, one day, I noticed a card under the glass top of my dresser. I recalled seeing it there for the first time after my mother went to the hospital. But I did not bother to read it. Now I pulled it out and read it:

For ev'ry pain we must bear,
For ev'ry burden, ev'ry care,
there's a reason.

For ev'ry grief that bows the head,
for ev'ry teardrop that is shed,
there's a reason.

For ev'ry hurt, for ev'ry plight,
For ev'ry lonely, pain-racked night,
there's a reason.

But if we trust God, as we should,
It will work out for our good.
He knows the reason. AUTHOR UNKNOWN

After reading the prayer the student said, "I could picture my mother coming into my room and slipping the card beneath the glass, as if to say, 'It's all right, God knows the reason.' From that moment on I was able to accept my mother's death."
JON CACCITORE

■ ***Recall an episode that gave you an insight into the faith of one or both of your parents.***

190 STAGE 2: CHAPTER 14

parents found a poem she had written during her illness. A portion of it reads:

■ *O God, I'm free! . . .*
Your hand came through the dark,
A faint spark; but it lit my soul.
My fire is burning, Lord.
No one can put it out.
O God, I'm free! MISSION MAGAZINE

You might share this prayer that someone wrote after reading the girl's prayer.

■ *O God, show me what I can do*
to help your hand come through the dark
and light a spark in another's life.

SCRIPTURE Journal

QUESTION ***Pick one of the passages. Read it prayerfully and write a short statement to Jesus expressing your feelings about it.***

NOTES

PRAYER Journal

In the movie *Little Big Man*, Old Lodgeskin made a final prayer to God before dying:

I thank you for making me a human being.
I thank you for my defeats.
I thank you for my sight.
And I thank you for my blindness
which has helped me see even further.

■ *Reflect on the final sentence of the prayer and recall an example (preferably from your own life) to illustrate it.*
■ *Imagine you are alone and have only minutes to live. Compose a prayer you would like to make to God at that critical moment of your life.*

SCRIPTURE Journal

1 Jesus heals the sick — Luke 7:1–10
2 Jesus shares his power — Luke 10:1–9
3 Disciples heal the sick — Luke 10:17–24
4 Church heals the sick — Acts 5:12–16
5 Church urges healing — James 5:13–20

■ *Pick one of the above passages. Read it prayerfully and write out a brief statement to Jesus expressing your feelings about it.*

STAGE 2: CHAPTER 14 191

You may simply wish to read this passage from the fourth reading and have the students express their feelings about it to Jesus:

> *As a result of what the apostles were doing, sick people were carried out into the streets and placed on beds and mats so that at least Peter's shadow might fall on some of them as he passed by. . . .*
> *And they were all healed.*

Here's what one student wrote. You might want to share it with the students.

> ■ *Jesus, when I read things like this in your holy book, I stop and pray:*
> *"Lord, let Peter walk my way.*
> *Let his shadow fall on me, heal me, and help me be what I want to be."*
> *Do you ever hear my prayer?*
> *How come you don't answer it?*

Classroom Resources

CATECHISM

Catechism of the Catholic Church *Second Edition*

For further enrichment, you might refer to:

1. Anointing	Index	p. 756
	Glossary	p. 866
2. Viaticum	Index	p. 856
	Glossary	p. 902

See also: Healing, Grace.

—AVAILABLE FROM THE UNITED STATES CATHOLIC CONFERENCE, WASHINGTON DC

VIDEOS

No One Cries the Wrong Way

Eight 15-minute segments. The mystery of suffering and dying through the eyes of faith. 1998

—AVAILABLE FROM BROWN-ROA, DUBUQUE IA

Walks with Jesus: Anointing of the Sick

Mark Link, S.J.

Three seven-minute meditations. Includes the stories of the Vietnam vet and Fr. Keller's anointing of the young man in Wyoming. 1998.

—AVAILABLE FROM CHRISTIAN CLASSICS, A DIVISION OF THOMAS MORE PUBLISHING, ALLEN, TX

NOTE

For a list of (1) General resources for professional background and (2) Addresses, phone/fax numbers of major publishing companies, see Appendix B of this Resource Manual.

CHAPTER 15
Marriage

CHAPTER at a Glance

The aim of this chapter is to give the students a deeper appreciation of the:

1 *Beauty and seriousness of marriage*
2 *Church's teaching concerning the sanctity of marriage*
3 *Challenges and dangers of the phases through which most marriages pass*

ACTIVITY—Have a student read aloud the scriptural introduction, which begins, "Then God said, 'And now let us . . .' "

Have a second student read aloud the commentary. It begins: "The story of the human race . . ."

Now read the following statement to the class:

■ *Psychologist Eugene Kennedy recommends this "test of friendship." If we don't enjoy being with someone unless we are doing something— like bowling or going to a movie— then that person may not be as good a friend as we think.*

The true test of friendship is that we can do nothing together and still be happy. In other words, we enjoy each other so much that we don't need the glue of activity to hold us together.

On a scale of one (not at all) to ten (totally), to what extent do you agree with Kennedy's "friendship test"?

After the students have committed themselves in writing, have them call out their responses while a "secretary" tallies them on the chalkboard. If there is a significant disparity in the responses, have the students discuss it.

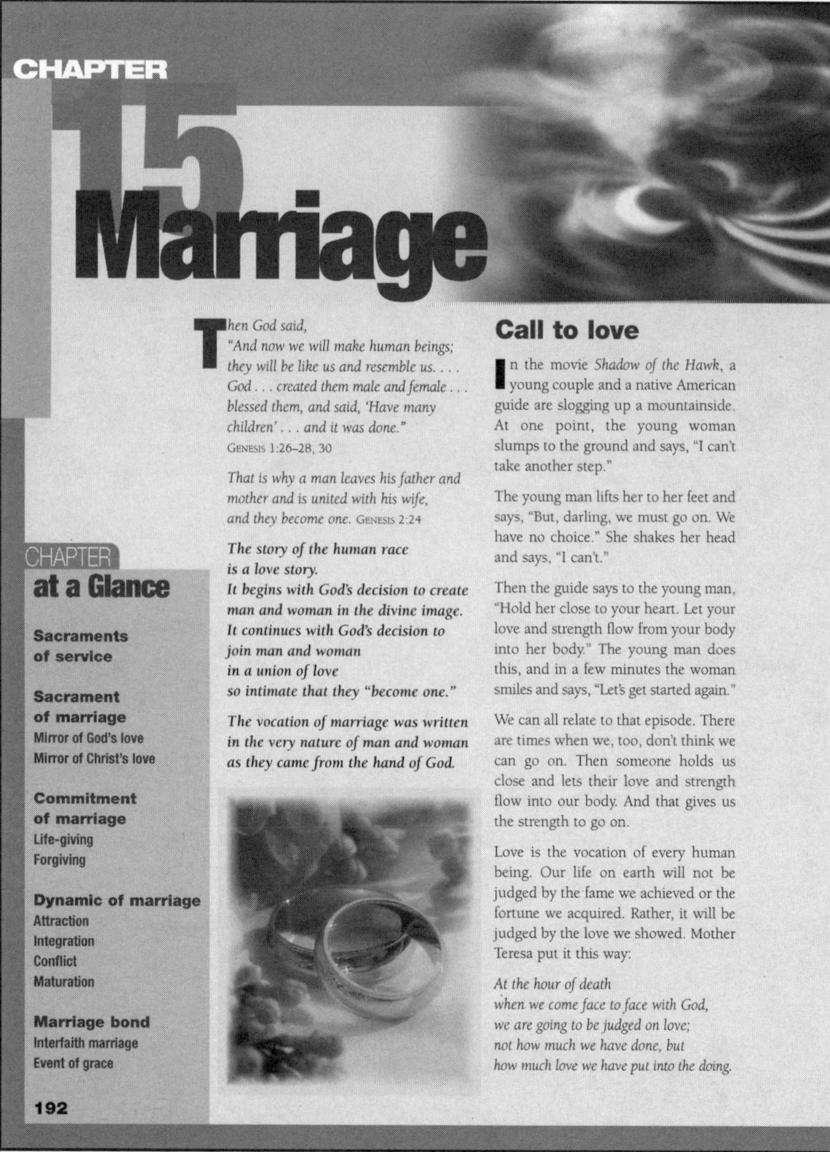

CHAPTER 15 Marriage

Then God said,
"And now we will make human beings;
they will be like us and resemble us. . . .
God . . . created them male and female . . .
blessed them, and said, 'Have many
children' . . . and it was done."
GENESIS 1:26–28, 30

That is why a man leaves his father and
mother and is united with his wife,
and they become one. GENESIS 2:24

The story of the human race is a love story. It begins with God's decision to create man and woman in the divine image. It continues with God's decision to join man and woman in a union of love so intimate that they "become one."

The vocation of marriage was written in the very nature of man and woman as they came from the hand of God.

CHAPTER at a Glance

Sacraments of service

Sacrament of marriage
Mirror of God's love
Mirror of Christ's love

Commitment of marriage
Life-giving
Forgiving

Dynamic of marriage
Attraction
Integration
Conflict
Maturation

Marriage bond
Interfaith marriage
Event of grace

192

Call to love

In the movie *Shadow of the Hawk*, a young couple and a native American guide are slogging up a mountainside. At one point, the young woman slumps to the ground and says, "I can't take another step."

The young man lifts her to her feet and says, "But, darling, we must go on. We have no choice." She shakes her head and says, "I can't."

Then the guide says to the young man, "Hold her close to your heart. Let your love and strength flow from your body into her body." The young man does this, and in a few minutes the woman smiles and says, "Let's get started again."

We can all relate to that episode. There are times when we, too, don't think we can go on. Then someone holds us close and lets their love and strength flow into our body. And that gives us the strength to go on.

Love is the vocation of every human being. Our life on earth will not be judged by the fame we achieved or the fortune we acquired. Rather, it will be judged by the love we showed. Mother Teresa put it this way:

At the hour of death
when we come face to face with God,
we are going to be judged on love;
not how much we have done, but
how much love we have put into the doing.

Call to love

CLARIFY—Recall the question Ann Landers put to her women readers:

"Would you be content to be held close and treated tenderly and forget about 'the act' [intercourse]?"

Of the 90,000 who responded, nearly three-fourths said yes. Even more surprising, 40 percent of those who said yes were under 40 years old.

Recall, also, the example of author Ardis Whitman in the previous chapter:

She was having trouble adjusting to her son's death. One night, her young granddaughter and her granddaughter's boyfriend took her to a nightclub.

NOTES

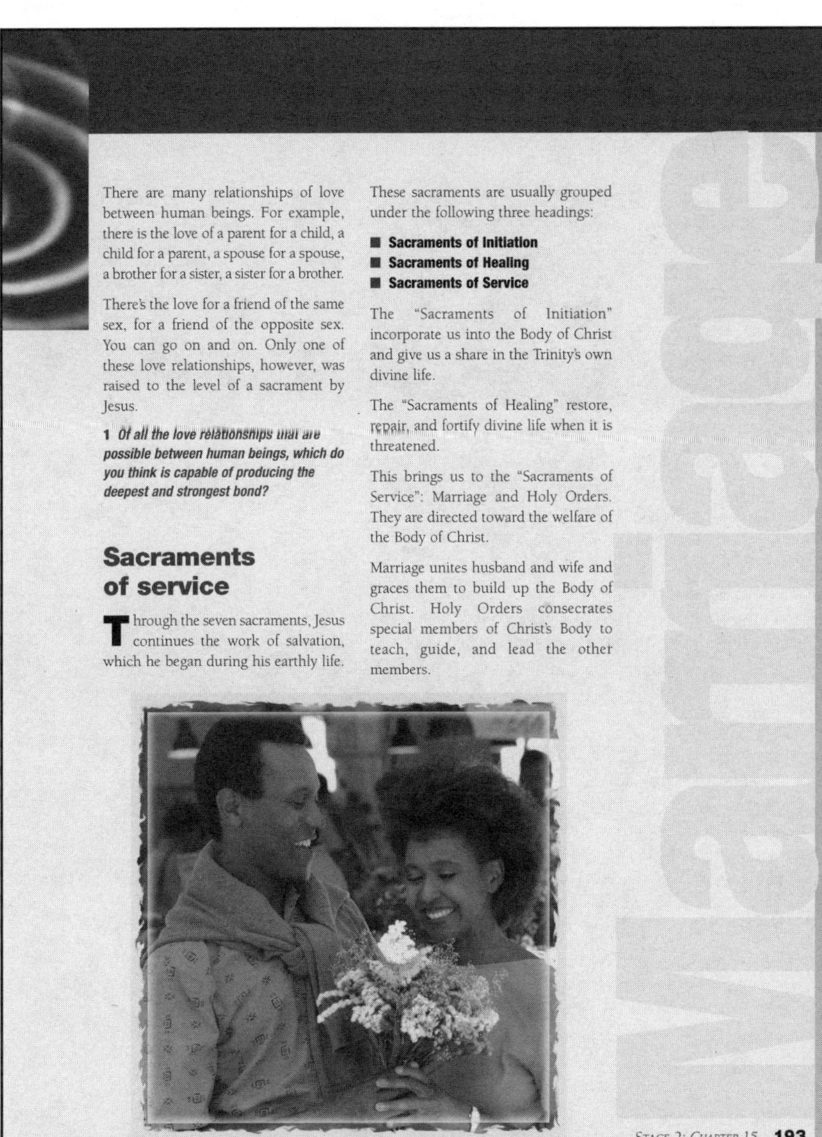

There are many relationships of love between human beings. For example, there is the love of a parent for a child, a child for a parent, a spouse for a spouse, a brother for a sister, a sister for a brother.

There's the love for a friend of the same sex, for a friend of the opposite sex. You can go on and on. Only one of these love relationships, however, was raised to the level of a sacrament by Jesus.

1 ***Of all the love relationships that are possible between human beings, which do you think is capable of producing the deepest and strongest bond?***

Sacraments of service

Through the seven sacraments, Jesus continues the work of salvation, which he began during his earthly life.

These sacraments are usually grouped under the following three headings:

- **Sacraments of Initiation**
- **Sacraments of Healing**
- **Sacraments of Service**

The "Sacraments of Initiation" incorporate us into the Body of Christ and give us a share in the Trinity's own divine life.

The "Sacraments of Healing" restore, repair, and fortify divine life when it is threatened.

This brings us to the "Sacraments of Service": Marriage and Holy Orders. They are directed toward the welfare of the Body of Christ.

Marriage unites husband and wife and graces them to build up the Body of Christ. Holy Orders consecrates special members of Christ's Body to teach, guide, and lead the other members.

When the orchestra played a song that reminded Ardis of her son, tears welled up in her eyes.

Spontaneously, the young couple took her hands in theirs. She said this gesture of intimacy and love not only gave her strength, but brought God "very close" to her.

CLARIFY—Stress the point that "love is the vocation of every human being." Reread to the class Mother Teresa's observation. She captures the point perfectly, saying:

When we die, God won't be interested so much in the great things we did in life, but how much love went into doing them.

CLARIFY—Stress another point about love. We need to show it in a concrete way. (Recall the Mark Chapman interview in Dr. Lee Salk's book, *My Father, My Son*, page 9.)

One of the author's students told this story to illustrate the importance of showing love. You might share it with the students:

■ *It's sad how we take those we love for granted. I do this especially with my parents. I am often too busy to show them that I love them—even though I care about them a lot.*

For example, when I went to work in my father's restaurant, I saw my dad sitting in a chair and I said "Hi" and walked on by. I looked back and saw a frown on his face. So I walked back and kissed him on the cheek. You wouldn't believe the glow and the smile I received—it really made me realize that parents need to be shown that we love them.

QUESTION **1** ***Of all the love relationships that are possible between human beings, which do you think is capable of producing the deepest and strongest bond?***

■ *An interesting scriptural "love bond" is the one between David and his close friend Jonathan. 1 Samuel 18:1 says Jonathan loved David more than he loved himself. And in 2 Samuel 1:26 David says of Jonathan, "How wonderful was your love for me, better even than the love of women."*

Sacraments of service

NOTEBOOK—Review the three groups of sacraments. Develop the following diagram on the chalkboard for entry into the students' notebooks:

1 Initiation:

Baptism	*Communicates life*
Confirmation	*Enriches life*
Eucharist	*Nourishes life*

2 *Healing:*

Reconciliation	*Restores life*
Anointing	*Fortifies life*

3 *Service:*

Marriage	*Builds up Christ's Body*
Orders	*Ministers to Christ's Body*

PRACTICAL Connection

***CLARIFY*—Stress that interviews can be tremendously helpful for the young couple. Many couples have found these interviews to be an unanticipated "blessing." You might share these two examples with your students:**

- *Mary and Marty had been living together since high school and had not practiced their faith since grade school. During their interviews, as part of their marriage preparation, they said that they wanted a church wedding for "social reasons" and to "please their parents."*

  As the interviews progressed, Mary and Marty began talking about their faith seriously for the first time. Both felt the desire to learn more about the religion in which they had been raised.

  They enrolled in a program for returning Catholics and became active again in the Church. Marty said later, "I can't tell you how much those interviews blessed us."

Consider the second example:

- *Ron and Sandra were both in their late teens when Sandra became pregnant. Their parents, who were good friends, urged them to get married, offering them financial help. (Both wanted to go to college.)*

  Ron and Sandra had reservations. Neither one was ready to settle down. But the parents prevailed, and the couple set up an appointment for a premarriage interview with the pastor of Sandra's parish.

  After talking with the young couple, the pastor agreed with the couple that marriage would be a mistake at this point in their lives. With the pastor's help, they were able to get their parents to see their point of view. They also arranged to put the child up for adoption.

PRACTICAL Connection

Marriage is one of the most important steps we will ever take. Therefore, we should prepare for it spiritually and psychologically. Under normal conditions, most dioceses require up to six months' preparation. This includes:

Interviews with a priest or deacon; presentation of recent certificates of Baptism, Communion, and Confirmation; and personal and liturgical preparation.

A baptismal certificate affirms one's Catholic identity. It may be obtained by contacting the parish where the baptism took place.

Most dioceses provide a variety of preparation options, such as Pre-Cana conferences and Engagement Encounters.

Sacrament of marriage

Of all the love relationships among people, the marriage between husband and wife is special. It has its origin in the God who created them.

The vocation of marriage was written in the nature of man and woman as they came from God's hand. CCC 1603

With the coming of Jesus, God raises married love to the dignity of a sacrament. And through the sacrament God blesses the lives of married people so profoundly that their love has the potential of mirroring God's own love for the human race.

Mirror of God's love

God's love for the human race has two distinguishing characteristics that stand out like the sun and the moon in the sky. God's love is:

- **Creative** **Life-giving**
- **Redemptive** **Forgiving**

It is *creative* or *life-giving* in the sense that God's love gave birth to the human family. It is *redemptive* or *forgiving* in the sense that when the human family sinned, God forgave and redeemed it. CCC 1602–11

Married love mirrors God's creative and redemptive love. It, too, is life-giving and forgiving.

It is *life-giving* in the sense that the love of husband and wife brings forth life, just as God's love did. CCC 2366–70 It is also life-giving in the sense that it provides a climate of love in which this life can grow and mature, into adulthood. CCC 1652–55

Married love is *forgiving* in the sense that husband and wife forgive the hurts they cause one another, either intentionally or unintentionally. CCC 1644 They do not stop loving.

194 STAGE 2: CHAPTER 15

Sacrament of marriage

***CLARIFY*—Children form their initial idea of God from their parents. The *Catechism of the Catholic Church* (1666) puts it this way:**

- *Children receive their "first proclamation of the faith" in the family home. Thus it has been called "the domestic church. . . . ."*
  The domestic Church acts as the "sacrament" (tangible manifestation) of God's love in the home. The universal Church acts as the "sacrament" (tangible manifestation) of God's love in the world.

NOTES

Mirror of Christ's love

Paul carries the image of married love a step further. He compares it to Christ's love for the Church, saying, "Husbands, love your wives just as Christ loved the church and gave his life for it." Ephesians 5:25

We pray to God in the liturgy of the Wedding Mass:

All-powerful and ever-living God . . .
the love of husband and wife . . .
bears the imprint
of your own divine love.

In brief, God elevated married love to the dignity of a sacrament, mirroring:

- **God's love for the human family**
- **Christ's love for the Church**

2 If married love is so richly blessed, why do so many marriages fall short of what God intended a marriage to be?

Commitment of marriage

There is an ancient story about a young man who knocked at the door of a house. A voice from inside said, "Who is it?"

The young man said, "It is I. I've come to ask permission to marry your daughter."

The voice from inside said, "You're not ready; come back in a year."

3 What made the "voice" say, "You're not ready yet"?

A year later, the young man returned and knocked again.

The voice from within said, "Who is it?" The young man said, "It is your daughter and I. We've come to ask your permission to marry."

The voice from within said, "You are now ready. Please come in."

This story illustrates how important it is that both marriage partners are ready. This readiness can be achieved only by:

- **Extended courtship**
- **Serious reflection**
- **Honest discussion**
- **Mutual prayer**

Marriage covenant

Today, much is said about "marriage contracts." But this is not what marriage is all about—each partner protecting her or his material possessions, time, career, and so on. Marriage is a covenant.

A *contract* protects the parties in advance. It spells out what is expected of each party. A *covenant* does not.

A *covenant* is an unconditional, mutual pledge to love and serve the other forever: in good times and in bad times, in sickness and in health, for better or for worse.

4 Why do you think it is essential that the marriage covenant be "unconditional" and "forever"?

PRAYER **hotline**

Lord,
place your hand
on his shoulder.
Whisper your voice in his ear.
Put your love in his heart.
Help him fulfill
your plan in life.

Author unknown: "Prayer for one's husband"

THINK about it

Marriages are
made in heaven,
but they are lived on earth.

George P. Weiss

Stage 2: Chapter 15 **195**

Mirror of God's love

NOTEBOOK—Develop the following diagrams on the chalkboard. They expand upon two distinguishing characteristics of God's love and married love:

Creative love is fruitful	*Life-giving*
Redemptive love is faithful	*Forgiving*

Mirror of Christ's love

QUESTION **2 *If married love is so richly blessed, why do so many marriages fall short of what God intended a marriage to be?***

■ *An analogy may help. Pointing to a gang of street toughs, Susan said to her Christian friend, Kay: "It's been 2,000 years since your Jesus came into the world, and it's still filled with evil people."*

Five minutes later, the two friends came upon a group of dirty-faced kids. Kay turned to Susan and said, "It's been 2,000 years since soap came into the world, and it's still filled with dirty faces."

As long as we have free will, we will have "dirty faces" and "disappointing marriages." Soap and Jesus are not the problem.

Commitment of marriage

QUESTION **3 *What made the "voice" say, "You're not ready yet"?***

■ *Before two people are ready for marriage, they must be "thinking as one," because marriage makes them "one flesh." As long as they're "thinking as two," they aren't ready for marriage. And "thinking as one" does not mean that one must suppress his or her individuality. If they think this, they're still "thinking as two."*

Marriage covenant

NOTEBOOK—The following diagram sums up the essential difference between a contract and a covenant:

Contract	*Conditional agreement*
Covenant	*Unconditional pledge*

QUESTION **4 *Why do you think it is essential that the marriage covenant be "unconditional" and "forever"?***

God said of a married couple. "They became one." Genesis 2:4 Jesus said, "No human being must separate, then, what God has joined together. Matthew 19:16 Divine wisdom decreed the marriage covenant to be "forever" and "unconditional."

Dynamic of marriage

CLARIFY—For a colorful description of the four phases, consider the following descriptive names that Father Andrew Greeley gives to the four stages in his book, *The Bottom Line Catechism*:

1	*"Falling in love"*	*Attraction*
2	*"Settling down"*	*Integration*
3	*"Bottoming out"*	*Conflict*
4	*"Beginning again"*	*Maturation*

NOTEBOOK—Construct the following diagram on the chalkboard. It sums up the key ideas concerning the four phases through which most marriages pass.

1 *Nature*	*Attraction (4 levels)*
Challenge	*Keep attraction balanced*
Danger	*Imbalance of attraction*
2 *Nature*	*Integration (love and life)*
Challenge	*Give love top priority*
Danger	*Take love for granted*
3 *Nature*	*Conflict (Problems arise)*
Challenge	*Make conflict constructive*
Danger	*Suppress conflict*
4 *Nature*	*Maturation (Love matures)*
Challenge	*Forgive and rediscover love*
Danger	*Give up and let love die*

Attraction

QUESTION **5** ***Can you give a concrete example of what is meant by letting "one level roam out of control and overwhelm the other"?***

■ *The most common danger is that the physical attraction is allowed to overwhelm all other considerations and the couple never does grow—much less grow toward a balanced attraction.*

Integration

QUESTION **6** ***What do you understand by the statement "integrating the excitement of love with the ordinariness of everyday life"?***

Dynamic of marriage

Most marriages go through a four-phase cycle. An understanding of this cycle can spell the difference between a happy marriage or a painful one. The four phases are:

- **Attraction**
- **Integration**
- **Conflict**
- **Maturation**

Attraction

First, there is the *attraction* phase. It is the thrilling experience of being drawn to one another in a way that makes life pulsate with excitement. This phase takes place at four human levels: physical, emotional, intellectual, and spiritual.

The *challenge* of this phase is to keep the four levels of attraction in harmony and balance. The danger is to let one level roam out of control and overwhelm the others.

5 Can I give a concrete example of what is meant by letting "one level roam out of control and overwhelm the other"?

If a couple meets the challenge and survives the danger, their attraction will flower into a commitment to marry.

Integration

Second, is the *integration* phase. Once a couple marry, they begin the important process of integrating the excitement of love with the ordinariness of everyday life.

6 What do I understand by the statement "integrating the excitement of love with the ordinariness of everyday life"?

The *challenge* of this phase is to retain love as the couple's top priority. It is to keep love from becoming routine. The *danger* is to begin to take love for granted and subordinate it to other things.

Conflict

Third, there is the *conflict* phase. It begins when marriage partners fail the *challenge* or fall into the danger of the second phase. When this happens—and it does to *some degree* in most marriages—the relationship enters a critical stage. Faults that were

■ *You begin to discover your partner's faults, hang-ups, and whims. Along with trying to juggle work schedules, this requires give-and-take and genuine integration.*

Conflict

QUESTION **7** ***How would you counsel a couple to handle problems that arise in this stage?***

■ *Don't let anger and frustration build up. Deal with it before it reaches the explosive stage. Realize that it takes two to make up, but only one to take the initiative.*

NOTES

once overlooked now ignite sharp conflict. The "adoring spouse" becomes a "nagging adversary."

7 *How would I counsel a couple to handle problems that arise in this stage"?*

The *challenge* of this phase is to steer conflict into constructive directions. The *danger* is to avoid or suppress conflict rather than deal with it. If it is suppressed, communication breaks down and resentment builds.

Maturation

The fourth phase is the *maturation* phase. It begins when the partners resolve to deal constructively with conflict and rediscover love. It can be the most beautiful period in a marriage.

To understand how this phase works, think of human intimacy as having a "rubber band dimension." Father Andrew Greeley explains it this way:

The two lovers drift apart. . . .
but the residual power of their affection
(pair bonding) is often,
indeed usually, sufficiently strong
to impel them back to one another.

Awkwardly, clumsily, blunderingly,
they stumble into one another's arms,
forgive each other, and begin again
in a new burst of romantic love.
The Bottom Line Catechism

The *challenge* of this phase is to forgive the other's faults and to rediscover his or her goodness. The danger is to give up and let love die, rather than let it be reborn.

If marriage partners meet the challenge and avoid the *danger*, the residual power of their affection will launch them into a new dimension of married love. And it will be more beautiful and more romantic than the love they first shared.

8 *Why will it be more beautiful and more romantic than the love they first shared?*

This brings us to a question of which we are all too painfully aware of in our modern world.

Marriage bond

From earliest times, the Church has taught that the marriage bond cannot be broken or dissolved. It bases its teaching on Jesus' words: We "must not separate, then, what God has joined together." Mark 10:9

In other words, by divine law, the marriage bond is "perpetual and exclusive." CCC 1606–08

9 *What is meant by "perpetual and exclusive"?*

Tom Anderson

Tom rented a seaside cottage for a two-week vacation with his wife. He resolved that for two weeks he'd be the ideal husband: caring and thoughtful.

Everything went well, until the last day. Then Tom caught his wife staring at him through tear-filled eyes:

"Tom," she said,
"Do you know something I don't?"
"What ever do you mean?"
he replied.
"Well," she said,
"just before our vacation,
I went to the doctor
for my checkup.
Ever since then,
you've been so kind to me.
Did the doctor tell you
something about me?
Do I have cancer?
Am I going to die?
Is that why you're so kind to me?"

It took a minute
for her words to sink in.
Then Tom broke into a laugh,
threw his arms around her,
and said,
"No dear, you're not going to die.
I'm just beginning to live."

Retold from *Guideposts* magazine

Stage 2: Chapter 15 **197**

Maturation

QUESTION 8 *Why will it be more beautiful and more romantic than the love they first shared?*

■ *Often it is more rewarding, romantic, and beautiful, because it involves a familiar, trusted lover instead of someone new.*

Up Close & Personal

ACTIVITY—To bring this down to a practical level for the students, you might have them list: (1) One thing they like about their family situation, (2) One thing that could be better.

After studying them, categorize them, present them to the class anonymously, and discuss them.

Marriage bond

QUESTION 9 *What is meant by "perpetual and exclusive"?*

■ *By nature the marriage bond binds two people forever. "The consent . . . is sealed by God himself. . . . The Church does not have the power to contravene this disposition of divine wisdom."* CCC 1638–40

QUESTION 10 *In what sense is an annulment totally different from a divorce or separation?*

■ *A divorce or a separation is a civil process that involves two married people. An annulment is an ecclesiastical process that involves two people who were thought to be validly married but, because of some essential defect (e.g., lack of maturity to be married), were, in fact,* not validly married.

NOTEBOOK—With the help of the students, construct the following diagram on the chalkboard.

Annulment —
- *Not "breaking up" an existing marriage*
- *But a judgment that no marriage ever existed.*

CLARIFY—Contrary to what people may think, the legal process for seeking an annulment of an "essentially defective" first marriage is normally neither difficult nor expensive.

■ *Commenting on this, one official of the Archdiocese of Chicago said that the paperwork and legal work involves about three hundred dollars in Chicago, if the person can afford it. If he or she can't afford it, the fee is waived.*

CLARIFY—Both Church and civil law consider the children of an annulled marriage to be legitimate, providing at least one of the partners believed at the time that the marriage was real.

QUESTION **11 *Give one concrete example of each of the above.***

***DISCUSS*—**A young man said to a friend after a marriage ceremony, "That whole ceremony was just a formality for me, because no two people can promise to live with each other for the rest of their lives."

Ask the students: Did a marriage really take place or not, given the remarks of the young man? Do you see any grounds for a future annulment of that marriage?

- *There was no marriage for lack of consent. He feigned consent, therefore there are ample grounds for a declaration of nullity (annulment).*

***CLARIFY*—**Stress that a divorced person who remarries without an annulment of their previous marriage—and while their previous partner remains alive—remains in the Church.

They should also consult the pastor to see if there are grounds for "declaration of nullity" (annulment) of the first marriage.

Such a person is encouraged to continue to worship with the Catholic community and be active in the parish, but he or she is not free to receive Holy Communion.

QUESTION **12 *Why are they not free to receive Communion?***

- *Remarriage without an annulment of the previous marriage—and while their previous partner is alive—is a grave or mortal breach of God's law.*

QUESTION ***Why do difficulties bring some couples closer together, but have just the opposite effect on other couples?***

SHARE YOUR meditation

In ancient times, a town fort in Weinsberg, Germany, was surrounded by an enemy. The enemy commander, who prided himself on being honest and noble, agreed to let all the women and children leave the fort.

He also agreed to let the women take with them their most precious possession.

When the moment of evacuation came, the commander couldn't believe what he saw: a long line of children and women leaving the fort. On the back of each woman was her most precious possession: her husband.

Retold from Ruth Youngdahl Nelson: *A Grandma's Letters to God*

- ***Why do difficulties bring some couples closer together, but have just the opposite effect on other couples?***

The Church recognizes, however, that living out the lofty vocation of marriage involves "good times and bad." And sometimes the "bad times" overpower the "good times." Marriage partners begin to admit things they denied before being married. Problems that they hoped marriage would solve grow even worse. CCC 1606–08

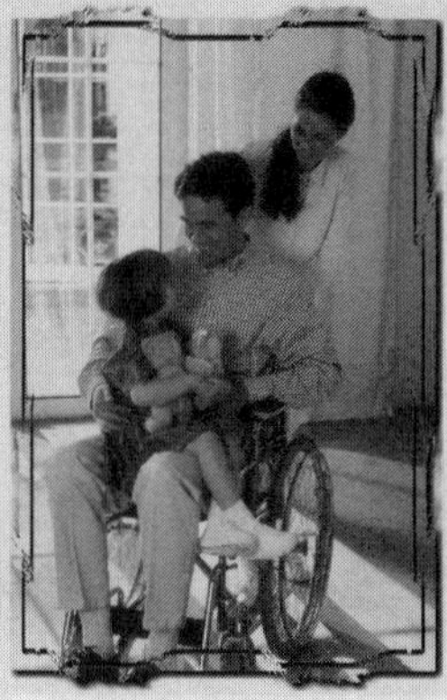

When harsh realities like this set in, the couple can best express genuine marital love in two ways, especially by:

- **Praying together for God's help**
- **Consulting a professional counselor**

Often this twofold expression of love bears remarkable fruit, leading to a deeper, more mature love for one another.

But sometimes it doesn't. And so the Church recognizes the reality of failed marriages:

There are some situations in which living together becomes practically impossible for a variety of reasons.

In such cases the Church permits the physical separation of the couple and their living apart. CCC 1649

Remarriage, however, is possible only when one's spouse dies or an *annulment* is granted.

An annulment is a judgment by the Church that what seemed a marriage, was not. CCC 1625–29 Therefore, it is *not* a divorce or separation.

10 *In what sense is an annulment totally different from a divorce or separation?*

Some grounds for the annulment of a marriage are the following. One or both parties:

- **Lack maturity to marry**
- **Lack the freedom to marry**
- **Feign consent**
- **Hide a defect to gain consent**

11 *Give one concrete example of each of the above.*

Catholics who remarry, when they are *not* free to do so, should continue to worship with the community and seek its support, even though they may not receive Communion. CCC 1648–51

12 *Why are they not free to receive Communion?*

198 STAGE 2: CHAPTER 15

- *In many cases, it is a question of disposition or maturity. Are the two people positively or negatively disposed? Are they mature and balanced individuals?*

There is also the question of what kind of support the couples get from friends, relatives, and family members. In other words, are they "stepping-stones" or "stumbling blocks" to reconciliation of the two?

You might shed some light on the situation by bringing the issue closer to the students. Ask them: Why do some teenagers continue to do well in the face of a divorce in their family, while others do not?

NOTES

Interfaith marriage

All religions recognize that a marriage between persons of different faiths is a serious step. Some religions discourage it on principle.

13 *What are some of the problems connected with an interfaith marriage?*

An interfaith marriage should be entered into only after profound reflection, frank communication, and mutual prayer for guidance.

There are many issues that need to be faced honestly in advance.

Catholic partners in an interfaith marriage must affirm commitment to their own faith and to sharing it with their children.

Their partners, in return, must respect this twofold commitment.

An interfaith marriage may take place in either a Catholic church or the place of worship of the other partner.

Since marriage partners confer marriage on each other (their mutual consent is the basis of their marriage), a priest, deacon, rabbi, or minister (with the Church's approval) may perform the ceremony.

One final point.

A Catholic who married outside of the Church and wants to be reunited with the Church should consult a priest about the possibility of validating the marriage (marrying within the Church) in a private ceremony.

Event of grace

The sacrament of marriage is an "event of grace." But it is not a "one-time event" that takes place on a couple's wedding day and ends there.

Rather, it is an "ongoing event" that continues throughout the couple's entire life. It is something the couple must never stop working at.

A fitting conclusion to our reflection on the marriage vocation is Paul's beautiful description of mature love:

Love is patient and kind;
it is not jealous or conceited or proud;
love is not ill-mannered
or selfish or irritable;
love does not keep a record of wrongs;
love is not happy with evil,
but happy with truth.
Love never gives up . . .
Love is eternal. 1 Corinthians 13:4–8

14 *Why do you think couples fail to work hard at their marriage? What suggestion would you have for them?*

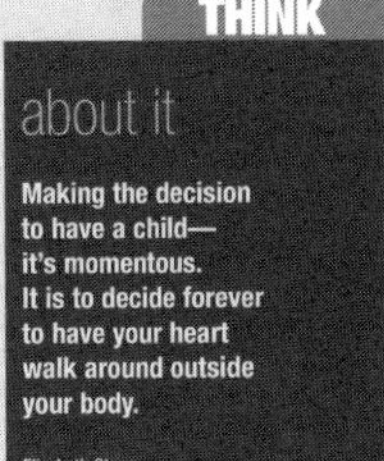

THINK
about it
Making the decision to have a child—it's momentous.
It is to decide forever to have your heart walk around outside your body.
Elizabeth Stone

Interfaith marriage

CLARIFY—Stress that all religions acknowledge the difficulties and challenges of an interfaith marriage.

CLARIFY—Stress that the Church is particularly sensitive to circumstances that may surround a given marriage. Thus, with the Church's approval, an interfaith marriage may be performed by a priest, a deacon, a rabbi, or a minister.

Likewise, with the Church's approval, an interfaith marriage may take place either in a Catholic church or the church to which the other party belongs.

In the case of a non-Christian person and a Catholic person, the Church may grant permission for the marriage to be held in a place other than a synagogue or a church, for example, a hall or a hotel.

This is true if a church or a synagogue wedding would appreciably disrupt the unity of the newly married couple. The Church seeks to listen to all sides and then make an evaluation.

QUESTION **13 *What are some of the problems connected with an interfaith marriage?***

- *A couple contemplating an interfaith marriage is strongly advised to consult with two or three couples of interfaith marriages (where both parties are genuinely happy and take their faith seriously).*

Such consultation will alert them to problems that may never otherwise occur to them. Being aware of such problems in advance will allow them to anticipate and discuss them, before being surprised and caught off guard by them. The value of all this foreknowledge is incalculable.

Event of grace

QUESTION **14 *Why do you think couples fail to work hard at their marriage? What suggestion would you have for them?***

Here are a few excellent suggestions people have given young married couples:

- *Let there be spaces in your togetherness.*
Kahlil Gibran

Chains do not hold a marriage together.
It is threads, hundreds of tiny threads,
which sew people together.
French actress Simone Signoret

Love is an act of endless forgiveness,
a tender look which becomes a habit.
Peter Ustinov

The important thing in marriage is not so much a question of thinking alike, but rather, thinking together. Similarly, being the right person in a marriage is, literally, as important as finding the right person.

When marriage works, nothing on earth can take its place. Helen Gahagan Douglas

Recap

Jesus delighted in visiting homes. Consider a few examples:

1 Peter's sick mother-in-law MARK 1:29
2 Jarius's mortally ill daughter MARK 5:41
3 Simon the Pharisee LUKE 7:41
4 Mary and Martha JOHN 12:2
5 Zacchaeus the tax collector LUKE 19:5
6 The Emmaus disciples LUKE 24:31
7 The young newlyweds of Cana JOHN 2:12

There's something especially beautiful about Jesus choosing as his first miracle the changing of water into wine—especially for the two newlyweds who badly underestimated the celebrating capacity of their guests.

It is this kind of divine courtesy that makes Jesus so approachable.

The conclusion we may draw is clear. A good marriage is not simply a contract between two people. It is infinitely more. It is a sacred covenant between three. But too often one is left out.

Too often
Christ is never invited to the wedding and finds no room in the home. Why?
It is because we have misrepresented him and forgotten his joyful outlook on life.
DONALD T. KAUFFMAN

Review

DAILY QUIZ—The review questions may be assigned (one or two at a time) for homework or a daily quiz.

CHAPTER TESTS—Reproducible chapter tests are found in Appendix A. For consistency and ease in grading, quizzes are restricted to (1) "Matching," (2) "True/False," and (3) "Fill in the Blank."

TEST ANSWERS—The following are the answers to the test for Chapter 15. (See Appendix A, page 326.) Each correct answer worth 4 points.

Recap

Of all the loves two people can enjoy, only one was raised by Jesus to the level of a sacrament: married love. It mirrors:

- **God's love for the human family**
- **Christ's love for the Church**

Married love mirrors God's love in that it, too, is both:

- **Creative**
- **Life-giving**
- **Redemptive**
- **Forgiving**

The dynamic of most marriages involves four critical stages:

- **Attraction**
- **Integration**
- **Conflict**
- **Maturation**

Because marriage is such an important step in life, it should be preceded by:

- **Extended courtship**
- **Serious reflection**
- **Honest discussion**
- **Mutual prayer**

Review

1 List (a) four love relationships people can enjoy, and (b) the only one Jesus elevated to the dignity of a sacrament.

2 List, and briefly explain, how married love mirrors God's love for the human family.

3 Upon what words of Jesus does the Church base its teaching that there can be no remarriage after a divorce while both parties are alive?

4 List the four steps that should precede the commitment that marriage involves on the part of both people.

5 List and briefly describe (a) the four phases through which most marriages pass, and (b) the challenge and the danger that each phase presents.

6 What is an annulment? Give three examples of "grounds for an annulment."

7 What does the Church teach about (a) separation, (b) divorce without remarriage?

8 What is (a) the attitude of all religions toward interfaith marriages, and (b) what do they recommend for those considering such a marriage?

9 What is the obligation of a Catholic partner concerning interfaith marriage?

10 Where may an interfaith marriage take place, and who may perform it?

True/False

1 = T	2 = F	3 = T	4 = T
5 = F	6 = F	7 = T	8 = T
9 = F	10 = F	11 = T	12 = T
13 = F	14 = T	15 = T	16 = T

Fill in the Blanks

Answers must be given in this order:
1. (a) Attraction (b) Integration
(c) Conflict (d) Maturation

Answers may be given in any order:
2. (a) Physical (b) Emotional
(c) Intellectual (d) Spiritual

NOTES

Reflect

1 Barbara Walters was interviewing a famous couple on *60 Minutes*. She asked them:

"How have you managed
to keep your love alive
across 35 years of married life?"
When they didn't answer right away,
she tried to help them, saying,
"Was it because both of you
were so willing to give and take
on a 50–50 basis?"

The wife broke into a gentle laugh
and said, "Oh my!
Married life never breaks that evenly.
Sometimes it's more like 90–10."

That was a high point of the interview, because it made such an important point: When it comes to love, you can't keep score. The day a husband and wife begin to do so is the day the marriage begins to die.

■ ***Explain the statement, "When it comes to love, we can't keep score."***
■ ***To what extent does the statement apply to (a) brothers and sisters, (b) two friends?***

2 In his book *You Are the Light of the World*, John Catoir writes:

Studies conducted over a seven-year period
at the University of Virginia
found that within one year of their divorce,
60 percent of the husbands
and 73 percent of the wives
felt that they might have made a mistake.

Even those who thought
their marriages
were destructive relationships
said that maybe they could have
worked out their marital problems
if they had tried harder.

■ ***From your own family experience, make a list of four or five reasons why husbands and wives run into marriage problems.***
■ ***Show your list to a married friend or to one or both of your parents and ask them to critique the reasons. What reasons would they delete or modify? What reasons would they add?***

3 In his book *Born Again*, Charles Colson said of himself and his wife: "In the ten years we've been married, I realized we'd never discussed . . . the living God, the faith deep down inside each one of us."

■ ***To what extent does your family discuss such things at home? Recall a good discussion you had in your home recently. What did you find especially good about it?***

Reflect

1 ***a) Explain the statement, "When it comes to love, we can't keep score."***
b) To what extent does the statement apply to (a) brothers and sisters, (b) two friends?

■ *It is easier to illustrate what we mean by "keeping score" than it is to explain it. For example, someone says, "I did such-and-such for you. Now it's your turn to do something for me." Jesus had some chilling words about "keeping score": "The measure you use for others is the one that God will use for you."* LUKE 6:38

A recently married young man told the author that Barbara Walters' interview kept his marriage from getting off on the wrong foot. He had begun to "keep score" and was becoming resentful of his wife because he thought he was currently giving more than he was getting in return.

2 ***a) From your own family experience, make a list of four or five reasons why husbands and wives run into marriage problems.***
b) Show the list to a married friend or to one or both of your parents and ask them to critique the reasons. What reasons would they delete or modify? What reasons would they add?

■ *This makes a good written assignment. It "gives permission" to the students to engage their parents in meaningful communication about meaningful things. Many students—and parents—need this kind of "permission." Unfortunately, unless opportunities are provided, such communication often does not occur.*

3 ***To what extent does your family discuss such things at home? Recall a good discussion you had in your home recently. What did you find especially good about it?***

■ *Recall the background on Colson. See page 170: "Prayer hotline."*

Colson finally broke the ice one night and began to discuss these things with his wife, Patty. (His wife was Catholic; he was not.) The discussion went long "into the night." He said, "We ended by deciding to get out the family Bible when we returned home [from vacation] and begin reading it."

PRAYER TIME with the Lord

QUESTION ***Write a similar blessing of your own.***

Engraved on the fireplace of the White House State Dining Room is a blessing. It was found in a letter by John Adams, who was the second president of the United States, serving from 1797 to 1801. His son, John Quincy Adams, became the sixth president and served from 1825 to 1829.

President Franklin D. Roosevelt saw the blessing and ordered it engraved on the fireplace. Roosevelt was the 23rd president, serving four terms from 1933 to 1945. The blessing reads (Copy it on the board):

I pray Heaven
bestow
the best of blessings on this house,
and on all
that shall hereafter
inhabit it.
May none but honest and wise men
ever rule
under this roof.

You might suggest that the students write a similar blessing and ask their parents to place it over the fireplace.

PRAYER TIME with the Lord

Lord, enter our house.
Bless it and make it a home.

Bless our roof
that it may shelter us
on good days and bad days.

Bless our doors
that they may stand open
to friend and foe alike.

Bless our rooms
that they may be places
of love and peace.

Above all, bless our family.
Bless us one and all.

Bless our minds
that they may be open to your Word—
and to the words of each other.

Bless our arms
that they may reach out to the needy—
and to the needs of each other.

Bless our hearts
that they will be filled with love for you—
and with love for each other. M.L.

■ ***Write a similar blessing of your own.***

202 Stage 2: Chapter 15

PRAYER Journal

QUESTION ***Compose two verses of your own. Replace*** **bitterness, love,** ***and*** **life** ***with one of the following sets (or a set of your own).***

1	*Criticism*	*Praise*	*Self-esteem*
2	*Suspicion*	*Trust*	*Friendship*
3	*Cheating*	*Honesty*	*Character*

Thus, one of your verses might read:

Criticism blows up self-esteem;
Praise builds self-esteem;
Criticism shipwrecks relationships;
Praise keeps them afloat.

NOTES

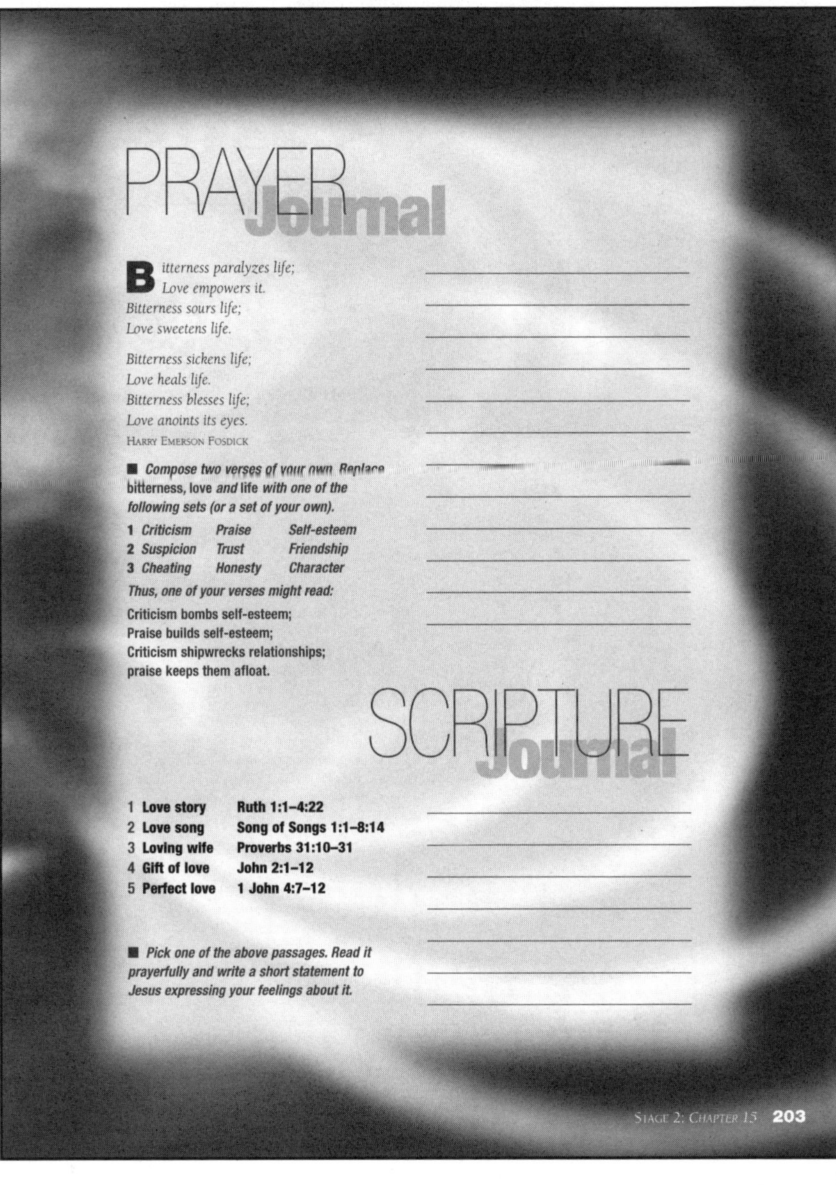

PRAYER Journal

Bitterness paralyzes life;
Love empowers it.
Bitterness sours life;
Love sweetens life.

Bitterness sickens life;
Love heals life.
Bitterness blesses life;
Love anoints its eyes.
HARRY EMERSON FOSDICK

■ *Compose two verses of your own. Replace bitterness, love and life with one of the following sets (or a set of your own).*

1	*Criticism*	*Praise*	*Self-esteem*
2	*Suspicion*	*Trust*	*Friendship*
3	*Cheating*	*Honesty*	*Character*

Thus, one of your verses might read:

Criticism bombs self-esteem;
Praise builds self-esteem;
Criticism shipwrecks relationships;
praise keeps them afloat.

SCRIPTURE Journal

1	Love story	Ruth 1:1–4:22
2	Love song	Song of Songs 1:1–8:14
3	Loving wife	Proverbs 31:10–31
4	Gift of love	John 2:1–12
5	Perfect love	1 John 4:7–12

■ *Pick one of the above passages. Read it prayerfully and write a short statement to Jesus expressing your feelings about it.*

STAGE 2: CHAPTER 15 203

SCRIPTURE Journal

QUESTION ***Pick one of the passages. Read it prayerfully and write a short statement to Jesus expressing your feelings about it.***

You may simply wish to read this passage, which is a favorite reading at marriage ceremonies, and have the students express their feelings to Jesus about it.

Wherever you go, I will go;
wherever you live, I will live.
Your people will be my people,
and your God will be my God.
Wherever you die, I will die,
and there is where I will be buried.
RUTH 1:16–17

Classroom Resources

CATECHISM

Catechism of the Catholic Church *Second Edition*

For further enrichment, you might refer to:

1. Marriage	Index	p. 822
	Glossary	p. 877
2. Covenant	Index	p. 779
	Glossary	p. 873
3. Commitment	Index	p. 774–75

See also: Service, Grace.
—AVAILABLE FROM THE UNITED STATES CATHOLIC CONFERENCE, WASHINGTON DC

VIDEO

Marriage

Four 30-minute segments. This series explores every stage of marriage, including wedding plans, the early years of marriage, establishing careers, children, and communication.
—AVAILABLE FROM BROWN-ROA, DUBUQUE,IA

BOOKS

A Marriage Sourcebook

Robert Baker, Joni and Kevin Charles Gibley

A look at the mystery of marriage through scripture, prayer, poetry, fiction, and music.
—AVAILABLE FROM LITURGY TRAINING PUBLICATIONS, CHICAGO, IL

Sex and the Teenager: Choices and Decisions

Kieran Sawyer, S.S.N.D.

Practical presentation of a Catholic perspective on sexuality, moral values, and personal choices. 1999.
—AVAILABLE FROM AVE MARIA PRESS, NOTRE DAME, IN

NOTE

For a list of (1) General resources for professional background and (2) Addresses, phone/fax numbers of major publishing companies, see Appendix B of this Resource Manual.

CHAPTER 16
Holy Orders

CHAPTER at a Glance

The aim of this chapter is to give students a perspective and an understanding of:

1. *Christian ministry in general*
2. *Ordained ministry in particular*

READ—Have a student read aloud the scriptural introduction, which begins: "Every high priest . . ." Have another student read the commentary following the scriptural instruction. It begins: "Baptism makes every Christian . . ."

NOTEBOOK—With the help of the students, develop the following diagram of the "three priesthoods" referred to in the commentary. Have the students enter it into their notebooks:

Priests	*Christ*	*By Sonship*
	Common	*By Baptism*
	Ordained (Min.)	*By Orders*

Christ—*"We have a great High Priest who has gone into the very presence of God—Jesus, the Son of God."* HEBREWS 4:14

Common—*"Jesus Christ . . . freed us from our sins and made us a kingdom of priests."* REVELATION 1:5–6

Ordained (Ministerial)—*"A bishop . . . must have a firm grasp of the word so that he may be able to preach . . . and refute those who contradict it."* TITUS 1:7–9 NRSV

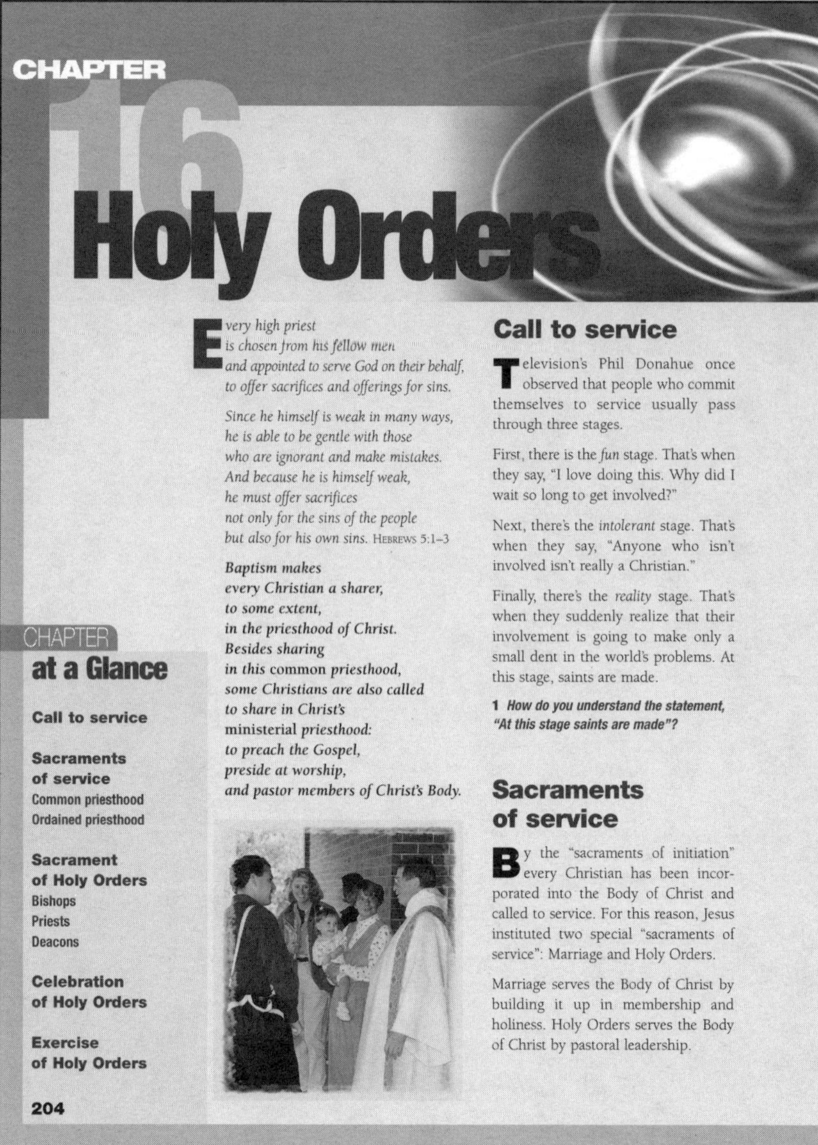

CHAPTER 16

Holy Orders

Every high priest
is chosen from his fellow men
and appointed to serve God on their behalf,
to offer sacrifices and offerings for sins.

Since he himself is weak in many ways,
he is able to be gentle with those
who are ignorant and make mistakes.
And because he is himself weak,
he must offer sacrifices
not only for the sins of the people
but also for his own sins. HEBREWS 5:1–3

Baptism makes
every Christian a sharer,
to some extent,
in the priesthood of Christ.
Besides sharing
in this common priesthood,
some Christians are also called
to share in Christ's
ministerial priesthood:
to preach the Gospel,
preside at worship,
and pastor members of Christ's Body.

CHAPTER **at a Glance**

Call to service

Sacraments of service
Common priesthood
Ordained priesthood

Sacrament of Holy Orders
Bishops
Priests
Deacons

Celebration of Holy Orders

Exercise of Holy Orders

204

Call to service

Television's Phil Donahue once observed that people who commit themselves to service usually pass through three stages.

First, there is the *fun* stage. That's when they say, "I love doing this. Why did I wait so long to get involved?"

Next, there's the *intolerant* stage. That's when they say, "Anyone who isn't involved isn't really a Christian."

Finally, there's the *reality* stage. That's when they suddenly realize that their involvement is going to make only a small dent in the world's problems. At this stage, saints are made.

1 ***How do you understand the statement, "At this stage saints are made"?***

Sacraments of service

By the "sacraments of initiation" every Christian has been incorporated into the Body of Christ and called to service. For this reason, Jesus instituted two special "sacraments of service": Marriage and Holy Orders.

Marriage serves the Body of Christ by building it up in membership and holiness. Holy Orders serves the Body of Christ by pastoral leadership.

Call to service

QUESTION **1** ***How do you understand the statement, "At this stage saints are made"?***

■ *In the "fun" stage and in the "intolerant" stage, we often enjoy a warm glow from helping others. It gives us a "sense of joy" and a "feeling of satisfaction."*

The true test of service is whether we continue to serve after the joy and the "feeling" of satisfaction subside.

When "fun" and "feeling" subside or diminish considerably, the "realistic" stage begins.

CLARIFY—The following example provides a concrete illustration of the "realistic" stage:

■ *Years ago, Dr. Lloyd Judd practiced medicine in rural Oklahoma. Many people in his area were poor and had no private transportation of their own.*

He often had to drive out to their ramshackled homes to treat someone who was sick or injured.

One day, Dr. Judd himself became sick. When his condition worsened, he checked

NOTES

Common priesthood

When we think of Holy Orders, we think immediately of the *priesthood,* and rightly so.

On the other hand, we must keep in mind that by our baptism we all participate in the priesthood of Christ. Peter writes to the Christians of his day:

You are the chosen race,
the King's priests, a holy nation,
God's own people, chosen
to proclaim the wonderful acts of God,
who called you out of darkness
into his own marvelous light.
1 PETER 2:9

Every baptized Christian, therefore, participates in the priesthood of Christ.

We call this participation the *common* priesthood of the faithful to distinguish it from the *ordained* priesthood.

Ordained priesthood

The *ordained* priesthood differs in an essential way from the *common* priesthood. It is not something that you choose, in the sense that it is an option for all Christians. CCC 1591–2

Rather, it is something that you are "called" to by God. Thus, we frequently speak of someone having a *vocation* ("calling") to the priesthood.

Whereas the common priesthood is conferred by the sacrament of Baptism, the *ordained* priesthood is conferred by the sacrament of Holy Orders.

The *ordained* priesthood is also called the *ministerial* priesthood. This title stressed its special ministry to the Church.

Let us take a closer look at the "call" to the ordained priesthood and the service or "ministry" it performs.

STAGE 2: CHAPTER 16 **205**

into a hospital. There he learned he had terminal cancer.

His thoughts immediately turned to his young children. There was so much he wanted to tell them. But they were too small to understand.

So he arranged to record a set of tapes, which his children could play back when when they reached their late teenage years. Here's an excerpt from one of them. It provides us with a concrete example of the realistic stage (when fun and feeling subside):

"Are you willing to get out of a warm bed on a cold night and drive 20 miles to see a sick person, knowing that they can't pay you and that they could wait until morning to be treated? If you can answer yes to this question, you are ready to study medicine."

Sacraments of service

NOTEBOOK—Summarize the two sacraments of service—and how they relate to the various members of the Body of Christ:

Service
- *Marriage* — *Builds membership*
- *Orders:* — *Pastors members*

Common priesthood

CLARIFY—Baptism and Confirmation call, empower, and perfect in us a share in the three missions of Jesus. (See page 144.)

Prophetic	*Teach and witness to Gospel*
Priestly	*Offer selves with Christ*
Kingly	*Build up God's Kingdom*

Ordained priesthood

CLARIFY—Stress that the ordained priesthood is essentially different from the common priesthood.

Stress, also, that it is a "special" call to the ministry of pastoral service to the common priesthood.

NOTEBOOK—Sum up the two forms of Christian priesthood as follows:

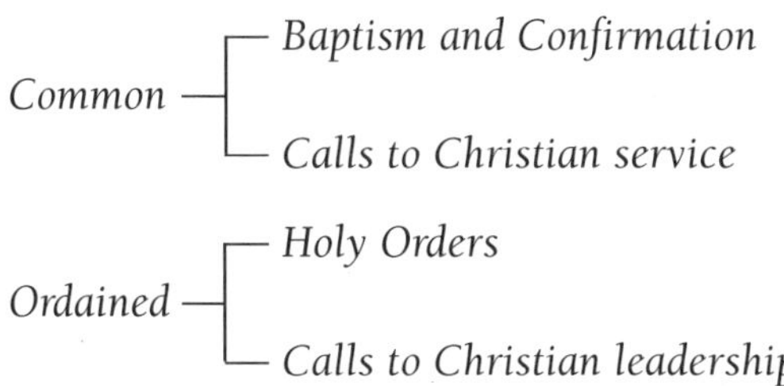

Up Close & Personal

DISCUSS—List pros and cons for pursuing the priesthood right after high school.

Here are typical bios of three young men who entered the seminary in the year 2000. The first names have been changed. All else is correct:

Mike, 22. Has BA's in philosophy and theology from Loyola University, Chicago. Taught religion to children in his parish, worked with the disabled at Chicago's Misericordia Center, and toured Europe with a dancing group. His hobbies are reading and running.

Jason, 22. Has a BA in religious studies from Indiana University, taught math at Xavier High School in New York City. Enjoys weight-lifting, running, and chess.

Todd, 26. Holds a degree in general studies from Warner Pacific College. Did a hitch in the Marine Corps for two years right after high school, and worked as a security guard. He also enjoys running.

THINK about it

DISCUSS—What does it mean to "place yourself in the hands of God"?

- *Mother Teresa is a good example. She felt called to work among the poor of India. She began her ministry by renting an old building and using it as a school for small children. She had no desks, no chairs, no table. Her chalkboard was the building's dirt floor, which she wrote on with a pointed stick and rubbed smooth with an old rag.*

By 1990 the dirt-floor school had multiplied into 100 schools, 120 leprosy clinics, 750 mobile dispensaries, and 150 homes for homeless people. The point is that Mother Teresa placed herself in the hands of Jesus and he placed himself in her hands. Mother Teresa did what the boy in the Gospel did. JOHN 6:1–13 *She gave her "five loaves" and "two fish" to Jesus, and he "multiplied" them beyond all imagining.*

Up Close & Personal

John Catoir

As a young man
I felt a strong attraction
for the priesthood, but I held back.
I was afraid to assume
the many burdons;
afraid of all the alligators
in the swamp of life;
afraid of failing. . . .

It took me about seven years
of inner turmoil,
from high school
through college and
military service,
before I had the courage
to say 'yes' to God's call.
I never regretted my decision.

John Catoir: *That Your Joy May Be Full*

THINK about it

Blessed are they who place themselves in the hands of Jesus. He will place himself in their hands.

Anonymous

Sacrament of Holy Orders

Father John Eagen writes in his inspiring spiritual autobiography:

There's a marvelous line
in Alan Paton's book
Cry, the Beloved Country:

When someone tries to thank
the old black preacher for his kindness
and tells him, "You are a good man,"
the old man says simply:
"No. I'm just a weak sinful man,
but the Lord has laid his hands on me
and that is all."

To me that says it exactly.
The Lord has laid his hands on me.
When I was a freshman at Campion
in the first closed retreat of my life,
unexpectedly God . . .
touched my life deeply . . .
and that is all.

A TRAVELLER TOWARD THE DAWN (condensed)

2 What is a "closed retreat"? Have you ever made one? How do you think God decides on whom to "lay hands"?

Besides participation in the *common* priesthood, to which all Christians are called, some Christians are called to special service within the Church. This call is to the *ministerial* or *ordained* priesthood. CCC 1547

The special call to the *ordained* priesthood is rooted in the Old Testament.

There God chose the twelve tribes of Israel to be a *priestly* people. EXODUS 19:3 But within the twelve tribes, God chose one tribe, Levi, for liturgical service to the other tribes. NUMBERS 47:53, JOSHUA 13:33

This special call of the tribe of Levi helps us to understand the special call of the *ordained* priesthood in the New Testament. It is at the service of the *common* priesthood. CCC 1547

The *ordained* priesthood is conferred by the sacrament of Holy Orders and exercised in three different degrees:

- **Bishops** CCC 1593–94
- **Priests** CCC 1595
- **Deacons** CCC 1596

206 STAGE 2: CHAPTER 16

Sacrament of Holy Orders

QUESTION ***2a What is a "closed retreat"? Have you ever made one?***

A retreat can be "open" or "closed." An "open" retreat usually involves a series of presentations related to our Christian calling, along with periods of reflection, discussion, and recreation.

A "closed" retreat is usually made at a retreat house, under the direction of a retreat master. It can be made individually, with a small group of six or seven, or in much larger groups. It is usually done over a weekend, in an atmosphere of silence, and with scheduled periods for presentations and reflection.

NOTES

Bishops

As successor of the Apostles, the bishop receives the "fullness" of the sacrament. CCC 1555–61

This "fullness" gives him both the authority and the responsibility to carry out the threefold, apostolic mission. CCC 939 It involves:

- **Teaching** **Preaching the Gospel**
- **Sanctifying** **Presiding at worship**
- **Leading** **Pastoring spiritually**

The "fullness" of Holy Orders unites the bishops into a college of bishops," under the leadership of the bishop of Rome.

Just as Peter held a special leadership role among the Apostles, so his successor, the "Bishop of Rome," holds a special leadership role among the "college of bishops." CCC 880–82

Scripture gives a number of examples that reflect Peter's leadership role. For example, he:

- **Heads list of Apostles** Lk 6:14
- **Speaks for Apostles** Acts 2–5
- **Holds keys** Mt 16:19
- **Instructs leaders** Gal 1:18

This special leadership role of the "Bishop of Rome" prompted eleventh-century Christians to give him a special title: *Pope*, which means "Father of the fathers."

Christians continue to call him by this title.

Priests

As the early Church grew in numbers, the bishop could no longer serve all the people entrusted to his care. He therefore ordained co-workers. CCC 1562–68

Given the name "presbyters" (priests), they were put in charge of smaller units (parishes) of the bishop's assigned territory (diocese). They exercised their ministry only with permission of the bishop and in communion with him.

3 ***What do I look for most in a priest?***

Deacons

Deacons are single or married men who have felt God's call to ordained ministry. CCC 1569–71 They serve the Catholic community in a variety of ways. CCC 1569–71 For example, they:

- **Baptize new members**
- **Assist at and bless marriages**
- **Preside over funerals**
- **Perform ministries of charity**

4 ***Why would/wouldn't I consider a call from God to Church ministry as a deacon?***

PRACTICAL Connection

The practice of Roman Catholic bishops and priests to remain celibate (not marry) dates back to early Christian times. But it didn't become a universal practice until the twelfth century. Two reasons recommend it.

First, from a *spiritual* viewpoint, celibacy models itself on Jesus, who was celibate. Thus, it acts as a sign of Jesus' continued presence in his Church.

Second, from a *practical* viewpoint, it frees the priest from family demands and makes him more available for service to the Church.

Stage 2: Chapter 16 **207**

QUESTION **2b** *How do you think God decides on whom to lay hands?*

- *If you have the following, you are a candidate on whom God might decide to "lay hands": (1) A desire to serve, (2) At least average intelligence, (3) Moral integrity, and (4) Satisfactory health.*

After discussing the topic, direct the students to "Share your meditation" on page 208. What is said of the Jesuits, holds for all (men and women) contemplating a vocation.

NOTEBOOK—Sum up the ordained ministry for entry into notebooks as follows:

Ordained	*Bishops*	*Apostles' successors*
	Priests	*Bishops' assistants*
	Deacons	*Priests' assistants*

Bishops

CLARIFY—Stress their calling to the "fullness of Orders," calling and empowering them to teach, sanctify, and lead.

NOTEBOOK—With the help of the students, construct the following diagrams on the board. They document how Jesus authorized the Apostles to teach in his name and assured them of the Spirit's assistance.

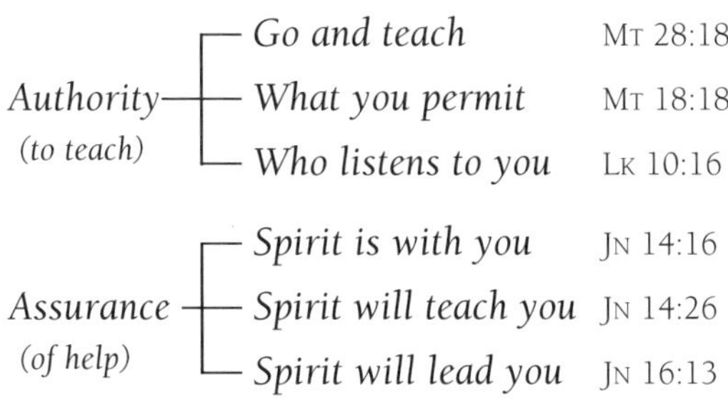

Priests

QUESTION **3** *What do you look for most in a priest?*

Have the students write out their responses in private and share them in a small group.

Deacons

QUESTION **4** *Why would/wouldn't you consider a call from God to Church ministry as a deacon?*

Perhaps you might wish to hold up with this question until the students have done their interviews of deacons. (See "Reflect," #1, page 211.)

PRACTICAL Connection

NOTEBOOK—*Stress the fact that celibacy did not become universal in the Western Church until the twelfth century. Sum up the two purposes that celibacy serves as follows.*

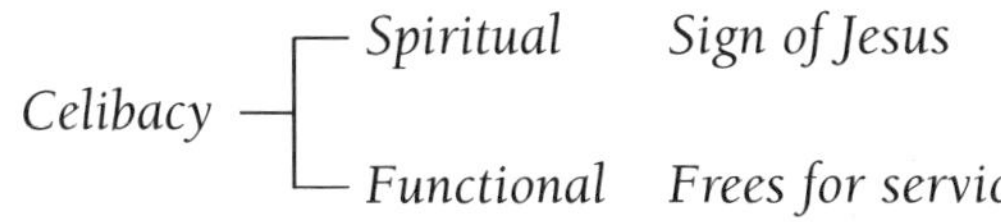

Share Your meditation

You might use this "meditation" as an opportunity to say a few words about religious communities of priests, sisters, and brothers.

> *Members of religious communities often take vows or promises of poverty (foregoing ownership of goods), chastity, and obedience to their religious superior.* CCC 925–927
>
> *Taking vows or promises does not elevate them into a position in the Church that is higher and holier than other Christians. It carves out for them a different Christian lifestyle—a different way of striving for the same perfection to which every Christian is called.* MATTHEW 5:48
>
> *Religious communities have their own particular spirit or spirituality. It is tailored to help their members carry out the particular ministry to which the community has committed itself in a special way: educating the young, working among the poor, preaching the Gospel in mission countries, etc.*

Celebration of Holy Orders

CLARIFY—Recall that the "fullness" of the sacrament gives the bishop the authority and responsibility of:

1	*Teaching*	*Preaching the Gospel*
2	*Sanctifying*	*Presiding at worship*
3	*Leading*	*Pastoring spiritually*

In this section we focus on the difficult task of teaching in the name of Jesus. Because of the difficulty, Jesus gave his successors the special help of the Holy Spirit.

SHARE YOUR **meditation**

To a young man who wishes to be a Jesuit, I would say:

Stay at home if this idea makes you unsettled or nervous. Do not come to us if you love the Church like a stepmother, rather than a mother, Do not come if you think that in so doing you will be doing the Society of Jesus a favor.

Come if serving Christ is at the very center of your life. Come if you have an open spirit, a reasonably open mind and a heart larger than the world. Come if you know how to tell a joke and can laugh with others and . . . on occasions you can laugh at yourself.

Pedro Arrupe, General of the Society of Jesus

■ ***Why would this statement make you more/less attracted to the priesthood?***

PRAYER **hotline**

"I will go! Send me!"

Isaiah 6:8

Celebration of Holy Orders

The celebration of the sacrament of Holy Orders follows the same liturgical movement for all three degrees. CCC 1597 It consists of two essential elements:

- **Imposing hands**
- **Prayer of consecration**

The prayer of consecration asks God to give to the ordinand (one being ordained) the graces of the Holy Spirit needed to carry out his ministry.

Exercise of Holy Orders

Let us now take a closer look at how the "college of bishops," under the leadership of the pope, the bishop of Rome, carry out the ministry conferred upon them by Holy Orders.

One day, Jesus was instructing his disciples. In the course of the instruction, he turned to Peter and said to him:

"You are a rock,
and on this rock foundation
I will build my church. . . .
I will give you
the keys of the Kingdom of heaven;
what you prohibit on earth
will be prohibited in heaven,
and what you permit on earth
will be permitted in heaven."
MATTHEW 16:18–19

And just before ascending to his Father, Jesus commissioned Peter and the Apostles to teach all nations, saying, "I will be with you always to the end of the age." MATTHEW 28:20

To assist the Apostles and their successors in this awesome task, Jesus promised them the help of the Holy Spirit:

I will ask the Father,
and he will give you another Helper,
who will stay with you forever.
He is the Spirit. . . .
whom the Father will send in my name,
will teach you everything
and make you remember
all that I have told you. JOHN 14:16–17, 26

It is against this background that we must consider the teaching office of the bishops, under the leadership of the pope.

We sometimes refer to this teaching office as the *magisterium* of the Church. A much misunderstood dimension of this teaching office is *infallibility.* CCC 888–92

Infallibility

Simply put, infallibility means that God will not allow his Church to depart from the teachings of Jesus in matters of faith and morals.

Somewhat as the Holy Spirit guided the authors of Scripture in matters relating to salvation, so the Holy Spirit guides the teachers of the Church in matters relating to faith and morals.

Consider two ways infallibility is exercised.

Exercise of Holy Orders

CLARIFY—A detailed discussion of the magisterium, along with the formation of conscience, will be discussed on pages 282 and 283 in connection with moral decision making.

Infallibility

NOTEBOOK—Review the two ways in which the pope enjoys the charism of infallibly by virtue of his office. Have students list them in their notebooks.

The first is when the Holy Father, acting in his capacity as:

NOTES

First, the pope, as head of the college of bishops, teaches infallibility when, by virtue of his office as supreme pastor and teacher of the faithful, he proclaims, by a definitive act, a doctrine relating to faith and morals to be infallible.

Second, it is also present when the "college of bishops," acting together with the pope, exercise their official teaching office (magisterium), especially in an ecumenical council.

Therefore, when the Church, in one of these two situations, proposes a doctrine for belief as being divinely revealed" and as the teaching of Christ, the doctrine "must be adhered to with the obedience of faith. CCC 891

In brief, then, the charism of infallibility is simply the carrying out of Jesus' promise to his Apostles.

5 Why is the charism of infallibility so essential when it comes to interpreting Scripture and truths relating to matters of faith and morals?

Commenting on the need for some way of settling disputes, such as those regarding biblical interpretation, one Protestant writer candidly observes:

The conference of Luther and Zwingli . . .
to unify the German and Swiss
Reformation, broke down . . .
over the failure of the two leaders
to agree on the interpretation
of a single Biblical text:
"This is my Body."

From that day on the misuse of the Bible
has vitiated the spirit of Protestantism . . .
and divided it into sects.
CHARLES CLAYTON MORRISON:
PROTESTANT MISUSE OF THE BIBLE

PRACTICAL **Connection**

Saint Ignatius of Antioch writes about A.D. 110:

Let everyone revere. . . .
the bishop as the image
of the Father and
the presbyters [priests]
as the senate of God.

AD TRALL 3,1

Bishops of the world gathered in Rome.

1 *Head of the "college of bishops" and*
2 *Supreme pastor-teacher of the faithful,*
3 *Proclaims by a "definitive act" a doctrine pertaining to faith or morals.*

The second is when:

1 *The "college of bishops,"*
2 *Acting with the pope,*
3 *Exercises their official teaching office, especially in an ecumenical council.*

Therefore, when the Church, in one of these situations,

1 *Proposes a doctrine for belief*
2 *As being divinely revealed and as the teaching of Christ,*
3 *The definitions must be adhered to with the obedience of faith.*

QUESTION **5** ***Why is the charism of infallibility so essential when it comes to interpreting Scripture and truths relating to matters of faith and morals?***

■ *A Protestant minister told the author that the older he got, the more sympathetic he became to the idea of a "pope" (who could speak authoritatively on matters of faith and morals).*

He was deeply saddened that disputes over faith and morals were splintering the Protestant community. His point is echoed by the Morrison quote, from the Christian Century, *cited on page 209 of the student book.*

PRACTICAL **Connection**

Saint Ignatius was bishop of Antioch, a city that ranked next to Rome as one of the great cities of its time.

Ignatius was born around A.D. 50, about the time Paul and Barnabas were preaching in Antioch. Luke tells us in Acts 11:26:

For a whole year the two met
with the people of the church and
taught a large group.
It was at Antioch that the believers
were first called Christians.

It is significant that the Church was already so organized (bishops and priests) at such a very early date.

Ignatius was arrested during the persecution of Christians under the emperor Trajan and condemned to be fed to wild beasts in the arena in Rome.

He was paraded through town after town, as his captors took him by an overland route to Rome.

Along the way Ignatius wrote a series of letters exhorting Christians. A famous line from one of the letters is:

I am God's wheat and I am being
ground by the teeth of wild beasts
to make a pure loaf for Christ.

He was martyred in Rome around A.D. 110.

Recap

■ *Jesus prayerfully called an initial twelve Apostles whose sole desire was to spend their lives in his presence. Thus, Jesus formed a permanent community of leadership, a sort of "college" with them.*

They were eventually sent out to teach, heal, and minister to the people of that age. They were sent to spread the faith to all the world. And they were confirmed in their mission by the Holy Spirit at Pentecost, as the Acts of the Apostles tells us.

Eventually, they came to be called "bishops."

These first ones appointed by Christ soon added others, and down through history such appointments continued so that since the time of Christ there has been a steady succession of bishops, passing on the mantle of ministry and leadership, continuing the work of Christ. With priests and deacons to help them, the bishops preside over the People of God, taking the place of the apostles in doing so. Whoever listens to them is listening to Christ.

THE DOGMATIC CONSTITUTION ON THE CHURCH, CHAPTER 3: ON THE HIERARCHICAL STRUCTURE OF THE CHURCH, IN PARTICULAR THE BISHOPS. VATICAN II IN PLAIN ENGLISH: THE CONSTITUTIONS BY BILL HUEBSCH WITH PAUL THURMES, THOMAS MORE, ALLEN, TX, 1997

Review

DAILY QUIZ—The review questions may be assigned (one or two at a time) for homework or a daily quiz.

CHAPTER TESTS—Reproducible chapter tests are found in Appendix A. For consistency and ease in grading, quizzes are restricted to (1) "Matching," (2) "True/False," and (3) "Fill in the Blanks."

TEST ANSWERS—The following are the answers to the test for Chapter 16. (See Appendix A, page 327.) Each correct answer worth 4 points.

Recap

By our Baptism into the Body of Christ we become a priestly people. This priesthood is called the "common priesthood of the faithful." Besides this priesthood, some are called to special service within the Church. This call is to the "ordained priesthood." Conferred by Holy Orders, it is exercised in three degrees: bishops, priests, deacons.

The bishops, successors of the Apostles, receive the fullness of the sacrament, empowering them to:

- **Teach** — **Preach the Gospel**
- **Sanctify** — **Preside at worship**
- **Lead** — **Pastoral guidance**

The sacrament of Holy Orders is conferred by the:

- **Imposition of hands**
- **Prayer of Consecration**

Peter held a special leadership role among the apostles. For example, he:

- **Heads all lists of Apostles**
- **Speaks for the Apostles**
- **Holds the "Keys of the Kingdom"**
- **Instructs others in leadership**

The bishop of Rome is the successor of Peter and holds a special leadership role within the "college of bishops."

Jesus commissioned the Apostles and their successors to "hand on the faith," promising them the guidance of the Holy Spirit. A part of that promise is the "charism of infallibility." Simply put, it means that God will not allow his Church to err in matters relating to salvation.

Review

1 Briefly explain (a) "common priesthood of the faithful," (b) *ordained* priesthood.

2 List (a) the three degrees of the ordained priesthood, (b) the four ways, mentioned in the text, by which deacons serve the Catholic community.

3 List (a) four examples from Scripture that reflect Peter's leadership role among the Apostles, (b) the biblical reference and words by which Jesus conferred the leadership authority of his Church upon Peter, (c) the name we give Peter's successor.

4 Cite biblical passages that show that Jesus (a) commanded the Apostles to teach in his name, (b) promised them that the Holy Spirit would guide them in this task.

5 Briefly explain (a) infallibility, (b) two ways infallibility is exercised, (c) what is required of us when it is exercised concerning some doctrine, (d) what we mean by "magisterium."

6 How did the conference between Luther and Zwingli illustrate the practical need for the charism of infallibility?

7 Briefly explain (a) what is meant by "celibacy," (b) when the practice became universal in the Roman Catholic Church, (c) two reasons for it.

Matching

1 = e	2 = a	3 = b	4 = i
5 = g	6 = h	7 = j	8 = f
9 = d	10 = c		

True/False

1 = T	2 = F	3 = T	4 = T
5 = T			

Fill in the Blanks

1. (a) Bishop (b) Priest (c) Deacon
2. (a) Heads all lists of the Apostles
   (b) Speaks for the other Apostles
   (c) Holds the Keys of the Kingdom
   (d) Instructs the other Apostles
3. (a) Teach *or* Preach the Gospel
   (b) Sanctify *or* Preside at worship
   (c) Lead *or* Guide pastorally

NOTES

Reflect

1 John Eagan, S.J., writes in his spiritual journal, *A Traveller Toward the Dawn*:

At the Our Father, holding hands and singing,
suddenly the beauty of it all struck me,
and I almost lost it with a rush of emotion.

And then at Communion time
as I broke and folded over the host
and then held it up: insight.
This is Jesus, God's own Son,
the one who stands before each human being
the Great God of the stars and skies.

The people come up, hundreds of them,
and suddenly in the midst of it all
a wave of gladness comes over me.
I'm so glad to be here today.
For a moment I choke and can't say
the simple words: "The Body of Christ." (CONDENSED)

■ **Interview (in person or by phone) a priest, sister, brother, or deacon about their calling:**
(a) When they first experienced the call.
(b) What their first response to it was.
(c) What moved them to say "Yes."
(d) If they have ever regretted their decision.
(e) What do they think is the best age for a decision of this type and why.

2 Imagine that you have been hired by a team of professional advertising consultants. The team has been commissioned to design a one-minute television commercial to run just before half-time of the Super Bowl. Its purpose is to invite young people to consider the religious ministry.

■ ***What "gimmick" would you suggest the team use to get the attention of the young viewers they want to reach? What would you suggest they say to them once they had their attention?***

3 Saint Francis Xavier was a talented athlete at the University of Paris. There he felt the call to the priesthood, responded to it, and became a missionary to India. He wrote to a friend:

The native Christians here have no priests.
There is nobody to say Mass for them,
nobody to teach them. . . .

Many people are not becoming Christian
for one reason only: there is nobody
to make them Christians.

Again and again,
I have thought of going around to
the universities of Europe and crying out
like a madman [for young people
to come to help me].

■ ***List some reasons why you think there is an even greater shortage of vocations to the priesthood, sisterhood, brotherhood, and deaconate in our day.***

STAGE 2: CHAPTER 16 **211**

Reflect

1 ***Interview (in person or by phone) a priest, sister, brother, or deacon about their calling:***
a) ***When they first experienced the call.***
b) ***What their first response to it was.***
c) ***What moved you to say, "Yes."***
d) ***If they have regretted their decision.***
e) ***What they think is the best age for a decision of this type and why.***

Have two students work together as a team on this project.

2 **a)** ***What "gimmick" would you suggest the team use to get the attention of the young viewers they want to reach?***
b) ***What would you suggest they say to them once they had their attention?***

Have small groups work at this. Have each group come up with a concrete proposal.

3 ***List some reasons why you think there is an even greater shortage of vocations to the priesthood, sisterhood, brotherhood, and diaconato in our day.***

■ *Formerly, most priestly vocations came from teenagers right out of high school. Now this has changed. Only a few teenagers are entering directly from high school. A new source of vocations is older men.*

Special seminaries are now being set up specifically for older men. Pope John XXIII National Seminary in Weston, Massachusetts, enrolls men between the ages of thirty and sixty studying for the priesthood.

At Holy Apostles Seminary in Cromwell, Connecticut, its seminarians average 45 years of age. The advertising copy for the seminary in Cromwell notes that all of Jesus' Apostles (with the possible exception of John) were adults beginning a "second career." The new seminarians include former lawyers, doctors, managers, army officers, and the like.

PRAYER TIME with the Lord

QUESTION ***Identify a priest who influenced or impacted your life in some way and what it was that he said or did.***

A priest who impacted the lives of many was Father Damien De Veuster (1840–1899), a young Belgian priest.

■ *His story begins when a terrifying epidemic of leprosy broke out on the Hawaiian Islands in the mid 1880s. That was a time when modern medicine was decades away from any remedy for the disease.*

To arrest the spread of the disease, authorities did something they hated to do but felt that they had to do. They set up a leper settlement on the remote and almost inaccessible island of Molokai. Robert Ellsburg writes in his book All Saints:

"Hawaiians . . . suffering from the disease were snatched by force from their families and communities and sent to this island. . . Patients were literally dumped in the surf and left to make their way ashore, seek shelter in caves or squalid shacks, and cling to life as best they could."

Father Damien heard of their plight and volunteered to go to Molokai and minister to them. Once on the island, he organized them into a community, built a church in which to worship, worked beside them, walked with them, and ate with them. After 12 years, the inevitable happened. He contracted the unthinkable disease. He lived four more years, dying in 1889. Pope John Paul II beatified him in 1995, which is a preparatory step toward sainthood.

PRAYER Journal

QUESTION ***Compose a prayer for someone who has played an important role in your life: a priest, a teacher, a parent, a friend.***

PRAYER TIME with the Lord

Jane Austen was an acclaimed eighteenth-century British novelist. One of her most popular novels, *Pride and Prejudice*, was made into a Hollywood film. She also wrote a prayer that needs to be repeated again and again. It reads:

Grant us grace, Almighty Father,
so to pray as to deserve to be heard.

Pray the following "Prayer for Priests" in a way "as to deserve to be heard":

O Jesus, I pray
for your faithful and fervent priests;
for your unfaithful and tepid priests;
for your priests laboring at home
or abroad in distant mission fields.
for your tempted priests . . .
for your young priests . . .
for your dying priests. . . .

But above all I recommend to you
the priests dearest to me;
the priest who baptized me;
the priests who absolved me from my sins;
the priests at whose Masses I assisted. . . .

O Jesus, keep them all close to your heart,
and bless them abundantly in time and
in eternity. AUTHOR UNKNOWN

■ ***Identify a priest who influenced or impacted your life in some way and what it was that he did or said.***

212 STAGE 2: CHAPTER 16

Here's a sample prayer for a friend. You might share it with your students to give them a concrete idea of what to do.

Lord, bless my friend, Kelly.

Bless her mind
with the light of your truth
that she may continue walking
in your footstep.

Bless her heart
with the fire of your love
that she may radiate your love,
even more than she does now.

And, Lord,
after you have blessed Kelly,
let her be an even greater blessing
to me and to everyone she meets.

NOTES

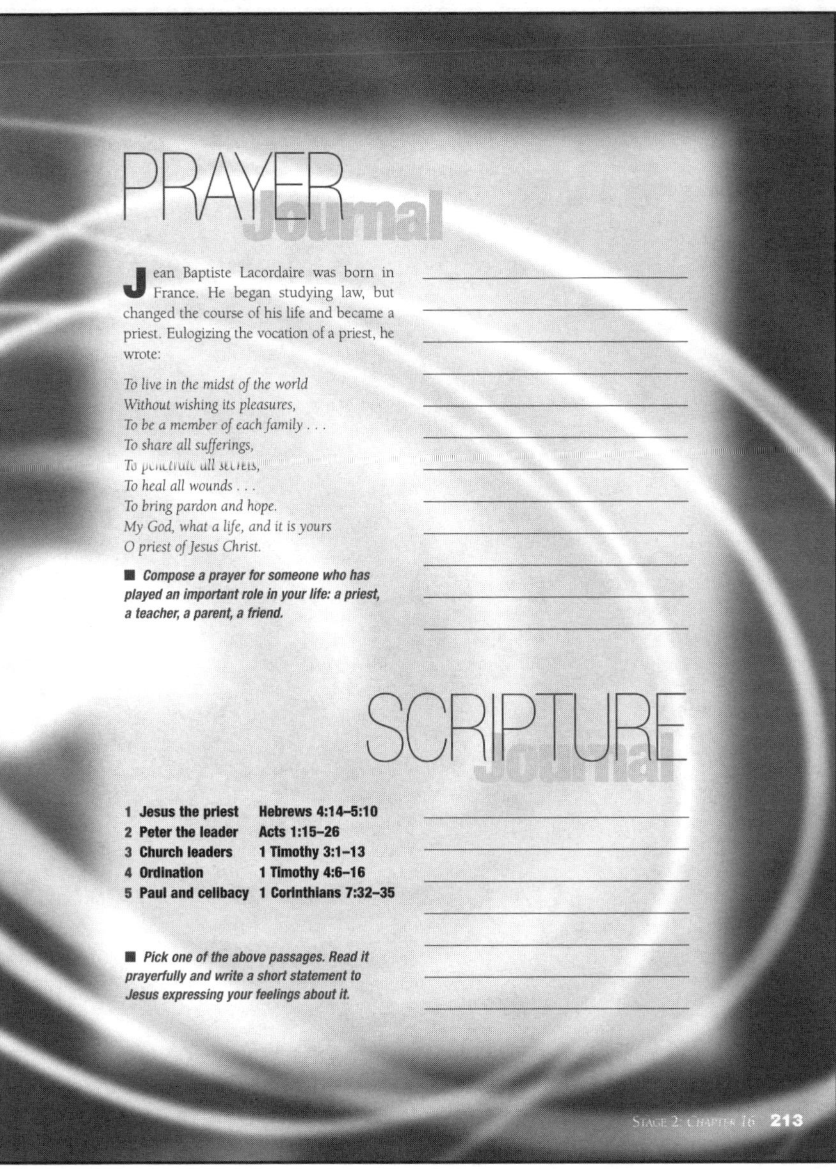

PRAYER Journal

Jean Baptiste Lacordaire was born in France. He began studying law, but changed the course of his life and became a priest. Eulogizing the vocation of a priest, he wrote:

To live in the midst of the world
Without wishing its pleasures,
To be a member of each family . . .
To share all sufferings,
To penetrate all secrets,
To heal all wounds . . .
To bring pardon and hope.
My God, what a life, and it is yours
O priest of Jesus Christ.

■ ***Compose a prayer for someone who has played an important role in your life: a priest, a teacher, a parent, a friend.***

SCRIPTURE Journal

1	Jesus the priest	Hebrews 4:14–5:10
2	Peter the leader	Acts 1:15–26
3	Church leaders	1 Timothy 3:1–13
4	Ordination	1 Timothy 4:6–16
5	Paul and celibacy	1 Corinthians 7:32–35

■ ***Pick one of the above passages. Read it prayerfully and write a short statement to Jesus expressing your feelings about it.***

STAGE 2: CHAPTER 16 **213**

SCRIPTURE Journal

QUESTION ***Pick one of the above passages. Read it prayerfully and write a short statement to Jesus expressing your feelings about it.***

You may wish to read to the students a passage from the fourth reading and have them write a short statement to Jesus expressing their feelings about it:

> *Do not let anyone look down on you*
> *because you are young,*
> *but be an example for the believers*
> *in your speech, your conduct,*
> *your love, faith, and purity.* 1 TIMOTHY 4:12

CLARIFY—Paul met Timothy in Lystra. He liked the young man, accepted him as a co-worker, and ordained him to the ministry. 2 TIMOTHY 1:6.

Classroom Resources

CATECHISM

Catechism of the Catholic Church *Second Edition*

For further enrichment, you might refer to:

1. Holy Orders	Index	pp. 804–05
	Glossary	p. 890
2. Priesthood	Index	pp. 837–38
	Glossary	p. 895

See also: Pastor, Bishop, Deacon.
—AVAILABLE FROM THE UNITED STATES CATHOLIC CONFERENCE, WASHINGTON DC

CD-ROM

Dogmatic Constitution on the Church (*Lumen Gentium*)

especially chapters 1–4
—AVAILABLE ON THE WELCOME TO THE CATHOLIC CHURCH CD-ROM FROM HARMONY MEDIA INC., CERVAIS, OR

CIRCULAR LETTER

The Priest and the Third Christian Millennium: Teacher of the Word, Minister of the Sacraments, and Leader of the Community

Vatican Congregation of the Clergy Focuses on the roles of preaching, celebrating the sacraments, and leadership.
—AVAILABLE IN *ORIGINS*, SEPTEMBER 9, 1999, VOL 29: NO. 13, CNS DOCUMENTARY SERVICE

VIDEO

Understanding the Sacraments

Thirty-three-minute presentation. Insight and inspiration for the celebration of the sacraments. 1996.
—AVAILABLE FROM ST. ANTHONY MESSENGER PRESS, CINCINNATI, OH

NOTE

For a list of (1) General resources for professional background and (2) Addresses, phone/fax numbers of major publishing companies, see Appendix B of this Resource Manual.

STAGE 3 WITNESS
We journey together

CLARIFY—John Ruskin (1819–1900) was considered one of England's finest writers. His primary focus went from art and the writing of such books as *The Seven Lamps of Architecture* (1849) to social issues and the writing of such books as *Letters to the Workmen* and *Laborers of Great Britain* (1871–1884).

A college which bears his name was founded in 1899 at Oxford. Its purpose was to make education available to the working class through correspondence courses.

CLARIFY—The story of the lamplighter (spelled out a bit more on page 144) occurred when Ruskin was an old man.

DISCUSS—Read the following two excerpts to the students and ask:
(a) "What is the point of each?" and
(b) "How does each one relate to the Ruskin quote?"

1 *The early followers of Francis of Assisi wanted to know what to say when he sent them forth into towns and villages. He said, "Preach the gospel. If necessary use words."*

2 *Not the cry, but the flight of the duck leads the flock to fly and follow.* CHINESE PROVERB

■ *Both questions may be answered with another saying: "Christian witness is a lot like perfume. It works best if you don't have to call attention to it."*

LOOKING**Back**

CLARIFY—Give the students a few minutes to reflect on the following two questions:

1 *One period in my life*
when I felt good about the way
I was living out my faith was . . .

2 *One reason I felt good*
about the way I was living was . . .

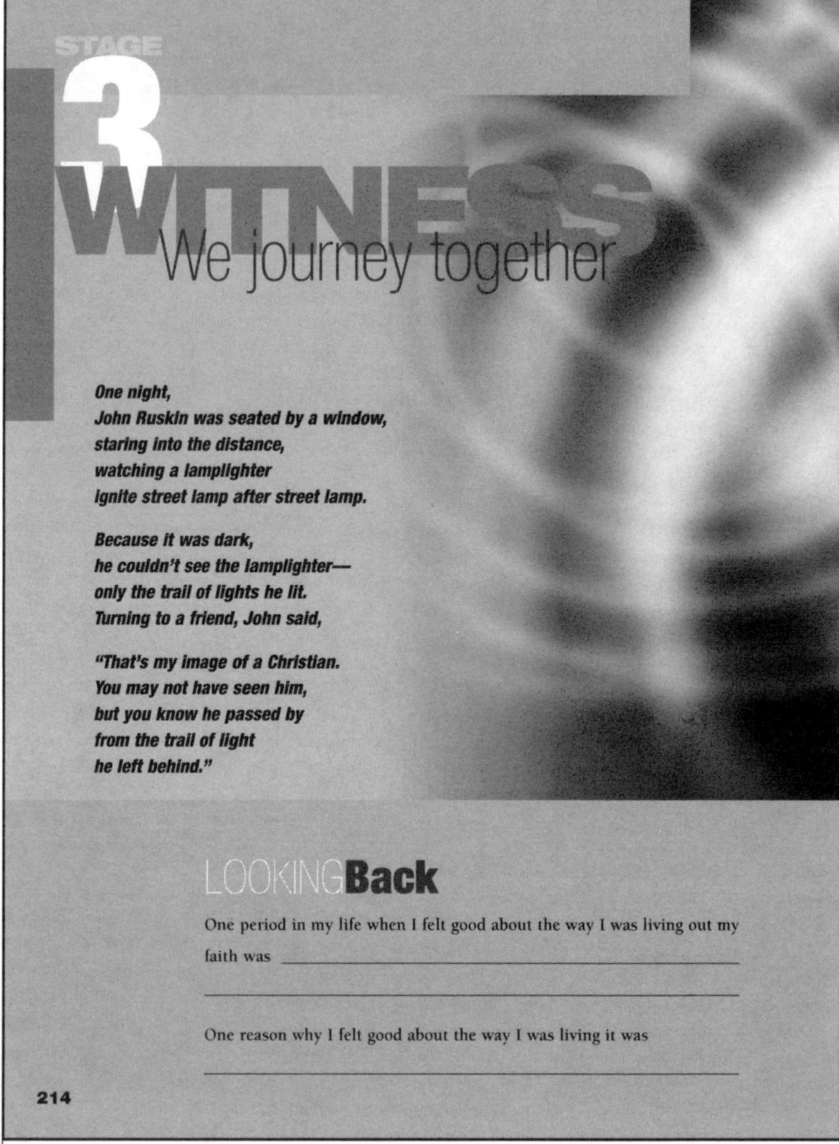

STAGE
3
WITNESS
We journey together
One night,
John Ruskin was seated by a window,
staring into the distance,
watching a lamplighter
ignite street lamp after street lamp.
Because it was dark,
he couldn't see the lamplighter—
only the trail of lights he lit.
Turning to a friend, John said,
"That's my image of a Christian.
You may not have seen him,
but you know he passed by
from the trail of light
he left behind."
LOOKINGBack
One period in my life when I felt good about the way I was living out my faith was
One reason why I felt good about the way I was living it was
214

Have a few volunteers give their responses.

DISCUSS—Father Joseph Girzone, an author of several spiritual books, said that after he made his first Communion he felt close to Jesus at all times—even though he was not particularly holy. When he was only 14 he shocked his parents by asking to go to a high school seminary. He wrote:

The seminary was heaven
until the presence of Jesus left me
after my second year.

To find out why the "feeling" of the "presence of Jesus" left him, he started reading books on the spiritual life. He writes:

■ *I learned that God had not left me but was drawing me to a deeper relationship*

NOTES

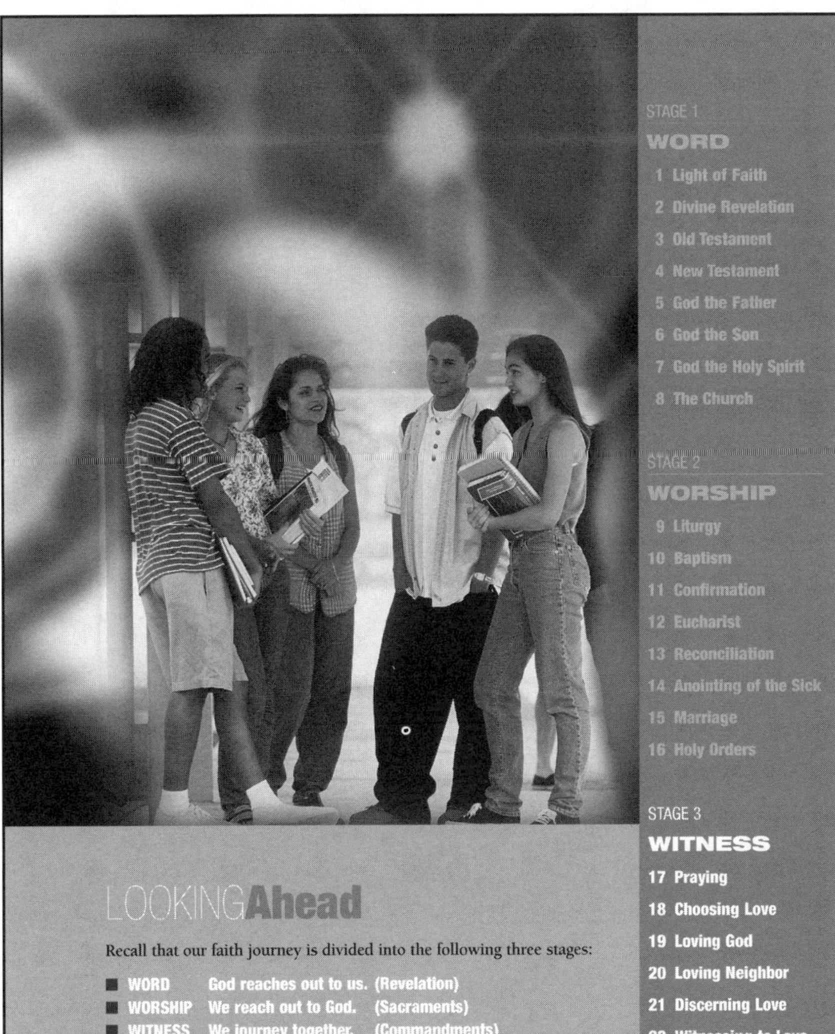

STAGE 1

WORD

1 Light of Faith
2 Divine Revelation
3 Old Testament
4 New Testament
5 God the Father
6 God the Son
7 God the Holy Spirit
8 The Church

STAGE 2

WORSHIP

9 Liturgy
10 Baptism
11 Confirmation
12 Eucharist
13 Reconciliation
14 Anointing of the Sick
15 Marriage
16 Holy Orders

STAGE 3

WITNESS

17 Praying
18 Choosing Love
19 Loving God
20 Loving Neighbor
21 Discerning Love
22 Witnessing to Love
23 Rejoicing in Love

LOOKING**Ahead**

Recall that our faith journey is divided into the following three stages:

- **WORD** God reaches out to us. (Revelation)
- **WORSHIP** We reach out to God. (Sacraments)
- **WITNESS** We journey together. (Commandments)

In the first two stages, we saw how God reached out to us and invited us to journey with him through life. In this final stage, we take a look at what God's invitation involves.

215

beyond the senses. . . . Daily Mass and Communion comforted me, but were not the overwhelming experiences they had once been.

Ask the students: What does he mean by the statement: "I learned that God had not left me but was drawing me to a deeper relationship beyond the senses?" Refer the students back to chapter 1. Review two points especially:

1 *The reference to John Kirvan's book* The Restless Believers *(page 10 of the text, under the subtitle "Adolescent stage"). It parallels what Girone experienced.*

2 *The reference to "Darkness" (the loss of a sense of Jesus' presence) that occurs on the faith journey. Review what was said on pages 14 and 15 of the text, under "Suffering Darkness." Recall, also, for the students the story of Marion Bond West (page 15 of this Resource Manual).*

Periods of darkness are simply a stage in the spiritual growth process. Therefore, we should not be disturbed if we don't "feel" as close to God as we once did—unless, through negligence, we've let our faith deteriorate. God is simply "drawing us" from childhood to an adult faith.

Nevertheless, in our adult years, we are sometimes "gifted" in prayer with a "feeling of deep and warm closeness to God." When this happens we simply "savor" the gift gratefully, allowing God to hold us lovingly as a loving mother holds her child.

LOOKING**Ahead**

***CLARIFY*—If we take the spiritual journey seriously, we are in for a spiritual adventure that will be anything but boring. A good description of what we can expect is the following poem, quoted earlier on page 85:**

■ *Jesus and I were riding a tandem bicycle.*
At first, I sat in front; Jesus in the rear.
I couldn't see him, but I knew he was there.
I could feel his help when the road got steep.

Then, one day, Jesus and I changed seats.
Suddenly, everything went topsy-turvy.
When I was in control,
the ride was predictable, even boring.

But when Jesus took over, it got wild!
I could hardly hold on.
"This is madness!" I cried.
But Jesus just smiled and said, "Pedal!"

So I learned to shut up and pedal—
and trust my bike companion.
Oh, there are still times
when I get scared and I'm ready to quit.
But Jesus turns around,
touches my hand, smiles, and says,
"Pedal!" M.L. INSPIRED BY AND MODELED AFTER AN UNKNOWN AUTHOR

***CLARIFY*—Preview the titles of the seven chapters under "Stage 3: Witness" (bottom right-hand corner of this page).**

CHAPTER 17
Praying

CHAPTER at a Glance

The goal of this chapter is to give students an overview of prayer. Specifically, to introduce them to the:

1. *Reasons we pray*
2. *Three settings of prayer*
3. *Four preparatory steps*
4. *Four ends of prayer*
5. *Three forms prayer takes*
6. *Two prayer attitudes*

Sadhu and the boy

CLARIFY—Stress that the first step in learning to do anything is the desire to learn. This is especially true of prayer.

■ *Saint Augustine never ceased to stress the importance of desire when it came to prayer. In fact, the desire to pray is a great prayer in itself.*

QUESTION **1** ***What do you think is the primary reason we should pray to God?***

■ *Thomas Merton explained it this way: "Prayer is an expression of our incompleteness. We are a gap, an emptiness that calls for fulfillment."*

In other words, without God's love for us and our love for God, we are incomplete. Saint Augustine put it this way: "Our hearts were made for you, O God, and they will not rest until they rest in you."

Prayer is the way we express (1) our love of God and (2) our need for God.

Prayer purpose

QUESTION **2** ***For what reason do you find yourself praying mostly? Explain.***

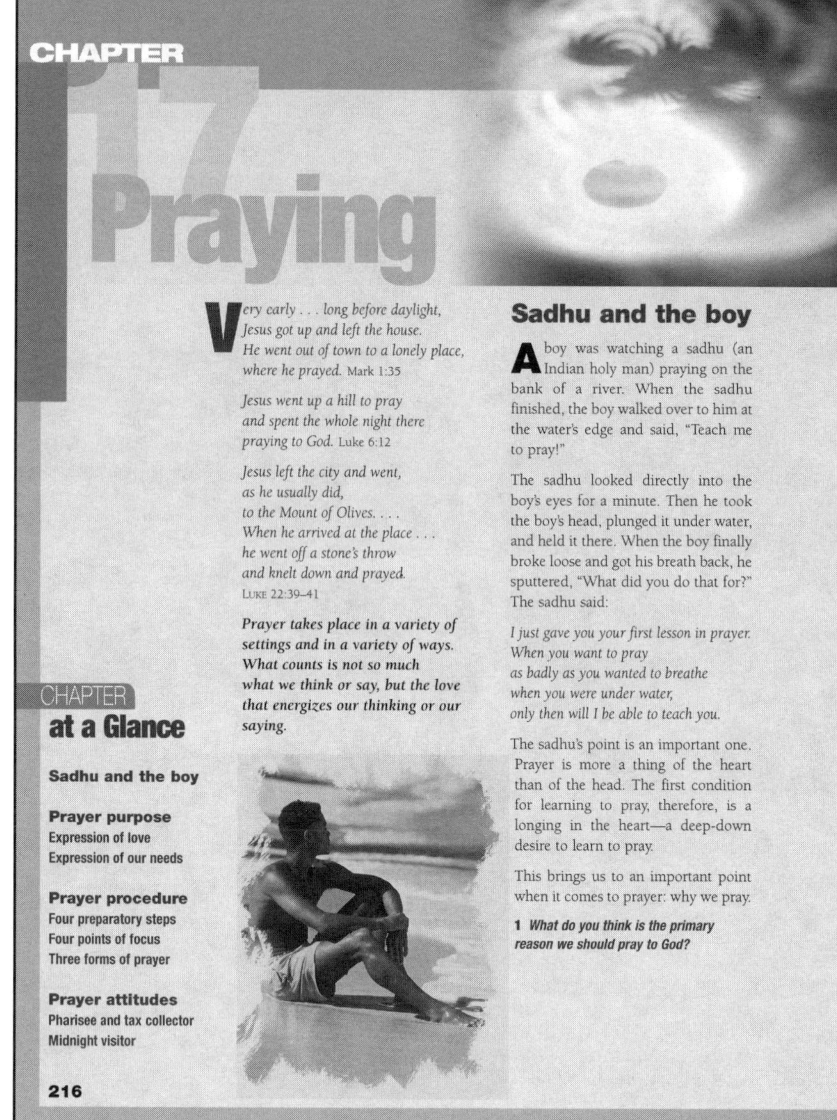

CHAPTER 17 Praying

Very early . . . long before daylight,
Jesus got up and left the house.
He went out of town to a lonely place,
where he prayed. Mark 1:35

Jesus went up a hill to pray
and spent the whole night there
praying to God. Luke 6:12

Jesus left the city and went,
as he usually did,
to the Mount of Olives. . . .
When he arrived at the place . . .
he went off a stone's throw
and knelt down and prayed.
Luke 22:39–41

Prayer takes place in a variety of settings and in a variety of ways. What counts is not so much what we think or say, but the love that energizes our thinking or our saying.

CHAPTER at a Glance

Sadhu and the boy

Prayer purpose
Expression of love
Expression of our needs

Prayer procedure
Four preparatory steps
Four points of focus
Three forms of prayer

Prayer attitudes
Pharisee and tax collector
Midnight visitor

216

Sadhu and the boy

A boy was watching a sadhu (an Indian holy man) praying on the bank of a river. When the sadhu finished, the boy walked over to him at the water's edge and said, "Teach me to pray!"

The sadhu looked directly into the boy's eyes for a minute. Then he took the boy's head, plunged it under water, and held it there. When the boy finally broke loose and got his breath back, he sputtered, "What did you do that for?" The sadhu said:

I just gave you your first lesson in prayer.
When you want to pray
as badly as you wanted to breathe
when you were under water,
only then will I be able to teach you.

The sadhu's point is an important one. Prayer is more a thing of the heart than of the head. The first condition for learning to pray, therefore, is a longing in the heart—a deep-down desire to learn to pray.

This brings us to an important point when it comes to prayer: why we pray.

1 ***What do you think is the primary reason we should pray to God?***

CLARIFY—First, have the students assign a priority number to each of the reasons (1 = most; 5 = least).

Second, have them share their reasons in small groups of three or four.

Third, have the group agree on a priority.

Fourth, tally the results on the chalkboard and discuss.

Expression of love

CLARIFY—Stress that the surest sign that our prayer is an "expression of love" for God is if it bears fruit and leads to a love of our neighbor. Consider an example.

■ *The film* The Bridge Over the River Kwai *dealt with a Japanese prison camp*

NOTES

Prayer purpose

If we asked people walking out of a church on Sunday morning why they pray, they would probably give us a menu of reasons. Prayer gives us:

- **Peace that the world can't give**
- **Wisdom that no education can give**
- **Strength to live as we ought**
- **Forgiveness for something we did**
- **Help that only God can give**

2 For what reason do you find yourself praying mostly? Explain.

Expression of love

The above reasons are excellent ones for praying; but they cannot be the *primary* reasons for praying. Why? It's because they all deal with the usefulness of prayer.

Prayer is a lot like friendship. A friendship can serve many useful purposes. For example, our friend is always ready to help us. But usefulness can never be the primary reason for the friendship. Why not?

If that is the primary reason for befriending someone, then there is no true friendship. We don't "use" a friend. The same is true of God. We don't use God.

But there is another reason usefulness can't be the primary reason for praying. It is this. The day may come when the prayer may no longer seem useful.

For example, the time may come when, for some reason or another, it seems that God no longer answers our prayers. If this is our main rea--- for praying, we may be tempte[d] give it up.

What, then, is the *primary* reason for praying? Prayer is an *expression of love to God*, who is love. It is an expression of love to God, who created us, redeemed us, and continually graces us.

Expression of our needs

Does this mean that we shouldn't pray to God for useful things, such as peace, wisdom, or help in an exam? Of course not! Jesus himself taught us to pray for such things, saying:

Ask, and you will receive;
seek, and you will find;
knock, and the door will be
opened to you. LUKE 11:9

Not only did Jesus teach us to pray things, he did it himself. For exam he prayed in the garden Gethsemane:

Praying

STAGE 3: CHAPTER 17 217

in Thailand during World War II. It was based on an actual event.

Some 12,000 Allied prisoners died there from starvation, brutality, and disease, building a railroad. Working in heat that reached 120 degrees, husky men became walking skeletons in a matter of weeks. Their worst enemy, however, was not the Japanese, but themselves.

Fear of the Japanese made them paranoid. The law of the jungle took over. They began to steal from one another and to betray one another to win favors from their guards. Something had to be done. Two prisoners began organizing Bible study groups.

Through their study and prayer, they began to realize that Jesus was not dead. He was alive in their midst and understood their situation. He too was bone-weary from too much work. He too was hungry from not enough food. He too was betrayed by one of his own. Ernest Gordon writes:

"We began to grasp the truth that suffering comes from human avarice and stupidity, not from God. . . .

"We learned to pray for others more than for ourselves. When we did pray for ourselves, it was not to get something, but to release some power within us. Gradually we learned to pray that hardest of all prayers: for our enemies. LUKE 6:28

During the final months of the war, an incident occurred that showed how far they had come spiritually. A trainload of wounded Japanese soldiers arrived. They were in pitiful shape: dirty, starving, wounds filled with maggots.

"With no order from me my men moved over to clean the soldier's wounds, and give them our own ration of rice. . . . They were no longer enemies, but fellow sufferers. . . . We'd found life—life with meaning and purpose. . . . We yearned to share our discovery."

"IT HAPPENED ON THE RIVER KWAI": ERNEST GORDON WITH CLARENCE HALL IN *READER'S DIGEST,* JUNE 1960

Prayer (expressing love for God) must also lead to action (expressing love for neighbor). John writes:

True love . . . shows itself in action. . . . If we say we love God, but hate others, we are liars. 1 JOHN 3:18, 4:19

Expression of our needs

***NOTEBOOK*—With the help of the students, develop the following diagram on the board.**

Prayer	*Love*	*Primary purpose*
	Needs	*Secondary purpose*

HISTORICAL Connection

CLARIFY—**Lincoln refers to the prayer Solomon prayed, when he succeeded his father David as king:**

■ *"I am very young*
and don't know how to rule. . . .
So give me the wisdom I need to rule. . . .
Otherwise, how would I ever be able
to rule this great people of yours?"

The Lord was pleased
that Solomon had asked for this,
and so he said to him,
"Because you have asked
for wisdom to rule justly,
instead of long life for yourself or riches
or the death of your enemies,
I will give you what you have asked for."
1 KINGS 3:7–12

Prayer procedure

CLARIFY—**Thoreau (1817–1862) lived in his hut from July 1845 to September 1847. It was an experiment to see how simply he could live.**

■ *His two-year stay was interrupted for one day, which he spent in jail because he refused to pay the poll tax in his native town, Concord, Massachusetts. He said the money was being used to support the Mexican War, which he regarded a "land grab" by Southern slaveholders.*

Thoreau's jail stint was in keeping with his belief in nonviolent resistance (spelled out in his essay, "Civil Disobedience").

When Ralph Waldo Emerson (1803–1882) visited Thoreau in jail, Emerson said, "Henry, why are you here?" Thoreau retorted, "Waldo, why are you not here?"

Thoreau's justification for civil disobedience was that it was obedience to a higher law. He wrote in Walden, "I march to a different drummer."

HISTORICAL Connection

James Murdoch spent three weeks in the White House as the guest of President Abraham Lincoln. One night, before the Battle of Bull Run, Murdoch couldn't sleep. Suddenly, he heard moaning. He went to see what it was. He writes:

I saw the President
kneeling beside an open window.
His back was toward me. . . .
Then he cried out
in tones so pleading
and sorrowful:

"O thou God that heard Solomon
on the night when he prayed
for wisdom, hear me;
I cannot lead this people,
I cannot guide the affairs
of this nation without thy help.
I am poor, and weak, and sinful.
O God! . . .
hear me and save this nation."

Lincoln Talks: A Biography in Anecdote, Emanuel Hertz, ed.

Father, if you will
take this cup of suffering from me.
Not my will, however,
but your will be done. LUKE 22:42

Our reason for praying is twofold. It is the way we express to God our:

- **Personal love**
- **Personal needs**

This brings us to the question of how to pray.

Prayer procedure

Henry David Thoreau was a nineteenth-century naturalist. He lived a part of his life in a tiny hut on Walden Pond outside of Concord, Massachusetts. Describing its simple furnishings, he wrote in his book *Walden*:

I had three chairs in my small hut:
one for solitude, two for friendship,
and three for society.

Thoreau's description points to an important psychological fact about our human nature. It has three dimensions:

■ **Personal**	**Solitude**
■ **Interpersonal**	**Friendship**
■ **Social**	**Community**

In other words, there are times when we need to be alone. There are times when we need the support of family and close friends. And there are times when we need the support of the total community.

What is true of our psychological makeup is true also of our spiritual makeup.

Sometimes we need to pray alone, sometimes we need to pray with family and friends CCC 2685, 2689, and sometimes we need the support of the community.

3 Give a concrete example to illustrate a time when we might feel the need to pray in each of these three settings.

CLARIFY—**A good way to illustrate the three dimensions of our human nature (and need to express each in prayer) is our reaction to the death of a loved one. The author experienced this firsthand when his brother Tony died.**

■ ***Interpersonal dimension (group prayer)***: *As Tony lay dying, the author felt the need to pray with the family, keeping vigil at Tony's bedside during the final hour of his life.*

Personal dimension (solitary prayer): *After Tony died, the author felt a need to spend time alone in prayer, to comprehend what had happened and to speak to God about it.*

Social dimension (community prayer): *Finally, the author and his family felt a need to pray together with the community*

NOTES

The Gospel portrays Jesus praying in all three of these settings:

- **Alone** MARK 1:35
- **With friends** LUKE 9:28
- **With the community** LUKE 4:16

Praying daily to God alone is as important as eating and sleeping. We need spiritual food as much as we need physical food.

Furthermore, unless we learn to relate to God in solitude, we will find it next to impossible to relate to God in small group or community prayer. Praying in private is the key that unlocks the door to praying with others.

4 Why do you think praying in solitude is the key to praying with meaning in a small group or community setting?

Four preparatory steps

When we want to get to know someone better, we agree on places and times to meet. We don't leave these things to chance. Getting to know each other is too important for that.

It is the same with getting to know God better through prayer. Four steps are involved in preparing for serious prayer:

- **Finding a place**
- **Scheduling a time**
- **Choosing a posture**
- **Entering God's presence**

The first step is finding a place to pray. CCC 2691 Some people can pray anywhere. But it usually helps to have

privacy or solitude. Jesus sought solitude. For example, he "went up a hill to pray" LUKE 6:12 and "out of town to a lonely place" MARK 1:35.

The important thing about a prayer place is that we feel comfortable there, for example, a "prayer chair" in our own room.

5 Where do you usually pray? Explain.

The second step in serious prayer is scheduling a *time* to meet God on a brief daily basis. Some people pray best in the morning; others pray best at night. Jesus prayed at both times. The Gospel says, "Very early the next morning Jesus prayed" and "Jesus spent the whole night praying." MARK 1:35; LUKE 6:12.

Finding a time for prayer is important. It might be that we will have to experiment for a week or so to find the time that fits us best.

6 When do you usually pray and how do you pray?

PRAYER hotline

Lord,
help me be the person
my dog thinks me to be.

Charles S. Martin

(funeral Mass) to mourn the loss of a member of the community.

CLARIFY—You may wish to read to the students the exact passages in Scripture that refer to Jesus praying alone, with friends, and with the community. Here they are:

Solitude — *Jesus went out of town to a lonely place, where he prayed.* MARK 1:35

Friendship — *Jesus took Peter, John, and James with him and went up a hill to pray.* LUKE 9:28

Community — *On the Sabbath Jesus went as usual to the synagogue.* LUKE 4:16

QUESTION **3** ***Give a concrete example to illustrate a time when we might feel the need to pray in one of these three settings.***

Share this example by a high-school student.

One winter night a friend and I
were driving down an icy road.
We noticed something on the roadside.
It turned out to be an old man who had
fallen on the ice and hurt himself.

We put the man in the car.
While my friend ran to a nearby house
to call paramedics, I asked the man,
"Do you believe in God?" He nodded.

With that I prayed the Our Father
a sentence at a time, pausing to
let him repeat the words after me.
That Our Father was the most
meaningful prayer of my life.

Four preparatory steps

QUESTION **5** ***Where do you usually pray ? Explain.***

Dag Hammarskjold was Secretary General of the United Nations from 1953 to his death in a plane crash in 1961.

He is responsible for building a "meditation room" in the UN building and never went on any important mission without visiting the room first.

QUESTION **6** ***When do you usually pray and how do you pray?***

George Washington Carver (1864–1943) was famous African-American botanist. He rose daily at four o'clock to pray, explaining:

I go out into the woods.
There in the early morning stillness,
I listen to God and to his plan for me.
At no other time
have I so sharp an understanding. . . .
Then I hear God best and learn his plan.

QUESTION 7 *What posture do you usually use when you pray?*

Three ministers were discussing the best posture for prayer. One said, "I pray best walking." The second said, "I pray best kneeling." The third said, "I pray best lying down."

A repairman overheard the conversation and could not contain himself. "Hey, fellas," he blurted out, "for what it's worth, the best prayer I ever made was while dangling upside down by one foot from a telephone pole in the midst of a thunderstorm."

We all have our favorite posture in prayer. But in the end, posture remains only an "aid" to prayer. When push comes to shove, you can pray in almost any posture.

QUESTION 8 *Why do you think trying to feel God's presence will usually always be wrong?*

Prayer is a gift, especially when it comes to "feeling" God's presence.

THINK about it

***CLARIFY*—**Stress that God wants us to pray to him with the confidence of a child. This is the point of the Lord's Prayer:

- *In Jesus' day, no Jew dared speak God's name. Spelled YHWH in Hebrew and pronounced "Yahweh," it is translated into English as* LORD.

  And no one ever dreamed of speaking of God the way Jesus did. CCC 209 *The word he used to address God was "Abba."* MARK 14:36 *Literally, it means "Daddy."*

  Early Christians imitated Jesus and used the word "Abba," also. This means they addressed the all-powerful Creator of the universe with the tender trust and intimacy of a child addressing a parent.

***NOTEBOOK*—**The Lord's Prayer contains two sets of petitions: three "your" petitions and three "our" petitions

The third step is taking a posture for praying. Some people prefer sitting, some kneeling, others lying down. Jesus used different postures. For example, he "knelt down" LUKE 22:41 and prayed "face downward on the ground" MATTHEW 26:39.

The best posture for prayer is the one that helps you to pray. Again, this often requires experimentation.

7 What posture do you usually use when you pray?

THINK about it

You are a child of God. Please call home.

Bumper Sticker

The fourth and final step for serious prayer is entering into God's *presence*. One method people have found helpful for doing this is the following:

After taking our prayer posture—for example, sitting in a chair—we spend a minute or so becoming aware of our clothes gripping our legs, our shoes gripping our feet, and the chair gripping our body.

When we are ready, we recall how present God is to us. We pray in words like this:

Lord, you embrace me
infinitely more firmly
than the clothes on my body,
the shoes on my feet,
and the chair in which I sit.
May my awareness of their embrace
deepen my awareness of your embrace.

Here it is important to realize that a sensible awareness of God's presence is a gift. God gives us this awareness from time to time.

When this happens, we simply remain in God's presence, savoring it.

An awareness of God's presence is a profound prayer in itself. Any effort, however, to try to feel it is usually wrong.

8 Why do you think trying to feel God's presence will usually be wrong?

Four points of focus

Our prayer can take different points of focus. Four widespread ones are:

- **Adoration** CCC 2626–28, 2639–43
- **Contrition** CCC 2629–31
- **Thanksgiving** CCC 2637–38
- **Supplication** CCC 2629–36

The focus of *adoration* is the mystery of God's glory. An example of this form of prayer is the Apostle Thomas. He falls on his knees before the risen Jesus and prays, "My Lord and my God!" JOHN 20:28

220 STAGE 3: *CHAPTER 17*

(combining the last two): Have students enter the following in their notebooks. (Omit listing the CCC [*Catechism of the Catholic Church*] reference.)

	Your petitions	CCC 2804
1	*Hallowed be your name*	CCC 2858
2	*Your Kingdom come*	CCC 2859
3	*Your will be done*	CCC 2860
	Our petitions	CCC 2804
1	*Give us our daily bread*	CCC 2861
2	*Forgive us our trespasses*	CCC 2862
3	*Lead us not into temptation but deliver us from evil*	CCC 2863 CCC 2864

The three "your" petitions focus on the coming of God's Kingdom. The three "our" petitions focus on our needs as we work and pray for its coming.

NOTES

Up Close & Personal

The focus of *contrition* is the mystery of God's mercy. An example of this form of prayer is the tax collector in Jesus' Parable of the Pharisee and the Tax Collector. Jesus says of the tax collector:

He stood at a distance and
would not ever raise his face to heaven,
but beat on his breast and said,
"God, have pity on me, a sinner!"
LUKE 18:13

The focus of *thanksgiving* is the mystery of God's goodness to us. An example is Jesus himself. One day his disciples returned all excited about preaching and healing people. Upon seeing this, Jesus thanked his Father in heaven, saying:

Father, Lord of heaven and earth!
I thank you because
you have shown to the unlearned
what you have hidden from the wise
and learned. LUKE 10:21

Finally, the focus of *supplication* (petition) is the mystery of God's loving concern for us. Jesus told his disciples:

Ask, and you will receive;
seek, and you will find;
knock, and the door will be
opened to you." LUKE 11:9

Jesus referred to the "prayer of petition" frequently in the Gospels. He himself used this prayer in the garden, praying, "Father, if you will, take this cup of suffering away from me."

9 Which prayer form do you find yourself using most frequently?

Prayer of petition

The prayer of petition is probably the most popular focus of people's prayers. It is important, therefore, to make a few special comments about it. Two points deserve special mention.

First, it presumes that what we ask for is for our greater spiritual welfare and in harmony with God's will.

Second, it presumes that God often answers our prayers in ways different from what we expect or in ways that we may not recognize until much later in our life. An anonymous poet refers to this latter point when he writes:

I asked for health,
that I might do greater things;
I was given infirmity,
that I might do better things. . . .

I asked for riches,
that I might be happy;
I was given poverty,
that I might be wise.

I asked for power,
that I might have the praise of men;
I was given weakness,
that I might feel the need of God. . . .

I asked for all things,
that I might enjoy life;
I was given life,
that I might enjoy all things. . . .

I got nothing I asked for,
but everything I hoped for.
Almost despite myself,
my unspoken prayers were answered.

I am among all men
most richly blessed.

Piri Thomas

Piri Thomas was a convict, a drug pusher, and an attempted killer. He was sharing a prison cell with the "thin kid." One night he was moved to repentance for his sinful life.

He waited until the thin kid was asleep. Then he knelt down and prayed out loud. He writes in *Down These Mean Streets:*

I told God
what was in my heart. . . .
I talked to him plain. . . .
I talked to him of my wants
and lacks, of my hopes
and disappointments.

After Piri finished praying, a voice said, "Amen." It was the thin kid. Thomas writes:

No one spoke for a long time.
Then the kid whispered,
"I believe in Dios also."

The two young men talked a long time. Finally, Piri climbed back into his bunk, saying:

"Good night, Chico, I'm thinking
that God is always with us.
It's just that we aren't
always with him."

I fell asleep thinking that
I heard the kid crying softly.
Cry kid, I thought.
I hear even Christ cried.

STAGE 3: CHAPTER 17 221

Four points of focus

Forms—
- Adoration (Thos: "My Lord and God!")
- Contrition (Tax man: "Pity me.")
- Thanksgiving (Jesus: "thanked God")
- Supplication (Jesus: "Ask, and receive.")

These four prayer forms (also called purposes or ends of prayer) are easily memorized. The first letter of each of the four forms spells the word ACTS.

QUESTION **9 *Which prayer form do you find yourself using most frequently?***

Prayer of petition

CLARIFY—Years ago, a man named Bruno Hagspiel lived in a rural area where clothing stores carried only the bare essential items: underwear, socks, work clothes. So he used to buy his dress clothes from a mail-order house. At the bottom of each order form was this question: "If we don't have the article you ordered in stock, may we substitute?"

On one of his orders, Bruno wrote "yes." A week later, he was thrilled to death when the mail-order house sent him a beautiful substitute at no extra cost—and listed at double the price of the one he ordered.

From that point on, Bruno always printed a big, bold "YES" after that question "May we substitute?" He even hoped they didn't have the item in stock, so they would send him something better.

Bruno compared the mail-order episode to prayer to God, saying:

- *When we pray to God, we should never omit telling him that we will gladly accept a substitute. In fact, every time God does substitute something, it is always far better than what we asked for—or thought we needed.*

Up Close & Personal

CLARIFY—Few descriptions of how to enter into prayer are as beautiful and solid as this one. Piri Thomas did everything right.

1 *He waited until the thin kid was asleep. (He scheduled his prayer for an appropriate time to give him privacy.)*

2 *He knelt down. (He assumed an humble posture for his prayer.) In his book, he explains that he knelt down because he couldn't "play it cheap." In other words, the sincerity of his prayer was reinforced by his kneeling posture.*

3 *In his book, he says, "I made like God was there in the flesh with me." In other words, he entered into God's presence.*

4 *He spoke to God "plain" from the heart, and as one friend speaks to another.*

Three forms of prayer

SHARE YOUR
meditation

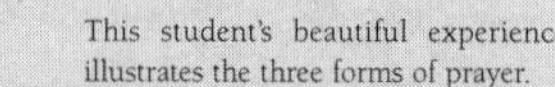

In his book *God Calling*, A. J. Russell has God say something like this:

Have you ever thought
what it means
to be able to visit me
any time you wish?

Even important people
can't visit heads of state
like that.
They must make an
appointment months in advance.

But I invite you
to visit with me
any time you wish.

I do more, I will visit
with you at any hour
of the day or night,
should you invite me.

■ ***Why don't I invite God into my life more often?***

Three forms of prayer

A high school student wrote the following reflection in a homework assignment. It is a beautiful illustration of the three forms prayer ordinarily takes.

One day after playing in the park,
I went to a nearby fountain for some water.
The cool water tasted good,
and I felt refreshment enter my tired body.

Then, I lay down and began to think.
"We need water to drink.
But where does water come from?"
"Clouds!" I thought, "but where do clouds
come from?" "Vaporized moisture."
This went on until I was left
with just one answer: God!

Then I kind of talked to God
for a little bit in my own words.

For the next couple of minutes,
I just lay on the grass,
looking up at the sky,
in awe of what God must be like.
SLIGHTLY ADAPTED

This student's beautiful experience illustrates the three forms of prayer.

- ■ **Meditation** — **Thinking about God**
- ■ **Conversation** — **Conversing with God**
- ■ **Contemplation** — **Resting in God**

10 ***Recall a time when you had an experience somewhat like the student above.***

Often, the above three forms of prayer are so closely interwoven in one and the same prayer that it is hard to say where one stops and the other begins.

Let's take a closer look at each.

First, *meditation.* CCC 2705–8 Its focus is the *mind.* It involves a prayerful probing of the idea of God—or some other spiritual truth. In other words, it is doing what the student did:

Then, I lay down and began to think.
"We need water to drink.
But where does water come from? . . ."
This went on until I was left
with just one answer: God!

Second, *conversation.* CCC 2700–2704, 2607–10 Its focus is the *heart.* It involves talking to God from the heart, as the student did, "Then I talked to God . . . in my own words."

Third, *contemplation.* CCC 2709–19 Its focus is the *soul.* It involves resting quietly in God's presence, open to whatever God may wish to say to me in the depths of my being. The student said:

For the next couple of minutes,
I just lay on the grass, looking up at the
sky, in awe of what God must be like.

11 ***Which of these three prayer forms do you normally find yourself using most? Explain.***

222 STAGE 3: CHAPTER 17

QUESTION **10** ***Recall a time when you had an experience somewhat like the student above.***

Sir Alister Hardy was an internationally known marine biologist. He also had a deep faith in God. That faith was nourished in his youth by his love and reverence for nature:

■ *I especially liked walking*
along the banks of various streams,
watching, as summer developed,
the sequence of wild flowers . . .
I wandered along their banks, at times
almost with a feeling of ecstasy. . . .

Occasionally,
when I was sure no one could see me . . .
I fell on my knees . . . thanking God,
who felt so very real to me,
for the glories of his kingdom
and for allowing me to feel them.
QUOTED IN DAVID HAY: *RELIGIOUS EXPERIENCE TODAY,* MOWBRAY, LONDON, 1990

As Hardy grew older, he never forgot these experiences. Moreover, he encountered other people who had similar experiences. These "graced moments" took the form of:

1 *a burst of light in a moment of darkness*
2 *an influx of strength in a moment of need*
3 *an unseen presence in a moment of joy*

CLARIFY—A good illustration of meditation is Psalm 139. Notice how it prayerfully explores the idea of God from every angle, as a jeweler might explore the facets of a diamond.

The psalmist begins by exploring God's mysterious *knowledge.* He prays:

■ *LORD, you have examined me*
and you know me.
You know everything I do;
from far away
you understand all my thoughts. . . .

Even before I speak,
you already know what I will say. . . .
Your knowledge of me is too deep;
it is beyond my understanding. 139:1–2, 4, 6

Then the psalmist explores God's presence:

Where could I go to escape from you?
Where could I get away from
your presence? . . .
If I flew away beyond the east
or lived in the farthest place in the west,
you would be there to lead me,
you would be there to help me. 139:7, 9–10

CLARIFY—Conversation involves not only "speaking" to God, but also "listening" to God. We don't listen with physical ears, but with spiritual ears. An illustration: Shortly before the Battle of Gettysburg, Abraham Lincoln said:

NOTES

SHARE YOUR
meditation

Two prayers

Jesus told two parables to illustrate two important attitudes that we should have when we pray. CCC 2613 The first one reads:

Once there were two men
who went up to the Temple to pray:
one was a Pharisee,
the other a tax collector.

The Pharisee . . . prayed,
"I thank you, God . . .
that I am not like that
tax collector over there.
I fast two days a week and give you
one tenth of all my income."

But the tax collector stood at a distance
and wouldn't even raise his face to heaven,
but beat on his breast and said,
"God have mercy on me a sinner!"

"I tell you," said Jesus,
"the tax collector, and not the Pharisee,
was in the right with God
when he went home.

For those who make themselves great
will be humbled,
and those who humble themselves
will be made great." LUKE 18:10–14

Night visitor

A second prayer attitude that Jesus said we should strive to have in prayer is referred to in his Parable of the Night Visitor. It reads:

Suppose one of you should go
to a friend's house at midnight and say,

"Friend,
let me borrow three loaves of bread.
A friend of mine who is on a trip
has just come to my house,
and I don't have any food for him!"

And suppose
your friend should answer from inside . . .
"The door is already locked,
and my children and I are in bed.
I can't get up and give you anything."
Well, what then?

"I tell you
that even if he will not get up
and give you the bread
because you are his friend,
yet he will get up
and give you everything you need
because you are not ashamed
to keep asking.

"And so I say to you:
Ask, and you will receive;
seek and you will find;
knock, and the door
will be opened to you." LUKE 11:5–9

12 *Why do you think so many people begin a prayer program, but fail to persevere in it?*

At this moment, millions of invisible TV signals swirl around us in living color and sound. But the only way we can prove this fact is to tune them in on a TV set.

Just as a TV world swirls about us invisibly, so does the faith world in which God lives. And just as we need a TV set to get in touch with the TV world, so we need prayer to get in touch with the faith world.

■ ***What is one reason, right now in your life, why you'd really like to get in touch with the faith world and God?***

THINK
about it

Turn to the LORD and pray now that he is near.

Isaiah 55:6

STAGE 3: CHAPTER 17 **223**

■ *I went to my knees in prayer.*
Never before had I prayed
with so much earnestness. . . .
I prayed that God
would not let the nation perish. . . .
I felt my prayer was answered. . . .
I had no misgivings about the result.

The final line led Lincoln into contemplation, just resting peacefully in God's presence.

QUESTION **11 *Which of these three prayer forms do you normally find yourself using most? Explain.***

If you wish, you might want to change this question to read as follows: Which of these prayer forms do you find easiest to pray?

Two p

CLARIFY—B
collectors. They
for Rome. They a
collect taxes by bid

Once they got the job,
to get back their investme
profit besides. Because the
worked for Rome, they could
Roman cooperation.

Biblical scholar William Barclay say
tax collectors were not above "overtaxing" the people. Moreover, there was not a whole lot the victims could do.

Stress that, by eating with tax collectors, Jesus put himself in a very unfavorable light, especially with the Pharisees.

Night visitor

QUESTION **12 *Why do you think so many people begin a prayer program, but fail to persevere in it?***

It's the way human nature is. A lot of people begin *physical fitness* programs and fail to persevere. It's that way with *spiritual fitness* programs as well.

Over and above this, a low level of faith and and a low level of motivation or desire, also, enter in.

Share Your **meditation**

CLARIFY—The graphic imagery in this meditation has helped a lot of people grasp the idea of what prayer is all about. Be sure the students understand the point.

THINK **about it**

CLARIFY—One of the underlying premises of this book and course is that we must lead students to prayer.

A course that does not move down from the head to the heart (the greatest distance in the human body, according to AAs) misses the point: faith.

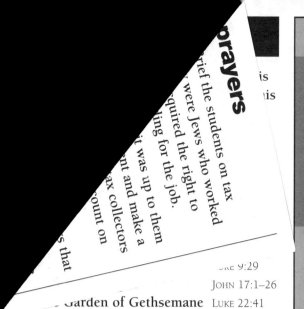

... 9:29

... JOHN 17:1–26

... Garden of Gethsemane LUKE 22:41

On the cross on Calvary LUKE 23:34

Review

DAILY QUIZ—Just a reminder: Review questions may be assigned (one or two at a time) for homework or a daily quiz.

CHAPTER TESTS—Reproducible chapter tests are found in Appendix A. For consistency and ease in grading, quizzes are restricted to (1) "Matching," (2) "True/False," and (3) "Fill in the Blanks."

TEST ANSWERS—The following are the answers to the test for Chapter 17. (See Appendix A, page 328.) Each correct answer worth 4 points.

Matching

1 = f	2 = d	3 = c	4 = g
5 = b	6 = a	7 = e	

True/False

1 = T	2 = F	3 = T	4 = F
5 = F	6 = T	7 = T	8 = F
9 = T			

Fill in the Blanks

1. (a) Humility (b) Perseverance
2. (a) Finding a place
   (b) Scheduling a time
   (c) Choosing a posture
   (d) Entering into God's presence

Recap

The first condition for learning to pray is the desire to pray. Prayer is, above all, an expression of love to God, who is love. Prayer takes place in one of three settings:

- **Alone**
- **Family or friends**
- **Large community**

Four preparatory steps to any serious prayer program involve:

- **Finding a place**
- **Scheduling a time**
- **Choosing a posture**
- **Entering God's presence**

Four points of focus that are commonly found in people's prayers are:

- **Adoration** — **Focus on God's glory**
- **Contrition** — **Focus on God's mercy**
- **Thanksgiving** — **Focus on God's goodness**
- **Supplication** — **Focus on God's concern**

Prayer normally follows the following three styles or forms:

- **Meditation** — **Thinking about God**
- **Conversation** — **Conversing with God**
- **Contemplation** — **Resting in God**

Two attitudes we should have in praying are:

- **Humility**
- **Perseverance**

Review

1 Explain (a) the first condition for learning to pray, (b) two reasons the useful benefits of prayer can't be the primary reason we pray, (c) the primary reason we pray.

2 List and briefly explain (a) the three settings of prayer, (b) the four preparatory steps of prayer.

3 List and briefly explain (a) the four points of focus common in most people's prayer, (b) two points to keep in mind when it comes to asking God for things.

4 List and briefly explain (a) the three forms that prayer normally takes, and (b) how these forms normally appear in most prayers.

5 List and briefly explain the two prayer attitudes that we should have and what parable Jesus used to teach and illustrate each.

224 STAGE 3: CHAPTER 17

3. (a) Alone
   (b) With friends
   (c) With the community

Reflect

1 **a)** ***On a scale of one (little) to ten (lots), how much confidence do you have that God answers prayers?***
b) ***How do you explain the fact that some prayers do not seem to be answered?***

CLARIFY—Refer the students back to the reflection of the anonymous poet on page 221. His point is that God does answer every prayer, but not always the way that we expect it.

Refer them back to the story of the man who used to indicate on the mail order forms that they could substitute if what he

NOTES

Reflect

1 A lay minister headed for Room 201. A nurse told her a patient was there from her hometown. When she got to the room, however, the expected patient was not there. The lay minister apologized to the occupant, saying she probably got her numbers mixed up. But the patient said, "Please stay! It's no mistake that you came here today. I've been praying for the courage to talk with someone like you, but I couldn't bring myself to do it."

- ***On a scale of one (little) to ten (lots), how much confidence do you have that God answers prayers?***
- ***How do you explain the fact that some prayers do not seem to be answered?***

2 Charlie Rumbaugh grew up in reform schools, jails, and hospital wards. At the age of seventeen, he escaped from a manic depressive ward, found a gun, and held up a jewelry store. A scuffle followed and the jeweler was killed.

A Texas judge sentenced Charlie to death. During his stay on death row, guards treated Charlie badly on several occasions. Shortly before being executed, Charlie asked a friend to pray that he'd be able to forgive the guards before he died. Moments before he received the lethal injection, Charlie said to all involved, "You may not forgive me, but I forgive you." Then he said to the warden, "I'm ready."

- ***How did Charlie's final moments resemble Jesus' final moments?***
- ***Describe a time when you found it hard to forgive someone.***

3 One winter night a high school student and her friend were driving down an icy road. They noticed something on the side of the road. It turned out to be an old man who had fallen on the ice. They put the man in the car.

While her friend ran to a nearby house to call the paramedics, the other student asked the man, "Do you believe in God?" The injured man nodded. With that, the student prayed the Our Father a sentence at a time, pausing to let the old man repeat the words after her.

Later, the student said, "That Our Father was the most meaningful prayer of my life."

- ***Describe a time when you and a friend helped someone as the two friends did.***
- ***Recall one of the most meaningful prayers you ever prayed.***

4 Bryon Dell grew up on a farm in Nebraska. One morning when Bryon was herding the cows, his pony, Frisky, became frightened and bolted off at breakneck speed. Bryon held on for dear life and remained unhurt. That night his father knelt with him to thank God that he was not hurt. That incident took place over 50 years ago, and Bryon has never forgotten it. It inspired him to make prayer a regular part of his daily life.

- ***Describe a happening from your childhood that continues to have an impact on you.***
- ***Did any of your parents ever pray with you? Explain.***

ordered was not in stock (page 221). He always ended up with something better. God knows what's best. Recall the words of Jean, "I have lived to thank God that my prayers have not been answered."

2 ***a) How did Charlie's final moments resemble Jesus' final moments?***
b) Describe a time when you found it hard to forgive someone.

■ *Charlie imitated Jesus by forgiving those who had sinned against him. You might share with students a time when you yourself found it hard to forgive someone.*

3 ***a) Describe a time when you and a friend helped someone as the two friends did.***
b) Recall one of the most meaningful prayers you ever prayed.

The high-school student described in this exercise shared this incident with the author. The student showed great sensitivity by: (1) first asking the man if he believed in God, and (2) the way she paused to let the man participate more fully in the prayer.

4 ***a) Describe a happening from your childhood that continues to have an impact on you.***
b) Did any of your parents ever pray with you? Explain.

This is a fairly sensitive exercise. It should be done as a written assignment. The best responses could be shared anonymously with the class.

PRAYER TIME with the Lord

QUESTION ***Would you say Mike's prayerful experience during his sky dive is an example of contemplation, meditation, or conversation? Explain.***

Mike's prayerful experience is a good example of what was said on page 222 about meditation, conversation, and contemplation:

> ■ *Often these three prayer forms are so closely interwoven in one and the same prayer that it is hard to say where one stops and the other begins.*

Have the students pick out lines from Mike's prayerful experience that speak of each of the three prayer forms. For example:

1 Conversation: *"Tears blur my eyes. I thank God out loud."*
2 Meditation: *"Wow! What a beautiful place the sky is! It's like a giant cathedral."*
3 Contemplation: *"It's God's place! And more beautiful than I ever dreamed."*

An alternative exercise would be to have students write out a prayer experience of their own.

PRAYER TIME with the Lord

Mike Valentino, a junior in a Chicago high school, describes his first sky dive:

The plane door opens.
The spotter pats my back. I jump!

I strive for stability—the poetic arch.
I have it! I have it! I'm poetry in motion.
It's great! It's great!
I feel a jolt. My chute has opened up.
Tears blur my eyes. I thank God out loud!

Wow! What a beautiful place the sky is!
It's like a giant cathedral! It's God's place!
And more beautiful than I ever dreamed of!

It's a heaven here. Yes, a heaven!
I feel I'm dreaming.
But no dream has ever been so real.

I look down—to prepare for landing.
I ride the wind. I'm holding—facing the wind.
My landing is great!

Joy and pride well up inside me.
I'm a sky diver;
and I'll never again be the same.

■ ***Would you say Mike's prayerful experience during his sky dive is an example of contemplation, meditation, or conversation? Explain.***

226 STAGE 3: CHAPTER 17

PRAYER Journal

QUESTION ***List seven "natural highs" that "raise your mind and heart to God and move you to want to give thanks."***

If writing out "seven natural highs" would be too much for the level of your students, you might have them write our three or four.

The important thing is to get the students to become aware of and reflect on the many "prayerful experiences" that they have and fail to recognize or appreciate.

NOTES

PRAYER Journal

Prayer often occurs after we experience a "natural high." Here are seven "natural highs" that one girl said "raise my mind and heart to God and move me to want to give thanks."

- *Having my last class canceled on a spring day*
- *Listening to my headphones as I jog along on a sunny fall afternoon*
- *Watching my baby brother do something for the first time after I taught him*
- *Seeing a falling star on a clear night*
- *Enjoying a hot shower after a strenuous workout on a winter day*
- *Skiing or sledding down a hill while big snowflakes are falling*
- *Watching my dog jump around because he's so glad to see me*

■ ***List seven "natural highs" that "raise your mind and heart to God and move you to want to give thanks."***

SCRIPTURE Journal

1	**Pray with humility**	**Luke 18:9–14**
2	**Pray with generosity**	**2 Chron. 1:7–12**
3	**Pray with simplicity**	**Matthew 6:5–13**
4	**Pray with vigor**	**Luke 11:5–13**
5	**Pray with perseverance**	**Luke 18:1–8**

■ ***Pick one of the above passages. Read it prayerfully and write a short statement to Jesus expressing your feelings about it.***

STAGE 3: CHAPTER 17 **227**

SCRIPTURE Journal

QUESTION ***Pick one of the above passages. Read it prayerfully and write a short statement to Jesus expressing your feelings about it.***

Number 1, Pray with humility (LUKE 9–14), is quoted on page 223. Have the students read it there.

Instruct them to imagine they are the boy in the red cap (pictured on page 223) and give imaginative answers to the following two questions:
(1) Why is he feeling so badly?
(2) Write out the prayer he is making to God.

Classroom Resources

CATECHISM

Catechism of the Catholic Church *Second Edition*

For further enrichment, you might refer to:

1.	Witness	Index	p. 859
2.	Prayer	Index	pp. 835–36
		Glossary	p. 895

See also: Love, Disciple, Mass
—AVAILABLE FROM THE UNITED STATES CATHOLIC CONFERENCE, WASHINGTON DC

CD-ROM

The Life of Christ

A visual journey through the four Gospels. 1995.
—AVAILABLE FROM HARMONY MEDIA, INC., CERVAIS, OR

VIDEO

Questions of the Soul: What Is Prayer?

Father Michael Himes

Thirty minutes. Thought-provoking insights into effective approaches to prayer. 1995.
—AVAILABLE FROM OBLATE MEDIA, ST. LOUIS, MO

BOOKS

One-Day Retreats for Senior High Youth

Geri Braden-Whatenby and Joan Finn

Practical ideas for retreats on prayer, peace, self-esteem. 1997.
—AVAILABLE FROM ST. MARY'S PRESS, WINONA, MN

Vision: Year A, Mission: Year B, Action: Year C

Mark Link, S.J.

Meditations on the daily readings and Sunday readings of the Lectionary. 1992, 1993, 1994.
—AVAILABLE FROM THOMAS MORE, ALLEN TX

NOTE

For a list of (1) General resources for professional background and (2) Addresses, phone/fax numbers of major publishing companies, see Appendix B of this Resource Manual.

CHAPTER 18
Choosing Love

CHAPTER at a Glance

The aim of this chapter is to give the students an insight into Jesus' teaching on morality:

1 *How it is beautifully consistent with what science tells us about the emergence and development of life on our universe*
2 *How moral growth develops and matures by way of definable stages*

READ—Have a student read aloud the scriptural introduction, which begins: "The command I am giving you . . ." Have a second student read aloud the commentary. It begins: "Christian morality may be described . . ."

CLARIFY—The "commentary reading" is from Deuteronomy ("second law"). It is not a "second" law in the sense that it is "new," but in the sense that it reviews and explains the main laws of the Old Covenant.

■ *The Book of Deuteronomy takes the form of a series of instructions by Moses to the people—as they stand on the heights of Moab, overlooking the Promised Land. The "commentary reading" sums up his message to them.*

REVIEW—Use the overview of Deuteronomy as an opportunity to do a quick overview of the basic structure of the Bible. Students need mini-reviews of this sort from time to time. Ask the students:

1 Into what two major divisions is the Bible divided? (See following chart or refer back to page 34.)

2 Into what four groups do we traditionally divide the OT and the NT and how many books are in each group? (See table below or page 34.)

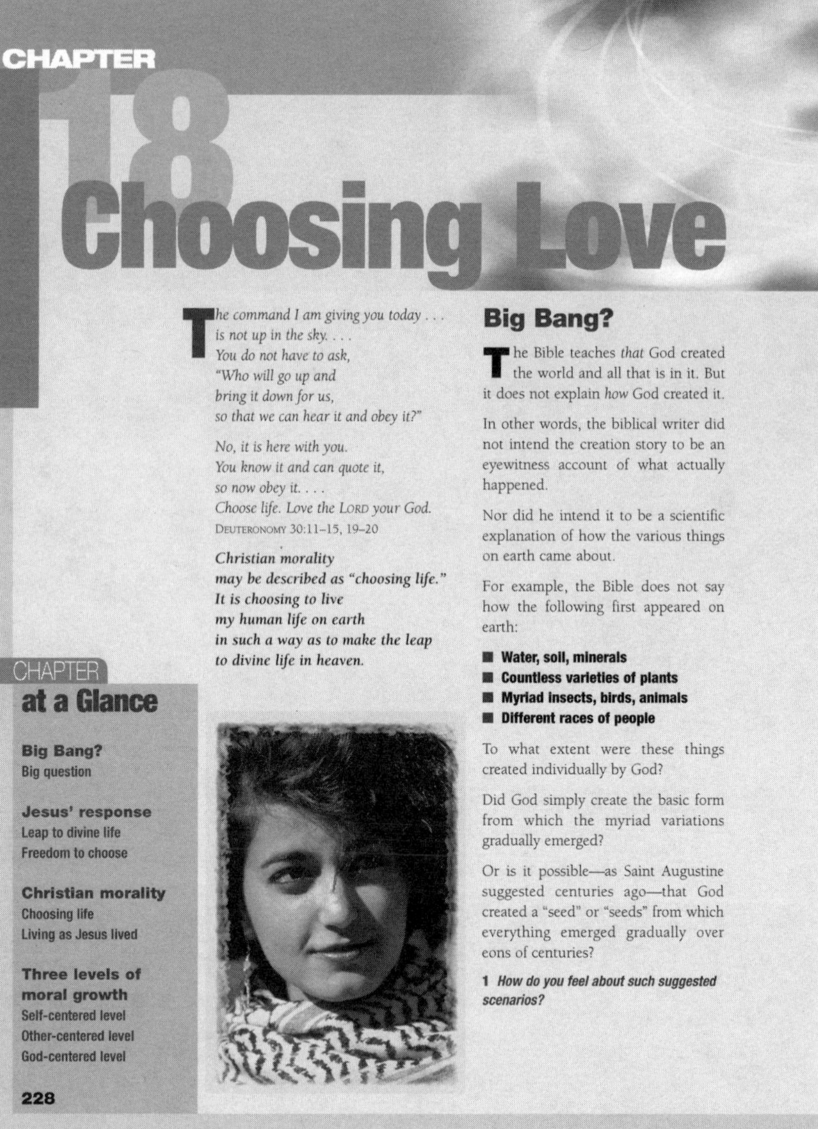
CHAPTER 18

Choosing Love

The command I am giving you today . . .
is not up in the sky. . . .
You do not have to ask,
"Who will go up and
bring it down for us,
so that we can hear it and obey it?"

No, it is here with you.
You know it and can quote it,
so now obey it. . . .
Choose life. Love the LORD your God.
DEUTERONOMY 30:11–15, 19–20

Christian morality may be described as "choosing life." It is choosing to live my human life on earth in such a way as to make the leap to divine life in heaven.

Big Bang?

The Bible teaches *that* God created the world and all that is in it. But it does not explain *how* God created it.

In other words, the biblical writer did not intend the creation story to be an eyewitness account of what actually happened.

Nor did he intend it to be a scientific explanation of how the various things on earth came about.

For example, the Bible does not say how the following first appeared on earth:

- **Water, soil, minerals**
- **Countless varieties of plants**
- **Myriad insects, birds, animals**
- **Different races of people**

To what extent were these things created individually by God?

Did God simply create the basic form from which the myriad variations gradually emerged?

Or is it possible—as Saint Augustine suggested centuries ago—that God created a "seed" or "seeds" from which everything emerged gradually over eons of centuries?

1 How do you feel about such suggested scenarios?

CHAPTER at a Glance

Big Bang?
Big question

Jesus' response
Leap to divine life
Freedom to choose

Christian morality
Choosing life
Living as Jesus lived

Three levels of moral growth
Self-centered level
Other-centered level
God-centered level

228

3 To which group of OT books does the Book of Deuteronomy belong?

NOTEBOOK—Both the OT (46 books) and NT (27 books) have four parts. Have students record them.

Old Testament	New Testament
Pentateuch 5 (+3 spec)	*Gospels 4*
Wisdom 7	*Acts 1*
Historical 13	*Letters 21*
Prophetic 18	*Revelation 1*

The Greek word *Pentateuch* means "five scrolls.") The Pentateuch is also called the *Books of Moses* and the *Torah*, the Hebrew word meaning "the law." (The word "Bible" comes from the Greek word *biblia*, meaning "books."

NOTES

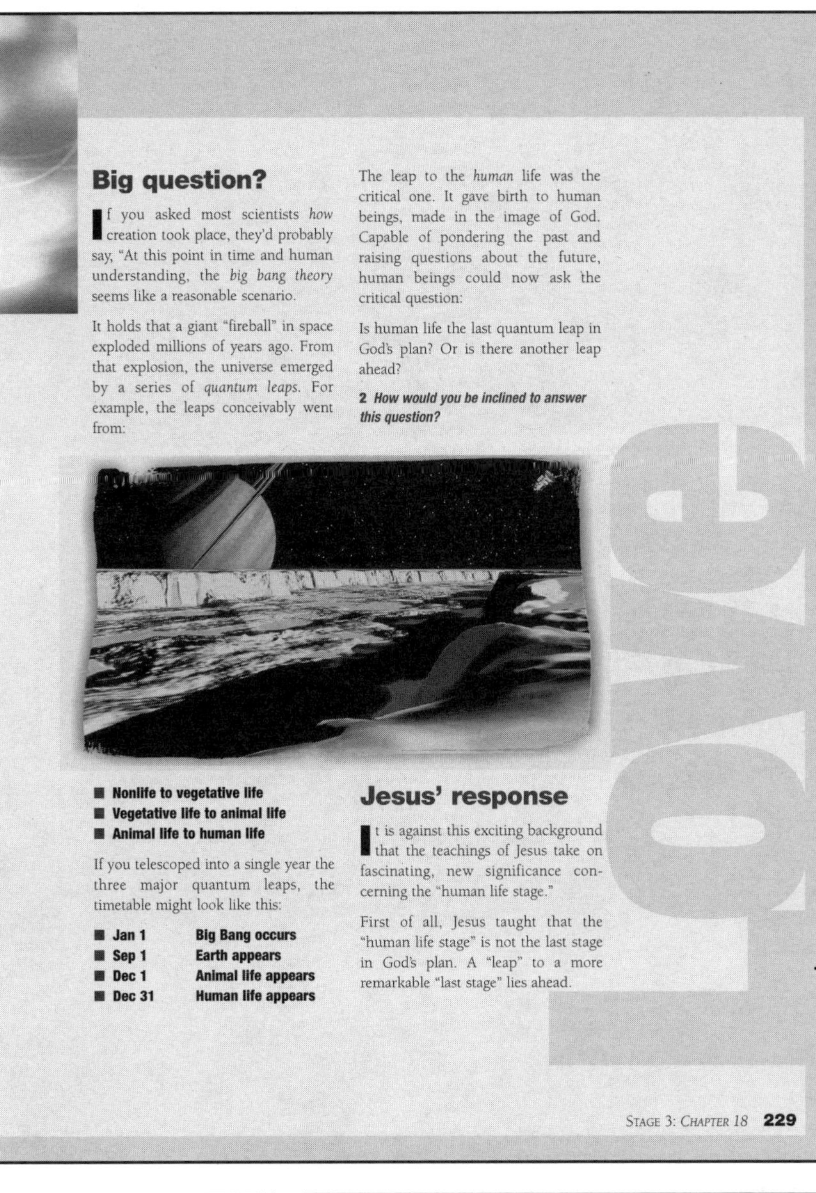

Big question?

If you asked most scientists *how* creation took place, they'd probably say, "At this point in time and human understanding, the *big bang theory* seems like a reasonable scenario.

It holds that a giant "fireball" in space exploded millions of years ago. From that explosion, the universe emerged by a series of *quantum leaps*. For example, the leaps conceivably went from:

- **Nonlife to vegetative life**
- **Vegetative life to animal life**
- **Animal life to human life**

If you telescoped into a single year the three major quantum leaps, the timetable might look like this:

- **Jan 1** **Big Bang occurs**
- **Sep 1** **Earth appears**
- **Dec 1** **Animal life appears**
- **Dec 31** **Human life appears**

The leap to the *human* life was the critical one. It gave birth to human beings, made in the image of God. Capable of pondering the past and raising questions about the future, human beings could now ask the critical question:

Is human life the last quantum leap in God's plan? Or is there another leap ahead?

2 How would you be inclined to answer this question?

Jesus' response

It is against this exciting background that the teachings of Jesus take on fascinating, new significance concerning the "human life stage."

First of all, Jesus taught that the "human life stage" is not the last stage in God's plan. A "leap" to a more remarkable "last stage" lies ahead.

Stage 3: *Chapter 18* **229**

Big Bang?

QUESTION **1** ***How do you feel about such suggested scenarios?***

■ *Evolutionists suggest that we are part of a process that has been going on for billions of years—and is still going on.*

Evolutionists include both theists and nontheists. Nontheists do not, necessarily, see God involved in the evolutionary process. Theists see God involved in the process in an intimately personal way.

Saint Augustine (early 5th century) seems to have had a sense of God's personal, intimate involvement in such a process.

He suggested that God could have created a primeval form or seed from which our universe and life emerged. Though Augustine's theory was rejected in his day, many modern scientists think along similar lines.

For the Church's position on all of this, recall the reference to *Humani generis* on page 11 of this manual.

Big question?

CLARIFY—Scientists, like Carl Sagan, think the "big bang" occurred about fifteen billion years ago.

British astronomer Sir Bernard Lovell says the "critical" moment of the "big bang" came "one second" after the explosion.

In that incredibly brief window of time, the amounts of helium and hydrogen were established. Lovell writes:

> *Had the forces of attraction between the protons been minutely stronger, all the hydrogen in the primeval condensate would have turned to helium.*

Had this happened, no galaxies or life would have emerged.

The "big bang" theory delights theologians. Why? It points to a beginning: to creation. Robert Jastrow, director of NASA's Goddard Institute for Space, in his book *Have Scientists Found God*?, writes:

> *The scientist has scaled the mountains of ignorance; as he pulls himself over the final rock, he is greeted by a band of theologians who have been sitting there for centuries.*

The biblical story of creation suggests the same progressive life-leaps:

Human (conscious) life	*Gen 1:27*
Animal (sense) life	*Gen 1:20, 24*
Vegetative (plant) life	*Gen 1:11*
Nonlife	*Gen 1:10*

QUESTION **2** ***How would you be inclined to answer this question?***

This question prepares the students for "Jesus' response": The "human life" stage is not the last; a more remarkable "leap" lies ahead.

THINK about it

CLARIFY—This saying makes an important point. Whether it is in the area of sports, academics, or the spiritual life, the heart must take the lead, or nothing will happen.

Jesus' response

CLARIFY—The "final leap" in God's plan is the leap to eternal life. One scripture scholar says of John's Gospel:

> ■ *The mission of Jesus in John is often conceived as the bringing of life. This is eternal life, primarily viewed as an eschatological [end-time] reality. . . .*
>
> *John's conception [of eternal life as an end-time reality] should not be taken as implying that there is no present transformation of the Christian through faith and sacramental participation in the life of Jesus.*
>
> *Rather, it emphasizes more than Paul the difference between the inchoate ["growing" or "emerging"] life in the believing Christian and the fullness of eschatological realization.* JOHN L. MCKENZIE: DICTIONARY OF THE BIBLE

In other words, the "seed" of eternal life is in us now. The "harvest" or "final leap" will not be "fully" realized until heaven.

Freedom to choose

CLARIFY—Stress the idea that we choose eternal life, that is, we must freely choose to take the next quantum leap.

> ■ *Formerly, the leap was random. With the advent of consciousness, the leap is a matter of conscious, free choice.*

QUESTION **3 *Why do you think God gives to each human the awesome choice to accept or reject the invitation to divine life?***

> ■ *The simple answer is that this is the way God chose to set the whole thing up. Theologically, love demands that we be free to accept or reject it. A loss of freedom means a loss of love.*

Christian morality

CLARIFY—There are many people today who believe the "parable" described in this section is moving toward "reality" with each passing century. Regardless of your take on this, the parable illustrates in a contemporary way our task in this world.

CLARIFY—Stress the last three paragraphs of this section:

> ■ *Old age and illness make it impossible for human beings to live indefinitely on planet Earth. Jesus has revealed, however,*

NOTES

Leap to divine life

I have come
in order that you might have life—
life in all its fullness. . . .

For what my Father wants is that all
who see the Son and believe in him
should have eternal life.
And I will raise them to life
on the last day. JOHN 10:10; 6:40

Jesus teaches that another "leap" lies ahead. It is the leap to *eternal, divine life*. Or to put it another way, it is the leap from a human life to a share in the very life of the Holy Trinity.

We explicitly affirm our faith in this final stage of our destiny in every Mass. When the priest pours a few drops of water into the wine, he prays silently:

By the mystery of this water and wine
may we come to share
in the divinity of Christ
who humbled himself to share
in our humanity.

This brings us to a second thing that Jesus makes clear about the human life stage of creation.

THINK about it

The hand will not reach out for what the heart does not long for.

German proverb

Freedom to choose

Prior to human life, all leaps to a new life took place randomly and blindly.

In other words, prior to the human stage, no other stage of development possessed the ability or the freedom to choose to leap to the next stage.

With the arrival of human life, all this changed. God gave to human beings the awesome responsibility of taking control of their destiny.

God gave them the power and the freedom to choose to make the leap to eternal, divine life or not.

So the teaching of Jesus makes two points clear about human beings. God:

- **Invites us to share in the divine life**
- **Leaves us free to accept or reject it**

3 *Why do you think God gives to each human the awesome choice to accept or reject the invitation to divine life?*

Christian morality

Imagine that the deterioration of planet earth made it impossible for human life to survive beyond ten more years. What would happen?

Scientists would begin a frantic search for another planet that would be capable of supporting human life. Suppose they found one. What then? We would be ecstatic!

230 STAGE 3: CHAPTER 18

But there is *bad* news and *good* news. The bad news is that life on the new planet is significantly different from life on planet Earth. The *good* news is that human beings have the ability to adapt to life on the new planet. It is not easy; but it is possible.

What do you think would happen at this point? Scientists would learn everything they could about life on the new planet. Then they would build centers on earth reproducing the exact conditions of the new planet.

At these centers, they would conduct programs to teach people how to adapt to the new life. Obviously, only people who persevered in adapting to the new life would be shuttled to the new planet.

This parable gives us an insight into what Christian morality is all about. Think of it this way.

Old age and illness make it impossible for human beings to live indefinitely on planet Earth. Jesus has revealed, however, that there is another planet, so to speak, beyond this one: heaven. But life in heaven is totally different from life on earth.

But there is *good* news. Jesus taught us how to live in this life in a way that will adapt us and prepare us for life in heaven.

Viewed this way, Christian morality is simply choosing to live in this life in a way that prepares us for the leap to divine life.

4 To what extent does this view of Christian morality differ from the one you have had up to this point in your life?

Sheila Cassidy

England's Doctor Sheila Cassidy spent four years working among the very poor in Chile. One day she was arrested for treating a political enemy of the state. For four days she was tortured and questioned. She wrote later:

For the first time in my life
I thought I was going to die. . . .
I was experiencing
in some slight way
what Christ had suffered. . . .

I suddenly felt
enormously loved . . .
because I felt I had in a way
participated in his suffering. . . .
I remembered the prayer
Dietrich Bonhoeffer wrote
while he was waiting execution:

"In me there is darkness,
but in Thee there is light. . . .
Lord, whatsoever this day
may bring
Thy name be praised."

"Prayer Under Duress"

After three weeks in solitary and five weeks in a detention camp, she was expelled from Chile and returned safely to England.

that there is another planet, so to speak, beyond this one: heaven. But life in heaven is totally different from life on earth.

But there is good news. Jesus taught us how to live in this life in a way that will adapt us and prepare us for life in heaven.

Viewed this way, Christian morality is simply choosing to live in this life in a way that prepares us for the leap to divine life.

QUESTION ***4 To what extent does this view of Christian morality differ from the one you have had up to this point in your life?***

DISCUSS—After sharing with the class the following comments of a young man, ask them: Why do/don't you agree with him?

I wish I had been born atheistic, rather than Catholic. Then I could have done everything I ever wanted to do. And I wouldn't have committed a single sin, because I wouldn't have known better.

Finally, in my old age, I'd get converted, be baptized on my death bed and go straight to heaven. Wow! What a scenario!

The boy's view of morality is just the opposite of the view in the text. His view comes down to this: "Something is bad because it is a sin, rather than something is a sin because it is bad." (A fuller discussion of this issue will be treated in the third reflection on page 237. You might want to check it now.)

Up Close & Personal

Sheila Cassidy quotes a prayer by Dietrich Bonhoeffer (1906–1945). A brilliant Lutheran pastor and theologian, his life was cut short when he was accused and convicted of conspiring to topple Hitler. A prison doctor described his execution:

Between 5 and 6 o'clock the prisoners . . . were taken from their cells and the verdict of the court martial read to them.

Through the half-open door in one room of the huts I saw Pastor Bonhoeffer . . . kneeling on the floor, praying fervently. . . .

I was most deeply moved by the way
this loveable man prayed, so devout
and so certain that God heard his prayer.

At the place of execution,
he . . . climbed the steps of the gallows,
brave and composed.
His death ensued after a few seconds.

In the almost 50 years
that I have worked as a doctor,
I have rarely seen a man die so submissive
to the will of God.

E. BETHGE: *DIETRICH BONHOEFFER*

THINK about it

ACTIVITY—Have the students respond to the following anonymously:

1 *What is the meaning of the billboard sign?*
2 *How would you answer God's question?*
3 *Explain your answer to God.*

Choosing life

QUESTION **5** ***Explain how the average person might attempt to sow: (a) love where there is hatred, (b) pardon where there is injury, (c) faith where there is doubt, (d) hope where there is despair.***

■ *This is the kind of Christian ministry that every average person is called to by Baptism and Confirmation. Here are some examples initiated by ordinary people.*

(1) One day Philadelphia housewife Rita Schiavone visited a bedridden blind person. She was shocked to find that the woman had barely enough food to keep her alive. She was even more shocked to learn that other shut-ins were in similar situations.

Rita began "Aid for Friends." Soon her organization numbered over 3,000 volunteers who cook, transport, and deliver food to shut-ins. It also arranges visits to shut-ins to give them regular companionship.

(2) Massachusetts teacher Bob Anastas was outraged when two of his students were killed by a drunken driver.

He organized SADD (Students Against Drunk Drivers). It is now a nationwide organization and is becoming a powerful force in the fight to get drunken drivers off the road.

(3) Ruth Colvin was appalled by the number of adults, especially immigrants in her area, who could not read or write

Choosing life

The choice that Moses set before each Israelite is the same choice that God sets before each human being:

I am now giving you
the choice between life and death . . .
and I call heaven and earth
to witness the choice you make.
Choose life. DEUTERONOMY 30:19

Our Christian calling in this life is to choose to live in a way that prepares us to make the leap to *divine* life in the next.

Or, to put it in biblical imagery, it is to "plant the seeds" in this life that will produce a "harvest of eternal life" in the next life. Paul puts it this way:

You will reap exactly what you plant.
If you plant
in the field of your natural desires,
from it you will gather
the harvest of death.

If you plant in the field of the Spirit,
from the Spirit you will gather
the harvest of eternal life.
GALATIANS 6:7–8

What I say is this:
let the Spirit direct your lives. . . .
The Spirit has given us life . . .
[and] must also control our lives.
GALATIANS 5:16, 25

Here we should point out what "planting in the field of the Spirit" involves. It involves letting the Spirit make us instruments of God's love. The "Peace Prayer" of Saint Francis expresses it in these memorable words:

Lord,
make me an instrument of your peace.

Where there is hatred, let me sow love;
where there is injury, pardon;
where there is doubt, faith;
where there is despair, hope;
where there is darkness, light;
where there is sadness, joy.

Grant that I may not so much
seek to be consoled as to console;
to be understood as to understand;
to be loved as to love;
for it is in giving that we receive;
it is in pardoning that we are pardoned;
and it is in dying
that we are born to eternal life.

5 ***Explain how the average person might attempt to sow (a) love where there is hatred, (b) pardon where there is injury, (c) faith where there is doubt, (d) hope where there is despair.***

THINK about it

God asks . . .

"Will the road you're on get you to my place?"

Billboard sign

Living as Jesus lived

This brings us to yet an even more personal way of describing Christian morality.

At the Last Supper Jesus washed the feet of his Apostles. When he finished, he sat down at table again and said to them:

I have set an example for you,
so that you will do
just what I have done for you. . . .
Love one another, just as I love you.
JOHN 13:15, 15:12

232 STAGE 3: CHAPTER 18

English. She decided that something should be done about the situation.

So she founded "Literacy Volunteers of America," a program to teach adults to read. It now operates in most of our states and has taught over 100,000 adults.

Living as Jesus lived

CLARIFY—Trying to live and love as Jesus did is not easy in today's world. In fact, sometimes it is downright hard. Someone compared it to trying to "walk on water."

Recall the story in Matthew 14:22–31. Jesus invited Peter to come to him across the stormy waters of the lake. Peter stepped out of the boat and began to walk.

NOTES

A more personal way of describing Christian morality is as follows: It is saying "yes" to Jesus' invitation to live and love as he did, that we may be raised to life by Jesus on the last day.

Living and loving as Jesus did is not easy. This is because original sin has flawed the human intellect and will. As a result, we are not always able to do what we would like to do.

Paul speaks for all of us when he writes:

Even though the desire to do good
is in me,
I am not able to do it.
I don't do the good I want to do; instead,
I do the evil that I do not want to do. . . .

Who will rescue me from this body
that is taking me to death?

Thanks be to God,
who does this
through our Lord Jesus Christ.
ROMANS 7:18–19, 24–25

Christian morality is a challenge. We can meet it only by remaining united with Jesus, who said:

A branch cannot bear fruit of itself;
it can do so only if it remains in the vine.
In the same way you cannot bear fruit
unless you remain in me.

I am the vine,
and you are the branches. . . .
You can do nothing without me.
JOHN 15:4–5

6 *What is meant by "union with Christ"? What is there about modern life that makes it difficult to remain in union with Christ?*

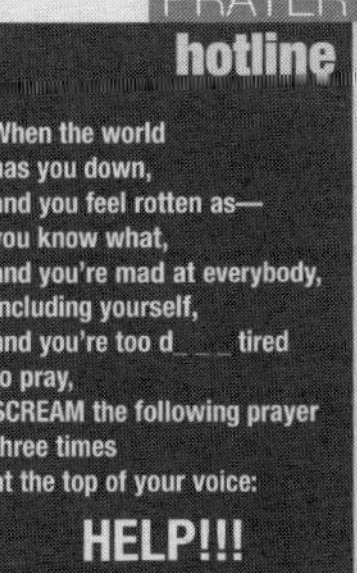

PRAYER
hotline
When the world
has you down,
and you feel rotten as—
you know what,
and you're mad at everybody,
including yourself,
and you're too d___ tired
to pray,
SCREAM the following prayer
three times
at the top of your voice:
HELP!!!

STAGE 3: *CHAPTER 18* **233**

But then Peter became alarmed at the high winds and the high waves. For a brief moment he took his eyes off Jesus. And that was his fatal mistake. He began to sink.

Christian life is like that. Jesus has invited us to come to him across the stormy waters of life.

As we walk toward Jesus, we become alarmed. For a brief moment we take our eyes off him and focus on the high winds and the high waves (difficulties of this life).

And this is our fatal mistake. We begin to sink. When this happens, we must do what Peter did. We must call out to Jesus for help.

QUESTION **6 *What is meant by "union with Christ"? What is there about modern life that makes it difficult to remain in union with Christ?***

■ *It means remaining in union with Jesus (the vine). Unless the branch remains united to the vine, it dies. We remain in union with Christ especially through the sacraments, prayer, and good works.*

PRAYER hotline

DISCUSS—When the humor of this prayer subsides, we begin to realize that it makes a very important point about prayer.

Ask the students: What point does it make? (Prayer must come from the heart.)

John Bunyan (1628–88) was the author of *Pilgrim's Progress* in 1678. It is said that for the next 200 years, next to the Bible, it was the most widely read book.

It dealt with our search for God through trial and tribulation, it condemned religious "formalism," and it assured simple, uneducated people that they had value in God's sight.

Ask the students: What do we mean by religious "formalism"?

■ *It is all show and no soul. God says to the people through the prophet Isaiah:*

"When you lift your hands in prayer,
I will not look at you.
No matter how much you pray,
I will not listen,
for your hands are covered with blood.

"Wash yourselves clean.
Stop all this evil that I see you doing.
Yes, stop doing evil and learn to do right.
See that justice is done—
help those who are oppressed,
give orphans their rights,
and defend widows."

"I, the LORD, have spoken." ISAIAH 1:17, 20

Share Your meditation

CLARIFY—You cannot make the leap to divine life (become a butterfly) until you are willing (to stop crawing) to open your heart to divine grace and live and love as Jesus did.

LIFE Connection

CLARIFY—This inspiring statement spells out in a concrete, everyday approach how to begin to live and love as Jesus did.

Moral growth

CLARIFY—The model of moral growth followed here is based on one by Soren Kierkegaard (1813–1855). He was a Danish theologian and philosopher. A prolific writer, he frequently signed his works with pen names.

■ *Stress that "every human being follows a unique path that has its own twists and turns, its own dips and rises. What a formulation like Kierkegaard's does is to help us better understand the general dynamic involved in moral growth."*

Kierkegaard once said that there was no such thing as "being Christian," only "becoming Christian." This is another way of saying that moral growth is an ongoing process. It is a never-ending journey.

Self-centered level

CLARIFY—Kierkegaard referred to these three stages as the aesthetic (self-centered) stage, the ethical (other-centered) stage, and the religious (God-centered) stage.

■ *The word "aesthetic" comes from the Greek word* aesthetikos, *which pertains to "sense perception." Recall that at this stage we "live largely under the influence of our senses and our emotions."*

SHARE YOUR meditation

The butterfly was happy because it was her birthday. So she called over to the caterpillar.

"It's my birthday. Ask me anything and if I can, I will grant it.

The caterpillar thought and thought until his head hurt. Then he said, "Tell me how to become a butterfly."

The butterfly said, "That's very difficult. There is only one way to do it. You must want to fly so badly that you're willing to stop crawling." The same is true of love.

■ **What point does the above story make?**
■ **How do you see it applying to your life?**

Moral growth

Learning to live and love as Jesus did is a growth process that continues all of our life. It involves three stages or "levels of growth."

■ **Self-centered**
■ **Other-centered**
■ **God-centered**

Let's take a closer look at each of these three levels of moral growth.

Self-centered level

During this first level, we live largely by our senses and emotions. Our main concern is our own needs and enjoyment.

At this level we are basically selfish. We want to be free to do whatever we want. We don't realize it, but we are anything but free.

We are slaves of our prejudices and passions. We pursue one fleeting pleasure after another.

We see Jesus' teaching as a *restriction* (to our freedom). It forbids us to do what we want to do. It is something that cramps our style. At this level, we see *sin* merely as *violation* (of a restriction).

As long as we remain at this level, we are doomed to unhappiness.

Other-centered level

We advance to the next level when we begin to shift our focus from ourselves to others.

We do this by assuming social obligations, such as friendships and commitments. By accepting these responsibilities, we take a giant step toward personal freedom.

LIFE Connection

DO a little more
than you're paid to do;

GIVE a little more
than you have to;

TRY a little harder
than you want to;

AIM a little higher
than you think is possible.

Art Linkletter (slightly adapted)

234 STAGE 3: CHAPTER 18

The prime example of the self-centered stage is a small child. But this stage is not restricted to childhood. Some adults never quite emerge from it.

DISCUSS—Ask the students: At what age would you say a person (under normal conditions) begins to break out of the self-centered stage and progress to the other-centered stage?

■ *People would probably debate this. Children begin the "breakout" when they begin to become aware of the rights of others. The "breakout" takes a giant step forward in adolescence.*

Other-centered level

CLARIFY—Stress the relationship between law and love. Law is love's servant.

NOTES

At this stage, we see Jesus' teaching not as a restriction and as something negative. Rather, we see it as something freeing and positive.

Only in this light can we appreciate the psalmist when he prays to God: "How I love your law!" PSALM 119:97

The psalmist saw God's law as "freeing us from" our own ignorance and passion and "freeing us for" happiness and service to God and neighbor.

At this level, we see Jesus' teaching as a *guide* (to growth and happiness). And we see *sin* as *infidelity* (to growth). It is living irresponsibly and stupidly.

God-centered level

We advance to the final level when we discover our personal relationship with God. This discovery develops out of an awareness of our true *identity* (we are God's children) and our true *destiny* (we are called to eternal life).

At this level, we see Jesus' teaching as concrete signs of God's love for us. God wants us to be happy. God wants to share his own divine life with us.

At this level, we also discover Jesus and why he came into the world: to "free us from sin" and to "free us to love God and neighbor." To put it another way, Jesus came to bring us the "fullness" of life: eternal, divine life.

Finally, at this level, we discover the true relationship between Jesus' teaching and love. *Jesus' teaching* is an invitation (to love). Jesus said:

Those who accept
my commandments and obey them
are the ones who love me. JOHN 14:21

And so, at the God-centered level we see Jesus' teaching as an *invitation* (to love). We see sin as a *refusal* (to love).

Sin is saying "no" to Jesus' invitation to live and love as he did.

Viewed this way, Christian morality is choosing to live as Jesus modeled and taught: in a way that prepares us to make the leap to divine life with him in the world to come.

FAITH Connection

We may sum up the way that people at each level of moral growth view Jesus' teaching and sin as follows:

	Jesus' teaching
Self	**Restriction to freedom**
Other	**Guide to growth**
God	**Invitation to love**
	Sin
Self	**Violation of restriction**
Other	**Infidelity to growth**
God	**Refusal to love**

■ *First, law serves as an invitation to action when we are not as responsive to love's invitation as we should be. In other words, just as Mother's Day or Thanksgiving Day reminds us that a love response should be made, so does law.*

Second, law serves as a guide to action (growth) when we are not certain what love invites us to do.

DISCUSS—The relationship between law and love puts a heavy burden on lawmakers and law enforcers. They must always remember that love does not do away with law, but that law can do away with love. Ask the students: What does this sentence mean?

■ *The first half of the sentence, "love does not do away with law," means we need laws to invite and guide us in loving. We are flawed human beings who still suffer from the effects of original sin.*

The second half of the sentence, "law can do away with love," means we can start doing things in a "legalistic" way. We can keep the "letter of the law" and lose sight of the "spirit of the law."

This happened to some of the Pharisees and occasioned this scathing rebuke from Jesus: "Outside you appear good to everybody, but inside you are full of hypocrisy and sins."
MATTHEW 23:28

God-centered level

REVIEW—Have the students recall the conditions that must be present before a sin becomes mortal (See page 172).

Mortal sin
- *Grave matter*
- *Sufficient reflection*
- *Full consent of the will*

CLARIFY—Review three important things concerning sin in general:

1 *Venial sin occurs when one of the above three conditions is only partially fulfilled.*

2 *Sufficient reflection does not mean "meditating" on what I am about to do. It is enough that my conscience tells me in a general way that an action is a mortal sin.*

3 *Full consent of the will is impeded by such things as significant fear and significant pressure.*

FAITH Connection

This tiny table contains a concise summary of the entire section on "Moral growth" (pages 234–35). Have the students memorize and be able to explain clearly each of the three levels under (1) Jesus' teaching and (2) Sin, as outlined in the table.

Recap

A fitting recap to Christian morality is this paraphrased statement from *The Spiritual Exercises of St. Ignatius.* It is called "The Principle and Foundation."

Read it slowly, stopping after each statement and asking: Do you agree with it? If not, reword it to so that you can agree with it.

1 *I believe that God created me to share my life and love with him and other people forever.*

2 *I believe that God created all the other things to help me achieve this lofty goal.*

3 *I believe, therefore, that I should use the other things God created insofar as they help me attain my goal and abstain from them insofar as they hinder me.*

4 *It follows therefore that I should not prefer certain things to others. That is, I should not value, automatically, health over sickness, wealth over poverty, honor over dishonor, or a long life over a short one. My sole norm for valuing and preferring a thing should be this: How well does it help me attain the end for which God created me?*

Review

DAILY QUIZ—The review questions may be assigned (one or two at a time) for homework or a daily quiz.

CHAPTER TESTS—Reproducible chapter tests are found in Appendix A. For consistency and ease in grading, quizzes are restricted to (1) "Matching," (2) "True/False," and (3) "Fill in the Blanks."

TEST ANSWERS—The following are the answers to the test for Chapter 18 (see Appendix A, page 329). Each correct answer worth 4 points.

Recap

If you asked most scientists how creation took place, they'd probably say, "The *big bang theory is a reasonable scenario.*" In any event, the leap to the *human* life was the critical one. It gave birth to human beings, who could now ask the critical question: *Is human life the last quantum leap in God's plan? Or is there another leap ahead?*

Jesus taught that another "leap" lies ahead. It is the leap from human life to a share in the divine life of the Trinity. Jesus also taught that we are free to accept or reject God's invitation to divine life.

In this context, Christian morality is accepting God's invitation to live life on earth in such a way as to make the leap to this awesome life.

Christian morality involves a journey of growth that begins in childhood and never ends. It moves forward gradually through three levels:

- **Self-centered**
- **Other-centered**
- **God-centered**

Our view of *law* and *sin* is conditioned by the growth level at which we find ourselves.

Review

1 Explain briefly (a) the "big bang" theory, (b) the "critical leap" in this theory and why, (c) the "critical question" human beings could now ask.

2 Explain Jesus' twofold teaching about whether or not the "human life stage" is the final stage in God's plan.

3 Describe (a) our Christian calling in this life, (b) what "planting in the field of the Spirit" involves, (c) a *personal* way of describing Christian morality.

4 Explain (a) why Christian morality is a difficult challenge, (b) the image Jesus used to teach us how we can successfully meet this difficult challenge.

5 List and briefly describe (a) the three levels of moral growth, (b) how people in each level view Jesus' teaching, (c) how people in each level view sin.

Matching

1 = b	2 = c	3 = b	4 = b
5 = a	6 = a	7 = c	8 = b
9 = a			

True/False

1 = F	2 = F	3 = T	4 = T
5 = T	6 = T	7 = F	8 = T
9 = T	10 = F	11 = T	12 = T
13 = F	14 = T	15 = F	16 = T

NOTES

Reflect

1 In his novel *The Source*, James Michener recreates a time in history when people worshiped many gods.

In one scene, he portrays the people of Makor sacrificing infants and young children to their new god, Melak. Then Michener explains why the people threw out their old gods and adopted a new god.

It was partly because
his demands on them were severe
and partly because
they had grown somewhat contemptuous
of their local gods
precisely because
they were not demanding enough.

A Gallup poll shows that many modern Christians are like the people of Makor. They do not think their religion is very demanding. That poll raises a question: Why do many modern Christians think Jesus' teachings are not demanding?

■ ***Why do you think many people feel that Jesus' teachings are not very demanding?***
■ ***On a scale of one (not very) to ten (very), how demanding do you think Jesus' teachings are?***

2 One girl answered the two questions above this way: Concerning the first question she said, "Either they don't understand it or they don't take it seriously."

She gave this example of a demanding teaching which she feels many people don't take seriously: "Love your enemies, do good to those who hate you." Luke 6:27

The girl answered the second question by giving Christianity a rating of "seven."

■ ***Why do you agree/disagree with her answer to (a) the first question, (b) the second question?***

3 In her book *Pilgrim at Tinker Creek*, Annie Dillard writes:

I read about an Eskimo hunter
who asked the local missionary priest,
"If I did not know about God and sin,
would I go to hell?"
"No," said the priest,
"not if you did not know."
"Then why," asked the Eskimo earnestly,
"did you tell me?"

■ ***How would you answer the hunter?***

Reflect

1 a) *Why do you think many people feel Jesus' teachings are not very demanding?* b) *On a scale of one (not very) to ten (very), how demanding do you think Jesus' teachings are?*

■ *Have the students write out their "personal conclusions," share them in groups, and come to a "group conclusion." Next, have the groups share their conclusion with the class and come to a "class conclusion."*

2 *Why do you agree/disagree with her answer to (a) the first question, (b) the second question?*

■ *Some people have a cafeteria mentality, when it comes to the Gospel. Ask the students: What is a "cafeteria" mentality? (People take what they like and leave what they dislike.) Commenting on this approach, Saint Augustine said centuries ago: "If you believe what you like and reject what you don't like, you don't believe in Jesus, but in yourself."*

Ask the students: What did he mean by that? (You set yourself up as judge over Jesus' teachings, deciding where you think he was right—and where he was wrong.)

3 *How would you answer the hunter?*

The Eskimo hunter's question implies that a thing is bad because it is a sin. The opposite is true: A thing is a sin because it is bad. (Be sure the students understand this critical distinction.)

The Eskimo hunter is at the first stage of moral growth. He views law as a restriction that God has placed on the human race. He views sin simply as a violation of a restriction. He is not even close to the second stage (seeing law as a guide to his growth—and happiness), much less to the third stage (seeing law as an invitation to love). To better illustrate, imagine this dialogue:

HUNTER: If I did not know about sin, for example, that drugs, theft, murder, and sexual abuse of children were wrong, would I go to hell if I did these things?
PRIEST: No, not if you did not know.
HUNTER: Then why did you tell me?
PRIEST: Because God wants you to know that doing these things will destroy you and your loved ones. They will never bring you happiness.

Seen from this viewpoint, God's law is a great gift: a guide to growth and happiness. This explains why the psalmist could sing: "I have greater wisdom than old men, because I obey your commands. . . .
I love them with all my heart."
Psalm 119:100, 167

PRAYER TIME with the Lord

QUESTION **_Compose a brief prayer to Jesus explaining what threatens to keep you from having this vision of the world. End by asking Jesus to help you acquire it._**

To help your students get started, you might share this excerpt from *Desiderata* by Max Ehrmann with your students. It contains the same upbeat spirit of the Fra Giovanni excerpt. According to Sam McGarrity, associate editor of *Guideposts* magazine:

> ■ *Its message . . . has comforted and inspired millions of people. . . . In the sixties hippies passed it out on street corners. In 1972, it was recorded as a narrative song that sold more than a million copies. It has been recited at weddings and funerals and . . . used in drug rehabilitation programs:*
>
> *"Be gentle with yourself.*
> *You are a child of the universe,*
> *no less than the trees and the stars;*
> *you have a right to be here.*
>
> *"And whether or not it is clear to you,*
> *no doubt the universe*
> *is unfolding as it should.*
>
> *"Therefore be at peace with God . . .*
> *[and] keep peace with your soul. . . .*
> *With all its sham, drudgery,*
> *and broken dreams,*
> *it is still a beautiful world."*

PRAYER Journal

QUESTION **_Compose (a) an e-mail to Jesus explaining your situation and (b) an e-mail that Jesus may send to you in reply._**

To help the students get started, share with them this sample e-mail:

Dear Jesus,

> *I'll bet you're surprised to hear from me! Yeah! It's really me. I'll get to the point. I used to be a tugboat, but I've run out of gas. I don't know what's happened to me. I know you're busy, but could you take a minute to tell me how I can shake whatever it is that's making me like this. I'm not a real good follower, but I am*
>
> *One of your fans,*
> *Todd*

Here's Jesus' e-mail back:

Dear Todd,

> *I've been wondering when you'd get in touch with me. I'm aware of your case. It can't be solved by e-mail. It will take a series of face-to-face sessions. Let's begin tonight in your room, just before you turn in. I'm glad you're a fan.*
>
> *Your best friend,*
> *Jesus*

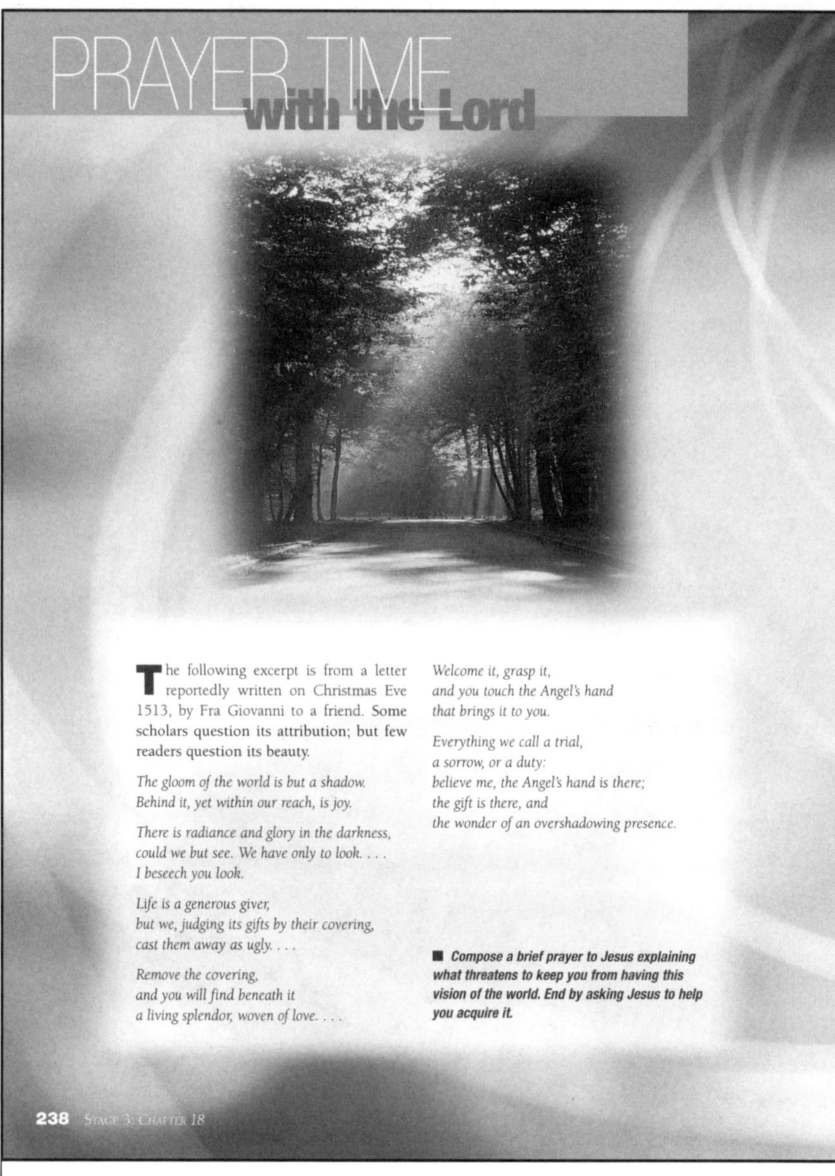

PRAYER TIME with the Lord

The following excerpt is from a letter reportedly written on Christmas Eve 1513, by Fra Giovanni to a friend. Some scholars question its attribution; but few readers question its beauty.

The gloom of the world is but a shadow.
Behind it, yet within our reach, is joy.

There is radiance and glory in the darkness,
could we but see. We have only to look. . . .
I beseech you look.

Life is a generous giver,
but we, judging its gifts by their covering,
cast them away as ugly. . . .

Remove the covering,
and you will find beneath it
a living splendor, woven of love. . . .

Welcome it, grasp it,
and you touch the Angel's hand
that brings it to you.

Everything we call a trial,
a sorrow, or a duty:
believe me, the Angel's hand is there;
the gift is there, and
the wonder of an overshadowing presence.

■ **_Compose a brief prayer to Jesus explaining what threatens to keep you from having this vision of the world. End by asking Jesus to help you acquire it._**

238 STAGE 3: CHAPTER 18

NOTES

PRAYER Journal

Christians come in three models: rafts, sailboats, and tugboats.

Rafts follow Jesus only when someone pulls or pushes them.

Sailboats follow Jesus only in good weather. When stormy weather comes, they go with the wind and the waves. In other words, they follow the crowd more than they follow Jesus.

Tugboats follow Jesus in all weather. They don't always travel fast; but they always travel straight.

■ ***Compose (a) an e-mail to Jesus explaining your situation and (b) an e-mail that Jesus may send to you in reply.***

SCRIPTURE Journal

1	**I am in the Father**	**John 14:1–14**
2	**Remain in me**	**John 15:1–11**
3	**You are like light**	**Matthew 5:1–16**
4	**Seek heaven**	**Colossians 3:1–17**
5	**Share God's glory**	**Romans 8:18–30**

■ ***Pick one of the above passages. Read it prayerfully and write a short statement to Jesus expressing your feelings about it.***

Stage 3: Chapter 18 239

SCRIPTURE Journal

QUESTION ***Pick one of the above passages. Read it prayerfully and write a short statement to Jesus expressing your feelings about it.***

You may simply wish to read the following excerpt from the second reading and have the students write on it:

> *I am the vine, and you are the branches. Those who remain in me, and I in them, will bear much fruit.* John 15:5

Classroom Resources

CATECHISM

Catechism of the Catholic Church *Second Edition*

For further enrichment, you might refer to:

1. Morality	Index	p. 826
	Glossary	p. 888
2. Duties, (Religious)	Index	p. 785
3. Life	Index	pp. 815–17
	Glossary	p. 886

See also: Law, Love, Creation.

—Available from the United States Catholic Conference, Washington DC

CD-ROM

The Way of the Lord Jesus

Germaine Grisez

A two-volume resource work on Church moral teachings.

—Available on the Welcome to the Catholic Church CD-ROM from Harmony Media Inc., Cervais, OR

VIDEOS

A Case of Conscience

Twenty-minute, award-winning drama about making choices.

—Available from Brown-Roa, Dubuque IA

Godspell

This wonderful Broadway musical reenacts the parables, the Last Supper, and the Passion in modern-day New York City. 105 minutes.

—Available from Oblate Media, St. Louis, MO

NOTE

For a list of (1) General resources for professional background and (2) Addresses, phone/fax numbers of major publishing companies, see Appendix B of this Resource Manual.

CHAPTER 19
Loving God

If we obey God's commands,
then we are sure that we know him.
If we say that we know him,
but do not obey his commands . . .
there is no truth in us.

But if we obey his word,
we are the ones whose love for God
has been made perfect. . . .
Those who obey God's commands
live in union with God
and God lives in union with them.
1 JOHN 2:3, 5–6, 3:24

The first three commandments invite us to make love of God the center of our lives; and they provide us with concrete guidelines for doing this.

CHAPTER **at a Glance**

The Ten Commandments
Jesus and the commandments
Jesus fulfills commandments
Gift of the commandments

1st commandment
Superstition
Divination
Spiritism

2nd commandment
Curses
Oaths

3rd commandment
Holy days
Precepts of the Church

240

The Ten Commandments

How might a television news crew file a report from Mount Sinai shortly after Moses received the Ten Commandments from God? Here's one imaginative scenario:

ANCHOR	*This is Joel ben Isaac reporting from Mount Sinai.* *The Hebrew leader Moses just came down the mountain with a lightning bolt: ten commandments from God. Our roving reporter, Rebecca, is at the scene. What's the mood there, Rebecca?*
REPORTER	*Ugly, Joel! Really ugly! That lightning bolt has this crowd up in arms. Pro-choicers call it a criminal attack on human freedom.*
ANCHOR	*How are these laws likely to affect the average people, Rebecca?*
REPORTER	*That's hard to say, Joel. But one camel trader put it this way: "It's going to take more than ten rules to reverse habits that have been built up over the centuries."*

CHAPTER at a Glance

The aim of this chapter is twofold in scope: 1) to show how Jesus redefined and transformed the commandments into:

1. *Signs of love*
2. *Invitations to love*
3. *Guides to love*

2) to present an overview of the first three commandments.

1. *Worship no God but me*
2. *Do not use my name for evil purposes*
3. *Observe the Sabbath and keep it holy*

DISCUSS—Have a student read aloud the three introductory paragraphs. They begin with, "If we obey God's commands . . ." and end with ". . . guidelines for doing this." Ask the students: Can you name the first three commandments?

The Ten Commandments

ACTIVITY—Dramatize the "live" report from Mount Sinai. Have one student sit at your desk and be the anchor person. Have a second student stand at the window and look out (as if viewing the situation at Mount Sinai), acting as the roving reporter.

(Caution: Be sure to adjust the names in the dialogue to the actual names of the students involved in the dramatization.)

ACTIVITY—Consider having a group of four drama students (or creative ones) do three on-the-spot, "unrehearsed" interviews:

Cast of characters

Student 1	*TV reporter*
Student 2	*Pro-choice Israelite*
Student 3	*God-fearing Israelite*
Student 4	*Camel trader*

The TV reporter should be warned in advance in order to prepare (in writing) three or four questions that they will ask. The questions might revolve around how they see the Ten Commandments impacting:

1. *Their personal lives*
2. *The lives of the Israelite people*
3. *The future of the world*

> *QUESTION* **1** ***How do you think the Israelites* really *reacted to God's Ten Commandments?***

Exodus 24:3 reads:

Moses went and told the people
all the LORD's commands

NOTES

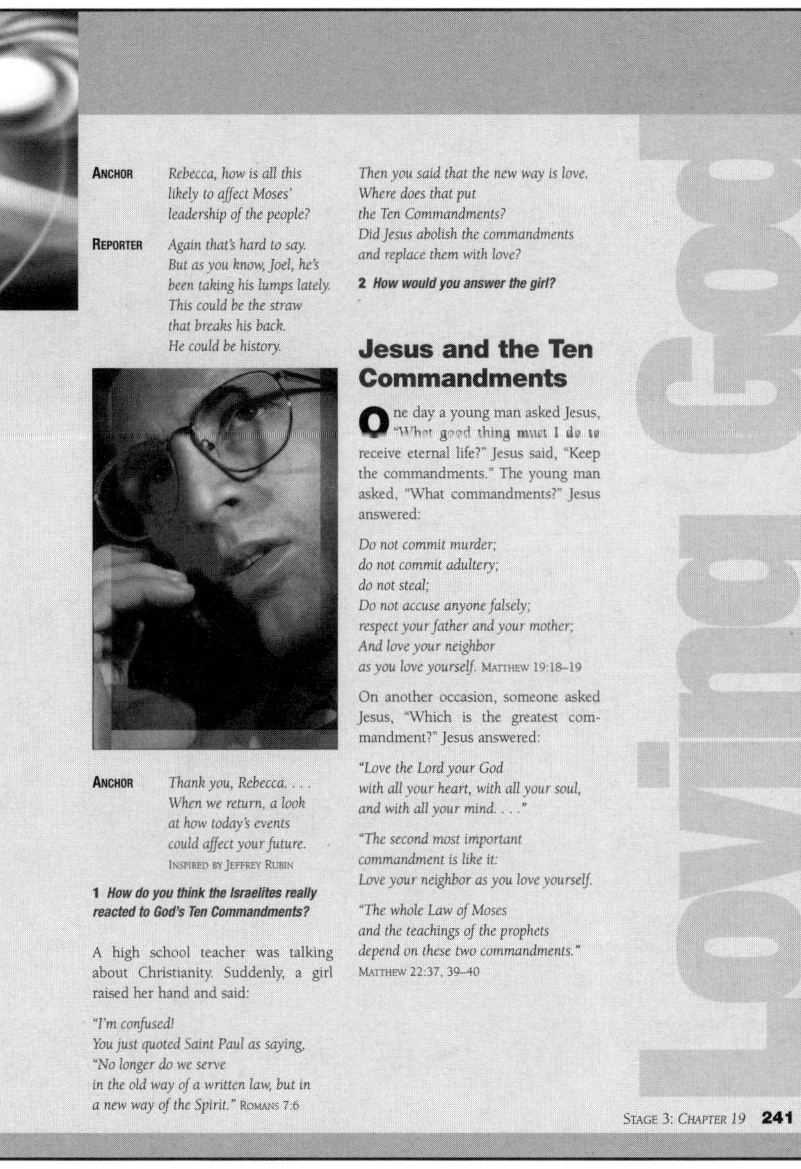

ANCHOR *Rebecca, how is all this likely to affect Moses' leadership of the people?*

REPORTER *Again that's hard to say. But as you know, Joel, he's been taking his lumps lately. This could be the straw that breaks his back. He could be history.*

ANCHOR *Thank you, Rebecca. . . . When we return, a look at how today's events could affect your future.*

INSPIRED BY JEFFREY RUBIN

1 *How do you think the Israelites really reacted to God's Ten Commandments?*

A high school teacher was talking about Christianity. Suddenly, a girl raised her hand and said:

"I'm confused!
You just quoted Saint Paul as saying,
'No longer do we serve
in the old way of a written law, but in
a new way of the Spirit.'" ROMANS 7:6

Then you said that the new way is love.
Where does that put
the Ten Commandments?
Did Jesus abolish the commandments
and replace them with love?

2 *How would you answer the girl?*

Jesus and the Ten Commandments

One day a young man asked Jesus, "What good thing must I do to receive eternal life?" Jesus said, "Keep the commandments." The young man asked, "What commandments?" Jesus answered:

Do not commit murder;
do not commit adultery;
do not steal;
Do not accuse anyone falsely;
respect your father and your mother;
And love your neighbor
as you love yourself. MATTHEW 19:18–19

On another occasion, someone asked Jesus, "Which is the greatest commandment?" Jesus answered:

"Love the Lord your God
with all your heart, with all your soul,
and with all your mind. . . ."

"The second most important
commandment is like it:
Love your neighbor as you love yourself.

"The whole Law of Moses
and the teachings of the prophets
depend on these two commandments."
MATTHEW 22:37, 39–40

Loving God

STAGE 3: CHAPTER 19 241

and all the ordinances,
and all the people answered together,
"We will do everything
that the LORD has said."

Psalm 119:97, 103, 105 reads:

How I love your law!
I think about it all day long. . . .
How sweet is the taste of your
instructions—sweeter than honey! . . .
Your word is a lamp to guide me
and a light for my path.

QUESTION **2 *How would you answer the girl? (Namely, did Jesus abolish the commands or replace them with love?)***

■ *The purpose of this question is not necessarily to get a correct response from the students, but to start them thinking and to prepare them for the material ahead.*

CLARIFY—Point out that the first three commandments refer to our relationship with God; and the last seven refer to our relationship with our neighbor.

In the Book of Deuteronomy, Moses says to the people: "The LORD gave me the two stone tablets on which he had written the covenant." 9:11

NOTEBOOK—Traditionally, artists have placed the three commandments referring to our relationship with God on the first tablet and the seven referring to our relationship with our neighbor on the second tablet, as follows. Have the students copy the schema below in their notebooks.

	God		*Neighbor*
I	Worship only me	IV	Respect parents
II	Keep my name holy	V	No murder
III	Keep Sabbath holy	VI	No adultery
		VII	No stealing
		VIII	No false witness
		IX	Covet not another's wife
		X	Nor another's property

Jesus and the Ten Commandments

CLARIFY—Referring to commandments dealing with our neighbor, Saint Paul echoes Jesus' words, saying:

■ *The commandments,*
"Do not commit adultery;
do not commit murder;
do not steal;
do not desire what belongs
to someone else"—all these,
and any others besides,
are summed up in the one command,
"Love your neighbor
as you love yourself."
If you love someone,
you will never do them wrong;
to love, then, is to obey the whole Law.
ROMANS 13:9-10

CLARIFY—Stress the focus of the young man's question: eternal life. We may rephrase it as follows: What must I do to make the "leap" from *this life* to *eternal life?*

Share Your meditation

■ *This was probably the man's saying to Jera, in effect: "I wouldn't blame God if he returned to heaven for a while, until, like the Prodigal Son, we came to our senses."*

The man had touched Jera deeply. He hadn't come to church to fulfill an obligation, ask a favor, or complain about the world—but simply to sing to God.

THINK about it

CLARIFY—Mohandus Gandhi was killed in 1948 by a Hindu extremist. The assassin was waiting with his hands folded, palms together in the Hindu gesture of a friendly greeting. Hidden in his hands was a revolver. The man fired three shots at close range.

As Gandhi fell, he put his hand to his forehead in the Hindu gesture of forgiveness. Pandit Nehru, who took over the leadership of India, said of Gandhi's death:

> *The light has gone out of our lives*
> *and there is darkness everywhere.*
> *I do not know*
> *what to tell you and how to say it. . . .*
> *The father of our nation, is no more.*

Gandhi had worked tirelessly to bring the light of hope to India's Untouchables, the downtrodden people of Hindu society.

An insight into this great-souled man came one day, as he was boarding a moving train. One of his sandals slipped off and fell on the track. Gandhi quickly took off the other one and threw it back to the fallen one, saying, "The poor man who finds the other sandal will now have a pair."

During his student days in South Africa, Gandhi was moved by Jesus' teachings, convinced that Christianity was the antidote to India's caste system.

One day he went to a Catholic Church to attend Mass and get instructions. He was stopped at the door and told gently that if he desired to attend Mass he was welcome to do so in a church reserved for blacks.

Gandhi left disheartened and never returned. He saw that Christians in South Africa had their own caste system.

One can only speculate what Gandhi might have done for the conversion of India, had he not met with that episode of discrimination.

Jesus fulfills the commandments

NOTEBOOK—Stress that Jesus redefined and refocused the Ten Commandments in terms of love, transforming them into:

SHARE YOUR meditation

Osborne Jera was startled to hear someone singing at the top of his voice in an empty church in the middle of the day. Looking around, he saw a man, hat in hand, eyes closed, facing the altar. When his song ended, the man opened his eyes. Seeing Jera, he said:

I just felt like singing to God—
if he's still here.
Such awful things
happening' in the world. Felt like
a little song might cheer him up.

Then the man flashed empty hands, saying, "I haven't touched anything." Jera thought, "How wondrously wrong he was to say, 'I haven't touched anything!'"

■ ***Explain the following two comments:***
(a) "I felt like singing to God—if he's still here";
(b) "How wrong he was to say, 'I haven't touched anything!'"

THINK about it

Our armaments have failed already. Let us now be in search of something new; let us try the force of love and God.

Mohandus K. Gandhi

Jesus fulfills the commandments

Jesus did not abolish the commandments. He brought them to fulfillment and redefined them in terms of love:

- **God** **Commandments 1–3**
- **Neighbor** **Commandments 4–10**

In redefining the Ten Commandments, Jesus gave them an entirely new focus. He transformed them into:

- **Signs of love**
- **Invitations to love**
- **Guides to love**

First, Jesus transforms the commandments into *signs of love:* our love for Jesus, Jesus' love for us, and our love for one another. Jesus said:

If you love me,
you will obey my commandments. . . .
My commandment is this:
love one another just as I have loved you.
JOHN 14:15; 15:12

If you have love for one another,
then everyone will know
that you are my disciples. JOHN 13:35

Second, Jesus transforms the commandments into *invitations to love.*

Because we are Jesus' disciples, and desire to remain so, the commandments become invitations to love. That is, they summon us to love when we forget to do so, or are tempted not to do so.

Finally, Jesus transforms the commandments into *guides to love.* They point out a loving course of action, when it is not clear what love invites us to do in a given situation.

Gift of the commandments

After the Israelites escaped from Egypt, Moses led them through the desert to Mount Sinai. At the foot of the mountain, Moses instructed them to pitch camp.

On the morning of the third day,
there was thunder and lightning . . .
The LORD. . . called Moses
to the top of the mountain . . .
Moses then went down to the people
and told them what
the LORD had said. . . .

These were his words:
"I am the LORD your God who brought
you out of Egypt." EXODUS 19:16; 20:2, 25

1. Worship no god but me. . . .
2. Keep my name. . . .
3. Keep holy the Sabbath. . . .
4. Respect your father and mother. . . .
5. Do not commit murder.
6. Do not commit adultery.
7. Do not steal.
8. Do not accuse anyone falsely.
9. Do not desire another's wife . . .
10. nor anything else that he owns.

DEUTERONOMY 5:7, 11, 16–21

By his gift of the Ten Commandments to them, God entered into a covenant ("sacred agreement") with Israel. By that covenant, they became God's "chosen people," which means they became God's "chosen instrument" for re-creating the world.

Here's how one modern Jew describes what the covenant did for Israel:

Israel is not a "natural" nation;
it is, indeed, not a nation at all
like the nations of the world.

NOTES

It is a supernatural community,
called into being by God
to serve his eternal purposes in history.

It is a community
created by God's special act of covenant . . .
Apart from the covenant,
Israel is as nothing and Jewish existence
is a mere delusion.
The covenant is at the very heart
of the Jewish self-understanding
of its own reality.
WILL HERBERG: "JEWISH EXISTENCE AND SURVIVAL: A THEOLOGICAL VIEW"

Let us now take a closer look at each of the first three commandments.

First commandment

A reporter asked Cecil B. DeMille, the director of the film *The Ten Commandments*, "What commandment do you think that people today break most?"

The director answered, "The very first commandment: 'Worship no God but me.' It's the one that Israel broke first, and it's the one that we still break most."

DeMille hastened to explain that we do not fashion idols out of metal and bow before them. "Rather, we make idols of flesh and money and bow before them."

Jesus warned people about this very danger in his Sermon on the Mount. He explained why they must worship God alone, saying:

"Your heart
will always be where your riches are. . . .
You cannot be a slave of two masters;
you will hate one and love the other;
you will be loyal to one
and despise the other.
You cannot serve both God and money."
MATTHEW 6:21–24

Thus, the first commandment is an invitation to make God the focus of all our energies and desires. It is an invitation to:

- **Believe in God** CCC 2087–89
- **Hope in God** CCC 2090–92
- **Love God** CCC 2093–94
- **Serve God** CCC 2095–2109

That brings us to some specific ways we violate the first commandment.

STAGE 3: CHAPTER 19 **243**

1 *Sign* — *Your love for one another will be the sign that you are my disciple.*

2 *Invitation* — *If you want to show your love for me keep my commandment.*

3 *Guide* — *Love one another just as I have loved you.*

Gift of the commandments

CLARIFY—Stress that the covenant ("sacred agreement" with God) transformed Israel from a band of ex-slaves into an assembly of chosen people ("God's instrument for re-creating the world").

CLARIFY—Stress the point made in the last chapter: Israel viewed the commandments not as something negative but as something positive. They were a concrete sign of God's love for them. Specifically, the Israelites viewed the Ten Commandments as freeing them:

1) *From a life of ignorance and passion*
2) *For a life of love and service*

First commandment

NOTEBOOK—The first commandment calls for fidelity to the infused virtues of faith, hope, and charity. Called the *theological* (theo = "God") virtues, they were given to us in Baptism, relate us to the Trinity in a personal way, and are the foundation of our spiritual life. Each virtue invites and empowers us in a special way:

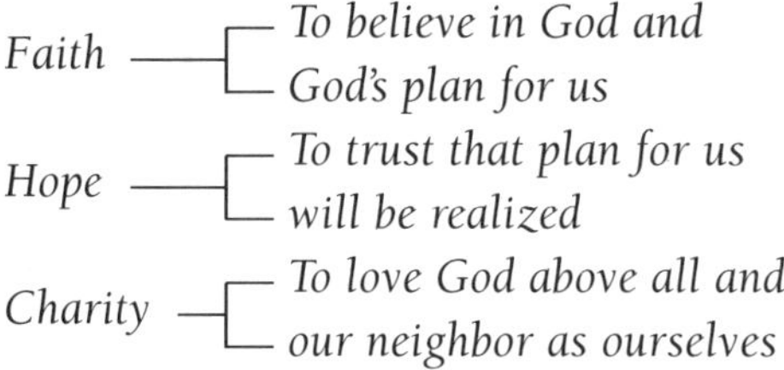

Faith
To believe in God and God's plan for us
Hope
To trust that plan for us will be realized
Charity
To love God above all and our neighbor as ourselves

In gratitude for this incredible gift we pledge:

Service — *To make God the priority and focus of our life*

NOTEBOOK—The first commandment forbids practices such as:

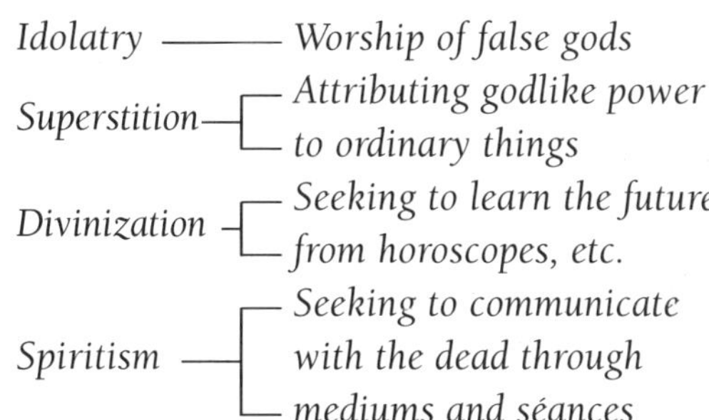

Idolatry
Worship of false gods
Superstition
Attributing godlike power to ordinary things
Divinization
Seeking to learn the future from horoscopes, etc.
Spiritism
Seeking to communicate with the dead through mediums and séances

ACTIVITY—Have students explain DeMille's point: "We make idols of money and flesh and bow before them."

- *When we choose money over God's law, we make it an idol. When we choose wrongful pleasure over God's law, we make it an idol.*

Superstition

ACTIVITY—Have students take a dollar bill. Tell them, "If you're superstitious, a dollar bill is the most unlucky item you can possibly carry around."

Take the right circle containing the eagle on the back of the bill. It has six groups of 13 items.

Have the students identify them:

1) 13 stars in the circle above the eagle
2) 13 stripes on the eagle's shield
3) 13 arrows in the eagle's left claw
4) 13 leaves on olive branch (right claw)
5) 13 olives on the same branch
6) 13 letters in the motto (eagle's mouth) (E Pluribus Unum = One from Many)

Ask the students: Why the number 13? (The 13 colonies of our infant nation.)

QUESTION **3 *What are some other examples of superstition today? What do you think accounts for superstition among many people, even in our day?***

■ *Good luck = carrying a rabbit's foot, finding a four-leaf clover, etc. Bad luck = having a black cat cross our path or walking under a ladder.*

Divination

DISCUSS—What is being depicted in the photograph at the top of page 244?

■ *The "signs of the zodiac." They are the basis for many astrological charts and forecasts. The word "zodiac" comes from a Greek word meaning "circle of animals." It is an imaginary path followed by the sun, moon, and principle planets.*

Ancient people divided the path into twelve 30-degree arcs or "houses" that correspond to the twelve divisions of the calendar year. Each contains a star pattern (sign), after which it is named (Aries: ram; Taurus: bull; Gemini: twins; Cancer: crab; Leo: lion; Virgo: virgin; Libra: balance; Scorpio: scorpion; Saggitarius: archer; Capricornus: goat; Aquarius: water carrier; Pisces: the fish.)

Superstition

In an age of science and reason, it is incredible that some airplanes have no row 13, or seat 13. And some hotels skip from the twelfth floor to the fourteenth, all because some people feel uneasy about the number 13.

This is evidence that *superstition* still plays a surprising role in some people's lives.

3 *What are some other examples of superstition today? What do you think accounts for superstition among many people, even in our day?*

Divination

Somewhat related to superstition is *divination,* which seeks to learn the future from palm readers, fortune-tellers, and horoscopes. Such practices are specifically forbidden in both the Old Testament and in the New Testament. DEUTERONOMY 18:10–11, ACTS 16:16, CCC 2116

Spiritism

A third practice that relates to the first commandment is *spiritism.* CCC 2117 It involves such things as seeking to communicate with the dead through mediums and seances. Again, the Bible prohibits such practices. LEVITICUS 20:27. Commenting on spiritism, Thomas Higgins says in *Man As Man:*

While most spiritistic mediums may be laughed at as frauds . . . not all the phenomena of modern spiritism may be dismissed as hokum.

Some truly genuine effects are wrought. The explanation of some of these effects may be traced to occult, but natural causes, whereas others . . . can be due only to diabolical intervention.

4 *Why do you think people who claim psychic powers are able to command such a following over television and the Internet?*

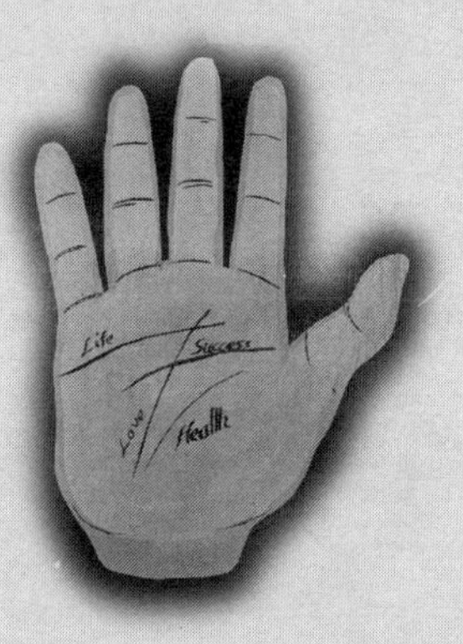

244 STAGE 3: CHAPTER 19

As the earth circles the sun, the sun appears to go from one arc to the next. A person born when the sun occupies a given arc is, supposedly, influenced by its star pattern.

At the time of the astrologer Hipparchus (c. 150 B.C.) the signs corresponded closely with the constellations. Owing to precession, the whole system is off by a full sign or house; e.g., the sign Aries is now occupied by the constellation Pisces.

CLARIFY—The book *Astrology Disproved* by L. E. Jerome contains a statement signed by 192 scientists (19 Nobel prize winners). It protests publishing of astrological forecasts and horoscopes in newspapers: "We believe the time has come to challenge directly and forcefully the pretentious claims of astrological charlatans."

NOTES

Second commandment

The second commandment reads: "Do not use my name for evil purposes." Commenting on this commandment, someone said, "When I misuse God's name, I don't mean anything by it. It's just a *bad habit* I have."

Try using that excuse when a traffic officer stops you for speeding or when your supervisor catches you arriving late for work.

The second commandment "governs our use of speech in sacred matters." CCC 2142–54 It summons us to keep holy God's name, as Jesus taught us in the Lord's Prayer: "Hallowed be thy name."

Deliberate or careless misuse of God's name offends God, but also our neighbor. Consider two examples.

Cursing

Cursing calls upon God to inflict harm on someone. It dishonors God gravely, because it attempts to make God a partner to evil. CCC 2148

Damning someone in God's name is more often a careless expression of frustration or irritation than a genuine intention to curse.

Misuse of God's name, by one of the above two ways, can lead to scandal, especially where young people are concerned. Scandal is "an attitude or behavior which leads another to do evil." CCC 2284–87 Jesus spoke about it bluntly, saying:

Things that make people fall into sin
are bound to happen,
but how terrible for the one
who makes them happen!

It would be better for him
if he were thrown
into the bottom of the sea
than for him to cause
one of these little ones to sin.
So watch what you do.
LUKE 17:1–3

5 *List some ways that scandal can be given to "little ones" by (a) adults, especially parents, (b) young people.*

Oaths

A second example of an abuse of God's name is the misuse of *oaths*. Oaths call upon God to witness that we speak the truth. In a society where lying is common, courts require people to swear to their testimony. In grave cases like this, therefore, oaths are permitted.

To lie under oath is a sin of *perjury*. CCC 2149–55 It dishonors God gravely by asking God to witness to a lie.

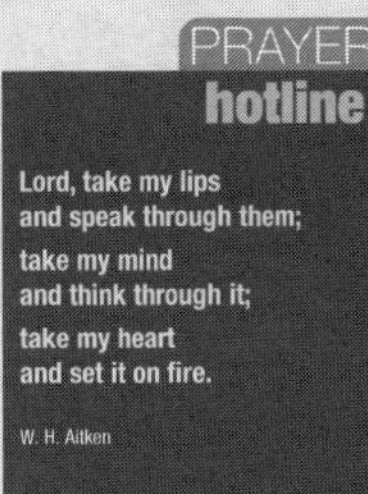

PRAYER
hotline
Lord, take my lips
and speak through them;
take my mind
and think through it;
take my heart
and set it on fire.
W. H. Aitken

Spiritism

QUESTION **4 *Why do you think people claiming psychic powers are able to command such a following over television and the Internet?***

■ *A good "general" explanation is this one: "When we stop believing in God, we start believing in anything."*

Second commandment

NOTEBOOK—The second commandment forbids the misuse of God's name, e.g., by:

Cursing	*Asking God to inflict evil*
Oaths	*Asking God to witness to truth*
Perjury	*Lying under oath*

Cursing

CLARIFY—The phrase "God damn you," as used by people today, is not a curse, but an expression of anger or frustration.

QUESTION **5 *List some ways that scandal can be given to "little ones" by (a) adults, especially parents, (2) young people.***

■ *Here are three excellent observations that may come in handy in the discussion of this important topic.*

1) If you Christians
in India, in Britain, or in America
were like your Bible,
you would conquer India in five years.
INDIAN BRAHMAN TO A MISSIONARY

2) One person practicing sportsmanship is far better than fifty preaching it.
KNUTE ROCKNE

3) The worst danger that confronts the younger generation is the example set by the older generation. E. C. MCKENZIE

Oaths

CLARIFY—Jesus said, "Do not swear (take an oath) . . . Say 'Yes' or 'No'—anything else you say comes from the evil one." MATTHEW 5:34-37

■ *Following Paul who says, "I call God as my witness"* (2 CORINTHIANS 1:23), *Jesus' words are interpreted "not to exclude oaths made for grave and right reasons" (public office or courtroom).* CCC 2154

PRAYER **hotline**

The "Peace Prayer" of Saint Francis (page 232) spells out what this prayer is asking of God.

Up Close & Personal

Students will be able to relate to this episode. You might ask them to pause, reflect, and recall a similar episode in their own lives.

Third commandment

CLARIFY—Refer the students back to Saint Justin's description of how the early Christians celebrated the Eucharist "on the day of the sun" around A.D. 100:

On the day of the sun,
all who dwell in the city or country
gather in the same place.
HISTORICAL CONNECTION, PAGE 160

Refer the students to Revelation 1:10–11 where John writes about an experience that took place on the "Lord's Day":

On the Lord's Day,
the Spirit took control of me
and I heard a loud voice, that sounded
like a trumpet, speaking behind me.
It said, "Write down what you see,
and send the book to the churches
in these seven cities: Ephesus. . . ."

Henry Ford once said that it is not only good religion but also good business to relax on the Lord's Day. He said that his company would have had the famous Model-A car in production six months earlier had he not forbidden his engineers to work on Sunday.

Observance of the Lord's Day

CLARIFY—Peter charged the Christian community to bear witness to the world:

You are . . . God's own people,
chosen to proclaim
the wonderful acts of God,
who called you out of darkness
into his own marvelous light. 1 PETER 2:9

Up Close & Personal

Jacques Braman

One day a young lady asked James Martin, "How can I find God?" This question inspired him to ask people of all ages, religions, and occupations how they found God.

The result was a fascinating book called *How Can I Find God?* One entry in it is by Jacques Braman. It reads:

It was a peaceful evening.
My mom and brother and
sister and I were on our
way to a high school
basketball game . . .

It was quiet in the car. . . .
I was just looking out the window
at the still night, enjoying
the stars . . . happy to be
on my way to the game.

The happiness that I was feeling
grew deeper and . . .
I noticed that tears
were rolling down my cheeks.
This was really weird. . . .

Then I understood.
This was how full joy
could be . . .
a joy that comes only from God.

Third commandment

It is not uncommon to find a pamphlet by some religious sect saying that Christians violate the third commandment. They observe Sunday, and not the Sabbath, as the commandment reads. A few early Jewish converts to Christianity made the same point.

This raises a question. If the third commandment says we should "observe the Sabbath and keep it holy," why did the first followers of Jesus change their observance to Sunday?

Observance of the Lord's Day

There are many reasons. Two major ones are that Jesus rose on Sunday JOHN 20:1 and the Holy Spirit descended upon the followers of Jesus on a Sunday. ACTS 2:1–4

These events gave new significance to this day. They signaled the sunset of the Old Testament era and the sunrise of the New Testament era.

Guided by the Holy Spirit, the followers of Jesus chose Sunday as the day to celebrate the Lord's Supper ACTS 20:7–11 and referred to it as the Lord's Day. REVELATION 1:10

246 STAGE 3: CHAPTER 19

One of the most powerful ways of doing this is by worshipping together each Sunday at Mass.

DISCUSS—An old Jew, named Samuel, stopped going to the synagogue because someone there had publically humiliated him.

■ *One day an old rabbi from the synagogue visited Samuel. He asked to come in and sit with him in front of the fireplace.*

And so the two men sat together in complete silence, watching the fire burn. After twenty minutes the old rabbi picked up a pair of tongs, took a glowing coal from the fireplace, and set it on Samuel's hearth. As they watched in silence, the coal slowly lost its glow. Then it died completely.

NOTES

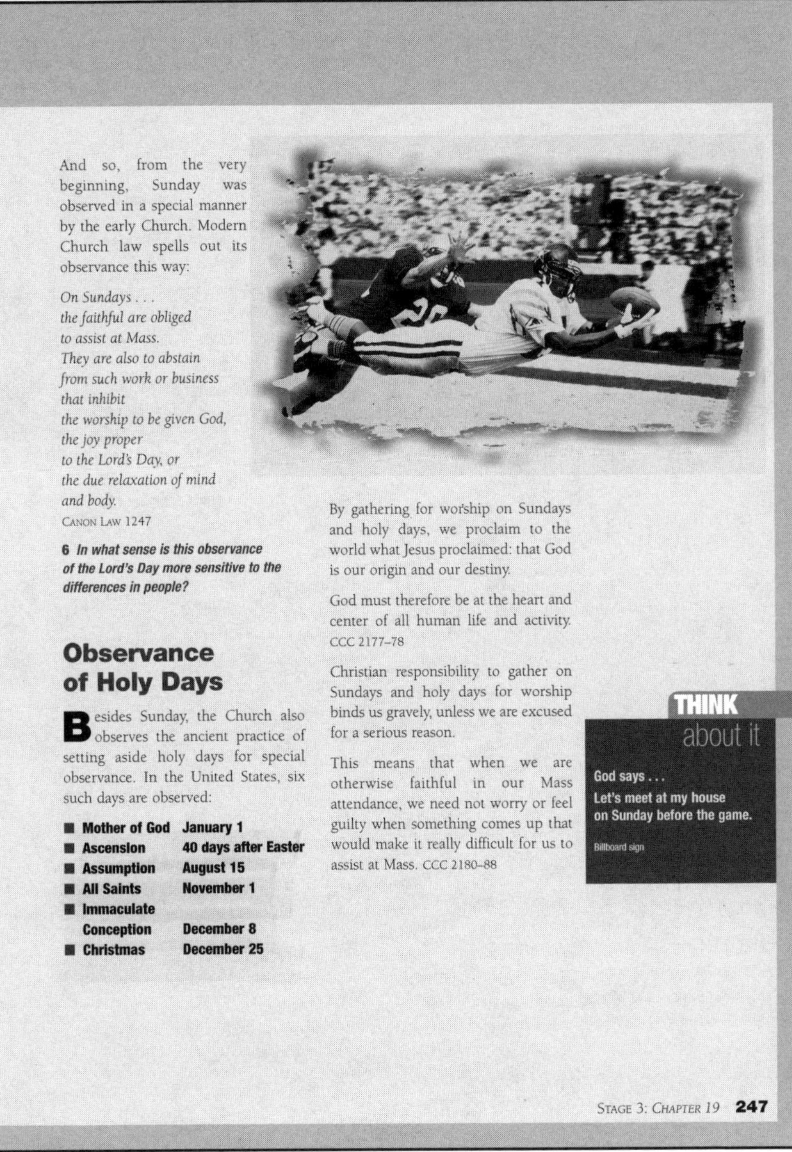

And so, from the very beginning, Sunday was observed in a special manner by the early Church. Modern Church law spells out its observance this way:

On Sundays . . .
the faithful are obliged
to assist at Mass.
They are also to abstain
from such work or business
that inhibit
the worship to be given God,
the joy proper
to the Lord's Day, or
the due relaxation of mind
and body.
CANON LAW 1247

6 *In what sense is this observance of the Lord's Day more sensitive to the differences in people?*

By gathering for worship on Sundays and holy days, we proclaim to the world what Jesus proclaimed: that God is our origin and our destiny.

God must therefore be at the heart and center of all human life and activity. CCC 2177–78

Observance of Holy Days

Besides Sunday, the Church also observes the ancient practice of setting aside holy days for special observance. In the United States, six such days are observed:

- **Mother of God** — **January 1**
- **Ascension** — **40 days after Easter**
- **Assumption** — **August 15**
- **All Saints** — **November 1**
- **Immaculate Conception** — **December 8**
- **Christmas** — **December 25**

Christian responsibility to gather on Sundays and holy days for worship binds us gravely, unless we are excused for a serious reason.

This means that when we are otherwise faithful in our Mass attendance, we need not worry or feel guilty when something comes up that would make it really difficult for us to assist at Mass. CCC 2180–88

THINK about it

God says . . .
Let's meet at my house on Sunday before the game.
Billboard sign

STAGE 3: *CHAPTER 19* **247**

A few minutes later, Samuel turned to the old rabbi and said, "I understand. I'll come back to the synagogue."

Ask the students: What did Samuel understand?

■ *When we stop going to church, we run the risk of losing our faith.*

Just as the coal slowly lost its heat when it got separated from the "coal community," so we risk losing our faith if we get separated from the "Christian community."

ACTIVITY—Have the students interview someone who has stopped practicing the faith. It is important to begin the interview by telling the person the story of Samuel. After telling/reading it, ask them the following questions:

1 What did Samuel understand?
2 Why did you stop going to Church?
3 What keeps you from returning?
4 What do you miss most?
5 What have you put in place of church attendance to keep your faith alive?
6 How open are you to begin practicing your faith again? Explain.

QUESTION **6 *In what sense is this observance of the Lord's Day more sensitive to the differences in people?***

■ *Under previous observance, hard manual labor was not permitted. For some people who worked in an office all week, getting out and chopping wood was a joy and truly relaxing in body and spirit.*

CLARIFY—Objectively, Catholics have a grave obligation to assist at Mass on Sundays and holy days.

■ *Subjectively, a serious reason (for example, sickness) removes this obligation.*

In discussing the obligation to assist at Mass, we need to be extremely sensitive, especially with young people who are in a state of confusion—even alienation—about their faith.

Therefore, we should be careful not to load a crippling guilt trip on them and alienate them further by a negative or heavy-handed approach.

We should keep in mind the words of Isaiah, who said of the Lord's servant: "He will not break off a bent reed nor put out a flickering lamp." ISAIAH 42:3

THINK about it

DISCUSS—Ask the students: What is the point of the billboard sign and why do/don't you think the sign is an effective one to get across the point?

ACTIVITY—Have the students compose or design their own billboard sign to get across the same point.

Recap

It is fitting to recap this chapter in a highly personal way. Ultimately, that's where every chapter should end: down from the head into the heart—and then letting the heart lead the way from there.

Years ago, Fulton Oursler was a prominent author and senior editor of *Reader's Digest*. Reflecting on his spiritual journey to God, he said:

> *It is through prayer*
> *that we know there is a God.*
> *Through prayer we know God—*
> *as Father. . . .*
>
> *As we come to know God,*
> *the urge to serve God personally*
> *becomes overpowering.*
>
> *We feed the hungry, visit the sick . . .*
> *clothe the naked. . . .*
> *That is where the human being comes*
> *closest to God and knows God best.*
>
> *Isn't it strange that*
> *it should have taken me so many years*
> *to find the key to the mystery? . . .*
> *I have much lost time to make up.*
> LIBERTY, MARCH 1949

Recap

Jesus did not abolish the commandments. Rather, he brought them to fulfillment and redefined them in terms of love:

- **Commandments 1–3** **Love of God**
- **Commandments 4–10** **Love of neighbor**

In redefining the Ten Commandments, Jesus gave them an entirely new focus. He transforms them into:

- **Signs of love**
- **Invitations to love**
- **Guides to love**

The first three commandments that God gave Moses and the Israelites at the foot of Mount Sinai invite them to make God the focus of all their energies and desires.

Violations of the first three commandments may be summed up as follows:

- **First** **Superstition, divination, spiritism**
- **Second** **Curses and rash oaths**
- **Third** **Failure in Sunday worship**

Review

1. List the Ten Commandments that God gave gave to Moses at the foot of Mount Sinai.
2. Briefly explain how Jesus redefined (a) the first three commandments, (b) the last seven commandments.
3. List and briefly describe the new threefold focus that Jesus gave the commandments.
4. Briefly explain what God's gift of the covenant did for Israel.
5. Identify (a) superstition, (b) divination, (c) spiritism.
6. Briefly explain what we mean by (a) curses, (b) oaths, (c) why oaths are permissible in grave situations, (d) perjury, (e) scandal.
7. List two major reasons why Christians, guided by the Holy Spirit, observe Sunday rather than the Sabbath.
8. List the six holy days and when they are observed by Catholics in the United States.

248 STAGE 3: CHAPTER 19

Review

DAILY QUIZ—The review questions may be assigned (one or two at a time) for homework or a daily quiz.

CHAPTER TESTS—Reproducible chapter tests are found in Appendix A. For consistency and ease in grading, quizzes are restricted to (1) "Matching," (2) "True/False," and (3) "Fill in the Blanks."

TEST ANSWERS—The following are the answers to the test for Chapter 19. (See Appendix A, page 330.) Each correct answer worth 4 points.

Matching

1 = h	2 = d	3 = e	4 = b
5 = f	6 = g	7 = a	8 = c

True/False

1 = T	2 = T	3 = F	4 = T
5 = F	6 = F	7 = T	8 = F
9 = F	10 = T		

Fill in the Blanks

1. (a) Mother of God: January 1
   (b) Ascension: 40 days after Easter
   (c) Assumption: August 15
   (d) All Saints: November 1
   (e) Immaculate Conception: December 8
   (f) Christmas: December 15
2. (a) signs of love
   (b) invitations to love
   (c) guides to love

NOTES

Reflect

1 Ann Landers received a letter from a young woman who had gone to a fortune-teller. The fortune-teller told her that she would never have a child of her own. The young woman was devastated. She said, "I cried all the way home."

Then to the young woman's great joy, she became pregnant. But her joy soon turned to fear when she recalled what the fortune-teller had said. But the baby arrived on schedule and healthy.

■ ***You may have heard the statement, "Something is not bad because it's a sin; it's a sin because it's bad." Explain how the woman's experience illustrates the point of the statement.***

■ ***What are two concerns that you have about the future? Explain.***

2 Eugene O'Neill was one of America's great playwrights. He won both the Pulitzer prize and the Nobel prize. The last play he wrote was entitled *Long Day's Journey into Night*.

In it, he has the leading character describe a mystical experience he has. Actually, it was an experience O'Neill himself had in connection with the sea.

It occurred one night when he was lying on the bow of a small boat. The water was spraying and foaming under him and the the white sails of the boat were shining in the moonlight, beautiful and bright above him. He writes:

For a moment, I lost myself. . . .
I became the white sails and flying spray,
became the beauty and rhythm,
became the moonlight and the ship and
the dim-starred sky!
I belonged . . . within something
greater than my own life.

■ ***How do you interpret O'Neill's words, "I belonged within something greater than my own life"?***

■ ***Can you think of a time when you felt the way O'Neill did? Explain.***

3 Marion Bond West lost her father when she was about four years old. This made it necessary for her mother to take a job to support her.

So her mother arranged to have a neighbor baby-sit Marion. Each lunch hour Marion's mother hurried home to eat with her. But when she left after lunch, Marion grew hysterical.

One day Marion's mother stopped coming. Years later, Marion learned why.

Her mother still came each noon, sat at the window, watched her play, and longed to hold her close—especially when she fell and cried. But for Marion's own good, she didn't.

"Close By," Guideposts, June 1979

■ ***How does this true story have application to God's personal, loving relationship to you?***

Reflect

1 a) *You may have heard the statement, "Something is not bad because it's a sin; it's a sin because it's bad." Explain how the woman's experience illustrates the point of the statement.*

■ *Recall what was said about the statement on page 237. It's an important concept for young people to grasp.*

Going to a fortune-teller is a sin because its bad. The woman's experience shows that in a graphic way: She cried all the way home and was filled with fear.

b) *What are two concerns that you have about the future? Explain.*

■ *Have the students do this question anonymously. The results can then be collected, tallied on the chalkboard, and discussed.*

2 a) *How do you interpret O'Neill's words, "I belonged within something greater than my own life"?*

b) *Can you think of a time when you felt the way O'Neill did? Explain.*

■ *Eugene O'Neill interpreted the "moment" as a possible experience of God. He added that he had experienced other moments: "Several other times in my life, when swimming far out, or lying alone on the beach, I have had the same experience."*

3 *How does this true story have application to God's personal, loving relationship to you?*

■ *After planting corn, farmers pray for rain, lots of rain. Once the corn starts to grow, they do something strange, very strange. They pray for a period of "stress and dryness." The reason is to force the corn roots to grow downward in search of water, rather than stay on the surface. Unless the tap root of the corn grows downward to the "water level," the corn will wither and dry when the heat of summer sets in—it will have no way to draw up water.*

Our spiritual life, especially our prayer life, is like that. God gives us a good start. Then God lets a period of "stress and dryness" set in to force our spiritual roots to grow downward to the faith level, rather than stay on the surface at the feeling level.

Ask the students: Why must our spiritual life, especially our prayer life, be an exercise of faith, rather than feeling?

■ *If we pray solely to experience a good feeling, prayer can become an exercise of sophisticated self-indulgence and is doomed to disaster.*

PRAYER TIME with the Lord

QUESTION **a) *After studying the above six reasons (why the author prays) number them from one to six, in the order that best describes why you pray.***
b) *Briefly explain your "first" choice.*

PRAYER TIME with the Lord

I pray because I am a Christian,
and to do what a Christian must do,
I need strength.

I pray because there's confusion in my life,
and to know what is right,
I need light.

I pray because I have questions,
and to keep growing in the faith,
I need help.

I pray because I must make decisions,
and the choices are not always clear,
so I need guidance.

I pray because most of what I have
has been given to me,
and I ought to give thanks.

I pray because Jesus prayed,
and if he considered it important,
so should I. M.L.

■ ***After studying the above six reasons, number them from one to six, in the order that best describes why you pray.***
■ ***Briefly explain your "first" choice.***

250 STAGE 3: CHAPTER 19

■ *French philosopher Blaise Pascal says God created us in his "image and likeness."*

One way God created us in his "image and likeness" is by sharing his divine power with us. He did this two ways; by making us intellectual ("thinking") persons and spiritual ("praying") persons.

Because we are thinking persons we can impact people's lives. (For example, a doctor can diagnose illnesses and prescribe cures—dramatically impacting the person's health and lifespan.)

On the other hand, because we are praying persons, we can impact people's live just as powerfully—if not more powerfully.

In the words of Dr. Alexis Carrel: "Prayer is the most powerful form of energy we can generate."

And in the words of Lord Tennyson:
"More things are wrought by prayer
Than this world dreams of.
Wherefore let thy voice
Rise like a fountain for me night and day."

PRAYER Journal

QUESTION ***Describe briefly where you find God.***

You might share with the students how Wernher von Braun answered this question.

Wernher von Braun has been called the "twentieth-century Columbus." More than any other scientist, he is responsible for putting us on the moon.

Born in Germany, he surrendered to the Allies near the end of World War II, when the Russians marched on Berlin. He was sent to the United States and eventually became the director of Alabama's Marshall Space Flight Center. He said in a lecture:

■ *The natural laws of the universe are so precise that we have no difficulty building a spaceship to fly to the moon, and we can time the flight with the precision of a fraction of a second. . . . Anything . . . so precisely balanced . . . can only be the product of a Divine Idea.* UNPUBLISHED LECTURE

SCRIPTURE Journal

QUESTION ***Pick one of the above passages. Read it prayerfully and write a short statement to Jesus expressing your feelings about it.***

You may simply wish to read the following excerpt from the fifth reading and have the students express their feelings about it.

NOTES

PRAYER Journal

Daniel Harrington, S.J., is a biblical scholar. When asked where he finds God, he said:

"I stutter. . . .
As a young boy I read in a newspaper
that Moses stuttered.
I looked it up in the Bible, and sure enough
in Exodus 4:10 Moses says to God:
'I am slow of speech and slow of tongue.'"

But Harrington found much more than this. He found the story of God's self-revelation to Moses and of God's missioning of Moses to speak that self-revelation to the world.

Harrington ended, "I found God in the Bible, and I have continued to do so ever since."

■ ***Describe briefly where you find God.***

SCRIPTURE Journal

1	**Worship God only**	**Deuteronomy 4:15–20**
2	**Keep the Sabbath**	**Nehemiah 13:15–22**
3	**Keep Temple holy**	**Matthew 21:12–16**
4	**Prayer in the Temple**	**1 Kings 8:22–30**
5	**Praise God**	**Psalm 150**

■ ***Pick one of the above passages. Read it prayerfully and write a short statement to Jesus expressing your feelings about it.***

STAGE 3: *CHAPTER 19* **251**

Before reading it, you might point out that it will take only 10 seconds to read, but it would have taken, perhaps, 25 minutes to perform.

For example, after the emcee shouted, "Praise him with drums and dancing," a whole company of performers leaped into action with drums and dancing. The Hebrews were uninhibited in their worship. (Recall David dancing before the Ark. 2 SAMUEL 6:16)

Praise the LORD*! Praise him*
for the mighty things he has done. . . .
Praise him with trumpets. . . .
Praise him with drums and dancing.
Praise him with harps and flutes.
Praise him with cymbals. . . .
Praise the LORD*!*

Classroom Resources

CATECHISM

Catechism of the Catholic Church *Second Edition*

For further enrichment, you might refer to:

1. Commandment	Index	p. 774
	Glossary	p. 871
2. Law (Moral)	Index	p. 814
	Glossary	p. 886

See also: Sabbath, Worship, Good, Evil.

—AVAILABLE FROM THE UNITED STATES CATHOLIC CONFERENCE, WASHINGTON DC

CD-ROM

The Way of the Lord Jesus

Germaine Grisez

A two-volume resource work on Church moral teachings.

—AVAILABLE ON THE *WELCOME TO THE CATHOLIC CHURCH* CD-ROM FROM HARMONY MEDIA INC., CERVAIS, OR

BOOK

The Challenge of Faith

John Powell, S.J.

Examines what authentic spirituality is from the viewpoint of our ongoing interaction and dialogue with God. 1998.

—AVAILABLE FROM THOMAS MORE PUBLISHING, ALLEN, TX

BOOK

God the Father: Meditations for the Millennium

Mark Link, S.J.

A twenty-week daily meditation program built around seven themes: "Search for the Father," "Touch of the Father," etc.

—AVAILABLE FROM THOMAS MORE PUBLISHING, ALLEN, TX

NOTE

For a list of (1) General resources for professional background and (2) Addresses, phone/fax numbers of major publishing companies, see Appendix B of this Resource Manual.

CHAPTER 20
Loving Neighbor

CHAPTER at a Glance

The aim of this chapter is to give the students an overview and deeper awareness of:

1 *How the last seven commandments invite and guide us as we strive to live as members of Christ's Body*

2 *How this provides us with a special challenge in today's world*

READ—Have a student read aloud the scriptural introduction, which begins, "Jesus said: 'I love you just as . . .'" Have another student read aloud the commentary. It begins: "Jesus redefined and gave new focus to the Ten Commandments . . ."

DISCUSS—Jesus says in the scriptural instruction: "Love one another, just as I love you." Ask the students: "Isn't it impossible for us to love others as Jesus loved us?"

Somewhere in the discussion, be sure to stress that the Gospel contains five references to the fact that what is impossible for us to do is possible for God.

The classic example is the angel's word to Mary that she is to bear a son, even though she is a virgin. LUKE 1:37 The four other references are: MATTHEW 17:20, 19:26, MARK 10:27, and LUKE 18:27. Stress, also, that every command or call from God carries with it the grace to carry it out. 2 CORINTHIANS 12:9

> QUESTION **1** ***Why do people tend not to get involved in cases like Steve's, saying, "It's none of my business?" Evaluate their reasons. Why would/wouldn't you be inclined to get involved in a case like Steve's?***

Three questions are at issue here:

1 *Why do people tend to not get involved?*
2 *Evaluate their reasons.*
3 *Why would/wouldn't you be inclined to become involved?*

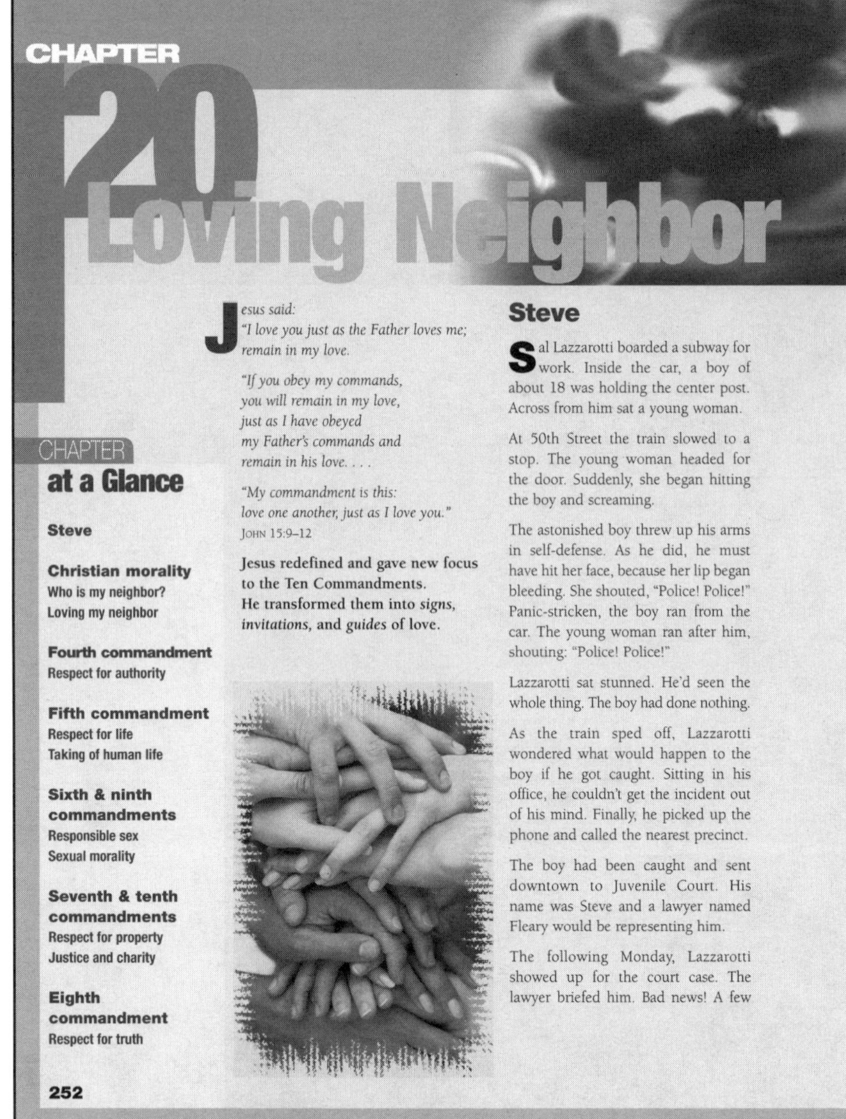

CHAPTER 20 Loving Neighbor

Jesus said:
"I love you just as the Father loves me;
remain in my love.

"If you obey my commands,
you will remain in my love,
just as I have obeyed
my Father's commands and
remain in his love. . . .

"My commandment is this:
love one another, just as I love you."
JOHN 15:9–12

Jesus redefined and gave new focus to the Ten Commandments. He transformed them into *signs, invitations*, and *guides* of love.

CHAPTER at a Glance

Steve

Christian morality
Who is my neighbor?
Loving my neighbor

Fourth commandment
Respect for authority

Fifth commandment
Respect for life
Taking of human life

Sixth & ninth commandments
Responsible sex
Sexual morality

Seventh & tenth commandments
Respect for property
Justice and charity

Eighth commandment
Respect for truth

Steve

Sal Lazzarotti boarded a subway for work. Inside the car, a boy of about 18 was holding the center post. Across from him sat a young woman.

At 50th Street the train slowed to a stop. The young woman headed for the door. Suddenly, she began hitting the boy and screaming.

The astonished boy threw up his arms in self-defense. As he did, he must have hit her face, because her lip began bleeding. She shouted, "Police! Police!" Panic-stricken, the boy ran from the car. The young woman ran after him, shouting: "Police! Police!"

Lazzarotti sat stunned. He'd seen the whole thing. The boy had done nothing.

As the train sped off, Lazzarotti wondered what would happen to the boy if he got caught. Sitting in his office, he couldn't get the incident out of his mind. Finally, he picked up the phone and called the nearest precinct.

The boy had been caught and sent downtown to Juvenile Court. His name was Steve and a lawyer named Fleary would be representing him.

The following Monday, Lazzarotti showed up for the court case. The lawyer briefed him. Bad news! A few

252

Steve

DISCUSS—Ask students: "Had the artist not come to Steve's defense, what effect do you think this failure would have had on:

1 the outcome of the trial,
2 Steve's future,
3 the girl's future,
4 Sal Lazzaroti's future?

1 *The outcome of the trial was sealed had Sal Lazzaroti not taken the trouble to inquire about Steve and to take time from work to testify on his behalf.*

2 *Steve would have probably ended up in prison for a crime of which he was innocent. It may have embittered him and started him on a crime career. On the other hand, Sal may have inspired him to help others, as Sal had helped him.*

NOTES

years ago Steve had been picked up with other boys on suspicion of stealing a car, but wasn't charged.

When the judge began questioning the girl, Lazzarotti couldn't believe what she was saying. At that point the judge asked her to be more specific, saying, "A witness is present and will be testifying." When she heard this, she grew nervous and and started contradicting herself.

The judge stopped. He called both lawyers forward and huddled with them. Both nodded in agreement; the young woman probably needed psychiatric help. The judge dismissed the case.

Steve grasped Lazzarotti's hand in gratitude, too choked to speak. On his way home, Lazzarotti thought to himself, "How close I came to not getting involved, saying 'It's none of my business.'"

RETOLD FROM SAL LAZZAROTTI: "WHY SHOULD I GET INVOLVED?" GUIDEPOSTS MAGAZINE

1 Why do people tend not to get involved in cases like Steve's, saying, "It's none of my business"? Evaluate their reasons. Why would/wouldn't you be inclined to get involved in a case like Steve's?

Christian morality

Making my neighbor's *need* "my business" is at the very heart of what Christian morality is all about.

One day a man asked Jesus, "Who is my neighbor?" Jesus responded by telling him this parable.

There was once a man who was going down from Jerusalem to Jericho when robbers attacked him, stripped him, and beat him up, leaving him half-dead.

It so happened that a priest was going down that road; but when he saw the man, he walked on by on the other side. In the same way a Levite also came there, went over and looked at the man, and walked on by on the other side.

But a Samaritan who was traveling that way came upon the man, and when he saw him, his heart was filled with pity.

The Good Samaritan, Van Gogh.

He went over to him, poured wine on his wounds and bandaged them;
then he put the man on his own animal and took him to an inn, where he took care of him.

The next day he took out two silver coins and gave them to the innkeeper.
"Take care of him . . .
and when I come back this way,
I will pass you whatever else
you spend on him."

STAGE 3: CHAPTER 20 253

3 *The girl needed help badly. Thanks to Sal's testimony at the hearing, she got it. It could have saved her life.*

4 *Finally, had Sal not done what he did, he may have spent his life regretting the missed opportunity to make a major difference in the lives of several people, including himself.*

Van Gogh, "The Good Samaritan"

CLARIFY—Spend some time on Vincent Van Gogh (1853–1890). His story is well worth it.

■ *He was born in the Netherlands. At 22, he became somewhat of a religious fanatic and began preaching. His unconventional, enthusiastic style did not move people.*

At the age of 27, he began to paint, creating some 1,700 drawings and paintings (referred to as postimpressionistic in style). Again, he met with apparent failure, selling only one painting in his lifetime: "Cypress and Flowering Tree" for $80. (That same painting sold for $1.3 million in 1970.)

Van Gogh went to Paris in 1886. Three years later, he ended up in Auvers, where a Dr. Gachet treated him for "oncoming insanity." In 1890, he took his own life. A century later, his painting, "Portrait of Dr. Gachet," sold for $82.5 million.

Van Gogh painted over 40 self-portraits. (Someone said, "What a vain creature to paint that many paintings of himself. The truth was he could not afford a model.) A year before his death, he painted a self-portrait entitled "Portrait of the Artist Without Beard" which sold for $71 million in the 1990s.

In 1972, a four-story art museum was built in Amsterdam to house Van Gogh's works exclusively. Only a handful of artists have been so honored.

Besides leaving behind a museum full of art, he left behind a series of letters to his brother Theo. A brief excerpt from one letter contains more wisdom than some entire books:

I always think the best way
to know God is to love many things.
Love a friend, a wife . . . whatever. . . .
Then, you will know there is a God.
Then, you will believe.

Christian morality

CLARIFY—The road from Jerusalem to Jericho twists downward through narrow passes, making travelers especially vulnerable to bands of outlaws.

A letter from A.D. 171 complains of the banditry along the road. Historical records testify that merchants who traveled the road regularly often had to pay protection money to local thugs for safe passage.

This infamous road provided Jesus with a realistic setting for his parable.

QUESTION **2 *Why do you think the priest and the Levite bypassed the man? Why do you think Jesus chose a Samaritan to be the hero of the story?***

We begin with the second question, which is the most important of the two:

- *Making a Samaritan the hero would have shocked and even angered some of his Jewish hearers. They regarded Samaritans as renegades and heretics. The rift between the two groups was rooted in Assyria's conquest of Israel (10 tribes who occupied the territory of Samaria (722 B.C.).*

  Those Jews who survived the conquest—and were not sent off as slave laborers—intermarried with the Gentile foreigners brought in by the Assyrians. The rift between Jews and Samaritans widened with time, to the point that Samaritans were banned from Jewish Temple and synagogue worship.

  The Samaritans retaliated. They made common cause with Jewish enemies, often not permitting Jews to enter their towns and villages. LUKE 9:52

  By making a Samaritan the hero of his parable, Jesus made it crystal-clear that love has no boundaries. Neighborliness is not limited to neighborhoods. This is why Jesus reworded the question so as to shift the focus of the discussion from "defining" a neighbor to "being" a neighbor.

  Jesus says, in effect, "Every member of the human family is my neighbor, including my enemies." LUKE 6:27

This brings us to the first question: "Why do you think the priest and the Levite bypassed the man?" Before taking it up in "Who is my neighbor?" take up the "Historical Connection."

HISTORICAL **Connection**

A regiment of German prisoners was being marched in single column through the streets of Moscow during World War II.

First came the Nazi officers—well fed, well dressed, heads held high. Their demeanor was one of superiority to their ill-clothed onlookers—mostly angry, Russian women who had lost sons and husbands in the fierce fighting.

Next came the German soldiers—young, thin, ill-clothed, hobbling on crutches, heads hanging in pain and shame. The street went deathly silent at the sight.

Then an old woman took a crust of dry bread from her pocket and gave it to a young soldier who could hardly walk. (It may have been her own evening meal.)

Then other women began giving the wounded soldiers bread, cigarettes, and kerchiefs. These soldiers were no longer enemies. They were suffering human beings.

Reported by Donald Nicholl
in *Triumphs of the Spirit in Russia*

And Jesus concluded,
"In your opinion, which of these three acted like a neighbor toward the man attacked by the robbers?"

The teacher of the law answered,
"The one who was kind to him."
Jesus replied, "Go, then, and do the same." LUKE 10:26–37

2 *Why do you think the priest and the Levite bypassed the man? Why do you think Jesus chose a Samaritan to be the hero of the story?*

Who is my neighbor?

The priest was probably on his way to Jerusalem to worship in the Temple. Apparently, he feared the man was dead. To touch a dead man would make him unclean and ban him temporarily from temple worship.

A Levite was somewhat like a modern deacon. He assisted the priests. 1 CHRONICLE 23:3–5 But Levites were under a different cleanliness code than priests. They could touch dead bodies.

Possibly the Levite's concern was that the robbers may have been hiding in the underbrush. Perhaps they were using the wounded man as bait to attract and rob another man.

Finally, there was the Samaritan. Jews regarded Samaritans as heretics. In Jesus' day, they were banned from the Temple and the synagogue. Their religious contributions were refused and their testimony in courts was not accepted.

Samaritans were also hostile to Jews. They made common cause with Jewish enemies, often not letting them into their towns. LUKE 9:52

Jesus chose a Samaritan as his hero to teach his listeners that love of neighbor has no boundaries. Every member of the human family is my neighbor, including my enemies. LUKE 6:27

Loving my neighbor

This brings us back to the Ten Commandments. Jesus did not abolish them, but brought them to fulfillment and redefined them in terms of love:

- **God** **Commandments 1–3**
- **Neighbor** **Commandments 4–10**

In redefining the Ten Commandments in terms of love, Jesus gave them an entirely new focus and transformed them into:

- **Signs** **Of Jesus' love for us**
- **Invitations** **To love as Jesus did**
- **Guides** **On how to love**

In the last chapter we covered the first three commandments; in this chapter we will take up the final seven: love of neighbor. We will treat them under three headings, respect for:

- **Authority and life**
- **Property and truth**
- **Conscience and Church teaching**

254 STAGE 3: CHAPTER 20

HISTORICAL **Connection**

CLARIFY—If you were looking for a modern example to illustrate how Jesus intended the Parable of the Good Samaritan to be applied to life, you could hardly find a better one than this. One courageous woman began the whole process.

Loving my neighbor

CLARIFY—Review how the commandments are a guide, an invitation, and a sign. Toward the end of his teaching ministry, Jesus made three remarkable statements:

1 *Love the Lord your God . . .*
This is the greatest . . . commandment.

NOTES

Share Your meditation

A speaker was giving a talk to parents. He stressed the need for them to reach out more to children, especially teenagers. After he finished, a mother said:

You've talked a lot
about our failure
to reach out to our children.

I've reached out again and again
to my teenage son,
but he rejects my efforts—
often coldly and cruelly.
Tell me what I'm supposed
to do now.

■ ***How would you answer that mother?***

Fourth commandment

Years ago, a popular Hollywood actor, Ricardo Montalban, wrote a highly publicized, fatherly letter to his son. It reads:

We are father and son
by the grace of God,
and I accept that privilege
and awesome responsibility. . . .
I am not your pal. . . .
I am your father.
This is 100 times more
than what a pal is. . . .
Whatever I ask you to do
is motivated by love.
This will be hard for you to understand
until you have a son of your own.
Until then, trust me.
—Your Father

3 ***Why would/wouldn't you like to receive such a letter as a daughter or son?***

Familial authority

The fourth commandment deals with respect for authority within the building block of society: the family. CCC 2207–13 It also deals with civil authority within society itself. We begin with respect for familial authority.

Years ago, Alvin Toffler made this sobering statement about the family in his book *Future Shock:*

The family has been called
the "giant shock absorber"of society—
the place to which
the bruised and battered individual returns
after doing battle with the world,
the one stable point
in an increasingly flux-filled environment.
As the superindustrial revolution unfolds,
the "shock absorber" will come in
for some shocks of its own.

PRAYER hotline

O Lord, bless all who love me,
and keep 'em lovin me.
And, Lord,
for those who don't love me,
turn their hearts,
or at least turn their ankles
so I can recognize them
by their limping.

Irish blessing

The second is . . . Love your neighbor
as you love yourself. MATTHEW 22:37–39

2 *If you love me, you will obey my commandments.* JOHN 14:15

3 *If you have love for one another . . .*
everyone will know
that you are my disciples. JOHN 13: 35

NOTEBOOK—Have the students enter this summary of the commandments in their notebooks:

- *Guide* (*to eternal life*)
  - *Love God*
  - *Love neighbor* MT 22:37-39
- *Invitation*
  - *If you love me, keep my commandments* JN 14:15
- *Sign*
  - *If you have love for one another, then everyone will know you are my disciples* JN 13:25

Fourth Commandment

QUESTION **3** ***Why would/wouldn't you write such a letter to a daughter or son?***

For those who would not like to receive such a letter from a parent, ask them to reword it so that they would like to receive it from a parent.

Share Your meditation

■ *Ask why a son or daughter would reject their efforts "coldly and cruelly."*

PRAYER hotline

Other Irish blessings:

1 *"May you live as long as you want and never want as long as you live."*

2 *"May the Good Lord take a liking to you, but not too soon."*

3 *"May you be in heaven a full half-hour afore the devil knows you're dead."*

An Irish saying: "The reason the Irish are fighting each other is that they have no other worthy opponent."

Familial authority

CLARIFY—One of the clearest summaries of the family's relationship to the state and its purpose is this statement by Pope Pius XI in his encyclical *Casti connubii:*

The family is more sacred than the state,
and members are begotten
not for the earth and for time,
but for heaven and eternity.

A summary of the family's relationship to the Church is this one by Pope Leo XIII:

The family . . . was before the Church,
or rather the first form of the Church
was the family.

QUESTION **4** ***What do you think is one of the greatest threats to the family today? Explain.***

Give students time to reflect.

CLARIFY—It's interesting to reflect upon the impact of Haven's decision. Had he not made it, this story would never have happened and millions of people would have been deprived of one of the most inspirational stories ever to come out of the Olympics.

Civil authority

CLARIFY—Father Mike Pfleger is pastor of Saint Sabina's, a Chicago inner-city parish with drug and gang problems. He listed 118 billboards advertising tobacco and alcohol within a ten-block radius of his parish. He went to the white neighborhood where he grew up, just west of Sabina's, and listed only three.

Talks with Chicago's city council and billboard owners (who admitted targeting minorities) didn't change things. So Father Pfleger and others embarked on predawn forays to paint out the product names advertised on the billboards. When he was arrested, he said, "I hate being arrested and I hate jail, but I believe you have to fight for what's right."

CLARIFY—Stress the idea that citizens have not only the *right* but also the *obligation* to refuse to obey unjust laws and governments. In his famous *Letter from a Birmingham Jail*, Martin Luther King Jr., says that there are two kinds of laws: just and unjust. As we have a moral responsibility to obey just laws, so we have a moral responsibility to disobey unjust laws. King writes:

> *I would agree with Saint Augustine that an unjust law is no law at all. . . . An unjust law is a human law that is not rooted in eternal and natural law.*

Up Close
& Personal

Bill Havens

Bill Havens was a member of the U.S. Olympic canoe team. He was scheduled to compete in the Olympics in Paris. Then he learned that his wife was expecting to give birth to their first child at the very time he was scheduled to compete.

The more Bill pondered the question, the more he thought his place was with his wife, though she urged him to compete. So he dropped from the team.

As it turned out, his wife was late giving birth to a son, and the U.S. team won the gold medal. Bill could have made both events. He never said anything to his son about being disappointed that he missed the Olympics.

Years later, a cablegram arrived from Helsinki, Finland, where the Olympics were in progress. It read: "Dad, I won. I'm bringing home the gold medal you lost while waiting for me to be born." Bill's son Frank had just won the Olympic single's canoe competition.

What Toffler predicted has come to pass. And the shocks to the family community have been so great that some social critics fear it may be heading toward "complete extinction."

Not everyone agrees with these critics; but all *do* agree that the situation is serious. Therefore, all agree that family members have an obligation—more than ever before in history—to contribute to family stability. CCC 2214–33

Concretely, parents must take to heart—more than ever—Saint Paul's words to raise their children "with Christian discipline and instruction." EPHESIANS 6:4; CCC 2221–31

And children must take to heart—more than ever—his words to respect parents. EPHESIANS 6:1–2; CCC 2214–20

God intended the family to be one of God's greatest blessings and gifts. Our gift back to God is to help the family become what God made it to be: the sign and instrument by which human society matures into the Kingdom of God. CCC 2232–33

4 What do you think is one of the greatest threats to the family today? Explain.

Civil authority

Closely related to respect for familial authority is respect for civil authority: the authority of the wider civil community. CCC 2234–46

Because we share the blessing of the civil community, we owe it special loyalty and we share in its responsibilities.

Jesus made this clear when he told his disciples "Pay to the Emperor what belongs to the Emperor." LUKE 20:25

Paul made a similar point in his letter to the Romans, saying:

> *Everyone must obey*
> *state authorities, because no authority*
> *exists without God's permission,*
> *and the existing authorities*
> *have been put there by God.* ROMANS 13:1

Conversely, the state must also respect the rights of citizens. Citizens do not exist for the state; the state exists to provide a social order in which "we may live a quiet and peaceful life with all reverence toward God and with proper conduct." 1 TIMOTHY 2:2

256 STAGE 3: *CHAPTER 20*

> *Any law that uplifts the human personality is just. Any law that degrades the human personality is unjust.*

Rory McCormick carries the whole process a step further, writing:

> *To disobey the law openly, formally, and nonviolently can be a moral act of the highest kind. . . . This is quite different from furtive disobedience to the law.*

QUESTION **5** ***Before engaging in civil disobedience, what are some things you should consider?***

CLARIFY—In November 1999, 12,000 demonstrators—including *students*—joined the yearly protest aimed at shutting down the U.S.-run military training school for South American soldiers at Fort Benning, Georgia.

NOTES

No state may trample on the God-given rights of individuals and families. If it does, citizens have not only the right but also the obligation to refuse to obey. With Saint Peter they protest, "We must obey God, not men." ACTS 5:29

5 Before engaging in civil disobedience, what are some things you should consider?

Fifth commandment

Albert Diianni has traveled widely in such places as South America, Central America, and the Philippine Islands. These travels have had a profound effect on him. Writing in *America* magazine, he says:

In my visits
to Peru, Brazil, Mexico, and the Philippines,
I have seen peoples and lands
ravaged by the corruption of political
leaders and the uncaring greed
of multinational corporations.

I have shivered at the burials of infants
who died because their parents lacked
the rudimentary education to provide
them simple hygienic or medical care.

Diianni's words put flesh and blood on these otherwise cold statistics about the people of the world:

- **Millions are illiterate**
- **Millions have no full-time job**
- **Millions suffer from hunger**

It was with these millions of human lives in mind that the bishops of the Second Vatican Council wrote:

There must be made available to all . . . what is necessary to lead a truly human life: food, clothing, and shelter. . . . We must help the poor, and do so not merely out of our abundance. . . .

This sacred Council urges all . . . to remember the early Christian saying . . . "If you don't feed those dying of hunger, you have killed them."
THE CHURCH IN THE MODERN WORLD, 26, 69

This shocking statement jolts us out of our complacency. It makes us realize that when brothers or sisters are dying of hunger, we have a grave obligation to feed them, inasmuch as we are able.

It is against this disturbing background that we take up the fifth commandment God gave Moses at Mount Sinai: "Do not commit murder." CCC 2258–62

THINK about it

If you can't feed a hundred people, feed just one.

Mother Teresa

HISTORICAL Connection

During the Great Depression, New York's former mayor, Fiorello La Guardia, sometimes presided at court.

Once, an unemployed man was brought before him for stealing bread for his family. La Guardia said, "Sir, I'm sorry! The law excepts no one. I fine you $10."

Then La Guardia opened his wallet, gave the man $10, remitted the fine, and levied a 50-cent fine on everyone in the courtroom for living in a city where a person had to steal to feed his family.

The man left the courtroom with tears in his eyes and $47.50 in his pocket.

Retold from *Reflections for Peace of Mind:* Maurice Nassan, S.J.

Ten protesters were convicted and face up to 12 months in prison and $10,000 in fines for trespassing. Each act of civil disobedience, therefore, should only be planned and carried out after parental and legal consultation.

Fifth commandment

CLARIFY—President John F. Kennedy said: "If a free society cannot help the many who are poor, it cannot save the few who are rich." We could help the poor immeasurably simply by curtailing the grotesque waste of food and energy.

British economist Barbara Ward noted that people in wealthy nations throw away about 15 percent of all the food they buy. She pointed out that "one B-1 bomber uses as much gasoline in one year as the entire bus fleet of the United States."

Statistics like this were a source of grave concern to General Dwight D. Eisenhower (1890–1969). He was the commander in chief who directed the successful D-day invasions of Normandy (June 1944) and the conquest of western Germany (by May 1945). In 1952 he was elected the 34th president of the U.S.

Toward the end of his life he made this surprising statement:

Every gun that is made, every warship
that is launched, every rocket that is fired,
signifies in the final sense a theft from
those who hunger and are not fed,
those who are cold and not clothed.

THINK about it

Some people dismiss this statement as ridiculous. Perhaps they should think again.

- *At the age of 40, Mother Teresa went into the slums of Calcutta, bought a tiny old building with no floor, and started a school for poor children. She had no chairs, desks, or tables. Her chalkboard was the dirt floor, which she rubbed smooth with an old rag. Her chalk was a stick with a pointed end.*

Now, after her death, there are 100 fully equipped schools, 750 mobile dispensaries, 120 leprosy clinics, 150 homes for the dying, 30 homes for abandoned children, and 40,000 volunteer helpers worldwide.

Like the boy who gave his loaves and fishes to Jesus (read John 6:5–13 to the students), she did the same. And Jesus multiplied them beyond her wildest dream.

HISTORICAL Connection

Fiorello La Guardia (1882–1947) served as mayor of New York City for 11 years, from 1934 to 1945. Historians regard him as the greatest reform mayor the city ever had. The story told here is typical of his remarkable vitality and creativity.

Murder

ACTIVITY—The murder of innocent human life by senseless shootings in schools in the late 1990s has fueled the debate about the over-the-counter sale of handguns and rapid-fire assault rifles.

The powerful National Rifle Association holds that Americans have a moral and constitutional right to own guns for various reasons, such as protection against unjust aggressors, and opposes any tampering with that "right."

On the other hand, easy access to handguns and assault rifles is a continuing and growing threat to innocent life in America.

Have the students do a private ballot on whether they favor the NRA position or legislative change. Tally and discuss.

War

CLARIFY—Consider just one example:

- *In March 1988, Iraq dropped chemical bombs on the city of Halabjah. The* London Daily Telegraph *described the city as an "open grave." Estimates of the dead ranged up to 5,000. The people who did not die were covered with mustard gas burns and will be "pulmonary cripples the rest of their lives." Japan used poison gas against China (1937–45). Egypt used mustard against Yemen (1963–67). Poison gas is called the "poor man's atomic bomb." Libya, Iraq, Iran, and Syria are all producing it. Western security services feel it is only a matter of time before terrorists begin using it to terrorize governments and create mass panic.*

RALPH KINNEY: "THE GROWING MENACE OF CHEMICAL WEAPONS," *READER'S DIGEST*, JULY 1989

Suicide

CLARIFY—The case of hunger strikes is one of the best ways to illustrate the difference between indirect (not intending) and direct taking of one's life. Be sure the students understand when the indirect taking of one's life is morally permissible and when it is not. This is key.

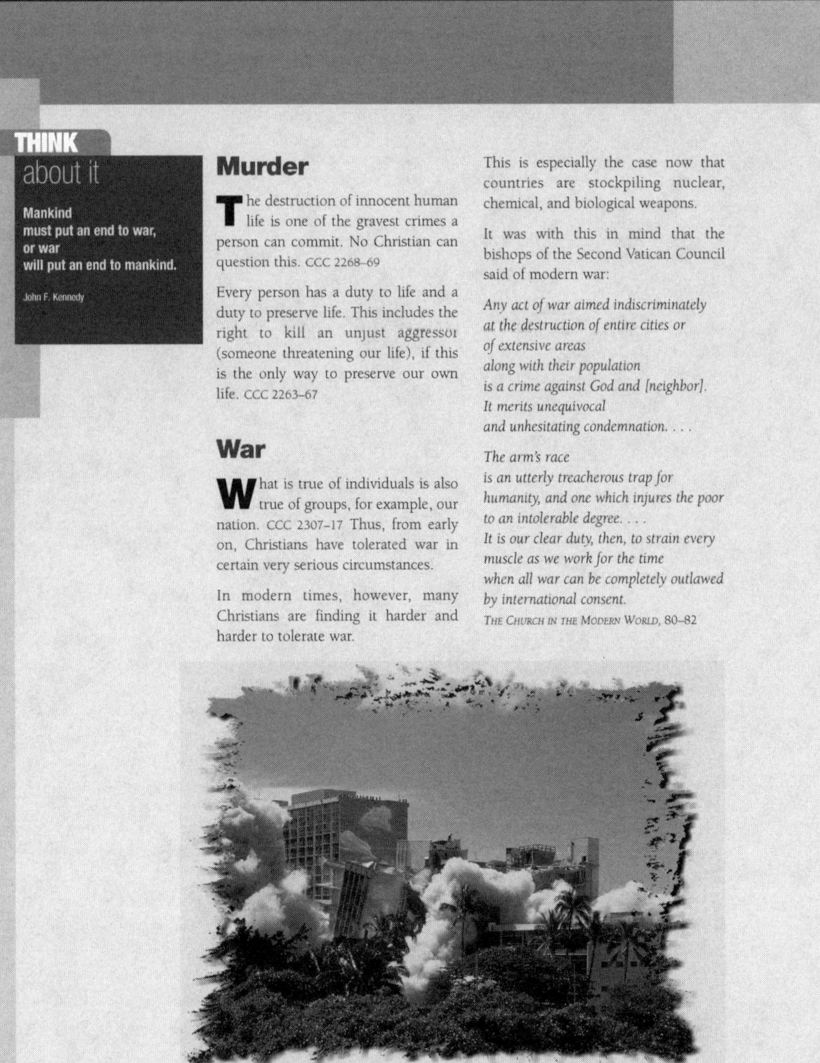

THINK about it

Mankind must put an end to war, or war will put an end to mankind.

John F. Kennedy

Murder

The destruction of innocent human life is one of the gravest crimes a person can commit. No Christian can question this. CCC 2268–69

Every person has a duty to life and a duty to preserve life. This includes the right to kill an unjust aggressor (someone threatening our life), if this is the only way to preserve our own life. CCC 2263–67

War

What is true of individuals is also true of groups, for example, our nation. CCC 2307–17 Thus, from early on, Christians have tolerated war in certain very serious circumstances.

In modern times, however, many Christians are finding it harder and harder to tolerate war.

This is especially the case now that countries are stockpiling nuclear, chemical, and biological weapons.

It was with this in mind that the bishops of the Second Vatican Council said of modern war:

Any act of war aimed indiscriminately
at the destruction of entire cities or
of extensive areas
along with their population
is a crime against God and [neighbor].
It merits unequivocal
and unhesitating condemnation. . . .

The arm's race
is an utterly treacherous trap for
humanity, and one which injures the poor
to an intolerable degree. . . .
It is our clear duty, then, to strain every
muscle as we work for the time
when all war can be completely outlawed
by international consent.

THE CHURCH IN THE MODERN WORLD, 80–82

258 STAGE 3: *CHAPTER 20*

NOTEBOOK—The following diagram sums up the difference between the direct (intended) and the indirect (not intended) taking of one's life.

- *Indirect*
  - *Accepts death if necessary*
  - *Uses possibility of death to "push" others*
- *Direct*
  - *Uses death*
  - *as a means to an end*

QUESTION **6** ***Can you give an example of an end that is "proportionate to the risk to the striker's life"?***

- *Political prisoners who go on a hunger strike as a last resort to stop torture that leads to maiming and death.*

NOTES

As never before, Christians are becoming aware of their responsibility to be peacemakers in the spirit of the Sermon on the Mount:

Happy are those who work for peace;
God will call them his children!
MATTHEW 5:9

Suicide

Closely related to taking another's life is taking one's own life. CCC 2280–83 A question arises, however, concerning such actions as hunger strikes, which involve the possibility of taking one's own life. There are three kinds of strikes.

The first kind is where the striker *intends* his death as a means to an important end. In other words, it involves the *direct* killing of oneself. This is gravely wrong, no matter how lofty the motive.

The second kind is where striker does *not* intend his or her death, but will accept it, if necessary.

The third kind is where the striker does *not* intend death, but uses the possibility of death to "push" the other side.

These latter two cases involve *indirect* killing of oneself. We say indirect because in neither case does the striker intend death. In fact, the striker hopes and prays it won't occur. Both cases, therefore, are morally permissible when the importance of the end is proportionate to the risk to the striker's life.

6 *Can you give an example of an end that is "proportionate to the risk to the striker's life"?*

Capital punishment

Sister Helen Prejean wrote a book entitled *Dead Man Walking* upon which the movie of the same title is based. In it she lists a number of cases of people sent to death row and later found to be innocent.

One innocent man was Randall Adams. The Texas Court of Criminal Appeals overturned his murder conviction in 1989 when it was proven that prosecutors fabricated evidence and used the perjured testimony of the actual murderer.

People have tended to view capital punishment as a "last resort" measure taken by society to defend itself against hard-core criminals. Today, however, many Christians are finding capital punishment harder and harder to justify.

First of all, it risks executing the innocent, especially the poor who cannot afford quality defense (over half death-row inmates are minorities, most of whom are poor and poorly represented by counsel).

Second, it tends to erode respect for life and dehumanize all concerned.

Third, it frustrates the primary purpose of punishment: rehabilitation.

Finally, it leads to incredible court delays that diminish its effectiveness as a deterrent (major reason given for justifying it). CCC 2263–67

7 *How do you feel about capital punishment and why?*

THINK about it

Capital punishment is as fundamentally wrong as a cure for crime as charity is wrong as a cure for poverty.

Henry Ford

LIFE Connection

Ours is a world of nuclear giants and ethical infants.

We know more about war than we know about peace, more about killing than we know about living.

We have grasped the mystery of the atom and rejected the Sermon on the Mount.

General Omar Bradley

THINK about it

It is easier to put on slippers than to carpet the earth.

Anthony de Mello, S.J. (slightly adapted)

Capital punishment

CLARIFY—In March 2000, Governor George Ryan of Illinois declared a halt on death penalties. Among the reasons: in recent years, 85 people on death rows nationwide have been released for wrongful convictions.

A recent study by the American Bar Association lists a series of horror stories involving defense counsel in capital cases. These included "sleeping through the proceedings and failing to call witnesses for the defense of the accused."

In his 1995 encyclical *Evangelium vitae*, Pope John Paul opposed capital punishment, saying that cases where this penalty is necessary "are very rare, if not practically nonexistent." The revised *Catechism of the Catholic Church* includes this quotation.

NOTEBOOK—The following diagram sums up reasons why Christians are finding it next to impossible to justify capital punishment.

Cap. Pun.
- *Erodes respect for life*
- *Risks executing innocent*
- *Frustrates rehabilitation*
- *Ceases to deter crime*

QUESTION **7 *How do you feel about capital punishment and why?***

■ *Have students vote "For" or "Against" by secret ballot. Tally and discuss.*

THINK about it

DISCUSS—Ask: What is Ford's point?

■ *We need preventative proaction, such as education, e.g. "Give a man a fish, and you feed him for a day. Teach a man to fish and you feed him for a lifetime"?*

LIFE Connection

CLARIFY—Dr. Martin Luther King put it perhaps even more clearly, saying:

■ *Our scientific power has outrun our spiritual power. We have guided missiles and misguided men.*

THINK about it

CLARIFY—Take pornography. The best protection against it is to help people "put on slippers" —acquire a faith-mind-set that it's a:

1 *Grave abuse of one of God's most beautiful and wonderful gifts to us*

2 *Deadly evil capable of destroying our human personality and our human integrity.*

This does not mean we do nothing to "carpet the world" (try to stamp out its existence). We do both; but we give priority to "putting on spiritual slippers."

Abortion

***CLARIFY*—Testifying before Connecticut's House-Senate Judiciary Committee, Dr. Paul Byrne, chairperson of the pediatric department at Saint Vincent's Medical Center in Bridgeport, Connecticut, said:**

A new human life begins at conception, when the sperm providing half the chromosomes penetrates the ovum, [enabling] the other half of the chromosomes to form a new set of chromosomes. The new DNA, the new set of chromosomes, is different from the DNA or the chromosomes of the father [and mother]. . . .

At conception the external characteristics used later for identification of the individual person—namely the color of hair, the color of skin, the color of the eyes, the sex, and the fingerprints—are already determined. . . .

At eight weeks, when all the organs are present, the medical name of the human being changes from embryo to fetus. The medical name remains fetus until changed to infant at birth.

***CLARIFY*—Judge William J. Campbell of the U.S. District Court for the Northern District of Illinois, Eastern Division, pointed out the following:**

Seven weeks after conception the fertilized egg develops into a well-proportioned, small-scale baby. It bears all of the familiar external features and all the internal organs of an adult human being. It has muscles; hands with fingers and thumbs. . . .

Brain waves have been noted at forty-three days. The heart beats; the stomach produces digestive juices.

***ACTIVITY*—You might check with the local "Right-to-Life" organization and have a representative come out to speak to the class.**

***NOTEBOOK*—Have the students enter this concise summary on abortion in their notebooks:**

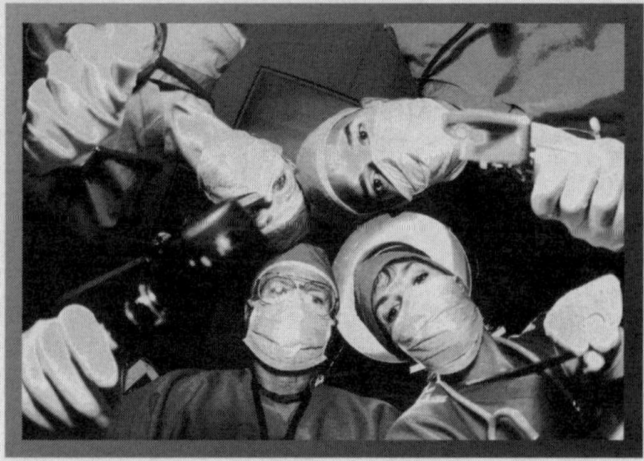

Abortion

Abortion was widespread in ancient pagan society. Early Christian response to abortion was one of militant opposition.

For example, around A.D. 80, the Didache, the oldest known Christian document apart from the Christian Scriptures, says bluntly, "You shall not practice abortion."

Under the influence of Christianity, abortion was eventually outlawed by civil authorities. Not until the twentieth century did it become widespread again.

Today, the Christian response to abortion is still one of militant opposition. CCC 2270–75 This opposition is based on the belief that the fertilized egg will develop into a human person and must therefore be protected. In dealing with the issue of abortion, however, we need to make an important distinction.

First, there is *direct* abortion, which is an action whose direct intent is to kill an unborn fetus. Direct abortion is forbidden by the fifth commandment.

Second, there is *indirect* abortion, which is an action whose direct intention is not to kill the fetus but to save the life of the mother.

For example, let us suppose that to save a pregnant mother's life, a doctor must remove a diseased uterus. The abortion of the fetus that follows indirectly from this operation is totally unwanted and uncontrollable.

To underscore the intent of *indirect* abortion, we might add that every effort to preserve the life of the fetus is made. Removing the uterus in this case is permissible, even though it leads indirectly to the fetus' death.

8 *How do you explain the statement that "abortion affects virtually every person in this country to some extent"?*

FAITH Connection

The family is more sacred than the state, and human life is created not for the earth and for time, but for heaven and eternity.

Pope Pius XI

260 STAGE 3: CHAPTER 20

Direct abortion	*Death intended*
Indirect abortion	*Death unintended*

QUESTION **8 *How do you explain the statement that "abortion affects virtually every person in this country to some extent"?***

Vice President Hubert Humphrey touched upon it, saying: "The moral test of government is how it treats those who are in the dawn of life, the children; those who are in the twilight of life, the aged; and those who are in the shadows of life, the sick, the needy and the handicapped."

Euthanasia

***NOTEBOOK*—Have the students sum up the distinction between direct euthanasia and passive euthanasia:**

NOTES

SHARE YOUR **meditation**

Euthanasia

The word *euthanasia* comes from the Greek word *euthanatos*, which means "easy death." As with abortion, the Christian response to euthanasia is one of militant opposition. CCC 2276–83 But, as with abortion, an important distinction has to be made here.

First, there is direct euthanasia (traditionally referred to as "mercy killing"). This is a deliberate act that brings about the death of someone.

The person is usually someone who is suffering greatly from old age or an incurable illness. Direct euthanasia is always gravely wrong, no matter how noble the motives.

Second, there is what some people refer to as passive euthanasia, which is totally different from direct euthanasia.

It is allowing an aged or incurably ill patient to die naturally, rather than prolonging their death needlessly and indefinitely through the use of *extraordinary* means. In such a situation it is morally permissible to allow the death to occur naturally.

9 ***Can you think of a concrete example when so-called "passive euthanasia" would be morally permissible?***

Drugs and alcohol

The danger of alcohol comes when the user abuses or misuses it. CCC 2288–91 It is gravely sinful to deliberately drink to excess, seriously impairing one's ability to function both physically and mentally. The pain and suffering brought on by such irresponsible behavior can be seen daily.

It must be noted, however, that the abuse of alcohol often stems from alcoholism, which the medical profession lists as a disease. Those suffering from this disease have a grave obligation to seek help. Moreover, we have a duty to help them in any way we can.

Related to the abuse of alcohol is the abuse of drugs. Again, the tremendous suffering brought about by drug abuse is one of the horrendous tragedies of our times.

A serious abuse of drugs for mind-altering or recreational purposes is gravely wrong.

As with those who suffer from alcoholism, those who suffer from drug addiction are gravely obliged to seek help, if they are aware of their affliction.

I watched them tear
a building down;
A gang of men in a busy town.
With a mighty heave
and lusty yell,
They swung a beam
and a side wall fell.

I said to the foreman,
"Are these men as skilled
as the men you'd use
if you had to build?"

He laughed and said, "No indeed!
Any worker is all I'd need.
And I can wreck in a day or two
what it took the builder
a year to do."

And I thought to myself
as I went my way,
"Just which of these roles
have I tried to play?"

Am I a builder
who works with care,
measuring life
by the rule and square,
Or am I a wrecker
as I walk the town,
content with the labor
of tearing down?

Author unknown

■ ***Why does there seem to be a tendency to "tear down" (reputations, ideas, etc.)?***

Direct	*Cause death:*	*Lethal injection*
Passive	*Allow death:*	*Withhold medicine*

QUESTION **9** ***Can you think of a concrete example when so-called "passive euthanasia" would be morally permissible?***

■ *A terminally ill person is dying. Rather than use extraordinary means simply to delay death for a short time for no reasonable purpose, the doctor allows nature to take its course.*

CLARIFY—Related to euthanasia is "assisted suicide." It's been publicized in books, like Lonny Shaelson's *A Chosen Death: Dying Confront Assisted Suicide* (1995), and by Dr. Jack Kevorkian, who was in attendance at the deaths of dozens in the 1990s. Oregon voters passed the Death with Dignity Act in 1994.

Concerning assisted suicide, Pope John Paul II wrote in *Evangelium vitae* (1995):

■ *To concur with the intention of another person to commit suicide and to help in carrying it out . . . means to cooperate in and at times be the actual perpetrator of an injustice which can never be excused even if requested.*

Drugs and alcohol

Alcoholics Anonymous, founded in 1935, is the "best therapy" ever devised for helping alcoholics. The heart of the program is its "Twelve Steps," by which millions of recovering alcoholics have gained and maintained sobriety.

(You might wish to review the first five steps discussed on page 173 in reference to the sacrament of Reconciliation.)

CLARIFY—Cocaine Anonymous also uses the same program to help cocaine addicts kick their addiction. In 1990, the National Institute on Drug Abuse estimated that some three million Americans use cocaine.

Programs costing up to $12,000 per addict per month have had minimal practical success. The only really successful program is Cocaine Anonymous. An estimated 50 percent of those who remain faithful to the CA program for at least a year stay off drugs completely. Over 1,600 CA groups are operating in the United States and Canada.

As mentioned earlier, you might check the AA listings for speakers to youth groups.

Share Your **meditation**

You might prefer to hold off on this meditation until you discuss "Detraction" on page 271. It is especially powerful in connection with that topic.

Sixth and ninth commandments

QUESTION **10** ***How would you answer this question? (What do we mean when we say of a young husband and wife: They truly love each other deeply?)***

■ *The purpose of this question is to get the students to probe more deeply into what constitutes "true love" and " responsible sex. In other words, the purpose is to prepare them for the material ahead. Let the discussion continue as long as it is fruitful.*

Love versus feeling

NOTEBOOK—Sum up the characteristics of feeling and love for entry into notebooks.

Feeling is
- *High-voltage infatuation*
- *Intoxication of being desired*
- *The thrill of taking a leap*
- *An emotional sprint*

Love is
- *Enduring commitment*
- *Disciplined work*
- *An act of the will*
- *A marathon of the heart*

You might wish to connect these points with the "Dynamic of marriage" and its four phases on pages 196–97.

QUESTION **11** ***How would you answer that question? (How should we understand the expression* responsible sex*?")***

Responsible sex celebrates
- *Love*
- *Life*
- *Faith*

Sex celebrates love

CLARIFY—Stress the idea that "sex is not the only expression of love between two people. Rather, it is the crowning expression of a marathon of prior expressions."

Stress, also, that a sexual expression of love involves far more than sexual intercourse. Recall and review the "sex poll" cited in the discussion of the power of touch (page 185).

Remember once more that columnist Ann Landers asked her women readers to respond to this question:

■ *Would you be content*
to be held close and treated tenderly
and forget about "the act"?
Answer yes or no
and please add one sentence:
I am over (or under) 40 years of age.

Sixth and ninth commandments

Some people view sex as recreation and sex partners as instruments of pleasure. Today, there is growing rejection of this attitude. More and more, people are agreeing that sex must be responsible: it must be based on love.

But this brings up the question: What is love? In other words, what do we mean when we say of a young husband and wife: "They really love each other deeply"?

10 How would you answer this question?

Love versus feeling

There is a lot of confusion about what people mean by love. One writer alludes to part of this confusion, saying that love is not a *feeling* but a commitment.

Feeling
is the high-voltage, circuit-blowing
infatuation we've all experienced
when we connect with someone new.
It is the intoxication
of being accepted and desired.
It is the thrill of taking a leap,
shedding clothes and inhibitions,
being dazzled by the private
magnificence of another. . . .
but in the end, sadly,
it is an emotional sprint. . . .

Commitment,
by contrast, is a marathon of the heart.
It requires training, discipline,
endurance and work.
It is not a spectator sport or an event
whose outcome can be decided in
seconds.

It is pushing up hills and suffering pain
and resisting the temptation to drop out. . . .
When love is viewed as an act of will . . .
it can survive as long as your heart beats.
Art Carney

This brings us to the big question: How should we understand the expression *responsible sex?*

11 How would you answer that question?

Responsible sex is not yielding to a "circuit-blowing" feeling. It is not taking a "leap" and "shedding inhibitions" because we find each other "exciting."

262 Stage 3: Chapter 20

NOTES

Nor is it engaging in an "emotional sprint," just to prove to the other that we do really like them very much.

Responsible sex is something much more precious. It is, indeed, "a marathon of the heart." It is the "crown" of a shared commitment that has been won after a journey of mutual discipline, sacrifice, and fidelity.

Responsible sex is a celebration of three great God-given gifts: love, life, and faith.

Sex celebrates love

Responsible sex is a celebration of the mystery of love. It celebrates the flowering of love that is committed to "pushing up hills and suffering pain" as long as the heart beats.

Here we need to keep in mind that sex is not the only expression of love between husband and wife. Rather, it is the *crowning* expression of many expressions of love between the two. These prior expressions take a variety of forms. Saint Paul lists some of them:

Love is patient and kind;
it is not jealous or conceited or proud;
love is not ill-mannered
or selfish or irritable;
love does not keep a record of wrongs;
love is not happy with evil,
but is happy with the truth.
Love never gives up.
1 CORINTHIANS 13:4–7

In other words, Paul is saying that love expresses itself in a multitude of everyday, concrete ways. The crowning expression, however, is the sexual union.

Sex celebrates life

Responsible sex also celebrates the mystery of life. Concerning this point, someone once said that every birth begins with a love story. This is simply another way of describing responsible sex. It is a way of saying that sex joins together in the same loving embrace the two purposes for which God ordained it. God intended the sexual union to be:

- **Unitive**
- **Procreative**

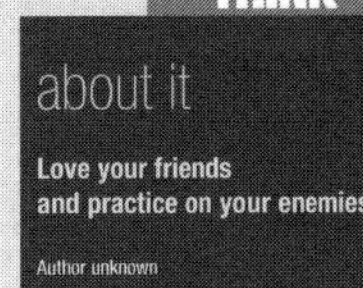

THINK
about it
Love your friends and practice on your enemies.
Author unknown

The responses were amazing:

More than 90,000 women cast their ballots. Seventy-two percent said yes. . . .
Of those 72 percent who said yes,
40 percent were under 40 years old.
That was the most surprising aspect
of the survey. . . .

[One woman wrote:]
The best part is the cuddling and caressing and the tender words that come from caring. JANUARY 15, 1985

DISCUSS—Ask students: What point about sex does the Ann Landers survey make?

The key point is that a sexual expression
of love involves far more
than the act of sexual intercourse.

Sex celebrates life

CLARIFY—This section dovetails and reviews the key points made in "Mirror of God's Love" (chapter 15, page 194) which provides the relevant references to the *Catechism of the Catholic Church*.)

NOTEBOOK—After developing it on the board, have the students enter the following summary in their notebooks:

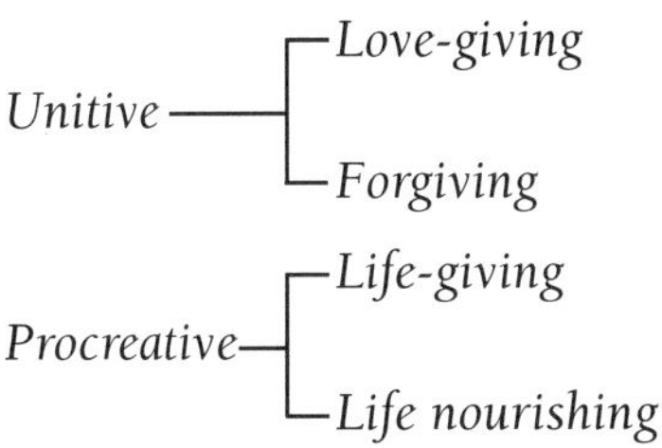

THINK about it

In a moment of humorous cynicism, Oscar Wilde (1856–1900), Irish poet, dramatist, and novelist said:

Always forgive your enemies.
Nothing annoys them so much.

Henry Wadsworth Longfellow (1807–82), the American poet, said, in a serious vein:

If we could read
the secret history of our enemies
we should find in each man's life
sorrow and suffering enough
to disarm all hostility.

Martin Luther King Jr., makes an even more sublime statement about loving your enemies:

Love is the only force
capable of transforming an enemy
into a friend.

An unknown author sums up the idea of loving one's enemies, saying:

No one needs love more
than someone who doesn't deserve it.

Share Your meditation

You might wish to share these thoughts of other people on mothers and children:

1 *Simply having children does not make mothers.* JOHN SHEDD

2 *The best thing a father can do for his children is to love their mother.* THEODORE HESBURGH

PRAYER hotline

■ *God put something noble and good in every human heart.* MARK TWAIN

Sex celebrates faith

CLARIFY—It is not uncommon for deeply loving couples to speak of a "faith experience of God" at the "height of sexual union."

Touching on the possibility of such an experience, Pope Saint Leo the Great made this statement:

■ *In the gospel of John, the Lord says: "Beloved, let us love one another, for love is from God". . . . The faithful should therefore enter into themselves and make a true judgment. . . .*

If they find some store of love's fruit [generosity, kindness, forgiveness] in their hearts, they should not doubt God's presence within them.

QUADRAGESIMA ANNO

QUESTION **12** ***What are some lesser ways you can celebrate these same three gifts? (Love, life, faith)***

1 *Love fully:*
Everything is full of beauty,
when your heart is full of love.
2 *Live fully:*
The creed of the true saint is
to make the most of life, and
to make the best of it. EDWIN HUBBELL CHAPIN
3 *Believe fully:*
Believe that life is worth living,
and your belief
will help create the fact. WILLIAM JAMES

SHARE YOUR meditation

When God
wants a great job done
in the world
or a great wrong righted,
he goes about it
in a very unusual way.

He doesn't stir up his earthquakes
or send forth his thunderbolts.
Instead he has
a helpless baby born,
perhaps in a simple home . . .
[to] some obscure mother.

And then God puts the idea
into the mother's heart,
and she puts it
into the baby's mind.
And then God waits.

E. T. Sullivan

■ ***After reading this, what thoughts occur to you?***

PRAYER hotline

Lord, help me to see what I looked like when you first dreamed of me.

Author unknown

First, God intended the sexual union to be *unitive*.

This means that God ordained sex to be the way for a married couple to celebrate and strengthen the love bond that unites them.

Second, God intended the sexual union to be *procreative*.

This means that God ordained sex to be the way a married couple cooperates with God to bring new life into the world.

The unitive and the procreative dimensions of the sexual union might be compared to the body and soul of a person.

God joined them together and intended them to work together. In this sense, responsible sex is not just a celebration of love.

It is also a celebration of life.

Sex celebrates faith

Many married couples testify that at the height of sexual union they sometimes soar beyond themselves. They are caught up in an experience that they can only describe as mystical: one that goes to the heart of their marriage.

This "mystical" experience is a deep faith experience of God—especially God's presence in the love bond that unites them.

It is a faith experience of the fact that Jesus blessed the love of a husband and wife in the most remarkable way imaginable. He raised their love to the level of a sacrament. Commenting on this, one author writes:

In Christian marriage
God covenants with the couple. . . .
God promises to stand by the couple . . .

264 STAGE 3: CHAPTER 20

Sexual morality

CLARIFY—The caution given in chapter 18 of the manual concerning the Sunday Mass obligation (third commandment) needs to be repeated again concerning sexual morality.

We need to be extremely sensitive in dealing with it. Many people (especially young people) are in a state of confusion—even alienation—in matters of faith.

■ *Therefore, we should be careful not to load a crippling guilt trip on them—or to alienate them further—by a heavy-handed, negative approach to sexual morality.*

We need to keep in mind the words of Isaiah, who described the gentle

NOTES

so that they can initiate a union . . .
and bring it to maturity in love.
LADISLAS ORSY

In brief, then, responsible sex is a "crowning" celebration of God's three greatest gifts: love, life, and faith.

12 ***What are some lesser ways you can celebrate these same three gifts?***

Sexual morality

Saint Paul likened the love of a husband for his wife to the mystery of God's love for Israel and Christ's love for his Church. EPHESIANS 5:25–33

It is only against the background of such a mystery that we can appreciate the sixth commandment ("Do not commit adultery") and the ninth commandment ("Do not desire another man's wife").

The traditional teaching of the Catholic Church on responsible sex is rooted in these two commandments. We may sum up this teaching in the following six statements:

1. Sex is a gift from God to be treasured exclusively as the celebration of love, life, and faith between a husband and a wife.

2. Sex involves giving of one's total self to the other. This gift demands such a deep commitment and dedication that it can be made only with the help of the grace that God gives through the sacrament of Marriage.

3. The sexual union between husband and wife must always respect both the unitive and the procreative purposes for which God ordained it.

4. All voluntary sexual activity or pleasure (thoughts, words, and actions) outside of the marriage is objectively and gravely wrong. Subjectively, however, the gravity of an act may be diminished because of circumstances.

For example, someone watching a movie may be caught by surprise by an unanticipated sequence that is sexually exciting. This could result in a powerful sexual reaction that was neither foreseen nor intended.

On the other hand, to watch a movie or read a book simply because it is sexually stimulating and exciting is objectively and gravely wrong.

sensitivity of the Lord's servant (the Messiah) in these terms:

"He will not break off a bent reed
nor put out a flickering lamp." ISAIAH 42:3

CLARIFY—One thing that complicates sexual morality for young people is the practice of social dating, a comparatively recent practice. Formerly, young people did not "date" until they were seriously thinking about marriage.

The term given to this immediate preparation for marriage was courtship (serious dating). Although marriage did not automatically follow, courtship was regarded as a definite prelude to marriage. Furthermore, courtship usually took place within the context of a protective setting.

■ *With the advent of modern technology (car, theater), social life and entertainment became less family centered. As a result, young adults began to develop a social life completely divorced from the home or family setting.*

This also led to social dating. Adding to the phenomenon was our modern educational process. School social activities and the fact that marriage was now delayed until a young person finished college made some form of social dating desirable, if not necessary.

■ *Today, social dating is aimed primarily at companionship and enjoyment, while serious dating (courtship) implies the further aim of selecting a marriage partner.*

ACTIVITY—Related to sex is the question of AIDS. Review a few basics to relieve any false fears. Have students write "True" or "False" to the following. Discuss as needed.

1 *Babies born of mothers infected with the AIDS virus can be infected by the AIDS virus in the mother's womb. (True)*
2 *It's good to avoid swimming in a widely-used public pool as a precaution against picking up the AIDS virus. (False)*
3 *It is somewhat dangerous to sit next to an AIDS-infected person for any length of time in a crowded area. (False)*
4 *Insects, like mosquitoes, have been known to carry the AIDS virus from one person to another. (False)*
5 *Sharing sexual fluids during sexual activity is the major way to become infected with the AIDS virus. (True)*
6 *Tragically, paramedics are exposed to the AIDS virus in giving mouth-to-mouth resuscitation to AIDS victims. (False)*
7 *It is remotely possible to pick up the AIDS virus from a public toilet just after it has been used by an AIDS victim. (False)*

THINK about it

The people who make a difference are not the ones with the credentials, but the ones with the concern. MAX LUCADO

THINK about it

■ *I'm going your way, so let us go hand in hand. . . . Let us help one another while we may.* William Morris

Seventh and tenth commandments

DISCUSS—Frank Mihalic credits sportswriter Bob Considine for the following story about the great heavyweight champion Joe Louis. It goes something like this:

> ■ *At one point, Joe invested some of his earnings in a 500-acre farm. One day, he decided to ride out alone on horseback to take a closer, leisurely look at it.*
>
> *In a secluded, wooded corner of the farm, he came upon a cottage. Since it clearly looked occupied, Joe decided to see who lived there. After all, everything on the property belonged to him now. So he knocked at the door.*
>
> *An elderly white man and his wife came to the door. "Whad'ya want?" snapped the man. Joe tipped his hat and said: "I just happened to be riding by and. . . ." "Well, keep riding!" snarled the old man. Joe was stunned by his hostile reaction. But he said calmly, "Something wrong?" The old man snarled, "You bet there is! Some nigger just bought this place."*

Ask the students, If you had been Joe, what would you say and do at this point?

After the students have discussed it, ask: What do you think Joe did say and do?

> ■ *Joe stayed cool and said in his typical, low-key way:*
>
> *"That's why I'm here. I have a message from the owner. He'd like you to stay, just as you're doing now. He also said there'd be no rent while he was owner."*

5. Young people, especially, should not lose heart or become discouraged when it comes to the problems and the moral failures they experience in matters related to sex. They should learn to speak maturely and frankly about these problems with a parent, a counselor, or a priest.

6. All Christians should realize that temptations against the sixth and the ninth commandments are not a sign of depravity.

Rather, they are a sign of our humanity and our need for the healing and the forgiveness that Jesus came to bring us.

Self-mastery is a long and exacting work.
One can never consider it acquired
once and for all.
It presupposes renewed effort
at all stages of life.
The effort required
can be more intense in certain periods,
such as when the personality
is being formed during childhood
and adolescence. CCC 2342

THINK about it

I vowed never to marry until I found the ideal woman. Well, I found her. But, alas, she was waiting for the ideal man.

Composer Robert Schumann

Finally, we should never forget that God is more compassionate and eager to forgive than we are to ask for forgiveness—no matter how often we fall victim to temptation and sin.

Seventh and tenth commandments

Martin Luther King, Jr., led the struggle for human and civil rights in the United States. A turning point came in 1963 at the Lincoln Memorial in Washington.

There, Dr. King delivered his famous "I Have a Dream" speech. A year later, he was awarded the Nobel Peace Prize. In his acceptance speech, he said:

We have learned
to fly in the air like birds
and to swim in the sea like fish.
But we have not learned
the simple act of living together
as brothers and sisters.

It is only against the background of such a disturbing reality that we can fully appreciate the seventh and tenth commandments (respect for property).

The traditional Catholic teaching on human and civil rights is rooted in these two commandments. It holds that we are all one family under God. And since we are one family, we should treat each other that way.

Treating each other as family means honoring the dignity and the rights of one another as children of God's family. It means treating one another with justice and charity.

> *Joe then remounted his horse and continued to check out his new farm.*
> Retold from *1000 Stories You Can Use*, Vol 2, 1987. Printed in the Republic of the Phillipines.

Ownership and stewardship

CLARIFY—When it comes to ownership, Christians should keep in mind two things: (1) the tendency to greed, (2) the responsibility to share. Here are two excellent quotations relating to both:

> *The Romans had a proverb which said that money was like seawater; the more you drank the thirstier you became.*
> William Barclay

NOTES

Ownership and stewardship

Treating another with *justice* means respecting their right to own property and respecting the property they own. Treating others with *charity* means opening our hearts to those who, for various reasons, do not have adequate material goods for a decent life.

These reasons may be linked to birth: mental limitations, handicaps, sickness, or lack of marketable talents. They may also be linked to culture, such as prolonged exploitation by richer nations. Finally, the reasons may be linked to geography, such as flooding, famine, and limited natural resources.

This brings us to Catholic teaching regarding ownership, stewardship, and the distribution of the material wealth. CCC 2401–14

Jesus recognized that inequality exists when it comes to material wealth. He recognized that some people are more talented and earn more money. Some have more luck and acquire more wealth. Some are simply born into a wealthy family, culture, or country.

But Jesus also made it clear that those who are blessed with wealth have an obligation to help those who are needy. CCC 2443–49 The Parable of Lazarus and the Rich Man makes this clear. LUKE 16:19–31 The Last Judgment narrative leaves no doubt about the gravity of this obligation. MATTHEW 25:31–46

Related to the obligation of those who enjoy material wealth is the responsibility or stewardship of those who operate companies. CCC 2426–36

Catholic teaching has always held the right of companies to make a profit. But it also recognizes the right of workers to make a just wage.

We may sum up Catholic teaching concerning the rights and responsibilities of the workplace in two very general statements:

1. Human labor has always held a special dignity in the Catholic perspective of life.

In the Old Testament, the creation narrative presents God in the role of a worker and an artisan.

And in the New Testament, Jesus himself works as a carpenter for thirty long years. So, too, Saint Paul works as a tent-maker, even while engaged in his preaching ministry.

2. Employers have an obligation to engage in businesses that are moral. In other words, it is morally wrong to engage in prostitution or pornography.

Employers also have an obligation to balance the welfare and needs of employees with their own corporate obligation and right to make a reasonable profit.

Similarly, employees have a moral obligation to work honestly and responsibly for their employers. In other words, they must give a fair day of work for fair pay.

13 *What is your experience concerning the above obligations?*

THINK about it

Life is not lost by dying; life is lost minute by minute, day by dragging day, in a thousand small uncaring ways.

Stephen Vincent Benet

LIFE Connection

I fear
that we are too concerned
with material things
to remember
that our real strength
lies in spiritual values.

I doubt
there is in
this troubled world today,
a single problem
that could not be solved
if approached in the spirit
of the Sermon on the Mount.

President Harry Truman

As long as anyone has the means of doing good to his neighbor, and does not do so, he shall be reckoned a stranger to the love of the Lord. SAINT IRENAEUS

A quote that sums up the Christian viewpoint on money is one from P. T. Barnum (1810–91). He established the circus in 1871, billing it as "The Greatest Show on Earth."

Money is a terrible master
but an excellent servant.

CLARIFY—The wealthy man in the Parable of Lazarus and the Rich Man lived in total disregard of Leviticus 25:23, which reminds wealthy landowners:

QUESTION **13 *What is your experience concerning the above obligations?***

DISCUSS—You might ask the students to share any experience of the following in their part-time jobs:

- *Lori Magraw was a college student working part-time in a Seattle shoe store. One day she was told to package defective shoes and return them to the manufacturer. She was told to use a knife to damage perfectly good shoes that had been returned by dissatisfied customers and could not be resold.*

  When she refused, she was fired. Lori filed a complaint with a city agency and received a small cash settlement and a promise from the shoe store that the practice of purposely damaging shoes would be stopped.

THINK about it

Two quotations are relevant here:

1 *The greatest of all faults is to be conscious of none.* THOMAS CARLYLE

2 *To be truly human is to be conscious of human weakness, but confident that it can be overcome.* ROMANO GUARDINI

LIFE Connection

DISCUSS—Ask the students: What's the point? How does it relate to the matter at hand?

Christian example is what is needed in today's world. "Example is not the main thing in life—it is the only thing." ALBERT SCHWEITZER

HISTORICAL Connection

■ *The wall was begun in 214 B.C. as a defense against northern tribes. It extends 1,500 miles over rolling terrain. It was said to have been the only man-made object on earth that the astronauts could identify from the moon.*

Stealing

DISCUSS—*Reader's Digest* (December 1995) carried an article entitled "How Honest Are We?" by Ralph Kinney Bennet. It led off with this question: "Would you return a wallet filled with money?"

Reader's Digest editors set up a test in cities coast-to-coast to see what Americans would do. They left 120 wallets in public places in 12 different cities across the nation, 10 in each city.

Ask the students: What percentage of the wallets with a sizeable amount of money do you think were returned?

Have the students commit themselves in writing.

The return was 67 percent, which means almost seven out of 10 were returned, on an average.

The city that led all cities was Seattle, with nine out of the ten "plants" being returned. What motivated the people to return the wallets? The article said:

A large number of returners cited their belief in God. And even those who don't regularly attend services often credited religious lessons as a moral prod.

CLARIFY—Stress the final point of this section: the obligation for restitution and the ways of making it.

QUESTION **14 *What would you recommend to cut down on shoplifting?***

CLARIFY—You might set up the discussion on this problem in the following way:

1 *How prevalent is shoplifting among the young people you know?*

Stealing

A camera store in New York City reduced thefts drastically by posting this sign for all customers to see: "Your picture has been taken four times in the last thirty seconds. We have a front view, two side views, and one from the rear."

Stealing is a disturbing problem that stores and banks face. It involves not only customers but also employees.

HISTORICAL Connection

The Great Wall of China is a gigantic structure which cost an immense amount of money and labor.

When it was finished, it appeared impregnable. But the enemy breached it. Not by breaking it down or going around it.

They did it by bribing the gatekeeper.

Harry Emerson Fosdick

For example, one reliable survey (documented by lie-detector tests) shows that over 70 percent of store employees and 80 percent of bank employees engage in some form of stealing (often minor).

Technically, stealing may be defined as taking something from another against his or her reasonable will. The phrase "against his or her reasonable will" is important, because it would not be stealing if, for example, we took food to stay alive.

Presumably, the owner of the food would not object if she or he knew of our circumstances. (To object under such circumstances would be "unreasonable.")

The gravity of stealing depends on the:

- **Circumstances involved**
- **Value of what is taken**

An example will clarify what this means. If an employee of a successful business steals five dollars from the cash register, the theft is sinful but not gravely so.

But if the employee intends to continue to steal over a period of time, the thefts can add up to grave matter. CCC 2408

Before we can be forgiven a sin of theft in the sacrament of Reconciliation, we must restore, or intend to restore, what we took. CCC 2487

In rare cases, however, we may be excused from restoring the stolen goods directly to the owner because it would cause hardship substantially graver than that inflicted upon the injured party.

In such rare cases, where it is extremely difficult or impossible to return what we wrongly took, we may give to charity the equivalent of what we stole. CCC 2412, 2487

The willingness to make restitution is a concrete sign of repentance.

14 *What would you recommend to cut down on shoplifting?*

268 STAGE 3: CHAPTER 20

2 *To what extent do you let it be known to them that you disapprove of such action?*

You might want to rephrase question 14 to read: What do you recommend to deter young people your age from shoplifting?

Cheating

DISCUSS—Paul DiNatale is a New York architect. One of his jobs is to inspect old city-owned buildings. He must determine whether they should be torn down or remodeled.

One day, after submitting a bill for $300, he received a check from the city for $3,000. He returned the check to the city.

NOTES

Cheating

A Cornell University study indicates that by the time children today are ten years old they have already developed a "non-condemning attitude" toward cheating. Experts say they pick up this attitude from adults and peers.

Cheating, "whether it be to acquire money, grades, or a scholarship," is doubly sinful. It involves, in some sense, both stealing and lying. We steal and answer from another (stealing) and claim it to be our own (lying).

The gravity of cheating depends on the circumstances of the situation. To knowingly and willingly cheat another out of a scholarship, for example, is clearly a grave sin. CCC 1459 On the other hand, to cheat on a quiz would fall into a lesser category of sinfulness.

15 ***What would you recommend to cut down on cheating?***

Gambling

State lotteries and betting on sports events are widespread today. They are so widespread that some sources estimate that up to 75 percent of the adult population engages in some form of gambling. We may describe gambling as betting or taking a chance on an uncertain outcome.

When gambling is comfortably within one's means, it may be considered entertainment and, therefore, morally permissible. CCC 2413 But gambling can quickly become immoral when it ceases to be comfortably within our means or out of our control.

When gambling goes beyond our means, it can bring incredible suffering upon people and families. The same is true when gambling ceases to be under our control. When we become aware that it has a compulsive hold on us, we have an obligation to seek help.

LIFE Connection

Our deepest fear is not that we are inadequate. Our deepest fear is that we are powerful beyond measure.

It is our light,
not our darkness,
that most frightens us. . . .

We are born
to make manifest
the glory of God
that is within us.
It's not just in some of us;
it is in everyone.

And when we let
our own light shine,
we subconsciously
give other people
permission to do the same.

Nelson Mandella

THINK about it

The path through light is often through sin.

Anonymous

When asked what motivated him not to keep it and cash it, he gave a list of reasons.

Ask the students: What would motivate you to return the check?

After giving several reasons, Paul concluded: "I also gave it back to show that there are still honest people around."

QUESTION **15** ***What would you recommend to cut down on cheating?***

You might prefer to hold off on this question and treat it together with Case #4 under "Reflect" on page 273.

Gambling

CLARIFY—A 200-page study of the National Gambling Study Commission (June, 1999) says state lotteries net $35 billion yearly. Fifty percent of adults spend $300 per person per year. This leaps to nearly $1,000 for black, usually male, school dropouts. Smith says that gamblers commonly fit three groups:

1 *Recreational—spend limited sum for gambling, rarely exceed it, and are open about their spending*

2 *Problem—often go beyond the limit they set and lie about their spending*

3 *Pathological—dip into family funds to support their addition*

GAMBLING-HELP HOTLINE: 800-522-4700; WWW.NCPGAMBLING.ORG

CLARIFY—Gamblers Anonymous has been around for over thirty years. Unfortunately, says Don Mitchell, executive director of the Illinois Council on Compulsive Gambling, compulsive gamblers usually do not admit their problem until they have "totally destroyed themselves or their family."

LIFE Connection

The things that count most in life are the things that can't be counted. E. C. McKenzie

THINK about it

Great occasions do not make heroes or cowards. They simply unveil them to the eyes of men. Silently and imperceptibly, as we wake or sleep, we grow strong or weak, and it last some crisis shows us what we have become. Bishop Westcott

QUESTION **16** ***What are some pros and cons when it comes to state lotteries?***

CLARIFY—Have the students conclude the discussion by balloting in writing whether they are "pro" or "con" when it comes to lotteries. Have them explain why. Collect, scan, and choose the better ones to comment on in the next class session.

THINK about it

In his play Hamlet, Shakespeare connected the two points in this quote as follows:

This above all: to thine own self be true,
And it must follow as the night the day,
Thou canst not then be false to any man.

Eighth commandment

QUESTION **17 *How do you account for such skepticism?***

CLARIFY—This question has been inserted to get the students thinking about this growing problem, especially in the light of scandals in recent years in the highest offices and departments of our government.

CLARIFY—In contrast to the honesty with regard to stealing reflected in the *Reader's Digest* experiment is a front-page story in the *Dallas Morning News* (OCTOBER, 1998).

It led off with this arresting headline: "But my child wouldn't life or cheat! Think again." The article went on to submit a *1998 Report Card on the Ethics of American Youth.* Here are excerpts from it:

- *The Josephson Institute of Ethics polled 20,000 middle and high school students across the nation. . . . Most of them said they cheat and lie to their parents. Nearly half admitted stealing, and a third said they would lie to get a good job. Yet most of these same students said they were satisfied with their own ethics and character.*

The article concluded:

You have to ask yourself, What is the next generation of paramedics, nuclear inspectors and journalists is going to be like? Said Michael Josephson, president of the California institute.

Ask the students: How would you answer that question?

Compulsive gambling is so widespread that numerous organizations, like Gamblers Anonymous, have been created to deal with the problem.

Describing the grip that compulsive gambling can hold on us, one person says:

The first time I had a dollar in my pocket
that I could call my own
was when I was forty-six years old.
By that time I had wrecked a business
and put out of work
a couple of hundred people
who depended on me for a living.

16 *What are some pros and cons when it comes to state lotteries?*

Yet, a few days later, the *Chicago Tribune* carried a front-page story about people who refused to believe that the event actually took place.

NASA said it was not surprised.

It routinely receives letters from skeptics, like the person who claimed that the first moon walk was "staged on a back lot at Warner Brothers."

17 *How do you account for such skepticism?*

This brings us to the eighth commandment: "Do not accuse anyone falsely."

This commandment forbids "misrepresenting the truth in our relations with others." CCC 2464, 2482–87

THINK about it

Integrity is telling myself the truth. And honesty is telling the truth to other people.

Spencer Johnson

Eighth commandment

Some years back, American and Soviet astronauts docked together 140 miles above the planet Earth. The event made spectacular television coverage.

Lying

Human society is built on mutual trust between individuals and nations. Nothing erodes or destroys trust more than lying. When trust breaks down, society breaks down.

270 STAGE 3: CHAPTER 20

Lying

DISCUSS—The *Chicago Tribune* ran a story about a twelve-year-old named Lisa, who had recently died of leukemia. Her parents did all they could to keep her from learning about her fatal disease. Instead of telling her the truth, they told her she had anemia.

After Lisa's death, her mother found a secret diary that her daughter had kept during her three-year illness. As she read it, she cried. The diary revealed that Lisa had known all along that she was dying. She had shared her worries and concerns with her diary, rather than upset her parents by letting them know that she knew she was dying.

Ask the students: How is Lisa's case another illustration of what is meant by the

NOTES

The Hebrew Scriptures were especially hard on liars. For example, the Book of Sirach says:

Lying
is an ugly blot on a person's character. . . .
A thief is better than a habitual liar.
SIRACH 20:24–25

Lying is especially destructive when it involves people who have a special claim to our trust, like family or friends.

One of the most destructive forms of lying, however, is lying to oneself. For example, we can deny that we sin. Commenting on the need to be truthful to ourselves, the great poet Shakespeare penned these memorable lines:

This above all— to thine own self be true;
And it must follow, as the night the day,
Thou canst not then be false to any man.
WILLIAM SHAKESPEARE: *HAMLET*

One of the most vicious lies is one that destroys another's good name. Concerning this lie, Shakespeare again writes:

Who steals my purse, steals trash;
'tis something, nothing;
Twas mine, 'tis his,
and has been slave to thousands;

But he that filches from me my name
Robs me of that which not enriches him
And makes me poor indeed.
WILLIAM SHAKESPEARE: *OTHELLO*

A person who injures another's name has an obligation to repair the damage, if possible. But trying to repair the damage is often as difficult as trying to unring a bell.

***18** How might you go about trying to repair the injury to another's good name?*

Detraction

A person's reputation or good name can also be destroyed by detraction. CCC 2477–79 Detraction may be described as broadcasting another's private faults, failures, or sins without sufficient reason.

The most common way this is done is by gossip. A fitting commentary on this sinful practice is this excerpt:

I maim without killing.
I break hearts and ruin lives. . . .
The more I am quoted
the more I am believed. . . .

My victims are helpless. . . .
I topple governments
and wreck marriages. . . .
I make innocent people cry
in their pillows. . . .
I am called Gossip.

Office gossip. Shop gossip. Party gossip. . . .
Before you repeat a story ask yourself:
Is it true? Is it fair? Is it necessary?
If not—SHUT UP. ANONYMOUS

***19** List two or three reasons why you think people engage in gossip.*

PRAYER hotline

Lord,
it's been a
fantastic morning so far.
I haven't lied, cheated,
or gossiped; but, in a minute,
I'll be getting out of bed;
and that's when
I'll really need your help.

LIFE Connection

Always
remember to forget,
The things that made you sad.
But never forget to remember,
The things that made you glad.

Always remember to forget,
The friends that proved untrue.
But don't forget to remember
Those that have stuck by you.

Always remember to forget
The troubles that passed away.
But never forget to remember
The blessings
That come each day.

Irish poem

statement: "Something is not bad because it is a sin; it is a sin because it is bad"?

DISCUSS—Years ago, CBS News commentator Eric Sevareid addressed a joint session of the Massachusetts State Legislature. He cited an example to show how the media can "lie" by telling the truth—but not the whole truth:

■ *A telecast from Vietnam showed Buddhists rioting in Saigon and Da Nang. "The riots," said Sevareid, "involved a tiny portion of the people in either city; yet the effect of the pictures in this country, including Congress, were explosive. People here thought Vietnam was tearing itself apart, that civil war was raging. Nothing of the sort was happening." In point of fact, "a block away from the Saigon riots the populace was shopping, chatting, sitting in restaurants in total normalcy."*

Ask the students: What alarms you most about this kind of "news media" lie? Give an example of how you, personally, can lie by "telling the truth—but not the whole truth."

CLARIFY—Pope Pius XII has been falsely accused of silence on the holocaust. Responding to this accusation, J. Sparks cited the Christmas 1941 issue of the *New York Times*. It reads:

> *The voice of Pius XII is a lonely voice in the silence and darkness enveloping Europe this Christmas. . . . He is about the only ruler left on the Continent of Europe who dares to raise his voice at all.*

Sparks also quotes one of the most prominent Jews of our time, Albert Einstein, who said:

■ *Only the Church stood squarely across the path of Hitler . . . the Church alone had the courage and persistence to stand for intellectual truth and moral freedom. I am forced thus to confess that what I once despised, I now praise unreservedly.*
"VIEWPOINTS": *DALLAS MORNING NEWS*: 10/1/99

QUESTION ***18 How might you go about trying to repair the injury to another's good name?***

An old story illustrates how hard it is to repair another's good name. It seems an old monk gave the following penance to the penitent: Take a pillow full of feathers. Go out to a field. Rip open the pillow case and throw the feathers into the wind. The next day, go out and collect the feathers and bring them back to me.

Detraction

QUESTION ***19 List two or three reasons why you think people engage in gossip.***

DISCUSS—How prevalent among young people is the kind of gossiping referred to in the commentary on detraction? Explain.

Recap

Burt Lancaster, one of Hollywood's greatest actors, grew up on the streets of New York in poverty. His most vivid boyhood memory was standing on a street corner in front of a bank:

■ *By sheer chance, he happened to glance at the gutter. What he saw made his heart leap.*

There lay a $20 bill. In those days that was a small fortune. Picking it up, he thrust it in his pocket. As he prepared to dash home to give the treasure to his mother, he saw a woman walking along slowly. Her face looked worried and upset. Her head was bent down, looking for something.

As she approached, she said to Burt, "Son, you didn't happen to see any money, did you?" She explained that she had just cashed a $20 check at the bank to buy some things she badly needed. As she spoke, Burt saw tears in her eyes.

He swallowed deeply, pulled the bill from his pocket, gave it to the lady, and said:

"This must be your $20 bill, ma'am. I just found it in the gutter." The tears of sorrow in the woman's eyes turned to tears of joy. The look of happiness on her face sent a warm glow through Burt's body. "That was the happiest moment of my life," the star said. Anne Heaney (adapted)

Review

DAILY QUIZ—Just a reminder: Review questions may be assigned (one or two at a time) for homework or a daily quiz.

CHAPTER TESTS—Reproducible chapter tests are found in Appendix A. For consistency and ease in grading, quizzes are restricted to (1) "Matching," (2) "True/False," and (3) "Fill in the Blanks."

TEST ANSWERS—The following are the answers to the test for Chapter 20. (See Appendix A, page 331.) Each correct answer worth 4 points.

Recap

Jesus did not abolish the Ten Commandments, but brought them to fulfillment and redefined them in terms of love:

■ **God**	**Commandments 1–3**
■ **Neighbor**	**Commandments 4–10**

In redefining them in terms of love, Jesus gave them a new focus and transformed them into—

■ **Signs**	**Of his love for us**
■ **Invitations**	**To love as he loved us**
■ **Guides**	**On how to love**

The latter seven commandments deal with matters relating to love of self and neighbor in areas of reverence for:

■ **Authority**	**Commandment 4**
■ **Life**	**Commandments 5, 6, 9**
■ **Truth**	**Commandment 8**
■ **Property**	**Commandments 7, 10**

Review

1 Explain briefly how love acts as a (a) sign, (b) invitation, (c) guide.

2 Briefly explain when we have a right and an obligation to oppose civil authority.

3 Explain (a) when it is permissible to kill in self-defense, (b) why Christians are finding it harder to justify capital punishment.

4 Using the example of a hunger strike, explain (a) the difference between direct and indirect taking of one's life, (b) when the indirect taking of one's life is permissible.

5 Explain the difference between (a) direct abortion and indirect abortion, (b) direct euthanasia and passive euthanasia, and when they are permissible.

6 List and briefly explain (a) when the misuse of drugs or alcohol is gravely sinful, (b) the twofold end of the sexual union, (c) the six statements that summarize traditional Catholic teaching on responsible sex.

7 Explain briefly what it means to treat another with (a) justice and (b) charity; and give three reasons that may keep people from having the adequate material needs for a decent life.

8 List and explain (a) the technical definition of stealing, (b) the two factors that determine the gravity of stealing, (c) restitution and when we are obliged to make it.

9 Explain (a) when cheating becomes gravely sinful, (b) two conditions that make gambling immoral, (c) the difference between lying and detraction, (d) the obligation we have to repair this injury from lying or detraction.

Matching

1 = b	2 = b	3 = a	4 = a
5 = a	6 = a	7 = a	8 = b

True/False

1 = T	2 = F	3 = T	4 = F
5 = T	6 = F	7 = T	8 = T
9 = T	10 = F		

Fill in the Blanks

1. (a) Unitive (b) Procreative
   (c) Body (d) Soul
2. (a) Life (b) Love (c) Faith

NOTES

Reflect

1 Sexual curiosity, questions, and fantasies can plague us. The healthy way to deal with these common problems is to discuss them with a counselor or confessor. But the Internet is easier. At first, we are tempted to explore everything available, rationalizing that we're "educating" ourselves. Inevitably, however, it ends up generating all kinds of problems.

■ ***How serious a problem among your friends is Internet pornography?***
■ ***What advice would you give a friend who is concerned about spending a lot of time visiting unhealthy sites on the Internet?***
■ ***Why do these unhealthy sites tend to erode faith?***

2 A high school boy was working for a drugstore. He got caught stealing. He writes:

The owner called my parents
and I got killed.
Worse yet, they won't trust me anymore.
How can I get my parents
to believe me and to trust me again?
I just don't feel like I belong
if I'm not trusted.
I want to be trusted again,
but how do I go about it?

■ ***If this student were a friend, what advice would you give him?***
■ ***Recall a time when something similar happened to you.***

3 A report in *USA Today* says that "alcohol claims 100,000 lives a year" and costs our nation "more than $117 billion a year in everything from medical bills to loss of time in the work place." Commenting on ancient abuse of alcohol, poet William Shakespeare said:

O God.
That man should put an enemy
in their mouths to steal away their brain.

■ ***On a scale of one (not much) to seven (very much), how big a problem is alcohol abuse among your friends? Drug abuse?***

4 A survey of over one hundred universities showed that over half of the students cheated regularly. Even more alarming was that they seldom had any sense of wrongdoing. This raises a question: Besides being against the seventh commandment, why is cheating wrong?

■ ***Answer on an unsigned sheet of paper: (a) how often you cheat on quizzes: (i) never, (ii) occasionally, (iii) whenever the opportunity arises; (b) why you cheat.***
■ ***On a scale of one (not very) to ten (very), how guilty do you feel when you cheat? Explain.***

STAGE 3: CHAPTER 20 273

Reflect

1 a) *How serious a problem among your friends is Internet pornography?*

■ *Perhaps the best approach is to have the students respond on a scale of 1 (no problem at all) to 10 (really serious).*

b) What advice would you give a friend who is concerned about spending a lot of time visiting unhealthy sites on the Internet?

■ *Get help. Talk to a parent, a counselor. Make a decision once and for all to abstain from this practice.*

c) Why do these unhealthy sites tend to erode faith?

■ *Visiting them sets up a conflict between our* belief *and our* behavior. *We believe one thing (It's wrong to do this), but we do it anyway. We realize we must resolve this conflict. If we don't, we won't be at peace with ourselves.*

So we try to change our behavior. *If we can't, we may begin to question our faith destructively. (See the difference from constructive questioning, pages 10–11) In other words, we try to adjust our* belief *to fit our* behavior. *We say: "What's wrong with it? Nothing! Everybody does it!"*

Result? Our faith erodes. We feel guilty. We can't pray. We are tempted to give up our faith and God.

2 a) *If this student were a friend, what advice would you give him?*
b) Recall a time when something similar happened to you.

■ *Have the students write out their responses to both questions, share them in small groups, and prepare a group report to the class.*

3 *On a scale of one (not much) to seven (very much), how big a problem is alcohol abuse among your friends? Drug abuse?*

■ *Use same procedure in Question 2.*

4 a) *Answer on an unsigned sheet of paper: (a) how often you cheat on quizzes: (i) never, (ii) occasionally, (iii) whenever the opportunity arises; b) Why do you cheat?*
b) On a scale of one (not very) to ten (very), how guilty do you feel when you cheat? Explain.

■ *Collect the responses, tally on the chalkboard and discuss. After the survey and discussion have each student write out their personal feelings about the exercise, e.g. were they (surprised/not surprised somewhat surprised by what they heard? Explain.*

PRAYER TIME with the Lord

Compose a similar blessing for a very special person

You might give the students an option: to do a blessing for several people (friends or family).

■ *Lord, bless, my dad. He seems to be having a lot of stress put on him at work. He comes home looking tired. Sometimes he's really short tempered. He's a great guy, Lord! He just needs your blessing in a special way.*

Lord, bless my mother. She's really an inspiration to me. She works hard. Sure, she has her moments of impatience, but who wouldn't in her situation. The big thing is she really cares a lot about all of us. I can honestly say, "I love her a lot!"

Bless my older brother, Aaron. He's in the midst of something. I'm not sure what it is. I used to ask him what was bothering him, but he kept telling me: "I got it under control. Quit bugging me." I don't think he has. Bless him real good, Lord.

Bless one other person. Her name is Donna and I really like her a lot. Help her to stay the way she is. She's one person I trust and thank you for putting in my life.

As the book says, "God, take care of yourself, because if anything happens to you, we're all sunk."

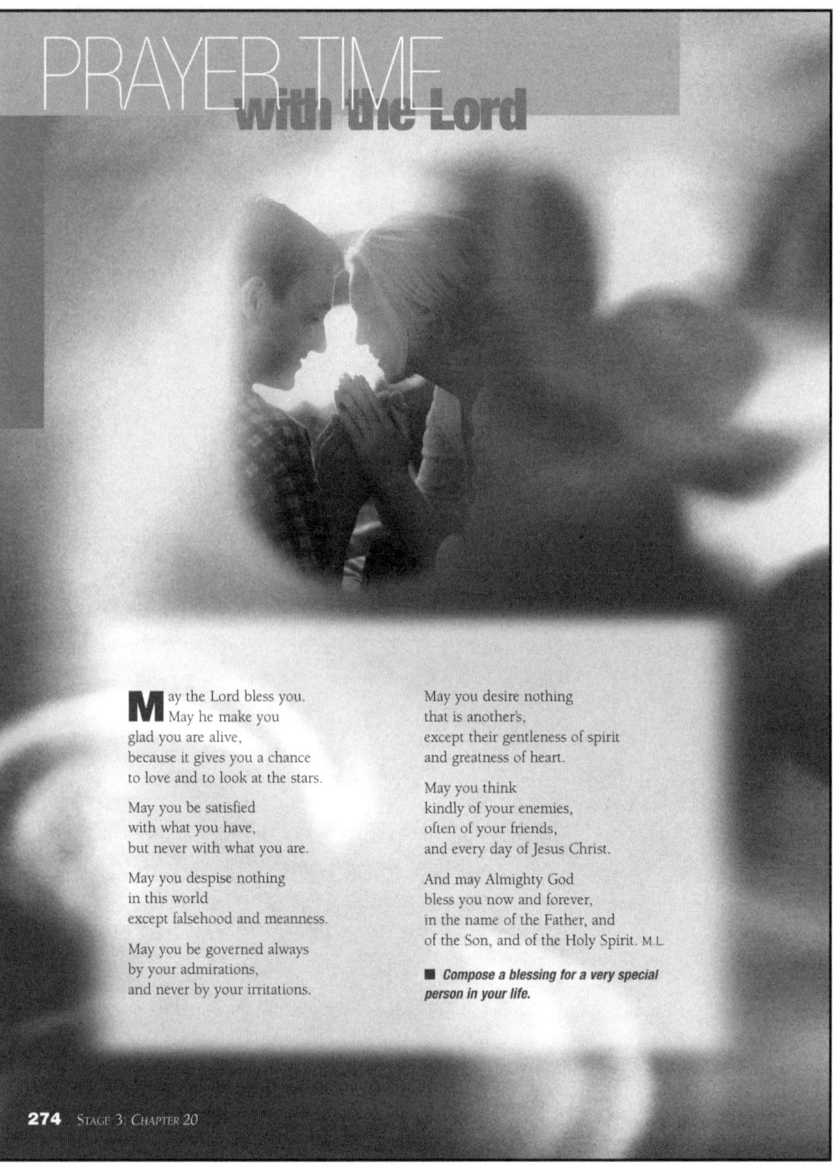

PRAYER TIME with the Lord

May the Lord bless you.
May he make you
glad you are alive,
because it gives you a chance
to love and to look at the stars.

May you be satisfied
with what you have,
but never with what you are.

May you despise nothing
in this world
except falsehood and meanness.

May you be governed always
by your admirations,
and never by your irritations.

May you desire nothing
that is another's,
except their gentleness of spirit
and greatness of heart.

May you think
kindly of your enemies,
often of your friends,
and every day of Jesus Christ.

And may Almighty God
bless you now and forever,
in the name of the Father, and
of the Son, and of the Holy Spirit. M.L.

■ ***Compose a blessing for a very special person in your life.***

274 STAGE 3: CHAPTER 20

PRAYER Journal

QUESTION **List one or two concrete things you have done recently to help (a) your family or a family member, (b) someone outside your circle of family and friends?**

Instruct the students to be concrete and detailed. Here's an example:

■ *At my mother's suggestion, I asked a friend to double date, and take my sister to the Grant Park outdoor concert. I knew my sister like him. We had a really great time and plan to do something together again this week. I never thought I'd double date with my sister, but it turned out great.*

NOTES

PRAYER Journal

Albert Schwietzer was a concert pianist who gave up his career in music to become a missionary doctor in Africa. He once said,

It's not enough to say,
"I'm a good father.
I'm a good husband." . . .

You must do something . . .
for those who have need of help,
something for which you get no pay
but the privilege of doing it.

For remember,
you don't live in a world all your own.
Your brothers and sisters are here too.

■ ***List one or two concrete things you have done recently to help (a) your family or a family member, (b) someone outside your circle of family and friends.***

SCRIPTURE

1	**Lying**	**Ezekiel 13:6–16**
2	**Cheating**	**Amos 8:4–10**
3	**Stealing**	**Exodus 22:1–14**
4	**Illicit sex**	**Deuteronomy 22:13–30**
5	**Adultery**	**John 8:1–11**

■ ***Pick one of the above passages. Read it prayerfully and write out a brief statement to Jesus expressing your feelings about it.***

SCRIPTURE Journal

QUESTION ***Pick one of the above passages. Read it prayerfully and write out a brief statement to Jesus expressing your feelings about it.***

Suggest that the students do the fifth reading. JOHN 8:1–11. You might have it read aloud in class by one of the students. Discuss what Jesus may have written "on the ground with his finger."

Classroom Resources

CATECHISM

Catechism of the Catholic Church *Second Edition*

For further enrichment, you might refer to:

1. Faith	Index	p. 807
2. Authority	Index	p. 759
3. Respect	Index	p. 841
4. Sexuality	Index	p. 848

See also: Morality, Sin, Detraction, Chastity.

—AVAILABLE FROM THE UNITED STATES CATHOLIC CONFERENCE, WASHINGTON DC

CD-ROM

The Way of the Lord Jesus
Germaine Grisez
A two-volume resource work on Church moral teachings.
—AVAILABLE ON THE *WELCOME TO THE CATHOLIC CHURCH* CD-ROM FROM HARMONY MEDIA INC., CERVAIS,

VIDEOS

The Neighbor: The Parable of the Good Samaritan
Twelve-minutes. A young, multi-cultural cast re-enacts the parable of the Good Samaritan—sure to spark lively discussion about compassion, forgiveness, violence, and hatred. 1998
—AVAILABLE FROM BROWN-ROA, DUBUQUE, IA

My Brother's Keeper *Rick Doyle*
Thirty-six minutes. Gripping story about two brothers and the use and misuse of freedom. 1998.
—AVAILABLE FROM TWENTY-THIRD PUBLICATIONS, MYSTIC, CT

Who Is My Neighbor *Rick Doyle*
Forty-five minutes. This award winning drama explores acceptance, human dignity, and respect for others.
—AVAILABLE FROM TWENTY-THIRD PUBLICATIONS, MYSTIC, CT

NOTE

For a list of (1) General resources for professional background and (2) Addresses, phone/fax numbers of major publishing companies, see Appendix B of this Resource Manual.

CHAPTER 21
Discerning Love

CHAPTER at a Glance

The aim of this chapter is to give the students a better understanding of the:

1 *Three kinds of moral decisions that we are called on to make;*
2 *The nature of the twofold teaching charism that Jesus bestowed on his Church to assist it in its teaching mission;*
3 *The right and responsibility of forming and following our own conscience in accord with right reason and divine law.*

READ—Have a student read aloud the scriptural introduction, which begins: "Jesus said: 'Gentiles do not have the Law . . .'" Have another read aloud the commentary. It begins: "All of us—from a talk show host . . ."

DISCUSS—John Cardinal Newman writes: "Conscience praises, it blames, it promises, it threatens. . . ."

Ask the students: From your own personal experience, give an example of how you have experienced your conscience praise, blame, promise, threaten. Here are some actual examples:

1 *Praises—"It visits me with a deep satisfaction after I help someone or resist a temptation."*
2 *Blames—"It lets me know (after I've shouted at my mother or father) that I was wrong to do so."*
3 *Promises—"It tells me in my heart that, if I apologize for shouting or lying, it will, in the long run, be a blessing for me and my parents."*
4 *Threatens—"It warns me in advance that if I cheat on an exam I'm not going to be proud of myself for doing so."*

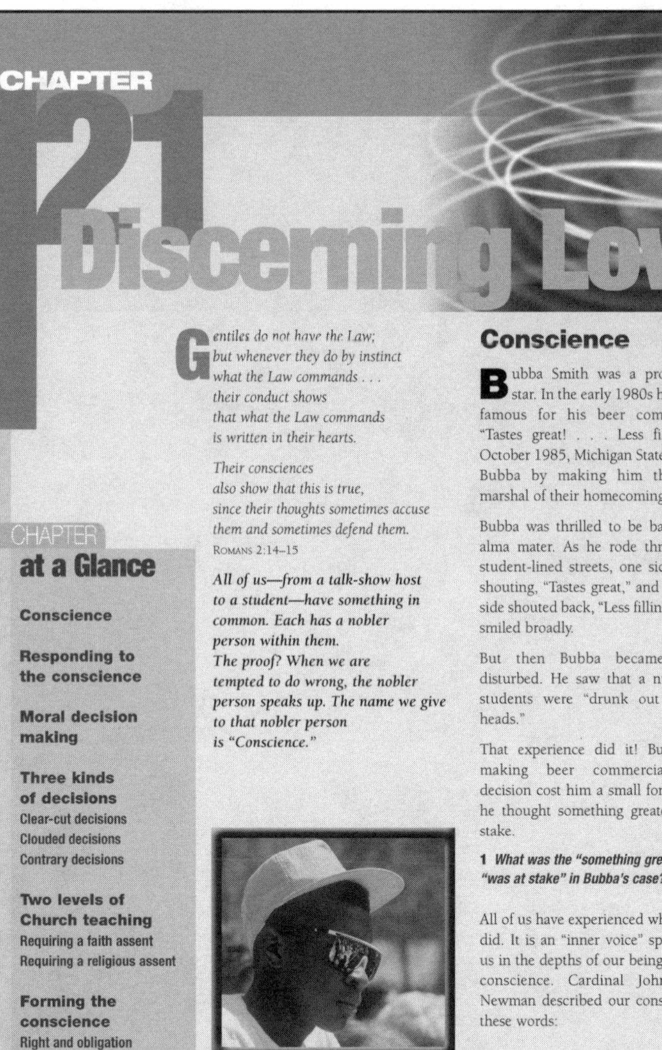

CHAPTER 21 Discerning Love

Gentiles do not have the Law;
but whenever they do by instinct
what the Law commands . . .
their conduct shows
that what the Law commands
is written in their hearts.

Their consciences
also show that this is true,
since their thoughts sometimes accuse
them and sometimes defend them.
ROMANS 2:14–15

All of us—from a talk-show host to a student—have something in common. Each has a nobler person within them. The proof? When we are tempted to do wrong, the nobler person speaks up. The name we give to that nobler person is "Conscience."

CHAPTER at a Glance

- **Conscience**
- **Responding to the conscience**
- **Moral decision making**
- **Three kinds of decisions**
  - Clear-cut decisions
  - Clouded decisions
  - Contrary decisions
- **Two levels of Church teaching**
  - Requiring a faith assent
  - Requiring a religious assent
- **Forming the conscience**
  - Right and obligation
  - Vincible ignorance
  - Invincible ignorance

276

Conscience

Bubba Smith was a pro football star. In the early 1980s he became famous for his beer commercials: "Tastes great! . . . Less filling!" In October 1985, Michigan State honored Bubba by making him the grand marshal of their homecoming parade.

Bubba was thrilled to be back at his alma mater. As he rode through the student-lined streets, one side started shouting, "Tastes great," and the other side shouted back, "Less filling." Bubba smiled broadly.

But then Bubba became deeply disturbed. He saw that a number of students were "drunk out of their heads."

That experience did it! Bubba quit making beer commercials. The decision cost him a small fortune, but he thought something greater was at stake.

1 What was the "something greater" that "was at stake" in Bubba's case?

All of us have experienced what Bubba did. It is an "inner voice" speaking to us in the depths of our being. It is our conscience. Cardinal John Henry Newman described our conscience in these words:

Conscience

QUESTION 1 *What was the "something greater" that "was at stake" in Bubba's case?*

■ *Bubba's conscience told him that it was wrong for him (a celebrity, whom young people idolized) to take advantage of his status and lend his name to a product that leads to the type of thing he was seeing on both sides of the street: substance abuse. His conscience told him that to continue to do so would be irresponsible.*

QUESTION 2 *In what sense may we speak of conscience as a "voice"? As God's "voice"?*

■ *The word "voice" is used here in a metaphorical sense. It is called "God's" voice*

NOTES

It praises,
it blames, it promises, it threatens. . . .
It is more than man's own self.
The man himself has no power over it,
or only with extreme difficulty;
he may not make it,
he cannot destroy it,
he may refuse to use it, but it remains.
Its very existence
throws us out of ourselves,
to go see him in the heights and depths,
whose Voice it is.
APOLOGIA PRO VITA SUA

2 In what sense may we speak of conscience as God's "voice"?

Responding to the conscience

Our conscience is a judgment of our reason. It empowers us to determine whether a certain act is morally good or evil. And it obliges us to follow faithfully its verdict.

If we are to hear and follow the voice of conscience, we must place ourselves in God's presence, and listen. Saint Augustine puts it this way:

Return to your conscience, question it. . . .
Turn inward . . . and in everything you do, see God as your witness.

When we make every effort to hear the "voice" of conscience clearly and correctly, we have *both the obligation* and the *right* to follow the judgment of our conscience. The Church assures us:

Man has the right to act in conscience
and in freedom so as personally
to make moral decisions.
He must not be forced to act contrary
to his conscience.
Nor must he be prevented from acting
according to his conscience."
VATICAN II, DIGNITATIS HUMANAE

Let us now take a look at the process of moral decision making. It will show how our conscience and the Church's authority work together.

Moral decision making

A 15-year-old boy and his father were driving past a tiny airport in Ohio. Suddenly, a low-flying plane spun out of control and nose-dived onto the runway. The boy yelled, "Dad! Dad! Stop the car!"

Minutes later, the boy was pulling the pilot out of the plane. It was the boy's twenty-year-old friend. He had been practicing takeoffs and landings. He died in the boy's arms.

That night, the boy was too crushed to eat supper. He went to his room, closed the door, and lay on his bed. He had been working part-time in a drugstore. Every penny he made he spent on flying lessons. His goal was to get his pilot's license when he turned 16.

The boy's parents wondered what effect the tragedy would have on his decision to continue flying. They discussed it with him, but they told him that the decision had to be his.

3 Recall a time when your parents left a final decision up to you.

Discerning

STAGE 3: CHAPTER 21 **277**

in the sense that it has its origin in God—not from our imagination. Some compare it to a kind of "built-in walkie-talkie set" by which God speaks to us. Others compare it to a "spiritual instinct" akin to the instinct that guides the migration of birds. More biblically, others see it in terms of God's words to Jeremiah: "I will put my law within them and write it on their hearts." 31:33

Responding to the conscience

NOTEBOOK—We may sum up this section as follows: Our conscience gives us the:

1. *Power—to discern right from wrong*
2. *Responsibility—to listen to it prayerfully*
3. *Responsibility and right—to obey it*

Moral decision making

QUESTION **3** ***Recall a time when your parents left a final decision up to you.***

■ *Give students time to think. Let them share in small groups, then have the group pick one example to share with the class.*

CLARIFY The story of Neil Armstrong's boyhood experience was told by his mother Viola in *The Guideposts Treasury of Faith*. Neil, a native of Wapakoneta, Ohio, stepped onto the moon July 20, 1969, at 10:56 P.M. (E.D.T.). His two flight companions were Ed "Buzz" Aldrin and Mike Collins.

CLARIFY—Recall Aldrin's Communion service while Neil Armstrong was preparing for his moon walk. (Exercise 1, page 163). Months later, on a world tour, the three astronauts visited Pope Paul VI. Aldrin called the visit one of the most "stirring moments" of the tour. In his book *Return to Earth*, he writes:

■ *His Holiness unveiled three magnificent porcelain statues of the Three Wise Men. He said that these three men were directed to the infant Christ by looking at the stars and that we three also reached our destination by looking at the stars.*

CLARIFY—The moon missions had a remarkable spiritual impact on several of the astronauts. Jim Irwin says his trip to the moon on Apollo 15 changed his life forever. In *To Rule the Night*, he writes:

■ *It has remade my faith. . . .*
I felt an overwhelming sense
of the presence of God on the moon. . . .
Ed Mitchell was the Lunar Module Pilot
on Apollo 14, and he and I have
talked freely about the thing we felt
on the moon. . . . As a result Ed has
founded the Mind Science Foundation
for the purpose of pursuing scientific
explanations of the presence of God.

Refer the students back to similar comments made by astronaut James Irwin in chapter 2 on page 21.

DISCUSS—Ask: How would you explain Dulles's point that the search for God can appropriately begin from a reflection on the voice of conscience?

- *Refer the students to "Think about it" on page 282 and ask: How does Kant's statement suggest the explanation of Dulles's point?*

As the "starry skies above"(Creation) point to a Creator who fashioned them, so the "moral law within" (Conscience) points to a Law-giver who fashioned it.

The German philosopher Immanuel Kant (1724–1804) has been called one of the most influential thinkers of modern times.

Three kinds of decisions

NOTEBOOK—Have the students enter the three kinds of decisions in their notebooks:

Clear-cut	*It is clear what to do*
Clouded	*It is unclear what to do*
Contrary	*It involves acting against traditional authority (Church)*

QUESTION **4** ***Cite an example to illustrate each kind of decision.***

Clear-cut	*I am tempted to steal*
Clouded	*Our family doesn't know whether it's best to put Granny in a nursing home.*
Contrary	*My sister is tempted to marry a divorced man who refuses to file for an annulment.*

Up Close & Personal

Avery Dulles

Avery Dulles was the son of John Foster Dulles, Secretary of State under President Eisenhower. A convert to Catholicism, Avery became a Jesuit priest. He writes:

The search for God can appropriately begin from a reflection on the voice of conscience.

Anyone who has experienced the fact of moral obligation has the makings of a belief in God and has the prerequisites for hearing God's word fruitfully.

But the hearing of that word will not result in faith unless it is accompanied by prayer.

Quoted in *How Can I Find God?* edited by James Martin

Two days later the boy's mother noticed an open notebook in her son's room. It was one he had kept from childhood. Across the top of the page was written, "The Character of Jesus." Beneath it was listed a series of qualities:

- **Jesus was humble**
- **Jesus was a champion of the poor**
- **Jesus was unselfish**
- **Jesus was close to his Father**

The mother realized that in her son's hour of decision he was turning to prayer and to Jesus for guidance. Later, she asked him what he had decided. He responded, "With God's help, I must continue to fly."

That boy was Neil Armstrong. And on July 20, 1969, he became the first human being to walk on the moon.

The millions of people who watched him on television had no idea that one reason why he was walking on the moon was Jesus. They had no idea that it was from Jesus that he drew the strength and guidance to make the decision that was responsible for what he was now doing.

The story of Neil Armstrong illustrates an important point. Responsible moral decisions are not always easy to make. There are times when we are not sure what love invites us to do. When such a decision arises, we should do what Neil Armstrong did. We should:

- **Consult Jesus' teaching**
- **Seek competent advice**
- **Pray for guidance**

Three kinds of decisions

In general, there are three different kinds of moral decisions. We may describe them as:

- **Clear-cut decisions**
- **Clouded decisions**
- **Contrary decisions**

A *clear-cut* decision is one in which it is clear what we must do. A *clouded* decision is one in which the right decision is not clear to all. A *contrary* decision is one that involves acting contrary to traditional authority

4 ***Cite an example to illustrate each kind of decision.***

278 STAGE 3: CHAPTER 21

Clear-cut decisions

CLARIFY—Henry VIII's involvement reads:

1509 Became king at age 18

1527 Pope refused to annul his marriage so he could marry Anne Boleyn

1529 Made Thomas More Chancellor of England

1534 Henry left Catholic Church, formed Church of England, and arrested More for refusing to swear that his first marriage was invalid

1535 Beheaded Thomas More

1536 Beheaded Anne Boleyn and married four more times before death in 1547

1935 Thomas More canonized and made patron saint of lawyers

NOTES

Clear-cut decisions

The movie *A Man for All Seasons* is based on the life of Saint Thomas More. He rose to prominence when King Henry VII appointed him chancellor of England in 1529. But tragedy soon struck his life.

Henry divorced his queen and remarried. To combat civil and religious opposition to his remarriage, he ordered high dignitaries of the state to sign a document swearing that the marriage was valid.

Henry also let it be known that if they refused to sign the document, they would be tried for treason.

A dramatic scene occurred when Lord Norfolk asked Thomas More to sign. When he refused, Norfolk appealed to him to reconsider in the light of his love for his family and his friends.

But Thomas More knew that a more important love was at stake: his love of God. He could not swear to something he knew to be false.

Shortly afterward, he was arrested, imprisoned for 15 months in the Tower of London, and then executed for treason.

The decision More faced was as clear-cut as it was difficult. He was aware of the facts of the case. He knew the Church's teaching on divorce and remarriage. He knew what God's love invited him to do.

Meeting the challenge

More's greatest need, therefore, was for the moral courage to do what his conscience told him he must do.

The role that prayer played in More's decision is clear from a letter he wrote to his daughter Meg. In it he described what he would do if fear threatened his resolve:

I shall remember how Saint Peter
at a blast of wind began to sink
because of his lack of faith,
and I shall do as he did:
call upon Christ. . . .

And then I trust
he shall place his holy hand on me
and in the stormy seas
hold me up from drowning.
And therefore my dear daughter,
do not let your mind be troubled.

The first kind of moral decision, therefore, is one that is clear-cut. It is one in which it is perfectly obvious what we must do.

Such a decision, however, can be extremely hard to make because it can exact such a great personal price from us, as it did for Thomas More. As such, it requires great moral courage.

5 ***Can you give examples to illustrate the difference between moral courage and physical courage? Which would be the harder for you? Explain.***

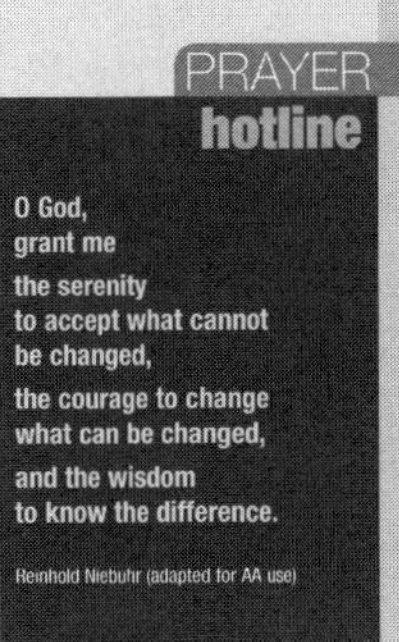

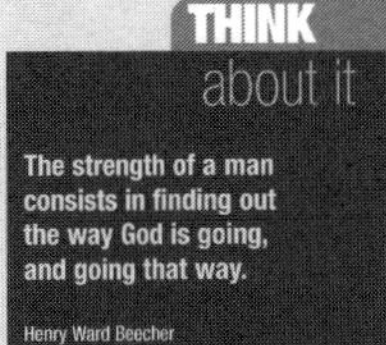

THINK
about it
The strength of a man
consists in finding out
the way God is going,
and going that way.
Henry Ward Beecher

STAGE 3: CHAPTER 21 **279**

Meeting the challenge

DISCUSS—Ask students: What episode in Peter's life is More referring to?

■ *Read the "water-walking" episode of Peter in Matthew 14:22–33.*

QUESTION **5** ***Can you give examples to illustrate the difference between moral courage and physical courage? Which would be the harder for you? Explain.***

■ *Refer the students back to "Up Close & Personal" focusing on Dr. Sheila Cassidy, page 231. Ask them:*

What part of her story illustrates moral courage (treats an enemy of the state, knowing what arrest would mean) and physical courage (withstands four days of torture under questioning)?

PRAYER hotline

Ask: What kind of courage is being referred to here: moral and/or physical? (moral: agree to do something difficult; physical: withdrawal from alcohol can be painful.)

THINK about it

■ *Years ago, Joe Paterno, football coach of Penn State, got a "big-money" offer to coach the New England Patriots.The night before signing, he couldn't sleep. He felt uneasy about his decision, reasoning that the "unrest" in his soul indicated that this was not the way God wanted him to go.*

The next morning, he phoned the Patriots and called off the meeting. He explained to the press that he suddenly realized that the opportunity to impact the lives of college students was more important to him than the money and the prestige of being a pro coach. With that decision, a deep inner peace entered his soul.

The case of Paterno makes an important point about decision making. When a person who is prayerfully seeking God's will makes a decision that causes him "unrest" as it did Paterno, it's almost always a sign that it's not God's will.

Contrary to this, when a person seeking to do God's will makes a decision that results in peace, as it did when Paterno reversed his decision, it's almost always clear confirmation that it is the right decision.

Share Your **meditation**

Have the students recall and review the answer we gave to Question 2 on page 277.

Clouded decisions

QUESTION **6** ***Why do/don't you think Franz made the right decision?***

■ *In hindsight, Franz was absolutely right. The only adequate explanation for what he did is the one he himself gives, saying:*

"I guess they (the others) don't have the grace to see it. But I do have the grace to see it, so I cannot serve in the army."

The case of Granny

NOTEBOOK—The three steps involved in making a moral decision are important. List them on the chalkboard as follows to facilitate memorizing:

PONDER	*Teaching of Church*
PURSUE	*Advice of competent people*
PRAY	*For guidance of Spirit*

DISCUSS—Refer the students back to the story of Neil Armstrong and his teen-age decision about flying. Ask the students which of the following categories it fit under:

CLEAR-CUT	*It is clear what to do*
CLOUDED	*It is unclear what to do*
CONTRARY	*It involves acting against the teaching of Jesus*

CLARIFY—Armstrong instinctively followed the 3 key steps of the decision-making process:

PONDER	*Teaching (example of Jesus)*
PURSUE	*Consulted (parents)*
PRAY	*Prayed for help (GOD)*

QUESTION **7** ***Create a list of pros and cons for assisted living in Granny's case. What advice and guidance will you seek?***

SHARE YOUR **meditation**

All of us—whether we are a child, an astronaut, or the Holy Father himself—have something remarkable in common. As noble as we may be, we have a "nobler person" within us.

When we are tempted to do something less than noble, the nobler person "speaks" to us. The name we give to this "nobler person" is *Conscience.*

The "voice" of our conscience speaks to us in our most inner core or "sanctuary" of our being. It calls us to love, to do what is good and avoid what is evil. When we listen to it, in a real sense, we hear God "speaking" to us through it.

■ ***In what sense do we hear God speaking to us through our conscience?***

Clouded decisions

When Hitler came to power in Nazi Germany, Franz Jägerstatter was a young Austrian farmer. He had a wife and two small children.

Franz also had the distinction of being the only man in his village to vote against Austria's political merger with Nazi Germany.

In February 1943, Franz was ordered to report for military service in the German army. He faced a dilemma. How could he fight in what he believed to be an immoral war?

Franz consulted his parish priest and his bishop. Both suggested the possibility of serving in the medical corps. It would excuse him from bearing arms.

But Franz felt that just wearing a uniform could be interpreted as a sign that he approved of the Nazis and the war.

When a state-appointed lawyer asked Franz why he was having such a problem with military service, when millions of German Christians had no problem, he responded:

I guess they don't have the grace to see it.
But I do have the grace to see it,
so I cannot serve in the army.

So it happened that, after pondering Jesus' teaching, seeking competent advice, and praying for guidance, Franz felt compelled to follow his own conscience.

On August 9, 1943, Franz was executed. History has since honored him as a hero and a saint.

Franz's decision is a good example of what is meant by a clouded decision. Commenting on this kind of decision the *Catechism of the Catholic Church* says:

Man is sometimes confronted
by situations
that make moral judgments less assured
and decisions difficult.
But he must always seriously seek
what is right and good and discern
the will of God expressed in divine law.

To this purpose,
man strives to interpret the data
of experience and the signs of the times
assisted by the virtue of prudence,
by the advice of competent people,
and by the help of the Holy Spirit
and his gifts. CCC 1787–88

6 ***Why do/don't you think Franz made the right decision?***

Consider yet another example, closer to home, of a *clouded* decision.

The case of Granny

Imagine you are the mother of three children, ages six, nine, and eleven. Your eighty-eight-year-old grandmother lives with you. She is mentally alert and loved by your children.

But she has severe arthritis and is beginning to need more and more attention. It is also making her more and more demanding. This is starting to take its toll on you, your husband, and the children.

One day, after a very trying experience, your husband reluctantly suggests it might be time to move Granny to a

280 STAGE 3: CHAPTER 21

The case of Granny illustrates an important point when it comes to the second step in the decision-making process. It is this:

■ *Pursuing competent advice includes consulting not only professionals (e.g., doctor and pastor), but also everyone involved: Granny, your children, you, and your husband.*

DISCUSS—Consider another clouded moral decision. The Academy Award-winning movie *Chariots of Fire* dealt with the 1924 Olympic games in Paris. Specifically, it dealt with England's Eric Liddell.

■ *Known in the track and field world as the "Flying Scot," he was an odds-on favorite to win the gold in the 100-meter event.*

NOTES

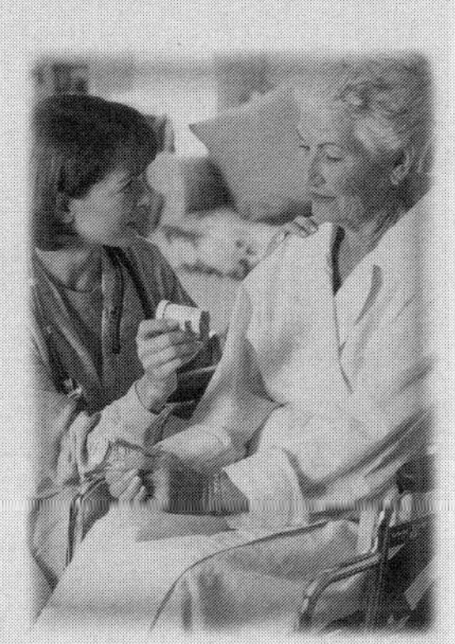

home that offers assisted living. Now, you are faced with a clouded moral decision. It is not clear what love invites you do.

The correct procedure for making such a decision is to follow the three steps mentioned earlier. You should:

- **Ponder the Church's teaching**
- **Pursue competent advice**
- **Pray for guidance**

The second step in this process is especially critical in Granny's case. It involves consulting not only with Granny and the children, but also with professionals, like the family doctor, and your pastor.

Once you have taken these three steps, you may choose with a clear conscience whatever your intellectual judgment, guided by grace, seems to indicate.

7 Create a list of pros and cons for assisted living in Granny's case. What advice and guidance will you seek?

Contrary decisions

The most difficult and serious moral decision of all is one that puts us at odds with the traditional moral teaching of the Church on a particular point. To illustrate why it is so serious, consider two of Jesus' statements to his disciples:

I tell you, Peter: you are rock,
and on this rock foundation
I will build my church. . . .

I will give you
the keys of the Kingdom of heaven;
what you prohibit on earth
will be prohibited in heaven,
and what you permit on earth
will be permitted in heaven.
MATTHEW 16:18–19

On another occasion, Jesus makes this statement to his disciples:

I have much more to tell you,
but now it would be too much
for you to bear.
When, however, the Spirit comes,
who reveals the truth about God,
he will lead you into all truth.
JOHN 16:12–13

These two passages illustrate why a moral decision that is contrary to the official teaching of the Church is so serious. It is because of the twofold charism that Jesus bestowed upon his Church.

First, he authorized and empowered his Church to teach in his name. Second, he assured his Church that the Holy Spirit would guide it in its teaching role.

THINK about it

Put your heart right. . . . Your life will be brighter than sunshine at noon.

Job 11:13, 17

STAGE 3: CHAPTER 21 **281**

When the Olympic schedule came out, the 100-meter event was scheduled for Sunday. Eric found himself face-to-face with a clouded moral decision.

He was extremely religious. His "fundamentalist" conscience made him uneasy about running such an important race on the Lord's Day.

He pondered the situation, consulted with people, and prayed over it. He finally came to the conclusion that "for him," at least, running the event would be wrong.

Everyone from the Prince of Wales on down tried to dissuade Eric. English newspapers even called him a traitor. But he refused to go against his personal conscience.

Eric met with his coaches and suggested that a teammate run the 100-meter dash in his place. He would enter the 400-meter dash (run on a weekday), even though he had never run this race in his entire life.

To make a long story short, Eric won the 400-meter event and his teammate, Abrams, won the 100-meter event. Instead of winning just one gold medal, thanks to Eric, England won two.

Ask the students: What kind of courage did it take for Eric to follow his conscious? (moral)

Contrary decisions

NOTEBOOK—Be sure the students understand why a contrary decision is so serious.

It involves acting in opposition to the twofold teaching charism that Jesus conferred on his Church:

Charism — *Power to teach in his name* / *Assurance of the Spirit's help*

DISCUSS—Refer the students back to the case of Joe Paterno (Penn State football coach) on page 279 of this manual. Ask the students: What kind of moral decision did it involve: clear-cut, clouded, contrary? Explain.

- *It was clouded. There is some basis, however, for saying that it was also contrary in the sense that we are to use our talents in the way that best serves God and God's plan for us. Guiding the lives of young people would, therefore, seem to take precedence.*

Next, refer the students back to Olympic hopeful Bill Havens on page 256. What kind of a decision did it involve?

- *The answer to the Paterno decision applies here, also. Significantly, both men made the right decision and both were blessed immensely.*

THINK about it

Recall and review the discussion of Kant's quotation, as treated under "Up Close & Personal" (Avery Dulles) on page 278.

Two levels of Church teaching

CLARIFY—An example of second-level teaching that moral theologians give is the Church's teaching on birth control. It is spelled out in *Humanae Vitae* ("Of Human Life") and was restated in the *Catechism of the Catholic Church.* CCC 2370 Traditionally, the Church has taught, and continues to teach, that artificial birth control is gravely immoral.

The Church has the responsibility to give guidance on this issue and other moral issues, just as Paul had the responsibility to give guidance to the Corinthians on a question that was bothersome to them.

Likewise, we have the responsibility to give "religious assent" to these teachings of the Church. Giving religious assent means we should accept the reliability of the Church's teachings on such subjects because Jesus authorized his Church to teach in his name, and assured it that the Spirit would guide it in its teaching role.

NOTEBOOK—Have the students place in their notebooks the following summary of the two levels of teaching:

1st —
- *Church teaches with absolute certitude*
- *We give a faith assent; to do other would be to cease being Catholic*

2nd —
- *Church teaches with less than absolute certitude*
- *We give a religious assent because of the Church's teaching charism*

CLARIFY—An analogy may help us understand the Church's position regarding the second level (the analogy is admittedly far-out, but illustrates the point well).

In other words, to act contrary to the official teaching of the Church is to act in opposition to the twofold charism that Jesus bestowed upon it.

Having said this, however, we must understand that the Church is made up of human beings, and the Holy Spirit guides it accordingly.

This means that the Holy Spirit does not short-circuit human intelligence, insight, and learning. The Holy Spirit guides the Church in keeping with the laws of human nature.

Thus, it happens that the Church receives clarity on certain moral and doctrinal matters gradually and by stages.

THINK about it

**Two things fill the mind with ever new and increasing wonder and awe—
the starry heavens above me and the moral law within me.**

Immanuel Kant

Two levels of Church teaching

Because the Church does not enjoy the same clarity on all moral and doctrinal matters, it teaches at different levels.

At one level, the Church teaches as one with full certitude. For example, when it teaches that the Eucharist is really the Body of Christ, it does so with absolute certainty.

Consequently, we give this teaching a full *faith assent.* If we did not, we would no longer be Catholic. CCC 891

At the second level, the Church teaches as one possessing less than absolute certitude on a particular matter. A kind of biblical parallel to this second level teaching occurs in Paul's First Letter to the Corinthians. He writes:

Now, concerning what you wrote
about unmarried people:
I do not have a command from the Lord,
but I give my opinion as one
who by the Lord's mercy
is worthy of trust. 1 CORINTHIANS 7:25

An example of this level of teaching is one "that leads to a better understanding of Revelation in matters of faith and morals." To this level of teaching, we must give a *religious assent.* CCC 892

The Church has the responsibility to give guidance on moral issues—just as Paul had the responsibility to give guidance to the Corinthians on a question that was bothering them.

Likewise, we have the responsibility to give *religious assent* to these teachings

282 STAGE 3: CHAPTER 21

- *A father is an amateur chemist. He spends his nights working on a deadly poison that looks, smells, and tastes like a certain brand of cola. One night he puts the deadly poison in a cola bottle, recaps it, and puts it in the refrigerator, next to a recapped bottle of normal cola.*

  The next morning the man's wife finds their little son pouring a drink from a recapped cola bottle. Fearing it might be the deadly poison, she screams at the child, "Don't drink that!" Then she snatches the drink from the child's hand.

  The woman calls her husband at work and asks which bottle contains the poison. Her husband says, "It's the one with a white X on the bottom."

NOTES

Vincible ignorance can occur when we "take little trouble to find out what is true and good." It can also occur when, through sin, we allow our conscience to become "blind" to truth. In both of these cases, we are morally responsible for the evil we commit.

Invincible ignorance occurs when an "erroneous judgment" is not due to our fault. For example, it could be due to incorrect information given us by another.

If this be the case, we are not responsible for the error. In other words, we are not guilty of any sin when we do what we thought was morally right.

Nonetheless, it remains an evil or disorder. It becomes important, therefore, to "work to correct errors of moral conscience." CCC 1793

In conclusion, to act contrary to the Church's moral teaching is a grave matter. For it means we act in opposition to the twofold teaching charism that Jesus bestowed on his Church to assist its teaching ministry.

It is also a grave matter because it is so easy for us to delude ourselves into believing what we would like to believe.

The Church's teaching is a "light for our path," given to us by Jesus himself. Therefore, we should strive by faith, study, and prayer to make it a part of our every moral decision. CCC 1802

of the Church. Giving a *religious assent* means we accept the reliability of the Church's teaching.

It was Jesus himself who authorized his Church to teach in his name, and assured it that the Holy Spirit would guide it in its teaching role. For these two religious reasons, we accept the reliability of this teaching—hence, the expression "religious assent."

Forming our conscience

Nonetheless, the Church also teaches that individuals have not only a right, but also an obligation to form our own moral conscience in accord with right reason and divine law.

A human being must always obey
the certain judgment of his conscience.
If he were deliberately to act against it,
he would condemn himself. CCC 1790

The Church also recognizes that we could make an "erroneous judgment" in forming conscience. CCC 1790–94 Such an error could result from either:

- **Vincible ignorance** **Our fault**
- **Invincible ignorance** **Not our fault**

LIFE Connection

At one point in the movie, *The Alamo,* "showdown time" comes and the defenders have to vote their consciences. John Wayne stands up and says:

Now I might sound like a Bible-
beater yelling up a revival
at a river-crossing
camp-meeting,
but that don't change
the truth none.

There's a right and there's wrong.
You gotta do one or the other.
You do the one and you're living.
You do the other,
and you may be walking around
but you're dead as a beaver hat.

- ***Describe a time in your life when "showdown time" came, and you had to choose between the hard right and the easy wrong.***

The mother checks the bottle from which her son has poured his drink. She sees that it does not have an X on it. So she returns the drink to the child. The child is confused. "Something's wrong with Mother," the child thinks. "First she screams and forbids me to drink the cola. Now she says it's okay. Why can't Mother make up her mind?"

The child did not understand that the mother was doing exactly what a mother should do, because she did not have absolute certitude that the child's drink was safe. Until she acquired that degree of certitude, she had to forbid the child to drink it.

The Church's position on second-level moral teachings is something like that. The Church does not have absolute certitude that it will be destructive to the individual's and society's well-being. Until that certitude is acquired, the Church must follow the safer course.

Another example may help:

- *Two people are out hunting deer. They decide to separate and go their own way for a while. Ten minutes later, one of the hunters sees movement in a clump of bushes. This could indicate the presence of a deer or his friend. Until he has absolute certitude that the movement is a deer (not his friend), he would never and should never fire into the bushes.*

Forming our conscience

CLARIFY—Stress that it is a grave matter to act contrary to the Church's teaching for two reasons. First, it involves acting against the teaching charism that Jesus gave his Church. Second, it is so easy to con ourselves into believing what we would like to believe.

But stress also that we have a right and a responsibility to form and follow our own conscience (CCC 1783, 1789, 1790, 1798) —even at the risk of making an "erroneous judgment."

If we are *not* responsible for the error in judgment ("invincible ignorance"), we are not guilty of any sin, because we did what we thought was the morally right thing to do.

The following basic guidelines must be observed in forming our conscience:

1. *We've unsuccessfully sought alternative solutions to our moral problem;*
2. *We have a grave reason for acting;*
3. *We've prayed diligently for guidance;*
4. *We've pondered the Church's teaching and consulted with the competent people.*

LIFE Connection

Have the students discuss in small groups and then select one example to share with the entire class.

Recap

An appropriate recap of the importance of the price we can and must pay when it comes to following our conscience is Victor Hugo's *Les Miserables.*

Jean Valjean concealed his past life of crime and became a new man—an honored, prominent citizen. Everybody admired him. Then he learned that an innocent man had been condemned to die from some of the crimes he himself had committed in his sinful past.

Jean was faced with a hard clear-cut decision. Should he keep silent and let an innocent man die for what he had done?

After a great struggle of conscience, he decided he could not do this.

Review

DAILY QUIZ—Just a reminder: Review questions may be assigned (one or two at a time) for homework or a daily quiz.

CHAPTER TESTS—Reproducible chapter tests are found in Appendix A. For consistency and ease in grading, quizzes are restricted to (1) "Matching," (2) "True/False," and (3) "Fill in the Blanks."

TEST ANSWERS—The following are the answers to the test for Chapter 21. (See Appendix, page 332.) Each correct answer is worth 4 points.

Matching

1 = d	2 = b	3 = e	4 = g
5 = c	6 = f	7 = a	

True/False

1 = T	2 = F	3 = T	4 = F
5 = F	6 = T	7 = T	8 = T

Recap

Moral decision making has to do with deciding what is the morally right thing to do in a given situation.

A *clear-cut* decision is like the one Thomas More had to make. A *clouded* decision is like the one Franz Jägerstatter had to make. A *contrary* decision is one that puts us at odds with the twofold charism that Jesus bestowed on his Church.

The Church teaches at two levels. At one level, the Church teaches as one having full certitude on a matter. Consequently, we give this teaching a full *faith assent.*

At the second level, the Church teaches as one possessing less than absolute certitude on a particular matter. We give this teaching a *religious assent.* That is, we accept the reliability of this teaching because Jesus gave to his Church the charism (gift) to teach in his name and the assurance that the Holy Spirit would assist it.

Nevertheless, the Church teaches that we have the right and the obligation to form our moral conscience in accord with right reason and divine law.

The Church also recognizes that we may make an "erroneous judgment" in forming our conscience. CCC 1790-94 Such an error could result from vincible ignorance (our fault) or invincible ignorance (not our fault).

In the latter case, we would not be morally responsible for the evil we commit. It nonetheless remains an evil and we need to work to correct it.

Review

1 List, briefly explain, and give an example of the following moral decisions: (a) clear-cut, (b) clouded, (c) contrary.

2 List and briefly explain, the threefold procedure for making a clouded decision.

3 List and briefly explain the twofold charism Jesus bestowed upon his Church to assist it in its teaching ministry.

4 List and briefly explain (a) the two levels at which the Church teaches, (b) the kinds of assent we must give to each level.

5 List and briefly explain (a) the two kinds of "erroneous judgments" that could result from forming our conscience, (b) which one we would not be morally responsible for and why.

6 List and briefly explain the twofold reasons why acting contrary to the official moral teaching of the Church is a grave matter.

Fill in the Blanks

1. (a) Clear-cut (b) Clouded
   (c) Contrary
2. (a) Ponder Church's teaching
   (b) Pursue competent advice
   (c) Pray for guidance
3. (a) Absolute (b) Faith
   (c) Less than absolute
   (d) Religious

NOTES

Reflect

1 The *Louisville Courier-Journal* carried a story about a seven-year-old who accidentally swallowed a crayon while playing on a school bus. It lodged in the windpipe and was slowly choking the child.

Seeking a speedier ride to the hospital, the driver tried to flag down a motorist. When no one stopped, the driver blocked the traffic lane, forcing the next car to stop. The motorist replied, "I don't want to be late for work."

When the child finally reached the hospital, surgery was ordered. But it was just minutes too late to save the youngster.

■ ***Into which of the three groups of moral decisions did the motorist's decision fall? Explain.***

2 You are the mother of three children, ages five, seven, and nine. Your eldest has a poor self-image and needs a lot of support. Your husband Bob spends about 10 hours a day at the office just to make ends meet. You are offered an excellent 40-hour-a-week job.

■ ***Why would/wouldn't you take the job?***

3 Bill Quinlan and his 18-year-old nephew David sailed out of San Diego Harbor for Ecuador. Ten days later, a tropical hurricane destroyed their sailboat, leaving them with a rubber raft that began losing air.

It became clear that the two together had no chance of survival. Bill scratched a message to his wife and children on an empty water can. Then he handed his wedding ring to David, saying, "Give this to my son when he's old enough to understand." David accepted the ring, too exhausted to argue.

Bill slipped into the water and swam off. David became overwhelmed with guilt and began to cry hysterically. Then he lapsed into a deep sleep. Sometime later a fishing boat spotted him and picked him up.

■ ***Granted that Bill's action was courageous, was he guilty of suicide? Explain.***

■ ***In which of the three groups of moral decisions did Bill Quinlan's action fall?***

STAGE 3: CHAPTER 21 285

Reflect

1 ***Into which of the three groups of moral decisions did the motorist's decision fall? Explain.***

■ *It is a clear-cut moral decision. Clearly, it is difficult in that the motorist may end up paying a high personal price.*

2 ***Why would/wouldn't you take the job?***

■ *This is the kind of discussion that can take place either in small groups or in class with everyone involved in it.*

3 **a)** ***Granted that Bill's action was courageous, was he guilty of suicide? Explain.***
b) ***In which of the three groups of moral decisions did Bill Quinlan's action fall?***

■ *Bill did not intend his death. He hoped against hope that he would be picked up by a passing fishing boat. In other words, he did not intend his death but was willing to accept it. (Recall the discussion of "hunger strikes" on page 259.)*

Risking his life was simply the price he was willing to pay to help his nephew's chances of survival. Bill's decision seems to fall into the category of a clouded moral decision. It was not clear that his action would save his nephew's life.

Bill's decision recalls a classic case that is sometimes cited in textbooks on morality.

■ *A man and a woman are trapped on the top floor of a burning building. Both have handguns. The man decides to shoot himself rather than suffer the agony of slowly burning to death. The woman feels it is wrong to shoot herself to keep from suffering the same fate. She decides to jump, praying that she will miraculously survive.*

Again, refer the students to the three kinds of hunger strikes.

Ask: Which of the three kinds of hunger strikes is closest to the example of the man's decision? The woman's decision?

The man's decision resembles the first kind. He intends his death as a means to an end. The woman's decision resembles the second kind. She does not intend her death. In fact, she hopes against hope that she will survive (land on something that will break her fall, etc.).

PRAYER TIME with the Lord

QUESTION **What are one or two things you have complained about recently? What might you do to set these things right, rather than complain about them?**

To start students thinking, you might suggest complaints dealing with the following areas:

1. *A certain course and how it is taught*
2. *Certain students and how they act*
3. *A teacher you don't connect with*
4. *Things you are asked to do at home*
5. *Things your parents won't let you do*

Have the students share their conclusions in small groups.

PRAYER Journal

QUESTION **Compose a prayer asking for the courage to stand up and be counted on the side of people who build, not tear down.**

Refer the students back to the "Life Connection" on page 283. Have them use John Wayne's style of down-to-earth speaking to ask God's help in one of the following cases:

1. *To pray that your class will have the courage to be honest in quizzes and exams.*
2. *To pray that your friends will have the courage for Christian witness when it comes to drugs and/or alcohol.*
3. *To pray that you will have the courage to treat your parents with the respect you think you would like from children.*

PRAYER TIME with the Lord

Father, grant that I may be a bearer
of Christ Jesus, your Son.
Allow me to warm
the often cold, impersonal scene
of modern life
with your burning love.

Strengthen me, by your Holy Spirit,
to carry out my mission
of changing the world or
some definite part of it, for the better. . . .

Make me more energetic
in setting to right
what I find wrong in the world
instead of complaining
about it or myself.

Nourish in me a practical desire
to build up rather than tear down,
to reconcile more than polarize,
to go out on a limb,
rather than crave security.

Never let me forget
that it is far better to light one candle
than to curse the darkness,
and to join my light, one day, with yours.

CHRISTOPHER PRAYER: AUTHOR UNKNOWN

- **What are one or two things I have complained about recently?**
- **What might I do to set these things right, rather than complain about them?**

286 STAGE 3: CHAPTER 21

SCRIPTURE Journal

QUESTION **Pick one of the above passages. Read it prayerfully and write out a brief statement to Jesus expressing your feelings about it.**

You might choose this excerpt from the fourth reading and have the students express their feelings to Jesus about it:

- *[The Jewish authorities wanted to put the apostles to death for refusing to stop their preaching about Jesus. But a wise and respected Jewish authority said:]*

NOTES

PRAYER Journal

Pearl S. Buck won the Nobel Prize in literature for her novel *The Good Earth.* Deeply concerned about the direction of our nation, she wrote:

This country is divided into two halves:
the people who build,
and the people who break down.

It's time for each of us to stand up and
be counted on the side of the people
who add to our spiritual health
rather than subtract from it.

Each day things happen
which make the wheel turn.
And it's up to each one of us
which way it goes.

■ ***Compose a prayer asking for the courage to stand up and be counted on the side of people who build, not tear down.***

SCRIPTURE Journal

1	**Clear-cut decision**	**1 Corinthians 5**
2	**Clouded decision**	**1 Corinthians 8**
3	**Clouded decision**	**Romans 14**
4	**Postponing a decision**	**Acts 5:27–39**
5	**Landmark decision**	**Acts 15:1–21**

■ ***Pick one of the above passages. Read it prayerfully and write out a brief statement to Jesus expressing your feelings about it.***

"Leave them alone! If what they have planned and done is of human origin, it will disappear, but if it comes from God you cannot possibly defeat them. You could find yourselves fighting against God."

Classroom Resources

CATECHISM

Catechism of the Catholic Church *Second Edition*

For further enrichment, you might refer to:

1. Conscience	Index	p. 777
	Glossary	p. 872
2. Responsibility	Index	p. 842
3. Obedience	Index	p. 828
	Glossary	p. 889

See also: Obligation, Faults, Law.

—AVAILABLE FROM THE UNITED STATES CATHOLIC CONFERENCE, WASHINGTON DC

VIDEO

High Powder

Sixty minutes. Compelling story of young man who discovers use of drugs by his ski team and decides what to do about it. 1995

—AVAILABLE FROM PAULIST PRESS, MAHWAH, N.J.

BOOKS

Waking Up Bees

Jerry Daoust

True-to-life stories about facing important issues such as love, work, vocation, suffering. 1999

—AVAILABLE FROM ST. MARY'S PRESS, WINONA, MN.

Challenge 2000

A Daily Meditation Program based on The Spiritual Exercises of Saint Ignatius.

Mark Link, S.J.

Divided into four parts—(1) Challenge, (2) Decision, (3) Journey, and (4) Victory—these daily meditations leads to a practical, prayerful discernment of God's will.

—AVAILABLE FROM THOMAS MORE, ALLEN, TX.

NOTE

For a list of (1) General resources for professional background and (2) Addresses, phone/fax numbers of major publishing companies, see Appendix B of this Resource Manual.

CHAPTER 22
Witnessing to Love

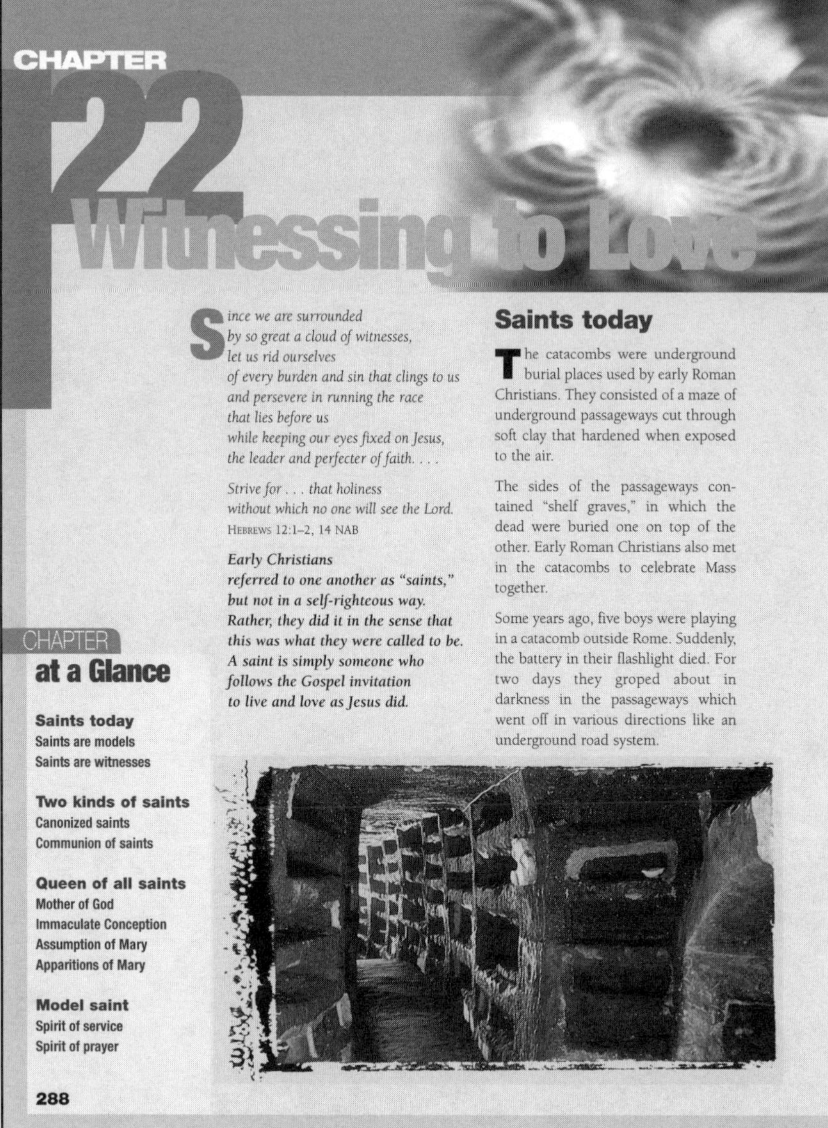

CHAPTER 22 Witnessing to Love

Since we are surrounded
by so great a cloud of witnesses,
let us rid ourselves
of every burden and sin that clings to us
and persevere in running the race
that lies before us
while keeping our eyes fixed on Jesus,
the leader and perfecter of faith. . . .

Strive for . . . that holiness
without which no one will see the Lord.
HEBREWS 12:1–2, 14 NAB

Early Christians referred to one another as "saints," but not in a self-righteous way. Rather, they did it in the sense that this was what they were called to be. A saint is simply someone who follows the Gospel invitation to live and love as Jesus did.

Saints today

The catacombs were underground burial places used by early Roman Christians. They consisted of a maze of underground passageways cut through soft clay that hardened when exposed to the air.

The sides of the passageways contained "shelf graves," in which the dead were buried one on top of the other. Early Roman Christians also met in the catacombs to celebrate Mass together.

Some years ago, five boys were playing in a catacomb outside Rome. Suddenly, the battery in their flashlight died. For two days they groped about in darkness in the passageways which went off in various directions like an underground road system.

CHAPTER **at a Glance**

Saints today
Saints are models
Saints are witnesses

Two kinds of saints
Canonized saints
Communion of saints

Queen of all saints
Mother of God
Immaculate Conception
Assumption of Mary
Apparitions of Mary

Model saint
Spirit of service
Spirit of prayer

288

CHAPTER at a Glance

The aim of this chapter is to extend the students' understanding of:

1 *Saints: their role and witness*
2 *Communion of saints*
3 *Canonized saints*
4 *Queen of all saints*
  a) Mother of God
  b) Immaculate Conception
  c) Assumption
  d) Model disciple

READ—Have a student read aloud the scriptural introduction, which begins: "Since we are surrounded by so great a cloud . . ." Have a second student read aloud the commentary. It begins: "Early Christians . . ."

Saints today

CLARIFY—Around the second century, Jews in Rome began burying their dead in underground cemeteries called catacombs. Consisting of a maze of corridors, some catacombs had as many as six levels.

The combined length of these corridors is estimated to be 600 miles. The dead were placed in niches along the walls and then sealed up with bricks or marble slabs.

■ *Because many early Christians were converts from Judaism, it was logical for them to continue this burial practice.*

In A.D. 64, a huge fire left vast sections of Rome in ashes. Rumors spread that Nero started the fire, hoping to burn the old city, rebuild a new one, and rename it for himself.

When the rumors persisted, Nero blamed the Christians of Rome for the fire. This touched off 300 years of persecution. No longer free to worship in public, Christians began to worship in secrecy in the catacombs.

While digging outside Rome in the 16th century, a workman accidentally rediscovered the catacombs, opening up a lost world.

A valuable historical aspect of the catacombs is the thousands of paintings, epitaphs, and graffiti that covered the surface of the tombs: fish, keys of Peter, anchors of hope, names of saints, and references to Jesus' parables and miracles.

DISCUSS—This brings us to the story of the boys who were lost in a catacomb. Their story makes a good parable showing how ancient saints still act as guides to modern Christians.

Many people today are like the lost boys. They started off believing the teachings

NOTES

Then one of the boys felt a smooth path running along the rough floor of the passageway. He reasoned that it had been worn smooth by the feet of ancient Christians filing in and out of the tunnels for Mass. The boys followed the path. It led to safety.

This story might be used as a kind of parable to illustrate the fact that saints who lived centuries ago can still serve as guides for modern Christians.

1 ***What are some examples of how saints of centuries ago serve as guides to us today?***

After Francis was released, it took him a good year to regain his health. Then he left the wealthy surroundings of his family, put on a peasant's garb, and set out to find God. His new home was an abandoned church on the outskirts of Assisi. There he spent hours alone in prayer.

Two biblical teachings, especially, began to haunt Francis. The first was that every person is created in God's image. The second was that whatever we do for the least person, we do for Jesus himself. MATTHEW 25:45

Witnessing

Saints are models

Saint Francis of Assisi was born into a wealthy Italian family. As a youth, he was free-spirited and somewhat irresponsible.

In 1202 he became a soldier and marched off to battle. He was taken prisoner and spent the next year of his life in prison. That experience changed his outlook on life forever.

2 ***Why would such an experience change someone's whole outlook on life?***

As a result of profound meditation on these two teachings, Francis developed a deep love for the outcasts of society.

One day, he came upon a leper. Although Francis had a dreadful fear of leprosy, he embraced the man. This moving incident dramatized the extent to which the teachings of Jesus had taken root in his heart.

Not long afterward, Francis was attending Mass. The Gospel reading recalled Jesus' instruction to his disciples to go forth into the surrounding towns

STAGE 3: CHAPTER 22 **289**

of Jesus (the "flashlight of their faith" burned brightly). Then for some reason the "flashlight of their faith" went out. They groped in "spiritual darkness."

Then one day they discovered the saints: people who led caring, loving lives. Inspired by these people they rediscovered the "light" of their faith again and their lives took on new meaning.

Ask the students: Can you recall some examples of people we read about who rediscovered their faith? (After identifying the person, ask for a brief description of how they rediscovered their faith and changed.)

Dorothy Day P. 11	*John Eagen* P. 174
Linda Marshall P. 135	*Tommy* P. 9
Thomas Merton P. 54	*Piri Thomas* P. 221
Margaret Mehren P. 23	*Terry Anderson* P. 24
Eugene O'Neill P. 249	*Chuck Colson* P. 170

NOTEBOOK—The following "cast of characters" summarizes the parallel between the story of the boys and many modern Christians:

Boys in Story	*Modern Christians*
Flashlight failure	*Faith failure*
Groping blindly	*Groping faithless*
Finding path	*Finding saints*
Following path	*Following saints*

QUESTION **1** ***What are some examples of how saints of centuries ago serve as guides to us today?***

■ *Some spent their lives working for peace* CF. GANDHI: RESOURCE MANUAL, P. 242
Some devoted their lives working with the poor and sick CF. SCHWIETZER:TEXT, P. 275
Some worked for renewal in the Church CF. FRANCIS OF ASSISI: TEXT AND MANUAL P. 289
Some gave us their lives in martyrdom CF. ST. JUSTIN, TEXT, P. 160. (WHEN HE REFUSED TO SACRIFICE TO IDOLS, HE WAS SCOURGED AND BEHEADED.)

CLARIFY—Stress that not all saints were outstanding intellects or talented. Recall the case of Saint Joseph Cupertino CF TEXT: P. 96.

Saints are models

QUESTION **2** ***Why would such an experience change someone's whole outlook on life?***

■ *Imprisonment has converted a lot of people. It shows us how vulnerable life is and gives us time to think about what is really important in the long run.*

CLARIFY—Saint Francis was born in Assisi (Italy) in 1182 and died forty-four years later in 1226. He was canonized two years later in 1228. Francis remained a deacon all his life, feeling he was unworthy to be a priest.

■ *Francis is credited with popularizing the Christmas "crib." He had a crib set up at Grecchio in 1223 as part of the town's celebration of midnight Mass. The people loved it. From that Christmas on, the popularity of the crib spread.*

THINK about it

The early followers of Francis of Assisi wanted to know what to do when they went out into the streets. Francis replied, "Preach the gospel at all times. If necessary use words."

■ *The most powerful preaching is done not by word, but by example. Poet Edgar A. Guest expressed it this way:*

"It is all in vain to preach the truth,
To the eager ears of trusting youth. . . .
Fine words may grace the advice you give,
But youth will learn from the way you live."

Witness to Jesus is like perfume. If it's really good, you don't have to call attention to it with words.

HISTORICAL Connection

CLARIFY—The word "stigmata" comes from the Greek word meaning "marks."

■ *In September 1224, while praying in a small hut under a beech tree at the foot of Mount Alvernia, Francis had a vision of the crucified Jesus. When the vision had ended, the hands, feet, and side of Francis bore the stigmata of Jesus' wounds. They remained imprinted in Francis's body until his death.*

QUESTION **3** ***What passage or story in Scripture ranks as one of your favorites? What do you like about the story?***

Recall the Gospel passage that became one of Saint Augustine's favorites. It led to his conversion.

■ *Throw off the works of darkness . . . and make no provision for the desires of the flesh.* ROMANS 13:12–14

A favorite parable of Albert Schweitzer led him to give up the concert stage in Europe and become a medical doctor to the poor in Africa. It was the Parable of Lazarus and the Rich Man. LUKE 16:19–31

THINK about it

Every Christian occupies some kind of pulpit and preaches some kind of sermon every day.

Author unknown

to preach the Good News. Jesus told his disciples not to take any money with them, but to trust in God for their material needs. MATTHEW 10:5–15

This instruction touched Francis deeply. He lived in a time like our own, when people were drifting from the teachings of Jesus. So Francis went forth into the towns of Italy to preach the Gospel anew.

His charismatic personality inspired other young people to follow his example. And so it happened that the Franciscan order was born.

3 What passage or story in Scripture ranks as one of your favorites? What do you like about the story?

HISTORICAL Connection

Ultimately, Francis attempted no more than to live out the teachings of Christ and the Spirit of the Gospel.

His identification with Christ was so intense that in 1224, while praying . . . he received the "stigmata," the physical marks of Christ's passion. . . .

He died October 3, 1226. His feast is observed on October 4.

Robert Ellsberg: *All Saints*

Saints are witnesses

Besides being guides and models for us to follow and imitate, saints are witnesses of what we are called to be.

In the novel *Anthony Adverse*, Hervey Allen says of Francis and of other faith-witnesses like him:

Brother Francis and his kind . . .
have always made Christianity
a dangerous religion.
Just when the Church
is about to be taken as a decorative
and snugly woven cocoon . . .
poof!—that cocoon bursts
and the beautiful psyche
of Christianity emerges.

4 What do you think Hervey means by "beautiful psyche of Christianity"?

A saint may be described as a person who follows the Gospel's invitation to love and live as Jesus did.

A saint is a living witness to the fact that God's grace can work miracles in us, if we but open our hearts to it.

Two kinds of saints

The word "saint" derives from the Latin word *sanctus*, which means "holy." Literally, the word *saint* means "holy one" and is translated that way in some Bibles.

The words *holy one* recall God's command: "Keep yourselves holy, because I am holy." LEVITICUS 11:44

290 STAGE 3: CHAPTER 22

■ *Schweitzer reasoned that he was the rich man and that his African brothers were Lazarus. How could he enjoy applause in Europe, while Lazarus suffered in Africa?*

ACTIVITY—You might have the students check their Scripture journals for a passage they like or find helpful. Have them read it to the class.

Saints are witnesses

QUESTION **4** ***What do you think Hervey means by "beautiful psyche of Christianity"?***

■ *Saint Paul is making a reference to the "Christian psyche" when he writes: "Let God transform you inwardly by a complete change of your mind.*

NOTES

Early Christians referred to one another as "saint." They did this not in a smug, self-righteous sense, but in the sense that this was what they are *called* to be.

Thus, we find the word *saints* used over sixty times in the New Testament. Saint Paul used it frequently in the salutation of his letters. An example is his Letter to the Colossians:

Paul, an apostle of Christ Jesus
by the will of God,
and Timothy our brother,
to the holy ones . . . in Colossae:
grace to you and peace from
God our Father. COLOSSIANS 1:1–2 NAB

Canonized saints

With the passage of time, however, the word *saint* was reserved exclusively for those Christians who were martyred for their faith or who had lived extraordinary, holy lives.

At first, a person was declared to be a saint by those who had seen the person martyred or who had witnessed the person's holy life.

Around the year 1000, Pope John XV set up a more exacting and objective process for declaring a person a saint. Called *canonization*, it involves an investigation of every aspect of a person's life. CCC 828, 1173

Communion of Saints

A question that people not of the Catholic faith sometimes have is this: "Why do you Catholics pray to saints? Why don't you pray directly to God?"

5 How would you respond to these two questions?

Catholics do pray directly to God in every Mass celebrated daily in every nation throughout the world. No relationship is more important than our relationship with God.

But our relationship with one another is also tremendously important. We profess this since earliest Christian times in the Apostle's Creed: "I believe in . . . the communion of saints." This phrase refers to two things:

SHARE YOUR meditation

Many rural villages in India are totally without electricity. People use tiny oil lamps, much like those used in Jesus' time, to light their homes.

The temple in one of these rural villages has a large frame hanging from its ceiling. Cut into the frame are a hundred slots into which tiny oil lamps can be placed.

When the people go to the temple after dark, they carry their oil lamps from their homes to guide them through the darkness.

Upon arriving in the temple, they place the lamp in one of the slots in the frame. By the time the last villager arrives, the darkness of the temple has been transformed into a glorious sea of light.

■ ***What important spiritual point does this story make?***
■ ***What might it be saying to our world, right now?***

THINK about it

The blood of martyrs is the seed of the Church.

Tertullian

Then you will be able to know . . .
what is good and pleasing to God."
ROMANS 12:2

In other words, the "beautiful psyche of Christianity" is the mind and heart of Christ.

Two kinds of saints

CLARIFY—The New Testament speaks exclusively of "uncanonized" people. The process of canonization came centuries later.

■ *A New Testament saint was simply (as the textbook says) "a person who follows the Gospel's invitation to love and live as Jesus did.*

Canonized saints

CLARIFY—Canonization came about when cults developed around certain martyrs and others. There was a need for true discernment, which was lacking in the popular mind of certain people "promoting" this or that "saint."

■ *The present process of canonization dates back to 1588. Pope Sixtus V designed a rigorous procedure for beatifying (first step to sainthood) and canonizing (final step) saints. The first papal canonization was a German bishop, Ulrich (890–973), canonized in 993 by Pope John XV.*

Communion of Saints

QUESTION ***5 How would you respond to these two questions?***

■ *Discuss the questions right in class. The ideal responses follow in the paragraphs following this question.*

CLARIFY—Stress the point that the communion of saints involves not only the members of the Church but also their "gifts," which they share with the entire Church.

Share Your meditation

CLARIFY—It took the lights of everyone in the community—not just a few—to transform the temple into a "sea of light." So, too, our world needs not just a few isolated saints, but a "community" or "communion of saints" to transform it.

THINK about it

Historically, persecutions foster Church growth. Why? (An outpouring of grace and truly inspiring witness.)

CLARIFY—Refer the students to the "haloes" on the wall in the background in the photo.

> ■ *British TV celebrity Malcolm Muggeridge, who was not a Catholic, went to India to film Mother Teresa's nuns working with dying patients. He describes the situation in his book* Something Beautiful for God.
>
> *His camera crew didn't anticipate the poor lighting in the building and failed to bring extra lights. So they thought it useless to film the sisters at work. But someone suggested they do it anyway. Maybe some footage would be usable.*
>
> *To the crew's amazement, it was illumined by a mysterious light. Muggeridge believed that it was a "glow" of love radiating from the sister's faces. He sensed this "glow" himself when he first entered the building. He says it was "like the haloes that artists have seen and made visible round the heads of saints," adding: "I find it not at all surprising that the luminosity should register on photographic film."*

Eventually, Muggeridge did what he swore he'd never do. He became a Catholic. Concerning his surprise conversion, he explained that his change of heart was brought about by Mother Teresa. He said:

> ■ *Words cannot express how much I owe her. She showed me Christianity in action. She showed me the power of love. She showed me how one loving person can start a tidal wave of love that can spread to the entire world.*

THINK about it

Another quote is relevant here. It reads:

> ■ *Holy men and women serve this world by reflecting in it the light of another.*
> JOHN W. DONOHUE

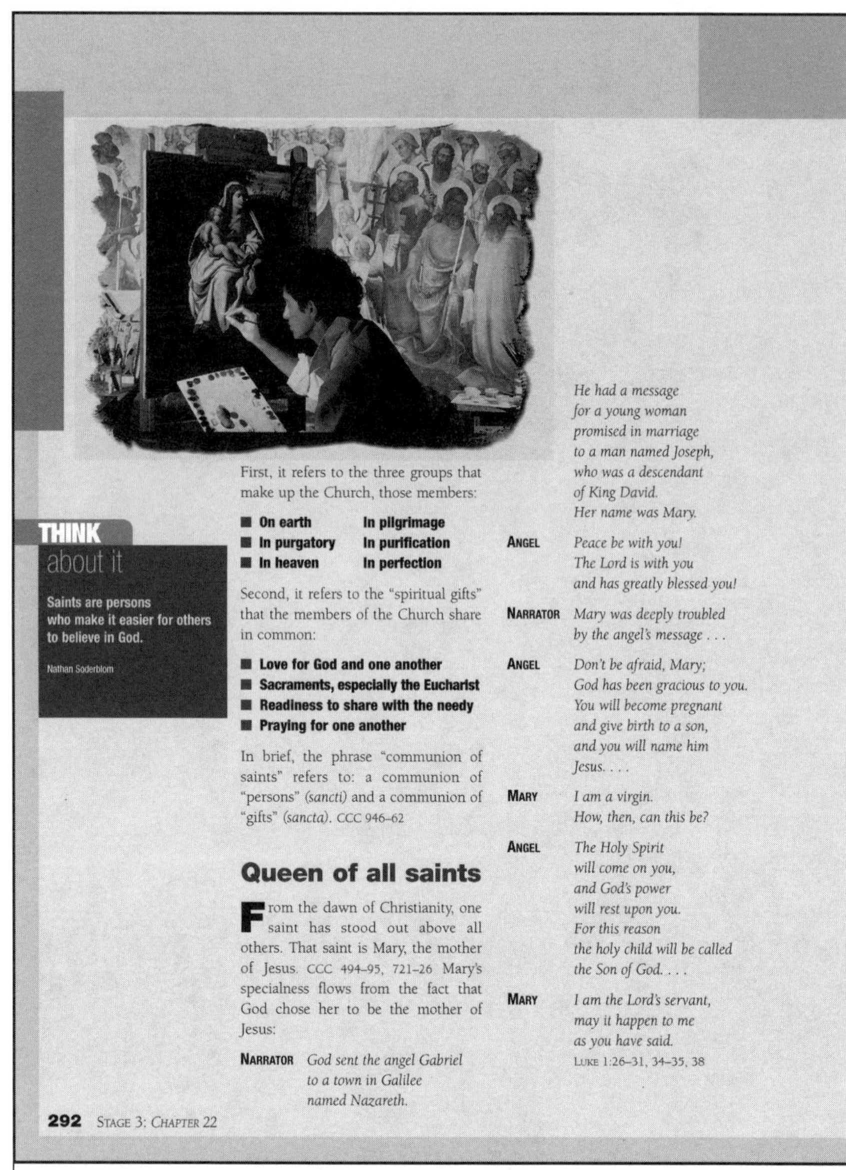

THINK about it

Saints are persons who make it easier for others to believe in God.

Nathan Soderblom

First, it refers to the three groups that make up the Church, those members:

- **On earth** — **In pilgrimage**
- **In purgatory** — **In purification**
- **In heaven** — **In perfection**

Second, it refers to the "spiritual gifts" that the members of the Church share in common:

- **Love for God and one another**
- **Sacraments, especially the Eucharist**
- **Readiness to share with the needy**
- **Praying for one another**

In brief, the phrase "communion of saints" refers to: a communion of "persons" (*sancti*) and a communion of "gifts" (*sancta*). CCC 946–62

Queen of all saints

From the dawn of Christianity, one saint has stood out above all others. That saint is Mary, the mother of Jesus. CCC 494–95, 721–26 Mary's specialness flows from the fact that God chose her to be the mother of Jesus:

NARRATOR *God sent the angel Gabriel to a town in Galilee named Nazareth. He had a message for a young woman promised in marriage to a man named Joseph, who was a descendant of King David. Her name was Mary.*

ANGEL *Peace be with you! The Lord is with you and has greatly blessed you!*

NARRATOR *Mary was deeply troubled by the angel's message . . .*

ANGEL *Don't be afraid, Mary; God has been gracious to you. You will become pregnant and give birth to a son, and you will name him Jesus. . . .*

MARY *I am a virgin. How, then, can this be?*

ANGEL *The Holy Spirit will come on you, and God's power will rest upon you. For this reason the holy child will be called the Son of God. . . .*

MARY *I am the Lord's servant, may it happen to me as you have said.*

LUKE 1:26–31, 34–35, 38

292 STAGE 3: CHAPTER 22

Queen of all saints

CLARIFY—Stress the point that Mary's "specialness" flows from the fact that she was chosen to be the mother of Jesus.

> ■ *Muslims have a great devotion to Mary as the mother of Jesus, whom they consider a great prophet. They believe in Mary's immaculate conception and in the virgin birth of Jesus. Muhammad called Mary the greatest of all women.*

Mother of God

CLARIFY—The idea of "virgin" birth has always fascinated people. It is called "parthenogenesis," after the Greek *parthenos* ("virgin"). In their book *Who Should Play God?*, Ted Howard and Jeremy Rifkin quote Dr. Helen Spurway,

NOTES

Mother of God

Mary's words, "I am a virgin," testify to her virginity. CCC 496–507 The child she conceived in her womb was not of human origin, but of the Holy Spirit. Thus, Mary is traditionally referred to as the "Virgin Mother of God."

6 *How can Mary, a human person, be called "Mother of God" in the literal sense of the title?*

The title "Mother of God" does not mean that Mary is God's mother from all eternity. It simply means that Jesus is God *according to the flesh*. It is in this sense that we honor Mary with the title "Mother of God." CCC 495, 507

Historically, the title "Mother of God" dates from the Council of Ephesus, A.D. 431. The council faced the problem of declaring that Jesus had two natures (divine and human) but was not two persons, as some theologians erroneously taught.

In stressing that Jesus was only "one" person, the council added that Mary, therefore, could be called the Mother of God. For, indeed, Jesus is God *according to the flesh*. CCC 495

Immaculate Conception

Catholics also honor Mary under the title "Immaculate Conception." To understand this title, we need to recall that the first sin "flawed" the human race. We refer to this flawed condition as the state of original sin. CCC 390–400

The title "Immaculate Conception" expresses Catholic belief, handed down by tradition, that, from the instant of her existence as a human person, God preserved Mary from original sin in preparation for her calling to be the mother of Jesus. CCC 488–94

Tradition also teaches that Mary remained sinless throughout her life. CCC 411 She was "most blessed of all women." Luke 1:42 In the words of the poet William Wordsworth, she is "our tainted nature's solitary boast."

Assumption of Mary

One of the Marian feasts celebrated in the Church is that of the Assumption. This feast celebrates Catholic belief—handed down by tradition—that Mary was taken up to heaven at the end of her life in the totality of her person. CCC 966

In other words, she went directly from an earthly state to a heavenly state, without her body undergoing decay, the penalty of sin. Genesis 3:19 Belief in Mary's assumption is a corollary of her Immaculate Conception. Because she was sinless, she did not fall under its penalty.

Mary's assumption is a beautiful reminder that we are all destined to be in heaven someday in the totality of our person, soul and body, just as Mary is now. CCC 966

HISTORICAL Connection

Mary is sometimes referred to as the "Mother of the Church." The wood carving below portrays Saint Peter Canisius and others striving to restore the unity of the Church at the time of the Reformation.

geneticist at the London University College, as suggesting that parthenogenesis may cause one in every 1.6 million pregnancies.

■ *The authors cite the example of a young German girl who collapsed on the streets of Hanover, Germany, during an allied bombing raid. Nine months later she gave birth to a baby girl. Blood tests, fingerprints, and other indicators showed the child to appear to be the "exact twin of the mother." Howard and Rifkin report that examining physicians theorized that "the shock of the bombing might have jarred a dormant body cell within the uterus to begin reproduction."*

QUESTION **6 *How can Mary, a human person, be called "Mother of God" in the literal sense of the title?***

■ *Stress that the title "Mother of God" does not mean that Mary is the mother of God from eternity. It means that Mary is the mother of Jesus, who is God "according to the flesh." In other words, insofar as Jesus is God (according to the flesh), to that extent Mary may truly be said to be the "Mother of God."*

Immaculate Conception

CLARIFY—How could Mary be born free from sin, although she belonged to the human race, which was enslaved by sin?

■ *An example throws light on this mystery. In ancient times, when slavery was widespread, children of slaves were doomed before they were born. A wealthy person, however, could liberate them from this doomed destiny by paying a ransom in advance of their birth. Thus, even though they were born of slave parents, they were born free of slave status.*

LIFE Connection

CLARIFY—The Reformation was the religious revolution in the 16th century, which led to the establishment of Protestant Churches. The Reformation proper began at about the same time in Germany (led by Martin Luther) and in Switzerland (led by Ulrich Zwingli).

Assumption of Mary

CLARIFY—The doctrine of the assumption was defined by Pope Pius XII in 1950, in the papal document *Munificentissimus Deus.*

From a practical viewpoint, Mary's presence in heaven, soul and body, reminds us that this is our destiny as well: to be in heaven, soul and body. We sometimes forget that in heaven we will have a body. An example may help to clarify this possibility:

■ *Take the tulip. In spring it has a colorful head and a lovely green body. Within a month, the tulip's body loses its beauty, dies, and decays. Only a bulb remains. When spring returns, a new body emerges from the bulb.*

So it is with us. When the "fall of our life" arrives, our body loses its beauty and dies. Soon nothing remains but our soul. But when "spring" comes (resurrection of the dead), a beautiful new body will emerge again from the "bulb" we call our soul. Listen to Saint Paul:

*"How can the dead be raised to life?
What kind of body will they have? . . .*

*"When you plant a seed in the ground,
it does not sprout to life unless it dies.
And what you plant is a bare seed . . .
not the full-bodied plant that will later
grow up. God provides that seed with the
body he wishes; he gives each seed its own
proper body. . . .*

"This is how it will be when the dead are raised to life." 1 CORINTHIANS 15:35–42

Apparitions of Mary

ACTIVITY—An account of Vittorio Micheli's cure appears in the *Reader's Digest* APRIL 1982, PAGES 65–69. You might have one of the students read it and report back to the class on it.

CLARIFY—Bernadette's life and story were popularized a number of years back by a book called *The Song of Bernadette.* It became a bestseller and was made into a popular movie. The story behind the writing of the book is almost as amazing as the book itself. It begins with World War II:

■ *A well-known Jewish writer, Franz Werfel, and his wife had slipped through the Nazi frontier. Working their way through France, they hoped to cross into Spain and set sail for the United States. But the Spanish border guards turned them back.*

Werfel and his wife sought shelter in nearby Lourdes, the site of Bernadette's apparitions, now a famous shrine. That night, the Jewish writer visited the shrine. Standing alone in the darkness, he spoke words to this effect:

*"I am not a believer,
and I must be honest and say so.
But in my extreme need, on the chance
that I could be wrong about God,
I ask for help for me and my wife."*

Werfel returned to the village. Never before, he told a friend later, did he experience such peace of mind as he did after making that prayer.

Within days, Werfel and his wife found a way to cross over into Spain. Shortly after, they were safely on board a ship, sailing to the United States.

The first thing he did in the United States was to write the story of Lourdes, calling it The Song of Bernadette.

LIFE
Connection

Marine Cyril J. O'Brien tells the following story:

*In my missal
there's a holy picture
to remind me
always to say a prayer
for the man who left it for me—
a Japanese
whom I saw only once,
as he died on Guam.*

*He was trying
to sneak into a bunker
behind a little knoll.
A patrol flushed him
and two companions
from the thicket.*

*They ran into us and were killed.
As a matter of routine,
the Marines searched them
for grenades,
intelligence material, souvenirs.
I put my hand into a wet,
sticky pocket.
It contained a picture
of our Blessed Mother.
It was the pocket over his heart.*

Catholic Digest, January 1, 1949

Touching on this mystery, Paul compares our body before death to a seed; he compares our body after death to the plant that emerges from the seed. 1 CORINTHIANS 15:36–38 Continuing this metaphor, Paul says:

*When the body is buried, it is mortal;
when raised, it will be immortal. . . .
When buried, it is a physical body;
when raised, it will be a spiritual body.*
1 CORINTHIANS 15:42, 44

Apparitions of Mary

In 1858 a fourteen-year-old French girl, Bernadette Soubirous, reported having a vision of Mary at a hillside in Lourdes, France. Civil and religious authorities scoffed at her claim. When she continued to visit the hillside to pray, she was threatened with punishment.

One day, Mary told Bernadette to dig into the ground with her hands. She did and a spring bubbled up. Miracles began.

One of the miracles involved a mother who bathed her paralyzed child in the spring waters; the child was restored to health. Fifty-four years after Bernadette died, that same child, then a 77-year-old man, was an honored guest at her canonization ceremony in Rome.

Today, the Medical Bureau of Lourdes has on file records of over 1,200 recorded cures that have taken place there. Before a cure is accepted by the bureau, it must be certified by an international commission of doctors and surgeons of all faiths.

A highly publicized cure took place in the 1970s.

It involved a former serviceman, twenty-three-year-old Vittorio Micheli of Italy. He had contracted bone cancer, and doctors had given up hope of his recovery.

In desperation, his family and friends took him to Lourdes.

There he was washed in the spring waters. Within a week, his pain vanished and the bone repaired itself.

There have been reports of other apparitions or visions of Mary over the centuries. Because of the possibility of deception, however, the Church exercises extreme caution in dealing with such reports.

Each case is investigated thoroughly (sometimes for years) before it is declared worthy of credibility.

7 ***Why do you think some people seem to be drawn more to apparitions and "messages" than to Scripture itself?***

Model saint

Catholics look upon Mary as the model disciple or saint. This means that they look upon her as being the model of what they should strive to imitate.

Two traits, especially, stand out in Mary's life, her:

- **Spirit of service**
- **Spirit of prayer**

294 STAGE 3: CHAPTER 22

NOTES

Up Close & Personal

Phyllis McGinley

Phyllis McGinley is a modern American poet. She wrote a book called *Saint-Watching*. In it she confesses:

When I was seven years old
I wanted to be
a tight-rope dancer
and broke my collarbone
practicing
on a child-size high wire.

At twelve
I planned to become
an international spy.

At fifteen
my ambition was the stage.

Now in my sensible
declining years
I would give anything . . .
to be a saint.

Spirit of service

A young believer said, "My life turned around when I stopped asking God to do things for me and asked God what I could do for him." Mary had this same kind of *spirit of service.*

Her spirit of service is illustrated in her response to the angel's announcement that she has been called to serve as the mother of Jesus. She answered, "I am the Lord's servant; may it happen to me as you have said." LUKE 1:38

Mary showed this kind of spirit when she learned that Elizabeth was pregnant with John the Baptist. She went immediately to help her cousin. LUKE 1:39

Mary's spirit of service also showed itself in a touching way at a wedding in Cana. When she learned that the newly married couple had run out of wine, she immediately sought Jesus' help. JOHN 2:1

Spirit of prayer

A second trait was Mary's spirit of prayer. It showed itself shortly after the birth of Jesus. Some shepherds showed up to tell Mary and Joseph what an angel had told them about the child.

[Mary and Joseph] were amazed
at what the shepherd said.
Mary remembered all these things
and thought deeply about them. LUKE 2:19

Mary's spirit of prayer also showed itself in her anticipation of Pentecost. Luke says that she and Jesus' disciples "gathered frequently to pray as a group" to prepare for the coming of the Holy Spirit. ACTS 1:14

In brief, then, Mary is an inspiration and a model to all believers, especially in her spirit of prayer and service. CCC 2673–82

8 What is one of the biggest obstacles that keeps me from making a more serious effort to make prayer a daily part of my life? To make service to others a part of my life?

PRAYER hotline

God grant me courage not to give up what I think is right even though I think it is hopeless.

Admiral Chester Nimitz

QUESTION **7** ***Why do you think some people seem to be drawn more to apparitions and "messages" than to Scripture itself?***

Many people seem to be insecure in their faith. They are constantly looking for some further assurance. Recall that this was also the case in Jesus' time. He said:

> ■ *The people of this day. . . ask for a miracle, but none will be given them except the miracle of Jonah.*
>
> *In the same way the prophet Jonah was a sign to the people of Nineveh, so the son of Man will be a sign for the people of his day.* LUKE 11:29–30

In other words, the preaching of God's word is sufficient. Just as Jonah preached it and people responded, so people today should respond to God's word in Scripture.

Model saint

CLARIFY—Stress the two traits: prayer and service. They are like two rails on a train track. Where you truly find one, you will find the other. If you don't, something is wrong.

Spirit of service

CLARIFY—Helen Keller (cf. this Resource Manual, p. 140) said of service:

> *I am only one; but still I am one. I cannot do everything, but still I can do something; I will not refuse to do the something I can do.*

Spirit of prayer

QUESTION **8** ***What is one of the biggest obstacles that keeps you from making a more serious effort to make prayer a daily part of your life? To make service to others a part of your life?***

Have the students discuss in small groups: obstacles to (1) prayer (2) service. Have them share the results with the class.

Up Close & Personal

> ■ *Saint Francis de Sales was born in France in the latter half of the 16th century. At one point in his youthful life, Francis feared that he had lost his friendship with God and was, therefore, predestined for hell for all eternity. (The Calvanists taught that we were predestined at birth for either heaven or hell.)*
>
> *That fear brought on a depression that tore his soul apart and affected his health deeply and adversely. In spite of his fear and depression, Francis promised God that, even if he were destined for hell, he would never resort to cursing God. He knelt at the statue of the Virgin Mary and recited a prayer called the Memorare. By the time he finished the prayer, his fear and depression had completely gone. It never returned.*

Recap

Nearly 3,000 saints are accepted as such by the Church. About another thousand men and women are being considered for eventual canonization. The first U.S. saint was Mother Frances Xavier Cabrini (1850–1917). She migrated from Italy to New York in 1889, became an American citizen in 1909, died in Chicago in 1917, and was canonized in 1946.

■ *It was common practice for early Christians to choose patron saints. A patron was a saint who was a special advocate before God. Early Christians often chose their namesake as their patron. They put themselves under their patron's protection, studied their patron's life, and tried to imitate their patron's virtue.*

Professions also had their patron saints. Fishermen chose Saint Andrew as their patron. Doctors chose Saint Luke, whom Saint Paul refers to as a "doctor." COLOSSIANS 4:14 *Carpenters chose Saint Joseph, whom Saint Mark refers to as being a carpenter.* MARK 6:3

In the Middle Ages, it became common practice to name towns and cities after saints. This explains city names like Saint Louis, Saint Paul, and San Francisco (Saint Francis).

Review

DAILY QUIZ—The review questions may be assigned (one or two at a time) for homework or a daily quiz.

CHAPTER TESTS—Reproducible chapter tests are found in Appendix A. For consistency and ease in grading, quizzes are restricted to (1) "Matching," (2) "True/False," and (3) "Fill in the Blanks."

TEST ANSWERS—The following are the answers to the test for Chapter 22. (See Appendix A, page 333.) Each correct answer worth 4 points.

Recap

A saint may be described as a person who follows the Gospel invitation to live and love as Jesus did. For this reason, saints become for us:

- **Models**
- **Witnesses**

There are two groups of people who enjoy the name "saint": canonized saints, and the communion of saints (members of Christ's Body, the Church):

- **Members in pilgrimage** — **On earth**
- **Members in purification** — **In purgatory**
- **Members in perfection** — **In heaven**

Of all the saints, the Virgin Mary is special. Her specialness flows from the fact that God chose her to be the mother of Jesus. We therefore give her the title "Mother of God."

We also honor her with the title "Immaculate Conception," because she was preserved from original sin.

Finally, because Mary was sinless, she did not fall under its penalty, but was assumed into heaven in the totality of her person.

Mary's assumption is a pledge that we too will join her in heaven in the totality of our person, if we strive to be like her, especially in her spirit of service and prayer.

Review

1 Explain (a) what ordeal changed the life of Saint Francis of Assisi, (b) what two Scripture readings gave him a love for society's rejects, (c) what Scripture reading inspired him to preach the Gospel, and (d) how the time in which Francis lived was similar to ours.

2 Explain (a) how a saint may be described, (b) the Latin word from which our word "saint" is derived and its meaning, (c) how the word "saint" changed in meaning over the passage of time, and (d) what the process for declaring a saint is called and what it involves.

3 Briefly explain: (a) the twofold meaning of the phrase "communion of saints," (b) the three groups of "persons" it includes, and (c) three groups of "gifts" it includes.

4 In what sense is (a) Mary "special," (b) the "Mother of God,"(c) the "Virgin Mother of God," (d) the "Immaculate Conception," and (e) the "model disciple" of her Son?

5 Explain (a) what we mean by Mary's "assumption," (b) how it is linked to the title "Immaculate Conception," and (c) how it speaks to us of our own destiny.

6 What two characteristics, especially, of Mary should we try to imitate? Give two examples from Scripture to illustrate each characteristic.

7 Explain (a) the origin of the springs at Lourdes and (b) how Lourdes became a place to which people came for healing.

Matching

1 = e	2 = f	3 = h	4 = b
5 = a	6 = i	7 = g	8 = j
9 = c	10 = d		

True/False

1 = F	2 = T	3 = F	4 = T
5 = T	6 = T	7 = F	8 = F
9 = T	10 = T	11 = T	12 = F
13 = T	14 = T	15 = T	

NOTES

Reflect

1 Some years ago, Dr. Alexis Carrel, a New York surgeon and Nobel Prize winner, went to Lourdes to investigate firsthand the cures that were being reported there. He himself had no religious faith at all.

While en route by train to the French village, Carrel was called several times to treat an extremely sick girl on the same train. He said that if she were cured at Lourdes, he would become a believer.

When the train arrived at Lourdes, Carrel accompanied the girl to the shrine. In his book *The Voyage to Lourdes*, he describes what happened at a prayer service after the girl was bathed in the famous spring waters. (For professional reasons, he changed all names and called himself Lerrac.)

Suddenly,
Lerrac felt himself turning pale.
The blanket which covered
Marie Ferrand's distended abdomen
was gradually flattening out.
He watched the intake of her breath
and the pulsing of her throat.
"How do you feel?" he asked her.
"I feel weak, but I feel I am cured."
Lerrac stood there in silence, his mind a blank.

Later, Carrel and two other doctors examined the girl carefully. Their conclusion was unanimous: she was cured.

Carrel still did not believe, even though he had seen everything with his own eyes. That night, he went for a long walk. He ended up in the back of a church and prayed for the gift of faith.

At about three o'clock in the morning, he returned to his hotel. As he sat down to record his thoughts before going to bed, he "felt the serenity of nature enter my soul. All intellectual doubts vanished."

At that moment Dr. Alexis Carrel became a believer. He went on to become a prominent Catholic.

■ ***Why do you think Dr. Carrel doubted, even after seeing the miracle?***
■ ***Why do you think fewer miracles are apparently taking place at Lourdes today than there once were?***

2 Elizabeth Ann Seton was the first native-born American saint. At nineteen, she married into a wealthy family. Before her husband died at the age of twenty-nine, they had five children.

Two years after her husband's tragic death, Elizabeth and the children embraced the Catholic faith. She became a teacher and opened a school for girls in Maryland in 1808.

The following year she founded the American Sisters of Charity, which pioneered the Catholic school system in the United States.

Elizabeth Ann Seton was canonized in 1975. Other U.S. saints include Mother Frances Xavier Cabrini, Bishop John Neumann, and Mother Katherine Drexel.

■ ***What made Elizabeth Seton an unlikely candidate for sainthood?***
■ ***Why do you think God often chooses unlikely candidates?***

Reflect

1 a) *Why do you think Dr. Carrel doubted, even after seeing the miracle?*

■ *We often hear people say, "If I could see just one miracle, I'd believe." Or, "If someone returned from the dead and spoke to me, I'd believe." Why do/don't you think they would believe?*

b) *Why do you think fewer miracles are apparently taking place at Lourdes today than there once were?*

■ *Various reasons are given. One is that people today lack the faith that people formerly had. You might ask the students: Do you think people today have less faith? If so, why?*

2 a) *What made Elizabeth Seton an unlikely candidate for sainthood?*

■ *Elizabeth Ann Seton (1774–1821) grew up as an Episcopalian. Her wealthy husband took the entire family to Italy for his health. There he died in December 1803. It was while in Italy that Elizabeth Ann became acquainted with Catholicism. She became a Catholic in 1805 upon her return to New York, after her husband's death in Italy.*

Her conversion caused her to be shunned by her family and friends. She was drawn to Catholicism by three things especially:
(1) Her belief in the Eucharist
(2) Her devotion to Mary
(3) Her conviction that the Catholic Church led back to the Apostles and to Jesus himself.

b) *Why do you think God often chooses unlikely candidates?*

■ *God purposely chose what the world considers nonsense in order to shame the wise, and he chose what the world considers weak in order to shame the powerful.*

He chose what the world looks down on and despises and thinks is nothing, in order to destroy what the world thinks is important. 1 CORINTHIANS 1:27–28

PRAYER TIME with the Lord

QUESTION ***Describe your special prayer place.***

To get students thinking, share with them some passages from Carlo Caretto's *Letters from the Desert*. That title says exactly what the book is about: reflections by a person who went to the desert to pray.

> ■ *The first nights spent in the desert made me send off for books on astronomy and maps of the sky. . . .*
>
> *Kneeling on the sand I sank my eyes for hours and hours in those wonders. . . .*
> *How dear were to me those stars;*
> *how close to them*
> *the desert had brought me.*
>
> *Through spending my nights in the open,*
> *I had come to know them by name. . . .*
> *Now I could distinguish their color,*
> *their size, their position, their beauty.*
> *I knew my way around them,*
> *and from them I could calculate the time*
> *without a watch.*

You might give the students an alternate exercise and have them describe a time when they prayed more fervently than they usually do.

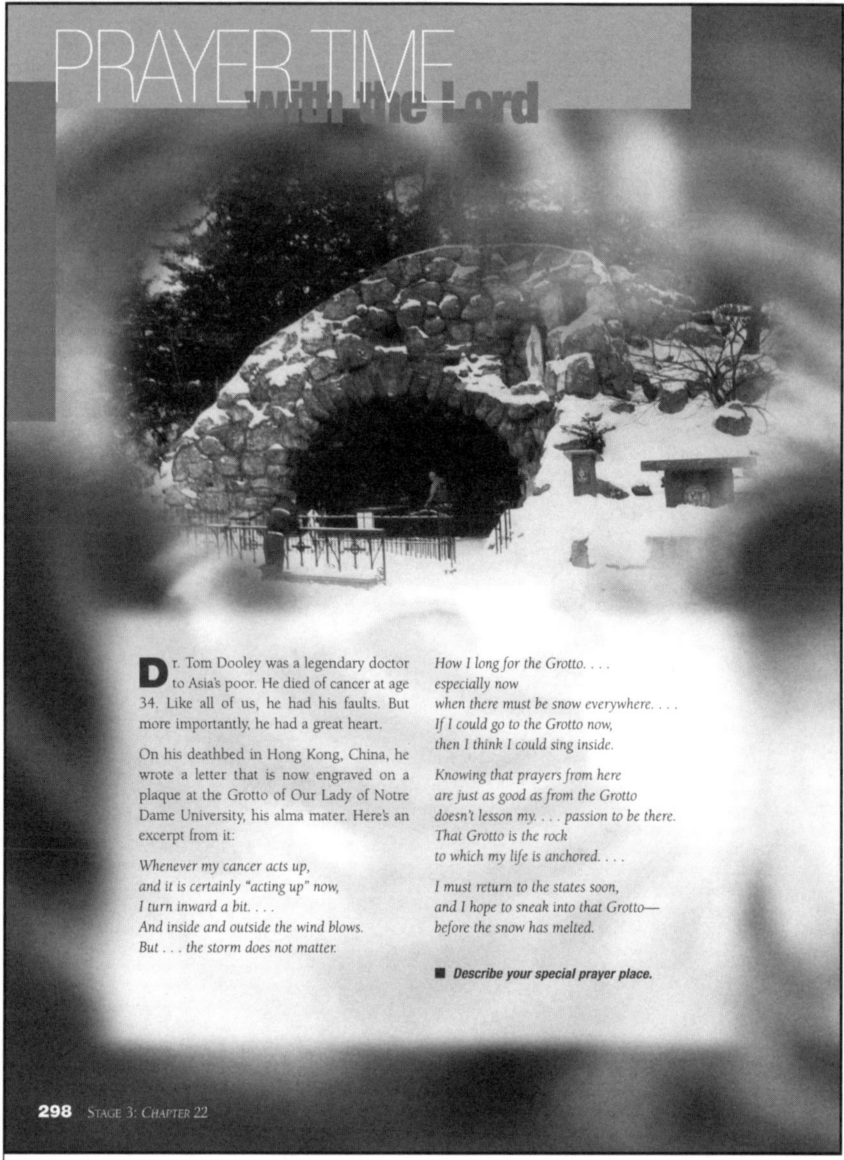

PRAYER TIME with the Lord

Dr. Tom Dooley was a legendary doctor to Asia's poor. He died of cancer at age 34. Like all of us, he had his faults. But more importantly, he had a great heart.

On his deathbed in Hong Kong, China, he wrote a letter that is now engraved on a plaque at the Grotto of Our Lady of Notre Dame University, his alma mater. Here's an excerpt from it:

Whenever my cancer acts up,
and it is certainly "acting up" now,
I turn inward a bit. . . .
And inside and outside the wind blows.
But . . . the storm does not matter.

How I long for the Grotto. . . .
especially now
when there must be snow everywhere. . . .
If I could go to the Grotto now,
then I think I could sing inside.

Knowing that prayers from here
are just as good as from the Grotto
doesn't lesson my. . . . passion to be there.
That Grotto is the rock
to which my life is anchored. . . .

I must return to the states soon,
and I hope to sneak into that Grotto—
before the snow has melted.

■ ***Describe your special prayer place.***

298 STAGE 3: CHAPTER 22

PRAYER Journal

QUESTION ***Do a "pencil meditation" on something you saw or heard recently.***

An alternate exercise might be to describe something that moved them deeply or made them think. Here are some suggestions:

1 *A homeless person you saw one day*
2 *A camping trip that put you in a prayerful mood*
3 *A storm they got caught it*
4 *A movie that made you really liked*
5 *A night with some friends*
6 *A son that you like a lot*
7 *A time when you sinned and sought God's forgiveness afterward*
8 *A time when you were deeply afraid*
9 *A person you admire very much*

NOTES

PRAYER Journal

Today I saw a water lily
growing in a pond.
It had the freshest yellow color I'd ever seen.
The lily—a precious treasure—
was unconcerned about whether
anyone noticed its astounding beauty.

As I sat there,
watching it unfold its petals noiselessly,
I thought of Mary pregnant with Jesus.
She, too, was a precious treasure.
She, too, was unconcerned about whether
anyone noticed her astounding beauty.

But to those who did, she shared a secret.
Her beauty came not from herself,
but from the Jesus life within her,
unfolding its petals noiselessly.

■ **Do a "pencil meditation" on something you saw or heard recently.**

SCRIPTURE Journal

1	You will bear a son	Luke 1:26–38
2	You will be called blessed	Luke 1:39–56
3	Your heart will break	Luke 2:22–35
4	Do what he tells you	John 2:1–12
5	Behold, your mother	John 19:23–27

■ ***Pick one of the above passages. Read it prayerfully and write a short statement to Jesus expressing your feelings about it.***

Stage 3: Chapter 22 299

SCRIPTURE Journal

QUESTION ***Pick one of the passages. Read it prayerfully and write a short statement to Jesus expressing your feelings about it.***

■ *Or you may read aloud to the students this passage from the third reading. Have them imagine they are either Mary or Joseph and write down their thoughts that night:*

Simeon said to Mary . . .
This child . . . will be a sign from God
which many people will speak against.
And sorrow, like a sword,
will break your heart. Luke 2:22–35

Classroom Resources

CATECHISM

Catechism of the Catholic Church *Second Edition*

For further enrichment, you might refer to:

1. Saint	Index	p. 846
	Glossary	p. 898
2. Mary	Index	p. 823
	Glossary	p. 887
3. Saints, Communion of	Index	p. 775
	Glossary	p. 871

See also: Sanctification, Witness, Prayer.

—Available from the United States Catholic Conference, Washington DC

BOOKS

All Saints: Daily Reflections on Saints, Prophets, and Witnesses for Our Time

Robert Ellsberg

Superb anthology of cameos of "mystics, martyrs, social activists, artists, writers, composers—who . . . mediate the many and surprising ways in which grace makes discipleship possible." Kenneth Woodward, 1997.

—Available from The Crossroad Publishing Co., New York, N.Y.

The Book of Eulogies: A Collection of Memorial Tributes, Poetry, Essays, and Letters of Condolence

Edited with Commentary by Phyllis Theroux

Entries range from Helen Keller's words about her dear friend Mark Twain to Cardinal Suenens' eulogy of Pope John XXIII. 1997.

—Available from Scribners, New York, N.Y.

NOTE

For a list of (1) General resources for professional background and (2) Addresses, phone/fax numbers of major publishing companies, see Appendix B of this Resource Manual.

CHAPTER 23
Rejoicing in Love

CHAPTER at a Glance

To help students explore and clarify Catholic teaching concerning life after death, especially the:

1 *End of the world: Return of Jesus and Resurrection of the dead*
2 *Two judgments: Particular and Last*
3 *Three destinies: Heaven, Hell, Purgatory*

READ—Have a student read aloud the scriptural introduction, which begins: "I saw a new heaven and a new earth . . ." Have a second student read aloud the commentary. It begins: "Is death a leap . . ."

End of the world

CLARIFY—Predicting the end of the world has held a perennial fascination for people, especially fundamentalist biblical groups. Here are a few examples:

■ *The Second Coming has been variously predicted for 1832, 1844, 1895, and 1900.*

The Jehovah's Witnesses, founded by Charles Taze Russell, predicted the beginning of the end in 1874—then in 1878, 1881, 1914, and 1918, with similar disappointing results.

Russell's successor, "Judge Joseph Rutherford selected 1925 and announced that millions now living will never die. He wasn't one of them, as he died in 1942."

ROBERT P. LOCKWOOD IN "ANYBODY HOME?" IN OSV, 1/2/2000, PAGE 23

QUESTION **1 *What would you do today, if you knew the world would end tonight? If you would do it then, why do you neglect doing it now?***

One college girl responded to the first half of this question this way:

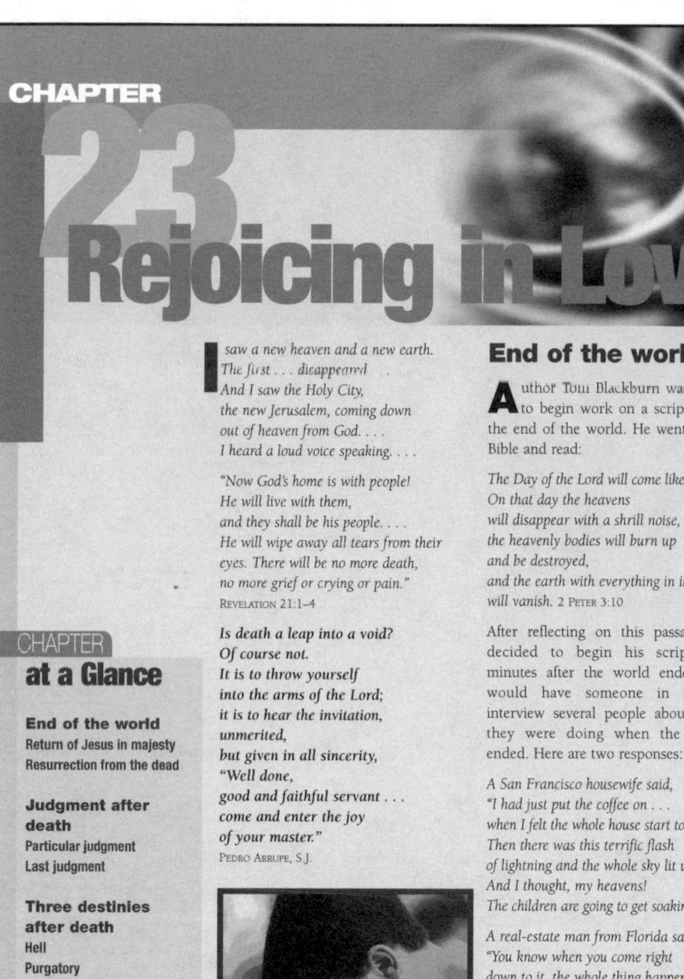

CHAPTER 23 Rejoicing in Love

I saw a new heaven and a new earth.
The first . . . disappeared . . .
And I saw the Holy City,
the new Jerusalem, coming down
out of heaven from God. . . .
I heard a loud voice speaking. . . .

"Now God's home is with people!
He will live with them,
and they shall be his people. . . .
He will wipe away all tears from their eyes. There will be no more death,
no more grief or crying or pain."
REVELATION 21:1–4

Is death a leap into a void?
Of course not.
It is to throw yourself
into the arms of the Lord;
it is to hear the invitation,
unmerited,
but given in all sincerity,
"Well done,
good and faithful servant . . .
come and enter the joy
of your master."
PEDRO ARRUPE, S.J.

CHAPTER at a Glance

End of the world
Return of Jesus in majesty
Resurrection from the dead

Judgment after death
Particular judgment
Last judgment

Three destinies after death
Hell
Purgatory
Heaven

Entry into glory
Life in God
Vision of God
Union with God

300

End of the world

Author Tom Blackburn was about to begin work on a script about the end of the world. He went to the Bible and read:

The Day of the Lord will come like a thief.
On that day the heavens
will disappear with a shrill noise,
the heavenly bodies will burn up
and be destroyed,
and the earth with everything in it
will vanish. 2 PETER 3:10

After reflecting on this passage, he decided to begin his script just minutes after the world ended. He would have someone in heaven interview several people about what they were doing when the world ended. Here are two responses:

A San Francisco housewife said,
"I had just put the coffee on . . .
when I felt the whole house start to shake.
Then there was this terrific flash
of lightning and the whole sky lit up.
And I thought, my heavens!
The children are going to get soaking wet!"

A real-estate man from Florida said,
"You know when you come right
down to it, the whole thing happened
just like they said it would."
SENSE AND INCENSE

1 *What would you do today, if you knew the world would end tonight? If you would do it then, why do you neglect doing it now?*

■ *I would contact*
all the people I had ever really loved,
and I'd make sure they knew
I really loved them.
I would play all the recordings
that meant the most to me. . . .
Then I would thank God
for the gift of life, and die in his arms.

Father Pedro Arupe, General of the Society of Jesus, used the same image of dying as the girl above. He writes:

■ *Is death a leap into a void?*
Of course not. It is to throw yourself
into the arms of the Lord;
it is to hear the invitation, unmerited,
but given in all sincerity, 'Well done, good
and faithful servant . . .
come and enter the joy of your master!' "

NOTES

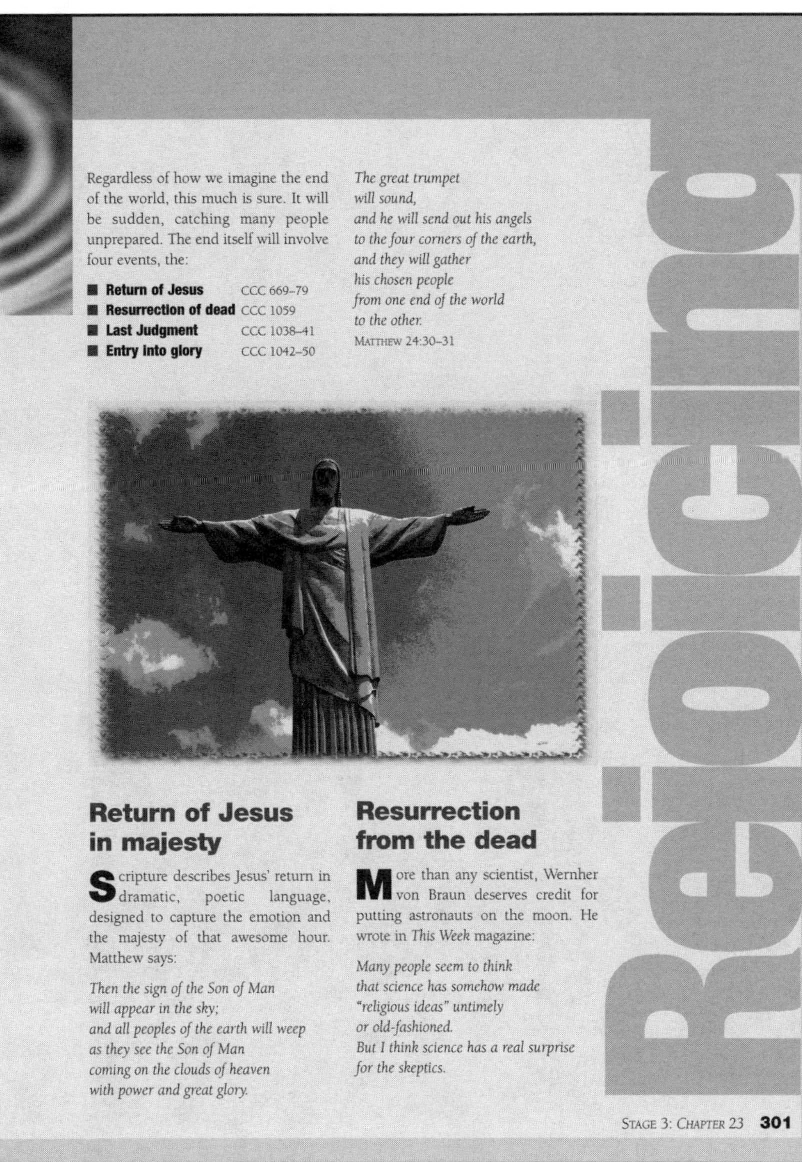

Regardless of how we imagine the end of the world, this much is sure. It will be sudden, catching many people unprepared. The end itself will involve four events, the:

- **Return of Jesus** CCC 669–79
- **Resurrection of dead** CCC 1059
- **Last Judgment** CCC 1038–41
- **Entry into glory** CCC 1042–50

The great trumpet
will sound,
and he will send out his angels
to the four corners of the earth,
and they will gather
his chosen people
from one end of the world
to the other.
MATTHEW 24:30–31

Rejoicing

Return of Jesus in majesty

Scripture describes Jesus' return in dramatic, poetic language, designed to capture the emotion and the majesty of that awesome hour. Matthew says:

Then the sign of the Son of Man
will appear in the sky;
and all peoples of the earth will weep
as they see the Son of Man
coming on the clouds of heaven
with power and great glory.

Resurrection from the dead

More than any scientist, Wernher von Braun deserves credit for putting astronauts on the moon. He wrote in *This Week* magazine:

Many people seem to think
that science has somehow made
"religious ideas" untimely
or old-fashioned.
But I think science has a real surprise
for the skeptics.

STAGE 3: CHAPTER 23 301

Have the students discuss the question in small groups and share the best response with the class.

CLARIFY—Stress the four events that will bring the world as we know it to an end:

1. *Glorious return of Jesus*
2. *Resurrection of the dead*
3. *Last judgment*
4. *Entry into glory*

Return of Jesus in majesty

CLARIFY—In Saint Paul's time, Christians of Thessalonica thought the return of Jesus (*parousia*) was imminent. When it didn't happen, they were dismayed. Why should their friends, who were dying, be deprived of seeing Jesus' return? Paul replied that they would see it.

■ *Those who have died believing in*
Christ will rise to life first;
then we who are living at that time
will be gathered up along with them
in the clouds to meet the Lord in the air.
And so we will always be with the Lord.
THESSALONIANS 4:16–18

This passage gave rise to what literalists (fundamentalists) call the "rapture." They interpret Paul's words as a literal description of how the world will end.

Contextualists say Paul never intended his description literally. He was simply employing symbolic imagery—as Matthew does in the passage cited in the textbook.

This kind of imagery burned itself in people's minds and called up awe and mystery. Isaiah used it in prophesying the destruction of Babylon, saying:

"Every star . . . will stop shining,
the sun will be dark when it rises,
and the . . . earth will be shaken
out of its place." ISAIAH 13:10, 13

You might wish to complete the literalist scenario of the end times.

They teach that "the rapture" will be followed by a seven-year "period of tribulation" (world misery).

The Antichrist (translated in some Bibles as "the enemy of Christ") will emerge from this period. 1 JOHN 2:18 Christ and the raptured saints will then return to earth to defeat the Antichrist and his army.

Their victory will usher in the millennium, 1,000 years of peace. It will be followed by the last judgment. REVELATION 20:1–15

Resurrection from the dead

CLARIFY—Before reading the von Braun quote from *This Week* magazine, have them turn to page 302 and read the thumbnail biography of von Braun under "Up Close & Personal."

QUESTION **2 *Explain von Braun's statement: "Nature does not know extinction. All it knows is transformation." How does it apply to the resurrection of the dead?***

■ *Von Braun explains it well when he says, "Not even the smallest particle can disappear without a trace." He then goes on to apply this principle to the resurrection, saying:*
"Now, if God applied this principle to the most minute and insignificant parts of his universe, doesn't it make sense to assume that he applied it also to the human soul? I think it does."

***CLARIFY*—Whenever the end of the world is mentioned, the name "Armageddon" is usually brought up. You might say a few words about this much misunderstood reference in the Book of Revelation.**

■ *Three general approaches of interpreting the Book of Revelation have emerged over the centuries:*

1 *The early history approach*
2 *The sweep-of-history approach*
3 *The end-of-history approach*

The early history approach holds that the original audience for which the book was written were the persecuted Christians of the first century. To them it says, "Persevere and remain faithful in your suffering! Christ has conquered; so will you!" (Catholic biblical scholars espouse this approach.)

The sweep-of-history approach holds that the original audience for which it was penned were people of all times. To them it says, "There will be times of testing and suffering, but persevere, God is in control." (Catholic scholars agree that—like all biblical books—the Book of Revelation has a "timeless" revelation for people of all time, but this was not the original historical audience for which it was written.)

Finally, the end-of-history approach holds that the primary audience of the book are those Christians who will be living when the world ends. Fundamentalists follow this approach. For them, it is a book of prophecies describing how the world will end. (All reputable biblical scholars reject this approach.)

This brings us back to Armageddon.

■ *The word "Armageddon" (har megiddon in Hebrew) means "Mount Megiddo." The city of Megiddo stood on this elevated site. Because of its strategic location, many important battles took place there.* Judges 5:19; 2 Kings 23:29 *As a result, the Book of Revelation used it as the site of a symbolic, final confrontation between the forces of good and evil.*

During the Cold War between the U.S. and U.S.S.R. (1980s), many fundamentalist preachers on TV heralded it as the first stage of the fulfillment of the prophecy of the "Armageddon battle."

Up Close
& Personal

Werner von Braun

Wernher von Braun's career began in Germany. He developed the famed V-2 rocket that devastated British cities during World War II. Toward the end of the war, as the Russians advanced toward Germany, von Braun and his staff fled to Bavaria, where they surrendered to the United States.

Toward the end of his life, von Braun wrote:

Science and religion are sisters.
Through science
we strive to learn more
of the mysteries of creation.
Through religion,
we seek to know the creator.

■ ***Why is religion often held in less regard than science?***

Science, for instance, tells us
that nothing in nature,
not even the tiniest particle,
can disappear without a trace.
Nature does not know extinction.
All it knows is transformation. . . .

Everything science has taught me—
and continues to teach me—
strengthens my belief in the continuity
of our spiritual existence after death.

2 *Explain von Braun's statement: "Nature does not know extinction. All it knows is transformation." How does it apply to the resurrection of the dead?*

Saint John says about life after death and the resurrection of the dead:

Time is coming
when all the dead will hear his voice
and come out of their graves;
those who have done good
will rise and live,
and those who have done evil
will rise and be condemned. John 5:28

Judgment after death

There's an ancient play called *Everyman.* In it God sends Death to the hero to tell him that his life is over.

When the hero recovers from shock, he asks Death to give him a few minutes to invite his friends—Money, Fame, Power, and Good Works—to accompany him into the afterlife. Death obliges.

To the hero's dismay, however, the only person who accepts his invitation is Good Works. The rest refuse.

The play makes an important point. As we pass through death from this life to the next, one thing alone will matter. Jesus alludes to it this way in his Sermon on the Mount:

Your light must shine before people, so that they will see the good things you do and praise your Father in heaven.
Matthew 5:16

ART
Connection

Michelangelo was an Italian poet, architect, sculptor, and painter. One of his greatest artistic achievements is the Sistine Chapel of the Vatican. Begun in 1508, it was completed in 1512. Shown here is a detail of the ceiling's "Last Judgment."

302 Stage 3: Chapter 23

NOTES

SHARE YOUR meditation

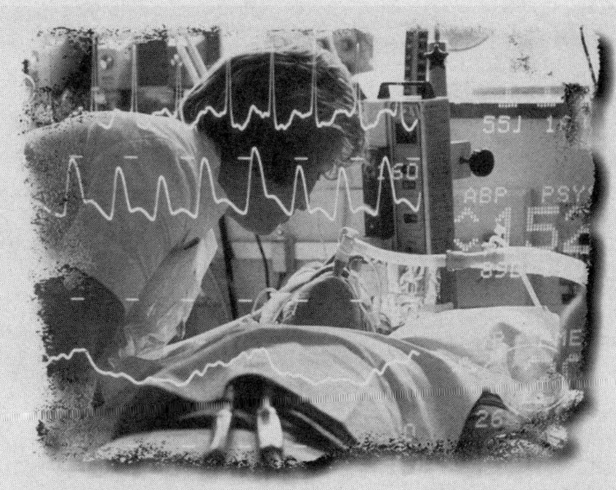

A prisoner in a Nazi death camp was standing next to a barbed-wire fence. Suddenly, the sun bloomed gold against a clear blue sky. Then it happened. His heart soared and he sang:

The sun has made a veil of gold
so lovely that my body aches.
Above, the heavens shriek
with blue—
Convinced I've smiled
by some mistake.
The world's abloom
and seems to smile.
I want to fly, but where, how high?
If in barbed wire
things can bloom
Why cannot I? I will not die.
Author unknown

■ ***When did the world "bloom" and wake within me new faith and new hope?***

Dr. Elisabeth Kubler-Ross of the University of Chicago has interviewed hundreds of people who have been declared clinically dead and then revived.

These people commonly report experiencing a kind of instant replay of their lives. Dr. Kubler-Ross quotes them as saying:

When you come to this point,
you see there are only two things
that are relevant:
the service you rendered to others,
and love.
All those things we think are important,
like fame, money, prestige, and power,
are insignificant.

3 *Can you think of any passages or parables in the Bible that suggest or state that "love" and "service" are, indeed, the only two relevant things that count in the end?*

The play *Everyman* and the research of Dr. Kubler-Ross lead us to a major theme of Scripture: judgment after death. Commenting on judgment after death, Saint Paul says:

All of us must appear before Christ,
to be judged by him.
Each one will receive what he deserves,
according to everything he has done,
good or bad, in his bodily life.
2 CORINTHIANS 5:10

The Scriptures speak of two judgments. They will take place at the end of:

- **Our life** **Particular** CCC 1021–22
- **Our world** **Last** CCC 1038–41

4 *Why do you think there will be two judgments, rather than just one at the end of each person's life?*

Let us now take a closer look at each judgment.

During the 1984 presidential debates, NBC's Marvin Kalb asked Ronald Reagan if he thought we might be headed toward a "nuclear Armageddon." Reagan said he did.

■ *People were shocked that: (1) a president of the United States took seriously a discredited approach to interpreting the Bible, and (2) by doing so, heated up the climate of hostility between Russia and the United States.*

ART Connection

Inspired by works like the *Divine Comedy* of Dante (1265–1321), Michelangelo does what Jesus did. LUKE 21:25 He portrays great "salvation" events in graphic, provocative imagery that "burns" itself into the soul. His painting of the Last Judgment is an example. He uses provocative imagery to try to help us come to grips with faith realities (like judgment and punishment) that we don't think about—or don't want to think about. But think about them, we must.

Judgment after death

QUESTION **3** ***Can you think of any passages or parables in the Bible that suggest or state that "love" and "service" are, indeed, the only two relevant things that count in the end?***

■ *LOVE: Jesus said, "Love the Lord your God with your whole heart . . . and . . . love your neighbor as you love yourself.*
The whole Law of Moses
and the teachings of the prophets
depend on these two commandments."
MATTHEW 22:37–39

SERVICE: Jesus said, "I was hungry and you did not feed me, thirsty but you would not give me a drink . . . naked but you would not clothe me." MATTHEW 25:42–43

QUESTION **4** ***Why do you think there will be two judgments, rather than just one at the end of each person's life?***

■ *It is fitting that in addition to a particular judgment, there should be some final closure to the entire work of salvation—when all creation, in unity and community, bears witness to the goodness and glory of God.*

Share Your meditation

Recall and review how international marine biologist Alister Hardy was walking along a riverbank one beautiful spring day. Suddenly, he dropped to his knees and gave thanks to God, who seemed to surround him and fill his heart with joy and love.

LITERARY Connection

DISCUSS—Ask the students: What point does the poem by John Keble make?

■ *Even though our words and deeds are past and even forgotten, some day they will revisit us. (See Exercise 2, page 309.)*

DISCUSS—French philosopher and Nobel Prize–winner for literature, Albert Camus (1913–60), makes the same point in a slightly different way:

I shall tell you a secret, my friend.
Do not wait for the last judgment,
it is taking place every day.

Ask the students: What is Camus's point?

■ *Every day of our life we are "casting ballots." At the Last Judgment we will simply "open the ballot box" and "count the ballots." In this sense our judgment by God is going on right now; but will not be revealed until the end of our lives.*

Particular judgment

CLARIFY—The movie *The Magnificent Ambersons* is still popular on TV film channels. You might share this scene from the story to help create the mood for talking about the "particular" judgment.

■ *The film centers around a family that enjoys enormous wealth and prestige. The leader of the clan is Major Amberson. He devotes his life to buying, selling, and banking. He is a man committed totally to worldly success.*

Near the end of the film, he is lying in bed, dying. His face is marked with concern. His eyes are those of a man not at peace with himself. The film narrator says:

"And now Major Amberson was engaged in the profoundest thinking of his life." He realizes that everything he worried about during his life was nothing compared to what he worries about now.

For Major Amberson knows that he must soon enter an unknown country where he is not even sure that he will be recognized and treated as an Amberson.

The scene recalls the words of mystic and Doctor of the Church, St. John of the Cross (1542–91). He writes:

■ *God will not judge us*
on our earthly possessions and successes,
but on how well we have loved.

QUESTION 5 *Why won't they be convinced?*

■ *Abraham was right in saying that even if Lazarus returned from the dead, his brothers would not believe. Later, and ironically, a man named Lazarus did return from the dead. And the opponents of Jesus would not believe. Rather, they sought to kill Jesus and Lazarus.* JOHN 11

LITERARY Connection

The deeds we do,
the words we say,
Into still air
they seem to fleet.

We count them ever past;
But they shall last—
In dread judgment they
And we shall meet.

John Keble

LIFE Connection

I shall pass through this world
but once.

Any good therefore
that I can do,
or any kindness
that I can show
to any human being,
let me do it now.

Let me not delay it
or defer it,
for I shall not pass
this way again.

Attributed to Stephen Grellet

Particular judgment

Each person will experience a particular judgment immediately after death. CCC 1020–22

Jesus refers to such a judgment in his Parable of the Rich Man and Lazarus. The rich man lived in a fine home and feasted on fine foods. The poor man, named Lazarus, used to be brought to the rich man's door to beg for food. But the rich man ignored him.

Eventually, both men died. The rich man ended up in a place of torment. Lazarus ended up in "the bosom of Abraham," a place of honor and comfort. The rich man pleaded with Abraham:

Take pity on me, and send Lazarus
to dip his finger in some water
and cool off my tongue,
because I am in great pain in this fire!
LUKE 16:24

Abraham explained that a "deep pit" separated them. Then the rich man pleaded with Abraham to send Lazarus back to earth to warn his family, saying, "If someone were to rise from death and go back to them, then they would turn from their sins." LUKE 16:30 But Abraham replied:

If they will not listen to Moses
and the prophets,
they will not be convinced
even if someone were to rise from death.
LUKE 16:31

5 *Why won't they be convinced?*

Last judgment

One day Jesus was talking to his disciples about the end of the world. He used this dramatic imagery to describe it:

"When the Son of Man comes as King
and all the angels with him,
he will sit on his royal throne,
and the people of all the nations
will be gathered before him.

"Then he will divide them into two groups,
just as a shepherd separates
the sheep from the goats. . . .

"The King will say
to the people on his right,

" 'Come, you that are blessed by my Father!
Come and possess the kingdom
which has been prepared for you
ever since the creation of the world.

" 'I was hungry and you fed me,
thirsty and you gave me a drink;
I was a stranger
and you received me in your homes,
naked and you clothed me;
I was sick and you took care of me,
in prison and you visited me.'. . .

"Then he will say to those on his left,

" 'Away from me. . . .
Away to the eternal fire
which has been prepared
for the devil and his angels! . . .

"I tell you, whenever you refused to help
one of these least important ones,
you refused to help me."
MATTHEW 25:31–32, 34–36, 41, 45

Jesus' dramatic description indicates that the entire human race will face a last judgment.

304 STAGE 3: CHAPTER 23

NOTES

THINK about it

From the voiceless lips
of the unreplying dead
there comes no word.
But in the night of Death,
Hope sees a star,
and listening Love can hear
the rustle of a wing.

Robert Green Ingersoll

Three destinies after death

In summary, then, a particular judgment will take place immediately after death. It will result in one of these three destinies.

Whatever the destiny, it will not be postponed, but will take effect immediately following the particular judgment:

■ **Hell**	CCC 1033–37
■ **Heaven**	CCC 1023–29
■ **Purgatory**	CCC 1030–32

Hell

One day Jesus told this Parable of the Weeds among the Wheat:

A man sowed good seed in his field.
One night, when everyone was asleep,
an enemy came
and sowed weeds among the wheat
and went away.

When the plants grew
and the heads of grain began to form,
then the weeds showed up.

The man's servants came to him. . . .
"Do you want us to go
and pull up the weeds?" they asked him.
"No," he answered,
"because as you gather the weeds
you might pull up some of the wheat
along with them.

"Let the wheat and the weeds
both grow together until harvest.
Then I will tell the harvest workers
to pull up the weeds first,
tie them in bundles and burn them,
and then to gather in the wheat
and put it in my barn."
MATTHEW 13:24–30

6 ***What is the point of this parable?***

The Parable of the Weeds and Wheat raises two questions. First, what did Jesus intend to teach about hell? About the punishment of hell?

THINK about it

Are you ready? Are you ready?
Ready for the Judgment Day?
When the saints and sinners
Shall be parted right and left
Are you ready
for the Judgment Day?

Old hymn

STAGE 3: CHAPTER 23 **305**

Last judgment

CLARIFY—In this Last Judgment parable Jesus uses a scene with which everyone in biblical times was familiar: sheep and goats grazing together. At night, however, they are separated, so that short-haired goats could be herded into a sheltered place to stay warm. In a similar way, good and bad people will be separated at the end of the world.

Three destinies after death

CLARIFY—The particular judgment and reward or punishment will take place immediately after death. (Recall the Parable of Lazarus and the Rich Man, where this is portrayed as the case.)

Hell

QUESTION **6** ***What is the point of this parable?***

■ *Sowing another's field with weeds or salt was a hated practice among ancients. Roman law punished it as a crime.*

Have the students identify the following "Cast of characters" in the parable:

1	*Sower*	*(Jesus)*
2	*Field*	*(World)*
3	*Wheat*	*(Good people)*
4	*Weeds*	*(Evil people)*
5	*Enemy*	*(Devil)*
6	*Harvest*	*(End of world)*
7	*Harvest workers*	*(Angels)*
8	*Separation*	*(Judgment)*
9	*Burning weeds*	*(Hell)*
10	*Storing of wheat*	*(Heaven)*

THINK about it

Ingersoll (1833–99) was a brilliant lawyer and orator. Although he was an outspoken agnostic, this lovely passage suggests that he was not too far from belief.

THINK about it

DISCUSS—The suddenness of death (and our need to be prepared at all times) is illustrated by the story of Buddy Holly.

■ *This 19-year-old Texan skyrocketed to fame in the 1950s. He was the first rock star to write, play, and sing his own music. Then a tragic plane crash cut short his life. At the moment TV commentators flashed the news of his death to the world, six of Buddy's songs were on the best-seller charts.*

Ask the students: Would you trade the rest of your life for two short years of fame, such as Buddy Holly enjoyed? Explain.

***CLARIFY*—Stress the three summary statements about hell: It exists, it's eternal, and it involves separation.**

QUESTION **7** ***Which of the interpretations of fire do you feel is correct?***

■ *In his book* Catholicism, *theologian Richard McBrien opts for the use of the word "fire" in a dramatic sense, saying:*

"Jesus used this imagery . . . to dramatize the urgency of his proclamation of the Kingdom and the seriousness of our decisions for or against the Kingdom. The stakes are as high as they can be. . . ."

THINK about it

Saint Irenaeus (c. 130–200) was a French bishop and theologian. He had a gift for getting to the point and expressing things clearly.

FILM Connection

This beautiful passage echoes Luke 21:22:

When things begin to happen (coming of the Son of Man on clouds of glory), stand up and raise your heads, because your salvation is near.

Purgatory

QUESTION **8** ***How do you feel about Samuel Johnson's conclusion?***

■ *There's a story that helps to visualize the spiritual reality of purgatory. It's about a boy and a girl who grew up together. They loved each other and promised to marry some day. Years passed and they went their separate ways. The boy became evil; the girl remained good. One day they met in a distant city.*

All the memories of their early love flooded back. The boy saw immediately that the girl had kept her goodness. With all his heart he regretted his sinful habits, because he was no longer capable of the kind of love that he once had for her.

At that moment, he would have joyfully endured any great pain if, through it, he could be "cleansed" of his evil habits.

Purgatory is something like that—a painful but joyful "purging" of our sins and sinful habits and ways.

QUESTION **9** ***How does the passage from the Book of Maccabees imply that purgatory exists, is temporary, and involves purification?***

■ *The full passage from Maccabees reads: "Judas did a noble thing because he believed in the resurrection of the dead. If he had not believed . . . it would have been foolish and useless to pray for them. In his firm and devout conviction that all of God's faithful people would receive*

THINK about it

Why shouldn't you believe you'll exist again after this existence, seeing you exist now after not being? . . .

Is it harder for God . . . who made your body when it was not to make it anew when it has been?

Saint Irenaeus

FILM Connection

Near the end of *The Great Dictator*, Charlie Chaplin cries out:

Look up, Hannah!
The clouds are lifting!
We are coming out
of the darkness
into the light. We are coming
into a new world—a kindlier
world, where men will rise
above their hate
and their greed and brutality.

Look up! Hannah!
The soul of man
has been given wings,
and at last he is beginning to fly.
He is flying to the rainbow . . .
into . . . the glorious future
that belongs to you—to me—
and to all of us!
Look up! Hannah! Look up!

Literal interpreters hold that Jesus intended to teach that hell is an actual *place*. Contextual interpreters hold that since hell exists outside of time and space, hell is best understood as a *state* of separation from God and the saved.

This brings us to the second question: How did Jesus intend us to understand the punishment of hell: fire? Bible interpreters tend to fall into groups in answering this question. Jesus meant the word *fire* in a:

- **Literal sense**
- **Dramatic sense**

Literal interpreters hold that Jesus used the word in a literal sense: real *fire*. Contextual interpreters hold that he used the word in a *dramatic* sense: to dramatize metaphorically, the urgency with which we should avoid hell. We should avoid it as we would eternal, physical fire.

In other words, the essence of hell is eternal separation from God and whatever suffering that involves, whether it be physical "burning" or spiritual "burning with shame and remorse."

This leads us to the traditional teaching of the Church about hell. It may be summed up in three brief statements. Hell:

- **Exists**
- **Is eternal**
- **Involves separation**

7 Which of the interpretations of fire do you feel is correct?

Purgatory

Someone once asked Samuel Johnson, the great British writer, what he thought about the Catholic teaching on purgatory.

He surprised them, saying that he thought it made good sense. He explained that it is obvious that most people who die aren't bad enough to be sent directly to hell; nor good enough to be sent directly to heaven.

So it makes sense to conclude that there must be a kind of middle state after death, in which a purgation, or purification, takes place.

8 How do you feel about Samuel Johnson's conclusion?

The traditional biblical passage cited as evidence of purgatory is in the Second Book of Maccabees. There Judas Maccabees takes up a collection for an "offering to set free from sin those who had died." 2 MACCABEES 12:45

This brings us to the traditional Catholic teaching on purgatory. CCC 1130-32 It may be summed up in three brief statements. Purgatory:

- **Exists**
- **Is temporary**
- **Involves purification**

9 How does the passage from the Book of Maccabees imply that purgatory exists, is temporary, and involves purification?

306 STAGE 3: CHAPTER 23

NOTES

Entry into glory

This brings us to heaven or "entry into glory." Scripture uses a variety of images to describe it. Consider just three:

- **Life in God**
- **Vision of God**
- **Union with God**

Life in God

In a beautiful letter to the Christians of his time, John exhorts them in these words:

Keep in your hearts the message
you have heard from the beginning.
If you keep that message,
then you will always live in union
with the Son and the Father.

And this is what Christ himself
promised to give us—eternal life.
1 John 2:24–25

Vision of God

Concerning the image of heaven as the vision of God, Saint Paul wrote to the Christian community at Corinth:

What we see now
is like a dim image in a mirror;
then we shall see face-to-face.
1 Corinthians 13:12

Theologians call the vision of God the "beatific vision." The word beatific comes from the Latin word *beatus*, meaning "happy." The heavenly vision of God results in happiness beyond words. CCC 1023–29

Union with God

Concerning the image of heaven as union with God, Saint Paul wrote to the Christian community at Colossae:

Your life is hidden with Christ in God.
Your real life is Christ
and when he appears,
then you too will appear with him
and share his glory! Colossians 3:3–4

Our union with God is the culmination of the destiny for which God made us. Saint Augustine expressed this destiny in these memorable words:

Our hearts are made for you, O Lord,
and they will not rest until they rest in you.

PRAYER hotline

[Lord God,
Creator of all things,]
If seeds in the black earth
can turn into such
beautiful roses, what might
the heart of man become
in its long journey to the stars.

Gilbert Kieth Chesterton

POETRY Connection

Do not stand at my grave
and weep
I am not there, I do not sleep
I am a thousand winds that blow
I am a diamond glint of snow
I am the sunlight
on ripened grain
I am the autumn rain
When you awake
in the morning hush
I am the swift uplifting rush
of birds circling in flight
I am the stars that shine at night
So do not stand at my grave
and cry
I am not there. I didn't die.

Author unknown

Stage 3: Chapter 23 307

a wonderful reward, Judas made provision for a sin offering to set free from their sins those who had died."

1 *Exists* — *Implied by Judas's action*
2 *Temporary* — *Destined for resurrection*
3 *Purification* — *Prayer & offering cleanse*

Entry into glory

DISCUSS—Joe Louis (1914-81) held the heavyweight boxing title for nearly 12 years. He once said, "Everyone wants to go to heaven, but nobody wants to die." You might ask the students: Why is this?

■ *A God-given "instinct" makes us value and hold onto life. Life is a gift from God. What we do with it is our gift back to God. There is, also, a fear of death that competes with our faith, especially if it is weak and still maturing.*

Life in God

CLARIFY—To give his congregation an idea of what eternal life is like, an old Baptist preacher said:

■ *Brethren and sisters, if a single sparrow hopped from the Atlantic Ocean to the Pacific Ocean, one hop a day, with a single drop of water in its bill, and then hopped back at the same speed and kept it up until all the water in the Atlantic Ocean was in the Pacific Ocean, then, brethren and sisters, it would only be a breakday [brief interlude] in eternity.*
Bennett Cerf, *The Sound of Laughter*

Vision of God

1 John 3:2 assures us that we shall see God and that vision will transform us into God's likeness. It is this vision that will inaugurate our new life—eternal life.

Union with God

CLARIFY—The celebrated philosopher, Confucius (550 B.C.–478 B.C.), defined heaven in five words "to be one with God." Understood correctly, you could hardly improve on that definition.

PRAYER hotline

Chesterton (1874–1936) was a prolific British author. He became a Catholic at 48. He was a huge man, who said one day: "I feel good. I stood up on the bus and gave my seat to three people who were standing."

POETRY Connection

See Resource Manual suggestions for Exercise 1 (page 309).

Recap

When you think about good gospel music, the name of John Peterson comes to mind. Since World War II, his musical creations number in the hundreds. They range from gospel songs to background music for films. When he was just getting started he wrote a hymn about heaven. It went like this:

Over the sunset mountains,
Heaven awaits for me.
Jesus, my Savior, I'll see.

A music critic said, "John, let me give you some advice, skip the notion of Jesus and spend more time on the joy of heaven."

Of course, Peterson refused, because the the joy of heaven is "standing face-to-face with Jesus."

Review

DAILY QUIZ—Just a reminder: Review questions may be assigned (one or two at a time) for homework or a daily quiz.

CHAPTER TESTS—Reproducible chapter tests are found in Appendix A. For consistency and ease in grading, quizzes are restricted to (1) "Matching," (2) "True/False," and (3) "Fill in the Blanks."

TEST ANSWERS—The following are the answers to the test for Chapter 23. (See Appendix A, page 334.) Each correct answer worth 4 points.

Matching

1 = e	2 = d	3 = b	4 = a
5 = c			

True/False

1 = T	2 = F	3 = F	4 = F
5 = T	6 = T	7 = F	8 = F
9 = T	10 = T	11 = F	12 = T

Recap Review

Regardless of how we imagine the end of the world, this much is sure. It will be suddenly catching many people unprepared. The end itself will involve four events:

- **Return of Jesus**
- **Resurrection of the dead**
- **Last judgment**
- **Entry into glory**

Scripture describes Jesus' return in dramatic, poetic language, designed to capture the majesty of that awesome hour.

Saint John says of the resurrection of the dead: "All the dead will hear his voice and come out of their graves." JOHN 5:28

Finally, Scripture speaks of two kinds of judgment after death:

- **Particular** — **End of our life**
- **Last** — **End of the world**

A particular judgment awaits each of us at the end of our life on earth. It will take place immediately after our death and result in one of these destinies:

- **Heaven** — **Union with God**
- **Hell** — **Separation from God**
- **Purgatory** — **Preparation for union**

A last judgment also awaits each one of us. It will manifest to the world what we have become and end with Jesus leading the faithful into glory, where there will be no more death, no more grief or crying or pain. REVELATION 21:4

1 List and briefly explain the four events that will take place at the end of the world.

2 List and briefly explain (a) the two kinds of judgments that will take place after death, (b) where and how Jesus refers to each, and (c) when each will take place.

3 List and briefly explain the two positions Bible interpreters take concerning Jesus' teaching on hellfire.

4 What three brief statements sum up the Church's teaching on (a) hell and (b) purgatory?

5 List and briefly explain three images that sum up the Church's teaching on heaven.

308 STAGE 3: CHAPTER 23

Fill in the Blanks

1. (a) Heaven: entry into glory; vision of God; union with God
   (b) Hell: eternal separation from God
   (c) Purgatory: temporary period of purification
2. (a) real fire: physical burning
   (b) metaphorical fire: burning with shame and remorse

NOTES

Reflect

1 There is a story of a merchant in ancient Baghdad who sent his servant to the market to buy supplies. The servant returned, trembling.

"Master!" he shouted. "Someone jostled me. When I looked, I saw it was Death. He gave me a threatening look. Lend me your fastest horse that I may flee to far-off Samarra. He will never think of looking for me there."

After giving his servant the horse, the merchant went to the market to buy the rest of the supplies. Who should he see but Death. He said to Death, "Why did you give my servant a threatening look this morning?"

"That wasn't a threatening look," said Death. "It was a surprise look. I was surprised to see him in Baghdad, for I had an appointment with him tonight in far-off Samarra."

■ ***What is the story's meaning? Suppose you knew that you had only 24 hours to live. What would you do and why?***
■ ***Compose a brief message you'd like read at your funeral Mass. Why choose this message?***

2 While operating on a woman, Dr. Wilder Penfield, a famous neurosurgeon, accidentally touched the temporal cortex of her brain with a weak electric current. The woman, who was under local anesthesia and able to talk, reported reliving the experience of bearing her baby.

Other similar experiments then followed. They confirmed what Dr. Penfield had discovered. Patients felt again the same emotion that the original situation produced and were aware of the "same interpretations" they gave the experience.

Some scientists are now convinced that the brain has recorded every sensation it has ever received.

■ ***Why is it significant that the patients were aware of the "interpretations" they gave to their experience at the time it occurred?***
■ ***What event would you like to relive in your life and why this event?***

3 A king with no heirs was conducting interviews for a gifted youth to become his son and rule after him. A peasant named Kriston felt "called" to apply.

He worked hard to buy good clothes for it. Putting them in his backpack, he began the week-long journey in tattered clothes. When he got to the palace, he saw a shivering old man in thin sack cloth sitting at the gate.

Moved to pity, Kriston gave the man his good clothes. As Kriston mounted the palace steps he began to panic. Had he ruined all chances of being chosen?

At first, the guards wouldn't admit him. But after consulting with the king, they took Kriston to the throne room. He was stunned at what he saw. On the throne sat the beggar in Kriston's clothes. Before Kriston could speak, the king embraced him and said, "Welcome, son!"

■ ***What Bible story does this story recall? Describe a time you sacrificed a good deal to help another.***

STAGE 3: CHAPTER 23 309

Reflect

1 a) *What is the story's meaning? Suppose you knew that you had only 24 hours to live. What would you do and why?*

■ *Recall the college girl's response in answer to Question 1 (page 300) of this Resource Manual.*

b) *Compose a brief message you'd like read at your funeral Mass. Why choose this message?*

■ *To get the students started, refer them back to the following:*

1 *"Life Connection," page 304 (Change the "I" to "We" and the "me" to "us.)*
2 *"Think about it," page 305*
3 *"Poetry Connection," page 307*

If you have any drama students (or really good readers) in class, have them each take one of the above and read them as they might do at someone's funeral.

Conclude by having the students create their own brief message, share it in small groups, and pick the best one to share with the class.

2 a) *Why is it significant that the patients were aware of the "interpretations" they gave to their experience at the time it occurred?*

■ *This is where the morality (moral goodness and evil of the act is to be found. e.g., Did I think that what I planned to do was sinful?*

b) *What event would you like to relive in your life and why this event?*

■ *Have the students write these out, so that you can go over them and select the better ones to be read in the next class meeting.*

3 *What Bible story does this story recall? Describe a time you sacrificed a good deal to help another.*

■ *I was naked and you clothed me.* MATTHEW 25:43 *Be sure to give the students time to think out or write out their response. "Think time" is really important for quality responses.*

PRAYER TIME with the Lord

QUESTION ***How is the situation of the twins in the womb parallel to our situation on earth?***

■ *We, too, fear to die, because we don't know what lies "on the other side." We may even question, at times, if there is an "other side."*

CLARIFY—You might share the following parable on dying by Henry Van Dyke:

■ *I am standing upon the seashore.*
A ship at my side spreads her white sails
to the morning breeze
and starts for the blue ocean.
She is an object of beauty and strength,
and I stand and watch until at last
she hangs like a speck of white cloud
just where the sea and sky
come down to mingle with each other.
Then someone at my side says,
"There! She's gone!" Gone where?
Gone from my sight that is all.
She is just as large
in mast and hull and spar
as she was when she left my side
and just as able to bear
her load of living freight
to the place of destination.
Her diminished size is in me, not in her.
And just at the moment when someone
at my side says, "There she goes!"
there are eyes watching her coming
and other voices
ready to take up the glad shout.
"Here she comes!"

And that is dying. Death is not the end of life. It is only a change of life.

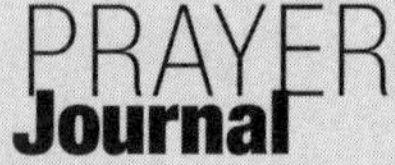

PRAYER Journal

QUESTION ***Compose a ten-line inscription for your gravestone that reflects your feelings about death and afterlife.***

CLARIFY—To get the students started, you might share with them this

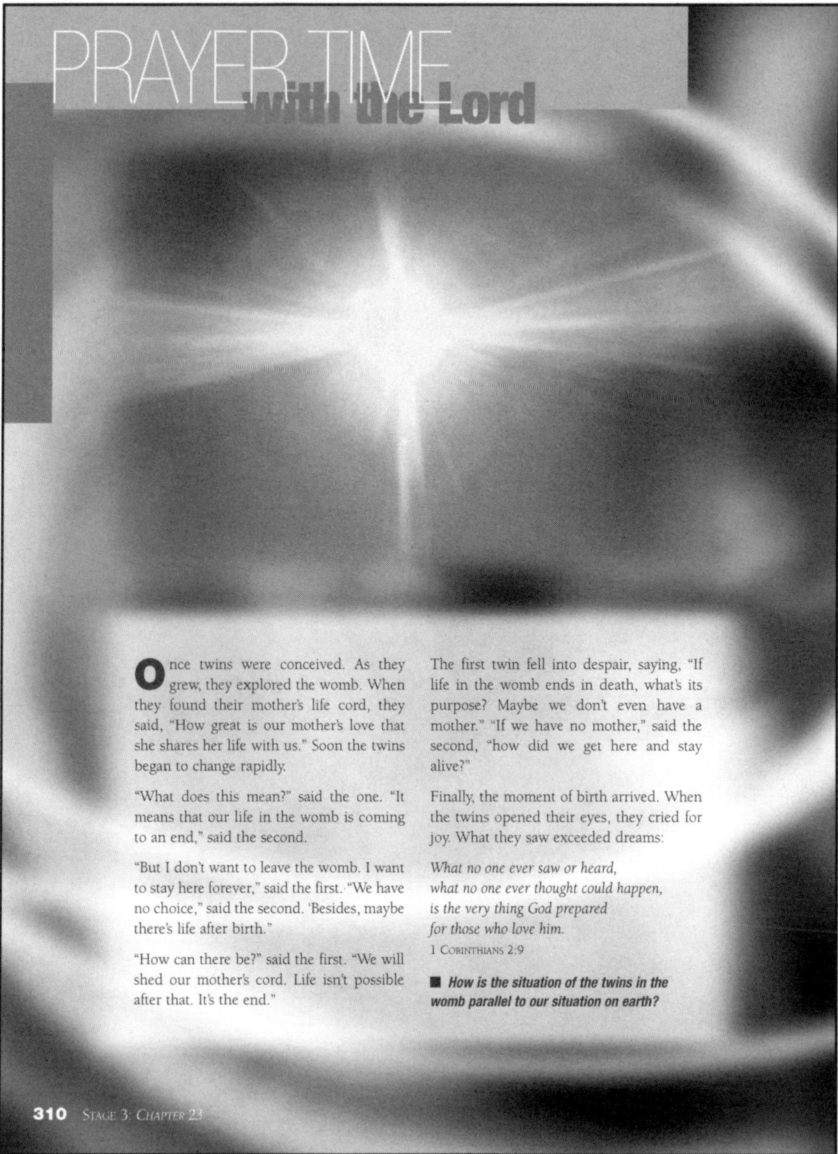

PRAYER TIME with the Lord

Once twins were conceived. As they grew, they explored the womb. When they found their mother's life cord, they said, "How great is our mother's love that she shares her life with us." Soon the twins began to change rapidly.

"What does this mean?" said the one. "It means that our life in the womb is coming to an end," said the second.

"But I don't want to leave the womb. I want to stay here forever," said the first. "We have no choice," said the second. 'Besides, maybe there's life after birth."

"How can there be?" said the first. "We will shed our mother's cord. Life isn't possible after that. It's the end."

The first twin fell into despair, saying, "If life in the womb ends in death, what's its purpose? Maybe we don't even have a mother." "If we have no mother," said the second, "how did we get here and stay alive?"

Finally, the moment of birth arrived. When the twins opened their eyes, they cried for joy. What they saw exceeded dreams:

What no one ever saw or heard,
what no one ever thought could happen,
is the very thing God prepared
for those who love him.
1 Corinthians 2:9

■ ***How is the situation of the twins in the womb parallel to our situation on earth?***

310 Stage 3: Chapter 23

inscription by one of the author's students:

■ *"Here lies Mike Henson.*
His body, which departed from the world
less than perfect,
has entered another world
in which he can finally be truly happy.

Now he is with the friend
he always had,
living the way he always wanted to
but never could.

Don't feel sorry for him.
Rather, rejoice with him."

NOTES

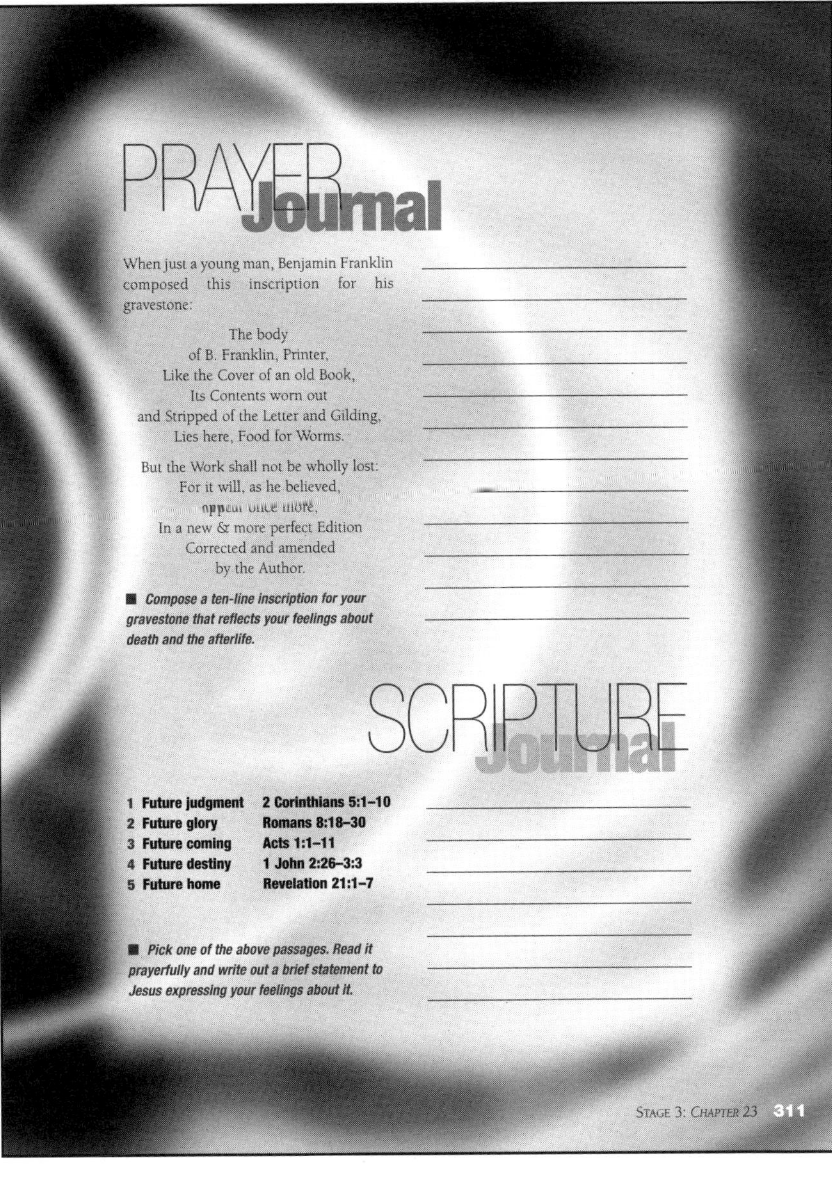

PRAYER Journal

When just a young man, Benjamin Franklin composed this inscription for his gravestone:

The body
of B. Franklin, Printer,
Like the Cover of an old Book,
Its Contents worn out
and Stripped of the Letter and Gilding,
Lies here, Food for Worms.

But the Work shall not be wholly lost:
For it will, as he believed,
appear once more,
In a new & more perfect Edition
Corrected and amended
by the Author.

■ ***Compose a ten-line inscription for your gravestone that reflects your feelings about death and the afterlife.***

SCRIPTURE Journal

1	**Future judgment**	**2 Corinthians 5:1–10**
2	**Future glory**	**Romans 8:18–30**
3	**Future coming**	**Acts 1:1–11**
4	**Future destiny**	**1 John 2:26–3:3**
5	**Future home**	**Revelation 21:1–7**

■ ***Pick one of the above passages. Read it prayerfully and write out a brief statement to Jesus expressing your feelings about it.***

Stage 3: *Chapter 23* **311**

SCRIPTURE Journal

QUESTION ***Pick one of the above passages. Read it prayerfully and write out a brief statement to Jesus expressing your feelings about it.***

CLARIFY—An alternate passage for students to express their feelings on is the concluding quote on the preceding page, page 310.

Classroom Resources

CATECHISM

Catechism of the Catholic Church *Second Edition*

For further enrichment, you might refer to:

1. Judgment	Index	p. 812
	Glossary	p. 884
2. Glory	Index	p. 797
3. Heaven	Index	p. 803
	Glossary	p. 881

See also: Exchatology, Resurrection, Hell

—Available from the United States Catholic Conference, Washington DC

CD-ROM

The Sources of Catholic Dogma

Denzinger

Scholarly, historical compendium of Church doctrine, councils, and documents.

—Available on the Welcome to the Catholic Church CD-ROM from Harmony Media Inc., Cervais, OR

VIDEO

No One Cries the Wrong Way

Eight 15-minute segments. The mystery of suffering and dying through the eyes of faith. 1998.

—Available from Brown-Roa, Dubuque IA

BOOK

The Book of Eulogies: A Collection of Memorial Tributes, Poetry, Essays, and Letters of Condolence

Edited with Commentary by Phyllis Theroux

Entries range from Helen Keller's words about her dear friend Mark Twain to Cardinal Suenens' eulogy of Pope John XXIII. 1997.

—Available from Scribners, New York, N.Y.

NOTE

For a list of (1) General resources for professional background and (2) Addresses, phone/fax numbers of major publishing companies, see Appendix B of this Resource Manual.

Name ______________________________

Each correct response is worth four points.

Matching (Use each response in the right-hand column only once.)

1. ____ Childhood stage of faith
2. ____ Adult stage of faith
3. ____ Destructive faith questioning
4. ____ Adolescent stage of faith
5. ____ Constructive faith questioning

a. Faith by choice
b. Faith by birth
c. Goal is to learn truth
d. Faith in transition
e. Goal is to disprove

True/False

1. ____ Faith is a mystery of *gift* (God's part) and *freedom* (our part).
2. ____ The adult stage of faith is normally the most painful stage.
3. ____ A conflict between belief and behavior can tempt us to question our faith destructively.
4. ____ Faith involves risk in the sense that God may abandon us if we enter into a life of sin.
5. ____ Faith is a one-time decision, not an ongoing process.
6. ____ An inability to find God is frequently traceable to an inability to open ourselves to love.
7. ____ Faith involves a team effort between God and ourselves.
8. ____ One of the biggest mistakes we can make is to think that some day we will "get the faith" and never have to worry about it again.
9. ____ Primarily, faith involves saying yes to a list of truths about God and Jesus.
10. ____ Because we are constantly evolving and changing as persons, faith involves a lifelong process of recommitment.
11. ____ The process of making the transition from a cultural to a convictional faith is usually fully complete by the time we reach twenty-one.

Fill In the Blanks

1. Every faith journey involves periods of darkness, when faith seems to go behind a cloud for a while. Three causes of this darkness are:

   (a) ____________________ **(b)** ____________________ **(c)** ____________________ .

2. The transition from a cultural to a convictional faith takes place at three levels. Each level requires a special openness on our part. The three levels and the special openness each requires are as follows:

   The **(a)** ________________ requires a special openness to **(b)** ________________.

   The **(c)** ________________ requires a special openness to **(d)** ________________.

   The **(e)** ________________ requires a special openness to **(f)** ________________.

Name ______________________________

Each correct response is worth four points.

Matching (Use each response in the right-hand column only once.)

1. ____ Canon
2. ____ Septuagint
3. ____ Wernher von Braun
4. ____ Scripture
5. ____ Terry Anderson
6. ____ Oral Tradition
7. ____ Tradition
8. ____ Inerrant

a. Experienced God in captivity
b. Mediate revelation
c. "20th century Columbus"
d. Word of God in the words of human beings
e. Revelation handed down by word of mouth
f. Official listing of inspired books
g. Free from error in matters related to salvation
h. Greek translation of the Old Testament

True/False

1. ____ Tradition is another name for immediate revelation.
2. ____ The word "revelation" comes from the Latin word meaning "to unveil."
3. ____ The Bible is not a single book, but a library of books.
4. ____ The events of Jesus' life may be compared to shells on the ocean floor.
5. ____ Catholics and Protestants agree on the canon of the Old Testament.
6. ____ Most Christian Churches agree on the canon of the New Testament.
7. ____ The biblical scrolls found in caves in the 1900s date from just after Jesus' birth.
8. ____ Parts of the Bible were passed on orally for a considerable length of time before being written down.
9. ____ The Church is the "mother" of the Bible, so to speak.
10. ____ The Bible is free from historical error.

Fill in the Blanks

1. Three ways by which we can know things:

(a) ______________________________
(b) ______________________________
(c) ______________________________

2. The three stages through which the Bible passed before reaching the form they now have:

(a) ______________________________
(b) ______________________________
(c) ______________________________

3. Name we give to the ancient biblical manuscripts found in caves between 1947 and 1956:

____

Name ______________________________

Each correct response is worth four points.

Matching (Use each response in the right-hand column only once.)

1. ____ Sin of commission
2. ____ Awareness of nakedness
3. ____ Abraham
4. ____ Sin of omission
5. ____ David
6. ____ Personal sin
7. ____ Expulsion from garden
8. ____ Snake
9. ____ Social sin
10. ____ Eating forbidden fruit
11. ____ Israelites
12. ____ Pollution of environment

a. Sin flawed the first couple
b. Experience of evil
c. Symbol of devil
d. Ancestor of Messiah
e. Father of nations
f. Sin involving a group
g. Not doing what we should do
h. Sin involving one person
i. God's chosen people
j. Physical de-creation
k. Stealing from another
l. Separation from God

True/False

1. ____ Muslims trace their origin to Abraham through Isaac, Abraham's son by Sarah.
2. ____ God's promise to David is especially important because it begins a series of promises that point to the coming of a Messiah.
3. ____ A literalist holds that the text is the only thing that needs to be considered in interpreting the meaning of a biblical passage.
4. ____ A contextualist holds that both the text and the context need to be considered in interpreting the meaning of a biblical passage.
5. ____ Most ancient peoples were monotheists; that is, they believed that there was only one God.
6. ____ God's covenant with David gave David a new identity and destiny.
7. ____ Some things that God created were not good.
8. ____ The tragic situation or state produced by the first sin of the first couple is sometimes referred to as the state of original sin.
9. ____ Literalists hold that the story of God creating the world in six days was intended to be a poetic story, not an eyewitness or scientific report of what happened.
10. ____ Scripture portrays angels as being God's servants and messengers.

Fill in the Blanks

The first sin of the first couple resulted in the following threefold impact on the human family and the world:

(a) ______________________________

(b) ______________________________

(c) ______________________________

Name ______________________________

Each correct response is worth four points.

Matching (Use each response in the right-hand column only once.)

1. ____ Dovelike form	***a.*** Signifies a "new era" is beginning
2. ____ Opening of sky	***b.*** Greek word meaning "sign"
3. ____ Heavenly voice	***c.*** Signifies a "new creation" is beginning
4. ____ Semeion	***d.*** This "word of God" is like television
5. ____ Dynamis	***e.*** Identifies the "new Adam" of "new creation"
6. ____ Resurrection	***f.*** Stresses Jesus, the "teaching Messiah"
7. ____ Old Testament	***g.*** Quantum leap to infinitely higher life
8. ____ New Testament	***h.*** This "word of God" is like radio
9. ____ John	***i.*** Greek word meaning "power"
10. ____ Matthew	***j.*** Wrote later than other gospel writers

True/False

1. ____ Matthew takes great pains to situate Jesus' birth against the background of the Old Testament prophecies.

2. ____ The novel *Father Malachi's Miracle* stresses the power of miracles to bring people to faith in God.

3. ____ Jesus' power over sin, sickness, and death are signs pointing to the demise of the Kingdom of Satan.

4. ____ Resuscitation means a quantum leap to an infinitely higher life form.

5. ____ The prophet Jeremiah foretold that certain signs would identify the arrival of the Messiah; for example, the eyes of the blind would be opened.

6. ____ The opening of the sky above Jesus must be understood against the people's prayers to God to "tear open the sky" and come down into the world to set things right.

7. ____ Thomas Merton, the trappist monk, designed a church door that contrasts the "tree of forbidden fruit" (de-creation) with the "tree of the cross" (re-creation).

Fill in the Blanks

1. The Magi present Jesus with three gifts. List each gift and explain what it points to in Jesus.

The gift of (**a**) ________________ points to (**b**) ________________

The gift of (**c**) ________________ points to (**d**) ________________

The gift of (**e**) ________________ points to (**f**) ________________

2. Jesus' miracles were signs announcing the arrival of:

(**a**) ______________________________________

(**b**) ______________________________________

Each correct response is worth four points.

Matching (Use each response in the right-hand column only once.)

1. ____ Matthew's Gospel	***a.*** "I love the sea, but I also fear it."
2. ____ Luke's Gospel	***b.*** Records best-known image of Trinity
3. ____ Rod McKeon	***c.*** Records most graphic image of Trinity
4. ____ Frank Borman	***d.*** Old Testament image of God as Father
5. ____ Shepherd	***e.*** Word Jesus used in addressing his heavenly Father
6. ____ Abba	***f.*** Image of God as Creator
7. ____ Movie projector	***g.*** Astronaut who helped read creation story

True/False

1. ____ If the movie *Laura* were used as a parable of God, Laura would represent God.
2. ____ We can get a detailed portrait of God from creation alone.
3. ____ One biblical image of God is an eagle who nourishes and teaches her young.
4. ____ The Scriptures use both male and female images of God.
5. ____ God may be compared to a movie screen and creation to the projector.
6. ____ Jesus used the image "Father" as God, rarely, but graphically.
7. ____ There is no contradiction in saying that we should fear God who loves us.
8. ____ God cannot love a person "a little" or "a lot," but only "totally."
9. ____ Early Christians hesitated to speak of God as "Father."
10. ____ Modern Palestinian children call their father "Abba."
11. ____ Jesus' first and last words, as recorded in Scripture, refer to God as Father.
12. ____ Jesus used the word "Father" of God over 170 times.

Fill in the Blanks

1. List three prominent ways God is present in our world in different ways and degrees:

(a) ______________________

(b) ______________________

(c) ______________________

2. Which person of the Holy Trinity corresponds to the following:

(a) ______________ Heat of the sun

(b) ______________ Energy of the sun

(c) ______________ Light of the sun

Name ________________________________

Each correct response is worth four points.

Matching (Use each response in the right-hand column only once.)

1. ____ YHWH — ***a.*** Hebrew word meaning "the anointed"

2. ____ Jesus — ***b.*** Hebrew proper name for God

3. ____ Messiah — ***c.*** Greek word meaning "fish"

4. ____ Christos — ***d.*** Greek word for "Messiah"

5. ____ ICHTHYS — ***e.*** He will save his people from their sins

True/False

1. ____ The title "Son of God" is used of Jesus in a literal sense of the word.

2. ____ The original meaning of YHWH is uncertain, but scholars suggest the translation "I am who I am."

3. ____ Cordell Brown was a Jew who fled Germany and became a Catholic.

4. ____ God's name was given to Moses by an angel.

5. ____ Scripture says Jesus was a blood descendent of Israel's first king.

6. ____ John's Gospel refers to Jesus as the "Word of God."

7. ____ By giving the name LORD to Jesus, early Christians affirmed that the same power, honor, and glory given to the Father is due to Jesus.

8. ____ The English name for the Italian who painted "The Baptism of Jesus" is Paul Waldeman.

9. ____ The name Jesus identifies him as having a saving mission from God.

10. ____ The title "Son of God" is always used in a literal sense in the Old Testament.

Fill in the Blanks

1. Two solemn moments when Jesus was given the title "Son of God" in a literal sense were ________________ and ________________.

2. We may think of Jesus as being the "Word of God" in the twofold sense that he tells us about ________________ and ________________.

3. The word ICHTHYS is linked to these four titles we give to the Second Person of God:

________________ , ________________ ,
________________ , ________________

4. Jesus had both a ______________ ___nature and a ________________ nature.

Name ________________________________

Each correct response is worth four points.

Matching (Use each response in the right-hand column only once.)

1. ____ RUAH	***a.*** Famous Italian painter
2. ____ Faithfulness	***b.*** One of the nine "fruits of the Spirit"
3. ____ Fortitude	***c.*** One of the seven "gifts of the Spirit"
4. ____ Hope	***d.*** Symbol of the Holy Spirit
5. ____ Babel	***e.*** British TV celebrity
6. ____ Pentecost	***f.*** Famous Franciscan priest
7. ____ Water	***g.*** One of three theological virtues
8. ____ Carravaggio	***h.*** Hebrew word meaning both "wind" and the "Spirit" of God
9. ____ Joseph of Cupertino	***i.*** Reversed what happened at Babel
10. ____ Malcolm Muggeridge	***j.*** Split people into hostile factions

True/False

1. ____ The Gospels make it clear that the Holy Spirit was active in Jesus' life long before Pentecost.

2. ____ The theological virtues are the foundation of our spiritual life.

3. ____ God the Father existed long before God the Son and God the Holy Spirit.

4. ____ The power to work miracles is listed as one of the seven "gifts of the Spirit."

5. ____ The "gifts of the Spirit" were exclusively for the personal good of the special person receiving them.

6. ____ The prophet Joel foretold the pouring out of the Spirit on Pentecost

7. ____ The gift of piety helps us discern the right path of action to take in difficult situations.

8. ____ Pentecost may rightly be referred to as the "birth of the Church."

9. ____ Peter experienced a remarkable conversion on the road to Damascus.

10. ____ The gift of "fear of God" is mentioned only in the the New Testament.

Fill in the Blanks

1. ______________ This virtue empowers us to love God and neighbor.

2. ______________ This virtue empowers us to trust that God's plan in us will be realized.

3. ______________ This "gift of the Spirit" begins our ascent up the spiritual ladder.

4. ______________ This New Testament writer refers to the nine "fruits of the Spirit."

5. ______________ This prophet refers to the seven gifts of the Spirit.

Name ____________________

Each correct response is worth four points.

Matching (Use each response in the right-hand column only once.)

1. ____	Holy Spirit	***a.***	Famous composer
2. ____	Creed	***b.***	Total and universal
3. ____	People of God	***c.***	Model of the Church
4. ____	Kingdom of God	***d.***	Mark of the Church
5. ____	Diocese	***e.***	Foreshadowed in creation
6. ____	Apostolic	***f.***	Power of God at work in the world
7. ____	Puccini	***g.***	Came to America to study our nation
8. ____	Church	***h.***	Cluster of parishes
9. ____	Catholic	***i.***	Summary of our faith
10. ____	De Toqueville	***j.***	Endowed Church with gifts and powers

True/False

1. ____ The Creed is said each Sunday at Mass by the entire congregation.
2. ____ Monsignor is an honorary title given to a bishop who has distinguished himself.
3. ____ The College of Cardinals elects the pope.
4. ____ The Church bears four distinguishing marks.
5. ____ The Church is a mixture of light and darkness.

Fill in the Blanks

1. The (**a**) _______ is to the human body what the (**b**) ____________ is to the Body of Christ.
2. The three basic models of the Church are (**a**) ________________ (**b**) ________________ (**c**) ________________
3. The Church was (**a**) ____________ for by the Old Testament, (**b**) ___________ by Jesus, revealed by the (**c**) _____________ has a (**d**) __________ dimension, and a (**e**) ____________ dimension.

Name ______________________________

Each correct response is worth four points.

Matching (Use each response in the right-hand column only once.)

1. ____ Lent
2. ____ Paschal mystery
3. ____ Anointing of the Sick
4. ____ Holy Orders
5. ____ Pentecost
6. ____ Acts of the Apostles
7. ____ Book of Revelation
8. ____ Epiphany
9. ____ Eucharist

a. Birthday of the Church
b. Occasionally the Second Reading of Mass
c. Sacrament of Service
d. Sacrament of sacraments
e. Spring
f. First reading of Mass during Easter season
g. Passover
h. Manifestation of Jesus to non-Jewish world
i. Sacrament of Healing

True/False

1. ____ The Lectionary contains all the most important Bible readings

2. ____ Easter begins with Ash Wednesday

3. ____ When the Church baptizes, it is Christ himself who baptizes.

4. ____ John Steinbeck was the Secretary of the Treasury under Presidents Nixon and Ford

5. ____ Through the liturgy, Jesus continues the work of our salvation.

Fill in the Blanks

1. These two readings set the theme of each Sunday Mass:

(a) ____________________ **(b)** ____________________

2. The following three sacraments are referred to as the sacraments of initiation:

(a) ____________________ **(b)** ____________________ **(c)** ________________

3. As Jesus once healed through the members of his **(a)** ________________ body,

he still heals through the members of his Church or **(b)** _______________ body.

4. The definition of a sacrament contains the following four essential elements:

(a) ____________________________ **(b)** ______________________________

(c) ____________________________ **(d)** ______________________________

Name ______________________

Each correct response is worth four points.

Matching (Use each response in the right-hand column only once.)

1. ____ White cloth		***a.*** Oil used in Baptism
2. ____ Water		***b.*** Wrote "Amazing Grace"
3. ____ Large Easter candle		***c.*** Symbol of Christ
4. ____ Heyerdahl		***d.*** Famous anthropologist
5. ____ Newton		***e.*** Placed upon the baptized
6. ____ Chrism		***f.*** Symbol of death and rebirth

True/False

1. ____ Baptism symbolizes our sacramental dying and rising in and with Christ.
2. ____ The Catholic Church forbids baptizing by total immersion in water.
3. ____ The name catechumen is given to someone who is just newly baptized.
4. ____ The ideal way to administer the Sacraments of Initiation is in a single ceremony.
5. ____ Besides "putting us right" with God, Baptism also puts us in possession of God's own eternal life.
6. ____ The waters of Baptism serve, symbolically, as a tomb and a womb.

Fill in the Blanks

1. The three ordinary ministers of Baptism are
   (a) ______________________
   (b) ______________________
   (c) ______________________
2. In an emergency, anyone can baptize;
   three minimal requirements need to be observed:
   (a) ______________________
   (b) ______________________
   (c) ______________________
3. We define a sacrament (e.g. Baptism) in the following fourfold manner. It is:
   (a) ______________________
   (b) ______________________
   (c) ______________________
   (d) ______________________
4. Baptism relates us to the Trinity in the following threefold way. We become:
   (a) ______________________
   (b) ______________________
   (c) ______________________

Name ______________________________

Each correct response is worth four points.

Matching (Use each response in the right-hand column only once.)

1. ____ Philip
2. ____ Pentecost
3. ____ Easter Vigil Service
4. ____ Peter and John
5 ____ Sealing
6. ____ Chrism

a. Adult Catholics usually enter Church
b. Used in Confirmation to anoint forehead
c. Preached to Samaritans
d. Imposed hands on Samaritans
e. Similar to ancient Roman military rite
f. Holy Spirit descends on disciples

True/False

1. ____ Samuel anointed Elisha a prophet.

2. ____ Moses conferred priesthood upon Aaron by anointing him with oil.

3. ____ Aaron conferred kingship on David by anointing him with oil.

4. ____ The "laying on of hands" had its origin in New Testament times.

5. ____ Through Confirmation we receive the same full outpouring of the Spirit as the disciples themselves received on Pentecost.

6. ____ The Apostles commissioned the first deacons by praying and placing their hands on them.

Fill in the Blanks

1. List and explain the threefold missions of Jesus to which the sacrament of Confirmation calls and empowers us.

(a) ______________ mission. Calls and empowers us to **(b)** ______________
(c) ______________ mission. Calls and empowers us to **(d)** ______________
(e) ______________ mission. Calls and empowers us to **(f)** ______________

2. The fourfold grace of the sacrament of confirmation includes the following:

(a) ______________________________
(b) ______________________________
(c) ______________________________
(d) ______________________________

3. The Liturgy of Confirmation involves the following three stages:

(a) ______________________________
(b) ______________________________
(c) ______________________________

Name ________________________________

Each correct response is worth four points.

Matching (Use each response in the right-hand column only once.)

1. ____ Shalom
2. ____ First reading
3. ____ Preface
4. ____ Eucharistic Prayer
5. ____ Letters of Saint Paul
6. ____ Responsorial Psalm

a. Meditation on First Reading
b. Usually found in the Second Reading
c. Hebrew word for "peace"
d. Ends with a reference to first Palm Sunday
e. Begins with a dialogue
f. Usually taken from the Old Testament

True/False

1. ____ When Jesus said "Do this in memory of me" he gave us a way to be present, in faith, to this great mystery just as truly as his apostles were 2000 years ago.

2. ____ To understand the Liturgy of the Eucharist, it helps to go back to the Jewish Passover meal.

3. ____ God promised through the prophet Jonah that a New Covenant would replace the Old Covenant.

4. ____ Each time the Mass is celebrated, Jesus is sacrificed again in a totally new sacrifice, totally different from the original sacrifice on Calvary.

5. ____ Both the Old Covenant and the New Covenant were "sealed" in blood.

6. ____ The Creed that we profess at each Sunday Mass is a summary of what we Catholics believe.

Fill in the Blanks

1. In Jesus' times there were two worship places in Israel. The first was found in every village and was called (**a**) ______________ . It was primarily a place of (**b**) ______________. The second worship place was found only in (**c**) ______________ and called (**d**) ______________. It was primarily a place of (**e**) ______________ .

2. The first part or movement of the Mass is called (**a**) ______________ It is begins with a (**b**) ______________. Its focal point is (**c**) ______________ The second part or movement of the Mass is called (**d**) ______________ It begins with a (**e**) ______________. Its focal point is (**f**) ______________

3. The "Institutional narrative" makes it clear that the Eucharist is not just a "memorial meal" but also a (**a**) ______________ meal and a (**b**) ______________ meal.

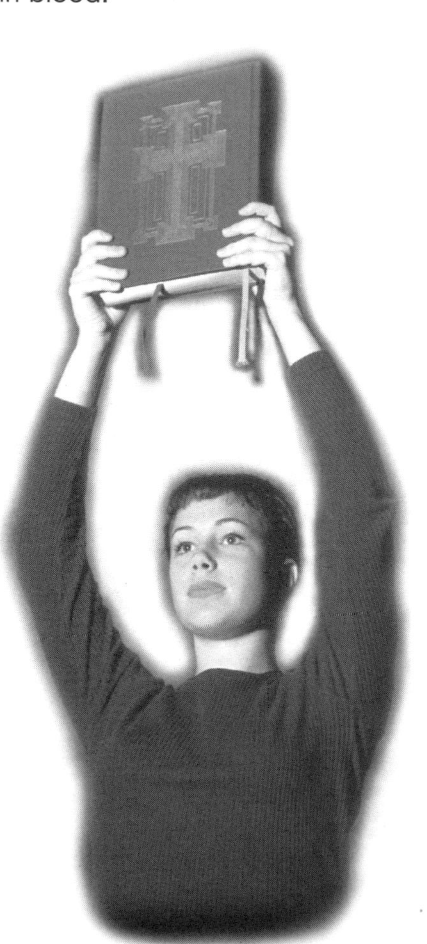

Each correct response is worth four points.

Matching (Use each response in the right-hand column only once.)

1. ____ Stealing a small article
2. ____ Adultery
3. ____ Imperfect contrition
4. ____ Serenity (peace) of conscience
5. ____ Sin of omission
6. ____ Perfect contrition

a. One of the graces of Reconciliation
b. Can forgive mortal sin
c. Involves a lesser motive than love of God
d. An example of grave matter
e. Failure to do something I should do
f. Example of venial sin

True/False

1. ____ Jesus showed he had the power to forgive sin in the course of healing a paralyzed man.

2. ____ The only way the Church forgives sins is in the sacrament of Reconciliation.

3. ____ If a priest assigns a penance that would prove difficult to perform, it would be appropriate to request that he change it to something else.

4. ____ Jesus shared his power to forgive sin in a specific way when he gave to Peter the keys of the Kingdom.

5. ____ Satisfaction has to do with making up for the harmful effects of our sins.

6. ____ It is good practice to introduce ourselves in the sacrament of Reconciliation (e.g., single or married, especially if we do not confess face-to-face.

7. ____ When the father in the Parable of the Prodigal Son hugs his son, it symbolizes he is restoring him again to full family status.

8. ____ Full consent of the will means we act voluntarily and freely.

Fill in the Blanks

1. To understand Reconciliation it helps to view it against the backdrop of the Parable of the Prodigal Son. The same four things the son did in the parable, we do in Reconciliation. They are:

(a) ______________________ **(b)** ______________________
(c) ______________________ **(d)** ______________________

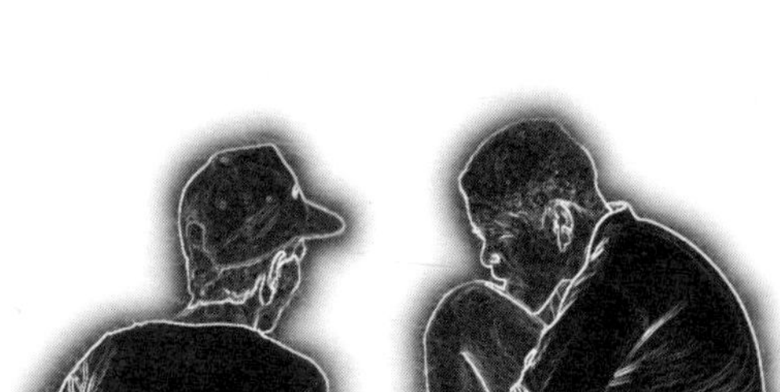

2. For a sin to be mortal these three conditions must be present:

(a) ______________________
(b) ______________________
(c) ______________________

3. What the father of the prodigal son did in the parable, the priest does in reconciliation. He:

(a) ______________________
(b) ______________________
(c) ______________________
(d) ______________________

Name ______________________

Each correct response is worth four points.

True/False

1. ____ The sacrament of the Anointing of the Sick may be celebrated anywhere.
2. ____ A person in a confused state of mind may not receive the sacrament of Anointing.
3. ____ The liturgy of the sacrament of Anointing normally involves anointing the sick person's hands.
4. ____ The liturgy of the sacrament of Anointing normally involves laying hands on the sick person's head.
5. ____ A person in a coma may not receive the sacrament of Anointing.
6. ____ The Bible portrays Jesus' followers continuing Jesus' healing ministry.
7. ____ Only a Catholic may receive the sacrament of Anointing.
8. ____ The ideal setting for celebrating the sacrament of Anointing is the sick person's bedroom.
9. ____ A heavily sedated person may never receive the sacrament of Anointing.
10. ____ The Bible clearly portrays Jesus sharing his healing power with his followers.
11. ____ The sacrament of Anointing involves anointing the sick person's lips.
12. ____ The sacrament of Anointing is a communal action involving the Body of Christ.
13. ____ Only a priest may lay hands on the sick person during the celebration of the sacrament of Anointing.
14. ____ A Jewish person may receive the sacrament of Anointing if the person does not believe that Christ acts through the sacrament.
15. ____ A grace of the sacrament of Anointing is preparation for entry into eternal life.

Fill in the Blanks

1. Four groups of people who should receive the sacrament of Anointing are:

   (a) ______________________

   (b) ______________________

   (c) ______________________

   (d) ______________________

2. The liturgy of the anointing of the sick follows a threefold format:

   (a) ______________________

   (b) that is ______________________

   (c) ______________________

   (d) that is ______________________

   (e) ______________________

   (f) that is ______________________

Name ________________________________

Each correct response is worth four points.

True/False

1. ____ Married love is the only love relationship that Jesus raised to the level of a sacrament.
2. ____ Marriage is more of a contract than it is a covenant.
3. ____ One purpose of marriage is to cooperate with God in bringing new life into the world.
4. ____ Saint Paul compared the love of husband and wife to the love of Christ and his Church.
5. ____ Under no circumstances may a Catholic couple who were married in a church ceremony get a divorce.
6. ____ An annulment is the "breaking up" of a true marriage.
7. ____ Faking consent in a marriage ceremony is grounds for annulment.
8. ____ Hiding a serious defect (for example, several convictions of child molestation) is grounds for an annulment.
9. ____ If a divorced Catholic remarries, the Church recognizes both marriages, even though the second one is sinful.
10. ____ The Church recommends interfaith marriages to foster better relationships between other religions.
11. ____ If a Hindu marries a Catholic, the Hindu must agree to raise all children to be Catholic.
12. ____ It is possible for a Catholic to marry a Lutheran in a Lutheran ceremony, performed by a Lutheran pastor, in a Lutheran church.
13. ____ A Catholic may never be married by a Jewish rabbi.
14. ____ Most dioceses require about a six-month preparation period for marriage.
15. ____ Recently issued certificates of Baptism, First Communion, and Confirmation are required as part of a Catholic's marriage preparation.
16. ____ A divorced Catholic whose first marriage is not annulled may not remarry if the spouse of the first marriage is still living.

Fill in the Blanks

1. Most marriages pass through the following phases in the following order:
   (a) ____________________ (b) ____________________
   (c) ____________________ (d) ____________________
2. Four levels at which two prospective marriage partners are usually drawn or attracted to each other are:
   (a) ____________________ (b) ____________________
   (c) ____________________ (d) ____________________

Name ______________________________

Each correct response is worth four points.

Matching (Use each response in the right-hand column only once.)

1. ____ Diocese
2. ____ Celibate
3. ____ Pope
4. ____ Vocation
5. ____ Presbyter
6. ____ Celibacy
7. ____ Infallibility
8. ____ Ordained priesthood
9. ____ Magisterium
10. ____ Common priesthood

a. State of being unmarried
b. "Father of fathers"
c. Shared by every baptized Christian
d. Teaching office of the Church
e. Church territorial division
f. Ministerial priesthood
g. Priest
h. Didn't become universal until 12th century
i. "Calling"
j. Means God will not allow his Church to err in matters relating to salvation

True/False

1. ____ Bishops are successors to the Apostles.
2. ____ Deacons are empowered to preside over the sacrament of Reconciliation.
3. ____ God chose the tribe of Levi for liturgical service to the other tribes.
4. ____ The pope is the head of the "college of bishops."
5. ____ Deacons may assist at and bless marriages.

Fill in the Blanks

1. The sacrament of Holy Orders is exercised in the following three different degrees:
   (**a**) ____________________
   (**b**) ____________________ (**c**) ____________________
2. Peter held a special leadership role among the Apostles in the following four ways:
   (**a**) ______________________________
   (**b**) ______________________________
   (**c**) ______________________________
   (**d**) ______________________________
3. Bishops, the successors of the Apostles, receive the fullness of the sacrament of Holy Orders, empowering them to: (**a**) ____________________
   (**b**) ____________________ (**c**) ____________________

Name ______________________________

Each correct response is worth four points.

Matching (Use each response in the right-hand column only once.)

1. ____ Meditation
2. ____ Contemplation
3. ____ Conversation
4. ____ Supplication
5. ____ Thanksgiving
6. ____ Adoration
7. ____ Contrition

a. Focus is the mystery of God's glory
b. Focus is the mystery of God's goodness to us
c. Speaking/listening to God
d. Resting in God
e. Focus is the mystery of God's mercy
f. Thinking about God
g. Prayer of petition

True/False

1. ____ The prayer of petition presumes that what we ask for is for our greater spiritual welfare and in harmony with God's will.
2. ____ Strangely enough, Jesus rarely referred to the prayer of petition.
3. ____ The focus of meditation is the mind.
4. ____ The primary reason why we pray is that we need God's help.
5. ____ The point of the Parable of the Night Visitor is that we should pray with humility.
6. ____ The focus of contemplation is the soul.
7. ____ The three forms of prayer are so interwoven in one and the same prayer that it is sometimes hard to say where one stops and the other begins.
8. ____ Piri Thomas spent three weeks in the White House as the guest of Abraham Lincoln.
9. ____ A sensible awareness of God's presence is a gift.

Fill in the Blanks

1. Two attitudes we should have in prayer are:
(a) ______________________________
(b) ______________________________

2. Four preparatory steps to any serious prayer program should involve:
(a) ______________________________
(b) ______________________________
(c) ______________________________
(d) ______________________________

3. The Gospel portrays Jesus praying in all three of these settings:
(a) ______________________________
(b) ______________________________
(c) ______________________________

Name ________________________________

Each correct response is worth four points.

Matching (Use responses in the right-hand column as often as you wish.)

1. ____ Jesus' teaching is a guide to growth.
2. ____ Sin is a refusal to love.
3. ____ Sin is infidelity to growth.
4. ____ We advance to this stage by assuming social obligations, like commitments.
5. ____ We don't realize it, but at this level we area anything but free,
6. ____ Sin is a violation of a restriction.
7. ____ Jesus' teaching is an invitation to love.
8. ____ At this level, God's law frees us "from" ignorance and passion "for" service.
9. ____ Jesus' teaching is a restriction to freedom.

a. Self-centered stage
b. Other-centered stage
c. God-centered stage

True/False

1. ____ It is absolutely certain that God created everything as the Bible describes it.
2. ____ With the emergence of plant life, the creative process took a quantum leap forward; it became conscious of itself.
3. ____ Jesus taught that there is another quantum leap beyond the human stage.
4. ____ Higher forms of creation, like humans, seem to have emerged from lower forms.
5. ____ In terms of Paul's imagery, our task in this life is to "plant the seeds" that will produce a "harvest of eternal life" in the next life.
6. ____ An important question that surfaced with the emergence of human life was, Is there another quantum leap ahead of us?
7. ____ The "big bang" theory contradicts biblical teaching.
8. ____ Jesus said, "I have come in order that you might have life—life in all its fullness."
9. ____ Saint Augustine suggested some 1500 years ago that God simply created the "seed" or "seeds" from which creation gradually emerged.
10. ____ It is really not too difficult to love and live as Jesus did.
11. ____ Before life reached the human stage, creation seems to have advanced from one quantum leap to the next randomly.
12. ____ One way of describing Christian morality is as follows: "Accepting God's invitation to live life on earth in such a way as to make the leap to eternal life."
13. ____ At the self-centered stage we become keenly aware of our identity (we are God's children) and our destiny (we are called to eternal life).
14. ____ Christian moral growth begins in childhood and never ends.
15. ____ At the other-centered stage, Jesus Christ becomes the central figure of our life.
16. ____ A personal way of describing Christian morality is saying "yes" to Jesus' invitation to live and love as he did.

Name ______________________________

Each correct response is worth four points.

Matching (Use each response in the right-hand column only once.)

1. ____ Superstition
2. ____ Covenant
3. ____ Spiritism
4. ____ Cursing
5. ____ Swearing
6. ____ Perjury
7. ____ Oaths
8. ____ Scandal

a. Calling upon God to witness to truth
b. Calling upon God to inflict harm
c. Attitude or behavior that leads another to do evil
d. A sacred agreement or pact
e. Seeking to communicate with the dead
f. Permitted in court situations
g. Lying under oath
h. Giving such things as the number 13 the power to help us or hurt us.

True/False

1. ____ The first three commandments invite us to make love of God the center of our lives.
2. ____ Scripture says, "If we obey God's commands, then we are sure that we know God."
3. ____ Jesus abolished the last seven commandments and put in their place the command to love our neighbor as ourselves.
4. ____ Observance of Sundays and holy days binds us gravely, unless we are excused for a serious reason, for example, sickness.
5. ____ Divination deals with worshiping false gods.
6. ____ The Bible places no prohibition against trying to communicate with the dead through prayerful seances.
7. ____ Damning someone in God's name in our current culture is more often a careless expression of frustration or irritation than a genuine intention to curse.
8. ____ Doing hard labor on Sunday is always sinful, even if it relaxes the mind and body.
9. ____ The greatest commandment is to love our neighbor as ourselves.
10. ____ The second commandment governs our use of speech in sacred matters.

Fill in the Blanks

1. List the names and dates of two holy days observed by Catholics in the United States.

Name / Date

(a) ______________________ **(b)** ______________________

(c) ______________________ **(d)** ______________________

2. Jesus redefined and refocused the Ten Commandments in the sense that they become:

(a) ______________________ **(b)** ______________________

(c) 

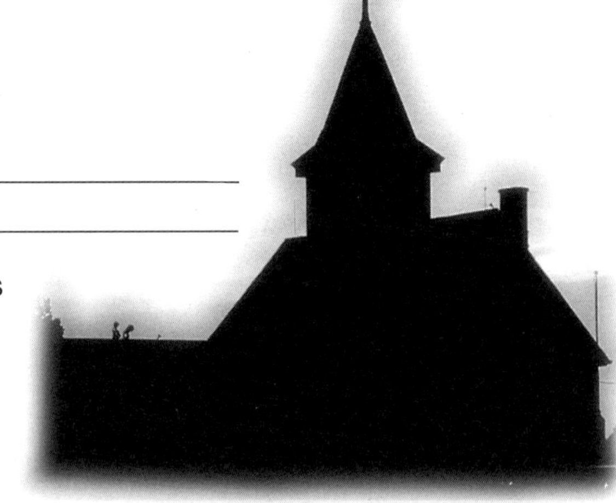

Name ______________________________

Each correct response is worth four points.

Matching (Use responses in the right-hand column as often as you wish.)

1. ____ Direct Euthanasia
2. ____ Cheating
3. ____ Capital punishment
4. ____ Detraction
5. ____ Stealing
6. ____ Gambling
7. ____ War
8. ____ Direct abortion

a. Permissible under certain conditions

b. Never permissible under any condition

True/False

1. ____ We owe the civil community special loyalty and share in its responsibilities.
2. ____ Because of the possible risk to life, all hunger strikes are immoral.
3. ____ Alcoholics and drug addicts have a grave obligation to seek help when they become aware of their addiction.
4. ____ Even those who are opposed to capital punishment agree that it is more justifiable today than ever.
5. ____ To watch a movie simply because it is sexually exciting and simulating is objectively and gravely wrong.
6. ____ If something is true about a person, we always have a right to make it public, even it it would hurt the other person.
7. ____ Passive euthanasia is permissible.
8. ____ Sexual temptation is not a sign of depravity so much as it is a sign of our humanity.
9. ____ Jesus made it clear that those who are blessed with wealth have an obligation to help the needy.
10. ____ Restitution means we resolve in our heart never to sin again.

Fill in the Blanks

1. The (**a**) ______________ and (**b**) ______________ dimensions of the sexual union may be compared to the (**c**) ______________ and (**d**) ______________ of the human person
2. Sex celebrates (**a**) ______________ (**b**) ______________ and (**c**) ______________.

Name ______________________

Each correct response is worth four points.

Matching (Use each response in the right-hand column only once.)

1. ____ Invincible ignorance
2. ____ Vincible Ignorance
3. ____ Conscience
4. ____ Franz Jaegerstatter
5. ____ Neil Armstrong
6. ____ Thomas More
7. ____ Erroneous judgment

a. An error in forming my conscience
b. A conscience error due to my carelessness
c. Faced a major decision as a teenager
d. A conscience error due to incorrect information
e. Empowers us to know right from wrong
f. Refused to swear to what he knew was false
g. Refused to participate in what his conscience told him was an immoral war.

True/False

1. ____ Our conscience may be described as a judgment of our reason.
2. ____ We could deny the Eucharist is really the Body of Christ and still be a good Catholic.
3. ____ If the Church pronounces some teaching to be divinely revealed, this means we must accept it as a matter of faith.
4. ____ An invincible error makes us morally responsible for our act.
5. ____ A charism is another word for conscience.
6. ____ Jesus assured the Church that the Holy Spirit would guide it in its teaching role.
7. ____ We have both an obligation and a right to follow our conscience.
8. ____ Sometimes the Church receives clarity on moral and doctrinal matters gradually and by stages.

Fill in the Blanks

1. There are three kinds of moral decisions. We may describe them as: **(a)** ______________ decisions, **(b)** ______________ decisions, and **(c)** ______________ decisions.

2. Sometimes we must make a moral decision in which it is not clear what the right decision is. In such a case we should follow these three steps:
(a) ______________________ **(b)** ______________________
(c) ______________________

3. There are two levels of Church teaching when it comes to moral and doctrinal matters. The first and most important is when the Church teaches with **(a)** ______________ certitude. We must give this teaching a full **(b)** ______________ assent. The second level is when it teaches with **(c)** ______________. We must give this teaching a **(d)** ______________ assent.

Name ______________________________

Each correct response is worth four points.

Matching (Use each response in the right-hand column only once.)

1. ____ Lourdes
2. ____ Bernadette Soubirous
3. ____ Mary
4. ____ Immaculate Conception
5. ____ Assumption
6. ____ Jesus
7. ____ Catacombs
8. ____ Canonization
9. ____ Sanctus
10. ____ Mother of Jesus

a. Belief that Mary entered heaven body and soul
b. Belief that Mary was preserved from sin from conception
c. Origin of word "saint"
d. Origin of Mary's specialness
e. Site of many modern miracles
f. Reported vision of Mary
g. Ancient burial grounds
h. Model disciple
i. God according to the flesh
j. Saint-making process

True/False

1. ____ The "communion of saints" refers to Holy Communion.
2. ____ The Church in pilgrimage refers to the Church on earth.
3. ____ Saint Francis was very "saintly" from early childhood onward.
4. ____ A saint may be described as a living reminder that God's grace can work miracles in us, if we open our hearts to it.
5. ____ The word "saint" means "holy one."
6. ____ Early Christians referred to one another as "saints."

7. ____ Canonization is no longer used by the Church.
8. ____ Catholics rarely pray to God directly, usually only through the saints.
9. ____ Tradition teaches that Mary remained a virgin all her life.
10. ____ Tradition teaches that Mary remained sinless all her life.
11. ____ The Church exercises extreme caution when it comes to reported apparitions of Mary.
12. ____ When we call Mary the "Mother of God," we mean that she was, in some mysterious way, God's mother from all eternity.
13. ____ Because Mary was sinless, she did not fall under the penalty of sin, and was assumed into heaven body and soul.
14. ____ The teaching concerning Mary's assumption into heaven was handed down by tradition.
15. ____ Scripture calls Mary "most blessed of all women."

Name ______________________________

Each correct response is worth four points.

Matching (Use each response in the right-hand column only once.)

1. ____ Heaven
2. ____ Purgatory
3. ____ Hell
4. ____ Last judgment
5. ____ Individual judgment

a. Occurs at the end of the world
b. Eternal separation from God
c. Occurs at the end of life
d. Preparation for union with God
e. Eternal union with God

True/False

1. ____ Before ascending to heaven, Jesus said he would return again.

2. ____ Our individual judgment by God will take place at the end of the world.

3. ____ We will not be rewarded or punished until the last judgment.

4. ____ The parable of Lazarus and the Rich man relates primarily to the last judgment

5. ____ Purgatory makes sense because most people die neither good enough for heaven nor bad enough for hell.

6. ____ The Parable of the Weeds and the Wheat concerns the separation of good people and bad people and their reward and punishment.

7. ____ The Church teaches that hell involves real, physical fire.

8. ____ The Church teaches that hell is a real, physical place.

9. ____ The Second Book of Maccabees implies the existence of Purgatory.

10. ____ Theologians call the vision of of God the "beatific vision."

11. ____ The parable of the Separation of the Sheep and the Goats relates primarily to the particular judgment.

12. ____ Heaven is better described as a state of being rather than a place.

Fill in the Blanks

1. List and briefly explain the three destinies associated with individual judgment.

Destiny *Explanation*

(a) ______________________________

(b) ______________________________

(c) ______________________________

2. When Jesus spoke of hell fire, some Christians think he meant fire in a literal sense; others in a dramatic sense. Briefly explain each of these senses.

(a) Literal: ______________________________

____

(b) Dramatic: ______________________________

____

Resource Guide

Resources for Professional Background

The Art of Catechesis by Maureen Gallagher. Mahwah, NJ: Paulist Press, 1998. Easy-to-read overview of catechesis with suggestions for making it more effective.

The Catechetical Documents: A Parish Resource. Chicago: Liturgy Training Publications, 1996. A handy collection of the major catechetical documents promulgated since the Second Vatican Council.

Catechism of the Catholic Church: Second Edition. United States Catholic Conference, Inc. 2000. The revised CCC presents the essential and fundamental contents of Catholic doctrine, with glossary and analytical index.

The Collegeville Pastoral Dictionary of Biblical Theology edited by Carroll Stuhlmueller. Collegeville, MN: The Liturgical Press, 1996. An accessible and comprehensive guide for gaining a deeper understanding of the Bible and its central place in the life of the Church.

General Directory for Catechesis: Congregation for the Clergy. Washington, DC: United States Catholic Conference, 1997. Addressed primarily to those who have responsibility for catechesis, the new Directory offers reflections and principles to guide the ministry of the word and, concretely, catechesis.

The Modern Catholic Encyclopedia edited by Michael Glazier and Monika Hellwig. Collegeville: The Liturgical Press, 1994. A popular reference book to help put readers in touch with modern scholarship.

Religious Education at the Crossroads by Francoise Darcy-Berube. Mahwah, NJ: Paulist Press, 1998. A clear and concise summary of the current trends in religious education.

Church History

A Popular History of the Catholic Church by Carl Koch. Winona: St. Mary's Press, 1997. This concise history of the Catholic church tells the story of the 2000-year relationship between Jesus and the believers who have followed him and the Spirit who dwells with us always.

A Short History of American Catholicism by Martin Marty. Allen, TX: Thomas More Publishing, 1995. The dramatic highpoints of American Catholicism over the past 500 years.

Liturgy

Liturgy with Style and Grace by Gabe Huck and Gerald Chinchar. Chicago: Liturgy Training Publications, 1998. This informative book is a basic requirement for anyone who wishes to learn more about the Mass, the sacraments, and the seasons of the church year.

Prayer and Spirituality

Crossing the River: Daily Meditations for Women by Carol Gura. Allen, TX: Thomas More Publishing, 1998. An inspiring approach to daily prayer focusing on women's spirituality, their dreams, their hopes, their concerns.

God Hunger: Discovering the Mystic in All of Us by John Kirvan. Notre Dame, IN: Soring Books, 1999. Presents 50 experiences for the soul built around the core insights of ten great mystics.

God in the Moment: Making Every Day a Prayer by Kathy Coffey. Chicago, IL: Loyola Press, 1999. Filled with practical ideas abut prayer and ways to respond to God's grace in our lives.

Lectio Divina: Renewing the Ancient Practice of Praying the Scriptures by M. Basil Pennington. New York: Crossroad, 1998. This informative and practical guidebook for today's Christian describes the time-tested method of praying with the Scriptures for wisdom, guidance, and joy.

Saints

All Saints: Daily Reflections on Saints, Prophets, and Witnesses for Our Time by Robert Ellsberg. New York: Crossroad, 1997. This wonderful treasury combines traditional saints with other spiritual giants whose lives speak to the meaning of holiness for our time.

The Second Vatican Council

Destination Vatican II:CD-ROM. Allen, TX: Thomas More Publishing, 1997. Here is technology that touches the heart—extensive coverage of the Council includes two version of 16 official council documents, extensive council documentary, and 4,000 of informative and inspiring text (PC and MAC versions available).

Vatican II: The Faithful Revolution. Allen, TX: Thomas More Publishing, 1997. This award-winning video presents the history of the Council by combining news clips and interviews.

Vatican II in Plain English by Bill Huebsch. Allen, TX: Thomas More Publishing, 1997.

Slipcase set of three books explains what happened at the council, why it was call, and all 16 council documents in readable sense lines.

Spiritual Foundations of Catholic Education

Educating for Life: A Spiritual Vision for Every Teacher and Parent by Thomas Groome. Allen, TX: Thomas More Publishing, 1997. A bold vision that gets to the heart of how and why we educate. Indispensable for all teachers.

Resources for Use in Classroom

1 Light of Faith

In Search of Belief by Joan Chittister. Liguori, MO: Liguori. Fresh and contemporary way to pray the Creed.

Romero. Available at most video rental stores. Absorbing feature film (1989) about El Savador's Archbishop Oscar Romero whose fight against social injustices lead to his assassination.

What Makes Us Catholic: Discovering Our Catholic Identity. Catholic Update Video, 30 minutes. Cincinnati, OH: St. Anthony Messenger Press, 1998. Multifaceted resource that highlights what Catholic believe and how they share their faith with others.

2 Divine Revelation

Meeting the Living God by William O'Malley, S.J. Video, 60 minutes. Mahwah, NJ: Paulist Press. Rich and engaging way to convey to teenagers what it means to encounter God.

3 Old Testament / 4 New Testament

Path through Scripture by Mark Link, S.J. Allen, TX: Thomas More Publishing, 1995. Sharply focused, concisely written, and graphically illustrated presentation of God's Word.

5 God the Father / 6 God the Son / 7 God the Holy Spirit

Mystery of God: Father, Son, and Spirit. Three 30-minutes videos. Allen, TX: RCL. A fascinating and contemporary approach to the story of creation, salvation, and God's abiding presence in our lives.

8 The Church

The Faithful Revolution. Allen, TX: Thomas More Publishing, 1997. Five 60-minute videos and blackline masters. See above.

Models of the Church by Avery Dulles, S.J., New York, NY; Doubleday, expanded revised edition, 1991. Presents six different roles in the life of the church and it mission on earth.

9 Liturgy

Living Liturgy: Spirituality, Celebration, and Catechesis for Sundays and Solemnities by Joyce Ann Zimmerman, Thomas Greisen, Kathleen Harmon, and Thomas Leclerc. Collegeville, MN: The Liturgical Press, Year B (2000), Year C (2001), Year A (2002). Offers practical means for reflecting on, celebrating, and living the paschal mystery.

10 Baptism

New Life: A Parish Celebrates Infant Baptism. Chicago, IL: Liturgy Training Publications, 1997. This 30-minute video highlights the celebration of infant Baptism within the Sunday Eucharist.

11 Confirmation

Confirmation: Commitment to Life by Father Joe Kempf. St. Louis, MO: Oblate Media & Communication, 1996. This 60-minute video focuses on a group of high-school students who discover how God and the sacrament of Confirmation fit into the real world.

12 Eucharist

Eucharist: A Taste of God by Father Joseph Kempf. St. Louis, MO: Oblate Media, 1995 . Video, 114 minutes. This lively program explores the Eucharist as a source of spiritual growth.

A Teens Guide to Living the Mass by Father Dale Fushek. St. Louis, MO: Oblate Media Communication, 1997. This 45-minute video explains how teens can and should play a vital role in the Mass and in the life of the Church.

Walks with Jesus: Eucharist by Mark Link, S.J. Allen, TX: Christian Classics, 1998. This 21-minute video features three true stories that illustrate why the celebration of the Eucharist is of central importance in the life of the Church.

13 Reconciliation

The Church Celebrates the Reconciling God. Cincinnati, OH: St. Anthony Messenger Press, 1999. Catholic Update Video, 27 minutes. Focuses on the history, theology, and practice of the sacrament of Reconciliation.

Pardon and Peace Remembered. St. Louis, MO: Oblate Media, 1998. Video, 15 minutes. A marvelous story of reconciliation and healing between and old man and a trouble young woman.

14 Anointing of the Sick

No One Cries the Wrong Way. Dubuque, IA: Brown-Roa, 1998. Video, eight 15-minute segments. The mystery of suffering and dying through the eyes of faith.

15 Marriage

Marriage. Dubuque, IA: Brown-Roa. Video, four 30-minute segments. This series explores every stage of marriage, including wedding plans, the early years of marriage, establishing careers, children, and communication.

Sex and the Teenager: Choices and Decisions by Kieran Sawyer, S.S.N.D. Notre Dame, IN: Ave Maria Press, 1999. Practical presentation of a Catholic perspective on sexuality, moral values, and personal choices.

16 Holy Orders

Understanding the Sacraments. Catholic Update Video, 33 minutes. St. Anthony Messenger Press, 1996. Insight and inspiration for the celebration of the sacraments.

17 Praying

Challenge 2000 by Mark Link, S.J. Allen, TX: Thomas More Publishing, 1993. A 36-week prayer program based on *The Spiritual Exercises of Saint Ignites.*

Christodrama. Dubuque, IA: Brown-Roa. Video, 60 minutes. How to experience the Gospel in a way that relates to your own life story.

30 Days with a Great Spiritual Teacher by John Kirvan and Richard Chilson. Notre Dame, IN: Ave Maria Press. Open-ended series now features 14 titles on the great spiritual masters of the Christian tradition.

What Do I Want in Prayer? by William Barry, S.J. Mahway, NJ: Paulist Press, 1994. Includes reading and meditative exercises as a way for greater intimacy with God.

18 Choosing Love

The Bible Jesus Read by Philip Yancey. Grand Rapids, MI: Zondervan Publishing House, 1999. Wonderful prequel to the story of Jesus that shows how the Old Testament helps us understand Jesus.

Jesus 2000 by Mark Link, S.J. Allen, TX: Thomas More Publishing, 1997. A 34-week prayer program that relives and celebrates the key events of Jesus'—based on the liturgical year.

19 Loving God

Dreams Alive edited by Carol Koch. Winona, MN: St. Mary's Press, 1991. Prayers by and for teenagers that are honest and articulate as well as optimistic and humorous.

20 Loving Neighbor

Exploring Media with Today's Parables. Dubuque, IA: Brown-Roa. Video 20 minutes. How to evaluate the impact of media and make a personal difference.

The Neighbor: The Parable of the Good Samaritan. Dubuque, IA: Brown-Roa, 1998. Video, 12 minutes. A young multi-cultural cast re-enacts the parable of the Good Samaritan—sure to spark lively discussion about compassion, forgiveness, violence, and hatred.

Power Surge: Integrity. New York, NY: W. H. Sadlier, 1994. A look at lying, stealing, and cheating and what it does to a person's

21 Discerning Love

Meditations for the Millennium by Mark Link, S.J. Allen, TX: Thomas More Publishing, 1998. Three handy prayer journals that focus on grace, reflection, and hope: Father, Son, and Holy Spirit.

22 Witnessing to Love

Chariots of Fire. Available at most video rental stores. Academy-award winning (1981) film based on true story of two Olympic athletes. One who sees victory as way to give glory to God; the other who see victory as a challenge to anti-Semitism.

Companion to the Calendar by Mary Ellen Hynes. Chicago, IL: Liturgy Training Publications, 1993. A daily and seasonal guide to the saints and mysteries that make up the Christian calendar.

Joseph. St. Louis, MO: Oblate Media, 1998. Video, 60 minutes. This program explores the life of Saint Joseph and the way he reflects God.

Waking Up Bees by Jerry Daoust. Winona, MN: St. Mary's Press, 1999. True-to-life stories abut facing important life issues such as love, work, vocation, and suffering.

23 Rejoicing in Love

A Promise in the Story by Nancy Marrocco. Winona, MN: St. Mary's Press, 1996. Engages young people to reflect upon death and grief as integral parts of Christian faith.

Sister Thea: Her Own Story. St. Louis, MO, Oblate Media, 1990. Video, 50 minutes. Award-winning memoir of the renown gospel singer, teacher, and evangelist is a testament to the power of faith over adversity in the face of death.